Patent Case Management Judicial Guide

Third Edition

2016

Volume I

Pretrial Case Management

Chapters 1–6

Patent Case Management Judicial Guide

Third Edition

Peter S. Menell
Koret Professor of Law
Berkeley Center for Law & Technology
University of California, Berkeley School of Law

Lynn H. Pasahow
Fenwick & West LLP

James Pooley
Orrick, Herrington & Sutcliffe LLP

Matthew D. Powers
Tensegrity Law Group LLP

Steven C. Carlson
Kasowitz, Benson, Torres & Friedman LLP

Jeffrey G. Homrig
Latham & Watkins LLP

George F. Pappas
Covington & Burling LLP

Carolyn Chang
Fenwick & West LLP

Colette Reiner Mayer
Morrison & Foerster LLP

Marc David Peters
Morrison & Foerster LLP

in collaboration with

Anita Choi
Morrison & Foerster LLP

John Fargo
U.S. Department of Justice

Michael Sawyer
Covington & Burling LLP

Allison A. Schmitt
University of California, Berkeley

Michael R. Ward
Morrison & Foerster LLP

Patricia Young
Latham & Watkins LLP

Federal Judicial Center 2016

email: pmenell@law.berkeley.edu

A print version of *Patent Case Management Judicial Guide* (3d ed. 2016), including all appendices, is available through Clause 8 Publishing (Clause8Publishing.com). The treatise is also available through the Lexis online database.

Summary Table of Contents

Table of Contents

Chapter 5 Claim Construction

Chapter 6 Summary Judgment

Foreword to Third Edition

Patent cases present unique and often daunting challenges for federal judges. The statutory law is complex, and appellate authority interpreting the relevant statutes constantly is evolving. Patent cases have their own peculiar nomenclature in which even the most diligent judges typically require a considerable amount of time to become fluent. And the exponential growth of new technologies has made the subject matter of many patent cases difficult for judges without a technical background to understand, at least to the point at which they have confidence in their decisions.

In addition to these challenges, patent cases also can present significant issues with respect to case management. The financial and competitive stakes often are extraordinarily high, and counsel tend to be correspondingly talented, active, and numerous. The major elements of most patent litigation, including discovery disputes, claim-construction hearings, dispositive motion practice, and trial, usually are intense affairs that test both the intellect and interpersonal skills of the judges who preside over them.

This outstanding, comprehensive judicial guide to the management of patent cases is the latest product of an eighteen-year collaboration between the Federal Judicial Center and the Berkeley Center for Law and Technology at the University of California—Berkeley School of Law. In addition to three editions of the guide, the results of that collaboration have included an annual seminar that has trained hundreds of federal judges in the fundamentals of intellectual property law and frequent special-focus programs on relevant legal developments. Under the visionary leadership of Professor Peter Menell, and with the assistance of a superb group of distinguished practitioners, the Berkeley Center has provided an invaluable service to the federal judiciary.

Jeremy D. Fogel
Senior District Judge
Director, Federal Judicial Center (2011–)

Foreword to First Edition

This judicial guide on patent case management is a collaborative effort between the Federal Judicial Center and the Berkeley Center for Law & Technology of the University of California–Berkeley School of Law. This collaboration began in 1998 when the Berkeley Center and the Judicial Center conducted their first intellectual property seminar for judges. That seminar was structured to provide district judges with a background and understanding of the many areas of intellectual property law. From that initial program has evolved an annual intellectual property seminar for judges at the Berkeley Center as well as a range of innovative intellectual property programs at the Federal Judicial Center's national and local workshops.

Then and now, the driving force behind these judicial education efforts in intellectual property has been Professor Peter Menell, Director of the Berkeley Center. Building on the enormous success of these programs, Professor Menell approached the Center several years ago with the idea of collecting materials on patent case management that had been compiled for the intellectual property seminars. With coauthors Lynn Pasahow, James Pooley, and Matthew Powers, along with the assistance of a distinguished group of collaborators and advisors, Professor Menell prepared this comprehensive guide. I believe this guide will be a valuable aid to judges handling the complex arena of patent cases

Barbara J. Rothstein
District Judge
Director, Federal Judicial Center (2003–2011)

Preface to the Third Edition

The patent system and patent case management continue to evolve rapidly. This edition encompasses implementation of the America Invents Act (AIA), the emergence of review proceedings at the Patent Trial and Appeal Board (PTAB), the Supreme Court's many recent patent decisions (patent eligibility, claim construction, claim indefiniteness, infringement analysis (rejecting "joint infringement"), the intent requirement for induced infringement liability (rejecting a defense of good-faith belief of a patent's invalidity), and attorneys' fees), and the Federal Circuit's damages jurisprudence, including damage awards for standard essential patents (SEP) licensed pursuant to fair, reasonable, and nondiscriminatory (FRAND) terms. It also includes case-management checklists, model case-management orders, and other materials developed by district judges and advisory bodies for streamlining patent case management. Finally, this volume adds a chapter on patent litigation at the Court of Federal Claims.

Preface to the Second Edition

As indicated in the preface to the First Edition of the Patent Case Management Judicial Guide (PCMJG), we committed to revise this volume on a biennial basis. And indeed, the patent system experienced substantial change during the ensuing two years. The Supreme Court and the Federal Circuit had issued a raft of important patent law decisions. In addition, many district courts had adopted and revised Patent Local Rules and begun implementation of the Patent Pilot Program.

Just as we were about to release the Second Edition of the PCMJG last fall, Congress passed the America Invents Act (AIA). By the time that we had written up the ramifications of that multi-faceted law for patent case management, the Supreme Court had rendered its decision in *Mayo Collaborative Servs. v. Prometheus Labs., Inc.*, 132 U.S. 1289 (2012). Other important decisions from the courts have continued apace.

These developments amply demonstrate that the patent system operates in an active seismic zone. This should not be surprising in view of the rapid advances in information and biomedical technologies and the desire of the various patent institutions to adapt patent law in response to the shifting tectonic plates.

As a result, this volume substantially updates and expands the coverage and analysis of patent case management practices. We remain committed to updating the volume on a biennial basis, although we and the courts need to be mindful of the unpredictability of living in an earthquake-prone environment.

Preface to the First Edition

As the number, size, and complexity of patent cases have grown throughout the United States over the past several decades—paralleling expansion in the role of high technology enterprises in the U.S. economy—the need for a comprehensive, user-friendly, and practical judicial guide for managing patent cases has become increasingly apparent. Although similar in many respects to other forms of complex civil litigation, patent cases pose distinctive case-management challenges. Patent cases feature complex and dynamic technological facts to a degree rarely encountered in most other areas of litigation. Furthermore, they employ unique procedures (such as claim construction hearings) that affect and interact with other aspects of the case (such as summary judgment motions and expert reports) in ways that create unusual scheduling and substantive complexity. In addition, patent cases often entail distinctive and difficult discovery issues, extensive use of experts, and particularly complex dispositive and pretrial motion practice.

Because of the decentralized, general jurisdiction structure of federal courts in the United States, much of the experience relating to managing patent cases is siloed in particular judicial chambers. As one jurist aptly noted, best practices for patent case management have been transmitted largely through word of mouth. Given the crowded, diverse dockets of federal courts, the accessibility and reliability of such knowledge is far from ideal. Judges in some districts have partially codified recommended practices in the form of Patent Local Rules, standing orders, and patent jury instructions, but these documents do not address the full range of distinctive challenges posed by patent litigation. Furthermore, such judicial wisdom continues to evolve.

Recognizing these patterns, the authors undertook in 2006 to survey the range of approaches and perspectives on patent case management, foster discussion and analysis of patent case management techniques, and develop an authoritative guide for judges, law clerks, practitioners, and patent and civil procedure professors and scholars. This project grew out of an annual series of intellectual property education programs that Professor Peter Menell has organized since 1998 for the Federal Judicial Center. It began by collecting available materials relating to patent case management and constructing a comprehensive outline. Over the next year, the team drafted, revised, and edited the principal chapters of the guide. They first vetted a draft at the FJC intellectual property conference in June 2007. They then undertook a substantial revision of the manuscript. Between December 2007 and August 2008, the authors met with district judges and magistrate judges in the most active patent jurisdictions around the nation—the Northern District of California, the Central District of California, the District of Delaware, the Northern District of Illinois, the District of New Jersey, the Southern District of New York, the Eastern District of Texas, and the Eastern District of Virginia—as well as the Federal Circuit to discuss the overall project and refine the specific case-management recommendations. Such sessions explored the range of practices and honed the best practices set forth in this Guide. The authors also assembled an advisory board of leading patent litigators and academics to provide input on the project.

Given the dynamism of the patent system and patent litigation, the authors plan to revise the guide on a biennial basis.

Acknowledgments

This project could not have reached fruition without the support and encouragement of the Federal Judicial Center and the Berkeley Center for Law & Technology. We are especially grateful to the many federal judges, practitioners, and professors who have provided insights and guidance on patent case management.

First Edition: We thank Nicholas Brown, Thomas Fletcher, and Sue Vastano Vaughan for their contributions; James Morando and Ted Sichelman for detailed comments; Ashley Doty, Blake Greene, Tamar Gubins, David Haskel, Justin Lee, Will McGinty, Hersh Reddy, and Jeff Thomas for excellent research assistance; David Grady and Jennifer Zahgkuni for their assistance in editing and formatting; and Laura Rochelois and the studio of By Design Legal Graphics for their assistance with figure illustrations.

Second Edition: We are grateful to David S. Bloch, Jeremy Bock, Anita Choi, Samuel Ernst, Thomas Fletcher, Rebecca Charnas Grant, Leeron G. Kalay, Clem Roberts, Kimberly N. Van Voorhis, Michael R. Ward, and Patricia Young for contributions; and Damion Jurrens, Benjamin Petersen, Roman A. Swoopes, Priscilla Grace Taylor, and Cecilia Ziniti for excellent research assistance.

Third Edition: We are grateful to Thomas Fletcher, Lisa Pirozzolo, and Mark Selwyn for comments; Danielle Goldstein, Nicholas Ham, Alexa Hansen, Alessa Phang, Brett M. Sandford, Gregory K. Sobolski, Ranganath Sudarshan, and Jonathan Tamimi for excellent research assistance; and LegalMetrics and Lex Machina for data.

JUDICIAL ADVISORY BOARD

Hon. Jeremy D. Fogel
District Judge
Northern District of California
Director, Federal Judicial Center

Hon. Cathy Ann Bencivengo
District Judge
Southern District of California

Hon. Susan G. Braden
Judge
Court of Federal Claims

Hon. James Rodney Gilstrap
District Judge
Eastern District of Texas

Hon. Paul Singh Grewal
Magistrate Judge
Northern District of California

Hon. Andrew J. Guilford
District Judge
Central District of California

Hon. Kathleen M. O'Malley
Circuit Judge
Court of Appeals for the Federal Circuit

Hon. Jerome Simandle
Chief Judge
District of New Jersey

Hon. Leonard P. Stark
Chief Judge
District of Delaware

Hon. Ronald M. Whyte
Senior District Judge
Northern District of California

ADR ADVISORY BOARD

Hon. Garrett Brown
District Judge (ret.)
District of New Jersey

Hon. David Folsom
District Judge (ret.)
Eastern District of Texas

Hon. Faith S. Hochberg
District Judge (ret.)
District of New Jersey

Hon. James F. Holderman
District Judge (ret.)
Northern District of Illinois

Hon. Edward Infante
Magistrate Judge (ret.)
Northern District of California

ACADEMIC AND PRACTITIONER ADVISORY BOARD

Jared Bobrow
Weil, Gotshal & Manges LLP

Colleen Chien
Santa Clara University School of Law

Morgan Chu
Irell & Manella LLP

Dennis Crouch
University of Missouri School of Law

Robin Feldman
Harry & Lillian Hastings Professor of Law
UC Hastings College of the Law

John M. Golden
Loomer Family Professor in Law
University of Texas School of Law

Michael A. Jacobs
Morrison & Foerster LLP

Mark D. Janis
Robert A. Lucas Chair of Law
Maurer School of Law
Indiana University

William F. Lee
Wilmer Cutler Pickering Hale & Dorr LLP

Mark A. Lemley
William H. Neukom Professor of Law
Stanford Law School
Durie Tangri LLP

Sonal Mehta
Durie Tangri LLP

Robert P. Merges
Wilson, Sonsini, Goodrich & Rosati Professor of Law
University of California, Berkeley School of Law

Arti K. Rai
Elvin R. Latty Professor of Law
Duke Law School

Clement S. Roberts
Durie Tangri LLP

David L. Schwartz
Northwestern University School of Law

Ted Sichelman
University of San Diego School of Law

Chapter 1
Overview of the Patent System and General Principles for Effective Patent Case Management

District court judges have extensive experience managing a wide range of complex litigation. Furthermore, multivolume treatises and law review articles comprehensively examine the substance of patent law. This guide does not attempt to replace either body of wisdom. Rather, it systematically explains and analyzes the judicial management of patent litigation.

Patent cases present distinctive management challenges and thus can benefit from a comprehensive framework of principles and methods tailored to contemporary practices. In addition to featuring complex and dynamic technological facts to a degree rarely encountered in most other areas of litigation, patent cases employ unique procedures (such as claim-construction hearings) that affect and interact with other aspects of the case (such as summary judgment motions and expert reports) in a way that creates unusual scheduling and substantive complexity. They also often proceed in parallel with proceedings involving the same patented technology in other tribunals—including the Patent Trial and Appeal Board (PTAB), International Trade Commission (ITC), other district courts, and courts outside of the United States. Patent cases also frequently raise difficult discovery issues, including patent-specific privilege and waiver questions. The number of potentially dispositive issues (both legal and equitable) makes patent case management particularly challenging. Furthermore, the landscape of patent litigation evolves rapidly due to advances in technology, shifts in the law, and changes in business strategy. The Supreme Court has been especially active in hearing patent cases over the past decade. Congress has also been active in reforming patent law, especially as it relates to case management.

Several of the Supreme Court's recent decisions have substantially expanded district judges' discretion in managing patent cases. The Court's decision in *eBay Inc. v. MercExchange, LLC*, 547 U.S. 388 (2006), interpreted the Patent Act to afford district judges significant leeway in awarding equitable relief. The Court's decisions in *Bilski v. Kappos*, 561 U.S. 593 (2010), *Mayo Collaborative Services v. Prometheus Laboratories, Inc.*, 132 S. Ct. 1289 (2012), *Association for Molecular Pathology v. Myriad Genetics, Inc.*, 133 S. Ct. 2107 (2013), and *Alice Corp. Pty. Ltd. v. CLS Bank Internation-*

al, 134 S. Ct. 2347 (2014), reinvigorate doctrines limiting patent eligibility, which has produced a raft of early dispositive motions. The Court's decisions in *Octane Fitness LLC v. Icon Health & Fitness, Inc.*, 134 S. Ct. 1749 (2014), and *Highmark Inc. v. Allcare Health Management System, Inc.*, 134 S. Ct. 1744, 1749 (2014), afford district judges greater discretion in awarding attorney fees. In *Teva Pharmaceuticals USA, Inc. v. Sandoz, Inc.*, 135 S. Ct. 831 (2015), the Court held that patent claim construction can entail subsidiary factual findings, expanding the role for evidentiary hearings in the claim-construction process. Furthermore, recent Federal Circuit decisions have expanded district judges' gatekeeping role in limiting damage theories and evidence. *See Apple, Inc. v. Motorola, Inc.*, 757 F.3d 1286 (Fed. Cir. 2014); *Uniloc USA, Inc. v. Microsoft Corp.*, 632 F.3d 1292 (Fed. Cir. 2011). At the same time, the rapid rise in streamlined postgrant review proceedings, established by the America Invents Act of 2011 (AIA), as well as the AIA's misjoinder provision (§ 299) have posed new challenges for managing patent cases. The contours of these doctrinal and procedural shifts are still being fleshed out through case-by-case adjudication.

This guide seeks to assist district court judges in surmounting the distinctive challenges of managing patent litigation. It combines the collective experience of leading patent jurists and attorneys from hundreds of patent cases and scores of patent trials to balance the perspectives of both patent holders and accused infringers. The rich variety of cases and rapidly evolving patent ecosystem require broad knowledge of the available tools. Rather than present a formulaic approach, this treatise sets forth and explores a wide range of options for the most common issues. It provides guidance on which factors make particular options preferable in certain circumstances. It also includes draft orders and exemplar case-management documents to illustrate case-management tools and strategies. It emphasizes and places in perspective those issues of greatest importance to trial courts.

1.1 Overview of the Patent System

Before turning to the details of patent case management, it is worthwhile examining the history, purposes, institutions, and economic factors that undergird the patent system and patent litigation.

1.1.1 Origins and Purposes

The U.S. patent system grows out of the early English Statute of Monopolies (1623), which prohibited the Crown from arbitrarily issuing letters patent "to court favorites in goods or businesses" while authorizing grants of exclusive rights to the "working or making of any manner of new Manufacture." 21 Jam. 1, c. 3, §§ 1, 6 (1623); *see also Graham v. John Deere Co. of Kan. City*, 383 U.S. 1, 5 (1966). In so doing, the Statute of Monopolies promoted free-market competition while addressing the appropriability problem that plagues technology markets: the difficulty in recovering the costs of research and development (R&D) and earning a fair return on the inherently risky investments in innovation.

In a competitive marketplace without protection for technological advances, inventors and entrepreneurs can encounter difficulty profiting from R&D investments. To the extent that they succeed in building a better device, process, or composition of matter, competitors can often quickly imitate the innovation without bearing the upfront R&D costs. These competitors can then undercut the innovator's price, pushing the market-clearing price toward the marginal cost of production (without consideration of R&D costs). Thus, unless the inventor/entrepreneur can protect their R&D costs in another way—for example, through trade secrecy—the motivation to engage in R&D will be below the social optimum. Trade secrecy, however, will only succeed for the limited set of technological advances—such as some process inventions—that do not reveal their inventive insights in the product that is sold in the marketplace. In addition, trade secrets can be difficult to enforce. Once the secret leaks, those who learn it through other than improper means are free to compete. Furthermore, trade secrecy slows dissemination of knowledge, which is vital to technological progress. The Statute of Monopolies sought to counteract this dilemma and thereby promote technological progress by affording exclusive rights to "working or making of any manner of new Manufacture" for limited times in exchange for disclosure of inventions.

Drawing on this framework, the founders of the United States authorized Congress to enact laws "[t]o promote the Progress of Science and useful Arts, by securing for limited Times to Authors and Inventors, the exclusive Right to their respective Writings and Discoveries." U.S. Const. art. I, § 8, cl. 8. In the nation's first State of the Union address, President Washington urged the Congress to exercise this power:

> The advancement of agriculture, commerce, and manufactures, by all proper means, will not, I trust, need recommendation. But I cannot forbear intimating to you the expediency of giving effectual encouragement as well to the introduction of new and useful inventions from abroad, as to the exertions of skill and genius in producing them at home . . .

George Washington, State of the Union Address, Journal of the Senate, 1st Cong., 2d Sess. 5 to 8 (Jan. 8, 1790). Congress enacted the first patent law soon after the nation was formed, declaring that anyone who had "invented or discovered any useful art, manufacture, engine, machine, or device, or any improvement therein not before known or used" shall have "the sole and exclusive right and liberty of making, constructing, using and vending to others to be used" for a term not to exceed fourteen years. Patent Act of 1790, Ch. 7, 1 Stat. 109-112. Although revised by Congress on several occasions over the next two and a quarter centuries, this terse formulation has remained the core of the patent system. Court decisions stretching back to the nineteenth century form an important source of patent law even today, as reflected in the Supreme Court's decision in *Mayo Collaborative Services v. Prometheus Laboratories, Inc.*, 132 S. Ct. 1289, 1293 (2012) (drawing on *Le Roy v. Tatham*, 55 U.S. (14 How.) 156 (1853), and *O'Reilly v. Morse*, 56 U.S. 62 (1853) to address the scope of patentable subject matter).

Therefore, it is important to understand the principles and policies undergirding the patent system. The most basic of these is the constitutional purpose: "To Promote Progress of . . . useful Arts." Patent law represents an important exception to the free-market system on which the United States of America was built. The founders were skeptical of government-bestowed privileges and monopolies. However, they recognized that without protection against unauthorized imitation, many inventors would lack adequate incentives to invest their resources and labors in inventive activities because second-comers could easily imitate successful discoveries without incurring the risk and cost of innovation. Patent law was enacted to ensure that those who make significant inventive contributions receive a reward that is at least roughly commensurate with the costs and risks of inventive activity. As President Abraham Lincoln, the recipient of U.S. Patent No. 6,469 ("A Device for Buoying Vessels Over Shoals"), would later remark, "the patent system added the fuel of interest to the fire of genius." *See* Abraham Lincoln, *Lecture on Discoveries and Inventions, Jacksonville, Illinois (Feb. 11, 1859), in* Lincoln: Speeches and Writings 1859–1865 3, 1011 (Don E. Fehrenbacher ed., 1989). The "fuel of interest" connotes the financial investment needed to stoke inventors' imagination and experimentation.

The founders also believed the ultimate beneficiary of such efforts should be the public, and thus limited the duration of patents to roughly the amount of lead time necessary to recoup the inventor's investment. In effect, the original term of fourteen years, borrowed from the English patent system, was double the seven-year term of trade guild apprenticeships dating back to the Middle Ages. Various other doctrines—such as the nonobviousness standard, disclosure requirements, infringement tests, statutory and judge-made defenses, the patent misuse doctrine, and remedy provisions—seek to ensure that the reward to the patentee is not disproportionate to the contribution to the prior art and maximizes the net public benefit.

A related principle of patent law is the notion that the patent represents a bargain between the inventor and the public. The public affords the patentee exclusive rights to prevent others from making, using, or selling the invention in exchange for fully and forthrightly disclosing the invention. In this way, the public can practice the invention following the patent's expiration and learn from the knowledge disclosed even during the term of the patent. Thus, U.S. patent law requires a sufficient disclosure to ensure that the inventor "possessed" the claimed invention and to enable others to build or use it later. This quid pro quo serves to promote progress by spurring cumulative innovation—enabling subsequent inventors to stand on the shoulders of their predecessors.

This bargain encourages inventors to disclose their inventions, which promotes the advancement of scientific knowledge and follow-on improvements and invention. In a world without patent protection, innovators would keep more innovative activity secret to discourage free riders, at least temporarily, thus depriving the public of the benefit of disclosure, which can help spur further innovation. Even before a patent expires, pioneering inventors and competitors can seek patents on improvements of patented technologies. They might have to license underlying patents or wait for those patents to expire to enter the market, but the public nonetheless can potentially benefit from more rapid technological advances and diffusion of knowledge.

The patent system also seeks to provide the public (including potential competitors and inventors) adequate notice of the boundaries of patent claims so that they can pursue competing projects without undue fear of encroaching upon the patentee's exclusive rights. In some areas of technology, this principle is especially difficult to apply owing to the inherent ambiguity of language. Unlike the metes and bounds of real property deeds—which can be objectively assessed by trained land surveyors—patent claims rarely trace intangible rights boundaries with complete precision. Advances in technology further complicate the delineation of patent boundaries. Courts have long sought to balance the incentive and notice purposes of the patent law. Requirements of clear and definite claiming further the notice goal but complicate other areas of patent law—such as determining the standards for nonliteral infringement where the "doctrine of equivalents" serves as a fulcrum of the incentives/notice balance.

Applying these principles in a complex patent dispute can be a challenging task. This guide seeks to rationalize and systematize the process of managing patent cases. Although many aspects of the patent statute are technical, patent adjudication involves many doctrines that demand the exercise of discretion. These larger purposes of the patent system provide the touchstone for interpreting the Patent Act and applying many patent doctrines.

1.1.2 Evolution of the Patent System

The nation's first patent act, enacted during the first congressional session, set forth terse general standards for protection, duration, rights, and remedies, but few details. This original institutional structure of the U.S. patent system was, however, short-lived for several reasons. It called upon the Secretary of State (Thomas Jefferson), the Secretary for the Department of War, and the Attorney General to examine patents, which, in light of their other responsibilities, proved untenable. Second, inventors were displeased with the high and vague threshold for protection: that inventions be deemed "sufficiently useful and important."

As a result, in 1793, Congress struck the requirement that inventions be "sufficiently useful and important" and replaced the examination process with a registration system, leaving the evaluation of patentability entirely to the courts. The Patent Act of 1793 retained a terse standard for patentability: an inventor could patent "any new and useful art, machine, manufacture or composition of matter, or any new and useful improvement on any art, machine, manufacture or composition of matter, not known or used before the application." Patent Act of Feb. 21, 1793, ch. 11, § 1, 1 Stat. 318. The inventor was still required to provide a written description of the invention and the manner of use "in such full, clear and exact terms, as to distinguish the same from all other things before known, and to enable any person skilled in the art or science, of which it is a branch, or with which it is most nearly connected, to make, compound, and use the same." *See id.*, § 3.

The courts fleshed out this lean statute. In the early years, they filled its gaps with English case law. *See generally* Peter S. Menell, *The Mixed Heritage of Federal Intellectual Property Law and Ramifications for Statutory Interpretation, in* Intellectual

Property and the Common Law 70–71 (Shyam Balganesh ed., 2013). In 1818, Justice Story, who wrote forty patent law opinions between 1813 and 1845, issued a paper stating that "[t]he patent acts of the United States are, in a great degree, founded on the principles and usages which have grown out of the English statute on the same subject." *See* On the Patent Laws, 16 U.S. (3 Wheat.) App. 13-29 (1818) (quoted in Edward C. Walterscheid, *To Promote the Progress of Useful Arts: American Patent Law and Administration, 1787–1836 (Part 1)*, 79 J. Pat. & Trademark Off. Soc'y 61 (1997)); *see also* Frank D. Prager, *The Influence of Mr. Justice Story on American Patent Law*, 5 Am. J. of Leg. History 254 n.1 (1961). In his first patent law opinion, Justice Story, sitting as a circuit justice, distinguished between unpatentable elements of motion and "the modus operandi, the peculiar device or manner of producing any given effect." The opinion recognized an experimental use defense based on the inference that "it could never have been the intention of the legislature to punish a man, who constructed such a machine merely for philosophical experiments, or for the purpose of ascertaining the sufficiency of the machine to produce its described effects." *See Whittemore v. Cutter*, 29 F. Cas. 1120, 1121–24 (C.C. Mass. 1813). In 1817, he expanded on the meaning of "useful invention" and novelty. *See Bedford v. Hunt*, 3 F. Cas. 37, 37–39 No. 1217 (C.C.D. Mass. 1817). In 1829, Justice Story interpreted the novelty requirement of "not known or used before the application" to pertain only to knowledge or use "by the public." *See Pennock v. Dialogue*, 27 U.S. 1, 19 (1829).

The courts also established standards for disclosure, requiring that the patent document identify the patented invention with specificity and distinguish it from the prior art. *See Lowell v. Lewis*, 15 F. Cas. 1018, No. 8568 (C.C.D. Mass. 1817); *Evans v. Eaton*, 20 U.S. 356, 434–35 (1822). In the absence of an ex-ante examination system, the patent bar developed the patent claim to reduce the risk of an invalidity ruling and to establish infringement more easily. *See* J. Jonas Anderson & Peter S. Menell, *Informal Deference: A Historical, Empirical, and Normative Analysis of Patent Claim Construction*, 108 Nw. U. L. Rev. 1, 8–21 (2014) (tracing the history of patent claiming).

Nonetheless, the lack of an examination system eroded faith in the patent system due to the proliferation of "unrestrained and promiscuous grants of patent privileges." *See* John Ruggles, Select Committee Report on the State and Condition of the Patent Office, S. Doc. No. 24-338, at 4 (1836). The Senate Report Accompanying the Patent Act of 1836 lamented that "[a] considerable portion of all the patents granted are worthless and void, as conflicting with, and infringing upon one another," the country had become "flooded with patent monopolies, embarrassing to bona fide patentees, whose rights are thus invaded on all sides," and that the "interference and collision of patents and privileges" had produced ruinous vexatious litigation. *See* Senate Report Accompanying Senate Bill No. 239, 24th Cong., 1st Sess. (Apr. 28, 1836).[1] In response, the Patent Act of 1836 instituted examination in a newly consti-

1. Analogous complaints have been made during the past two decades in reaction to the proliferation of business method and software patents. *See* Dan L. Burk & Mark A. Lemley,

tuted Patent Office, codified claiming conventions that grew out of jurisprudence, and introduced other procedural and institutional reforms, but perpetuated the standards of the 1793 Act as interpreted by the courts. *See* Patent Act of July 4, 1836, ch. 357, 5 Stat. 117.

In the century following the 1836 Act, the Supreme Court and lower federal courts established and explicated many of the key patent law doctrines: non-obviousness (*Hotchkiss v. Greenwood*, 52 U.S. 248 (1850)), limitations on patentable subject matter (*Le Roy v. Tatham*, 55 U.S. (14 How.) 156 (1853); *O'Reilly v. Morse*, 56 U.S. 62 (1853)), written description (*O'Reilly v. Morse*, 56 U.S. 62 (1853)), the doctrine of equivalents (*Winans v. Denmead*, 56 U.S. 330 (1854)), the doctrine of abandonment, suppression, or concealment as a limitation on prior art (*Kendall v. Winsor*, 62 U.S. 322, 328 (1858)), the best mode requirement (*Magic Ruffle Co. v. Douglas*, 16 F. Cas. 394, 396–97, No. 8948 (C.C.S.D. N.Y. 1863)), contributory infringement (*Wallace v. Holmes*, 29 F. Cas. 74 (No. 17,100) (C.C. Conn. 1871); *Thomson-Houston Elec. Co. v. Ohio Brass Co.*, 80 F. 712 (6th Cir. 1897)), experimental use exception to the statutory bar (*Elizabeth v. Pavement Co.*, 97 U.S. 126 (1877)), and accidental anticipation doctrine (*Tilghman v. Proctor*, 102 U.S. 707 (1880)).

As the patent system changed the dynamics of competition, concerns about economic concentration grew, contributing to the development of antitrust law. *See* Sherman Act, July 2, 1890, ch. 647, 26 Stat. 209. Courts became more skeptical of patent protection. Toward the end of the nineteenth century, the courts seemed "to become keenly aware that a patent could be used to stifle competition [and] they became stingy with preliminary injunctions against infringement." *See* Lawrence M. Friedman, A History of American Law 380 (1973). In 1883, Justice Bradley observed that, although inventors of substantial discoveries "are worthy of all favor,"

> [i]t was never the object of those laws to grant a monopoly for every trifling device, every shadow of a shade of an idea, which would naturally and spontaneously occur to any skilled mechanic or operator in the ordinary progress of manufactures. Such an indiscriminate creation of exclusive privileges tends rather to obstruct than to stimulate invention. It creates a class of speculative schemers who make it their business to watch the advancing wave of improvement, and gather its foam in the form of patented monopolies, which enable them to lay a heavy tax upon the industry of the country, without contributing anything to the real advancement of the art. It embarrasses the honest pursuit of business with fears and apprehensions of concealed liens and unknown liabilities to lawsuits and vexatious accountings for profits made in good faith.

Atl. Works v. Brady, 107 U.S. (17 Otto) 192, 200 (1883). These concerns contributed to judicial development of the exhaustion doctrine (*Adams v. Burke*, 84 U.S. 453 (1873)), the enablement doctrine (*The Incandescent Lamp Patent*, 159 U.S. 465 (1895)), the patent-misuse doctrine (*Motion Picture Patents Co. v. Universal Film*

The Patent Crisis and How the Courts Can Solve It (2009); James Bessen & Michael J. Meurer, Patent Failure: How Judges, Bureaucrats and Lawyers Put Innovation at Risk (2008); Adam B. Jaffe & Josh Lerner, Innovation and Its Discontents (2004).

Mfg. Co., 243 U.S. 502 (1917)), the reverse doctrine of equivalents (*Westinghouse v. Boyden Power Brake Co.*, 170 U.S. 537 (1898)), laches (*Woodbridge v. United States*, 263 U.S. 50 (1923); *Webster Elec. Co. v. Splitdorf Elec. Co.*, 264 U.S. 463 (1924)), and the inequitable-conduct defense (*Keystone Driller Co. v. General Excavator Co.*, 290 U.S. 240 (1933); *Hazel-Atlas Glass Co. v. Hartford-Empire Co.*, 322 U.S. 238 (1944); *Precision Instrument Mfg. Co. v. Automotive Maint. Mach. Co.*, 324 U.S. 806 (1945)).

1.1.2.1 Patent Act of 1952

Modern patent law dates to 1952, *see* Patent Act of 1952, Pub. L. No. 82-593, ch. 950, 82d Cong., 2d Sess., 66 Stat. 792, when Congress codified patent law in Title 35 of the U.S. Code and responded to pressure to correct court decisions from the prior two decades substantially raising the inventiveness bar. *See* P.J. Federico, *Origins of Section 103*, 5 APLA Q.J. 87 (1977). The House report characterized codification as the "principal purpose" of the bill. *See* H.R. Rep. No. 82-1923, at 5 (1952). One leading treatise observes that "[v]ery ancient statutory language was thus carried over, in a conscious effort to preserve existing statutory interpretations." Carl Moy, Moy's Walker on Patents § 1:23 (4th ed. 2010).

Much of the 1952 Act restated provisions from prior law while integrating, codifying, and in a few instances altering judicial doctrines. The 1952 Act retained the 1793 Act's text governing patentable subject matter virtually verbatim. The only pertinent difference between the 1793 and 1952 provisions is the substitution of the word "process" for "art." This alteration was not intended to effect any substantive change or to supplant more than a century of jurisprudence interpreting "art." *See* Peter S. Menell, *Forty Years of Wondering in the Wilderness and No Closer to the Promised Land:* Bilski*'s Superficial Textualism and the Missed Opportunity to Return Patent Law to its Technology Mooring*, 63 Stan. L. Rev. 1289, 1296–97 (2011). Rather, it was to avoid confusion with other meanings of the word "art."

The House report noted two "major" changes to the substantive patent law: "incorporating a requirement for invention in § 103 and the judicial doctrine of contributory infringement in § 271." *See* H.R. Rep. No. 82-1923, at 5 (1952). During the 1930s and 40s, the Supreme Court substantially tightened the judicially developed nonobviousness standard to require a "flash of genius." *See Cuno Eng'g Corp. v. Automatic Devices Corp.*, 314 U.S. 84, 91 (1941); *see also Great Atl. & Pac. Tea Co. v. Supermarket Equip. Corp.*, 340 U.S. 147, 152 (1950). In response, Congress formally codified the nonobviousness requirement. "[T]he manner in which the invention was made," whether "from long toil and experimentation or from a flash of genius" is immaterial to its patentability. It lowered the bar to what courts before 1930 had previously recognized as the appropriate level. *See* § 103; H.R. Rep. No. 82-1923, at 7, 18 (1952).

Congress also codified judicially developed, indirect liability doctrines, although with some adjustment to partially blunt recent expansion in the judicially developed patent misuse doctrine. The legislative history notes that "[t]he doctrine of contributory infringement has been part of our law for about 80 years," but that "[c]onsiderable doubt and confusion as to [its] scope" has resulted from recent patent misuse cases. *See* H.R. Rep. No. 82-1923, at 9 (1952) (referring principally to *Mercoid Corp. v. Mid-Continent Inv. Co.*, 320 U.S. 661 (1944)). In response, Congress expressly recognized the contributory infringement cause of action while codifying an express exclusion for the sale of staple articles of commerce suitable for noninfringing use. *See id.*; § 271(c). The 1952 Act also expressly authorized the use of means-plus-function claims, although with limitations on their scope. *See* § 112, ¶ 3, 66 Stat. at 798 (now codified at § 112(f)) (overturning *Halliburton Oil Well Cementing Co. v. Walker*, 329 U.S. 1, 12 (1946), which barred functional claiming).

Although the Patent Act of 1952 simplified and fleshed out the patent law, it left many important doctrines free-floating in jurisprudence. Even after this codification, the formal patent law still contained no mention of limitations on patent eligibility (or patentable subject matter), the experimental use exception to the statutory bar, the accidental anticipation doctrine, the doctrine of equivalents, the reverse doctrine of equivalents, the experimental use defense, the exhaustion doctrine, the patent misuse doctrine, the inequitable conduct doctrine, laches, or equitable estoppel.

1.1.2.2 America Invents Act of 2011

The vast expansion of patenting in the 1990s generated significant concerns about patent quality, anticompetitive patent thickets, and so-called patent "trolls"—nonpracticing entities principally in the information technology fields that pursued patent-assertion strategies against start-up and established technology companies. In addition, Congress heard calls for addressing the large and growing backlog of patent applications and promoting international harmonization. Comprehensive studies by the Federal Trade Commission (FTC) and the National Academies of Sciences (NAS) recommended comprehensive reforms—from tightening the nonobviousness standard to raising the bar for obtaining injunctive relief, clarifying (and tightening) the willfulness standard, rationalizing the determination of patent damages, shifting to a first-to-file system, and better funding Patent Office operations. *See* A Patent System for the 21st Century (Stephen A. Merrill, Richard C. Levin & Mark B. Myers eds., 2004); Fed. Trade Comm'n, To Promote Innovation: The Proper Balance of Competition and Patent Law and Policy (2003).

Beginning in 2005, Congress took up these and other recommendations, such as expanding postgrant review and moving to a first-to-file system, but it struggled to find common ground amidst the cacophony of competing interest groups. One of the greatest challenges faced by policymakers is making laws and rules that are fair both in the context of industries where the commercial products involve a single patent or a very small number of patents (e.g., pharmaceuticals, agriculture, chemicals) and in the context of industries where a large number of patents are involved in a single commercial product (e.g., mobile devices, semiconductors, software).

As Congress struggled to find common ground and to balance divergent industry concerns, the Supreme Court and the Federal Circuit have addressed much of the reform agenda through statutory interpretation and crafting of judicially created doctrines. The Supreme Court tightened the standard for obtaining injunctive relief, *see eBay Inc. v. MercExchange, LLC*, 547 U.S. 388 (2006), and the nonobviousness requirement, *see KSR Int'l Co. v. Teleflex Inc.*, 550 U.S. 398 (2007). The Federal Circuit has raised the bars for proving reasonable royalty. *See Uniloc USA, Inc. v. Microsoft Corp.*, 632 F.3d 1292 (Fed. Cir. 2011); *Lucent Techs., Inc. v. Gateway, Inc.*, 580 F.3d 1301 (Fed. Cir. 2009).

Only after the courts had resolved the most controversial issues dividing interest groups was there sufficient consensus for Congress to pass the America Invents Act in September 2011, *see* Pub. L. No. 112-29, 125 Stat. 284, a far less ambitious set of substantive patent reforms than those originally recommended and reflected in earlier patent reform packages. Although touted as the most significant change in patent legislation since the 1952 Act, the AIA did not ultimately address many of the concerns voiced in the FTC and NAS reports. The AIA principally addressed administrative changes to the patent system: shifting to a modified first-to-file system (retaining a grace period for inventor disclosure) and implementing a postgrant review process. The former change largely harmonized U.S. novelty provisions with those in place in most other patent systems around the world, while retaining a one-year grace period for inventor publication. The latter change reorganized the Board of Patent Appeals and Interferences (BPAI) into the Patent Trial and Appeal Board (PTAB) and established several new administrative postgrant review proceedings—postgrant review, covered business method review (CBMR), *inter partes* review (IPR), and derivation proceedings—offering those challenging patents a streamlined, participatory, and relatively rapid means for obtaining review of issued patents by panels of three administrative patent judges. In contrast to the often slow *inter partes* reexamination process, IPRs must be completed within eighteen months of the filing of a petition.[2]

The AIA has dramatically altered the patent litigation landscape, although not in ways that were fully anticipated at the time of its enactment. In its first full year of operation, the PTAB received over 1,000 petitions. The PTAB instituted review in over 80% of these petitions, and invalidated many of the reviewed claims. *See* Brian J. Love & Shawn Ambwani, *Inter Partes Review: An Early Look at the Numbers*, 81 Univ. of Chi. L. Rev. Dialogue 93 (2014) (reporting that the PTAB invalidated all claims in 77.5% of the first 160 petitions instituted). In light of these statistics, many accused patent infringers have predictably pursued IPRs upon being sued in district court, leading to many requests to stay district court proceedings pending PTAB re-

2. The AIA also expanded the prior user right for "method[s] of doing or conducting business" to all inventive fields, although the standards for establishing the right are high. *See* § 273 (the defendant must show by "clear and convincing evidence" that it commercially used the technology at least one year prior to the earlier of the effective filing date of the claimed invention or the date on which the claimed invention was disclosed to the public in a manner that qualified for the § 102(b) grace period). Congress added this defense in response to the Federal Circuit's 1998 decision rejecting the long-standing business method exception to statutory subject matter. *See State St. Bank & Tr. Co. v. Signature Fin. Grp., Inc.*, 149 F.3d 1368, 1375 (Fed. Cir. 1998); First Inventor Defense Act of 1999, Pub. L. No. 106-113, 113 Stat. 1536 (1999).

view. Although the institution and invalidation rates have dropped since the first year of the PTAB's operation, they remain substantial.

The White House and the U.S. Patent and Trademark Office (USPTO) have also played a significant role in addressing perceived problems with the patent system through administrative action. The USPTO has, for example, implemented the Prioritized Examination Program, issued § 112 guidance documents, and pursued patent quality initiatives aimed at improving claim clarity.

1.1.2.3 Deciphering and Interpreting Patent Law

Throughout the nineteenth century and into the twentieth century, courts fleshed out the skeletal early patent statute. They patched statutory gaps, integrated constitutional, antitrust, and pragmatic limitations, and drew on tort and equity principles to effectuate the enforcement of rights. Reflecting the jurisprudential style of those eras and the influence of their common-law roots, character, and responsibilities, the most influential intellectual property jurists—including Justice Joseph Story, Justice Benjamin Robbins Curtis, and later Judge Learned Hand—operated in a less formal, more common-law-oriented mode. *See* William C. Robinson, The Law of Patents for Useful Inventions 15, n.3 (1890) ("Our patent acts have always depended upon common-law principles for their construction and until recently have been uniformly treated as a part of that great body of theoretical and practical jurisprudence. Patent law is as truly though not so extensively a matter of historical development as the law of real property, and can no more be beneficially administered as a mere statutory system inoperative except where verbally declared, than any other of those ancient branches of the law which we have inherited from our Anglo-Saxon ancestors."). Their objective was to bring logic, consistency, and balance to the patent and copyright systems. As a consequence, they did not typically tie their interpretation tightly to statutory text. Through a pragmatic process drawing upon statutory, constitutional, and experiential sources as well as common sense, they forged patent law into a workable, dynamic system.

These patterns persist in the contemporary patent system as courts continue to play a critical role in evolving the patent system. The most significant changes to U.S. patent law in response to the calls for patent reform during the past decade took place in the courts—through tightening of the nonobviousness standard, raising the threshold for equitable relief, and reining in reasonable royalty determinations. More generally, the courts have made subtle adjustments to better accommodate differences among the broad range of technologies governed by a unitary patent system.

Courts will continue to play a substantial and critical role in developing patent law. Key features of patent law emerged as terse formulations during the early republic and have evolved through symbiotic processes of judicial, common-law-type development and legislative codification, correction, and addition. The rapidity and unpredictability of technological change have buffeted courts with new challenges, and they have employed common-law tools and functional reasoning to evolve the intellectual property system. This institutional mechanism, in the face of Congress's limited ability to act expeditiously and lack of sustained focus, has enhanced the courts' substantive imprint on patent law. The courts are currently struggling with the scope of patentable subject matter, a critical issue for the patent system and patent case management on which Congress has notably been silent.

The mixed heritage of patent law has important ramifications for statutory interpretation. To effectuate patent law's purposes, courts should be mindful of the source of the doctrines in play—whether common law or statutory. *See* Menell, *The Mixed Heritage of Federal Intellectual Property Law and Ramifications for Statutory Interpretation*, at 87–88. In assessing the provenance of statutory provisions, courts should remain open to examining legislative history—especially with regard to codification statutes and other amendments intended to explain the nature and purpose of judicially developed and crafted doctrines.

1.1.3 Patent Institutions

The district courts play a vital role in both enforcing patents and reviewing the validity of patent grants. This role should be understood within the larger patent system, which comprises the USPTO, the Court of Appeals for the Federal Circuit, and the International Trade Commission. In addition to these government institutions, there is a growing private marketplace for patent assets, which increasingly affects litigation.

1.1.3.1 The Patent Office

The Patent Office originates in the Patent Act of 1836 which reinstituted patent examination and established a formal agency. The Patent Office developed procedures for patent examination. Funding came principally from examination fees. Congress added trademark registration to the agency's responsibilities in 1881.

The USPTO today is an agency of the U.S. Department of Commerce. Nonetheless, federal law affords the USPTO greater independence over its operations and finances than most other subcabinet agencies.

> The United States Patent and Trademark Office is established as an agency of the United States, within the Department of Commerce. In carrying out its functions, the United States Patent and Trademark Office shall be subject to the policy direction of the Secretary of Commerce, but otherwise shall retain responsibility for decisions regarding the management and administration of its operations and shall exercise independent control of its budget allocations and expenditures, personnel decisions and processes, procurements, and other administrative and management functions in accordance with this title and applicable provisions of law. Those operations designed to grant and issue patents and those operations which are designed to facilitate the registration of trademarks shall be treated as separate operating units within the Office.

35 U.S.C. § 1(a). The Department of Commerce retains principal authority over policy matters, such as legislative positions, regulatory actions, and positions taken in interagency discussions relating to court cases. These decision processes are gov-

erned by a complex set of agreements and precedents between the Department of Commerce, the USPTO, and the Office of Management and Budget.

The USPTO is headquartered in Alexandria, Virginia. It is in the process of establishing satellite offices in four locations: Dallas, Texas; Denver, Colorado; Detroit, Michigan; and San Jose, California.

The Patent Office's primary function remains patent examination. It employs 12,000 people, including approximately 9,000 patent examiners and over 200 administrative patent judges (APJs). Examiners and APJs have technical backgrounds. Examiners are assigned to "art units" within "technology centers" based on their educational background and experience. They do not typically have law degrees but receive training in the requirements for patentability and patent prosecution.

Inventors filed over 578,000 utility patent applications in 2014, up from 164,558 utility patent applications in 1990. The USPTO granted over 300,000 in 2014, up from approximately 90,000 in 1990. The USPTO also received over 35,000 design patent applications and 1,000 plant patent applications in 2014, up from 11,288 and 418 respectively in 1990.

Section 14.2 provides general background about patent prosecution. The average pendency time for a utility patent application is approximately three years from the time of filing, although the time can vary significantly across technology fields. The USPTO is working to reduce a backlog of over one million patent applications.

Upon final rejection of a patent application, the applicant can seek continuing examination or appeal by the Patent Trial and Appeal Board (PTAB). *See* § 14.2.1.3. In addition, the PTAB conducts several new administrative review proceedings discussed in §§ 1.1.2.2, 14.2.1.3, 14.2.5.8.

Under § 282 of the Patent Act, issued patents enjoy a presumption of validity. Thus, the alleged infringer in a patent enforcement action (or a declaratory relief plaintiff) bears the burden of proving invalidity by clear and convincing evidence. *See Microsoft Corp. v. i4i Ltd. P'ship*, 131 S. Ct. 2238 (2011); § 14.2.6.

1.1.3.2 The Court of Appeals for the Federal Circuit

The Court of Appeals for the Federal Circuit, sitting in Washington, D.C., has exclusive jurisdiction over appeals of patent rejections from the USPTO as well as all appeals of patent decisions by the U.S. district courts and the U.S. International Trade Commission. In the former capacity, the Federal Circuit inherited the responsibilities of the U.S. Court of Customs and Patent Appeals.

Congress established the Federal Circuit in 1982 to provide greater doctrinal consistency and stability by creating a unified, specialized appellate court. *See* Rochelle Dreyfuss, *The Federal Circuit: A Case Study in Specialized Courts*, 64 N.Y.U. L. Rev. 1 (1989). Prior to its creation, there was substantial variation among the circuit courts of appeal in their attitudes toward patentability and enforcement. This new institution has significantly increased the rate at which patents have been upheld and has generally expanded patent protection. *See* William M. Landes & Richard A. Posner, *An Empirical Analysis of the Patent Court*, 71 U. Chi. L. Rev. 111, 112 (2004). It has also greatly increased the velocity of patent jurisprudence, speeding the responsiveness of all institutions governing patent protection to perceived problems.

The Federal Circuit's activity and internal divisions, as well as the greater salience of the patent system, have often captured the Supreme Court's attention over the past fifteen years. Whereas patent cases hovered between 1 and 2% of the Supreme Court's docket during the latter half of the twentieth century, the rate jumped to 3% in the 2000–2010 period. Since 2010, it has risen to over 5%, approaching the highest levels in U.S. history.[3] In addition, Congress and the USPTO have become far more active in adapting the patent system during the past decade.

1.1.3.3 The International Trade Commission

In 1974, Congress expanded the authority of the ITC to exclude unfair imports to the United States. *See* 19 U.S.C. § 1337; § 14.6.2.1. During the past decade, the ITC has emerged as one of the most salient patent enforcement venues in the United States. Its fast-track procedures—typically producing determinations within sixteen months of initiation of an investigation—and potent exclusion remedy have attracted an increasing number of patentees. *See Spansion, Inc. v. Int'l Trade Comm'n*, 629 F.3d 1331, 1358–59 (Fed. Cir. 2010) (interpreting the legislative framework governing the ITC as making injunctive relief "the normal remedy for a Section 337 violation" without a showing of irreparable harm).

The ITC now conducts more full patent adjudications on an annual basis than any individual district court in the nation. Since 2010, the ITC has instituted approximately 50 patent investigations per year, of which about 45% settle prior to a decision. *See* U.S. International Trade Commission, USITC Section 337 Investigations—Facts and Trends Regarding Caseload and Parties (June 2014 Update), *available at* http://www.usitc.gov/press_room/documents/featured_news/337facts2014.pdf. Its Section 337 administrative law judges (ALJs) focus almost exclusively on patent investigations, making the ITC the nation's only specialized, trial-level, patent-adjudication forum.

1.1.3.4 The Marketplace for Patents and Patent Litigation

The past two decades have witnessed the emergence of robust markets for patents and patent dispute resolution. Following the burst of the dot-com information-technology bubble in the late 1990s, a raft of information technology patents came onto the open market through bankruptcy and other transactions. This fueled what has come to be known as the "patent troll" problem—the assertion of often-vague patents by nonpracticing entities. Start-up companies can be particularly vulnerable because they do not have the time to litigate or seek reexamination of dubious patents during the precarious early business development phase. As the litigation over smartphones heated up, major technology companies spent billions of dollars to arm

3. During the industrial revolution—from 1840 through 1900—patent cases constituted between 3% to 8% of the Supreme Court's docket.

themselves with defensive and offensive patent portfolios. This arms race has spurred patent acquisition strategies that strain the resources of the USPTO and ultimately fuel patent litigation.

These factors have produced a complex strategic matrix for technology companies and patent litigators. Patent strategy has become integrated with business and litigation strategy in many technology markets. In the lead-up to initial public offerings, start-ups must navigate a bewildering maze of patent claims. They are under great pressure to settle disputes. District courts increasingly find themselves at the center of multifront battles over the hottest technologies.

It is important for district judges to recognize that the litigation in their courtrooms can be but one front in a complex, competitive war. The parties typically weigh a host of strategic options: inter partes or covered business method review at the PTAB; an ITC investigation; declaratory relief; alternative dispute resolution; and relief from foreign tribunals. Understanding this larger battleground is critical to managing the litigation in their courtroom.

1.2 A Preliminary Note About Settlement of Patent Cases

Patent litigation is expensive. Each side can expect to spend several million dollars in fees through trial in the simplest, single-patent case. Litigation costs quickly spiral in more complex patent cases. The high cost reflects in part the high stakes involved. For most businesses, this potential risk, coupled with the unpredictability of juries deciding complex technical questions, means that exploring settlement should be an imperative. Indeed, like other litigation, the vast majority of patent cases (more than 95%) ultimately resolve before trial—most through settlement and just under 10% through summary judgment rulings. But the timing of settlement varies widely. Approximately 30% of patent cases resolve before any court actions; approximately half resolve early in case management; and approximately 15% during or after pretrial proceedings. *See* FTI Consulting, Intellectual Property Statistics (May 2008) (based on data gathered by the Administrative Office of the U.S. Courts). Table 1.1 shows the median cost of resolving patent cases through the end of discovery and trial.

Table 1.1
Median Patent Litigation Costs: 2013

Amount in Controversy	Through End of Discovery	Through End of Trial
Less than $1 million	$530,000	$970,000
$1 million to $25 million	$1,700,000	$2,800,000
Over $25 million	$3,600,000	$5,900,000

Source: American Intellectual Property Law Association, Report of Economic Survey (2013).

Thus, early resolution offers substantial savings to the parties and the court in terms of resources and time. What are the impediments to earlier resolution, and what part can the district judge play to encourage it? Although we address this issue in detail in § 2.6, it is worthwhile highlighting key considerations for the outset of patent litigation.

The first barrier to settlement may be the relationship of the parties. For example, if the patent holder is not an operating entity but only holds its patents for assertion against potential infringers, it risks only the patents-in-suit and the cost of the litigation and faces no possibility of field-leveling counterclaims. For the defendant company accustomed to resolving disputes with competitors through compromise, this asymmetrical situation can lead to standoff. Just as challenging for different reasons is the case involving head-to-head competitors for whom litigation may be an important element in their competitive strategies.

The most effective approaches to settlement, therefore, require judicial intervention, early and often. This typically begins at the first case-management conference, where the court can relieve counsel (or one of them) of their natural reluctance to address the issue. The court should make it clear that cooperation and frequent reports on settlement are just as important as other aspects of case management. The type of process (e.g., early neutral evaluation, outside mediation, magistrate judge conference) and date for completion of the first phase should be set at this stage. The court should express its willingness to order in-person attendance by appropriate executives. To the objection that discovery will have to come first, the court should make clear that any information reasonably necessary to assess each side's position should be exchanged promptly. To the objection that settlement cannot usefully proceed until the court has construed the asserted claims, the court should point out that uncertainty often drives settlement, and early discussions will likely hasten the settlement process.

The best time for settlement is often at the outset of litigation, before vast amounts of time and resources are expended and positions harden. Apart from that, mediation can be most effective (a) after some initial discovery (when each side has presumably learned more about the merits), (b) just after a pivotal event, such as a claim-construction order, or a ruling on a preliminary injunction request or on summary judgment motions, or (c) just before such a high-risk, pretrial event, or just before trial itself (keeping in mind Samuel Johnson's oft-quoted observation that "when a man knows he is to be hanged in a fortnight, it concentrates his mind wonderfully").

Table 2.7 provides a practical guide for managing the underlying dynamics and pertinent settlement issues in the most common types of patent disputes:

- competitor versus competitor (regarding core technology)
- competitor versus competitor (noncore technology)
- large enterprise versus start-up/new entrant
- licensing company versus large enterprise
- licensing company versus start-up enterprise
- pharmaceutical versus pharmaceutical

- patent owner versus first alleged infringer (serial litigant)
- pharmaceutical versus generic
- medical device industry
- preliminary injunction motion

Here is a summary of general ways a district court can effectively encourage settlement of patent litigation:

1. Make clear to counsel that settlement is a process, not an event, and that it is extremely important to the court.
2. Get the settlement process moving early, dealing with objections that might cause delay. Appoint a mediator with experience in resolving patent disputes (this does not necessarily mean a patent lawyer).
3. Require frequent reports on the status of settlement efforts, requiring multiple mediation sessions if necessary.

Chapter 2
Early Case Management

Without close management, patent cases can consume a vastly disproportionate amount of court and staff time. High stakes often result in extensive, contentious motion practice. Keys to success lie in the early establishment of a case schedule and procedures for streamlining resolution of common issues, as well as creative approaches to settlement. Discovery requires special attention; it is treated separately in Chapter 4. However, discovery challenges (anticipating and avoiding them) are connected with many of the pretrial issues confronted by district courts.

This chapter examines pretrial case management. We begin with a review of typical timelines and specialized local rules from jurisdictions that have found them useful in handling a large number of patent cases. For courts outside these districts, these approaches will be helpful in understanding the management choices available.

We then describe specific issues connected to pleadings, including jurisdiction and venue, standing, declaratory judgment, special patent defenses (such as inequitable conduct and assignor estoppel), and common associated claims such as antitrust violations. The initial case-management conference (CMC) will be addressed, with particular attention to scheduling choices and their consequences. We consider the multipatent "mega case," processes for identifying (and narrowing) infringement and invalidity contentions, and whether and how to schedule a *Markman* hearing to determine what the patent claims mean. We revisit the latter issues in detail in Chapter 5.

We cover some of the common early motions, such as a motion for stay pending review of the patent by the Patent Trial and Appeal Board (PTAB) at the U.S. Patent and Trademark Office (USPTO), motions to dismiss for subject-matter ineligibility (§ 101), and motions directed at managing the issue of willful infringement, which is frequently asserted and is a predicate for an award of enhanced damages and attorneys' fees. We also discuss the critical process of encouraging resolution through mediation.

2.1 Patent Litigation Timelines and Specialized Local Rules

A patent case is, in many senses, like any other case. The plaintiff files a complaint alleging infringement. The defendant answers, alleging noninfringement and asserting various defenses, and potentially makes counterclaims of its own. The parties proceed to fact and expert discovery, motion practice, pretrial briefing, and trial. As in any litigation, the time necessary for each pretrial phase varies with the complexity and potential consequences of the issues presented.

However, there are certain unique aspects of patent litigation, the management of which will significantly affect the pretrial timeline. Key among these are the complexity of the legal issues, the complexity and difficulty of the technology at issue, and the large volume of highly sensitive technical documents, source code, and other information exchanged during discovery. Courts have implemented various mechanisms to help manage these and other issues efficiently and effectively, including the specialized case assignment rules in Patent Pilot Program districts, nearly universal use of protective orders, and patent local rules designed to facilitate discovery and frame claim construction.

2.1.1 Case Assignment—Patent Pilot Program

Concern over the challenges in handling patent cases led Congress to pass legislation in 2011 establishing the Patent Pilot Program. *See* Pub. L. 111-349 124 Stat. 3674, 28 U.S.C. § 137 (2011). The legislation established a ten-year project designed to enhance specialization and expertise in adjudicating patent cases and reduce the cost of patent litigation. Under the legislation, the Administrative Office of the United States Courts (AOUSC) designated fourteen district courts to participate. To be eligible, a district had to be among the fifteen district courts in which the largest number of patent and plant-variety protection cases were filed in 2010, or be district courts that adopted or certified to the director of the AOUSC the intention to adopt local rules for patent and plant-variety protection cases. From among the eligible courts that volunteered for the pilot program, the director was required by statute to select three district courts with at least ten authorized district judgeships in which at least three judges have made a request to hear patent cases, and three district courts with fewer than ten authorized district judgeships in which at least two judges have made a request to hear patent cases.

Under the legislation, patent cases filed in Patent Pilot Program districts are initially randomly assigned to all district judges, regardless of whether they have been designated to hear such cases. A judge who is randomly assigned a patent case but is not among the designated judges may decline to accept the case. That case is then randomly assigned to one of the district judges designated to hear patent cases. The Judicial Conference Committee on Court Administration and Case Management helps to implement the pilot program. The committee encourages the pilot courts in the project to use their case assignment system to ensure fairness in the distribution of the court's workload and to provide for the assignments of additional civil cases to those judges who decline patent cases. Appendix 2.2 lists the districts participating in the Patent Pilot Program and the judges opting into the specialized pool.

In most districts, nondesignated judges have thirty days to reassign the case. The Western District of Pennsylvania and the Northern District of Texas give judges only seven days to decide whether to keep the case. *See* W.D. Penn. Misc. Order No. 11-283, ¶ 3; N.D. Tex. Special Order No. 3-287. The Southern District of California gives judges twenty-eight days to decide whether to keep the case. *See* S.D. Cal. General Order No. 598, ¶ 3. In the Northern District of California, judges must make a declination *before* the patent case would have been assigned. If the nondesignated judge declines the case, it is then randomly assigned to one of the designated patent judges.

The Northern District of California has adopted a general order to augment the assignment procedure for patent cases. In the Northern District, nonpatent judges are allowed to decline no more than three patent cases in any given year. *See* General Order No. 67, ¶ B(3). The Northern District has also taken the "position that the patent pilot statute does not supersede statutes that allow Magistrate Judges to handle any case pursuant to consent by the parties." *See Patent Pilot Program Becomes Active January 1, 2012, available at* http://www.cand.uscourts.gov/news/63. Accordingly, the Northern District has designated magistrate judges who have an interest in patent cases. The Eastern District of New York has taken a similar position and also designated magistrate judges for the program. *See EDNY Implements Patent Pilot Program, available at* https://img.nyed.uscourts.gov/files/local_rules/PatentPilotProject-NYEDPressRelease.pdf.

The enabling legislation requires the FJC to study the extent to which the pilot program develops judicial expertise and efficiency in handling patent cases, the speed with which patent cases are resolved, reversal rates, and forum shopping. The pilot program also provides judges in non-pilot-program districts with readily identifiable resources (in the form of local rules, standing orders, and pilot-program judges themselves) and with substantial expertise on which to draw for guidance in managing patent cases.

Since its inception in 2011, only about one-third of patent cases originally assigned to nonpatent judges in district courts were reassigned to judges participating in the program. Thus, many judges within Patent Pilot districts that are not assigned to the program choose to retain their patent cases, but the patterns vary across districts. Owing to the relatively low referral rate, the Southern District of Florida discontinued its participation in the Patent Pilot Program in 2014.

2.1.2 Protective Orders

Patent litigation frequently presents situations where a party's most important trade secret information is alleged to be relevant to the resolution of the case. This is true of both technical data, such as source code and records of product development, and business information, such as financial statements and underlying records of sales and profit calculation. In many cases, both parties' sensitive information may be at issue.

As a result, the start of meaningful discovery in a patent case almost always requires the entry of a protective order—or, at a minimum, temporary provisions ensuring the confidentiality of discovery materials until a final protective order can be entered. Protective orders prevent disclosure of highly sensitive technical, financial, licensing, or business strategy information both to the public and to the parties' competitive decision makers. Therefore, courts should require parties to address the propriety of an umbrella protective order at the initial case-management conference if the parties have not already taken up the issue on their own initiative (or pursuant to local rule). The complexity and sensitivity of information produced in discovery may result in a request for a multitiered protective order governing discovery, in which some information is available to the opposing party but restricted to use in the specific litigation ("confidential"), and other, more sensitive information is given only to counsel of record and approved experts ("highly confidential" or "attorneys only"). Such orders are fairly common, and although they can be said to interfere with counsel's ability to advise their clients effectively, this objection can be addressed in a more specific context when a party seeks permission to share particular information that had been designated attorneys-only. *See, e.g.*, *Solaia Tech. LLC v. Jefferson Smurfit Corp.*, 2002 WL 1964761, 2002 U.S. Dist. LEXIS 15666, at *1–2 (N.D. Ill. Aug. 20, 2002).

The advantages of an umbrella protective order are that it reduces the number of times that the court is asked to resolve confidentiality issues, and it allows the information to be provided to opposing counsel in the first instance. Thus, when one side wants to change the designation of a particular document or set of data (for example, in order to prepare certain client representatives in advance of a settlement conference), the dispute can be informed by reference to actual documents, rather than abstractions.

The court should enter a protective order as soon as possible in the case. Often, key documents will not be produced until a protective order is entered to protect their confidentiality. The potential for opposition to entry of a protective order also weighs in favor of handling it at the outset of a case. In some litigation, the further the case develops, the harder it is for the parties to agree to confidentiality provisions. For example, in *Beech-Nut Nutrition Corp. v. Gerber Prods. Co.*, plaintiff Beech-Nut and defendant Gerber had jointly filed a stipulated protective order that the court rejected as overbroad. *See* No. CIV-S-01-1920-GEB-PAN, slip op. at 5 (E.D. Cal. Nov. 18, 2003). Beech-Nut opposed Gerber's subsequent motion for a protective order, despite originally agreeing to the stipulated protective order. *Beech-Nut*, No. CIV-S-01-1920-GEB-PAN (E.D. Cal. Mar. 16, 2004), slip op. at 1. However the terms of a protective order are determined, it is good practice to ensure that the protective order is in place before fact discovery begins in earnest.

2.1.2.1 Default Protective Orders

Many district courts implement default protective orders to avoid delays in patent litigation. Others provide default orders that give the parties advance guidance about the norms regarding protective order provisions for that district or judge, and provide judges with a neutral set of provisions that can be implemented in cases where the parties cannot agree on a joint protective order. Appendix 2.4 provides a catalog of default protective orders as well as a selection of default provisions. These approaches vary in terms of their timing and substance.

2.1.2.1.1 Timing

As noted, some districts have default protective orders that take effect automatically at the outset of the case. The Northern District of Illinois is one example. This district's approach recognizes that confidentiality issues abound in patent litigation. It prevents disputes or inaction regarding the protective order from delaying discovery, in particular, the exchange of patent-related contentions that the local rules require. After the default order is entered, the parties may, either at the outset of the case or later, seek a revised protective order that is more tailored to their case. Because the local rules provide for automatic entry of the default protective order, the desire to negotiate a more tailored version is not a basis to delay the disclosure and discovery schedule that the local rules contemplate. N.D. Ill. PLR 1.4. The Northern District of California takes a similar approach, requiring that "[d]iscovery cannot be withheld on the basis of confidentiality absent Court order. The Protective Order authorized by the Northern District of California shall govern discovery unless the Court enters a different protective order." N.D. Cal. Patent L. R. 2-2.

Another approach is to require that, in the absence of a protective order, materials produced in discovery be treated as "outside attorneys' eyes only" materials until a protective order is entered. *See, e.g.*, D. Del. LR 26.2 ("If any documents are deemed confidential by the producing party and the parties have not stipulated to a confidentiality agreement, until such an agreement is in effect, disclosure shall be limited to members and employees of the firm of trial counsel who have entered an appearance and, where appropriate, have been admitted *pro hac vice*. Such persons are under an obligation to keep such documents confidential and to use them only for purposes of litigating the case.").

Some districts have prepared default protective orders but stop short of entering them automatically when a case is filed. For example, the District of Delaware has adopted a set of guidelines for the exchange of electronic discovery and a separate set of guidelines for the inspection of source code, which implicate many of the same issues as umbrella protective orders. *See* D. Del. Electronic Discovery Default Standard and Default Standard for Access to Source Code. Parties are thus free to craft their own case-specific orders, but can do so with a clear understanding of what is likely to be implemented if they cannot agree on joint provisions. The District of Minnesota has taken a similar but more comprehensive approach by providing a sample protective order for the parties to work from in crafting an order tailored to the needs of their case. *See* D. Minn. Form 5. Appendix 2.4 contains default protective orders from the Northern District of California, the Northern District of Illinois, and the District of Minnesota, as well as the source code guidelines from the District of Delaware. They collectively illustrate the nuances of handling confidentiality issues in patent cases.

2.1.2.1.2 Substance—Tier Structure

The Northern District of California's multitiered default protective order illustrates the model. It distinguishes among three tiers: (1) "Confidential" information (information that qualifies for protection under Federal Rule of Civil Procedure

26(c)); (2) "Highly Confidential — Attorneys' Eyes Only" information (information that is "extremely sensitive," disclosure of which "would create a substantial risk of serious harm that could not be avoided by less restrictive means"); and (3) "Highly Confidential — Source Code" information ("extremely sensitive" information "representing source code and associated comments and revision histories, formulas, engineering specifications, or schematics that define or otherwise describe in detail the algorithms or structure of software or hardware designs"). *See* N.D. Cal. Patent L.R. 2-2 Interim Model Protective Order. While "Confidential" information may be disclosed to parties and their representatives who sign an acknowledgment of the protective order, so long as it is used only for the purposes of litigation, "Highly Confidential—Attorneys' Eyes Only" information may be disclosed only to in-house attorneys who are not involved in competitive decision making and whose identities are disclosed in advance. *Id.* "Highly Confidential—Source Code" information is made available for inspection pursuant to a strict set of guidelines, rather than produced, and is restricted to the same two in-house attorneys, as well as outside counsel and approved experts. *Id.*

Other courts have adopted a two-tier approach that does not explicitly identify source code. For example, the Northern District of Illinois adopted a default order that includes "Confidential" information ("information concerning a person's business operations, processes, and technical and development information within the scope of Rule 26(c)(1)(G), the disclosure of which is likely to harm that person's competitive position, or the disclosure of which would contravene an obligation of confidentiality to a third person or to a Court") and "Highly Confidential" information ("information within the scope of Rule 26(c)(1)(G) that is current or future business or technical trade secrets and plans more sensitive or strategic than Confidential Information, the disclosure of which is likely to significantly harm that person's competitive position, or the disclosure of which would contravene an obligation of confidentiality to a third person or to a Court"). *See* N.D. Ill. LPR Appendix B. While "Confidential" information may be disclosed to in-house counsel, "Highly Confidential" information may not, absent a court order. *Id.* The District of Minnesota has adopted a similar approach. *See* D. Minn. Form 5.

These and other default protective orders illustrate how courts commonly address the exchange of highly sensitive business and technical information in patent cases. Although some courts have adopted mandatory, default, or suggested protective orders, most districts allow the parties to negotiate and jointly propose the text of a stipulated protective order that the court then enters. Since confidentiality concerns vary from case to case, the court should be open to customizing provisions of default protective orders. Party disagreements on the substance of the protective order are usually limited to a few provisions, although there is potential in some cases for asymmetric interests in protecting confidentiality (such as when only one party is actively bringing new products to market). Courts can resolve such disputes by discussing with the parties the types of information they expect to produce and the confidentiality concerns that flow from that production. The court can then craft its protective order to address those specific issues in each case.

2.1.2.1.3 Prosecution Bars

In situations where an attorney represents a party both in litigation and in front of the Patent and Trademark Office in prosecution or postgrant review proceedings, it may be appropriate to include a "prosecution bar" in the protective order. This provision limits the ability of those who have seen designated material to engage in prosecution activities for a certain amount of time. Section 4.2.6.3 provides a detailed analysis of the considerations bearing on prosecution bars.

2.1.3 Managing Claim Winnowing and Construction of Claim Terms

Patent claims play a central role in patent cases, as they establish and delineate the intellectual property. Every patent ends with one or more claims (*see* § 112(b); § 14.1.1.3) and it is not uncommon for patents to contain a dozen or more claims. Each claim can support a patent infringement cause of action. Patent cases can allege infringement of multiple patents and multiple claims within each patent.

Disputes over the scope of patent claims can also complicate patent litigation. Parties often dispute the interpretation of words or "terms" within the claims. Disputes can arise as to the meaning of scientific and technical terms as well as common terms (such as "the" or "a") within the context of the particular patent.

Early patent case management provides a critical opportunity to address both the number of patents and patent claims asserted and the scope of those claims. The former issue tends to arise most often in especially complex patent assertions, but there have been examples of single patents with more than a hundred claims that presented case-management challenges. Should the number of patents or patent claims present an issue, a plan for winnowing the range of asserted patent claims should be developed relatively early in the case. Section 2.1.3.1 addresses the key considerations in patent and claim winnowing while § 2.1.3.2 addresses the far more critical issue of patent claim construction. Table 2.1 summarizes the practical advantages and disadvantages of the most common approaches to claim winnowing and claim construction.

Table 2.1
Advantages and Disadvantages of the Most Common Approaches to Claim Winnowing and Claim Construction

Approach	Strategy	Advantages	Disadvantages
Limiting number of patent claims to be litigated	Phased winnowing of patent claims asserted.	Avoids complexity and duplicative claims.	May have to be revisited if unique issues as to liability or damages arise relating to claims that were removed.
Identification of disputed claim terms	Parties identify to each other claim terms to be construed.	May help narrow disputed terms.	Requirement to confer may extend time required for claim construction.

Approach	Strategy	Advantages	Disadvantages
Identification of proposed constructions and evidence	Parties identify to each other their proposed constructions along with the intrinsic and extrinsic evidence on which they intend to rely, then confer.	May help narrow disputed terms.	Requirement to confer may extend time required for claim construction.
Claim term selection criteria	Limiting the number of claim terms.	May help focus the parties on the terms most likely to be critical to decisions on the merits. In some cases, a phased approach may mitigate the disadvantages.	May result in some important disputes remaining unresolved, thereby decreasing the parties' ability to evaluate their probability of success (and thus hindering settlement) until late in the case. *See O2 Micro Int'l Ltd. v. Beyond Innovation Tech. Co.*, 521 F.3d 1351, 1360–61 (Fed. Cir. 2008) (holding that all material claim-construction disputes must be resolved by the court prior to submission of the case to the jury).
Submission of joint statement of proposed constructions	Parties submit a joint claim-construction statement providing (a) a list of stipulated constructions; (b) the proposed constructions of each side for the disputed terms; and (c) the intrinsic and extrinsic evidence on which they intend to rely.	Forces the parties to identify the key disputed issues and evaluate the strength of the evidence in advance of burdening the court with briefing. Reduces the number of times parties change claim-construction positions during the briefing process. Provides the court with a useful roadmap of the upcoming briefing.	Extra submission may extend time required for claim construction and, depending on the schedule and the spillover from fact discovery, may force the parties to take positions before they have fully considered the issues.
Limiting the number of prior art references	Phased winnowing of prior art references that may be asserted at trial.	Reduces the cost and complexity of litigation and trial.	May unduly impair defendants' ability to challenge patent validity.

Approach	Strategy	Advantages	Disadvantages
Briefing	(a) Page limits, (b) simultaneous opening and opposing briefing without replies.	(a) May help focus issues and force the parties to avoid extraneous material; (b) can reduce the time needed for claim construction; and (c) gives both parties an equal chance to have the last word in a situation where neither side is really properly considered the movant.	(a) May prevent the parties from providing sufficient context into how the dispute over the proper construction is expected to influence the ultimate disputed issues of infringement and validity; and (b) can result in opening briefs that do not squarely address each other (generally the result of inadequate meeting and conferring in an earlier stage).
Technical Tutorial	Court receives an in-person or submitted (on paper or through multimedia) presentation regarding the technology. Recording the tutorial is useful.	Provides the court with context to help make better decisions about the meaning of highly technical and possibly unfamiliar terms. Submitted or recorded tutorials can be provided to new judicial clerks, as patent cases usually outlast any individual clerk's tenure. In addition, a recorded tutorial can be part of the appellate record.	Increases the burden on the court. Tutorials can be expensive for parties to produce. The parties will likely present information in a way that favors their view about the proper framework for approaching the technical issues.

2.1.3.1 Patent and Claim Winnowing

Claim winnowing has emerged in a relatively small, but growing, subset of cases in which patentees assert a large raft of patents and/or patent claims. *See, e.g., Hearing Components, Inc. v. Shure, Inc.*, 2008 U.S. Dist. LEXIS 109230, 2008 WL 2485426, at *1 (E.D. Tex. June 13, 2008) (limiting plaintiff to three claims per asserted patent); *Fenster Family Patent Holdings, Inc. v. Siemens Med. Sols. USA, Inc.*, 2005 U.S. Dist. LEXIS 20788, 2005 WL 2304190, at *3 (D. Del. Sept. 20, 2005) (limiting plaintiff to ten patent claims and five asserted products). In one notoriously complex case, the patentee asserted 1,975 claims from more than a dozen patents against 165 defendants in 50 groups of related defendants. *See In re Katz Interactive Call Processing Pa-*

tent Litig., 639 F.3d 1303, 1309 (Fed. Cir. 2011). Many of the patents and patent claims substantially overlapped. The district court ordered the patentee to winnow the number of patent claims being asserted—initially requiring selection of no more than forty claims per defendant group, with further winnowing down to sixteen claims per defendant group following discovery, subject to various provisos. The Federal Circuit condoned this practice provided that the district court's method for requiring the patentee to select claims allowed the patentee the opportunity to add claims that presented unique issues as to liability or damages. *Id.* at 1312–13; *see also Stamps.com Inc. v. Endicia, Inc.*, 437 F. App'x 897, 902–03 (Fed. Cir. 2011) (district court did not abuse its discretion by limiting a patentee to fifteen claims because the limit was not "immutable."). Some courts require some limitation of the number of asserted patent claims prior to claim construction, with a further limitation required after claim construction and yet a further limitation before trial. This step-wise approach allows the plaintiff to refine its theories as the case progresses through discovery, claim construction, and dispositive motions.

In 2013, the Federal Circuit Advisory Council promulgated a broader framework for streamlining patent cases, reducing the complexity of patent cases, and reducing litigation costs. *See* Model Order Limiting Excess Patent Claims and Prior Art (Fed. Cir. Advisory Council, 2013) (contained in Appendix D). The Model Order, which reflects the recommendations of the Federal Circuit Advisory Council, but not necessarily the views of all members of the Federal Circuit, and is not binding on district courts, provides a framework for managing the number of claims litigated, the number of prior art references that are presented, the number of claim terms that may be construed, and the number of accused products at issue.

The Model Order provides a phased process for winnowing the number of asserted patent claims:

- "Not later than 40 days after the accused infringer is required to produce documents sufficient to show the operation of the accused instrumentalities, the patent claimant shall serve a Preliminary Election of Asserted Claims, which shall assert no more than ten claims from each patent and not more than a total of 32 claims."
- "Not later than 28 days after the Court issues its Claim Construction Order, the patent claimant shall serve a Final Election of Asserted Claims, which shall identify no more than five asserted claims per patent from among the ten previously identified claims and no more than a total of 16 claims."

Model Order Limiting Excess Patent Claims and Prior Art §§ 2, 3 (Fed. Cir. Advisory Council, 2013) (contained in Appendix D).[1] The Model Order encourages parties to discuss lower limits based on "case-specific factors such as commonality among asserted patents, the number and diversity of accused products, the complexity of the technology, the complexity of the patent claims, and the complexity and number

1. The Model Order relaxes these limitations when only one patent is asserted, increasing the per-patent limits "by 50%, rounding up." Model Order Limiting Excess Patent Claims and Prior Art § 4 (Fed. Cir. Advisory Council, 2013).

of other issues in the case that will be presented to the judge and/or jury. In general, the more patents that are in the case, the lower the per-patent limits should be. The parties shall jointly submit any proposed modifications in their Federal Rule of Civil Procedure 26(f) Discovery Plan." *See id.* at n.1.

Not every patent case will need this formal, phased procedure to winnow its claims. However, for complex cases, the Model Order provides a framework to adapt to the circumstances of the particular case.

2.1.3.2 Claim Construction

Construing patent claim terms has long been a key aspect of patent litigation and arises in almost every patent case. Since the mid-1990s, a growing number of courts have opted to construe patent claim terms prior to trial. This was a reaction to the rise of jury trials to resolve patent cases in the 1980s, which created a problem for the district judge and Federal Circuit in reviewing a jury's determination. The scope of patent claims was often shrouded in the secrecy of jury deliberations. The district judge and the Federal Circuit had little basis on which to assess the jury's construction of patent claims.

The Supreme Court's seminal decision in *Markman v. Westview Instruments, Inc.*, 517 U.S. 370, 391 (1996), took claim construction out of the jury's hands and put the responsibility squarely on the district judge to construe patent claim terms. More recently, *Teva Pharmaceuticals USA, Inc. v. Sandoz, Inc.*, 135 S. Ct. 831 (2015), not only confirmed that district courts were authorized to resolve subsidiary factual issues underlying claim construction, but held that such findings of fact should be upheld unless they are clearly erroneous.

Given this allocation of decision-making authority, it often makes sense for the district judge to construe the patent claim terms significantly in advance of trial, for several reasons. This practice enables the parties to understand the key issues for trial more thoroughly and can guide the preparation of expert reports. In addition, claim construction can provide the basis for summary judgment, potentially simplifying or resolving the case. Early claim construction also enables the court and the parties to begin to prepare jury instructions.

We explore the early case-management aspects of claim construction in this chapter. Chapter 5 focuses on substantive issues relating to claim construction as well as the conduct of the hearing.

To structure and facilitate the claim-construction process, more than thirty districts have adopted patent local rules (PLRs) setting forth a standardized timeline and framework for disclosures and submissions leading up to a claim-construction or "*Markman*" hearing. Appendix D lists, and links to, these local rules as well as exemplars. While the specific timing, sequence, and content of disclosures and submissions vary among districts, patent local rules share a basic principle—they seek to present the court with a limited set of actual and meaningful disputes. *See generally* James Ware & Brian Davy, *The History, Content, Application and Influence of the Northern District of California's Patent Local Rules*, 25 Santa Clara Comp. & High Tech. L.J. 965 (2009) (providing a detailed account of the evolution of the Northern

District of California's patent local rules, the first and most influential local rule initiative).

The impetus for PLRs was a clash between the liberal notice pleading policy[2] underlying the Federal Rules of Civil Procedure and the need for patent litigants to receive more specific notice of the issues they were litigating. *See, e.g.*, *O2 Micro Int'l Ltd. v. Monolithic Power Sys.*, 467 F.3d 1355, 1365–66 (Fed. Cir. 2006). The plaintiff has not traditionally been required to specify which claims are infringed. Nor has the plaintiff needed to plead its theory of the meaning of the claim terms and the features of the defendant's products that are alleged to infringe. Because a plaintiff may assert infringement of multiple claims in multiple patents, a defendant reading a notice pleading complaint is typically left to guess the boundaries of a plaintiff's case and the available defenses.

A patent plaintiff reading a notice pleading answer and counterclaim is equally in the dark about the substance of the defendant's case. The defendant, for example, need not identify the prior art on which its invalidity defense relies. Nor does the defendant have to plead its theories of claim construction or which combinations of prior art references might invalidate each of the claims. Only the defense of unenforceability due to inequitable conduct in the procurement of the patent must be pled with particularity because it is viewed as a species of fraud. *See Exergen Corp. v. Wal-Mart Stores, Inc.*, 575 F.3d 1312, 1329 (Fed. Cir. 2009); *but cf.* D.N.H. SPR 2.1(a) (requiring any complaint (or counterclaim) for patent infringement to contain a list of all accused products or processes and at least one illustrative asserted patent claim (per asserted patent) for each product or process).

Initial disclosures required under Federal Rule of Civil Procedure 26 do not alleviate this problem. Implementing routine discovery procedures such as service of contention interrogatories or expert discovery could ultimately provide the necessary information. However, contention interrogatories are often not required to be meaningfully answered until the late stages of discovery. And expert discovery is most efficiently conducted after fact discovery makes it possible to narrow the issues.

As a result, absent forced, early substantive disclosure, patent litigants have been known to engage in a "shifting sands" approach to litigation based on "vexatious shuffling of positions." *See LG Elecs., Inc. v. Q-Lity Computer, Inc.*, 211 F.R.D. 360, 367 (N.D. Cal. 2002). Litigants may offer initial, substantially hedged, theories of infringement or invalidity, only to change those theories later by asserting different patent claims, different prior art, or different claim constructions, if their initial positions founder. Resulting extensions of fact and expert discovery can unduly prolong the litigation, unnecessarily sapping the court's and the parties' resources.

PLRs were developed to facilitate efficient discovery by requiring patent litigants to promptly disclose relatively specific bases underlying their claims. By requiring parties to disclose contentions in an orderly, sequenced manner, PLRs counter the

---

2. Note that changes to the Federal Rules of Civil Procedure, including the abolition of Rule 84 and the Appendix of Forms (including Form 18, the form patent infringement complaint), that took effect on December 1, 2015, will reduce this tension.

"shifting sands" tendencies. Neither litigant can engage in a strategic game of saying it will not disclose its contentions until the other side reveals its arguments. In discussing the Northern District of California's PLRs, the Federal Circuit explained that they are designed to require

> both the plaintiff and the defendant in patent cases to provide early notice of their infringement and invalidity contentions, and to proceed with diligence in amending those contentions when new information comes to light in the course of discovery. The rules thus seek to balance the right to develop new information in discovery with the need for certainty as to the legal theories.

O2 Micro, 467 F.3d at 1365–66; *see also Nova Measuring Instruments Ltd. v. Nanometrics, Inc.*, 417 F. Supp. 2d 1121, 1123 (N.D. Cal. 2006) ("The [patent local] rules are designed to require parties to crystallize their theories of the case early in the litigation and to adhere to those theories once they have been disclosed.").

PLRs adopted by a district, or by an individual judge as a standing order or a case-specific order, supplement the Federal Rules of Civil Procedure. Courts may modify the procedures dictated by PLRs as necessary to suit the issues presented in a particular case. *See, e.g.*, N.D. Cal. Patent L.R. 1.2. All modifications, as well as the rules or standing orders, must, of course, be consistent with Federal Circuit case law to the extent an issue "pertains to or is unique to patent law." *See O2 Micro*, 467 F.3d at 1364 (citing *Sulzer Textil A.G. v. Picanol N.V.*, 358 F.3d 1356, 1363 (Fed. Cir. 2004)). For example, Federal Circuit law was applied in cases addressing whether claim charts exchanged by parties pursuant to PLRs could be amended to add new statutory bases for invalidity and infringement. *See, e.g., Genentech, Inc. v. Amgen, Inc.*, 289 F.3d 761, 774 (Fed. Cir. 2002); *Advanced Cardiovascular Sys., Inc. v. Medtronic, Inc.*, 265 F.3d 1294, 1303 (Fed. Cir. 2001). In these situations, the Federal Circuit held that the sufficiency of notice regarding defenses or theories of liability under specific statutory provisions of patent law "clearly implicat[ed] the jurisprudential responsibilities of this court within its exclusive jurisdiction." *Advanced Cardiovascular*, 265 F.3d at 1303; *see also In re Spalding Sports Worldwide, Inc.*, 203 F.3d 800, 803–04 (Fed. Cir. 2000) (applying Federal Circuit law to a question of attorney–client privilege between patentee and patent attorney).

PLRs promote efficient case management by requiring the patentee to disclose the basis for its infringement contention and the accused infringer to disclose the basis for patent invalidity defense relatively early in the litigation process. In addition to advancing the claim-construction process, these disclosures set natural boundaries for discovery. They encourage settlement by providing parties with a reliable look at the specific accusations being presented and the evidence supporting them. In addition, some districts establish presumptive limits on the number of claim terms that will be construed to focus the litigation and streamline case management.

It should be noted that PLRs are merely presumptive and not mandatory. Judges in PLR districts retain authority to vary the rules to accommodate distinctive challenges or opportunities posed by particular cases. *See* N.D. Cal. Patent L.R. 1-3 ("The Court may modify the obligations or deadlines set forth in these Patent Local Rules based on the circumstances of any particular case, including, without limitation, the simplicity or complexity of the case as shown by the patents, claims, products, or parties involved. Such modifications shall, in most cases, be made at the initial case-management conference, but may be made at other times upon a showing of good cause."). Experience has shown that attorneys in districts with PLRs generally appreciate the balance and clarity that the rules provide. As a result, modification requests are relatively rare. In fact, attorneys familiar with such rules often propose similar parameters for managing cases in districts without formal PLRs.

Table 2.2 depicts a typical timeline for a patent case utilizing patent-specific initial disclosures, a structured claim-construction briefing process including a joint claim-construction statement, and a *Markman* hearing. The process depicted here is consistent with the requirements of local patent rules in districts such as the Northern District of California and the Eastern District of Texas.[3]

Table 2.2
Patent Local Rules Timetable,
Northern District of California

(1) Case-Management Conference	Set by Court	Patent Local Rule
(2) Disclosure of Asserted Claims and Infringement Contentions	Within 10 days of (1)	3-1 & 3-2
(3) Invalidity Contentions	Within 45 days of (2)	3-3 & 3-4
(4) Identify Claim Terms to be Construed	Within 10 days of (3)	4-1
(5) Preliminary Claim Constructions	Within 20 days of (4)	4-2
(6) Joint Claim-Construction Statement	Within 60 days of (3)	4-3
(7) Close of Claim-Construction Discovery	Within 30 days of (6)	4-4
(8) Opening Claim-Construction Brief	Within 45 days of (6)	4-5(a)
(9) Responsive Claim-Construction Brief	Within 14 days of (8)	4-5(b)
(10) Reply Claim-Construction Brief	Within 7 days of (9)	4-5(c)
(11) *Markman* Hearing	Within 14 days of (10)	4-6
(12) Claim-Construction Order	TBD by Court	N/A
(13) Produce Advice of Counsel, if any	Within 50 days of (12)	3-7

3. In March 2008, the PLRs for the Northern District of California were amended in two important respects, which are reflected in the text and table in this section. First, the concept of "preliminary" contentions has been eliminated in favor of reliance on the traditional practice of allowing amendments only for good cause. Second, in designating claim terms for construction, the parties are limited to ten terms, absent leave of court.

An accelerated timeline may be appropriate for less complex cases, for example where the technology is simple, or there is little dispute as to the structure, function, or operation of accused devices. Under a particularly streamlined plan, the parties would not make patent-specific initial disclosures or file joint claim-construction statements. The court might also forgo a *Markman* hearing and address claim construction as part of summary judgment. Table 2.3 provides an example of such a timeline. The decision to adopt an accelerated timeline is best made after discussing the substantive issues that will drive the case with the parties. *See* § 2.5; General Order 14-3 (E.D. Tex. Feb. 25, 2014) (creating a "Track B" accelerated discovery schedule for patent infringement suits in the Eastern District of Texas where the parties jointly agree such a schedule would be beneficial).

Table 2.3

Accelerated Patent Case-Management Timeline

(1) Case-Management Conference	Set by court
(2) Produce Opinion of Counsel, if any	Within 2 months after CMC
(3) Close of Fact Discovery	5 months after CMC
(4) Close of Expert Discovery	2 months after (3)
(5) Opening Briefs on Claim Construction and Summary Judgment	Within 30 days of (4)
(6) Responsive Briefs on Claim Construction and Summary Judgment	Within 14 days of (5)
(7) Reply Briefs on Claim Construction and Summary Judgment	Within 7 days of (6)
(8) Claim-Construction and Summary Judgment Hearing	Within 14 days of (7)
(9) Claim-Construction and Summary Judgment Order	TBD by court

Some districts, including several with substantial patent dockets (most notably Delaware,[4] Eastern Virginia, and Western Wisconsin), have not established a district-wide, rules-based approach to contention and claim-construction discovery. Instead, they address these issues on a judge-specific basis or through standard written discovery. The feasibility of the standard written discovery approach is improved when the court conducts claim construction after the close of fact discovery because both contentions and supporting evidence provided in interrogatory responses are often updated through the end of (and, at times, after) the fact discovery period.

4. Chief Judge Stark (D. Del.) has issued standardized procedures for managing patent cases, form scheduling order, and case-management checklists that parallel and go beyond district-wide patent local rules. Appendix 2.2 contains these documents.

Where a court intends to conduct claim construction earlier in the case (which might be especially advantageous where construction of a claim term could be case dispositive, *see* § 5.1.1), a court in a district that does not have patent local rules should nonetheless require the parties to exchange their burden-of-proof contentions, their claim-construction positions, and their supporting evidence well in advance of the claim-construction briefing.

2.1.3.2.1 Winnowing Claim Terms

As is more fully explored in § 5.1.2.1.3, district courts have wide discretion to limit the number of claim terms at issue, at least provisionally. Restricting the scope of the *Markman* hearing focuses the court's attention on the key issues (which may dispose of the case) and allows a more prompt and well-reasoned ruling on the central matters in the case. A substantial body of experience has shown that allowing the parties wide discretion to brief all claim terms that are potentially at issue invites false or inconsequential disputes. Parties reflexively seek to avoid the risk of a waiver finding, if they refrain from raising peripheral disputes.

To focus patent litigation on the most salient issues, a growing number of courts have established a presumptive limit on the number of claim terms—typically ten—that will be presented at the *Markman* hearing. Some districts have revised their PLRs to require the parties to jointly identify ten terms "likely to be most significant to resolving the parties' dispute, including those terms for which construction may be case or claim dispositive." *See* N.D. Cal. Patent L.R. 1.2; *see also* N.D. Ill. LPR 4.1(b) (requiring parties to limit terms submitted for construction to ten, absent a showing of good cause). The default ten-term limit can be increased or decreased depending on the circumstances of the case. In addition, some courts require parties to explain *why* particular terms are case-dispositive or otherwise significant so as to provide the court with context for the claim-construction dispute as well as the basis for deciding whether early construction of particular claim terms is warranted. *See, e.g.*, Magistrate Judge John D. Love (E.D. Tex.), Standing Order Regarding Letter Brief and Briefing Procedures for Early *Markman* Hearing/Summary Judgment of Noninfringement Requests, http://www.txed.uscourts.gov/cgi-bin/view_document.cgi?document=21674.

The ten-term limit does not fix the total number of terms that can be construed before trial. Parties can seek to construe additional terms at later phases in the case. However, for purposes of the principal *Markman* hearing, selecting the most significant terms allows courts to resolve the key disputes in the case most efficiently.

2.1.3.2.2 Claim-Construction Briefing and Oral Argument

Most district courts routinely utilize a *Markman* briefing coupled with a hearing, which typically consists of an argument of counsel and may include witness testimony, although this has been rare. Other courts do not hold a *Markman* hearing unless they determine from briefing that it would be helpful, such as when the experts sharply diverge on the perspective of a person of ordinary skill in the art. Many courts find it useful to have the parties first present a technology tutorial that sets the stage for the arguments that follow. Some courts will let the relevant claim terms emerge in briefing. Others do more to encourage the parties to reach agreement in advance on a set of disputed terms, for example, by requiring submission of joint claim-construction statements. *See* N.D. Cal. Patent L.R. 4-3. A district judge has broad discretion to manage the claim-construction process, which is reflected in the variety of mechanisms that courts have used. A court's decisions about claim timing and process should, however, consider the interrelation of claim construction with other aspects of the pretrial process, particularly discovery, summary judgment, and settlement.

The Supreme Court's decision in *Teva Pharmaceuticals USA, Inc. v. Sandoz, Inc.*, 135 S. Ct. 831 (2015), expressly recognizes that district courts might engage in fact-finding during claim construction and that the *Markman* process might involve evidentiary hearings and expert declarations. *See* J. Jonas Anderson & Peter S. Menell, *Restoring the Fact/Law Distinction in Patent Claim Construction*, 109 Nw. U. L. Rev. Online 185 (2015). Appreciating the ramifications of the *Teva* decision requires understanding the perspective from which patent claims are interpreted and the Federal Circuit's past application of the *Markman* decision.

> Courts interpret patent claims from the perspective of persons having ordinary skill in the art as of the time of the invention. *See Multiform Desiccants, Inc. v. Medzam, Ltd.*, 133 F.3d 1473, 1477 (Fed. Cir. 1998). Since few judges have such training and knowledge, they must step into the shoes of skilled artisans. As Professor William Callyhan Robinson explained more than a century ago, the court may look to: [T]estimony to explain the meaning of its language, or to expert evidence to ascertain the essential characteristics of the described invention and the differences between it and other patented inventions, or to papers in the Patent Office which are connected with the patent . . . to show the significance which [the inventor] attached to the terms.

3 William C. Robinson, The Law of Patents for Useful Inventions 248 (1890). In its *Markman* decision, the Supreme Court recognized the mixed fact/law character of claim construction. *See Markman*, 517 U.S. at 389–90 (characterizing claim construction as a "mongrel practice").

Yet following the *Markman* decision, the Federal Circuit heavily discounted the use of extrinsic evidence, warning that "[a]llowing the public record to be altered or changed by extrinsic evidence introduced at trial, such as expert testimony, would make this right meaningless." *Vitronics Corp. v. Conceptronic, Inc.*, 90 F.3d 1576, 1583 (Fed. Cir. 1996). The Federal Circuit reinforced that holding in ruling, en banc, that claim construction is a pure question of law. *Cybor Corp. v. FAS Techs., Inc.*, 138 F.3d 1448 (Fed. Cir. 1998) (en banc); *Lighting Ballast Control LLC v. Philips Elecs. N. Am. Corp.*, 744 F.3d 1272 (Fed. Cir. 2014) (en banc).

In overruling these decisions, the Supreme Court restored the fundamental principle, reflected in Federal Rule of Civil Procedure 52(a)(6), that courts of appeals uphold a district court's findings of fact unless they are clearly erroneous. *See Teva*, 135 S. Ct. at 835–38. As a result, district courts now have greater leeway to use traditional evidentiary techniques to determine how persons skilled in the technical arts relating to the claimed invention would have understood the claim terms at the time the invention was made. In the wake of the *Vitronics* and *Cybor* decisions, district courts avoided such evidentiary processes. Now, after *Teva*, district courts have leeway to use evidentiary hearings and other fact-finding techniques to resolve disputes as to how skilled artisans would have understood a claim term within the context of the patent at the time the invention was made.

It will be important, however, to recognize the primacy of the intrinsic evidence—the patent document and the prosecution history—in construing patent claims for two reasons. First, the Supreme Court emphasized that the intrinsic evidence overrides extrinsic evidence where the two diverge. This is consistent with the Federal Circuit's en banc decision in *Phillips*, which held that intrinsic evidence takes precedence over extrinsic evidence and dictionaries. *See Phillips v. AWH Corp.*, 415 F.3d 1303 (Fed. Cir. 2005) (en banc); § 5.2.2. Second, opening up the *Markman* process to evidentiary hearings whenever a party offers expert testimony could greatly complicate claim construction and waste resources.

Building on its *Markman* framework, the Supreme Court's *Teva* decision endorses a hybrid standard: factual determinations underlying claim-construction rulings are subject to the "clearly erroneous" (or "abuse of discretion") standard of review, while the Federal Circuit exercises de novo review over the ultimate claim-construction decision. In this manner, district judges can use their distinctive vantage point and evidentiary tools to ferret out factual underpinnings while the Federal Circuit can operate as a check on fidelity to the patent instrument. Therefore, even though the Federal Circuit retains de novo review of whether a trial court's construction of a patent claim comports with the intrinsic evidence, the appellate court must nonetheless sustain the trial court's subsidiary factual findings unless clearly erroneous. In cases where it is necessary to go beyond the intrinsic evidence to interpret claim meaning, the district court's resolution, if adequately grounded in extrinsic evidence, will control.

Where the court determines that a claim term warrants construction and subsidiary fact-finding would be valuable, the court should: (1) seek to delineate the disputed subsidiary factual questions prior to the *Markman* proceeding, (2) conduct focused briefing with supporting expert declarations and evidentiary hearings to create an adequate record for resolving such disputes, and (3) prepare a careful *Markman* order explaining the basis for their claim construction.

As noted above, the *Teva* framework presents the risk of greater cost and delay as parties engage in escalating battles of the experts. Such problems, however, are not unique to patent adjudication, although the technological complexity of patent cases creates greater opportunity for such tactics. District judges must not lose sight of intrinsic evidence's central role in claim construction, and must exercise due caution in entertaining extrinsic evidence.

It is important to recognize that parties dispute the construction of a variety of types of claim terms. Experience has shown that many of the disputed terms that are appealed to the Federal Circuit are not technical or scientific terms, but common terms whose meaning becomes disputed within the context of the particular patent claim.

Scientists and engineers usually have relatively clear understandings of many scientific or technical terms as used in their fields, even though such terms may be beyond a district judge's general experience. Scientists or engineers who take unjustified positions, particularly with respect to common terms, risk that federal judges will impugn their credibility. Since *Markman* testimony would not occur before a jury, district judges have substantial leeway to press the experts to clarify their positions. Over time, this possibility should help district judges understand any technical issues that underlie the parties' contentions and better determine whether the correct construction is one party's proposal, the other's, or neither party's.

The *Teva* decision arguably places a greater onus on district judges to understand and explain how they parse claim language. The decision affords them greater flexibility to use familiar tools for resolving factual disputes—presentation of evidence and expert testimony. At the same time, it may demand that they show how disputed subsidiary facts relate to the intrinsic evidence. Ultimately, this framework should add to the reliability of the dispute resolution process by bringing better evidence, more scrutiny, and fuller explication to bear on claim construction.

2.1.3.2.3 Claim Construction and Discovery

2.1.3.2.3.1 Discovery Prior to Claim Construction

As Chapter 5 explores more thoroughly, claim construction is based on the patent claims, specification, prosecution history, and, in some cases, on extrinsic evidence to reconstruct what patent claim terms would have meant to a person skilled in the art. In theory, therefore, discovery relating to the structure and function of accused devices or a patent holder's own products might seem unnecessary. *See SRI Int'l v. Matsushita Elec. Corp. of Am.*, 775 F.2d 1107, 1118 (Fed. Cir. 1985) (en banc). However, often, only by knowing the details of the accused product and the relevant prior art can the parties determine which claim terms need construction. Otherwise, the court might be asked to provide definitions for words and phrases that are unlikely to materially affect the outcome of the litigation. Likewise, an inventor's testimony as to what a patent means is typically seen as extrinsic evidence. The claim-construction process gives this testimony less weight, particularly when it is offered in a self-serving way. It can, however, help the court understand the context and background of an invention as well as what the inventor understood to be the point of novelty. In some cases, an inventor's deposition can also illuminate what happened during prosecution of the patent application, which in turn can shed light on the meaning of some terms.

The Supreme Court's *Teva* ruling has expanded the use of expert declarations and testimony in claim construction. As a result, it can be particularly useful to a court to ask the parties early in the claim-construction process if they intend to rely on expert testimony and, if so, what the substance of the testimony will be. The court will then be in a position to evaluate the need for such testimony. If the court already plans to have an expert tutorial in conjunction with the *Markman* hearing, it can leave its options open by informing the parties that it might take evidence from the experts should factual confusion or disputes arise. Since the *Markman* process does not involve juries, the court has greater flexibility in structuring the proceeding. For instance, the court can use the so-called "hot tub" method, in which the court asks the opposing technical experts to address directly each other's testimony and the judge's questions to sharpen and clarify the disputed issues and assess the credibility of the witnesses. Of course, depending on the case and the claim terms in dispute (e.g., technical versus common terms), claim construction may not benefit from expert testimony, and in those situations, the court may choose to exercise its discretion and not allow it, or limit it to the resolution of particular terms.

In practice, permitting fact discovery in advance of claim construction helps focus the claims and defenses in a case. For example, once a plaintiff has discovery on the structure and function of accused products or processes, it may eliminate certain claims that it initially intended to assert. It can prioritize the claim terms that will best bridge the gap between the parties' views regarding the value of the litigation. Accordingly, discovery in advance of claim construction is common. Indeed, the specialized local patent rules of most districts that have adopted them expressly provide for discovery prior to claim construction, including mandated early disclosures of infringement and invalidity contentions. It can be helpful for a court to discuss potential limits on or phasing of pre-claim-construction discovery with the parties. In some cases, it could be wasteful to devote substantial resources to discovery on issues unrelated to claim construction (e.g., damages, equitable defenses, and willfulness) when the claim-construction ruling could be dispositive or drive settlement.

2.1.3.2.3.2 Fact Discovery After Claim Construction

Often, as a result of a court's claim-construction order, issues arise which justify additional fact discovery. For example, the court's definition of a disputed claim term might implicate previously uninvestigated features of an accused device because a court is not limited to choosing between constructions proposed by the parties. Most courts, therefore, set fact discovery to proceed for some period after the expected ruling on claim construction. Courts managing cases in which an inventor is deposed for *Markman* purposes sometimes limit that initial deposition to claim-construction–related topics, and allow a more general deposition after the *Markman* process is complete.

2.1.3.2.3.3 Expert Discovery After Claim Construction

Expert reports on infringement, invalidity, and damages are central to almost every patent case. Technical experts opine on infringement and invalidity based on the meaning of the claim terms as determined by (or anticipated from) the court's claim-construction order. For this reason, claim construction should precede expert reports and depositions. Claim construction might also affect damage analyses. For example, as a result of the court's ruling, it might become apparent that certain accused devices or features do not infringe or that a hypothetical design-around might have been easier or more difficult. Many courts, therefore, schedule expert discovery and depositions to begin after claim construction. In other jurisdictions, courts set expert discovery before claim construction but require experts to write their reports in the alternative relative to each side's proposed constructions.

2.1.3.2.3.4 Legal Contentions After Claim Construction

In many cases, the legal theories on infringement or invalidity adopted by the parties may not work as well as a litigant expected after claim construction. In some cases or jurisdictions—especially those in which claim construction happens at the end of the case and/or in connection with summary judgment—the parties are provided only limited opportunities to change infringement and invalidity theories after claim construction. This forces the parties to think hard about their case early in the litigation and to settle on a particular theory. For that reason, it also prevents sandbagging. On the other hand, limiting the parties' ability to modify their legal theories after claim construction can result in a trap for the unwary and/or harshly deprive a party of an otherwise valid claim or defense. This is especially true when, as is often the case, the court adopts constructions that differ from *both* sides' proposals. The parties may not have anticipated the court's constructions and find that the construction has broken their theories.

For this reason, many courts allow parties to modify their infringement and invalidity contentions after claim construction, but require a "timely showing of good cause" to do so. *See, e.g.*, N.D. Cal. Patent L.R. 3-6; *see also O2 Micro*, 467 F.3d at 1366 (Fed. Cir. 2006) (affirming lower court's requirement that a party show diligence in order to establish "good cause" under local patent rules); *Finisar Corp. v. DirecTV Grp.*, 424 F. Supp. 2d 896, 901–02 (E.D. Tex. 2006) ("Invalidity is an affirmative defense, and the party which does not properly investigate applicable prior art early enough to timely meet disclosure requirements risks exclusion of that evidence.").

2.1.3.2.4 Claim Construction Generally Should Precede, but May Be Combined with, Summary Judgment

Claim construction is a critical predicate to the most common summary judgment motions. Indeed, the structure and operation of an accused device is often undisputed so that the determination of infringement will collapse into a question of claim construction. *Athletic Alternatives, Inc. v. Prince Mfg., Inc.*, 73 F.3d 1573, 1578 (Fed. Cir. 1996). The same can be true for invalidity. Claim construction is the foundation for analysis of both infringement (has the patentee claimed the technology practiced by the defendant?) and invalidity (does the patentee's claim "read on"[5] preexisting technology?). Most courts complete claim construction first, before allowing dispositive motions, on the theory that the parties need a definitive statement of claim scope before preparing summary judgment papers. It can be a significant burden to prepare a motion for summary judgment—including the supporting statements of undisputed material facts and declarations from fact and expert wit-

5. The phrase "read on" is a term of art in patent law. If an accused device, manufacture, composition, or process embodies each element of a patent claim (and hence infringes), the claim is said to "read on" it. Similarly, a patent claim "reads on" a prior art reference (and hence is invalid) if the prior art reference contains each of the claim limitations.

nesses—that takes into account multiple, potential constructions of key terms. Motions prepared with the claims already construed can be more focused on the reasons summary judgment is justified, and better fit within court-prescribed page limits. Other courts emphasize the risk that separate, isolated claim construction, done without a sufficient understanding of why and how the dispute about the meaning of a term *matters*, results in an abstract exercise that is more likely to be wrong. As a result, these courts combine the claim-construction and summary judgment proceedings. Alternatively, a few courts do not schedule dispositive motions for the same time as claim construction. They do, however, require the parties to explain the significance of the competing claim constructions and limit their ability to offer alternative theories of infringement or noninfringement that were not previously disclosed. Although there are substantial reasons to prefer an early claim construction (such as the ability to provide clarity and information on settlement value to litigants earlier in the case), it is also worth noting the Federal Circuit's position that claim constructions are not ripe for appellate review until the full factual record has been developed. *See, e.g.*, *Wilson Sporting Goods Co. v. Hillerich Bradsby Co.*, 442 F.3d 1322, 1327 (Fed. Cir. 2006). For that reason, early claim construction does not normally allow pretrial review of this interlocutory decision, even on a writ.

As explored more fully in Chapter 6, some experienced patent jurists have found it useful to distinguish between two kinds of summary judgment motions: (1) those that turn primarily or exclusively on claim construction—such as noninfringement (e.g., whether the claimed invention reads on the accused device)—and (2) those that turn principally on issues other than claim construction. These jurists have found that it is most efficient to combine the first set of summary judgment motions with claim construction. *See* § 6.1.2; *cf. MyMail, Ltd. v. Am. Online, Inc.*, 476 F.3d 1372, 1378 (Fed. Cir. 2007) ("Because there is no dispute regarding the operation of the accused systems, that issue reduces to a question of claim interpretation and is amenable to summary judgment."); *Gen. Mills, Inc. v. Hunt-Wesson, Inc.*, 103 F.3d 978, 983 (Fed. Cir. 1997) ("Where the parties do not dispute any relevant facts regarding the accused product . . . but disagree over possible claim interpretations, the question of literal infringement collapses into claim construction and is amenable to summary judgment."). These jurists address these motions either simultaneously with claim construction or immediately thereafter and consider the second category of summary judgment motions at another time, depending on other scheduling concerns, such as discovery.

2.1.3.2.5 Claim Construction May Encourage Settlement

One argument in favor of early, separate claim construction is that it may facilitate settlement. This may be more likely following the Supreme Court's *Teva* decision, which defers to district court claim constructions on subsidiary factual determinations. In some cases, it may be appropriate to conduct an early claim construction for a subset of the disputed claim terms that are deemed case-dispositive.[6] A court's rulings on claim scope can help the parties recalibrate their assessment of exposure and allow each side to take a fresh look at its case. As a result, it may be fruitful to schedule a settlement conference shortly after issuance of a claim-construction order. *See* § 2.4. This can be especially effective where one side (generally the defendant) identifies a single issue as its strongest argument for an outcome in its favor. If the defendant raises this issue during the initial CMC, and the court schedules an early claim construction followed by summary judgment on that single issue, it may substantially reduce the overall cost of the litigation. This procedure, however, should only be used where the defendant can convincingly explain *why* the case largely turns on a single disputed issue. Otherwise, there is potential for abuse in a request for limited claim construction and an early dispositive motion because defendants have an incentive to use the procedure to get the court to decide separately multiple attacks on the patent. On the other hand, it is also true that plaintiffs have an incentive to resist scheduling such a motion early in the case, not because the motion will not be dispositive, but because the plaintiff may hope to use the nuisance cost and disruption of the litigation to extract a larger settlement from the defendant. Thus, while this procedure can be very effective in the right cases, it should be deployed only after closely examining its potential positive and negative effects in the particular case.

2.1.3.2.6 Preliminary Injunction Motions Usually Require Preliminary Claim Construction

Preliminary injunction motions in patent cases typically require a court to construe claim terms on an accelerated schedule. Briefing usually includes the parties' positions on key claim terms (albeit less informed than they might have been through discovery, as explained above), and a court's decision to grant or deny the motion will often hinge on claim-construction issues. However, these preliminary constructions are not binding. *Sofamor Danek Grp., Inc. v. DePuy-Motech, Inc.*, 74 F.3d 1216, 1221 (Fed. Cir. 1996). Subsequent, more detailed briefing and analysis may lead a court to reconsider and revise constructions applied in a preliminary injunction motion. *See CVI/Beta Ventures, Inc. v. Tura LP*, 112 F.3d 1146, 1160 n.7

---

6. For example, the Eastern District of Texas invited a defendant to submit a letter brief requesting the court to construe no more than three case-dispositive terms. The court would then hold "an early *Markman* hearing on the identified case dispositive terms . . . . If the case is not resolved following the Court's claim construction summary judgment rulings, a *Markman* hearing, as set forth in the Docket Control Order or at the patent status conference, will occur as scheduled." *Glob. Sessions LP v. Travelocity.com, LP et al.*, 2011 U.S. Dist. LEXIS 155901 (E.D. Tex. Aug. 18, 2011); *see also Parallel Networks v. AEO, Inc.*, No. 6:20cv275-LED-JDL (E.D. Tex. Mar. 15, 2011) (ordering a *Markman* hearing on a small number of claim terms; reasoning that the hearing would "resolve several important issues at a beneficial time for each party to better evaluate its case").

(Fed. Cir. 1997); *see also* § 5.3.2.4.1. We explore the preliminary injunction stage of patent litigation in Chapter 3.

2.1.4 Managing the Parties' Claims, Defenses, Prior Art References, and Counterclaims

Patent local rules, standing orders, and the Federal Circuit Advisory Council's model order address a variety of more specific disclosure and case-management practices. This section explores several notable practices.

2.1.4.1 Early Document Production

The local patent rules of several districts require parties to produce infringement and/or invalidity-related documents with their initial disclosures or otherwise very early in a case. Several notable examples are the Northern District of Illinois Local Patent Rules 2.1–2.4 (requiring patent plaintiffs to produce invalidity-related documents with their initial disclosures and accused infringers to produce infringement and invalidity documents with their initial disclosures); the Western District of Tennessee Local Patent Rule 3.1 (requiring the party claiming infringement to produce infringement-related documents seven days after the initial response is filed, along with infringement contentions); and the Northern District of Ohio Local Patent Rules 3.1–3.2 (requiring patent plaintiffs to produce invalidity-related documents within fifteen days after the answer is filed). Patent plaintiffs often favor early production requirements but must not let their own early production obligations catch them off guard.

2.1.4.2 Ownership and Standing

A number of jurisdictions require plaintiffs to produce all documents relating to ownership of the asserted patents. *See, e.g.*, N.D. Cal. Patent L.R. 3-2(d); D. Idaho L. Patent R. 3.2(d); N.D. Ill. LPR 2.1(a)(4); D. Nev. LR 16.1-7(d); D.N.H. SPR 5.1(b)(4); D.N.J. L. Pat. R. 3.2(d); N.D.N.Y. L. Pat. R. 3.2(d): N.D. Ohio L. P.R. 3.2(d); W.D. Tenn. LPR 3.2(d). Others frame the obligation more broadly by requiring production of all documents relating to "[t]he standing of the party alleging infringement with respect to each patent upon which such allegations are based." *See* Maryland L.R. 804.1(b)(ii); *see also* S.D. Ohio Pat. R. 103.1(b)(5). More than just ownership documents, this requirement contemplates the production of licensing documents where an exclusive licensee may be bringing suit.

2.1.4.3 Joint Infringement

A majority of districts with local patent rules have provisions governing infringement contentions where joint direct infringement is alleged. Typically, a patentee plaintiff must describe "the role of each such party in the direct infringement." See the local patent rules for the following districts: N.D. Cal. Patent L.R. 3-1(d); D.

Idaho Loc. Patent R. 3.1(d); N.D. Ill. LPR 2.2(e); Maryland L.R. 804.1(a)(iv); E.D. Mo. Local Patent R. 3.1(a)(v); D. Nev. LR 16.1-6(d); D.N.H. SPR 5.1(a)(2)(B); D.N.J. L. Pat. R. 3.1(d); N.D.N.Y. L. Pat. R. 3.1(d); E.D.N.C. L. Civ. R. 303.2(a); N.D. Ohio L. P. R. 3.1(d); S.D. Ohio Pat. R. 103.2(a)(5); W.D. Tenn. LPR 3.1(d); E.D. Wash. LPR 120(d); W.D. Wash. Local Patent Rule 120(d).

2.1.4.4 Winnowing Prior Art References

Just as the assertion of myriad patent claims unduly complicates patent litigation for the defense, the assertion of myriad prior art references, many of which will not be pursued, can impose undue cost on the patentee and the court. In conjunction with its efforts to rein in excessive numbers of asserted patent claims, the Federal Circuit Advisory Council proposed a phased process for winnowing the number of asserted prior art references:

- "Not later than 14 days after service of the Preliminary Election of Asserted Claims, the patent defendant shall serve a Preliminary Election of Asserted Prior Art, which shall assert no more than twelve prior art references against each patent and not more than a total of 40 references."
- "Not later than 14 days after service of a Final Election of Asserted Claims, the patent defendant shall serve a Final Election of Asserted Prior Art, which shall identify no more than six asserted prior art references per patent from among the twelve prior art references previously identified for that particular patent and no more than a total of 20 references."

Model Order Limiting Excess Patent Claims and Prior Art §§ 2, 3 (Fed. Cir. Advisory Council, 2013);[7] *see also* D. Utah LPR 7.1 ("In its final pretrial disclosures, a party opposing infringement shall reduce the number of prior art references—and any combinations thereof—to be asserted in support of anticipation or obviousness theories to a manageable subset of previously identified prior art references. As a general rule, a manageable number of references per claim is no more than three (3) references.").

2.1.4.5 Other Practices

Less common PLR provisions that may be useful case-management tools include:

- Requiring parties to submit summary judgment motions as part of the claim-construction process. D. Utah LPR 6.2.
- Requiring parties to "[p]rovide a written summary of any oral advice and produce or make available for inspection and copying that summary and

7. The model order relaxes these limitations when only one patent is asserted, increasing the per-patent limits "by 50%, rounding up." Model Order Limiting Excess Patent Claims and Prior Art § 4 (Fed. Cir. Advisory Council, 2013) (contained in Appendix D).

documents related thereto for which the attorney–client and work product protection have been waived." S.D. Cal. Patent L.R. 3.7(b).

- Requiring patent owners to make a damages disclosure. S.D. Ind. Patent Case Management Plan III(E) (which requires that plaintiffs must serve a "statement of damages" within 30 days after a *Markman* order).
- Requiring a production of "license agreements for the patents-in-suit." S.D. Tex. P.R. 3-2(a)(4).
- Bifurcation is handled differently by different district courts. In the Southern District of Ohio, willful infringement is always bifurcated. *See* S.D. Ohio Pat. R. 107.2. The Northern District of Georgia expressly disfavors bifurcation of liability issues from damages issues. N.D. Ga. LPR 5.1. Most districts are silent on the issue, but the Western District of North Carolina suggests the parties should consider whether bifurcation is appropriate. W.D.N.C. P.R. 2.1(A)(7).

2.2 Complaint and Answer

Complaints and answers in patent cases are typically deceptively simple. Generally, the asserted patents are identified, and defendants are accused of infringing them. Complaints rarely detail the defendants' allegedly infringing activities and facts about the parties' interrelationships, although often critical to the practical resolution of the case, are not usually included absent allegations of inequitable conduct (which must be pled with particularity).

Nevertheless, a patent complaint may spawn a wide variety of early motion practice, including motions to dismiss relating to lack of standing, lack of actual case or controversy, necessary parties, and interactions with related legal actions. Motions to dismiss for failure to claim patentable subject matter are possible as well. *See In re Bilski,* 545 F.3d 943, 951 (Fed. Cir. 2008), *aff'd,* 561 U.S. 593 (2010); *see also* §§ 6.2.1.1.1, 14.3.1. To comprehend the underpinnings of the disputes that will be raised in these and subsequent motions, it often helps the court to understand the parties' prior dealings and connections, if any. For example, often patent litigants have had a prior business relationship, such as through licensing or licensing discussions. Some courts find it helpful to explore these issues, as well as other business and market considerations, in an early case-management or settlement conference. Further, as the content of the patent infringement complaint is so sparse, it might also be helpful to explore case-specific substantive issues, such as the nature and complexity of the technology, and whether adoption of some variation on the patent local rules will help manage the case. Section 2.5 provides an expanded checklist of potential topics that might usefully be explored at an early conference with the parties.

On December 1, 2015, the U.S. Supreme Court adopted a number of amendments to the Federal Rules of Civil Procedure. Among these is the abolition of Rule 84 and the Appendix of Forms, including Form 18, the form complaint for patent infringement. The pleading standards set forth in *Twombly* and *Iqbal* now govern patent cases. This is discussed in further detail below.

2.2.1 Plaintiff Standing Requirements

The plaintiff may be the patent rights holder suing for infringement, or an accused infringer who challenges liability under the Declaratory Judgment Act, claiming the patent is invalid, unenforceable, and/or not infringed. Every plaintiff must have standing to sue for the case to proceed. Although it is advisable for a court to address standing issues early, they can arise at any time—and cannot be waived, because standing is jurisdictional. *See Pandrol USA, LP v. Airboss Ry. Prods., Inc.*, 320 F.3d 1354, 1367–68 (Fed. Cir. 2003).

2.2.1.1 Infringement Plaintiff

2.2.1.1.1 Infringement Plaintiff Must Hold All Substantial Patent Rights

A party suing for infringement must hold exclusive rights to the patent being asserted. A patent issues in the name of the inventor(s) or their assignee (usually an employer), who is then the "patentee." Only a patentee can bring an action for patent infringement. § 281 (2012). The term "patentee" includes "not only the patentee to whom the patent was issued but also the successors in title to the patentee." § 100(d). Courts also permit exclusive licensees to bring suit in their own name, if the exclusive licensee holds "all substantial rights" in the patent, becoming, in effect, an assignee (and therefore a "patentee" within the meaning of § 281). *See Textile Prods., Inc. v. Mead Corp.*, 134 F.3d 1481, 1484 (Fed. Cir. 1998). "All substantial rights" usually include the right to sue for infringement (without leave of the patent owner) and the right to grant licenses; courts look to the intention of the parties and examine the substance of what was retained by the owner and what was granted to the licensee in order to determine whether the licensee has obtained all substantial rights. *See Vaupel Textilmaschinen KG v. Meccanica Euro Italia SPA*, 944 F.2d 870, 874–75 (Fed. Cir. 1991). Because patent assignments must be in writing, § 261, an oral agreement cannot grant "all substantial rights" in a patent sufficient to confer standing. *See Prima Tek II, L.L.C. v. A-Roo Co.*, 222 F.3d 1372, 1377 (Fed. Cir. 2000).

Another's infringement can still injure an exclusive licensee without all substantial rights. Therefore, they will have standing to sue, but only as a co-plaintiff with the patentee. *See Mentor H/S, Inc. v. Med. Device All., Inc.*, 240 F.3d 1016, 1017, 1019 (Fed. Cir. 2001); *cf. Propat Int'l Corp. v. Rpost US, Inc.*, 473 F.3d 1187 (Fed. Cir. 2007). A license that is not exclusive or that confers less than all the rights held under the patent cannot confer standing. *See Prima Tek II*, 222 F.3d at 1377–78.

2.2.1.1.2 Plaintiff Must Join All Joint Patent Owners

Ordinarily, all co-owners of a patent must consent for an infringement suit to be maintained. Where ownership of a patent is disputed, early motion practice may include an accused infringer's motion to dismiss for failure to join a purported third-party co-owner of the patent. This may happen, for example, when the patent resulted from a joint development project, *see Katz v. Lear Siegler, Inc.*, 909 F.2d 1459,

1462 (Fed. Cir. 1990), or where there is a dispute as to whether the asserted patent claims were included within an assignment agreement. *See Isr. Bio-Eng'g Project v. Amgen Inc.*, 475 F.3d 1256, 1265 (Fed. Cir. 2007).

In such cases, the court must first determine ownership of the patent. "Ownership depends upon 'the substance of what was granted' through assignment." *Id.* at 1265 (quoting *Vaupel Textilmaschinen*, 944 F.2d at 874). "In construing the substance of the assignment, a court must carefully consider the intention of the parties and the language of the grant." *Id.* The agreement must be interpreted according to applicable state law. *See id.* (interpreting contract under Israeli law). If it is determined that an owner of the patent is not included as a plaintiff, the complaint must be dismissed. *Id.* (affirming summary judgment that plaintiff lacked standing where plaintiff lacked complete ownership interest and co-owner was not joined). As described below (§§ 2.2.1.1.6–2.2.1.1.7), such a dismissal should be without prejudice to refile an action with the jurisdictional defect corrected.

In *STC.UNM v. Intel Corp.*, the Federal Circuit reaffirmed the rule that all co-owners of a patent must consent to join as plaintiffs for an infringement suit to proceed. 754 F.3d 940, 945–46 (Fed. Cir. 2014) (citing *Ethicon, Inc. v. U.S. Surgical Corp.*, 135 F.3d 1456, 1467 (Fed. Cir. 1998)). Because "one co-owner has the right to impede the other co-owner's ability to sue infringers by refusing to voluntarily join in such a suit," a co-owner cannot ordinarily be joined involuntarily as a plaintiff under Federal Rule of Civil Procedure 19. *Id.* at 946 (quoting *Schering Corp. v. Roussel-UCLAF SA*, 104 F.3d 341, 345 (Fed. Cir. 1997)). The court noted two exceptions to the rule against involuntary joinder: (1) when the plaintiff is an exclusive licensee and seeks to join the patent owner, and (2) when a co-owner has waived the right to refuse to join suit by agreement. *Id.*

2.2.1.1.3 An Exclusive Licensee Must Sometimes Join Its Licensor

Where an asserted exclusive licensee who has less than all substantial rights sues for infringement in its own name, a defendant will frequently move to dismiss for failure to join the licensor as a necessary party. *See, e.g., Propat Int'l*, 473 F.3d at 1189–93; *Fieldturf, Inc. v. Sw. Recreational Indus. Inc.*, 357 F.3d 1266, 1268–70 (Fed. Cir. 2004); *see also Intellectual Prop. Dev., Inc. v. TCI Cablevision of Cal., Inc.*, 248 F.3d 1333, 1339–40 (Fed. Cir. 2001). An exclusive licensee receives more rights in a patent than a nonexclusive licensee, but may receive fewer rights than an assignee of all substantial patent rights. For example, an exclusive licensee could receive the exclusive right to practice an invention within a given limited territory. *Id.* An exclusive licensee has standing to sue, but must join the patent owner as a necessary party. *Id.* at 1348; *Propat*, 473 F.3d at 1193; *Mentor H/S, Inc.*, 240 F.3d at 1019.

If an exclusive licensee with less than all substantial rights has failed to join the patent owner, the action may be dismissed without prejudice, in anticipation of its refiling with the patent owner named as a co-plaintiff. Indeed, the Supreme Court has explained that:

> [t]he owner of a patent, who grants to another the exclusive right to make, use, or vend the invention, which does not constitute a statutory assignment, holds title to the patent in trust for such licensee, to the extent that he *must allow the use of his name as plaintiff in any action brought at the instance of the licensee* in law or in equity to obtain damages for the injury to his exclusive right by an infringer, or to enjoin infringement of it.

Indep. Wireless Tel. Co. v. Radio Corp. of Am., 269 U.S. 459, 469 (1926) (emphasis added). Consequently, rather than dismissing the action, a court may grant a motion or cross-motion by the exclusive licensee for leave to amend to join the patent owner, either voluntarily or involuntarily. *See Intellectual Prop. Dev.*, 248 F.3d at 1347–48 (affirming district court's grant of plaintiff-exclusive licensee's motion for leave to amend to add patent owner as a party); *see also Abbott Labs. v. Diamedix Corp.*, 47 F.3d 1128, 1130–34 (Fed. Cir. 1995).

2.2.1.1.4 A Nonexclusive Licensee Has No Standing to Sue

> [A] nonexclusive license or "bare" license—a covenant by the patent owner not to sue the licensee for making, using, or selling the patented invention and under which the patent owner reserves the right to grant similar licenses to other entities—confers no constitutional standing on the licensee under the Patent Act to bring suit or even to join a suit with the patentee because a nonexclusive (or "bare") licensee suffers no legal injury from infringement.

Intellectual Prop. Dev., Inc. v. TCI Cablevision of Cal., Inc., 248 F.3d 1333, 1345 (Fed. Cir. 2001).

2.2.1.1.5 Patentee Can Only Convey Right to Sue by Transferring Substantially All Patent Rights

Assignment of a patent, or an exclusive license of a patent that conveys substantially all patent rights, conveys to the assignee or licensee the right to sue for present and future infringement of the patent. *See Propat Int'l*, 473 F.3d at 1189. A patent holder cannot, however, confer through assignment a right to sue for infringement—whether past, present, or future—separate from the conveyance of a proprietary interest in the patent. *Id.* at 1194 (citing *Crown Die & Tool Co. v. Nye Tool & Mach. Works*, 261 U.S. 24, 34–36 (1923)). As discussed above, to have standing to sue, a party must be an exclusive licensee or assignee of all substantial rights in a patent.

Further, because infringement harms only the owner of the patent at the time of the infringing acts, conveyance of the patent does not normally include the right to recover for injury occurring to the prior owner of the patent. *Minco Inc. v. Combustion Eng'g*, 95 F.3d 1109, 1117 (Fed. Cir. 1996). Thus, as a general rule, "the right to sue for *prior* infringement is not transferred unless the assignment agreement manifests an intent to transfer this right." *Id.* (emphasis added). To determine if patent assignment includes the right to sue for prior infringement, the court should analyze the assignment according to state contract law. *Id.* "Neither statute nor common law precedent, however, requires a particular formula or set prescription of words to express that conveyance." *Id.*

2.2.1.1.6 A Covenant Not to Sue or Similarly Binding Representations Can Moot a Controversy Between the Parties

A party's issuing a covenant not to sue or making a similarly binding representation such that it could not reasonably be expected to resume its enforcement efforts against a declaratory judgment plaintiff renders the case moot. *See Already, LLC v. Nike, Inc.*, 133 S. Ct. 721, 725 (2013) (trademark case); *Organic Seed Growers & Trade Ass'n v. Monsanto Co.*, 718 F.3d 1350, 1358 (Fed. Cir. 2013) (applying *Nike* to hold that Monsanto's judicially binding representations that it had no intent to enforce its patents against the declaratory judgment appellants mooted the case); *Danisco U.S. Inc. v. Novozymes A/S*, 744 F.3d 1325 (Fed. Cir. 2014) (citing *Nike* and noting that Novozymes had failed to offer "any assurance, such as with a covenant not to sue, that it will not accuse Danisco's [rapid starch liquefaction] products of [patent] infringement, which could potentially moot a controversy between the parties.").

2.2.1.1.7 Dismissal Based on Meritorious Standing Motions

If a case must be dismissed for lack of standing, it should ordinarily be dismissed without prejudice. *See Propat Int'l Corp. v. RPost US, Inc.*, 473 F.3d 1187, 1194 (Fed. Cir. 2007) (affirming district court's dismissal without prejudice even where non-exclusive licensee could not cure a standing defect by joining patent holder). If a plaintiff lacks standing, the court's jurisdiction cannot be invoked, and the plaintiff should not be penalized if it subsequently corrects the standing defect, for example, by joining all co-owners of the patent rights. Nonetheless, where the basis for dismissal cannot be rectified, such as where a covenant not to sue moots the controversy, *see* § 2.2.1.1.6, then the dismissal should be with prejudice.

2.2.1.2 Declaratory Judgment Plaintiff

A district court has subject-matter jurisdiction over a patent declaratory judgment action when an "actual controversy" exists between the plaintiff and defendant. *See* 28 U.S.C. § 2201(a) ("In a case of actual controversy within its jurisdiction . . . any court of the United States, upon the filing of an appropriate pleading, may declare the rights and other legal relations of any interested party seeking such declaration, whether or not further relief is or could be sought."). Where the patentee files for infringement, the defendant's answer will almost always plead a counterclaim for a declaration of noninfringement, invalidity, and sometimes unenforceability. This apparently superfluous pleading preserves the defendant's right to secure adjudication of claims that a plaintiff may later want to abandon for tactical reasons. For example, a plaintiff may decide to abandon claims in one asserted patent because the defendant raises strong invalidity defenses against that patent. A defendant's declaratory judgment counterclaim maintains its ability to adjudicate the patent's validity and avoid being threatened by that patent again. Although a plaintiff cannot avoid declaratory judgment counterclaims by dismissing its affirmative claims on the patent(s), a patentee can divest the district court of subject-matter jurisdiction of declaratory judgment counterclaims by offering the declaratory judgment plaintiff a covenant not to sue on the patent(s). *See Dow Jones & Co., Inc. v. Ablaise Ltd.*, 606 F.3d 1388 (Fed. Cir. 2010); *see also Already, LLC v. Nike, Inc.*, 133 S. Ct. 721 (2013) (upholding the voluntary cessation doctrine).

Timing is key. If a covenant not to sue is given prior to consideration or resolution of the underlying infringement claim, for example, at the outset of the litigation, it may be effective. *See Benitec Austl., Ltd. v. Nucleonics, Inc.*, 495 F.3d 1340, 1347 (Fed. Cir. 2007). A covenant not to sue will not result in dismissal if given after the resolution of the infringement claims. *Fort James Corp. v. Solo Cup Co.*, 412 F.3d 1340, 1348 (Fed. Cir. 2005).

Declaratory judgment actions may also arise where the accused infringer (as the plaintiff) disputes the patentee's extrajudicial assertion of infringement and seeks judicial resolution of the issue. These cases typically arise when the patent holder has sent a letter or otherwise given notice suggesting that the potential infringer may want to license the patent. Although patent holders attempt to craft letters with ambiguous language that avoids provoking declaratory judgment jurisdiction, there is no "safe harbor" form of notice. *See, e.g., Hewlett-Packard Co. v. Acceleron LLC*, 587 F.3d 1358, 1362 (Fed. Cir. 2009) ("The purpose of a declaratory judgment action cannot be defeated simply by the stratagem of a correspondence that avoids the magic words such as 'litigation' or 'infringement.'"). Frequently, the patent holder will respond to a declaratory judgment action by immediately filing an infringement complaint in another jurisdiction. These disputes will usually be controlled by the "first filed" rule and its exceptions, which aim to prevent forum-shopping. At least one district court has found an infringement lawsuit filed on a U.S. patent in a foreign country (Dubai) sufficient to create subject-matter jurisdiction for a declaratory judgment action in the United States. *See Juniper Networks Inc. v. Bahattab*, 2009 U.S. Dist. LEXIS 129765, No. 07cv1771 (PLF) (AK) (D.D.C. Aug. 14, 2009) (noting that the patent owner's action in Dubai appeared to be a novel forum-shopping attempt).

The Supreme Court has acknowledged that its precedent "do[es] not draw the brightest of lines between those declaratory judgment actions that satisfy the case-or-controversy requirement and those that do not." *MedImmune, Inc. v. Genentech, Inc.*, 549 U.S. 118, 127 (2007). The Court explained: "Basically, the question in each case is whether the facts alleged, under all the circumstances, show that there is a substantial controversy, between parties having adverse legal interests, of sufficient immediacy and reality to warrant the issuance of a declaratory judgment." *Id.* (quoting *Md. Cas. Co. v. Pac. Coal & Oil Co.*, 312 U.S. 270, 273 (1941)). The Supreme Court rejected the "reasonable apprehension of suit" test, holding merely that "the dispute be 'definite and concrete, touching the legal relations having adverse legal interests'; and that it be 'real and substantial' and 'admi[t] of specific relief through a decree of a conclusive character, as distinguished from an opinion advising what the law would be upon a hypothetical state of facts.'" *Id.* at 132 n.11 (quoting *Aetna Life Ins. Co. v. Haworth*, 300 U.S. 227, 240 (1937)) (alteration in original).

Interpreting *MedImmune*, the Federal Circuit held that declaratory judgment jurisdiction exists whenever "a patentee asserts rights under a patent based on certain identified ongoing or planned activity of another party, and where that party contends that it has the right to engage in the accused activity without license." *SanDisk Corp. v. STMicroelectronics, Inc.*, 480 F.3d 1372, 1381 (Fed. Cir. 2007); *see also Micron Tech., Inc. v. Mosaid Techs., Inc.*, 518 F.3d 897, 903 (Fed. Cir. 2008) (applying *Medimmune* and discussing the first-filed rule).

In *Arkema Inc. v. Honeywell International Inc.*, the Federal Circuit addressed the question of how far in advance the "planned activity" could occur to support declaratory judgment jurisdiction. 706 F.3d 1351 (Fed. Cir. 2013). Arkema intended to enter into long-term contracts to supply a product to be used in an alleged infringement. *Id.* at 1359. The commercial launch of the product in the United States was at least one year away, yet the Federal Circuit held that, under all the circumstances, Arkema was "in a *present* position of either committing to contracts that could expose it to liability for indirect infringement or abandoning its plans to supply [products] in the United States." *Id.* at 1359. Thus, the dispute was "of sufficient immediacy and reality to warrant the issuance of a declaratory judgment." *Id.* at 1360.

Another category of declaratory judgment actions is one in which a supplier files suit against a patentee who has sued (or threatened to sue) the supplier's customers based on the supplier's products or services. *See, e.g.*, Complaint for Declaratory Judgment, *Cisco Sys., Inc. v. Innovative Wireless Sols., LLC*, Case 1:13-cv-00492, 2013 WL 3130645 (W.D. Tex. June 12, 2013). These actions are often accompanied by a request to stay the customer suits in favor of the supplier's suit.

2.2.1.2.1 Defendant's Declaratory Judgment Counterclaims Are Not Mooted by Dismissal of Plaintiff's Infringement Claims

Accused infringers often file counterclaims for a declaratory judgment of invalidity as well as noninfringement. The Supreme Court has held that appellate affirmance of a judgment of noninfringement does not moot a declaratory judgment counterclaim of patent invalidity. *Cardinal Chem. Co. v. Morton Int'l, Inc.*, 508 U.S. 83, 98 (1993). In so holding, the Court again emphasized the importance to the public at large of resolving questions of patent validity, citing its opinion in *Blonder-Tongue Laboratories, Inc. v. University of Illinois Foundation*, 402 U.S. 313 (1971), and warned against "the danger that the opportunity to relitigate might, as a practical matter, grant monopoly privileges to the holders of invalid patents." *Cardinal Chem.*, 508 U.S. at 101. However, a district court in the exercise of its discretion may decline to resolve a declaratory claim of invalidity following its adjudication of noninfringement. *See MedImmune, Inc. v. Genentech, Inc.*, 549 U.S. 118, 136 (2007) (noting that the Declaratory Judgment Act, which provides that a court "may declare the rights and other legal relations of any interested party," 28 U.S.C. § 2201(a), "has long been understood 'to confer on federal courts unique and substantial discretion in deciding whether to declare the rights of litigants'" (quoting *Wilton v. Seven Falls Co.*, 515 U.S. 277, 286 (1995)).

2.2.1.2.2 Assignor Is Estopped from Seeking Declaratory Judgment of Invalidity

An inventor who assigns his patent rights to an employer and then leaves to join a competing company may find himself sued for infringement. Under the equitable doctrine of assignor estoppel, the former employee is estopped from raising invalidity as a defense or as the basis of a declaratory judgment claim. *Pandrol USA, LP v. Airboss Ry. Prods., Inc.*, 424 F.3d 1161, 1166–67 (Fed. Cir. 2005); *Diamond Sci. Co. v. Ambico, Inc.*, 848 F.2d 1220, 1224 (Fed. Cir. 1988). The underlying policy is that "an assignor should not be permitted to sell something and later assert that what was sold is worthless, all to the detriment of the assignee." *Pandrol*, 424 F.3d at 1167 (quoting *Diamond*, 848 F.2d at 1224).

The doctrine of assignor estoppel only applies to the defense in a patent infringement lawsuit and is not a separate federal cause of action. In *Semiconductor Energy Laboratory Co. v. Nagata*, the Federal Circuit rejected federal question jurisdiction over a case brought by a patent owner against the patent inventor. 706 F.3d 1365, 1368, 1370 (Fed. Cir. 2013). In an earlier infringement case brought by the patent owner, the inventor agreed to assist one of the defendants, and repudiated his signature on the patent application's declaration and assignment, in alleged violation of an alleged duty not to contend the patent he assigned was invalid or unenforceable. *Id.* at 1370. After the earlier case settled, the patent owner sued the inventor for various state-law causes of action and a declaratory judgment of "violation of federal patent law" premised on the offensive application of the doctrine of assignor estoppel. *Id.* at 1368. The Federal Circuit affirmed the district court's dismissal of the case for lack of federal question jurisdiction, holding that assignor estoppel "is a shield; it is an affirmative defense, not a claim for relief on its own," and that the state-law claims accordingly did not present a substantial question of federal patent law. *Id.* at 1370–71.

2.2.1.2.2.1 Parties in Privity with Assignor Are Also Estopped

Because assignor estoppel is an equitable doctrine "mainly concerned with the balance of the equities between the parties[,] [t]hose in privity with the assignor partake of that balance, hence, extension of the estoppel to those in privity is justified." *Intel Corp. v. U.S. Int'l Trade Comm'n*, 946 F.2d 821, 837 (Fed. Cir. 1991) (quoting *Shamrock Techs., Inc. v. Med. Sterilization, Inc.*, 903 F.2d 789, 793 (Fed. Cir. 1990)). Thus, the assignor's subsequent employer may also be estopped from asserting that the assigned patent is invalid. *Id.*; *Mentor Graphics Corp. v. Quickturn Design Sys.*, 150 F.3d 1374, 1379 (Fed. Cir. 1998) ("Assignor estoppel also prevents parties in privity with an estopped assignor from challenging the validity of the patent.").

In determining whether there is privity, the court should consider all contacts between the assignor and the alleged infringer, both direct and indirect, including the relationship between those contacts and the alleged infringement. *Intel Corp.*, 946 F.2d at 839.

> Privity, like the doctrine of assignor estoppel itself, is determined upon a balance of the equities. If an inventor assigns his invention to his employer company A and leaves to join company B, whether B is in privity and thus bound by the doctrine will depend on the equities dictated by the relationship between the inventor and company B in light of the act of infringement. The closer that relationship, the more the equities will favor applying the doctrine to company B.

Id. at 839–40 (quoting *Shamrock Techs.*, 903 F.2d at 793); *see also Checkpoint Sys. v. All-Tag Sec. S.A.*, 412 F.3d 1331, 1337 (Fed. Cir. 2005) ("Privity may be established where there is a close relationship among the relevant parties, such as where the ultimate infringer availed itself of the inventor's knowledge and assistance to conduct infringement."). Factors considered by other courts in assessing privity include: (1) the extent and nature of the parties' business relationships (e.g., whether a party challenging validity formed a joint venture with the assignor to manufacture the infringing product or whether a party challenging validity is a subsidiary of the assignor), (2) the financial dealings between the parties, including whether there is an indemnification agreement between the alleged infringer and the assignor, and (3) whether the ultimate infringer availed itself of the inventor's "knowledge and assistance" to conduct infringement. *Id.* (citing cases); *Checkpoint*, 412 F.3d at 1337; *Mentor Graphics*, 150 F.3d at 1379; *Dane Indus. v. Ameritek Indus., LLC*, 154 F. App'x 894 (Fed. Cir. 2005) (unpublished opinion).

2.2.1.2.3 Actual Case or Controversy Can Exist for Licensee in Good Standing Even in Absence of Material Breach

Patent licensees who are performing under their license agreement (e.g., paying royalties) may nevertheless present a controversy with their licensor sufficient to support a declaratory judgment action. This has not always been the case. Historically, courts held that patent licensees in good standing were unable to sue for a declaratory judgment that the licensed patent is invalid because (1) the licensee was not threatened with imminent injury and, therefore, had no standing and (2) no actual case or controversy existed so long as the license agreement was not breached. *See, e.g., Gen-Probe Inc. v. Vysis, Inc.*, 359 F.3d 1376, 1381 (Fed. Cir. 2004). The Supreme Court reversed this line of cases in 2007, holding that a patent licensee need not break or terminate its license agreement before seeking a declaratory judgment in federal court that the underlying patent is invalid, unenforceable, or not infringed. *MedImmune, Inc. v. Genentech, Inc.*, 549 U.S. 118, 136–37 (2007).

2.2.2 Defendant Standing Requirements

2.2.2.1 Infringement Defendants

A patent holder is not obligated to sue all accused infringers. It can select from alleged infringers—both direct and indirect. *See Giese v. Pierce Chem. Co.*, 29 F.

Supp. 2d 33, 40 (D. Mass. 1998) ("Courts have generally held that a patentee need not sue more than one infringer at a given time.") (quoting *Watkins v. Nw. Ohio Tractor Pullers Ass'n, Inc.*, 630 F.2d 1155, 1162 (6th Cir. 1980)).

While proof of direct infringement is a predicate to proving induced or contributory infringement, *Joy Techs., Inc. v. Flakt, Inc.*, 6 F.3d 770, 774 (Fed. Cir. 1993) (collecting cases), direct infringers do not have to be joined in a suit against a contributory infringer. *Refac Int'l, Ltd. v. IBM*, 790 F.2d 79, 81 (Fed. Cir. 1986) ("direct infringers need not be parties"); *see also Upjohn Co. v. Syntro Corp.*, 1990 U.S. Dist. LEXIS 11512, 1990 WL 79232 (D. Del. 1990).

2.2.2.1.1 Joinder Issues

Prior to the enactment of the America Invents Act (AIA) on September 16, 2011, Federal Rule of Civil Procedure 20(a)(2) governed the joinder of unrelated defendants in the same patent action. In some cases, the accused products differed drastically from one defendant to another, which could lead to many distinct theories of infringement. These cases commonly proceeded without severance or were consolidated on the theory that judicial resources would be conserved because the asserted patent was common to all the defendants. *See, e.g., MyMail Ltd. v. AOL, Inc.*, 223 F.R.D. 455, 456 (E.D. Tex. 2004) (reasoning that the "same transaction or occurrence" requires only "some connection or logical relationship between the various transactions or occurrences"). Although some issues, such as those relating to patent validity, would be the same for all of the defendants, the complexities in case management and discovery prompted some courts to reconsider this approach. *See Bender v. Exar Corp.*, CV 09-01140 (N.D. Cal. Aug. 3, 2009) (Alsup, J.) (refusing to relate twenty-four patent cases asserting the same patent); *Man Mach. Interface Techs., LLC v. Funai Corp., et al.*, CV 10-8629 (C.D. Cal. Apr. 7, 2011) (Walter, J.) (dismissing a defendant as improperly joined); *Interval Licensing LLC v. AOL, Inc.*, 2011 U.S. Dist. LEXIS 51195, 2011 WL 1655713 (W.D. Wash. Apr. 29, 2011) (holding that joinder was improper because "[p]laintiff has not alleged that the Defendants have engaged in the same transaction or occurrence"). In *In re EMC Corp.* (*In re EMC I*), 677 F.3d 1351, 1356 (Fed. Cir. 2012), the Federal Circuit clarified the law of joinder, holding that joinder is not appropriate merely because defendants face identical infringement claims or where different products or processes are involved. Instead, there must be "shared, overlapping facts that give rise to each cause of action, and not just distinct, albeit coincidentally identical, facts." *Id.* at 1359. "Unless there is an actual link between the facts underlying each claim of infringement, independently developed products using differently sourced parts are not part of the same transaction, even if they are otherwise coincidentally identical." *Id.*

Responding to concerns about joinder practices in patent cases, Congress enacted a special rule narrowing the joinder standards for patent cases in the AIA. Section 299 (a)(1) states that accused infringers may be joined only if

> any right to relief is asserted against the parties jointly, severally, or in the alternative with respect to or arising out of the same transaction, occurrence, or series of transactions or occurrences relating to the making, using, importing into the United States,

offering for sale, or selling of the same accused product or processes; and (2) questions of fact common to all defendants or counterclaim defendants will arise in the action.

Notably, the AIA specifically states that common infringement of the same patent, without more, is not enough to justify joinder in the same action. *See* § 299(b). The legislative history of the provision indicates that Congress intended to abrogate the interpretation of Federal Rule of Civil Procedure 20(a) adopted in *MyMail v. AOL* by more narrowly defining the parties who are properly joined in the same action for patent infringement. *See* H.R. Rep. 112-98 (2011). Note that § 299(c) provides that accused infringers may consent to joinder. Furthermore, the AIA's joinder rule does not stand in the way of consolidation of pretrial proceedings pursuant to 28 U.S.C. § 1407. *See* § 2.3.4.

Since the AIA joinder provision went into effect, several courts have held that joinder is proper where multiple alleged infringers of the same patent also share the same underlying accused product. *See, e.g., Vertical Comput. Sys., Inc. v. LG Elecs. MobileComm U.S.A., Inc.*, 2013 U.S. Dist. LEXIS 71561, 2013 WL 2241947 (E.D. Tex. May 21, 2013) (finding different defendants' common usage of Google's Android OS satisfied the "actual link" requirement in *In re EMC I*); *Steuben Foods, Inc. v. Oystar Grp.*, 2013 U.S. Dist. LEXIS 187536, 2013 WL 2105894, at *7 (W.D.N.Y. May 14, 2013) (denying motion to sever one defendant and transfer the infringement claims against it to a different forum, where the infringement claims against all the named defendants appeared to be based on the same accused product).

That said, "even if a plaintiff's claims arise out of the same transaction and there are questions of law and fact common to all defendants, district courts have the discretion to refuse joinder in the interest of avoiding prejudice and delay, ensuring judicial economy, or safeguarding principles of fundamental fairness." *In re EMC I*, 677 F.3d at 1360 (quoting *Acevedo v. Allsup's Convenience Stores, Inc.*, 600 F.3d 516, 521 (5th Cir. 2010)). "In a complicated patent litigation a large number of defendants might prove unwieldy, and a district court would be justified in exercising its discretion to deny joinder when different witnesses and documentary proof would be required." *Id.* (citations omitted). Because of § 299, some courts have denied joinder and severed defendants from the case, even where all defendants are accused of infringing the same product. *See Digitech Image Techs., LLC v. Agfaphoto Holding GmbH*, 2012 U.S. Dist. LEXIS 142034, 2012 WL 4513805 (C.D. Cal. Oct. 1, 2012) (severing forty-four defendants from the case because the relief sought did not arise out of the "same transaction" as required by § 299). While the AIA makes it easier for patent infringement defendants to challenge joinder, it has also led to a significant increase in "serially filed" cases that burden courts' dockets.

Even where the AIA's misjoinder provision bars formal joinder, some district courts have effectively consolidated serially filed cases involving the same patent or patents for claim construction. *See* § 5.1.3.8. Such treatment preserves the right of defendants to be tried separately while economizing on judicial and the parties' resources. Nonetheless, courts should be sensitive to the adverse effects on the parties of such effective consolidation of some pretrial issues. *See* § 5.1.3.8 (discussing effects on transfer motions). For example, a plaintiff could file a series of lawsuits timed to avoid having to meet substantive deadlines; when a deadline approaches, a new case could be filed along with a request to consolidate the cases and reschedule deadlines. This could disadvantage the first defendants in the series relative to the plaintiff and later defendants.

2.2.2.2 Declaratory Judgment Defendants

A declaratory judgment action seeking to invalidate or render unenforceable a patent must name as defendants all parties holding an interest in the patent. However, nonexclusive licensees are generally not thought to be necessary parties. *See In-Tech Mktg. Inc. v. Hasbro, Inc.*, 685 F. Supp. 436, 438–41 (D.N.J. 1988) (holding that a purported exclusive licensee was not a necessary party); *Meese v. Eaton Mfg. Co.*, 35 F.R.D. 162, 166–67 (N.D. Ohio 1964) (stating that, notwithstanding *Independent Wireless*, "[c]ourts have generally agreed that a mere licensee is not indispensable to an infringement suit by the patentholder"); *cf. Indep. Wireless*, 269 U.S. at 466 (describing a licensor and an exclusive licensee as "generally necessary parties in the action in equity"); *Arey v. Goodyear Tire & Rubber Co.*, 11 F.R.D. 209, 209 (N.D. Ohio 1951) (stating that an exclusive licensee was both necessary and indispensable).

2.2.3 Pleading

2.2.3.1 Infringement

Infringement complaints are usually sparse and conclusory. Typically, a patent holder will merely allege that a defendant is directly or indirectly infringing a patent. The asserted patents must be identified, and are often attached to the complaint. Some local rules require that they be attached. The complaint should also provide a statement of ownership of the asserted patent(s), identify the accused infringer(s), provide a brief statement of alleged infringing acts, and (if applicable) a statement regarding the patent owner's marking of a product with the patent number under § 287.

Historically, under the notice pleading requirement of Federal Rule of Civil Procedure 8(a), the patent holder has not been required to do more. Therefore, a defendant would not know which claims of the patents are being asserted against it and sometimes would not even know which of its products or processes are accused of infringing.

Past practices in pleading infringement, exemplified by Form 18, arguably conflict with recent Supreme Court precedent requiring greater specificity in complaints. In *Bell Atlantic Corp. v. Twombly*, an antitrust case, the Court held that "a plaintiff's obligation to provide the 'grounds' of his 'entitle[ment] to relief' requires more than labels and conclusions, and a formulaic recitation of the elements of a cause of action will not do." 550 U.S. 544, 555 (2007) (internal citations omitted). Even after *Twombly*, however, the Federal Circuit held that "a patentee need only plead facts sufficient to place the alleged infringer on notice as to what he must defend. . . . [A patentee] is not required to specifically include each element of the claims of the asserted patent." *McZeal v. Sprint Nextel Corp.*, 501 F.3d 1354, 1357

(Fed. Cir. 2007) (vacating dismissal of *pro se* plaintiff's complaint that conformed to Form 18 (then Form 16)). In 2009, the Supreme Court again addressed Rule 8(a), when it clarified that the holding of *Twombly* was not limited to antitrust cases. The Court held that "[t]o survive a motion to dismiss, a complaint must contain sufficient factual matter, accepted as true, to 'state a claim to relief that is plausible on its face.'" *Ashcroft v. Iqbal*, 556 U.S. 662, 678 (2009) (quoting *Twombly*, 550 U.S. at 555). "Where a complaint pleads facts that are 'merely consistent with' a defendant's liability, it 'stops short of the line between possibility and plausibility of 'entitlement to relief.'" *Id.* (quoting *Twombly*, 550 U.S. at 557).

Despite the Supreme Court's reiteration of heightened pleading standards, the Federal Circuit has so far held to its position that Form 18 controls the pleading requirements for direct patent infringement. *See In re Bill of Lading Transmission & Processing Sys. Patent Litig.*, 681 F.3d 1323 (Fed. Cir. 2012); *see also K-Tech Telecomms., Inc. v. Time Warner Cable, Inc.*, 714 F.3d 1277, 1283 (Fed. Cir. 2013) ("as we made clear in *R+L Carriers*, to the extent any conflict exists between *Twombly* (and its progeny) and the Forms regarding pleadings requirements, the Forms control"). In fact, the Federal Circuit does not even require the complaint to identify a specific accused product as long as it conforms to Form 18 and Rule 8(a). *K-Tech*, 714 F.3d at 1286.

District courts have struggled to reconcile Form 18 and Rule 84 with *Iqbal* and *Twombly*. Some courts have concluded that Form 18 applies only to claims of direct infringement, but that for claims of indirect infringement, more detailed allegations are required, such as the identity of the underlying direct infringer and the facts supporting the knowledge element of indirect infringement. *See, e.g., Elan Microelectronics Corp. v. Apple, Inc.*, 2009 U.S. Dist. LEXIS 83715, 2009 WL 2972374 (N.D. Cal. Sept. 14, 2009) (recognizing that Form 18 provides an example of how direct, but not indirect, patent infringement may be alleged); *Eolas Techs. Inc. v. Adobe Sys. Inc.*, 2010 U.S. Dist. LEXIS 58291, 2010 WL 2026627, at *3 (E.D. Tex. May 6, 2010) ("Form 18 does not expressly address indirect infringement claims, and courts are split on the pleading requirements of indirect infringement."). The Federal Circuit concurs: "In other words, because Form 18 addresses only direct infringement, we must look to Supreme Court precedent for guidance regarding the pleading requirements for claims of indirect infringement." *In re Bill of Lading*, 681 F.3d at 1337.

Aside from willful infringement, *see* § 2.2.3.2, defendants have increasingly challenged the sufficiency of allegations of induced and contributory infringement, particularly with respect to the specific intent requirement of induced infringement. Courts have generally required factual allegations not only of a defendant's knowledge of a plaintiff's patent at the time of the infringement, but also that the defendant knew the use of its product constituted infringement. *See, e.g., Versata Software, Inc. v. Cloud9 Analytics, Inc.*, 2014 U.S. Dist. LEXIS 19994, 2014 WL 631517, at *2 (D. Del. Feb. 18, 2014). However, there is not yet a consensus on whether the filing of the complaint is alone sufficient to satisfy the knowledge requirement of induced infringement. *Compare Bascom Research LLC v. Facebook, Inc.*, 2013 U.S. Dist. LEXIS 41429, 2013 WL 968210, at *4 (N.D. Cal. Mar. 12, 2013) (filing of the complaint held sufficient to establish defendant's postsuit knowledge for purpose of induced infringement, but that infringement was limited to postfiling conduct) *with Mallinckrodt Inc. v. E-Z-EM Inc.*, 670 F. Supp. 2d 349, 354 (D. Del. 2009) ("The Court is not persuaded by Plaintiffs' contention that the requisite knowledge [for induced infringement claim] can be established by the filing of the Plaintiffs' Complaint.").

Some courts require that pleadings identify which of a defendant's specific products or practices allegedly infringe. *See, e.g., Interval Licensing LLC v. AOL, Inc.*, No. 2010 U.S. Dist. LEXIS 131081, 2010 WL 5058620 (W.D. Wash. Dec. 10, 2010); *Bender v. LG Elecs., U.S.A., Inc.*, 2010 U.S. Dist. LEXIS 33075, 2010 WL 889541 (N.D. Cal. Mar. 11, 2010). In some cases, however, discovery may be necessary to identify how a defendant's product works and whether it infringes. Rule 11(b)(3) allows allegations that "will likely have evidentiary support after a reasonable opportunity for . . . discovery," but at least one district court has held that Rule 11(b)(3) does not affect the pleading standard under Rule 8(a). *Elan*, 2009 WL 2972374, at *3.

Despite Federal Circuit decisions upholding pleadings conforming to Form 18, some district courts continue to challenge the sufficiency of Form 18 and have required the heightened pleading standards set forth by the Supreme Court, even in cases of direct patent infringement. *See Macronix Int'l Co. v. Spansion Inc.*, 4 F. Supp. 3d 797 (E.D. Va. 2014) (holding that patent complaints are subject to the heightened pleading standard set forth in *Twombly* and *Iqbal*); *see also Regeneron Pharm., Inc. v. Merus B.V.*, 2014 U.S. Dist. LEXIS 84297, 2014 WL 2795461 (S.D.N.Y. June 19, 2014) ("This Court finds that the Federal Circuit's determination that *Twombly* is inapplicable to patent cases conflicts with significant Second Circuit precedent applying the principles of *Twombly* at the pleading stage of civil cases. This Court has found no basis in Second Circuit precedent to treat patent cases differently from other cases in which forms exist and to which *Twombly* applies. The principles set forth in *Twombly* apply to the evaluation of pleadings in patent infringement cases in this Circuit. Thus, the sufficiency of Regeneron's claim for patent infringement is assessed pursuant to the basic elements set forth in Form 18 as well as the guidance provided in *Twombly*.").

Other courts disagree with these challenges and question how the Federal Circuit's clear stance on Form 18 can be distinguished. *See JDS Uniphase Corp. v. Co-Adna Photonics, Inc.*, 2014 U.S. Dist. LEXIS 88031, 2014 WL 2918544 (N.D. Cal. June 26, 2014) ("As for *Macronix*, that opinion forcefully disagrees that *Bill of Lading* and *McZeal*, correctly applied the Supreme Court's decisions in *Twombly* and *Iqbal*. This court is unpersuaded by the opinion in *Macronix*, since it provides no argument for how *K-Tech*, which again reinforced the Federal Circuit's understanding of Form 18, can be distinguished. To the extent *K-Tech's* analysis rested on 'the applicable law of the regional circuit,' it was also applying the controlling law of the Ninth Circuit that this court is also bound to apply.") (citations omitted).

On December 1, 2015, the U.S. Supreme Court adopted a number of amendments to the Federal Rules of Civil Procedure. Among these is the abolition of Rule 84 and the Appendix of Forms, including Form 18. As a result, the pleading standards set forth in *Twombly* and *Iqbal* govern patent complaints.

Aside from heightened pleading requirements, some local rules require disclosure of additional information early in the case. *See, e.g.*, N.D. Cal. Patent L.R. 3-1 (requiring early disclosure of asserted claims and accused products). After that early disclosure, the asserted claims and accused products may not be amended without leave of court for good cause. *See* N.D. Cal. Patent L.R. 3-6. A plaintiff's diligence in investigating accused products may demonstrate good cause. *See O2 Micro*, 467 F.3d at 1366; *Abbott Diabetes Care Inc. v. Roche Diagnostics Corp.*, 2007 WL 2221029, 2007 U.S. Dist. LEXIS 59161, at *5–6 (N.D. Cal. July 30, 2007).

Courts also consider procedural matters in assessing good cause, including the impact of amendment on other case deadlines, whether the opponent already had sufficient notice of the added contentions, and whether there is prejudice or whether any prejudice may be mitigated through an award of costs. *Avago Techs. Gen. IP PTE Ltd. v. Elan Microelectronics Corp.*, No. C04-05385 JW (HRL), 2007 WL 1449758, 2007 U.S. Dist. LEXIS 39543, at *4 (N.D. Cal. May 15, 2007) (citing cases); *3COM Corp v. D-Link Sys., Inc.*, No. C 03-2177 VRW, 2007 WL 949596, 2007 U.S. Dist. LEXIS 26542, at *21–22 (N.D. Cal. Mar. 27, 2007) (finding good cause where amendment would occur before a *Markman* hearing and before the close of discovery; "[i]t is to be expected that a patent holder may find other product designations that infringe as discovery progresses"). Indeed, a decision on good cause may hinge on the timing of the amendments sought. *Compare Gen. Atomics v. Axis-Shield ASA*, No. C 05-04074 SI, 2006 WL 2329464, 2006 U.S. Dist. LEXIS 58939, at *5–6 (N.D. Cal. Aug. 9, 2006) (finding good cause where party "did not conceive of the infringement theory it seeks to add until the parties exchanged preliminary claim construction statements" and noting that the amendments were sought before claim construction) *with Atmel Corp. v. Info. Storage Devices Inc.*, No. C 95-1987 FMS, 1998 WL 775115, 1998 U.S. Dist. LEXIS 17564, at *5–9 (N.D. Cal. Nov. 5, 1998) (denying leave to amend based on "newly discovered facts" where claim construction was completed and summary judgment briefing had begun).

2.2.3.2 Willful Infringement

Like general infringement, willful infringement need not be pleaded with particularity. Nonetheless, some courts require greater specificity with regard to the advice of counsel defense that is often interposed in response to an allegation of willful infringement.

2.2.3.2.1 Opinions of Counsel

Defendants sometimes rely on opinions of counsel as part of a defense to an allegation of willful infringement—that is, a patent attorney's opinion as to whether the asserted patent is valid and/or infringed by the defendant's products or processes. A defendant need not plead in its answer that it will be relying on an opinion of counsel. However, in the interests of fair and efficient discovery, some courts require election of the advice-of-counsel defense by a specified date along with production of the attorney–client documents for which protection has been waived. *See, e.g.*, N.D. Cal. Patent L.R. 3-7.

2.2.3.2.2 Privilege Issues Relating to Opinions of Counsel

Where a party relies on an opinion of counsel, it waives privilege as to the opinion. *In re EchoStar Commc'ns Corp.*, 448 F.3d 1294, 1299 (Fed. Cir. 2006); *Informatica Corp. v. Bus. Objects Data Integration, Inc.*, No. C 02-3378 JSW, 2006 U.S. Dist. LEXIS 58976, at *5, 2006 WL 2329460 (N.D. Cal. Aug. 9, 2006).

The scope of that waiver is a knotty problem that often becomes the subject of motion practice. The problem is exacerbated when litigation counsel also gave the opinion. *Genentech, Inc. v. Insmed Inc.*, 442 F. Supp. 2d 838, 842–44 (N.D. Cal. 2006). Federal Circuit law is used to analyze the scope of the waiver in these cases. *EchoStar*, 448 F.3d at 1298. Waiver extends not only to opinions on which the party intends to rely but also to all related communications and documents relied on or considered in connection with the opinion. *Id.* at 1304.

The Federal Circuit clarified the scope of privilege waiver in *In re Seagate Tech., LLC*, 497 F.3d 1360 (Fed. Cir. 2007) (en banc), *overruled on other grounds by Halo Elecs., Inc. v. Pulse Elecs., Inc.*, 579 U.S. ___ (2016). The court found that the "significantly different functions of trial counsel and opinion counsel advise against extending waiver to trial counsel." *Id.* at 1373. The classic "sword and shield" argument does not apply, because of the very different types of legal advice offered by trial counsel (litigation strategy and adversarial representation) and opinion counsel (commercial "due care" taken before undertaking potentially infringing activity).[8] *Id.* at 1372–75. The same rationale applies to the work-product doctrine. *Id.* at 1375–76 (applying *Hickman v. Taylor*, 329 U.S. 495, 510–11 (1947), and *United States v. Nobles*, 422 U.S. 225, 239–40 (1975)).

Although *Seagate* provides courts with substantial guidance, they must continue to be attentive, in summary judgment practice and at trial, to attempts by a party to use evidence it previously argued was outside the scope of the waiver, particularly as the law in this area continues to evolve. The standard for determining willfulness remains the totality of the circumstances. *Halo Elecs., Inc. v. Pulse Elecs., Inc.*, 579 U.S. ___ (2016) (holding that "courts should continue to take into account the particular circumstances of each case in deciding whether to award [enhanced] damages, and in what amount"). Those circumstances, however, should not automatically include whether the accused infringer sought advice of counsel or presented it to the jury. Section 298, which was enacted as part of the America Invents Act in 2011, provides that "[t]he failure of an infringer to obtain the advice of counsel" or "the failure of the infringer to present such advice to the court or jury, may not be used to prove that the accused infringer willfully infringed . . . ." 35 U.S.C. § 298. Of course, defendants may waive the protection offered by Section 298 if they put reliance on advice of counsel at issue. *See, e.g., Ultratec Inc. v. Sorenson Commc'ns Inc.*, 2014 WL 4976596, at *1-2 (W.D. Wis. Oct. 3, 2014), amended, 2014 WL 5023098 (W.D. Wis. Oct. 8, 2014).

---

8. The Federal Circuit heavily discounted the value of post-litigation-commencement opinions for this same reason.

2.2.3.3 Defenses

2.2.3.3.1 Invalidity Defenses

Like plaintiffs' allegations of infringement, defendants' allegations of invalidity need not be pled with particularity. Defendants typically recite only that the patent is invalid, and may identify sections of the Patent Act, such as § 101, 102, 103, or 112. Although this sort of notice pleading has usually been held to satisfy the Federal Rules of Civil Procedure, in practice, it gives little notice to a patent holder about what grounds for invalidity a defendant will actually assert. For this reason, in a few instances, courts have applied *Twombly* and *Iqbal* to strike affirmative defenses and counterclaims for not providing sufficient detail in the pleadings. *See Cleversafe, Inc. v. Amplidata, Inc.* 2011 U.S. Dist. LEXIS 145995, 2011 WL 6379300 (N.D. Ill. Dec. 20, 2011) (dismissing affirmative defense of invalidity and counterclaim); *Groupon, Inc. v. MobGob LLC*, 2011 U.S. Dist. LEXIS 56937, 2011 WL 2111986 (N.D. Ill. May 25, 2011) (dismissing counterclaim); *Tyco Fire Prods. LP v. Victaulic Co.*, 777 F. Supp. 2d 921 (E.D. Pa. 2011) (dismissing counterclaim but not affirmative defense). *But see Pfizer v. Apotex, Inc.* 726 F. Supp. 921 (N.D. Ill. 2010) (notice of claim sufficient for invalidity counterclaim).

In addition, some district judges require that defendants disclose the specific grounds on which they assert invalidity early in a case, just as they require specific infringement contentions from a patent owner. Courts can require defendants to identify specific prior art references they intend to assert as invalidating and to disclose invalidity claims based on written description, indefiniteness, or enablement. *See, e.g.*, N.D. Cal. Patent L.R. 3-3. Following a specified time period for making these disclosures, they may be amended only upon a showing of good cause. *See* N.D. Cal. Patent L.R. 3-7.

2.2.3.3.2 Unenforceability Defenses

Unenforceability defenses include inequitable conduct, prosecution laches, equitable estoppel, and patent misuse (e.g., using patent rights to force tying agreements or compulsory licensing packages). With the exception of inequitable conduct, unenforceability allegations need not be pled with particularity.

2.2.3.3.2.1 Inequitable Conduct Pled with Particularity

Inequitable conduct is seen as a species of fraud, and must be pled with particularity. Fed. R. Civ. P. 9(b). Inequitable conduct must rest on specific allegations of intentional, material omissions or misrepresentations by the patentee during the application process for a patent—the "who, what, when, where, and how" of the alleged inequitable conduct. *Exergen Corp. v. Wal-Mart Stores, Inc.*, 575 F.3d 1312, 1327 (Fed. Cir. 2009); *see also Ferguson Beauregard/Logic Controls, Inc. v. Mega Sys., LLC*, 350 F.3d 1327, 1344 (Fed. Cir. 2003). The necessary knowledge and intent may be pled generally or on information and belief, but there must be sufficient allegations of underlying facts from which a court could reasonably infer that a specific person had such knowledge and intent. *Exergen*, 575 F.3d at 1328–29. Early in the case, any order granting dismissal for lack of specificity should be without prejudice. *See Sun Microsystems v. Dataram Corp.*, Civ. No. 96-20708 SW, 1997 WL 50272, 1997 U.S. Dist. LEXIS 4557, at *5–7, 12–14 (N.D. Cal. Feb. 4, 1997). Under recent Federal Circuit precedent, "[t]o prevail on the defense of inequitable conduct, the accused infringer must prove that the applicant misrepresented or omitted material information with the specific intent to deceive the PTO." *Therasense, Inc. v. Becton, Dickinson & Co.*, 649 F.3d 1276, 1287 (Fed. Cir. 2011). Furthermore, to prevail under the current standard, the accuser must prove that "but for" the withholding of a reference, the patent would not have issued. *Id.* at 1291.

Because of the particularity requirement, defendants often seek leave to amend or to add inequitable conduct allegations as they are developed during discovery. Assuming the defense is pled with sufficient particularity, such motions should be granted if brought early in the case. *Id.* However, as the case approaches trial, the potential for prejudice to the patentee from late-arising claims increases. *See, e.g., Cent. Admixture Pharm. Servs. v. Advanced Cardiac Sols., P.C.*, 482 F.3d 1347, 1357 (Fed. Cir. 2007).

To forestall unnecessary motion practice on inequitable conduct claims, courts often set a cut-off date for pleading such allegations. Under this approach, prior to that date, a defendant may add inequitable conduct allegations without seeking leave of court. Thereafter, such allegations may only be added upon a showing of good cause for delay. A typical time frame for cut-off is when fact discovery is approximately 60% complete (e.g., if fact discovery is scheduled for a five-month period, the cut-off date for asserting inequitable conduct would be at three months).

2.2.3.3.2.2 Privilege Issues Relating to Unenforceability

Unenforceability allegations typically relate to the prosecution of the patent (inequitable conduct and prosecution laches) or to decisions relating to misuse of the patent, such as conditioning a license agreement on the requirement to buy non-patented products (i.e., improper tying schemes). These issues typically involve attorney–client communications and may also involve attorney work product. As a result, discovery may generate disputes over privilege. Attorney–client privilege doctrine applies in these matters as it applies generally. Therefore, absent a showing under the crime-fraud exception doctrine, *In re Rhone-Poulenc Rorer*, 48 U.S.P.Q.2D (BNA) 1823, 1998 U.S. App. LEXIS 12829 (Fed. Cir. 1998), the privilege may be asserted, even where it appears to obstruct fact gathering critical to prosecuting an unenforceability claim. *Id.*

2.2.4 Counterclaims

The defendant typically asserts an array of counterclaims. In nearly every case, it seeks a declaratory judgment that the asserted patents are not infringed, invalid, and/or unenforceable. The defendant may also assert infringement of its own patents in a counterclaim.

2.2.4.1 Compulsory Counterclaims

Under Federal Rule of Civil Procedure 13(a), a counterclaim is compulsory if it arises out of the same transaction or occurrence as the opposing party's claim. Unsurprisingly, a counterclaim for infringement is compulsory in an action for declaration of noninfringement. *Vivid Techs., Inc. v. Am. Sci. & Eng'g, Inc.*, 200 F.3d 795, 802 (Fed. Cir. 1999). Similarly, counterclaims for declaratory judgment of noninfringement or invalidity are compulsory with respect to a claim of infringement.

2.2.4.2 Noncompulsory Counterclaims

In the most common noncompulsory counterclaim in a patent suit, the defendant/accused infringer alleges infringement of defendant's patent(s) by the plaintiff. Other arguably noncompulsory counterclaims may include antitrust claims, *Walker Process* claims (that the patentee asserts a fraudulently procured patent), *Walker Process Equip., Inc. v. Food Mach. & Chem. Corp.*, 382 U.S. 172 (1965), or *Handgards* claims (that the patentee seeks to enforce a patent it knows to be invalid or not infringed), *Handgards, Inc. v. Ethicon, Inc.*, 601 F.2d 986 (9th Cir. 1979). *See Tank Insulation Int'l, Inc. v. Insultherm, Inc.*, 104 F.3d 83 (5th Cir. 1997); *Hydranautics v. FilmTec Corp.*, 70 F.3d 533, 536–37 (9th Cir. 1995). Some courts have held that antitrust claims based on allegations of patent invalidity are compulsory, rather than permissive. *See Critical-Vac Filtration Corp. v. Minuteman Int'l, Inc.*, 233 F.3d 697, 702 (2d Cir. 2000). The Federal Circuit has observed the split of authority but has not resolved it. *See Nobelpharma AB v. Implant Innovations, Inc.*, 141 F.3d 1059, 1067 n.4 (Fed. Cir. 1998).

2.2.5 Potential Overlap with Nonpatent Claims; Choice of Law

Patent complaints may overlap with other forms of federal intellectual property claims (e.g., copyright, trademark), antitrust and sham litigation claims, and state-law claims such as unfair competition, trade secret misappropriation, or breach of a patent license agreement. Federal Circuit law governs issues within its "exclusive jurisdiction" (i.e., patent law issues). *See, e.g., Advanced Cardiovascular Sys., Inc. v. Medtronic, Inc.*, 265 F.3d 1294, 1303 (Fed. Cir. 2001) (holding that the Federal Circuit will apply its "own law to both substantive and procedural issues intimately involved in the substance of enforcement of the patent right.") (quotation omitted). The law of the regional circuit in which the district court sits governs issues outside of the Federal Circuit's exclusive jurisdiction. *Id.*

The question of whether federal patent law preempts other federal or state-law claims is decided based on Federal Circuit law, not regional circuit law. *See Midwest Indus., Inc. v. Karavan Trailers, Inc.*, 175 F.3d 1356, 1360–61 (Fed. Cir. 1999). *But see Gunn v. Minton*, 133 S. Ct. 1059 (2013) (applying *Grable & Sons Metal Prods., Inc. v. Darue Eng'g & Mfg.*, 545 U.S. 308, 314 (2005) to conclude "that state legal malpractice claims based on underlying patent matters will rarely, if ever, arise under federal patent law for purposes of 28 U.S.C. § 1338(a)").

2.2.6 Interaction with Other Types of Actions

2.2.6.1 Bankruptcy

Typically, when a debtor begins bankruptcy proceedings, all pending actions against the debtor, including actions in federal district courts, are stayed. Section 362(a)(3) of the Bankruptcy Code provides that a petition "operates as a stay, applicable to all entities of . . . any act to obtain possession of property of the estate or of property from the estate or to exercise control over property of the estate." The stay applies to pending patent litigation against a debtor, but not to claims by the debtor. *See Seiko Epson Corp. v. Nu-Kote Int'l, Inc.*, 190 F.3d 1360, 1364 (Fed. Cir. 1999). Such claims may proceed (e.g., if the debtor is the accused infringer, the debtor's counterclaims for patent invalidity may proceed). *See id.* Likewise, the automatic stay does not apply to non-bankrupt codefendants of a debtor. *Id.*; *but see In re Excel Innovations, Inc.*, 502 F.3d 1086, 1093–94, n.1 (9th Cir. 2007) (holding that on motion by debtor, bankruptcy court may enjoin ongoing proceedings against non-debtor; in most circuits, standard analysis for granting preliminary injunctive relief applies; some circuits do not require showing of irreparable harm). The district court may stay the entire case once the bankruptcy court automatically stays the claims against the debtor. Alternatively, it may proceed with those aspects of the case that are not subject to the automatic stay.

A party may petition the bankruptcy court for partial or full relief from the stay. *See Outlast Techs., Inc. v. Frisby Techs., Inc.*, 298 F. Supp. 2d 1112, 1113–14 (D. Colo. 2004) (modifying stay order to allow summary judgment motions already filed in the district court to be decided). If a district court believes that such relief is appropriate, for example because trial has commenced or a decision on summary judgment is pending, it may suggest such a motion for relief in its order staying proceedings in response to the bankruptcy court's automatic stay notice.

The bankruptcy court's disposition of the debtor's bankruptcy does not give the debtor a license to commit postpetition infringement. "A discharge in bankruptcy operates as an injunction against a plaintiff asserting a claim for a debt incurred, or a cause of action that arose, before the date of bankruptcy discharge. It does not act as an injunction against a plaintiff asserting a claim for a debt incurred, or a cause of action that arose, after the date of bankruptcy discharge." *Hazelquist v. Guchi Moochie Tackle Co.*, 437 F.3d 1178, 1180 (Fed. Cir. 2006). Therefore, if an accused infringer continues infringement after discharge of debts in bankruptcy court, it is subject to renewed patent litigation in federal district court. *Id.*

2.2.6.2 International Trade Commission Actions

In parallel with the district courts, the United States International Trade Commission (ITC) provides a forum for domestic industries to seek exclusion of goods that violate U.S. intellectual property rights. The ITC is an independent agency that, among other things, directs actions against unfair trade practices. Under § 337 of the Tariff Act of 1930, the ITC investigates complaints by domestic industries that goods imported into the United States violate U.S. intellectual property rights or through other methods of unfair competition. Thus, ITC investigations enable intellectual property owners that operate in domestic industries to enforce U.S. patent rights against infringing imports.

The ITC experienced a significant increase in patent enforcement actions after the Supreme Court's ruling in *eBay, Inc. v. MercExchange, L.L.C.*, 547 U.S. 388 (2006), owing to the greater availability of injunctive-type relief and rapid adjudication relative to district court proceedings. The ITC is not bound by *eBay*, which made injunctive relief less available in district court actions. *See Spansion, Inc. v. Int'l Trade Comm'n*, 629 F.3d 1331, 1359 (Fed. Cir. 2010) (holding the ITC "is not required to apply the traditional four-factor test for injunctive relief"). Where an ITC proceeding finds patent infringement, the ITC generally issues exclusion orders barring importation of the infringing articles into the United States. With regard to adjudication speed, the Trade Act directs the ITC to resolve cases "at the earliest practicable time," which generally translates into an eighteen-month process after commencement of the investigation. *See* Uruguay Round Amendments Act of 1994, Pub. L. 103-465, § 321, 103d Cong., 2d Sess., 108 Stat. 4809 (1994); Trade Act of 1974, Pub. L. No. 93-618, § 341, 88 Stat. 1978, 2053 (1975) (amending § 337(b) of the Tariff Act of 1930).

Patent holders often seek relief from the ITC and U.S. district courts simultaneously. This raises several case-management issues for district courts. We focus here on the granting of stays pending resolution of the ITC action and the effect of the ITC action on the district court's resolution of patent issues.

2.2.6.2.1 Stays Relating to Parallel ITC Proceedings

Under 28 U.S.C. § 1659(a), parties to a civil action that are also respondents in a parallel proceeding before the ITC can move for a stay of the district court proceedings as a matter of right:

> (a) Stay. — In a civil action involving parties that are also parties to a proceeding before the United States International Trade Commission under section 337 of the Tariff Act of 1930, at the request of a party to the civil action that is also a respondent in the proceeding before the Commission, the district court shall stay, until the determination of the Commission becomes final, proceedings in the civil action with respect to any claim that involves the same issues involved in the proceeding before the Commission, but only if such request is made within — (1) 30 days after the party is named as a respondent in the proceeding before the Commission, or (2) 30 days after the district court action is filed, whichever is later.

Id.; *see In re Princo Corp.*, 478 F.3d 1345, 1355 (Fed. Cir. 2007).

As noted in the statute, the stay remains in effect until the determination of the ITC becomes final. After the dissolution of the stay, § 1659(b) allows the parties to use the ITC investigation record in the district court proceeding.

> (b) Use of Commission Record. — Notwithstanding section 337(n)(1) of the Tariff Act of 1930, after dissolution of a stay under subsection (a), the record of the proceeding before the United States International Trade Commission shall be transmitted to the district court and shall be admissible in the civil action, subject to such protective order as the district court determines necessary, to the extent permitted under the Federal Rules of Evidence and the Federal Rules of Civil Procedure.

Id.

Although the stay provided for in § 1659(a) is mandatory, it only applies to "any claim that involves the same issues involved in the proceeding before the Commission." Usually this is interpreted as applying only to the patents that the ITC and judicial proceedings have in common. In cases involving additional patents not at issue in an ITC proceeding, courts are often asked to stay the entire proceeding. In deciding whether to grant such a stay, the district court will typically balance several factors. For example, in *FormFactor, Inc. v. Micronics Japan Co., Ltd.*, the district court granted a motion to stay pursuant to § 1659(a) only after considering "(1) possible damage which may result from the granting of a stay; (2) the hardship or inequity which a party may suffer in being required to go forward; and (3) the orderly course of justice measured in terms of the simplifying or complicating of issues, proof, and questions of law which could be expected to result from a stay." 2008 U.S. Dist. LEXIS 13114, 2008 WL 361128 (N.D. Cal. 2008). Only two of the four patents under consideration in the district court were at issue in the ITC proceeding. Nonetheless, the court ruled that the two remaining patents shared subject matter and common inventors with the patents at issue in the ITC proceeding, and therefore a stay of the action was warranted to avoid duplicative efforts in discovery. Similarly, the court in *ILJIN U.S.A. v. NTN Corp.* found that numerous factors weighed in favor of granting a stay, including the following:

> (1) the ITC claim was filed before the district court complaint;
>
> (2) the proceedings were more advanced in the ITC case than in the district court;
>
> (3) there had not been substantial discovery in the case;
>
> (4) indisputably, it would conserve judicial resources to allow the ITC investigation to at least narrow the issues before the district court case proceeded, with the added benefit of potentially avoiding conflicting decisions;
>
> (5) the ITC is more experienced in deciding patent disputes than the district court; and
>
> (6) the complainant did not present any persuasive reason why a stay should not issue.

2006 U.S. Dist. LEXIS 15389, 2006 WL 568351 (E.D. Mich. 2006).

A district court must also decide whether to stay its proceedings as to all of the claims at issue, even if only a portion of those claims are involved in a § 337 investigation. For example, in *Micron Technology, Inc. v. Mosel Vitelic Corp.*, the defendants moved to stay the district court proceedings for all the claims that were not at issue before the ITC. 1999 U.S. Dist. LEXIS 4792, 1999 WL 458168 (D. Idaho 1999). The defendants argued that because of the substantial overlap of legal and factual issues, a stay of all the claims, including those not at issue before the ITC, "would enhance judicial economy" as well as "provide the Court with the benefit of the findings, conclusions and views of the ITC." *Id.* at *4. Moreover, the defendants insisted that while they would be prejudiced by litigating in multiple forums, the plaintiff would not be prejudiced by a stay because it will obtain a timely resolution of the claims before the ITC. *Id.* Yet in denying the motion, the court concluded that the defendants failed to establish that a stay of the instant proceedings was "necessary to prevent undue hardship or injustice." *Id.* at *5. The court further noted that a party moving for a stay "must make out a clear case of hardship or inequity in being required to go forward, if there is even a fair possibility that the stay for which he prays will work damage to someone else." *Id.* at *4 (quoting *Landis v. N. Am. Co.*, 299 U.S. 248, 255 (1936)). In sum, the *Micron* court denied the motion to stay and ordered discovery with respect to the claims not before the ITC. *Id.* at *5.

In contrast, the court in *Alloc, Inc. v. Unilin Decor, N.V.* took the alternative approach and entered a stay for all the claims. 2003 U.S. Dist. LEXIS 11917, 2003 WL 21640372 (D. Del. 2003). The court noted that "even though the '579 patent does not contain precisely the same claims of the other patents that are under review or reexamination, there is a sufficient correlation among all of the patents for the court to conclude that a stay is appropriate." In this case, although the '579 patent was not part of the ITC proceeding, it claimed priority to and shared a specification with an earlier '621 patent that was part of the ITC proceeding. *Id.* at *1. In issuing the stay, the court noted that it "would benefit from a narrowing of the numerous complex issues relating to the claims." *Id.* at *2. Moreover, the court noted that discovery had not yet begun, nor had a trial date been set. *Id.* at *3. Indeed, neither party had incurred substantial, litigation-related expenses. *Id.*

Thus despite the statutory mandate of 28 U.S.C. § 1659(a), a respondent may still be required to make out a clear case of hardship or inequity before a stay will be entered. Where the patent before the district court is related to a patent before the ITC, however, a court might enter a stay to narrow complex issues and avoid duplicative discovery.

2.2.6.2.2 Effect of ITC Rulings on District Court Proceedings

The general intellectual property jurisdiction statute, 28 U.S.C. § 1338 grants federal courts original and exclusive jurisdiction of civil actions "arising under any Act of Congress relating to patents." As a result, ITC patent determinations—such as claim construction, validity, infringement, and defenses—do not have preclusive effect in subsequent district court litigation. *See Tex. Instruments, Inc. v. Cypress Semiconductor Corp.*, 90 F.3d 1558, 1568–69 (Fed. Cir. 1996); *but cf. Balt. Luggage Co. v. Samsonite Corp.*, 977 F.2d 571 (4th Cir. 1992) (affording preclusive effect to affirmative defenses raised during ITC investigation because the party raising the defense had a full and fair opportunity to litigate the defense before the ITC); *Union Mfg. Co. v. Han Baek Trading Co.*, 763 F.2d 42 (2d Cir. 1985) (holding that ITC *trademark* determinations have res judicata effect on subsequent federal court proceedings). Nonetheless, district courts can and do consider ITC rulings in assessing cases. *See, e.g., Glasstech Inc. v. AB Kyro O.Y.*, 635 F. Supp. 465, 468 (N.D. Ohio 1986); *Mentor Graphics Corp. v. Quickturn Design Sys.*, 999 F. Supp. 1388, 1393 (D. Or. 1997).

2.2.6.3 Parallel District Court Proceedings

It is not uncommon for patent holders to pursue infringement actions involving the same patent in different jurisdictions at the same time as a result of jurisdiction and venue considerations. Furthermore, co-pending litigations relating to the same patent can occur when companies under threat of patent enforcement pursue declaratory judgment of invalidity, noninfringement, or unenforceability in a jurisdiction other than where a patent holder is seeking to enforce the patent against other entities. The AIA will likely increase the likelihood of such proceedings by limiting joinder of unrelated defendants in patent cases. *See* § 2.2.2.1.1.

The co-pendency of litigation involving the same patent can result in duplicative expenditure of judicial resources and impose unnecessary burdens on parties. Litigants have several tools for addressing these concerns: (1) transfer of venue, addressed in § 2.3.3.1; (2) coordination of litigation across districts through provisions governing multidistrict litigation, addressed in § 2.3.4; and/or (3) requests to stay one or more proceedings pending resolution of common issues, particularly patent validity. The standards for stays parallel those for transfer of venue. Although the specific standards differ slightly among circuits, courts typically consider the following factors in evaluating a motion to stay: (1) whether a stay would cause undue prejudice to the nonmoving party; (2) whether a stay will simplify the issues for trial; and (3) whether discovery is complete and a trial date is set.

The public policy favoring expeditious resolution of disputes is of particular weight when dealing with wasting assets such as patents. *See Katz v. Lear Siegler, Inc.*, 909 F.2d 1459, 1464 (Fed. Cir. 1990). Nonetheless, when two actions involving nearly identical parties and closely related patent infringement questions are filed in separate districts, the general rule is that the case first filed takes priority. The subsequently filed suit should be dismissed, transferred, or stayed. *See Kerotest Mfg. Co. v. C-O-Two Fire Equip. Co.*, 342 U.S. 180 (1952); *Genentech, Inc. v. Eli Lilly & Co.*, 998 F.2d 931 (Fed. Cir. 1993); *see generally* 14D Charles Alan Wright & Arthur R. Miller, Federal Practice and Procedure § 3823 (3d ed. 1998). The first-to-file presumption applies to declaratory judgments as well. *See Wilton v. Seven Falls Co.*, 515 U.S. 277, 289 (1995) ("As a general rule, a first-filed declaratory judgment suit will be entitled to precedence over a later-filed patent infringement action."); *Sanofi-Aventis Deutschland GmbH v. Novo Nordisk, Inc.*, 614 F. Supp. 2d 772, 774 (E.D. Tex. 2009); *but cf. Uniroyal Engineered Prods., LLC v. Omnova Sols. Inc.*, 2009 U.S. Dist. LEXIS 22518, 2009 WL 736700, *1 (W.D. Wis. 2009) ("In general, when a declaratory judgment action and a patent infringement action are filed within days of each other, it is more appropriate to consider the convenience factors of 28 U.S.C. § 1404(a) rather than applying the rigid rule that the first-filed action trumps the later-filed action.").

The first-to-file rule "is a doctrine of federal comity, intended to avoid conflicting decisions and promote judicial efficiency, that generally favors pursuing only the first-filed action when multiple lawsuits involving the same claims are filed in different jurisdictions." *Merial Ltd. v. Cipla Ltd.*, 681 F.3d 1283, 1299 (Fed. Cir. 2012). "When two actions that sufficiently overlap are filed in different federal district courts, one for infringement and the other for declaratory relief, the declaratory judgment action, if filed later, generally is to be stayed, dismissed, or transferred to the forum of the infringement action." *Futurewei Techs., Inc. v. Acacia Research Corp.*, 737 F.3d 704, 708 (Fed. Cir. 2013). The first-to-file rule, however, "is not rigidly or mechanically applied—an ample degree of discretion, appropriate for disciplined and experienced judges, must be left to the lower courts." *Merial*, 681 F.3d at 1299. Exceptions may be made if justified by "considerations of judicial and litigant economy, and the just and effective disposition of disputes." *Futurewei*, 737 F.3d at 708. Resolution of whether the second-filed action should proceed presents a question sufficiently tied to patent law that the question is governed by the law of the Federal Circuit. *Id.* Although the forum of the first-filed action is favored, exceptions "are not rare, and are made when justice or expediency requires[.]" *Genentech, Inc.*, 998 F.2d at 937 (citing *Kahn v. Gen. Motors Corp.*, 889 F.2d 1078, 1081–83 (Fed. Cir. 1989)) (discussing the general rule, the "customer suit" exception, and other factors that overcome "the presumptive right of the first litigant to choose the forum). In weighing venue transfer or stay motions, courts have looked to:

- the status of the co-pending case, *Elite Licensing, Inc. v. Thomas Plastics, Inc.*, 2003 U.S. Dist. LEXIS 2439, 2003 WL 473669 (S.D.N.Y. 2003) (where the first-filed case was dismissed for improper venue); *Schnadig Corp. v. Collezione Europa U.S.A.*, 2001 U.S. Dist. LEXIS 9208, 2001 WL 766898 (N.D. Ill. July 3, 2001) (where the co-pending case is likely to be dismissed);
- harm caused by delaying the stayed issues, *see Kahn v. Gen. Motors Corp.*, 889 F.2d 1078, 1082–83 (Fed. Cir. 1989);
- whether the other forum lacks jurisdiction over all necessary or desirable parties;
- the possibility of consolidation, *see SAES Getters S.p.A. v. Aeronex, Inc.*, 219 F. Supp. 2d 1081, 1092 (S.D. Cal. 2002) (emphasizing the importance that related patents are construed consistently);
- convenience of the parties; and
- judicial economy, *see Serco Servs. Co., L.P. v. Kelley Co., Inc.*, 51 F.3d 1037, 1040 (Fed. Cir. 1995).

Nonetheless, that the first-filed claim anticipated the later-filed claim is not, without more, a sufficient ground to rebut the first-to-file presumption, *see Elecs. for Imaging, Inc. v. Coyle*, 394 F.3d 1341, 1347–48 (Fed. Cir. 2005), but it can be a factor in the broader balance governing whether to apply the first-to-file rule. *Serco Servs.*, 51 F.3d at 1040.

Stays of co-pending patent litigation involving different parties have been most commonly granted in "customer suit" situations. As the name implies, such litigation arises when the patent holder is engaged in one litigation against a provider of the accused technology and separate litigation against the purchaser of the accused technology. Based on language in *Katz v. Lear Siegler, Inc.*, 909 F.2d 1459, 1464 (Fed. Cir. 1990); *see also Codex Corp. v. Milgo Elec. Corp.*, 553 F.2d 735, 737–38 (1st Cir. 1977) (preference for a manufacturer's declaratory judgment action because the manufacturer is the true defendant), courts in some circumstances have stayed patent litigation against such customers pending the outcome of the supplier suit, principally, as in *Katz*, where resolution of liability with respect to the supplier will resolve liability with respect to the customer. Cases involving the same patent and same parties (e.g., a declaratory judgment action brought by the accused infringer and a patent infringement action brought by the patent holder) are typically resolved by the first-to-file rule: the earlier-filed case takes precedence, and the later-filed case is transferred, stayed, or dismissed.

Given the above-referenced proliferation of co-pending litigations involving the same patent, it seems likely that courts will increasingly be asked to decide whether some of those suits should be stayed. At least some such motions will be filed at the outset of the case, before any discovery occurs. Because the stay factors balance the specific benefits to be gained from the stay with the specific prejudice that is likely to be suffered by the nonmovant, as well as the stage of the litigation, the merits of such motions are fact-intensive and can vary substantially from case to case. That said, such motions raise several issues for courts to consider. First, because the plaintiff often files all, or many, of the co-pending litigations on the same day, it may be difficult or impossible for a court to identify a case or cases that naturally take precedence over others. Indeed, even if the various defendants agree that some cases should be stayed pending resolution of others, it is very likely that the defendants will disagree about whose case should proceed first. Thus, a California court may be asked to stay a case pending resolution of a Delaware case, while the Delaware court is asked to stay that same Delaware case pending resolution of the same California case. As a practical matter, many courts are likely to avoid wading into those murky waters.

Moreover, even where one case or a group of cases clearly takes precedence (e.g., first-filed), if the subsequent cases were filed soon after the case deemed to have precedence, the patent holder will likely argue that the stay will be prejudicial and that the possibility of case-narrowing is illusory—indeed, it may require the patent holder's claims against some defendants to sit for years while other litigation is resolved. In addition, the possibility that the case(s) deemed to have precedence will not actually resolve issues that narrow the case sought to be stayed (because of settlement, because the patent holder prevails, or otherwise) and that, even when the same patent claims are asserted, the claim-construction and invalidity issues may differ substantially (e.g., because the patent holder's infringement allegations against the various defendants differ) are also likely to be considered. For these reasons, where the request to stay is filed at the outset of the case, most courts will consider other options, such as MDL, to achieve efficiency, or elect to proceed with the case normally. Of course, the stage of the case deemed to have precedence can alter this analysis substantially—if, for example, a request seeks to stay a case in its infancy to await resolution of a case that is on the eve of a trial at which invalidity is at issue, the factors may weigh strongly toward stay; likewise, if the case deemed to have precedence is pending in a venue with a short time-to-trial, that may also weigh strongly in favor of a stay. Because of the nature of the stay factors, relevant considerations can vary widely. Courts should evaluate such motions carefully on a case-by-case basis.

2.2.6.4 PTO Review Proceedings—Reexamination, Reissue, and AIA Review

The Patent Office has long provided various forms of administrative review of patent validity and scope. Minor mistakes in a patent, such as typographical errors and misnamed or omitted inventors, can be corrected through a certificate of correction. *See* §§ 254–256. Since 1836, the Patent Act has provided for reissuance of defective patents. Under the 1952 Act, patentees can seek broadening reissues within a two-year window following issuance and can narrow patent claims at any time during the patent's duration. *See* §§ 251–252. Since 1981, the Patent Office has authorized any person—whether the patent owner, an accused infringer, or a third party—to seek ex parte reexamination of patents. *See* §§ 301–307. In 1999, Congress sought to bolster reexamination by establishing an inter partes option that allowed third-party requesters to participate in the reexamination process.

These procedures, however, had little effect on the vast majority of patent cases until recently. Correction and reissue processes typically took place before or outside of patent litigation. Because requesters are not permitted to participate in ex parte reexamination once granted, relatively few parties considered it worth pursuing unless they had an ironclad invalidity case. Their concern was that, if the attempt failed, the reexamination certificate would reinforce or "gold-plate" the patent's validity to a jury. Even with the establishment of inter partes reexamination, potential challengers worried about long delays, a perceived pro-patentee tilt, and severe estoppel effects on district court challenges.

The AIA's institution of three new review processes—inter partes review (IPR), covered business method review (CBMR), and postgrant review (PGR)—in 2011 has invigorated patent validity proceedings at the Patent Trial and Appeal Board (PTAB). The AIA mandates that these reviews proceed expeditiously in a streamlined process. As a result, a significantly higher percentage of defendants seek administrative review of patents asserted against them. The USPTO has hired more than 200 administrative patent judges (APJs) to review petitions. They sit in three-APJ panels to resolve validity challenges.

Recent Federal Circuit decisions regarding the effect of USPTO procedures on litigation are expected to increase their attractiveness to alleged infringers. In *Fresenius USA, Inc. v. Baxter Int'l, Inc.*, the court held that the cancelation of the asserted patent claims in a reexamination vitiated a judgment of infringement that had been stayed pending appeal. 721 F.3d 1330, 1332 (Fed. Cir. 2013). The decision rested on a holding that the judgment was not actually final, despite having been labeled as such. *Id.* at 1341–42, 1344. In *ePlus v. Lawson Software*, the Federal Circuit dissolved an injunction and contempt order that had been entered against an adjudged infringer because reexamination had canceled the patent claim on which they were based. 760 F.3d 1350, 1352 (Fed. Cir. 2014). It bears noting that in both *Fresenius* and *ePlus*, the Federal Circuit had earlier affirmed the USPTO's decision to cancel the claim in a separate appellate proceeding. Because defendants believe these cases give them "two bites at the apple" to show invalidity, district courts can expect parallel postgrant reviews and inter partes reviews to become common.

2.2.6.4.1 Stays Pending Review or Reexamination

Patent Office processes principally affect patent case management through stays pending Patent Office review. Stay requests were less common, and even less often granted, in the pre-AIA era. District courts were reluctant to trust the Patent Office to expeditiously reexamine patents. The situation could not be more different today. A high and growing percentage of patents in litigation are pursued in parallel at the PTAB and courts are far more inclined to stay litigation pending PTAB review.

District courts have wide discretion to stay litigation pending reexamination or reissue. *See Viskase Corp. v. Am. Nat'l Can Co.*, 261 F.3d 1316, 1328 (Fed. Cir. 2001) (citing *Patlex Corp. v. Mossinghoff*, 758 F.2d 594 (Fed. Cir. 1985)).[9] "In determining whether to grant a stay, courts routinely considered three factors: (1) whether a stay would unduly prejudice or present a clear tactical disadvantage to the nonmoving party; (2) whether a stay will simplify the issues in question and trial of the case; and (3) whether discovery is complete and whether a trial date has been set." *Magna Donnelly Corp. v. Pilkington N. Am., Inc.*, 2007 U.S. Dist. LEXIS 17536, at *6, 2007 WL 772891 (W.D. Mich. Mar. 12, 2007); *Fresenius Med. Care Holdings, Inc. v. Baxter Int'l, Inc.*, No. C 03-1431 SBA, 2007 U.S. Dist. LEXIS 44107, 2007 WL 1655625 (N.D. Cal. June 6, 2007); *see also MercExchange, L.L.C. v. eBay, Inc.*, 500 F. Supp. 2d 556, 563 (E.D. Va. 2007) (courts consider the stage of discovery, whether a trial date has been set, and whether a stay will unduly prejudice the nonmoving party). Stays are less appropriate when the USPTO proceedings are initiated late in the litigation. *See, e.g., IMAX Corp. v. In-Three, Inc.*, 385 F. Supp. 2d 1030, 1033–34 (C.D. Cal. 2005); *Gladish v. Tyco Toys*, No. S-92-1666 WBS, 1993 U.S. Dist. LEXIS 20211, at *6–8, 1993 WL 625509 (E.D. Cal. 1993).

Notwithstanding the potential benefits of staying litigation to receive the Patent Office's expertise in examining validity in reexamination, district courts were often skeptical that reexamination proceedings would conclude in a timely and effective manner. Patent Office statistics confirmed this perception. Concerns with both the slow processing of reexamination proceedings as well as the high costs of district court litigation led Congress to expand and expedite Patent Office review proceedings in the AIA. Beginning September 15, 2012, the AIA replaced inter partes reexamination with inter partes review (IPR), with a mandate that the Patent Office decide whether to institute an IPR petition within six months of the filing of a petition and render a decision within one year of institution. *See generally* § 14.2.5.6. The AIA also added a broader review for covered business methods (CBMR) and instituted a postgrant review (PGR) process to be undertaken during the first nine months after a patent issues. It also consolidated and expanded administrative resources within the Patent Trial and Appeal Board (PTAB).

---

9. A district court's discretion to stay proceedings does not, however, empower the court to direct that a party file a reexamination or reissue in the PTO, nor does it empower the court to place conditions on the stay that exceed its inherent power to manage its docket. *Emerson Elec. Co. v. Davoil, Inc.*, 88 F.3d 1051, 1053–54 (Fed. Cir. 1996) (reversing stay conditioned on party's agreement to submit to the PTO documents prepared by the patent litigation defendant).

The newly implemented PTAB review processes have effected a sea change in patent enforcement, review, and case management. The relatively low cost and swift processing of IPRs and CBMs in conjunction with both high review institution and invalidation rates have caused a veritable stampede by alleged infringers, potential defendants, and some nongovernmental organizations to the PTAB. From September 15, 2012, the effective date for IPR and CBMR proceedings, through March 15, 2015, parties have filed over 3,000 petitions—more than 2,700 IPRs and 300 CBMRs. *See* USPTO, AIA Progress (Apr. 9, 2015), http://www.uspto.gov/sites/default/files/documents/040915_aia_stat_graph.pdf. The PTAB has instituted review in approximately 80% of the petitions. As of April 2015, approximately one-third of the petitions have been terminated by settlement or decision. As of January 15, 2015, approximately 36% of claims for which IPR was instituted were found unpatentable. *See* USPTO, *Inter Partes* Review Petitions Terminated to Date (Jan. 15, 2015) http://www.uspto.gov/sites/default/files/documents/inter_partes_review_petitions_terminated_to_date%2001%2015%202015.pdf.

As a result, motions to stay litigation pending resolution of the IPR proceedings as well grant rates for litigation stays have risen sharply. District courts stayed litigation pending IPR in approximately 75% of cases through December 9, 2014. *See* Scott A. McKeown, *District Courts Increasingly Await PTAB Decision*, Patents Post-Grant Blog (Dec. 23, 2014) http://www.patentspostgrant.com/district-courts-increasingly-await-ptab-outcome; *see also Capriola Corp. v. La Rose Indus., LLC*, 2013 U.S. Dist. LEXIS 65754, 2013 WL 1868344 (M.D. Fla. Mar. 11, 2013) ("if the PTO declines *inter partes* review, little time is lost, but if PTO grants *inter partes* review, the promise is greater for an important contribution by the PTO to resolution of the governing issues in the litigation."). The rate of stay grants varies across districts and judges. The Northern District of California granted 85% of IPR stay motions through September 2014, while the Eastern District of Texas had granted 13% of stay petitions. *See* Goodwin Proctor, *The PTAB Second Anniversary: Reflections and Strategies for the Years Ahead*, IP Advisor (Sept. 2014) http://www.goodwinprocter.com/~/media/Files/Publications/Newsletters/IP%20Advisor/2014/Goodwin%20Procter%20IP%20Advisor%20PTAB%202nd%20Anniversary%20Edition.PDF.

2.2.6.4.2 Evaluating Stay Requests with Pending AIA Review

Most courts continue to evaluate stay motions according to the same three-factor test articulated prior to the passage of the AIA. *See Semiconductor Energy Lab. Co. v. Chimei Innolux Corp.*, 2012 U.S. Dist. LEXIS 186322, 2012 WL 7170593, at *1, n.1 (C.D. Cal. Dec. 19, 2012) ("The Court sees no reason why the three factor assessment would not still be relevant [to the new inter partes review proceeding]."). The decision remains based on the "totality of the circumstances" and the inquiry is not limited to the three factors commonly cited. *See Universal Elecs., Inc. v. Universal Remote Control, Inc.*, 943 F. Supp. 2d 1028, 1030–31 (C.D. Cal. 2013). Because the PTAB has six months to decide whether to institute an IPR proceeding after a petition is filed, § 314(b), and the scope of the proceeding will not be known until it is instituted, many courts have expressed reluctance to stay a case merely on the filing of a petition. *See, e.g.*, *Dane Techs., Inc. v. Gatekeeper Sys., Inc.*, 2013 U.S. Dist. LEXIS 117718, 2013 WL 4483355, at *4 (D. Minn. Aug. 20, 2013) ("Before the PTO makes this decision the Court can only speculate as to whether the PTO will review a patent and to what extent."); *Ultratec, Inc. v. Captel, Inc.*, 2014 U.S. Dist. LEXIS 120062 at *6–7 (W.D. Wis. Nov. 14, 2013) (stay pending the PTAB's decision on the petition "adds an additional layer of doubt whether the inter partes review will even occur, let alone whether it will simplify the issues or reduce the burden of litigation for the parties or the court"); *One StockDuq Holdings, LLC v. Becton, Dickinson & Co.*, 2013 U.S. Dist. LEXIS 36621, 2013 WL 1136726, at *3 (W.D. Tenn. May 6, 2013) (denying stay because "the PTO has not yet granted Defendant's Petition for reexamination and it is possible that the PTO will never grant Defendant's Petition" and "staying the case at this juncture could result in an unnecessary delay of six months").

One important issue in assessing a stay motion is whether the PTAB review would potentially resolve the full range of claims before the court. The stay motion presents the court with the opportunity to clarify the potential ramifications of the PTAB review. If a successful challenge would not resolve the outstanding questions, the court can explore the possibility of stipulations to streamline the district court litigation.

2.2.6.4.3 Special Case: Stay Request with Pending CBMR

Courts have shown greater willingness to stay litigation pending covered business method review (CBMR). The CBMR process was conceived as a transitional program for patents that claim "method or corresponding apparatus for performing data processing or other operations used in the practice, administration, or management of a financial product or service, [excluding patents for technological inventions]." AIA § 18(d)(1). The patentability of business methods has been especially controversial, with the Supreme Court substantially limiting eligibility for these claims. *See* §§ 14.3.1.2.4, 14.3.1.2.5, 14.3.1.3. Since the creation of CBMR, the PTO has interpreted the scope of the CBM procedure broadly. For instance, in *Salesforce v. VirtualAgility*, CBM 2013-00024, Paper No. 16 (P.T.A.B. Nov. 19, 2013), the PTAB instituted a CBMR for a patent even though the patent claim did not expressly refer to financial activity.

District courts have been lenient in granting stays pending CBMR, recognizing that the statutory language in the AIA regarding CBMRs was intended to encourage a higher rate of stays. *Market-Alerts Pty. Ltd. v. Bloomberg Fin. L.P.*, 922 F. Supp. 2d 486, 489, 496 (D. Del. 2013) (recognizing a fourth factor when considering a motion to stay pending CMBR—"whether a stay, or the denial thereof, will reduce the burden of litigation on the parties and on the court"—and acknowledging the addition of this factor was intended to encourage a higher rate of stays pending CBMR); *Versata Software, Inc. v. Volusion, Inc.*, 2013 U.S. Dist. LEXIS 182842, 2013 WL 6912688, at *2 (W.D. Tex. June 20, 2013) (instituting a stay pending CBMR based on the four-factor test and "Congress's clear preference in favor of stays"); *Progressive Cas. Ins. Co. v. Safeco Ins. Co.*, 2013 U.S. Dist. LEXIS 54899, 2013 WL 1662952 (N.D. Ohio Apr. 17, 2013) (reviewing the legislative history, which indicates the new CMBR is "designed to provide a cheaper, faster alternative to district court litigation over the validity of business-method patents"); *Zillow v. Trulia*, 2013 U.S. Dist. LEXIS 144919, 2013 WL 5530573, at *3 (W.D. Wash. Oct. 7, 2013) ("the fourth factor was added in order to ease the movant's task in demonstrating the need for a stay"). Section 18(b)(2) also provides that a party may make an interlocutory appeal from a district court's grant or denial of stay pending CBMR. *See VirtualAgility, Inc. v. Salesforce.com, Inc.*, 759 F.3d 1307 (Fed. Cir. 2014) (reversing district court decision to deny a stay even under an abuse-of-discretion standard). However, the Federal Circuit does "not have jurisdiction under § 18(b)(2) . . . to consider an interlocutory appeal from a decision on a motion to stay until the PTAB institutes a CBMR proceeding." *Intellectual Ventures II LLC v. JPMorgan Chase & Co.*, 781 F.3d 1372 (Fed. Cir. 2015).

2.2.6.5 Preemption of State-Law Unfair Competition Claims

Federal patent law preempts state tort law (e.g., for unfair competition) where the patentee has acted in good faith in its communications to others regarding alleged infringement. *See, e.g., Viskase Cos. v. World Pac. Int'l AG*, 710 F. Supp. 2d 754, 756 (N.D. Ill. 2010) (citing *Globetrotter Software, Inc. v. Elan Computer Grp., Inc.*, 362 F.3d 1367, 1374 (Fed. Cir. 2004)). "[T]o avoid preemption, bad faith must be alleged and ultimately proven, even if bad faith is not otherwise an element of the tort claim." *Globetrotter*, 362 F.3d at 1374 (internal quotation marks omitted).

2.2.7 Rule 11: Presuit Investigations—Objective Good-Faith Basis for Filing Pleading

Rule 11 requires that a party filing a complaint has sufficiently investigated to form a good-faith basis for its claims. Thus, a patentee must exercise reasonable diligence to ascertain infringement before filing suit. This process must include a reasonable investigation into the interpretation of the claims. *Judin v. United States*, 110 F.3d 780, 784 (Fed. Cir. 1997). Because patents are presumed valid under § 282, a patent holder has no obligation to assess validity prior to filing infringement claims. *See Q-Pharma, Inc. v. Andrew Jergens Co.*, 360 F.3d 1295, 1303 (Fed. Cir. 2004); *Vigil v. Walt Disney Co.*, 2000 U.S. App. LEXIS 6231, at *1–2, 2000 WL 353148 (Fed. Cir. 2000).

The level of inquiry may vary according to the nature of the allegedly infringing product or process since some infringement (for example, of software patents) is difficult to ascertain from publicly available information. *See Woods v. DeAngelo Marine Exhaust, Inc.*, 692 F.3d 1272, 1288–89 (Fed. Cir. 2012); *Judin*, 110 F.3d at 784. If an accused product is readily obtainable and easily examined, courts tend to hold that it is reasonable to expect the patent owner to examine it, or have a reasonable explanation for not doing so. *Judin*, 110 F.3d at 784 (holding that patent owner and attorney had acted unreasonably when they had not "attempted to obtain a device from the [defendant] or the manufacturer so that they could more closely observe the device, nor was any attempt made to dissect or 'reverse-engineer' a sample device"); *Refac Int'l Ltd. v. Hitachi Ltd.*, 141 F.R.D. 281, 286 (C.D. Cal. 1991); *c.f. Vista Mfg. Inc. v. Trac-4 Inc.*, 131 F.R.D. 134, 138 (N.D. Ind. 1990) (declining to "recognize a general rule that Rule 11 requires an infringement plaintiff to examine the defendant's product in all instances"). If it is not possible for a patent owner to fully investigate infringement (e.g., the invention is a patented method that the potential defendant practices in secret), Rule 11 permits a party to proceed by specifically identifying in its pleadings those factual contentions that will "likely have evidentiary support after a reasonable opportunity for further investigation or discovery," distinguishing them from those factual contentions that "have evidentiary support . . . ." Fed. R. Civ. P. 11(b)(3).

2.3 Jurisdiction and Venue

2.3.1 Personal Jurisdiction

Personal jurisdiction is analyzed under the familiar two-part test: whether the applicable state long-arm statute is satisfied and whether the exercise of personal jurisdiction is consistent with the Due Process Clause of the Constitution. *Silent Drive, Inc. v. Strong Indus., Inc.*, 326 F.3d 1194, 1200, 1201 (Fed. Cir. 2003); *Inamed Corp. v. Kuzmak*, 249 F.3d 1356, 1359–60 (Fed. Cir. 2001). Patent cases typically do not raise substantial issues of personal jurisdiction since the defendant is alleged to have sold or offered for sale infringing products within the district, which usually provides specific personal jurisdiction over the infringement dispute. Personal jurisdiction issues can arise, however, in ANDA cases (discussed in Chapter 10) or where non–U.S.-based parties are alleged to have infringed.

In *Daimler AG v. Bauman*, the Supreme Court held that a court's exercise of general jurisdiction is appropriate only when a defendant's affiliations with the forum state are so continuous and systematic as to render it "essentially at home" in that state. 134 S. Ct. 746, 755 (2014) (quoting *Goodyear Dunlop Tires Operations, S.A. v. Brown*, 131 S. Ct. 2846, 2851 (2011)). This ruling has particular implications for Hatch-Waxman Act–based ANDA cases, as more generic company defendants may elect to challenge personal jurisdictions in districts that are neither the generic company's principal place of business nor their place of incorporation. Chapter 10.2.1 discusses this case's impact on ANDA litigation in further detail.

Plaintiffs typically rely on the "stream of commerce" theory of personal jurisdiction advanced in *Asahi Metal Industry Co. v. Superior Court of California, Solano County*, 480 U.S. 102 (1987). *See, e.g.*, *Freescale Semiconductor, Inc. v. Amtran Tech. Co.*, 2014 U.S. Dist. LEXIS 58044, 2014 WL 1603665 (W.D. Tex. Mar. 19, 2014) (granting renewed motion to dismiss for lack of personal jurisdiction under the "stream of commerce" theory). *Asahi* includes two plurality opinions embodying two different tests for stream of commerce, the *O'Connor* test (defendant must perform some act with respect to its products purposefully directed towards the forum) and the *Brennan* test (sufficient if reasonably foreseeable products would enter the forum). The Supreme Court's later decision in *J. McIntyre Machinery Ltd. v. Nicastro*, 131 S. Ct. 2780 (2011), has not resolved the different tests, and the Federal Circuit has so far declined to take a position on either of the two tests. *See AFTG-TG, LLC v. Nuvoton Tech. Corp.*, 689 F.3d 1358, 1363 (Fed. Cir. 2012) ("the law [on stream of commerce] remains the same after *McIntyre*); *Beverly Hills Fan Co. v. Royal Sovereign Corp.*, 21 F.3d 1558, 1566 (Fed. Cir. 1994). Given the uncertainty surrounding the "stream of commerce" test, the Federal Circuit has emphasized the importance of jurisdictional discovery. *See Trintec Indus., Inc. v. Pedre Promotional Prods., Inc.*, 395 F.3d 1275, 1283 (Fed. Cir. 2005) (vacating trial court's dismissal for lack of personal jurisdiction and remanding for jurisdictional discovery, upon finding existing record was inadequate and jurisdictional allegations could be supplemented through discovery); *Commissariat a l'Energie Atomique v. Chi Mei Optoelectronics Corp.*, 395 F.3d 1315, 1319 (Fed. Cir. 2005) (vacating trial court's dismissal for lack of personal jurisdiction and remanding for jurisdictional discovery, upon a finding that the record sufficiently supported jurisdiction under the *Brennan* test, but was inadequate for a determination under the *O'Connor* test); *see also GrafTech Int'l Holdings Inc. v. G&CS Co.*, No. 2:12-cv-720, ECF No. 39 (E.D. Tex. Apr. 8, 2014) (denying without prejudice foreign defendant's motion to dismiss for lack of personal jurisdiction and ordering the parties to pursue jurisdictional discovery).

2.3.2 Subject-Matter Jurisdiction

2.3.2.1 Original Jurisdiction

Under 28 U.S.C. § 1338(a), federal district courts have exclusive original jurisdiction of "any civil action arising under any Act of Congress relating to patents." In *Christianson v. Colt Industries Operating Corp.*, the Supreme Court held that "cases fall within the Federal Circuit's patent jurisdiction in the same sense that cases are said to 'arise under' federal law for purposes of federal question jurisdiction." 486 U.S. 800, 814 (1988) (quotation omitted). *See also Warrior Sports, Inc. v. Dickinson Wright, P.L.L.C.*, 631 F.3d 1367 (Fed. Cir. 2011) (holding that a malpractice claim brought under Michigan law arose under federal law because it required the district court to resolve a substantive issue of patent law). The familiar "well-pleaded complaint" rule determines whether a case "arises under" federal law. Most decisions that address the rule have dealt with defenses, whether patent-specific (as in *Christianson*) or as a matter of general federal law. *See Holmes Grp., Inc. v. Vornado Air Circulation Sys., Inc.*, 535 U.S. 826, 831 (2002). In 2002, the Court clarified that whether a claim arises under an act "relating to patents" is to be determined solely on the basis of the complaint and not on any counterclaims, compulsory or otherwise. *Id.*

2.3.2.2 Supplemental Jurisdiction

The jurisdiction of federal district courts extends to state-law claims arising out of a patent dispute. A common example of such jurisdiction is a trade secrets cause of action relating to the same technology as the patent cause of action. The supplemental jurisdiction statute provides that "in any civil action of which the district courts have original jurisdiction, the district courts shall have supplemental jurisdiction over all other claims that . . . form part of the same case or controversy under Article III of the United States Constitution." 28 U.S.C. § 1367(a). Accordingly, if a district court has no underlying original jurisdiction (e.g., the plaintiff lacks standing to bring any federal claims), the supplemental state-law claims must be dismissed. *Textile Prods., Inc. v. Mead Corp.*, 134 F.3d 1481, 1485–86 (Fed. Cir. 1998). However, the district courts have discretionary authority to retain supplemental jurisdiction over state-law claims even when the federal claims giving rise to original jurisdiction have been dismissed on the merits. 28 U.S.C. § 1367(c); *Gaia Techs., Inc. v. Reconversion Techs., Inc.*, 104 F.3d 1296, 1297 (Fed. Cir. 1996) (citing *Baker v. Farmers Elec. Coop., Inc.*, 34 F.3d 274, 283 (5th Cir. 1994)), amending 93 F.3d 774, 781 (Fed. Cir. 1996).

2.3.3 Venue

Venue for patent cases is generally governed by 28 U.S.C. § 1391, permitting filing in any district in which infringing activity (broadly defined as making, selling, or offering for sale) has occurred.

2.3.3.1 Venue Transfer Motions

Because most patent cases involve products or services available nationally, the patent venue statute generally permits a plaintiff to bring suit in any district. Accordingly, defendants are often sued for infringement in a district in which they have no physical presence, and will often respond with a motion to transfer venue.

"For the convenience of parties and witnesses, in the interest of justice, a district court may transfer any civil action to any other district or division where it might have been brought." 28 U.S.C. § 1404(a). Federal Rule of Civil Procedure 72(a) requires that district courts "promptly conduct" venue transfer proceedings. *See In re EMC Corp.*, 501 F. App'x 973, 975, 976 (Fed. Cir. 2013) (stressing "the importance of addressing motions to transfer at the outset of litigation"); *see also In re Google, Inc.*, 2015-138 (Fed. Cir. 2015) (granting writ of mandamus to direct a magistrate judge to stay proceedings and decide a motion to transfer that had been pending for over nine months). Furthermore, motions to transfer venue are to be decided based on "the situation which existed when suit was instituted." *Hoffman v. Blaski*, 363 U.S. 335, 343 (1960) (quoting *Paramount Pictures, Inc. v. Rodney*, 186 F.2d 111, 119 (3d Cir. 1950) (Hastie, J., dissenting)). Thus, any familiarity that the district court has gained with the underlying litigation due to the progress of the case since the filing of the complaint is irrelevant when considering the transfer motion. *See In re EMC Corp.*, 501 F. App'x at 976.

To obtain a change of venue, the defendant must demonstrate why the forum should be changed. The difficulty of meeting that burden is the subject of some disagreement. In *Gulf Oil Corp. v. Gilbert*, a frequently cited case, the Supreme Court held that "unless the balance is strongly in favor of the defendant, the plaintiff's choice of forum should rarely be disturbed." 330 U.S. 501, 508 (1947), *superseded by statute*, 28 U.S.C. § 1404(a), *as recognized in Quackenbush v. Allstate Ins. Co.*, 517 U.S. 706 (1996). However, *Gilbert* is a *forum non conveniens* case, not a § 1404(a) case. In *Norwood v. Kirkpatrick*, decided after the enactment of § 1404(a), the Supreme Court held that § 1404(a)'s "words should be considered for what they say, not with preconceived limitations derived from the *forum non conveniens* doctrine," and that § 1404(a) was "intended to permit courts to grant transfers upon a lesser showing of inconvenience" than that required in the *forum non conveniens* context. 349 U.S. 29, 31, 32 (1955) (internal quotations omitted). The Fifth Circuit has further examined the difference between the *forum non conveniens* doctrine (which requires dismissal of a case) and § 1404(a) (which permits only transfers), and held that "the avoidance of dismissal through § 1404(a) lessens the weight to be given" to the plaintiff's choice of venue and that, consequently, "he who seeks the transfer must show good cause." *Humble Oil & Ref. Co. v. Bell Marine Serv., Inc.*, 321 F.2d 53, 56 (5th Cir. 1963). Sitting en banc, the Fifth Circuit held that

> to show good cause means that a moving party, in order to support its claim for a transfer, must satisfy the statutory requirements and clearly demonstrate that a transfer is "[f]or the convenience of parties and witnesses, in the interest of justice." Thus, when the transferee venue is not clearly more convenient than the venue chosen by the plaintiff, the plaintiff's choice should be respected. When the movant demonstrates that the transferee venue is clearly more convenient, however, it has shown good cause and the district court should therefore grant the transfer.

In re Volkswagen of Am., Inc., 545 F.3d 304, 315 (5th Cir. 2008) (en banc). The Fifth Circuit made clear that the "good cause" burden "reflects the appropriate deference to which the plaintiff's choice of venue is entitled." *Id.*

In determining whether to transfer venue, courts balance the convenience of the litigants and the public interest in the fair and efficient administration of justice. *Id.* The convenience factors include: (1) the relative ease of access to sources of proof; (2) the availability of the compulsory process to secure witnesses' attendance; (3) the willing witnesses' cost of attendance; and (4) all other practical problems that may interfere with the litigation being relatively easy, expeditious, and inexpensive. *In re TS Tech USA Corp.*, 551 F.3d 1315, 1319 (Fed. Cir. 2008) (applying Fifth Circuit law). The public factors include: (1) the administrative difficulties flowing from court congestion; (2) the local interest in having local issues decided at home; (3) the forum's familiarity with the governing law; and (4) the avoidance of unnecessary conflict-of-law problems involving the application of foreign law. *Id.* Although courts have traditionally also considered the plaintiff's forum choice (though that by itself was not conclusive or determinative, *In re Horseshoe Entm't*, 337 F.3d 429, 434 (5th Cir. 2003)), the Fifth Circuit in *Volkswagen* held that the plaintiff's forum choice was reflected in the moving party's burden to show good cause, and that no separate consideration need be given to the plaintiff's choice. *Volkswagen*, 545 F.3d at 315.

To correct "a patently erroneous denial of transfer," the Federal Circuit may grant a writ of mandamus, ordering a district court to transfer a case to a different venue. *In re Acer Am. Corp.*, 626 F.3d 1252, 1254 (Fed. Cir. 2010) (ordering transfer where plaintiff and five defendants were located in transferee venue and no party was located within 300 miles of courthouse where case was filed). "The writ of mandamus is available in extraordinary situations to correct a clear abuse of discretion or usurpation of judicial power." *In re Nintendo Co.*, 589 F.3d 1194, 1197 (Fed. Cir. 2009). In *Nintendo*, the Federal Circuit held that the district court abused its discretion "in a case featuring most witnesses and evidence closer to the transferee venue with few or no convenience factors favoring the venue chosen by the plaintiff." *See id.* at 1198.

Similarly, the Federal Circuit has granted mandamus relief in cases reflecting a variety of factual situations, especially out of the Fifth Circuit. *See, e.g., In re Microsoft Corp.*, 630 F.3d 1361 (Fed. Cir. 2011) (ordering transfer where U.K. plaintiff incorporated affiliate and established office without employees in Tyler, Texas, sixteen days before filing suit there); *In re Zimmer Holdings, Inc.*, 609 F.3d 1378, 1381 (Fed. Cir. 2010) (ordering transfer out of the Eastern District of Texas where "plaintiff is attempting to game the system by artificially seeking to establish venue by sharing office space with another of the trial counsel's clients"); *In re Hoffman-La Roche Inc.*, 587 F.3d 1333 (Fed. Cir. 2009) (ordering transfer from Eastern District of Texas where plaintiff's only connection to transferring district was storing electronic documents locally); *In re TS Tech USA Corp.*, 551 F.3d 1315, 1321 (Fed. Cir. 2008) (finding that the district court "clearly abused its discretion in denying transfer from a venue with no meaningful ties to the case"); *but cf. In re Apple Inc.*, 743 F.3d 1377, 1379 (Fed. Cir. 2014) (divided panel denied writ of mandamus seeking relief from Eastern District of Texas order denying transfer); *In re ASUS Comput. Int'l*, 537 F. App'x 928 (Fed. Cir. Sept. 11, 2014) (denying writ of mandamus, explaining that "[t]he clear abuse of discretion standard means that the district court has a 'range of choice' and that its decision will be upheld so long as it stays within reason." (quoting *In re Vistaprint Ltd.*, 628 F.3d 1342, 1347 (Fed. Cir. 2010)).

Notably, in applying Fifth Circuit law in these cases, the Federal Circuit held that the plaintiff's choice of forum need only be honored to the extent the plaintiff's connections to the forum are legitimate, rather than connections "made in anticipation of litigation and for the likely purpose of making that forum appear convenient." *See In re Microsoft Corp.*, 630 F.3d at 1361, 1364 (Fed. Cir. 2011); *see also In re Toyota Motor Corp.*, 474 F.3d 1338, 1340 (Fed. Cir. 2014) (applying Fifth Circuit law in affirming district court's transfer order, which found that the plaintiff's recent opening of an office in the district court's jurisdiction did not favor retention); *In re Nintendo*, 756 F.3d 1363 (Fed. Cir. 2014) (affirming Eastern District of Texas order denying transfer, noting that "decisions granting transfer have looked beyond the connection of the parties with the transferor venue when the disparity of convenience is so marked as to outweigh the plaintiff's right to choose the forum."). District courts beyond the Fifth Circuit have cited this rule to justify increased scrutiny of the plaintiffs' chosen forum. *See, e.g., Pragmatus AV, LLC v. Facebook, Inc.*, 769 F. Supp. 2d 991, 997 (E.D. Va. 2011) (citing *In re Microsoft* for the proposition that, for the plaintiff's choice to warrant substantial deference in the venue analysis, "[the] plaintiff must prove a legitimate connection to the district") (criticizing plaintiffs for selecting forum because of its reputation as a "rocket docket").

Another reason the Federal Circuit has ordered transfer is that "[i]n patent infringement cases, the bulk of the relevant evidence usually comes from the accused infringer. Consequently, the place where the defendant's documents are kept weighs in favor of transfer to that location." *In re Genentech, Inc.*, 566 F.3d 1338, 1345 (Fed. Cir. 2009) (quoting *Neil Bros. Ltd. v. World Wide Lines, Inc.*, 425 F. Supp. 2d 325, 330 (E.D.N.Y. 2006)); *but see In re Barnes & Noble, Inc.*, 743 F.3d 1381 (Fed. Cir. 2014) (divided panel denied writ of mandamus seeking relief from order refusing to transfer case even though party and nonparty witnesses resided in the transferee district because the movant failed to address how many such witnesses would be unavailable or unwilling to testify in the transferor district and other factors favored the transferor district). In addition, the Federal Circuit has played down the role of the defendant's place of incorporation, overturning a District of Delaware ruling that the defendant's nominal corporate domicile tipped the balance in favor of retaining venue in Delaware. *See In re Link_A_Media Devices Corp.*, 662 F.3d 1221 (Fed. Cir. 2011).

Nonetheless, the Federal Circuit has denied mandamus where remaining in a particular venue would significantly serve judicial economy. *See In re Vistaprint, Ltd.*, 628 F.3d 1452 (Fed. Cir. 2010) (denying writ of mandamus for transfer where there was past and co-pending litigation in the same court on the patent in suit); *In re Volkswagen of Am., Inc.*, 566 F.3d 1349 (Fed. Cir. 2009) (denying transfer where three lawsuits were pending in the same court on the same patents); *but see In re Verizon Bus. Network Servs.,* 635 F.3d 559 (Fed. Cir. 2011) (ordering transfer where convenience factors clearly outweighed the possible judicial efficiencies to be gained because the patent-in-suit had been previously construed by the same court in a separate action five years earlier, and prior to a reexamination proceeding).

Despite these denials of mandamus, recent writs issued by the Federal Circuit regarding transfer motions have made clear that certain facts, without more, are inadequate to maintain venue in a forum if there is another forum that is more convenient to witnesses in the action. For example, until recently, some district courts denied transfer on the ground that the forum was a centralized locale between many far-flung witnesses and documents. The Federal Circuit has rejected this rationale for maintaining venue. *See In re Genentech, Inc.*, 566 F.3d at 1348; *In re Nintendo Co.*, 589 F.3d 1194, 1199–1200 (Fed. Cir. 2009). Table 2.4 summarizes factual showings deemed insufficient to maintain venue.

Table 2.4
Facts, Standing Alone, Held Insufficient to Maintain Venue

District court deference to plaintiff's choice of forum.	*In re Nintendo*, 756 F.3d 1363 (Fed. Cir. 2014) *In re TS Tech USA Corp.*, 551 F.3d 1315 (Fed. Cir. 2008)
Presence of electronic documents in the forum.	*In re Hoffmann-La Roche Inc.*, 587 F.3d 1333 (Fed. Cir. 2009)
Plaintiff's presence in the venue was solely for purposes of litigation. For example: Incorporating in the venue 16 days prior to filing suit. Sharing office space in the forum with another client of trial counsel.	*In re Toyota Motor Corp.*, 474 F.3d 1338 (Fed. Cir. 2014) *In re Microsoft Corp.*, 630 F.3d 1361 (Fed. Cir. 2011) *In re Zimmer Holdings, Inc.*, 609 F.3d 1378 (Fed. Cir. 2010)
Past experience of the transferee forum with the patent in suit.	*In re Verizon Bus. Network Servs.*, 635 F.3d 559 (Fed. Cir. 2011)
Defendant sells allegedly infringing products in the forum.	*In re Nintendo Co.*, 589 F.3d 1194 (Fed. Cir. 2009)

"Central location" rationale.	*In re Genentech, Inc.*, 566 F.3d 1338 (Fed. Cir. 2009) *In re Nintendo Co.*, 589 F.3d 1194 (Fed. Cir. 2009)
Defendant is incorporated in the forum but maintains no other business presence there.	*In re Link_A_Media Devices Corp.*, 662 F.3d 1221 (Fed. Cir. 2011)

2.3.4 Multidistrict Coordination

There are a number of options for managing multiple patent cases between the same parties or involving the same patents. This issue takes on greater significance in the aftermath of the AIA's misjoinder provision. *See* § 2.2.2.1.1. Multiple cases pending in the same district are often consolidated (or at least coordinated) before a single judge. *See* § 5.1.3.8 (discussing claim construction in multidefendant cases). Related cases pending in multiple districts can be consolidated by a transfer of venue under 28 U.S.C. § 1404(a). In addition, the United States Judicial Panel on Multidistrict Litigation ("JPML") is authorized to transfer cases for coordinated or consolidated pretrial proceedings if transfer "will be for the convenience of the parties and witnesses and promote the just and efficient conduct of such actions." 28 U.S.C. § 1407.

Co-pending patent cases are eligible for coordination or consolidation through this process. For example, the JPML issued an order transferring seven patent actions relating to a patent on a system for spraying self-tanning solutions then pending in various districts for coordinated or consolidated pretrial proceedings. *See In re Laughlin Prods., Inc., Patent Litig.*, 265 F. Supp. 2d 525 (E.D. Pa. 2003). In *In re Bear Creek Techs., Inc.*, 858 F. Supp. 2d 1375 (2012) (MDL No. 2344), the JPML ruled that § 299(a) of the AIA does not alter its authority to order pretrial centralization of patent litigation. The JPML reasoned that there was "no overlap" between the AIA and § 1407, because of the different standards of the two statutes. It contrasted the AIA's focus on joinder and consolidation at trial with "Section 1407's express focus on transfer for pretrial proceedings." The JPML concluded that transfer and centralization was appropriate in *Bear Creek* because the separate actions shared "substantial background questions of fact" concerning the "validity and enforceability" of the patent-in-suit, as well as "claim construction." The JPML emphasized that "centralization offers substantial savings in terms of judicial economy by having a single judge become acquainted with the complex patented technology and construing the patent in a consistent fashion (as opposed to having six judges separately decide such issues)." When related cases or litigation between the same parties cannot be consolidated, district courts still have many available options to coordinate proceedings. Courts may designate one case as the "lead case," or even stay a case until the conclusion of another. Judges may conduct joint hearings or conferences, or jointly appoint special masters under Federal Rule of Civil Procedure 53. The parties may be required to prepare a joint discovery plan, and protective orders can be drafted to make discovery from one case available in another.

2.4 Scheduling

As in any litigation, the case-management conference and scheduling order under Federal Rule of Civil Procedure 26(f) and 16(b) form the starting point for managing the litigation. Scheduling and case management in a patent case must balance the need for efficient identification and resolution of key issues against the dangers of insufficiently comprehending those possibly complex, highly technical issues. As discussed above, in § 2.1, patent local rules adopted in some district courts reflect various approaches to striking this balance. Courts outside these districts should consider whether such rules can be adapted to the needs of a specific case, if not a standing order.

Regardless of any patent local rules, scheduling will be optimized if the scheduling order includes dates for:

- disclosure of invalidity and infringement contentions,
- last date to disclose intention to rely on advice of counsel as a defense,
- last date to add inequitable conduct allegations without leave of court,
- close of fact discovery,
- claim-construction hearing date,
- close of expert discovery,
- last date for filing and hearing dispositive motions (in most patent cases, both sides will want to file multiple summary judgment motions; *see* §§ 2.1.3.2.4 and 5.1),
- schedule for *Daubert* motions (*see* § 7.4.2),
- the possibility of staggering expert report deadlines with damages reports due before technical expert reports,
- requiring substantial disclosure of damages theories in initial disclosures (*see* §§ 2.6.4, 4.2.1), and
- setting an early date for motions to dismiss that would narrow the scope of the action (*see* § 6.1.3).

Case-specific factors will drive decisions regarding the time necessary to complete each of the above tasks. At the outset of the case, the parties will be more familiar with these unique factors. Therefore, to facilitate preparation of an effective case-management order, the court should ask the parties to address each of these issues and to provide a proposed calendar in their Rule 26(f) Joint Case Management Statement.

2.5 Case-Management Conference

Effective management of a patent case usually begins with a case-management conference pursuant to Rule 26(f). At the conference, the court and parties identify issues relating to the substance of the case and any business considerations that influence the dispute. The court should also establish ground rules that will encourage the parties to minimize acrimony and maximize communication and compromise.

In many districts, the conference is held off the record, with only counsel in attendance. Informality can promote more productive discussion and compromise. In particularly complex or obviously contentious cases, it may be necessary to conduct the proceedings on the record.

In advance of the initial conference, many courts will issue a form of standing order that applies to patent cases, addressing the matters to be covered in the Joint Case Management Statement, the agenda for the conference, certain aspects of local patent rules and attendant disclosures, and presumptive limitations on discovery.

Some courts have found it helpful in patent cases to distribute a very brief "advisory" document to address some of the special aspects of patent litigation, as well as expectations for conduct of the case, beyond what might be found in a typical standing order or local rules. This advisory document may be distributed at, or in advance of, the initial case-management conference. Appendices 2.3 and 2.4 contain examples. The court might consider in appropriate cases requiring that lead counsel provide a copy of this advisory to their respective clients.

The following charts identify subjects for initial and subsequent case-management conferences that guide preparations for discussing the case with counsel. Appendices 2.1 and 2.2a present this material as checklists that can be provided to the parties. Exploring these issues will provide insight into how counsel might be expected to conduct the litigation and whether the case is amenable to early settlement or summary judgment.

Table 2.5
Business and Market Considerations Checklist

Issue	Implications
What are the accused products?	Damages. Why certain terms are being disputed in claim construction and the effect of a given interpretation. This information may also affect the scope of discovery.
Do the accused products encompass the accused infringer's entire business, or are they part of a larger line of products?	Can be a factor in injunctions and stays: business-destroying judgments favor stays of execution.
How big is the market for these products (approximate annual sales figures)?	Willingness to litigate to trial. Justification for imposing private costs such as special masters.
Does the plaintiff make a competing product?	Relevant to consideration of injunctive relief. Can complicate damages because of plaintiff's loss of monopoly pricing.
Are there other competitors in the market?	Issue preclusion or stare decisis possible if patent owner loses. Damages affected if economic substitutes available.

Issue	Implications
Have the parties had a prior business relationship? If so, how and when did it end?	Partners who have a history together, or an ongoing relationship, are more amenable to settlement. May be helpful in understanding collateral motivations to sue, and possible avenues to settlement.
What is the financial state of the parties (e.g., what were the companies' prior-year profits and what are projected profits)?	See above.
Are the parties public companies?	See above.
Will injunctive relief put the accused infringer out of business?	See above.
How much time remains before the asserted patents expire?	Can affect equitable factors in injunctions and stays.

Table 2.6
Substantive Considerations Checklist

Issue	Implications
Is the party asserting the patent(s) the named inventor? If not, how did the party acquire the patent rights? If by license or assignment, when did this occur?	Standing.
Is there parallel litigation (e.g., ITC) or review at the PTAB?	Stay pending resolution of related actions.
Is there a dispute about the structure and function of the accused device?	If these points are undisputed, then infringement is effectively a question of claim construction, and the case may be handled on a more expedited basis.
Is the technology complex?	The court might require a tutorial or consider appointment of a special master or technical advisor.
Are there substantive issues amenable to early resolution (e.g., a few dispositive claim terms, patent eligibility)?	Narrowing the disputed issues early in the case can focus discovery and encourage settlement; timing of resolution; need for tutorial.
Have the asserted patents—or any related patents—been litigated in actions against other parties? If so, what was the outcome?	Other case discovery may be helpful to efficient handling of current litigation. Successful prior assertion of patent can affect validity analysis. Understanding how other courts handled claim-construction or summary judgment issues can be helpful, whether or not any decisions were final, vacated, or binding in the current case.

Issue	Implications
Have the asserted patents—or any related patents—been licensed to third parties? If so, is defendant asserting a license defense or patent exhaustion?	Patent owner's licensing activities can affect damages and consideration of injunctive relief.
Are the asserted patents connected with any industry standard? Are the asserted patents subject to a binding obligation to license?	Patent owner's participation in standard-setting organizations may affect damages and consideration of injunctive relief, as SSOs often impose patent disclosure obligations or obligations to license on fair, reasonable, nondiscriminatory terms.
Have the asserted patents—or any related patents—been reexamined in the USPTO? If so, what was the outcome? If not, is this something that either party is contemplating?	Outcome of USPTO proceedings can affect scope of claims and sometimes damages. Current or planned proceedings at USPTO may be grounds for stay of litigation. *See* § 4.6.4.
If the accused infringer intends to rely on opinion of counsel with attendant waiver of attorney-client privilege, what will be the scope of the waiver?	*See* § 2.2.3.2.2. Early discussion of waiver issues may obviate postwaiver disputes over scope.
Has litigation counsel for the patentee been involved in prosecution of the patents-in-suit or related patents?	May result in need to depose trial counsel or partners. Raises issues of privilege waiver and possible disqualification.
Discuss how the court intends to address the proper role for and limitations on expert witnesses. *See* § 7.4.1.	Raising these issues early can provide valuable guidelines for the parties in preparing for trial.
If the plaintiff has asserted indirect infringement (contributory or by inducement), discuss how plaintiff intends to prove accused infringer's required mental state.	Raising the issue early can help guide the parties to ensure that the necessary facts are developed in discovery.
How does the plaintiff expect to calculate reasonable royalty damages? Established royalty or hypothetical negotiation? Will the entire-market-value rule be applied? Are there comparable licenses?	Raising the issue early can help guide the parties to ensure that the facts necessary to support are developed in discovery.
Will any survey evidence be presented at trial (e.g., to show customer demand for the patented invention or support a damages theory based on the entire-market-value rule)?	May wish to require parties and their experts to discuss or agree on survey design before it is conducted, to save time and money and resolve admissibility problems in advance. *See* Manual for Complex Litigation, § 11.493 (4th ed. 2004); *see generally* Shari Seidman Diamond, *Reference Guide on Survey Research, in* Reference Manual on Scientific Evidence 359 (Federal Judicial Center, 3d ed. 2011).

Table 2.7
Managing Cooperation Between the Parties and the Potential for Early Resolution

Issue	Implications
Discuss potential parallel litigation and PTAB review.	Efficiency, timing, and cost of litigation. Whether to stay litigation depends in part on whether a stay would unduly prejudice or present a clear tactical disadvantage to the nonmoving party.
Discuss the parties' anticipated scope of discovery. Consider limiting the number of depositions, document requests and/or requests for admission. Consider whether the 25-interrogatory limit under the Federal Rules should be modified.	Efficiency and cost of litigation. More robust discovery planning generally means less call on the court to intervene later in discovery disputes.
Discuss electronic discovery issues.	Encourages early cooperation in complex and costly area; diminishes risk of inadvertent loss of electronic records.
Discuss the patents and claims being asserted. Consider imposing a limit on the number of claim terms to be construed.	Helps parties focus on narrowing issues in the case, reducing the burden on themselves and the court.
Discuss whether claim construction will turn on disputed subsidiary facts.	Helps to plan for *Markman* hearing—scope of tutorial; whether to have live testimony from experts or other witnesses.
Require the parties to meet and confer (at least telephonically) before bringing discovery disputes to the court. Provide stern warnings concerning cooperation and communication.	Reduces the need for court intervention to resolve discovery disputes, which can overwhelm a case if not controlled.
Consider limiting the number of discovery disputes the court will entertain without prior leave.	See above. The court may exercise even more control by requiring leave through a telephonic hearing, either directly or preceded by a very brief exchange of letters.
If the district does not have its own patent local rules, consider adopting the patent local rules of another district (e.g., Northern District of California). Discuss with the parties ways that such patent local rules might be adapted to the case.	Improves efficiency by eliminating most common discovery disputes. Generally improves forward progress of the case and assures that claim-construction and summary judgment motions will be informed.

Issue	Implications
Discuss the timing of summary judgment motions and their relationship to claim construction, and identify any other issues that could potentially give rise to dispositive motions. If so, do these issues require much discovery?	While claim construction may or may not have to be completed before the summary judgment process (*see* § 2.1.3), other issues may be dispositive. See § 6.1.1 for further discussion of issues that might be amenable to early adjudication.
Discuss any restrictions that the court will or might impose on the number of summary judgment motions.	Can greatly affect the parties' strategies and practices. See § 6.1 for guidance on summary-adjudication best practices for patent cases.
Discuss how the court will distinguish motions for summary judgment and motions *in limine*. *See* § 7.1.4.	Reduces burden of premature consideration of *in limine* motions and tardy consideration of summary judgment motions.
Discuss approaches to mediation. Appoint mediator, or initiate selection process. *See* § 2.7.	Establishes mediation as integral and continuous part of litigation process. Encourages parties to cooperate on information exchange. Enhances chance of early resolution.

2.6 Salient Early Case-Management Issues

This section addresses issues that can greatly influence the costs and complexity of patent litigation. The goal is to identify possible issues that can potentially lead to early resolution of some or all issues and/or greatly reduce the costs of patent litigation.

2.6.1 Multidefendant Litigations

An increasingly popular trend has been for patentees to sue large numbers of defendants in a single litigation. For plaintiffs, this approach is often less expensive and easier to coordinate than pursuing multiple different litigations. The AIA and the Federal Circuit's decision in *In re EMC Corp.*, 677 F.3d 1351 (2012), are likely to blunt this trend. For example, in those multidefendant cases where the conduct or products accused of infringement bear little resemblance from one defendant to another, there may be joinder issues. *See* § 2.2.2.1.1. But other types of multidefendant cases may be unaffected by these changes in the law. For example, the alleged infringement may stem from the defendants' compliance with an industry standard, or where the patentee has sued both the manufacturer of the accused products and its downstream customers (e.g., OEM companies).

The court's ability to efficiently manage such cases may be enhanced by identifying at an early stage the patentee's basis for including multiple defendants in the litigation.

2.6.1.1 Multidefendant Litigations Based on Standards Compliance

Standards regulate almost all modern manufacturing. For example, every wireless device must conform to a wide variety of standards set by industry-specific standard-setting organizations (SSOs). These standards ensure interoperability between devices. When practicing a mandatory feature of a standard infringes a patent, however, each manufacturer's compliance with the standard becomes an act of infringement. Recently, there has been enormous growth in patent litigations accusing whole industries of patent infringement based on the practice of standards. Identifying this underlying fact at the outset of the litigation can improve the court's management of the case.

For example, if the alleged infringing activity is purely the compliance with a mandatory feature of the standard, then discovery regarding the functional specifications of the accused products can be fairly limited.

However, these types of cases almost always also involve complicated defenses and counterclaims related to the patentee's potential noncompliance with the policies of the SSO that govern the adoption of the standard. For example, the defendant may bring claims or defenses alleging that the patentee participated in the development of the standard without timely disclosure of its patents that were essential to the standard, in violation of SSO policies. Alternatively, the defendant may allege that the patentee has failed to offer a license on fair, reasonable, and nondiscriminatory (FRAND) terms, as most SSO policies require for patents that patentees declare essential to the standard. These allegations may form the basis for equitable, contract-based, and/or antitrust claims and defenses. *See, e.g.*, *Qualcomm Inc. v. Broadcom Corp.*, 548 F.3d 1004, 1020 (Fed. Cir. 2008) (holding patent unenforceable for implied waiver where the patentee "organiz[ed] a plan of action to shield the '104 and '767 patents from consideration by the JVT (Joint Video Team) with the anticipation that (1) the resulting H.264 standard would infringe those patents and (2) Qualcomm would then have an opportunity to be an indispensable licensor to anyone in the world seeking to produce an H.264 compliant product."); *Broadcom Corp. v. Qualcomm Inc.*, 501 F.3d 297 (3d Cir. 2007) (holding that a claim for antitrust violations was stated based on a patentee's failure to offer a FRAND license). These additional claims and defenses can complicate the litigation and the scope of discovery.

Another consideration is that the defendants in these litigations are often competitors in the same industry (since they are all accused of practicing the same standards). Thus, confidentiality may be a significant consideration for certain issues, especially damages. This type of litigation lends itself well to bifurcating damages from liability, since the parties will likely share infringement and invalidity positions, but may vary on damages.

2.6.1.2 Customer/Manufacturer Multidefendant Litigations

To gain leverage over a manufacturer defendant, a patentee might join or separately sue the customers (e.g., OEM companies, distributors/resellers, etc.) of the manufacturer's allegedly infringing products. Because the manufacturer may be jointly and severally liable with the customers for the damages flowing from the infringement, these customers are generally superfluous to the litigation. Often, the court will stay the cases against the customer defendants pending the resolution of the litigation against the manufacturer defendants to decrease litigation costs and to streamline the case.

In a case involving only customer defendants, the parties will likely need to take third-party discovery from the manufacturers of the accused product to prove or defend against infringement. Such discovery can be difficult and time consuming, and may raise complicated protective-order issues. A lack of access to the details of the accused third-party technology may inhibit a defendant's ability to adduce evidence of and develop contentions for its noninfringement theory. The court should be cognizant of these discovery complications in a case involving only customer defendants.

Under Federal Rule of Civil Procedure 42(b), a district court can hold separate trials on various issues or claims "for convenience, to avoid prejudice, or to expedite and economize." In cases involving both customers and manufacturer defendants, manufacturer defendants may seek to stay the proceeding as to the customer defendants when the claims against customer defendants are merely peripheral to the main claim. The court will stay the cases against the customer defendants, sometimes subject to consent from the customer defendants to be bound by the judgment against the manufacturer defendant.

In a case involving only customer defendants, a manufacturer that wishes to protect its customers may adopt one of two approaches: (1) to seek leave from the court to intervene in the suits against the customers or (2) to file a declaratory judgment action of noninfringement in another forum. Under the former circumstance, courts frequently grant leave to intervene. Under the latter circumstance, the original plaintiff may seek to stay, dismiss or transfer the manufacturer defendant's declaratory judgment action based on the first-to-file rule. *See Futurewei Techs., Inc. v. Acacia Research Corp.*, 737 F.3d 704, 708 (Fed. Cir. 2013). A manufacturer defendant, on the other hand, may invoke the "consumer suit exception" and seek an injunction from the court presiding over its declaratory judgment action to enjoin the original plaintiff from prosecuting the customer suits. The determination under the first-to-file rule and the "customer suit exception" often turns on the consideration of judicial efficiency, including whether "the issues and parties are such that the disposition of one case would be dispositive of the other." *See, e.g., Proofpoint, Inc. v. InNova Patent Licensing, LLC*, 2011 U.S. Dist. LEXIS 120343, 2011 WL 4915847, at *7 n.5 (N.D. Cal. Oct. 17, 2011) (citing *Katz v. Siegler*, 909 F.2d 1459, 1463 (Fed. Cir. 1990)); *Contentguard Holdings, Inc. v. Google, Inc.*, 2014 U.S. Dist. LEXIS 51676, 2014 WL 1477670 (E.D. Tex. Apr. 15, 2014); *see also* Brian J. Love & James C. Yoon, *Expanding Patent Law's Customer Suit Exception*, 93 B.U. L. Rev. 1605 (2013) (proposing "resurrecting and expanding a forgotten patent law doctrine known as the 'customer suit exception,' which allows courts to stay patent suits filed against 'customer' defendants pending the outcome of litigation between the patentee and the accused technology's manufacturer").

2.6.2 Spoliation

Because of the potential penalties if a court finds that documents have been destroyed, the issue of spoliation and, specifically, whether the parties have taken reasonable steps to preserve relevant evidence often becomes a satellite litigation to the primary patent litigation. This issue is particularly prevalent where the plaintiff is a nonpracticing entity, who may have few documents to preserve and produce,[10] and the defendant is a large company with many documents that are potentially relevant to the litigation. Addressing this issue early in the litigation may allow the court to curb the issue before it consumes the court's time and the parties' resources. Section 4.4.2.1 discusses analyzing accusations of spoliation as the case progresses.

2.6.3 Early Claim Construction

Faced with the growing number of cases with tens (or hundreds) of defendants, some courts have taken an active case-management role by requiring the parties to identify claim terms, which if construed, they believe will dispose of all or a significant portion of the case. The court then proceeds to construe those claim terms on an expedited schedule. In some cases, the court orders parties to submit their claim-construction briefing via shorter than normal briefs and without any expert discovery. In the Eastern District of Texas, this approach has encouraged early resolution where it appears that the plaintiff only wants nuisance settlement values. *See, e.g.*, *Glob. Sessions LP v. Travelocity.com, LP et al.*, 2011 U.S. Dist. LEXIS 155901 (E.D. Tex. Aug. 18, 2011).

---

10. An NPE that has an established licensing campaign and/or past history of litigation may have many documents that it has a duty to preserve. *See, e.g.*, *Micron Tech., Inc. v. Rambus Inc.*, 645 F.3d 1311, 1315–19 (Fed. Cir. 2011) (finding spoliation on behalf of a nonpracticing entity).

Table 2.8
Issues Susceptible to Early Motions to Dismiss or Summary Judgment

Issue	Implications
Inequitable conduct defenses	See discussion of inequitable conduct at § 2.2.3.3.2.1. The standards set by the Federal Circuit in *Exergen Corp. v. Wal-Mart Stores, Inc.*, 575 F.3d 1312 (Fed. Cir. 2009) (pleading requirements), and *Therasense, Inc. v. Becton, Dickinson & Co.*, 649 F.3d 1276 (Fed. Cir. 2011) (proof of materiality and intent), will render this defense susceptible to an early motion to dismiss. If this issue is eliminated at an early stage, discovery will be narrowed (sometimes significantly).
Patentable subject matter	See discussion of § 101 of the Patent Act at § 6.2.1.1.1.
Extraterritoriality	It is increasingly common for plaintiffs to accuse acts committed abroad of infringement of U.S. patent law under either § 271(f) or § 271(g), either alone or in combination with § 271(b). Often, there are easily ascertainable facts regarding the contacts of the defendants with the United States that could lead to early resolution of claims or defenses on the basis of extraterritorial conduct.
Willfulness	Because "culpability is generally measured against the knowledge of the actor at the time of the challenged conduct," *Halo Elecs., Inc. v. Pulse Elecs., Inc.*, 579 U.S. ___ (2016), there may be evidence that can be produced early in the litigation that demonstrates no willful infringement (e.g., lack of pre-suit knowledge of the patent).
Is this a multidefendant litigation where the infringement theory is based on the defendants' compliance with certain industry standards? *See* § 2.6.1.1.	The court can sometimes significantly narrow the scope of fact discovery since infringement will largely rise and fall based on whether the standard infringes and whether the defendants assert that they comply with the standard.
Is this a multidefendant litigation where some of the defendants are customers accused of selling infringing products, and other of the defendants are manufacturers accused of making those same products? *See* § 2.6.1.2.	It may be possible to stay the cases against the customer defendants and allow the case to proceed against the manufacturer, who will be joint and severally liable with each of its customers.
Is this a multidefendant litigation that is not based on compliance with standards?	Case-management efficiency considerations may counsel in favor of breaking up the case into multiple cases based on similarity of accused products or relationships between the defendants.

2.6.4 Patentable Subject Matter

The Supreme Court's decisions in *Bilski v. Kappos*, 561 U.S. 593 (2010), *Mayo Collaborative Services v. Prometheus Laboratories*, Inc., 132 S. Ct. 1289 (2012), *Association for Molecular Pathology v. Myriad Genetics, Inc.*, 133 S. Ct. 2107 (2013), and *Alice Corp. Pty. Ltd. v. CLS Bank International*, 134 S. Ct. 2347 (2014), have invigorated patent eligibility limitations. *See* § 14.3.1.2.5. Since most extant patents were drafted and issued prior to these decisions, there has been a substantial rise in the number of motions to dismiss and seek summary judgment on patent eligibility grounds. Many of these cases have involved allegedly abstract business methods and diagnostic methods allegedly lacking inventive application of a law of nature. The courts have characterized patent eligibility as a question of law, which implies that patent eligibility could potentially be resolved through a motion to dismiss or summary judgment. *See, e.g., buySAFE, Inc. v. Google, Inc.*, 765 F.3d 1350 (Fed. Cir. 2014) (affirming grant of defendant's motion for judgment on the pleadings under Rule 12(c), concluding that asserted claims were not patent eligible); *see also Mayo Collaborative Servs.*, 132 S. Ct. at 1304 (rejecting government's suggestion to "substitute §§ 102, 103, and 112 inquiries for the better established inquiry under § 101").

Notwithstanding these indications that patent eligibility can be addressed early in cases involving simple business methods or broad claims to laws of nature or physical phenomena, it remains to be seen how courts will apply the "abstract ideas" and "inventive application" doctrines to more complex inventions. *See* § 14.3.1.3. District judges will need to understand the claimed invention, which could involve claim construction as well as learning the background science and technology. Disputes over scientific theories and what is an inventive, as opposed to a routine or conventional, application of scientific principles could well involve subsidiary factual determinations. It is unclear to what extent factual disputes surrounding these issues should be left to the jury. *Cf. Teva Pharms.*, 135 S. Ct. 831 (2015); *Markman*, 517 U.S. 370 (1996). At a minimum, the court might want to await discovery and a tutorial on the background science and technology before addressing complex patent eligibility questions.

2.6.5 Early Motions to Dismiss Indirect Infringement and Willfulness Claims

Indirect infringement and willfulness both require that the accused infringer knew of the asserted patents at the time of the infringement. Indirect infringement is also predicated on an act of direct infringement. *See* § 14.4.1.3. Claims of indirect infringement and willfulness, therefore, are susceptible to early determination, particularly in cases where there is evidence that the accused infringer did not know of the asserted patents before the suit was filed.

Indirect infringement claims frequently arise in cases involving patents with method claims. In these cases, a patentee's only practical cause of action will often be for indirect infringement against the manufacturer of a product alleged to practice the method claim. In these circumstances, there are numerous ways in which a court can surface early case-dispositive weaknesses. For example, if no single entity is responsible for the performance of each step of the claim, it may be fatal to the patentee's case. *Limelight Networks, Inc. v. Akamai Techs., Inc.*, 134 S. Ct. 2111 (2014). Alternatively, if the accused product is capable of many noninfringing uses and the manufacturer exerts no control over its customers, the claim will likely fail. Although the Federal Circuit has held that a method claim can be infringed where multiple parties combine to perform the claimed steps "if one party exercises 'control or direction' over the entire process such that every step is attributable to the controlling party, i.e., the 'mastermind,'" *see Muniauction, Inc. v. Thomson Corp.*, 532 F.3d 1318, 1329 (Fed. Cir. 2008), such "control or direction" requires a "principal–agent relationship or like contractual relationship." *Aristocrat Techs. Austl. Pty. Ltd. v. Int'l Game Tech.*, 709 F.3d 1348, 1363 (Fed. Cir. 2013).

2.6.6 Damages Theories and Proof

The damages-related aspects of patent infringement cases present special case-management challenges for the district court. In large part, this results from the fact that damages law is evolving rapidly in ways that alter or render obsolete methodologies for valuing patent damages (albeit often under protest from one of the parties). *See* § 14.4.3.2.1.4.1. It also results from the fact that the parties in most cases do not focus the same energy on damages that they do on liability issues, in part because districts that require comprehensive liability disclosures do not require them for damages. Another factor is that expert testimony concerning damages, unlike the typical expert opinion on patent liability issues, implicates and can draw from economic, mathematical, and financial valuation methodologies that are peer-reviewed and testable, as well as industry experience in patent valuation in the licensing and acquisition context. The interplay between this body of established non-patent-litigation valuation methodologies and the *Georgia-Pacific* factors commonly used to calculate damages in patent cases creates myriad disputes about the reliability of that testimony.

As a result of these and other factors, many patent cases involve challenges to the damages theories and evidence presented by one or both of the parties. This usually occurs in the context of *Daubert* challenges to damages-related expert testimony. *See* § 7.4. District courts have struggled to resolve disputes about whether the methodology used by a damages expert to reach his or her conclusions is both legally viable and reliable, or whether he or she applied that methodology reliably to the facts of the case before trial. Although courts have the tools to resolve such disputes early, they are rarely raised before the pretrial stage. As a result, a court that believes that a damages expert's opinions may not be reliable usually faces imperfect options: (1) excluding the expert and leaving the party with no expert testimony regarding damages at trial; (2) continuing the trial date and providing the party proffering the expert a do-over; or (3) allowing the testimony, despite its reservations, with the belief that the jury will see the weakness in the opinions and the intent that, if not, the court will correct the outcome through remittitur, JMOL, or a motion for new trial. *See, e.g., Intellectual Ventures I LLC v. Xilinx, Inc.*, 2014 U.S. Dist. LEXIS 54900, 2014 WL 1573542 (D. Del. Apr. 21, 2014) (refusing to allow patentee's expert to revise his report after determining the report was unreliable, forcing the patentee to rely on the defendant's expert testimony instead); *Golden Bridge Tech. Inc. v. Apple, Inc.*, 2014 U.S. Dist. LEXIS 67238, 2014 WL 1928977 (N.D. Cal. May 14, 2014) (striking damages expert's report but permitting a do-over on the eve of trial); *Golden Bridge Tech. Inc. v. Apple, Inc.*, 2014 U.S. Dist. LEXIS 76339, 2014 WL 4057187 (N.D. Cal. June 1, 2014) (striking damages expert's do-over report and denying a second do-over, as trial had begun).

Section 7.4.2 suggests effective ways to reduce the likelihood that fundamental disputes about damages theories and evidence are relegated to the eve of trial. Resolving such disputes about damages earlier in the case is difficult, in large part because the parties do not vet damages contentions as thoroughly as infringement and validity contentions. Under Federal Rule of Civil Procedure 26(a)(1)(3), a party claiming damages must provide as part of its initial disclosures "a computation of each category of damages claimed" and produce the documents and materials on which each computation is based. However, courts have not used this provision to compel a meaningful, early disclosure of the amount of damages claimed or the method by which they are computed in patent cases, apparently believing that claim construction and some damages discovery is necessary before a meaningful disclosure can fairly be compelled. *See* § 4.2.2. The parties usually exchange infringement and invalidity contentions during fact discovery, either in accordance with local rules or through interrogatory responses, which ensures that both parties are aware of the theories of infringement and invalidity in the early to middle stages of the case. By contrast, the parties' first disclosure of damages theories typically comes through the exchange of expert reports served after the close of fact discovery and concurrently with expert reports regarding infringement and invalidity. This creates two problems. First, because parties have not yet taken positions about damages, they cannot raise with the court in the early or middle portions of a case potential legal flaws or other issues that may render an expert opinion unreliable, as is commonly done with respect to disputes about infringement and invalidity theories. Second, *Daubert* challenges are necessarily relegated to the end of the case.

Recognizing this systemic problem, courts have begun experimenting with various mechanisms to encourage proper vetting of damages positions and opinions earlier in the case schedule. Here are several options:

Damages contentions. In jurisdictions that presently require parties to exchange infringement and invalidity contentions, the patentee could be required to provide damages contentions that (1) identify the type of damages sought (lost profits, reasonable royalty, or both); (2) provide an explanation of the specific theories and methodologies the patentee intends to use to value the infringement for which damages are sought; and (3) identify a range within which its ultimate damages number for each accused instrumentality is expected to fall. To enable the patentee to provide this information reliably, the accused infringer could be required to produce, along with its invalidity contentions, financial documents related to the accused instrumentalities (just as it is presently required to produce technical documentation concerning the accused instrumentalities). The patentee's deadline for serving such damages contentions could be set at a reasonable time (e.g., forty-five days) after the accused infringer's document disclosure. Although not specifically directed to expert testimony, these disclosures would require the patentee to identify its theories early in the case, would enable the accused infringer to disclose rebuttal damages theories in response to a contention interrogatory served during fact discovery, and would put parties in a position to challenge each other's legal and factual bases for damages positions earlier in the case.

Courts have elicited damages contentions in several ways. Judge Sue Robinson (D. Del.) requires the plaintiff to identify its damages model and accused products as part of its initial disclosures. *See* Patent Scheduling Order, § 1(c)(2) (Judge Sue Robinson, Feb. 15, 2015). Judge Cathy Ann Bencivengo (S.D. Cal.) has ordered preliminary damages disclosure in one of her patent cases:

> Preliminary Damages Disclosure
>
> Plaintiff will serve on each defendant a preliminary damages disclosure with the following information, no later than May 19, 2015 . . . :
>
> - Identifying the period for which it contends that defendant is liable for damages and the nature of the damages it will seek, lost profits and/or reasonable royalty;
> - If plaintiff is seeking a reasonable royalty, in whole or as part of its damages, plaintiff will identify the royalty base to which it contends a reasonable royalty may apply and whether any apportionment would be appropriate; and
> - Plaintiff will disclose and serve all license agreements it has entered into covering the patents at issue, whether entered into before or after the start of a litigation (i.e., licenses arising from settlement of litigation). The production of licenses is subject to the highest level of confidentiality (attorneys' eyes only) unless the plaintiff designates them otherwise. . . .

Case Management Order, *In re West View Research, LLC Patent Cases* (S.D. Cal. Apr. 25, 2015). Magistrate Judge Elizabeth Laporte (N.D. Cal.) encouraged the plaintiff to disclose its damages theory in answering defendants' request for additional information under Rule 26. *Eon Corp. IP Holding LLC v. Sensus USA Inc.*, 2013 U.S. Dist. LEXIS 32632, 2013 WL 3982994, *2–3 (N.D. Cal. Mar. 8, 2013). The court noted, however, that although early damages disclosure was ideal in theory, the many variables (type of defendant, product, availability of information" that courts and plaintiffs must consider in such disclosures makes their practice "challenging." Judge Laporte explained that

> [c]ourts must balance competing considerations when evaluating the extent and specificity of early damages disclosures that should be made in patent cases, including: the desirability of narrowing issues at an early stage versus the disclosure of strategically sensitive information; the possibility of settlement versus the early intrusion of expensive discovery requests and disputes; and the need for early disclosures versus the need for costly expert analysis that may be premature. . . . [A]n early estimate of the order of magnitude of damages at issue (e.g., less than $10 million; $25 million; more than $100 million) is important to the application of the principle of proportionality set forth in Federal Rule of Civil Procedure 26(b)(2)(C)(iii) to ascertain the burden and expense of discovery that is warranted.

Accelerated discovery schedule for damages. The court could elect to set an accelerated schedule for fact and expert discovery related to damages. For example, the court could require all damages-related discovery to be completed within two to three months before the fact-discovery deadline for other issues, and then require expert reports regarding damages to be served within a reasonable time thereafter (e.g., by applying the same gap between the close of damages discovery and service of the opening damages report as is set between the close of liability discovery and service of opening liability reports). Because it would allow the court to set a damages-related *Daubert* schedule that starts two to three months before summary judgment, this approach would provide sufficient time for the court to allow a one-time opportunity for a party whose proffered damages opinions are excluded to correct the deficiencies, if that opportunity is warranted, without moving the trial date. One notable example of an accelerated schedule for damages discovery is the so-called Track B in the Eastern District of Texas. The Track B Initial Patent Case Management Order was designed to complement the existing patent-case-management scheme (Track A). *See* General Order 14 – 03 General Order Regarding Track B Initial Patent Case Management Order (E.D. Tex. Feb. 25, 2014). Under Track B, the parties are required to submit a "good faith damages estimate" early in the case and are afforded significantly less discovery than under Track A. Track B, however, implements a much tighter schedule than Track A, presumably to facilitate early disclosure of infringement and invalidity contentions. Both parties can consent, or the court can order the case to be put on Track B. Table 2.9 summarizes Track B's schedule. During this initial phase of the case, discovery is limited to five interrogatories, five requests for production, and five requests for admission per side, absent leave or stipulation.

Table 2.9
Eastern District of Texas's Track B

Deadline	Event
14 days after answer	Patentee discloses infringement contentions and licensing disclosures.
44 days after answer	Initial disclosures and summary sales information for accused & "reasonably similar" products.
58 days after answer	Good-faith damages estimate + method of calculation.
72 days after answer	Accused infringer discloses invalidity contentions.
77 days after answer	Parties file notice of readiness for case-management conference.

Clear identification of "do-over" policy. Given the costs and time needed to prepare expert damage reports, the critical importance of such evidence to many patent cases, and the uncertainty surrounding the admissibility of damages evidence, courts should work with the parties to establish ground rules for allowing a party to rectify or substitute a damages report. Such a policy could deal with timing as well as scope.

At a minimum, such a discussion could surface the disputes that could arise and provide clues to the types of damages theories that are unlikely to be admissible and those that are. The Federal Circuit has moved away from formulaic damages theories (25% rule, Nash bargaining solution, entire market value rule) and moved toward other approaches (prior license agreements, smallest saleable patent-practicing unit as the basis for reasonable royalty calculations). Discussing how these doctrines apply to the particular facts and circumstances of the case could reduce the risks that the plaintiff will be left without a viable damages theory at the time of trial.

Early consideration of Daubert challenges and/or damages theories. Relatedly, the court could set an early schedule for consideration of *Daubert* challenges in appropriate cases. Alternatively, the court could vet the core damages theories early, leaving opportunity for narrower challenges after discovery and completion of the final expert report.

Judge Alsup's experience with early submission of an expert damages report in *Oracle America, Inc. v. Google Inc.*, however, was not regarded as a complete success. 798 F. Supp. 2d 1111, 1121–22 (N.D. Cal. 2011). Although the vetting process did not meet with his expectations, he was able to set some parameters on acceptable damages theories (foreshadowing the Federal Circuit's decision in *VirnetX, Inc. v. Cisco Sys., Inc.*, 767 F.3d 1308, 1332–34 (Fed. Cir. 2014) (questioning the Nash bargaining solution as an apportionment theory)) and warn the parties of the risks of questionable methodologies.

Bifurcation or reverse bifurcation. Depending on the circumstances and opportunities for settlement, the court could bifurcate liability and damages. *See* § 8.1.1.3. Trying damages first could be advantageous where the potential damages might be found to be modest and the liability issues are complex.

Independent or court-appointed damage experts. When the imprecise and speculative quality of economic methodology mixes with the polarizing nature of trial advocacy, the resulting economic testimony can be widely disparate and confusing. Courts might wish to appoint a respected and neutral expert to either present their own damages report or to comment on the reports of the parties' experts. *See* Fed. R. Evid. 706; J. Gregory Sidak, *Court-Appointed Neutral Economic Experts*, 9 J. Competition Law & Econ. 359 (2013) (discussing Judge Richard Posner's use of court-appointed damages expert); *cf. Gen. Elec. Co. v. Joiner*, 522 U.S. 136, 149–50 (1997) (Breyer, J., concurring) (encouraging, in a toxic torts case, the use of neutral experts to "overcome the inherent difficulty of making determinations about complicated scientific, or otherwise technical, evidence"); *In re Payment Card Interchange Fee & Merchant Discount Antitrust Litig.*, 2012 U.S. Dist. LEXIS 153637, 2012 WL 3932046 (E.D.N.Y. Mar. 19, 2013), ECF No. 1908 (Gleason, J.) (appointing a neutral economic expert to advise on "economic issues that may arise in connection with . . . final approval of a [$7.25 billion] proposed settlement" of an antitrust class action against Visa and MasterCard"); Joe S. Cecil & Thomas E. Willging, Court-Appointed Experts: Defining the Role of Experts Appointed Under Federal Rule of Evidence 706 (Federal Judicial Center 1993). Although it adds some additional costs and complexities at the front end of the process, such as defining the expert's role and compensation, an independent expert can solve problems that can emerge later in the litigation. Broaching this possibility early in the case-management process could unmask lurking problems and potentially elicit creative solutions to the economic damages quandary. It also offers the court some insurance of where the parties are contemplating speculative damages theories. *But see Oracle Am., Inc. v. Google Inc.*, 2012 U.S. Dist. LEXIS 132696, 2012 WL 4017808 (N.D. Cal. Apr. 10, 2012) (striking parts of court-appointed economic expert's report).

These approaches, or others, could be utilized alone or in combination, depending on the circumstances. In some cases, none of these approaches may be practical or warranted. Even in the best circumstances, these approaches can present the court and the parties with new challenges and unintended consequences. Nonetheless, they avoid relegating damages-related disputes to the end of the case, where the court has few practical options to resolve them equitably.

As is evident from the nature of these suggestions and this discussion, there is no one-size-fits-all approach to solving this problem. But courts should, in most patent cases, discuss with the parties the timing and nature of damages discovery and the timing of damages-related *Daubert* proceedings to determine whether these or other damages-specific provisions should be adopted. Moreover, case-management techniques that clarify the parties' damages positions and the theories supporting them early in the case have the side benefit of encouraging settlement. Once parties know the damages playing field, they will be better equipped to value the risk of the litigation and evaluate settlement positions. For all of these reasons, discussing the timing and nature of damages-related disclosures and discovery at the case-management conference stage is very important. If the parties and the court do not address these issues early in the case, they will be locked into a schedule that, in almost all cases, will limit the practical options that are available to resolve damages-related *Daubert* challenges and other disputes.

2.6.7 Nuisance-Value Litigation

In recent years, patent infringement cases that appear to have been filed simply to extract a nuisance-value settlement from a large number of defendants have proliferated. Such cases, if they are not resolved quickly, have the potential to clutter the court's docket and drain resources from other cases. However, given the highly technical nature of patent cases, it can be very difficult for a court to distinguish between nuisance-value cases and cases in which both parties genuinely seek resolution of the allegations by the court or a jury. Paradoxically, recent developments in venue-transfer law by the courts, and the joinder provisions enacted by the AIA, which intended to reduce nuisance-value litigation, can make it even more difficult to identify such cases. Under the AIA, fewer defendants are likely to be aggregated in any one case or judicial district. By engaging in active case management from the outset of the case, however, courts can drive the parties in such cases toward settlement. Moreover, requiring exchanges of contentions early in the case and permitting first-track summary judgment motions (as discussed fully in Chapter 6) allows the court to resolve such cases on the merits when they do not settle and, for that reason, also promotes settlement. Requiring the parties to participate in an early ADR process can help set the parties' expectations about the significance and costs of the case. Because these techniques are generally good practice, they do not require the court to identify and distinguish between nuisance-value cases and those with greater merit.

2.6.8 "Proportional" Scope of Discovery

On December 1, 2015, the U.S. Supreme Court adopted a number of amendments to the Federal Rules of Civil Procedure. Among these is an amendment to Rule 26(b) that limits the scope of discovery to "any nonprivileged matter that is relevant to any party's claim or defense and proportional to the needs of the case . . . ." The "proportionality" requirement is expected to better focus courts and litigants on the expected contribution of discovery to the resolution of the case, and is intended to help achieve the "just, speedy, and inexpensive determination" of litigation. Because one factor to be considered in determining proportionality is the amount in controversy, district courts can benefit from a reasoned conversation with the parties at the first case-management conference about the scope of the case, the nature and amount of the relief sought (as mentioned in the previous sections above), and how the case compares to other patent cases, with as much specificity as is possible. This discussion can then provide a useful baseline to judge proportionality as the case progresses, with the understanding that developments in the case or information obtained in discovery may warrant revision of what further discovery is considered "proportional."

2.7 Settlement and Mediation

The vast majority of patent cases (about 95%) settle, but often not until late in the case. In the meantime, the litigation can be extremely expensive for the parties. According to an industry survey, each side can expect to spend from $1.7 to $3.6 million in fees through the close of discovery, and between $2.8 and $5.9 million in total through trial. *See* § 1.2. Some cases can be substantially more expensive to litigate and try. Bringing the case to settlement on the eve of trial also squanders judicial and party resources. Consequently, early settlement is usually in everyone's best interest.

Most parties to patent litigation recognize the high economic stakes, uncertainty, and legal costs involved. Nevertheless, various impediments to settlement—ranging from the relationships between the particular parties to institutional issues arising out of the nature of some patent litigation—often prevent parties from settling cases without some outside assistance.

To overcome these impediments, courts should promote dialogue between the parties and, when the circumstances allow, settle them earlier in the litigation. Early judicial intervention, usually at the first case-management conference, can be a critical factor in bringing about settlement. Such initiative by the court emphasizes to the parties that the court wants them to actively consider settlement strategies as well as litigation strategies throughout the case.

Effective judicial encouragement of settlement involves several considerations: (1) appropriate initiation of mediation; (2) selection of the mediator; (3) scheduling of mediation; (4) delineating the powers of the mediator; (5) confidentiality of the mediation process; and (6) the relationship between mediation and litigation activities. Additional considerations come into play in multiparty and multijurisdictional cases.

2.7.1 Initiation of the Mediation Process

Many courts require, either by local rules or standardized order, that counsel for the parties discuss how they will attempt to mediate the case before the first case-management conference and that they report either their agreed plan or differing positions to the court at the conference. By requiring this early discussion, the court eliminates any concern that the party first raising the possibility of settlement appears weak. This can be particularly important at the outset of a case when attitudes may be especially rigid, posturing can be most severe, and counsel may know little about the merits of their clients' positions.

Whether or not the parties have agreed on a settlement discussion strategy, the court should address the subject at the conference and encourage the litigants to develop and evolve settlement strategies along with their trial strategies. The court should make it clear that it values the mediation effort and expects that the parties will give it similar importance. Thus, the court can assure that settlement efforts receive ongoing attention as the case progresses.

At the case-management conference, the court should order the parties to meet once with a specified mediator (or a mediator to be chosen according to a specified process) prior to a fixed deadline. If either party resists mediation, the court should order participation, as it is empowered to do. *See* 28 U.S.C. § 652(a) (Supp. 1998). A party's initial insistence that it will not consent to the mediation, will attend against its will, or has no interest in compromising its rights are positions that evidence more a lack of sophistication than a strategy. Experienced mediators routinely settle cases notwithstanding claims that "this case can't be settled."

2.7.2 Selection of the Mediator

Courts can identify successful mediators for patent cases from a variety of sources: other judges and magistrate judges, retired judges, professional mediators and practicing lawyers. In some courts, the trial judge serves as mediator, but this requires the express consent of the parties. Committee on Codes of Conduct, Judicial Conference of the United States, Code of Conduct for United States Judges Canon 3A(4) (1999). Many judges decline to act in this role because they believe that it is difficult to have the requisite candid discussion with parties and their counsel and later objectively rule on the many issues the court must decide. *See Fed. Trade Comm'n v. Freecom Commc'ns, Inc.*, 401 F.3d 1192, 1208 n.9 (10th Cir. 2005) (judges in nonjury cases should be especially hesitant to involve themselves in settlement negotiations); Wayne D. Brazil, Settling Civil Suits: Litigators' Views About Appropriate Roles and Effective Techniques for Federal Judges 84–99 (1985) (noting substantial attorney discomfort with trial judge's involvement in settlement negotiations).

The best choice is often a professional mediator with a record of successfully resolving patent litigation. A practicing patent attorney may have deeper knowledge of patent law, but that depth of knowledge, particularly in the details of patent prosecution, is unlikely to be useful in the mediation. The most useful attribute is the professional mediator's ability to diffuse discord and build consensus between the parties. It is important that the parties have confidence that the appointment was based on the mediator's skills and past success. Where the parties agree on a mediator, the court should usually appoint that person so that the authority of the mediator is clear.

To help judges choose mediators, some courts ask parties, attorneys, and mediators to evaluate the private mediation process confidentially at the conclusion of cases. This practice also has the advantage of putting mediators on notice that the court will monitor their performance. Forms used by the Northern District of Illinois for such an evaluation are attached as Appendices 2.4a, 2.4b, and 2.4c.

2.7.3 Scheduling the Mediation

In scheduling the first meeting with the mediator, the court should take into account the amount of time that the parties will need to become familiar with the principal issues, strengths, and weaknesses of the case as well as the risks and ramifications of the case for their businesses. Counsel typically reach this level of comprehension by the time that they file *Markman* briefs.

The mediator usually schedules the subsequent mediation sessions. The mediator has greater flexibility in arranging the meetings because, unlike a court, a mediator can consult with counsel, together or separately, to obtain their views and prepare for the next meeting.

In scheduling sessions, a mediator needs to take into account the progress of the case and how the stages of the litigation contribute to productive settlement discussions. For example, the mediator may conclude that a session should be held between briefing and hearing claim construction or summary judgment when positions are fully exposed, and the uncertainty of outcome can lead to compromise. *In limine*, *Daubert*, and other pretrial motions create similar opportunities. Substantive mediation preferably occurs before the intense and expensive period of trial preparation. Nevertheless, because many cases are settled only with the immediate uncertainty of trial, mediation efforts should continue through the pretrial process. Mediation after a jury verdict, but before the resolution of posttrial motions, can also be effective, especially in cases in which legal issues such as inequitable conduct and injunctive relief remain to be resolved.

2.7.4 Powers of the Mediator and Who Should Be Present During Mediation

To maximize the likelihood of successful mediation, the mediator must have the power to require certain actions. Most importantly, the mediator should be empowered to require, or the court should be prepared to order, that the parties participate in the mediation. Participation includes attendance by the most appropriate client representative. The common insistence that someone "with full settlement authority" attend the mediation is insufficient in patent cases because a person with authority does not necessarily have the requisite motivation to engage in meaningful compromise. For the typical corporate business entity, the person with the necessary authority and motivation may be a licensing executive; for the alleged infringer, it may be a manager of the operating unit responsible for the accused product or service whose budget will absorb the costs of the settlement and any judgment. Merely because in-house counsel oversees the litigation and has authority to settle does not mean that person is the most appropriate party representative.

The mediator may need to resolve disagreements about the relative seniority of party representatives. If litigants are of similar size, this usually is not a problem. But when one company is much smaller—for example, either a start-up competitor or a patent-holding company—it likely will be represented by its chief executive officer, and it may attempt to compel attendance of the chief executive of the larger entity. This approach can sometimes be counterproductive because it forces participation by someone who lacks sufficient knowledge and resents having to attend. It is more important that the representative of the large entity be someone with responsibility for and knowledge of the relevant portion of that entity's business.

The mediator may also need to address how to obtain approval of a settlement when no one person has settlement authority, and any outcome must be approved by a governing board. Where an entity requires board approval of a settlement, the entity is typically represented at the mediation by an individual. If the mediation is successful, the mediator should require that the representative commit to recommend the unconditional approval of the settlement to the board and require that the board act by a fixed date.

Another important power for a mediator is the right to exclude particular individuals from the process. For example, one or more of the parties' counsel or an individual, such as an inventor or a technical director, may be too deeply involved in the merits of the dispute to be constructive. Particularly for major cases, it can be useful to require the parties to be represented by attorneys other than lead litigation lawyers. They tend to be preoccupied with the merits and events of the litigation and sometimes find it difficult to communicate productively with each other.

2.7.5 Confidentiality of the Mediation

To maximize open communication and candor, everything submitted, said, or done during the mediation should be deemed confidential and not be available for use for any other purpose. Confidentiality is usually required by agreement of the parties or by court order or rule. *See, e.g.*, N.D. Cal. Patent L. R. 6-11 (broadly prohibiting disclosure or use outside the mediation of anything said or done in the mediation). Generally, the confidentiality requirements go beyond the evidentiary exclusion of Federal Rule of Evidence 408 and assure that the parties, their counsel, and the mediator can candidly discuss the facts and merits of the litigation without concern that statements might be used in the litigation or publicized. Given the importance of confidentiality to the mediation process, the court should be prepared to enforce these confidentiality guarantees strictly.

This same concern for confidentiality usually precludes reports to the trial judge of anything other than procedural details about the mediation, such as the dates of mediation sessions, or a party's violation of court rules or orders requiring participation. *See* Robert Niemic, Donna Stienstra & Randall Ravitz, Guide to Judicial Management of Cases in ADR 111–14, 163–64 (Federal Judicial Center 2001) [hereinafter *FJC ADR Guide*] ("An attorney-neutral should protect the integrity of both the trial and ADR processes by refraining from communicating with the assigned trial judge concerning the substance of negotiations or any other confidential information learned or obtained by virtue of the ADR process, unless all of the participants agree and jointly ask the attorney-neutral to communicate in a specified way with the assigned trial judge."); Am. Bar Ass'n, Civil Trial Practice Standards § 23e (2007) [hereinafter ABA Standards] ("The court should not communicate *ex parte* with any third-party neutral, including a senior, magistrate or other judge, involved in an alternative dispute resolution mechanism about the course of negotiations or the merits of the case."). "Public confidence in both the trial and settlement processes can be undermined if direct communication is permitted between the attorney/neutral and the assigned trial judge regarding the merits of the case or the parties' confidential settlement positions." *FJC ADR Guide* at 164.

In addition to being confidential, briefing and communications relating to mediation may be privileged against discovery in future litigation. *See, e.g.*, *Sheldone v. Pa. Tpk. Comm'n*, 104 F. Supp. 2d 511, 515 (W.D. Pa. 2000).

2.7.6 Relationship of the Mediation to the Litigation Schedule

Absent a final settlement, a case usually proceeds as scheduled without regard to mediation events. *See* ABA Standards § 23(f) (2007) ("The court ordinarily should not delay proceedings or grant continuances to permit the parties to engage in settlement negotiations.") This approach assures that the litigation is not unnecessarily delayed and encourages the parties to mediate diligently.

Arranging early discovery of needed information or scheduling early consideration of a potentially important summary judgment motion may make it possible for the parties to consider settlement earlier in the case. The patent owner, for example, may believe it needs software code, chemical formulation details, or other information not available by buying or using the infringing product or service. Alternatively, the parties may dispute the existence of an invalidating prior sale of the patented invention. This scheduling can be facilitated by the mediator at an early meeting with the parties.

Mediation is sometimes held while a critical case event is pending—for example, after the briefing and hearing of a preliminary injunction or summary judgment motion, but before the court decides the motion. In some courts, judges and mediators regularly communicate about scheduling to maximize these settlement opportunities. By providing the parties with an expected schedule for deciding the motion, the court can encourage them to focus on completing a settlement before the deadline. If the parties are productively engaged in mediation at the deadline, some judges continue to delay issuing a decision where the mediator and the parties so request.

2.7.7 Mediating Multiparty and Multijurisdictional Cases

Not all patent cases involve a single plaintiff and defendant in a single court. When in the typical multiparty case the patent owner asserts that the alleged infringers acted independently, separate mediation meetings can be scheduled for each alleged infringer. This allows the opportunity to negotiate settlements with each defendant based on the unique facts and market forces relevant to that party. It also allows the defendants interested in settling early to mediate without the interference of others who may wish to litigate the dispute through a later stage of the case.

Multijurisdictional cases often arise when a party sued on a patent brings a countersuit against the plaintiff in another court, asserting infringement of its own patent. In some circumstances, however, parties may find themselves in unrelated patent litigation in multiple courts because different business units of at least one of the parties have proceeded independently.

Settlement efforts normally should not be delayed in one court because of proceedings in another court. The parties should be required to comply with the court's usual mediation planning requirements. If the parties report active engagement in mediation in another jurisdiction, the court can delay ordering further mediation while they complete those efforts. In the mediation of multijurisdictional suits, the parties will make clear the scope of settlement they are prepared to negotiate. If the multiple cases are countersuits, cases in both courts will be settled. If the separate suits are the result of the independent actions of separate business units, one party may assert that the second suit will not be part of any settlement. Should its opponent disagree, the mediator will have to decide whether to force the discussion of the second suit—likely requiring the attendance of party representatives of the second business unit—or focus the discussions on the single case.

2.7.8 Factors Affecting the Likelihood of Settlement of Particular Categories of Cases

Like other aspects of patent litigation, settlement dynamics vary with the nature of the parties. While every case involves a multitude of individual settlement issues, categories of cases also reflect common traits and pathologies. The following chart summarizes the settlement issues and patterns associated with the most common types of patent disputes and provides insights into how and when settlement can be most effectively fostered:

Table 2.10
Settlement Considerations

Case Category	Settlement Issues
Competitor vs. Competitor—Core Technology	Difficult to settle absent a counterclaim or other significant risk to the patent owner or strategic opportunity available from business agreement. Meaningful mediation likely to require participation from senior officers of the parties. Agreement may present antitrust issues if the parties have large cumulative market share.
Competitor vs. Competitor—Noncore Technology	Likely to settle through mediation, potentially early in the litigation. Litigation may be the result of failed effort to negotiate license prior to litigation, with litigation intended to add additional negotiating leverage.
Large Enterprise vs. Start-Up/New Entrant	If no other competitor offers substantial equivalents of claimed patented technology, the established company may not settle without eliminating start-up's use of technology. The suit nevertheless may raise costs for the start-up to the point of forcing a settlement, potentially including acquisition of the start-up. If other competitors exist, settlement is likely, potentially early in litigation. Suit may be timed to critical event for start-up (e.g., new product offering, additional investment, public stock offering, or merger), in which case potential windows for settlement are very early in the litigation or just after the event.

Case Category	Settlement Issues
Licensing Company vs. Large Enterprise	The likelihood and timing of settlement depends on several factors: (1) the amount demanded—for example, the licensing company may intend future litigation against others and is seeking to build necessary funding through the current suit, in which case the demand may be modest and early settlement possible; (2) the size of the licensing company's portfolio—if the current suit likely is the first of several expected, a license to the patentee's entire portfolio can be an attractive settlement; (3) reputational effects: whether the large enterprise had or expects litigation with the patent owner or other licensing companies—several large companies believe, sometimes based on policy, that settling such suits encourages additional licensing company litigation, in which case settlement may not be possible until substantive rulings create a substantial risk of an adverse outcome for one of the parties or the enterprise has achieved its reputational goals; and (4) strategic alliances: whether the licensing company and large enterprise can join forces against the defendant's competitors—a settlement, potentially early in the litigation, may be based on an agreement allowing the enterprise to use the licensing company's portfolio against its competitors.
Licensing Company vs. Start-Up Enterprise	Such suits often are timed to critical events for the start-up. Very early settlement or settlement after the start-up accomplishes the event is likely. Obtaining participation from senior start-up company officers while the critical event is pending can be difficult and may justify telephone or other non-traditional participation in the mediation.
Serial Litigant: Patent Owner vs. First Alleged Infringer	Such patent owners face the collateral risk that an adverse *Markman* or other substantive ruling dooms not just this case, but the entire flotilla behind it. On the other hand, while a win cannot be used as collateral estoppel in subsequent suits, it can be persuasive in them, especially if they are brought in the same court. This may create settlement opportunities while important substantive rulings are pending.
Branded Pharmaceutical vs. Branded Pharmaceutical	Difficult, and often impossible, cases to settle, as industry economics are based on an exclusive position in marketing patent-protected drugs.

Case Category	Settlement Issues
Branded Pharmaceutical vs. Generic	Often based on Hatch-Waxman Act provisions that grant the generic a 180-day period of exclusivity after it enters the market. 21 U.S.C. § 355(j)(5)(B)(iv). Regarding Hatch-Waxman litigation generally, see Chapter 10. Because delaying actual market entry by the generic delays entry by all generics and because the economic loss to the pharmaceutical company after entry usually far exceeds profit to the generic, some of these cases have been settled by "reverse payments," payments by the pharmaceutical company to the generic to remain off the market for a period of time. Such settlements have been approved by appellate courts so long as the exclusion is no greater than the exclusionary potential of the pharmaceutical company's patent, but continue to be challenged by the Federal Trade Commission as anticompetitive. *See Joblove v. Barr Labs, Inc.*, 429 F.3d 370 (2d Cir. 2005), *amended*, 466 F.3d 187 (2006), *cert. denied*, 127 S. Ct. 3001 (2007); *Schering-Plough Corp. v. FTC*, 402 F.3d 1056 (11th Cir. 2005), *cert. denied*, 126 S. Ct. 2929 (2006).
Medical Device Industry	Historically an industry with a large amount of patent litigation, so it is likely the litigants have a history of litigation against each other; they may have other related or unrelated litigation in other courts, and they may have patent portfolios that threaten future litigation. Early settlement of the litigation is unlikely. Otherwise, like other "Competitor vs. Competitor" litigation (above), settlement will depend on whether the technology is "core" to a significant product.
Preliminary Injunction Motion	Motions for preliminary injunction present an opportunity for very early consideration of settlement: counsel quickly become knowledgeable, parties focus early on strengths and weaknesses, and there is a period early in the case while a potentially important ruling is pending.

Appendix 2.1
Initial Case-Management Conference Summary Checklist

Ask for an informal description of the technology.

Ask for a brief statement/summary of claims and defenses by each party and related background issues, including an informal and general description of the following:

- Identity of the accused products
- Whether the primary basis for asserted liability is direct or indirect infringement
- Whether there are there any third parties from which the parties expect to obtain substantial discovery
- Scope of accused products relative to the defendant's business
- Scope of the patented/embodying technology relative to the patentee's business
- Whether the parties are competitors
- Whether the patent(s)-in-suit have been, or are likely to be, the subject of reexamination proceedings
- Potential for parallel litigation and/or *inter partes* or covered business method review
  - Will a party seek a stay, consolidation, coordination, or transfer?
- Identify patent eligibility (§ 101) issues and discuss when they should be addressed
- What type of relief is being sought?
  - What damage theory(ies) will be pursued? How will they be proven?
  - What are the estimated damages?
  - Will injunctive relief be sought, and what kind?
  - What do the parties contend is the "smallest saleable patent practicing unit"?
  - Is the patentee licensing the technology and when will it produce licensing information?
  - Are any technology standards implicated?

Protective Order

- Is a protective order needed?
- Will a standard protective order suffice or will any party seek special requirements?
- Discuss known points of contention (e.g., prosecution bar, levels of confidentiality, access by in-house lawyers) and, if applicable, convey the court's general perspective on such issues

Discuss special issues related to willfulness (if asserted)

- Timing of the assertion of the claim
- Timing of the reliance on any opinion of counsel
- Possibility of bifurcation
- Possibility of disqualification of counsel

Discuss alternative dispute resolution (ADR)

- Usefulness
- Timing
- Mediation, arbitration, or other form

Discuss electronic discovery and consider limitations on discovery

- Format(s) for production of electronic discovery
- Limits on the scope of electronic discovery
- Source code – how will it be produced?
- Limits on the number of custodians
- Number of total hours for fact witnesses or number of depositions

Discuss contention disclosures and schedule therefor

- In patent local rule jurisdictions, discuss whether variance from the standard disclosure timelines is appropriate
- In jurisdictions without patent local rules, discuss whether the parties should exchange infringement, invalidity, unenforceability, and damages contentions and the appropriate schedule for such disclosures

Set timing and procedures for claim construction and dispositive motions

- Determine timing of summary judgment relative to claim construction
- If not addressed by local rule, set a schedule for exchanges of claim terms, proposed constructions, and supporting evidence
- Discuss whether a tutorial would be appropriate

How conducted: By counsel? By experts? Submissions (e.g., DVDs)?

- Discuss the number of patents and patent claims that would be tried and possible ways of winnowing
- Discuss limits on the number of claim terms submitted for construction
  - Require an explanation of the significance of the term (e.g., effect on infringement/validity)
  - Ask parties to rank the disputed claim terms based on their significance for resolving the case

Discuss claim construction hearing logistics

- Identify disputed subsidiary factual issues
- Discuss whether live witnesses should be called

- Encourage parties to use graphics, animations, and other visual displays to aid in understanding the technology and disputed claim terms
- Schedule a pre-claim-construction conference to finalize the logistics for the hearing (held after the parties' positions on claim construction have crystallized)

Discuss whether any summary judgment issues depend on claim construction or can otherwise be resolved with little or no discovery, including

- Is there a dispute about the structure/function of the accused products?
- Is there any claim term or claim construction issue that, once decided, will compel infringement or noninfringement?
- Are there territorial issues (e.g., location of allegedly infringing acts) that affect infringement?
- Are there any claims or defenses that are purely legal in nature?
  - If so, discuss whether a first-track and second-track schedule for summary judgment would be appropriate for the case (see Chapter 6)

Discuss whether any limits on the number of summary judgment motions (or number of pages of briefing) should be imposed or modified

Discuss limits on prior art references

Discuss issues related to *Daubert* and in limine motions

- Schedule *Daubert* motions well in advance of pretrial conference, for example concurrently with summary judgment
- Discuss scope of in limine motion practice and advise parties that the court will not consider dispositive motions disguised as in limine motions
- Damages
  - Discuss whether it would be appropriate to require damages contentions and/or an expedited damages discovery schedule, or to take other steps to facilitate the early resolution of challenges to damages-related theories or expert testimony.

Appendix 2.2a
Case Management Checklist

Honorable Leonard P. Stark, District of Delaware

Case Management Checklist

Case Name and Number ______________________________

Counsel
Lead Counsel for __________ ____________________
Delaware Counsel for __________ ____________________

Lead Counsel for __________ ____________________
Delaware Counsel for __________ ____________________

Meet and Confer

Counsel have met and conferred and have made good-faith efforts to discuss, in person and/or by telephone, each of the topics listed in the Checklist below, and will be prepared to address these topics at the Case Management Conference ("CMC").

Discovery

- What are the core technical documents?
- Does any party intend to request production of electronic mail? If so, why? How many custodians should be searched? What methods will be used to search for electronic documents (e.g., key word searches, predictive coding)?
- How can the Court best assist the parties to provide meaningful interrogatory responses to avoid discovery disputes over the adequacy of such responses?
- If source code is going to be produced, when, where, and how will it be made available?

Claim Construction

- What are the 1 or 2 most important claim terms requiring construction?
- Should the Court consider a "super-early" limited claim construction hearing on those most important terms?
- What is the maximum number of claim terms the parties will ask the Court to construe?
- How can the parties help the Court achieve its goal of ruling on claim construction disputes within 60 days of the claim construction hearing?

Narrowing the Case

- At what point(s) in the case will it be appropriate to limit/reduce the number of accused devices/functionalities, asserted patents, asserted claims, invalidity defenses (including obviousness combinations), and prior art references?
- Are there products that are not colorably different than the currently-accused products that Plaintiff expects or Defendant should expect will be added to the case?
- Should damages or any other portion of the case be bifurcated?

Related Cases

- What related cases are pending, in any Court, and what is their filing date and current status?
- Does Plaintiff plan to file additional related cases and, if so, on what schedule and how should that plan affect how this case will proceed?
- Has any patent-in-suit been litigated before and how soon is Plaintiff willing to produce the results of any such litigation, including settlement agreements?

Remedies

- What initial revenue/sales information does Plaintiff need to assess the value of the case and how soon is Defendant willing to produce such information?
- What type of relief is Plaintiff seeking: lost profits, reasonable royalties, injunction, and/or any other form of relief?
- What does Plaintiff contend is the "smallest saleable unit"?
- Has the patent been licensed or offered for any license and how soon is Plaintiff willing to produce licensing information?

Amendments

- What will be the deadline for proposed amendments to the pleadings, including adding allegations of indirect and/or willful infringement as well as inequitable conduct?
- What will be the deadline for adding or altering the accused devices/functionalities, asserted claims, and prior art?

Supplementation

- Will expert declarations/affidavits be permitted to be filed with case-dispositive and other motions, without other parties' agreement or leave of the Court?
- What will be the deadline for supplementing infringement, invalidity, damages, and other contentions?

Protective Order

- Are there any reasons this case requires provisions that are not typical of the protective order generally entered in this Court's patent cases?

Motions to Dismiss/Transfer/Stay

- Have any of these motions been filed and/or does any party anticipate filing such a motion?
- Will the parties consent to magistrate judge jurisdiction at least for the limited purpose of resolving these motions?[11]
- Should discovery and other exchanges of information (e.g., Default Standards ¶ 4 disclosures) be stayed during pendency of these motions?

Motions for Summary Judgment

- Are there any motions that are potentially fully case dispositive – or that would be dispositive of such a significant portion of the case that its resolution would greatly enhance the likelihood of a cost-effective pre-trial disposition – and that the parties agree the Court should hear early?
- If the Court is to hear any early summary judgment motion, which, if any, other parts of the case should be stayed?
- If the Court is to hear any early summary judgment motion, what is the moving party going to give up (e.g., the opportunity to file a motion on the same subject matter later in the case)?

Other Matters

- Are any postgrant review procedures underway or planned that might affect the manner in which this case should proceed?
- Would the Plaintiff be willing to stipulate to a maximum damages figure in exchange for restrictive discovery and an accelerated trial date?
- How soon can this case be ready for alternative dispute resolution?

Scheduling

- Address each matter listed in the Revised Patent Form Scheduling Order and submit, along with this Checklist, a joint proposed scheduling order, clearly identifying points of disagreement.

---

11. The identity of any party or parties declining to consent should not be disclosed to the Court at any point, only the fact that there is not unanimous consent.

Appendix 2.2b
Revised Procedures for Managing Patent Cases

Honorable Leonard P. Stark, District of Delaware
Revised Procedures for Managing Patent Cases
(June 18, 2014)

As a result of the invaluable discussions in which I participated as part of the District of Delaware's Patent Study Group, and as previewed in my presentation to our District's chapter of the Federal Bar Association last month, I describe below the Revised Procedures that I will follow in handling patent cases.

Applicability

Unless otherwise ordered, these Revised Procedures will govern all ***non-ANDA*** patent cases filed on or after July 1, 2014, that are assigned to me.

General Principles

Early investment of judicial resources, both from myself and Magistrate Judge Burke, will lead more often to identification of the "best" schedule for each case, promoting overall efficiency in the processing of cases on my docket.

Each patent case will initially be treated as its own case, even if it is related to a case or cases that have already been filed.

I have attempted to identify – and, as best as possible, reduce or eliminate – the areas that generally provide the highest likelihood for lengthy delays.

Referral Order

Within seven (7) days of a new patent case being assigned to me, my staff will docket the following Referral Order:

> This case will be governed by Judge Stark's Revised Procedures for Managing Patent Cases (see www.ded.uscourts.gov). In accordance with the Revised Procedures,
>
> IT IS HEREBY ORDERED that:
>
> 1. any and all matters relating to scheduling, including entry of a Scheduling Order, are referred to Magistrate Judge Burke;
>
> 2. any and all motions to dismiss, stay, and/or transfer venue, relating

to all or any part of the case, whenever such motions may be filed, are referred to Judge Burke for disposition or report and recommendation, to the full extent permitted by the Constitution, statute, and rule; and

3. within seven (7) days of the date of this Referral Order, the plaintiff(s) shall file the Procedures Order, which is found on Judge Stark's website (see www.ded.uscourts.gov).

Procedures Order

Within seven (7) days after the Court enters the Referral Order, the plaintiff(s) will be responsible for filing the following proposed Procedures Order, which the Court will then "so order" on the docket:

> IT IS HEREBY ORDERED that, subject to any subsequent order of the Court, the following procedures shall govern proceedings in this matter:
>
> 1. "Discovery Matters" Procedures.
>
> a. Any discovery motion filed without first complying with the following procedures will be denied without prejudice to renew pursuant to these procedures.
>
> b. Should counsel find, after good faith efforts - including ***verbal*** communication among Delaware and Lead Counsel for all parties to the dispute - that they are unable to resolve a discovery matter or a dispute relating to a protective order, the parties involved in the discovery matter or protective order dispute shall submit a joint letter in substantially the following form:
>
> Dear Judge Stark:
>
> The parties in the above-referenced matter write to request the scheduling of a discovery teleconference.
>
> The following attorneys, including at least one Delaware Counsel and at least one Lead Counsel per party, participated in a verbal meet-and-confer (in person and/or by telephone) on the following date(s): ________________

Delaware Counsel: ______________________________
Lead Counsel: ______________________________

The disputes requiring judicial attention are listed below: [provide here a non-argumentative list of disputes requiring judicial attention]

c. On a date to be set by separate order, generally not less than forty-eight (48) hours prior to the conference, the party seeking relief shall file with the Court a letter, not to exceed three (3) pages, outlining the issues in dispute and its position on those issues. On a date to be set by separate order, but generally not less than twenty-four (24) hours prior to the conference, any party opposing the application for relief may file a letter, not to exceed three (3) pages, outlining that party's reasons for its opposition.

d. Each party shall submit two (2) courtesy copies of its discovery letter and any attachments.

e. Should the Court find further briefing necessary upon conclusion of the telephone conference, the Court will order it. Alternatively, the Court may choose to resolve the dispute prior to the telephone conference and will, in that event, cancel the conference.

2. <u>Motions to Amend</u>.

a. Any motion to amend (including a motion for leave to amend) a pleading shall ***NOT*** be accompanied by an opening brief but shall, instead, be accompanied by a letter, not to exceed three (3) pages, describing the basis for the requested relief, and shall attach the proposed amended pleading as well as a "blackline" comparison to the prior pleading.

b. Within seven (7) days after the filing of a motion in compliance with this Order, any party opposing such a motion shall file a responsive letter, not to exceed five (5) pages.

c. Within three (3) days thereafter, the moving party may file a reply letter, not to exceed two (2) pages, and, by this same date, the parties shall file a letter requesting a teleconference to address the motion to amend.

3. Motions to Strike.

a. Any motion to strike any pleading or other document shall ***NOT*** be accompanied by an opening brief but shall, instead, be accompanied by a letter, not to exceed three (3) pages, describing the basis for the requested relief, and shall attach the document to be stricken.

b. Within seven (7) days after the filing of a motion in compliance with this Order, any party opposing such a motion shall file a responsive letter, not to exceed five (5) pages.

c. Within three (3) days thereafter, the moving party may file a reply letter, not to exceed two (2) pages, and, by this same date, the parties shall file a letter requesting a teleconference to address the motion to strike.

4. Scheduling Order. The foregoing procedures shall be repeated in the scheduling order to be entered in this case.

Scheduling and Case Management

As noted in the Referral Order, scheduling will be managed by Judge Burke, who will have full authority to work with the parties to craft a schedule appropriate to the particular circumstances of each patent case. Judge Burke's decisions with respect to scheduling are subject to reversal only for abuse of discretion.

Within ten (10) days after any defendant has filed a responsive pleading (e.g., answer, counterclaim, cross-claim) or a motion in lieu of (or in addition to) a responsive pleading, my staff or Judge Burke's staff will docket the following Case Management Order:

At least one defendant in this matter having filed a responsive pleading or a motion in lieu of (or in addition to) a responsive pleading,

IT IS HEREBY ORDERED that:

The parties shall meet and confer and discuss, in person and/or by telephone, each of the matters listed on the Court's Case Management Checklist ("Checklist"). Within thirty (30) days of the date of this Order, the parties shall jointly file the Checklist and their proposed scheduling order (consistent with the Court's Revised

> Patent Form Scheduling Order). Thereafter, the Court will schedule an in-person Case Management Conference/Rule 16 Scheduling Conference ("CMC") to be held with Judge Stark and/or Judge Burke. The Checklist and Revised Patent Form Scheduling Order can be found on the Court's website (www.ded.uscourts.gov).

A copy of the Checklist is available on the Court's website (www.ded.uscourts.gov). I recognize that some of the questions on the Checklist may relate to case strategy. Nonetheless, I expect counsel to make good faith efforts to discuss, in person and/or by telephone, each of the topics listed.

A copy of the Revised Patent Form Scheduling Order is available on the Court's website (www.ded.uscourts.gov).

The Case Management Conference ("CMC"), which also serves as the scheduling conference pursuant to Federal Rule of Civil Procedure 16, will be held in chambers or in the courtroom, on the record, with Judge Stark and/or Judge Burke. A court reporter will be present. At the CMC, each party must be represented by Lead Counsel and Delaware Counsel and be prepared to discuss each matter on the Checklist as well as any other matter that will be helpful or necessary to determining the most appropriate manner of managing the case. If there is a topic which a party thinks is inappropriate or premature to discuss, that party will have to explain its reasons for that view.

After the CMC, the Court may order the submission of a revised proposed scheduling order.

Where there are multiple related cases involving unrelated defendants, any party may request that the Court defer scheduling the CMC until a later date. Any party requesting such a deferral must accompany the request with a proposed order that, if entered, will require the parties to provide regular status reports advising the Court as to when they believe the case will be ready for a CMC and scheduling order. The greater the agreement among the parties to the related cases that deferral is appropriate, the more likely it is that deferral will be granted.

With rare exceptions, we will schedule trial upon entry of the scheduling order, setting a maximum number of trial days, double- and triple-tracking trials on my calendar as necessary.

If an early trial date is desired, the parties are reminded that if they unanimously consent to the jurisdiction of a Magistrate Judge, Judge Burke will almost always be able to proceed to trial more quickly than Judge Stark.

Where there are multiple related cases involving unrelated defendants, the Court will determine at some point (possibly as late as the pretrial conference) which defendant(s) will be tried first.

Motions to Dismiss, Transfer, or Stay

As noted in the Referral Order, any and all motions to dismiss, transfer, and/or stay will be referred to Judge Burke. Parties are reminded that they may consent to the jurisdiction of a Magistrate Judge for the limited purpose of final resolution of any motion, which has the effect of eliminating the right to file objections in the District Court, essentially giving the Magistrate Judge the same authority a District Judge would have with respect to that motion.

Generally, we will not defer the CMC and scheduling process solely due to the pendency of any of these motions.

Motions to Amend or Strike

As noted in the Procedures Order, any and all motions to amend (or motions for leave to amend) and/or strike will not be accompanied by full briefing but will, instead, be channeled into the "discovery matters" procedures.

Narrowing the Case

In order to manage my docket, and to ensure that litigation proceeds efficiently, I will be highly receptive to reasonable proposals to reduce, at an appropriate stage or stages of a case, the number of: patents-in-suit, asserted claims, accused products, invalidating references, combinations of invalidating references, invalidity defenses, and claim construction disputes.

Discovery

I have modified my discovery matters procedures in several ways, most notably as follows:

- there is no longer a requirement that counsel call chambers to request a discovery teleconference. Instead, counsel are required to submit a joint, non-argumentative letter, representing that Delaware Counsel and Lead Counsel have spoken about the issues in dispute, listing the issues on which counsel believe judicial intervention is required, and requesting the scheduling of a discovery dispute teleconference (a form for the letter is included with the Procedures Order)
- there is no longer a requirement that the parties submit copies of sealed documents within an hour after filing their letters
- parties are required to submit two (2) courtesy copies of their discovery letters and attachments

Discovery teleconferences will continue to be limited to approximately 30-45 minutes each.

Default Standards/Exchange of Contentions

Absent agreement among the parties or an order of the Court, the scheduling order will include dates for the exchange, in steps, of the following:

- Plaintiff shall identify the accused product(s), including accused methods and systems, and its damages model, as well as the asserted patent(s) that the accused product(s) allegedly infringe(s). Plaintiff shall also produce the file history for each asserted patent.
- Defendant shall produce core technical documents related to the accused product(s), sufficient to show how the accused product(s) work(s), including but not limited to non-publicly available operation manuals, product literature, schematics, and specifications. Defendant shall also produce sales figures for the accused product(s).
- Plaintiff shall produce an initial claim chart relating each known accused product to the asserted claims each such product allegedly infringes.
- Defendant shall produce its initial invalidity contentions for each asserted claim, as well as the known related invalidating references.
- Plaintiff shall provide final infringement contentions.
- Defendant shall provide final invalidity contentions.

Also absent agreement among the parties or an order of the Court, the scheduling order will include a date by which all parties must finally supplement, inter alia, the identification of all accused products and of all invalidity references.

The foregoing are the same procedures contained in Judge Robinson's recently issued "Patent Case Scheduling Order" ("SLR Order") (see ¶ 1.c, 1.f, 1.g).

Markman

I have set an aspirational goal of issuing all *Markman* rulings within 60 days after a *Markman* hearing. If I determine (due to, for example, an outsized number of claim disputes, deficiencies with the briefing, or scheduling congestion) that I will be unable to meet my goal, I will advise counsel of this fact.

Although I will continue to prefer having only a single *Markman* hearing in each case, and even just a single *Markman* hearing across all of any number of related cases, I do not plan to adhere rigidly to this preference. The parties should be prepared to discuss at the CMC whether a case or cases would be more efficiently handled by construing certain terms at an earlier point than other terms.

While I am not adopting Judge Robinson's requirement that "[f]or any contested claim limitation, each party must submit a proposed construction; i.e., 'plain and ordinary' meaning generally is not helpful to either the court or a jury" (SLR Order ¶ 5.b), I agree with her reasoning and am usually not persuaded that "plain and ordinary meaning" is an appropriate resolution of a material dispute over the scope of a claim term.

Summary Judgment/*Daubert* (Motions to Preclude/Exclude)

I will continue to permit parties to file as many summary judgment and *Daubert* (i.e., motions to exclude or preclude anticipated expert testimony, in whole or in part) motions as they wish, subject to the restriction that each side is limited to no more than a total of fifty (50) pages of combined opening briefs in support of any and all such motions, no more than fifty (50) pages of combined answering briefs in opposition to the motions, and no more than twenty (20) pages of combined reply briefs in support of their motions.

The parties must work together to ensure that the Court receives no more than a ***total*** of ***250 pages*** (i.e., 50 + 50 + 25 regarding one side's motions, and 50 + 50 + 25 regarding the other side's motions) of briefing on all case dispositive motions and Daubert motions that are covered by this scheduling order and any other scheduling order entered in any related case that is proceeding on a consolidated or coordinated pretrial schedule.

I will generally include in the scheduling order a date for argument on any motions for summary judgment and *Daubert* motions. Such a hearing will typically be held approximately two months prior to the pretrial conference. Generally, counsel should expect they will be given a total of no more than forty-five (45) minutes per side to present their arguments on all pending motions.

Pretrial Order

I have revised my form pretrial order. (See "Proposed Final Pretrial Order- Patent" at www.ded.uscourts.gov.) I note some of the more important changes below.

I have clarified that when parties estimate the anticipated length of trial, they must do so not only in terms of trial days but also in terms of a specific request for a number of hours they need for their trial presentations. In formulating such a request, counsel should assume that they will be charged time for: opening statements, examination of witnesses (including by playing or reading deposition testimony), closing arguments, arguing objections (including in the mornings before trial begins), and arguing motions (including for judgment as a matter of law). I usually do not charge time for jury selection, opening and final jury instructions, and arguments regarding jury instructions. Counsel should also assume that in a typical trial day we can usually get in 5 1/2 – 6 1/2 hours in a jury trial and 6 – 7 hours in a bench trial.

Counsel need to indicate whether, in connection with efforts to impeach a witness with prior testimony, they wish to permit objections for incompleteness and/or lack of inconsistency.

Counsel need to indicate whether, in connection with objections to expert testimony as being beyond the scope of previous expert disclosures, they request that the Court rule on such objections at trial or defer ruling unless and until the objections are renewed in connection with post-trial motions (with costs of the new trial to be charged entirely to the party whose trial conduct necessitates a new trial).

With respect to motions for judgment as a matter of law pursuant to Fed. R. Civ. P. 50, counsel need to indicate whether they request such motions: (i) be made at sidebar while the jury remains in the courtroom, (ii) be made immediately at the appropriate point during trial, and (iii) be supplemented in writing (and, if so, when).

Pretrial Conference

I expect to continue to conduct pretrial conferences largely as I have done to this point, although I will generally limit them to two (2) hours or less.

Jury Instructions, Voir Dire, Verdict Sheet

Where a case is to be tried to a jury, the parties must provide the Court with courtesy copies of the required documents – proposed voir dire, preliminary jury instructions, final jury instructions, and special verdict forms – as computer files. These courtesy copies may be sent by e-mail to my staff. The files may be in either WordPerfect or Microsoft Word format.

Trial

I expect to continue to conduct trials largely as I have done to this point.

After the jury returns a verdict, I will generally order the preparation of a joint status report, in which the parties should indicate, after meeting and conferring, how they believe the case should proceed, including whether (and when) additional briefing and/or in-court proceedings will be required.

The joint status report should identify the post-trial motions and issues on which any party intends to seek relief.

The joint status report should be accompanied by a proposed order to enter judgment on the verdict.

Post-Trial Motions

Unless otherwise ordered, briefing is according to Local Rules, no matter how many motions are filed by a party. That is, each side may file a maximum total of twenty (20) pages of opening briefing, twenty (20) pages of answering briefing, and ten (10) pages of reply briefing, ***regardless of how many motions are filed***.

Where possible, I will try to advise the parties as to my inclinations with respect to the issues that they plan to raise in their post-trial motions, so the parties may better assess whether I am likely to disturb the verdict of the jury.

Appendix 2.2c
Revised Patent Form Scheduling Order

Honorable Leonard P. Stark, District of Delaware

Revised Patent Form Scheduling Order

Revised June 2014

[NOTE: text in brackets is for guidance and should be deleted from proposed schedules submitted for the Court's consideration]

This ____ day of ____, 201_, the Court having conducted a Case Management Conference/Rule 16 scheduling and planning conference pursuant to Local Rule 16.2(a) and Judge Stark's Revised Procedures for Managing Patent Cases (which is posted at http://www.ded.uscourts.gov; see Chambers, Judge Leonard P. Stark, Patent Cases) on __________, 201_, and the parties having determined after discussion that the matter cannot be resolved at this juncture by settlement, voluntary mediation, or binding arbitration;

IT IS HEREBY ORDERED that:

1. Rule 26(a)(l) Initial Disclosures and e-Discovery Default Standard. Unless otherwise agreed to by the parties, the parties shall make their initial disclosures pursuant to Federal Rule of Civil Procedure 26(a)(1) within five (5) days of the date of this Order. If they have not already done so, the parties are to review the Court's Default Standard for Discovery, Including Discovery of Electronically Stored Information ("ESI") (which is posted at http://www.ded.uscourts.gov; see Other Resources, Default Standards for Discovery, and is incorporated herein by reference).

2. Joinder of Other Parties and Amendment of Pleadings. All motions to join other parties, and to amend or supplement the pleadings, shall be filed on or before __________, 201__.

3. Application to Court for Protective Order. Should counsel find it will be necessary to apply to the Court for a protective order specifying terms and conditions for the disclosure of confidential information, counsel should confer and attempt to reach an agreement on a proposed form of order and submit it to the Court within ten (10) days from the date of this Order. Should counsel be unable to reach an agreement on a proposed form of order, counsel must follow the provisions of Paragraph 8(g) below.

Any proposed protective order must include the following paragraph:

> Other Proceedings. By entering this order and limiting the disclosure of information in this case, the Court does not intend to preclude another court from finding that information may be relevant and subject to disclosure in another case. Any person or party subject to this order who becomes subject to a motion to disclose

another party's information designated "confidential" [the parties should list any other level of designation, such as "highly confidential," which may be provided for in the protective order] pursuant to this order shall promptly notify that party of the motion so that the party may have an opportunity to appear and be heard on whether that information should be disclosed.

4. Papers Filed Under Seal. In accordance with section G of the Administrative Procedures Governing Filing and Service by Electronic Means, a redacted version of any sealed document shall be filed electronically within seven (7) days of the filing of the sealed document. Should any party intend to request to seal or redact all or any portion of a transcript of a court proceeding (including a teleconference), such party should expressly note that intent at the start of the court proceeding. Should the party subsequently choose to make a request for sealing or redaction, it must, promptly after the completion of the transcript, file with the Court a motion for sealing/redaction, and include as attachments (1) a copy of the complete transcript highlighted so the Court can easily identify and read the text proposed to be sealed/redacted, and (2) a copy of the proposed redacted/sealed transcript. With their request, the party seeking redactions must demonstrate why there is good cause for the redactions and why disclosure of the redacted material would work a clearly defined and serious injury to the party seeking redaction.

5. Courtesy Copies. Other than with respect to "discovery matters," which are governed by paragraph 8(g), and the final pretrial order, which is governed by paragraph 20, the parties shall provide to the Court two (2) courtesy copies of all briefs and one (1) courtesy copy of any other document filed in support of any briefs (i.e., appendices, exhibits, declarations, affidavits etc.). This provision also applies to papers filed under seal.

6. ADR Process. This matter is referred to a magistrate judge to explore the possibility of alternative dispute resolution.

7. Disclosures. Absent agreement among the parties, and approval of the Court:

a. By ______, Plaintiff shall identify the accused product(s), including accused methods and systems, and its damages model, as well as the asserted patent(s) that the accused product(s) allegedly infringe(s). Plaintiff shall also produce the file history for each asserted patent.

b. By ______, Defendant shall produce core technical documents related to the accused product(s), sufficient to show how the accused product(s) work(s), including but not limited to non-publicly available operation manuals, product literature, schematics, and specifications. Defendant shall also produce sales figures for the accused product(s).

c. By ______, Plaintiff shall produce an initial claim chart relating each known accused product to the asserted claims each such product allegedly infringes.

d. By ______, Defendant shall produce its initial invalidity contentions for each asserted claim, as well as the known related invalidating references.

e. By ______, Plaintiff shall provide final infringement contentions.

f. By ______, Defendant shall provide final invalidity contentions.

8. Discovery. Unless otherwise ordered by the Court, the limitations on discovery set forth in Local Rule 26.1 shall be strictly observed.

a. Discovery Cut Off. All discovery in this case shall be initiated so that it will be completed on or before __________, 201__.

b. Document Production. Document production shall be substantially complete by _______, 201__.

c. Requests for Admission. A maximum of_ requests for admission are permitted for each side.

d. Interrogatories.

i. A maximum of _____ interrogatories, including contention interrogatories, are permitted for each side.

ii. The Court encourages the parties to serve and respond to contention interrogatories early in the case. In the absence of agreement among the parties, contention interrogatories, if filed, shall first be addressed by the party with the burden of proof. The adequacy of all interrogatory answers shall be judged by the level of detail each party provides; i.e., the more detail a party provides, the more detail a party shall receive.

e. Depositions.

i. Limitation on Hours for Deposition Discovery. Each side is limited to a total of_ hours of taking testimony by deposition upon oral examination.

ii. Location of Depositions. Any party or representative (officer, director, or managing agent) of a party filing a civil action in this district court must ordinarily be required, upon request, to submit to a deposition at a place designated within this district.

Exceptions to this general rule may be made by order of the Court. A defendant who becomes a counterclaimant, cross-claimant, or third-party plaintiff shall be considered as having filed an action in this Court for the purpose of this provision.

f. Disclosure of Expert Testimony.

i. Expert Reports. For the party who has the initial burden of proof on the subject matter, the initial Federal Rule 26(a)(2) disclosure of expert testimony is due on or before _________, 201__. The supplemental disclosure to contradict or rebut evidence on the same matter identified by another party is due on or before _________, 201__. Reply expert reports from the party with the initial burden of proof are due on or before ________. No other expert reports will be permitted without either the consent of all parties or leave of the Court.

Along with the submissions of the expert reports, the parties shall advise of the dates and times of their experts' availability for deposition.

ii. Expert Report Supplementation. The parties agree they [will] [will not] [CHOOSE ONE] permit expert declarations to be filed in connection with motions briefing (including case-dispositive motions).

iii. Objections to Expert Testimony. To the extent any objection to expert testimony is made pursuant to the principles announced in *Daubert v. Merrell Dow Pharm., Inc.,* 509 U.S. 579 (1993), as incorporated in Federal Rule of Evidence 702, it shall be made by motion no later than the deadline for dispositive motions set forth herein, unless otherwise ordered by the Court. Briefing on such motions is subject to the page limits set out in connection with briefing of case dispositive motions.

g. Discovery Matters and Disputes Relating to Protective Orders.

i. Any discovery motion filed without first complying with the following procedures will be denied without prejudice to renew pursuant to these procedures.

ii. Should counsel find, after good faith efforts - including ***verbal*** communication among Delaware and Lead Counsel for all parties to the dispute - that they are unable to resolve a discovery matter or a dispute relating to a protective order, the parties involved in the discovery matter or protective order dispute shall submit a joint letter in substantially the following form:

> Dear Judge Stark:
>
> The parties in the above-referenced matter write to request the scheduling of a discovery teleconference.
>
> The following attorneys, including at least one Delaware Counsel and at least one Lead Counsel per party, participated in a verbal meet-and-confer (in person and/or by telephone) on the following date(s):
>
> ______________________________
>
> Delaware Counsel: __________________________
>
> Lead Counsel: ______________________________
>
> The disputes requiring judicial attention are listed below: [provide here a non-argumentative list of disputes requiring judicial attention]

iii. On a date to be set by separate order, generally not less than forty-eight (48) hours prior to the conference, the party seeking relief shall file with the Court a letter, not to exceed three (3) pages, outlining the issues in dispute and its position on those issues. On a date to be set by separate order, but generally not less than twenty-four (24) hours prior to the conference, any party opposing the application for relief may file a letter, not to exceed three (3) pages, outlining that party's reasons for its opposition.

iv. Each party shall submit two (2) courtesy copies of its discovery letter and any attachments.

v. Should the Court find further briefing necessary upon conclusion of the telephone conference, the Court will order it. Alternatively, the Court may choose to resolve the dispute prior to the telephone conference and will, in that event, cancel the conference.

9. Motions to Amend.

a. Any motion to amend (including a motion for leave to amend) a pleading shall NOT be accompanied by an opening brief but shall, instead, be accompanied by a letter, not to exceed three (3) pages, describing the basis for the requested relief, and shall attach the proposed amended pleading as well as a "blackline" comparison to the prior pleading.

b. Within seven (7) days after the filing of a motion in compliance with this Order, any party opposing such a motion shall file a responsive letter, not to exceed five (5) pages.

c. Within three (3) days thereafter, the moving party may file a reply letter, not to exceed two (2) pages, and, by this same date, the parties shall file a letter requesting a teleconference to address the motion to amend.

10. Motions to Strike.

a. Any motion to strike any pleading or other document shall NOT be accompanied by an opening brief but shall, instead, be accompanied by a letter, not to exceed three (3) pages, describing the basis for the requested relief, and shall attach the document to be stricken.

b. Within seven (7) days after the filing of a motion in compliance with this Order, any party opposing such a motion shall file a responsive letter, not to exceed five (5) pages.

c. Within three (3) days thereafter, the moving party may file a reply letter, not to exceed two (2) pages, and, by this same date, the parties shall file a letter requesting a teleconference to address the motion to strike.

11. Tutorial Describing the Technology and Matters in Issue. Unless otherwise ordered by the Court, the parties shall provide the Court, no later than the date on which their opening claim construction briefs are due, a tutorial on the technology at issue. In that regard, the parties may separately or jointly submit a DVD of not more than thirty (30) minutes. The tutorial should focus on the technology in issue and should not be used for argument. The parties may choose to file their tutorial(s) under seal, subject to any protective order in effect. Each party may comment, in writing (in no more than five (5) pages) on the opposing party's tutorial. Any such

comment shall be filed no later than the date on which the answering claim construction briefs are due. As to the format selected, the parties should confirm the Court's technical abilities to access the information contained in the tutorial (currently best are "mpeg" or "quicktime").

12. Claim Construction Issue Identification. On _________, 201__, the parties shall exchange a list of those claim term(s)/phrase(s) that they believe need construction and their proposed claim construction of those term(s)/phrase(s). This document will not be filed with the Court. Subsequent to exchanging that list, the parties will meet and confer to prepare a Joint Claim Construction Chart to be submitted on _________, 201__. The parties' Joint Claim Construction Chart should identify for the Court the term(s)/ phrase(s) of the claim(s) in issue, and should include each party's proposed construction of the disputed claim language with citation(s) only to the intrinsic evidence in support of their respective proposed constructions. A copy of the patent(s) in issue as well as those portions of the intrinsic record relied upon shall be submitted with this Joint Claim Construction Chart. In this joint submission, the parties shall not provide argument.

13. Claim Construction Briefing. The parties shall contemporaneously submit initial briefs on claim construction issues on _________, 201__. The parties' answering/responsive briefs shall be contemporaneously submitted on _________, 201__. No reply briefs or supplemental papers on claim construction shall be submitted without leave of the Court. Local Rule 7.1.3(4) shall control the page limitations for initial (opening) and responsive (answering) briefs.

14. Hearing on Claim Construction. Beginning at ____ _.m. on _________, 201__, the Court will hear argument on claim construction. The parties shall notify the Court, by joint letter submission, no later than the date on which their answering claim construction briefs are due: (i) whether they request leave to present testimony at the hearing; and (ii) the amount of time they are requesting be allocated to them for the hearing.

Provided that the parties comply with all portions of this Scheduling Order, and any other orders of the Court, the parties should anticipate that the Court will issue its claim construction order within sixty (60) days of the conclusion of the claim construction hearing. If the Court is unable to meet this goal, it will advise the parties no later than sixty (60) days after the conclusion of the claim construction hearing.

15. Interim Status Report. On _________, 201__, counsel shall submit a joint letter to the Court with an interim report on the nature of the matters in issue and the progress of discovery to date. Thereafter, if the Court deems it necessary, it will schedule a status conference.

16. Supplementation. Absent agreement among the parties, and approval of the Court, no later than ________ the parties must finally supplement, inter alia, the identification of all accused products and of all invalidity references.

17. Case Dispositive Motions. All case dispositive motions, an opening brief, and affidavits, if any, in support of the motion shall be served and filed on or before ________, 201__. Briefing will be presented pursuant to the Court's Local Rules, as modified by this Order.

a. No early motions without leave. No case dispositive motion under Rule 56 may be filed more than ten (10) days before the above date without leave of the Court.

b. Page limits combined with *Daubert* motion page limits. Each party is permitted to file as many case dispositive motions as desired; provided, however, that each SIDE will be limited to a combined total of 40 pages for all opening briefs, a combined total of 40 pages for all answering briefs, and a combined total of 20 pages for all reply briefs regardless of the number of case dispositive motions that are filed. In the event that a party files, in addition to a case dispositive motion, a *Daubert* motion to exclude or preclude all or any portion of an expert's testimony, the total amount of pages permitted for all case dispositive and *Daubert* motions shall be increased to 50 pages for all opening briefs, 50 pages for all answering briefs, and 25 pages for all reply briefs for each ***SIDE***.[12]

c. Hearing. The Court will hear argument on all pending case dispositive and *Daubert* motions on _________ beginning at ____ . [The parties should propose a date approximately two months prior to the requested pretrial conference date.] Subject to further order of the Court, each side will be allocated a total of forty-five (45) minutes to present its argument on all pending motions.

18. Applications by Motion. Except as otherwise specified herein, any application to the Court shall be by written motion filed with the Clerk. Any non-dispositive motion should contain the statement required by Local Rule 7.1.1.

19. Pretrial Conference. On ________, 201__, the Court will hold a pretrial conference in Court with counsel beginning at ___ .m. [The parties should request a date approximately 2-4 weeks prior to their requested trial date.] Unless otherwise ordered by the Court, the parties should assume that filing the pretrial order satisfies the pretrial disclosure requirement of Federal Rule of Civil Procedure 26(a)(3). The parties shall file with the Court the joint proposed final pretrial order with the in-

12. The parties must work together to ensure that the Court receives no more than a total of 250 pages (i.e., 50 + 50 + 25 regarding one side's motions, and 50 + 50 + 25 regarding the other side's motions) of briefing on all case dispositive motions and *Daubert* motions that are covered by this scheduling order and any other scheduling order entered in any related case that is proceeding on a consolidated or coordinated pretrial schedule.

formation required by the form of Revised Final Pretrial Order- Patent, which can be found on the Court's website (www.ded.uscourts.gov), on or before ________, 201__. [The parties should insert a date no less than seven (7) days before the requested pretrial conference date.] Unless otherwise ordered by the Court, the parties shall comply with the timeframes set forth in Local Rule 16.3(d)(l)–(3) for the preparation of the joint proposed final pretrial order.

The parties shall provide the Court two (2) courtesy copies of the joint proposed final pretrial order and all attachments.

As noted in the Revised Final Pretrial Order- Patent, the parties shall include in their joint proposed final pretrial order, among other things:

a. a request for a specific number of ***hours*** for their trial presentations, as well as a requested number of days, based on the assumption that in a typical jury trial day (in which there is not jury selection, jury instruction, or deliberations), there will be 5 1/2 to 6 1/2 hours of trial time, and in a typical bench trial day there will be 6 to 7 hours of trial time;

b. their position as to whether the Court should allow objections to efforts to impeach a witness with prior testimony, including objections based on lack of completeness and/or lack of inconsistency;

c. their position as to whether the Court should rule at trial on objections to expert testimony as beyond the scope of prior expert disclosures, taking time from the parties' trial presentation to argue and decide such objections, or defer ruling on all such objections unless renewed in writing following trial, subject to the proviso that a party prevailing on such a post-trial objection will be entitled to have all of its costs associated with a new trial paid for by the party that elicited the improper expert testimony at the earlier trial; and

d. their position as to how to make motions for judgment as a matter of law, whether it be immediately at the appropriate point during trial or at a subsequent break, whether the jury should be in or out of the courtroom, and whether such motions may be supplemented in writing.

20. Motions *in Limine*. Motions *in limine* shall not be separately filed. All *in limine* requests and responses thereto shall be set forth in the proposed pretrial order. Each ***SIDE*** shall be limited to three (3) *in limine* requests, unless otherwise permitted by the Court. The *in limine* request and any response shall contain the authorities relied upon; each *in limine* request may be supported by a maximum of three (3) pages of argument and may be opposed by a maximum of three (3) pages of argument, and the side making the *in limine* request may add a maximum of one (1) additional page in reply in support of its request. If more than one party is supporting or opposing an *in limine* request, such support or opposition shall be combined in a single three (3) page submission (and, if the moving party, a single one (1) page

reply), unless otherwise ordered by the Court. No separate briefing shall be submitted on *in limine* requests, unless otherwise permitted by the Court.

21. Jury Instructions, Voir Dire, and Special Verdict Forms. Where a case is to be tried to a jury, pursuant to Local Rules 47 and 51 the parties should file (i) proposed voir dire, (ii) preliminary jury instructions, (iii) final jury instructions, and (iv) special verdict forms three (3) business days before the final pretrial conference. This submission shall be accompanied by a courtesy copy containing electronic files of these documents, in WordPerfect or Microsoft Word format, which may be submitted by e-mail to Judge Stark's staff.

22. Trial. This matter is scheduled for a __ day trial beginning at 9:30 a.m. on __________, 201__, with the subsequent trial days beginning at 9:00 a.m. Until the case is submitted to the jury for deliberations, the jury will be excused each day at 4:30 p.m. The trial will be timed, as counsel will be allocated a total number of hours in which to present their respective cases.

23. Judgment on Verdict and Post-Trial Status Report. Within seven (7) days after a jury returns a verdict in any portion of a jury trial, the parties shall jointly submit a form of order to enter judgment on the verdict. At the same time, the parties shall submit a joint status report, indicating among other things how the case should proceed and listing any post-trial motions each party intends to file.

24. Post-Trial Motions. Unless otherwise ordered by the Court, all SIDES are limited to a maximum of 20 pages of opening briefs, 20 pages of answering briefs, and 10 pages of reply briefs relating to any post-trial motions filed by that side, no matter how many such motions are filed.

____

UNITED STATES DISTRICT JUDGE

Appendix 2.3
Patent Pilot Program

District	Participating Judges
Central District of California	• District Judge Andrew J. Guilford • District Judge S. James Otero • District Judge Otis D. Wright II • District Judge George H. Wu • District Judge James V. Selna • District Judge John A. Kronstadt
Northern District of California	• District Judge James Donato • District Judge Lucy H. Koh • District Judge Jeffrey S. White • Senior District Judge Ronald M. Whyte • Magistrate Judge Laurel Beeler • Magistrate Judge Jacqueline Scott Corley • Magistrate Judge Nathanael M. Cousins • Magistrate Judge Elizabeth M. Laporte • Magistrate Judge Paul S. Grewal • Magistrate Judge Joseph C. Spero • Magistrate Judge Donna M. Ryu
Southern District of California	• District Judge Roger T. Benitez • District Judge Marilyn L. Huff • District Judge Dana M. Sabraw • District Judge Janis L. Sammartino • District Judge Cathy Ann Bencivengo
Northern District of Illinois	• Chief Judge James F. Holderman • District Judge Ruben Castillo • District Judge John W. Darrah • District Judge Gary S. Feinerman • District Judge Virginia Kendall • District Judge Matthew F. Kennelly • District Judge Joan Humphrey Lefkow • District Judge Rebecca R. Pallmeyer • District Judge Amy J. St. Eve • District Judge James B. Zagel
District of Maryland	• District Judge Marvin J. Garbis • District Judge William D. Quarles, Jr. • District Judge Roger W. Titus

District	Participating Judges
District of Nevada	• Chief Judge Robert C. Jones • District Judge Gloria M. Navarro • District Judge Philip M. Pro • District Judge Miranda Mai Du
District of New Jersey	• Chief Judge Jerome B. Simandle • District Judge Renee M. Bumb • District Judge Claire C. Cecchi • District Judge Noel L. Hillman • District Judge Peter G. Sheridan • District Judge Susan D. Wigenton • Senior District Judge Stanley R. Chesler • Senior District Judge Mary L. Cooper • Senior District Judge Joseph E. Irenas
Eastern District of New York	• District Judge Brian M. Cogan • District Judge John Gleeson • District Judge Kiyo A. Matsumoto • District Judge William F. Kuntz II • District Judge Joanna Seybert • Senior District Judge Jack B. Weinstein • Chief Magistrate Judge Steven M. Gold • Magistrate Judge Joan A. Azrack • Magistrate Judge Marilyn D. Go • Magistrate Judge Gary Brown • Magistrate Judge Cheryl L. Pollak • Magistrate Judge James Orenstein • Magistrate Judge Ramon E. Reyes, Jr. • Magistrate Judge A. Kathleen Tomlinson • Magistrate Judge William D. Wall
Southern District of New York	• District Judge P. Kevin Castel • District Judge Denise Cote • District Judge Katherine B. Forrest • District Judge John G. Koeltl • District Judge Colleen McMahon • District Judge Laura Taylor Swain • Senior District Judge Thomas P. Griesa • Senior District Judge Jed S. Rakoff • Senior District Judge Shira A. Scheindlin • Senior District Judge Robert W. Sweet

District	Participating Judges
Western District of Pennsylvania	• Chief Judge Gary L. Lancaster • District Judge Joy Flowers Conti • District Judge Nora Barry Fischer • District Judge Arthur J. Schwab • District Judge Cathy Bissoon • District Judge Mark R. Hornak
Western District of Tennessee	• Chief Judge Jon P. McCalla • District Judge S. Hardy Mays, Jr.
Eastern District of Texas	• Chief Judge Leonard E. Davis • District Judge Ron Clark • District Judge Rodney Gilstrap • District Judge Richard A. Schell • District Judge Michael H. Schneider, Sr.
Northern District of Texas	• District Judge David C. Godbey • District Judge Ed Kinkeade • District Judge Barbara M.G. Lynn

Appendix 2.4
Protective Orders

Many district courts have established default protective orders in conjunction with or in addition to Patent Local Rules (PLRs). This appendix catalogs the districts with default protective orders and contains several representative examples. The highlighted documents are contained herein.

California

Northern District (updated Aug. 20, 2014), two forms reprinted here:

Appendix 2.4a: (1) Patent Local Rule 2-2 Interim Model Protective Order

Appendix 2.4b: (2) Model Protective Order for Litigation Involving Patents, Highly Sensitive Confidential Information and/or Trade Secrets

Note that a Stipulated Protective Order for Standard Litigation is also available at http://www.cand.uscourts.gov/model-protective-orders

Southern District (updated Feb. 2, 2015) (Patent Local Rules)

Delaware

Appendix 2.4e: Default Standard for Access to Source Code, updated Dec. 8, 2011

Illinois

Northern District

Appendix 2.4c: Model Protective Order (Appendix B)

Minnesota

Appendix 2.4d: Form 5. Stipulation for Protective Order

Missouri

Eastern District (Appendix A)

New Jersey

General Discovery Confidentiality Order; Appendix S to Local Patent Rules

New York

Northern District (available at www.nynd.uscourts.gov)

Ohio

Northern District (effective Oct. 22, 2009) (Appendix A)
Southern District (effective June 1, 2010) (Appendix A)

Pennsylvania

Western District (effective Dec. 1, 2005) (Appendix LPR 2.2)

Tennessee

Western District (Patent Case Protective Order, Appendix A)

Texas

Eastern District (effective Feb. 22, 2005) (sample form)

Northern District, Dallas Division (effective May 1, 2007) (Appendix A)

Southern District (effective Jan. 1, 2008)

Appendix 2.4a
Northern District of California, Patent Local Rule 2-2
Interim Model Protective Order

UNITED STATES DISTRICT COURT
NORTHERN DISTRICT OF CALIFORNIA

Plaintiff,	
v.	Case No. C PATENT LOCAL RULE 2-2 INTERIM MODEL PROTECTIVE ORDER
Defendant.	

1. PURPOSES AND LIMITATIONS

Disclosure and discovery activity in this action are likely to involve production of confidential, proprietary, or private information for which special protection from public disclosure and from use for any purpose other than prosecuting this litigation may be warranted. This Order does not confer blanket protections on all disclosures or responses to discovery and the protection it affords from public disclosure and use extends only to the limited information or items that are entitled to confidential treatment under the applicable legal principles. As set forth in Section 14.4 below, this Protective Order does not entitle the Parties to file confidential information under seal; Civil Local Rule 79-5 sets forth the procedures that must be followed and the standards that will be applied when a party seeks permission from the court to file material under seal.

2. DEFINITIONS

2.1 Challenging Party: a Party or Non-Party that challenges the designation of information or items under this Order.

2.2 "CONFIDENTIAL" Information or Items: information (regardless of how it is generated, stored or maintained) or tangible things that qualify for protection under Federal Rule of Civil Procedure 26(c).

2.3 Counsel (without qualifier): Outside Counsel of Record and House Counsel (as well as their support staff).

2.4 Designated House Counsel: House Counsel who seek access to "HIGHLY CONFIDENTIAL – ATTORNEYS' EYES ONLY" information in this matter.

2.5 Designating Party: a Party or Non-Party that designates information or items that it produces in disclosures or in responses to discovery as "CONFIDENTIAL," "HIGHLY CONFIDENTIAL – ATTORNEYS' EYES ONLY," or "HIGHLY CONFIDENTIAL – SOURCE CODE."

2.6 Disclosure or Discovery Material: all items or information, regardless of the medium or manner in which it is generated, stored, or maintained (including, among other things, testimony, transcripts, and tangible things), that are produced or generated in disclosures or responses to discovery in this matter.

2.7 Expert: a person with specialized knowledge or experience in a matter pertinent to the litigation who (1) has been retained by a Party or its counsel to serve as an expert witness or as a consultant in this action, (2) is not a past or current employee of a Party or of a Party's competitor, and (3) at the time of retention, is not anticipated to become an employee of a Party or of a Party's competitor.

2.8 "HIGHLY CONFIDENTIAL – ATTORNEYS' EYES ONLY" Information or Items: extremely sensitive "Confidential Information or Items," disclosure of which to another Party or Non-Party would create a substantial risk of serious harm that could not be avoided by less restrictive means.

2.9 "HIGHLY CONFIDENTIAL – SOURCE CODE" Information or Items: extremely sensitive "Confidential Information or Items" representing computer code and associated comments and revision histories, formulas, engineering specifications, or schematics that define or otherwise describe in detail the algorithms or structure of software or hardware designs, disclosure of which to another Party or Non-Party would create a substantial risk of serious harm that could not be avoided by less restrictive means.

2.10 House Counsel: attorneys who are employees of a party to this action. House Counsel does not include Outside Counsel of Record or any other outside counsel.

2.11 Non-Party: any natural person, partnership, corporation, association, or other legal entity not named as a Party to this action.

2.12 Outside Counsel of Record: attorneys who are not employees of a party to this action but are retained to represent or advise a party to this action and have appeared in this action on behalf of that party or are affiliated with a law firm which has appeared on behalf of that party.

2.13 Party: any party to this action, including all of its officers, directors, employees, consultants, retained experts, and Outside Counsel of Record (and their support staffs).

2.14 Producing Party: a Party or Non-Party that produces Disclosure or Discovery Material in this action.

2.15 Professional Vendors: persons or entities that provide litigation support services (e.g., photocopying, videotaping, translating, preparing exhibits or demonstrations, and organizing, storing, or retrieving data in any form or medium) and their employees and subcontractors.

2.16 Protected Material: any Disclosure or Discovery Material that is designated as "CONFIDENTIAL," "HIGHLY CONFIDENTIAL – ATTORNEYS' EYES ONLY," or "HIGHLY CONFIDENTIAL – SOURCE CODE."

2.17 Receiving Party: a Party that receives Disclosure or Discovery Material from a Producing Party.

3. SCOPE

The protections conferred by this Order cover not only Protected Material (as defined above), but also (1) any information copied or extracted from Protected Material; (2) all copies, excerpts, summaries, or compilations of Protected Material; and (3) any testimony, conversations, or presentations by Parties or their Counsel that might reveal Protected Material. However, the protections conferred by this Order do not cover the following information: (a) any information that is in the public domain at the time of disclosure to a Receiving Party or becomes part of the public domain after its disclosure to a Receiving Party as a result of publication not involving a violation of this Order, including becoming part of the public record through trial or otherwise; and (b) any information known to the Receiving Party prior to the disclosure or obtained by the Receiving Party after the disclosure from a source who obtained the information lawfully and under no obligation of confidentiality to the Designating Party. Any use of Protected Material at trial shall be governed by a separate agreement or order.

4. DURATION

Even after final disposition of this litigation, the confidentiality obligations imposed by this Order shall remain in effect until a Designating Party agrees otherwise in writing or a court order otherwise directs. Final disposition shall be deemed to be the later of (1) dismissal of all claims and defenses in this action, with or without prejudice; and (2) final judgment herein after the completion and exhaustion of all appeals, rehearings, remands, trials, or reviews of this action, including the time limits for filing any motions or applications for extension of time pursuant to applicable law.

5. DESIGNATING PROTECTED MATERIAL

5.1 Exercise of Restraint and Care in Designating Material for Protection. Each Party or Non-Party that designates information or items for protection under this Order must take care to limit any such designation to specific material that qualifies under the appropriate standards. To the extent it is practical to do so, the Designating Party must designate for protection only those parts of material, documents, items, or oral or written communications that qualify – so that other portions of the material, documents, items, or communications for which protection is not warranted are not swept unjustifiably within the ambit of this Order.

Mass, indiscriminate, or routinized designations are prohibited. Designations that are shown to be clearly unjustified or that have been made for an improper purpose (e.g., to unnecessarily encumber or retard the case development process or to impose unnecessary expenses and burdens on other parties) expose the Designating Party to sanctions.

If it comes to a Designating Party's attention that information or items that it designated for protection do not qualify for protection at all or do not qualify for the level of protection initially asserted, that Designating Party must promptly notify all other Parties that it is withdrawing the mistaken designation.

5.2 Manner and Timing of Designations. Except as otherwise provided in this Order (see, e.g., second paragraph of section 5.2(a) below), or as otherwise stipulated or ordered, Disclosure or Discovery Material that qualifies for protection under this Order must be clearly so designated before the material is disclosed or produced.

Designation in conformity with this Order requires:

(a) for information in documentary form (e.g., paper or electronic documents, but excluding transcripts of depositions or other pretrial or trial proceedings), that the Producing Party affix the legend "CONFIDENTIAL," "HIGHLY CONFIDENTIAL – ATTORNEYS' EYES ONLY," or "HIGHLY CONFIDENTIAL – SOURCE CODE" to each page that contains protected material. If only a portion or portions of the material on a page qualifies for protection, the Producing Party also must clearly identify the protected portion(s) (e.g., by making appropriate markings in the margins) and must specify, for each portion, the level of protection being asserted.

A Party or Non-Party that makes original documents or materials available for inspection need not designate them for protection until after the inspecting Party has indicated which material it would like copied and produced. During the inspection and before the designation, all of the material made available for inspection shall be deemed "HIGHLY CONFIDENTIAL – ATTORNEYS' EYES ONLY." After the inspecting Party has identified the documents it wants copied and produced, the Producing Party must determine which documents, or portions thereof, qualify for protection under this Order. Then, before producing the specified documents, the Producing Party must affix the appropriate legend ("CONFIDENTIAL," "HIGHLY CONFIDENTIAL – ATTORNEYS' EYES ONLY," or "HIGHLY CONFIDENTIAL – SOURCE CODE") to each page that contains Protected Material. If only a portion or portions of the material on a page qualifies for protection, the Producing Party also must clearly identify the protected portion(s) (e.g., by making appropriate markings in the margins) and must specify, for each portion, the level of protection being asserted.

(b) for testimony given in deposition or in other pretrial or trial proceedings, that the Designating Party identify on the record, before the close of the deposition, hearing, or other proceeding, all protected testimony and specify the level of protection being asserted. When it is impractical to identify separately each portion of testimony that is entitled to protection and it appears that substantial portions of the testimony may qualify for protection, the Designating Party may invoke on the record (before the deposition, hearing, or other proceeding is concluded) a right to have up to 21 days to identify the specific portions of the testimony as to which protection is sought and to specify the level of protection being asserted. Only those portions of the testimony that are appropriately designated for protection within the 21 days shall be covered by the provisions of this Protective Order. Alternatively, a Designating Party may specify, at the deposition or up to 21 days afterwards if that period is properly invoked, that the entire transcript shall be treated as "CONFIDENTIAL" or "HIGHLY CONFIDENTIAL – ATTORNEYS' EYES ONLY."

Parties shall give the other parties notice if they reasonably expect a deposition, hearing, or other proceeding to include Protected Material so that the other parties can ensure that only authorized individuals who have signed the "Acknowledgment and Agreement to Be Bound" (Exhibit A) are present at those proceedings. The use of a document as an exhibit at a deposition shall not in any way affect its designation as "CONFIDENTIAL" or "HIGHLY CONFIDENTIAL – ATTORNEYS' EYES ONLY."

Transcripts containing Protected Material shall have an obvious legend on the title page that the transcript contains Protected Material, and the title page shall be followed by a list of all pages (including line numbers as appropriate) that have been designated as Protected Material and the level of protection being asserted by the Designating Party. The Designating Party shall inform the court reporter of these requirements. Any transcript that is prepared before the expiration of a 21-day period for designation shall be treated during that period as if it had been designated

"HIGHLY CONFIDENTIAL – ATTORNEYS' EYES ONLY" in its entirety unless otherwise agreed. After the expiration of that period, the transcript shall be treated only as actually designated.

(c) for information produced in some form other than documentary and for any other tangible items, that the Producing Party affix in a prominent place on the exterior of the container or containers in which the information or item is stored the legend "CONFIDENTIAL," "HIGHLY CONFIDENTIAL – ATTORNEYS' EYES ONLY," or "HIGHLY CONFIDENTIAL – SOURCE CODE." If only a portion or portions of the information or item warrant protection, the Producing Party, to the extent practicable, shall identify the protected portion(s) and specify the level of protection being asserted.

5.3 Inadvertent Failures to Designate. If timely corrected, an inadvertent failure to designate qualified information or items does not, standing alone, waive the Designating Party's right to secure protection under this Order for such material. Upon timely correction of a designation, the Receiving Party must make reasonable efforts to assure that the material is treated in accordance with the provisions of this Order.

6. CHALLENGING CONFIDENTIALITY DESIGNATIONS

6.1 Timing of Challenges. Any Party or Non-Party may challenge a designation of confidentiality at any time. Unless a prompt challenge to a Designating Party's confidentiality designation is necessary to avoid foreseeable, substantial unfairness, unnecessary economic burdens, or a significant disruption or delay of the litigation, a Party does not waive its right to challenge a confidentiality designation by electing not to mount a challenge promptly after the original designation is disclosed.

6.2 Meet and Confer. The Challenging Party shall initiate the dispute resolution process by providing written notice of each designation it is challenging and describing the basis for each challenge. To avoid ambiguity as to whether a challenge has been made, the written notice must recite that the challenge to confidentiality is being made in accordance with this specific paragraph of the Protective Order. The parties shall attempt to resolve each challenge in good faith and must begin the process by conferring directly (in voice to voice dialogue; other forms of communication are not sufficient) within 14 days of the date of service of notice. In conferring, the Challenging Party must explain the basis for its belief that the confidentiality designation was not proper and must give the Designating Party an opportunity to review the designated material, to reconsider the circumstances, and, if no change in designation is offered, to explain the basis for the chosen designation. A Challenging Party may proceed to the next stage of the challenge process only if it has engaged in this meet and confer process first or establishes that the Designating Party is unwilling to participate in the meet and confer process in a timely manner.

6.3 Judicial Intervention. If the Parties cannot resolve a challenge without court intervention, the Designating Party shall file and serve a motion to retain confidentiality under Civil Local Rule 7 (and in compliance with Civil Local Rule 79-5, if applicable) within 21 days of the initial notice of challenge or within 14 days of the parties agreeing that the meet and confer process will not resolve their dispute, whichever is earlier. Each such motion must be accompanied by a competent declaration affirming that the movant has complied with the meet and confer requirements imposed in the preceding paragraph. Failure by the Designating Party to make such a motion including the required declaration within 21 days (or 14 days, if applicable) shall automatically waive the confidentiality designation for each challenged designation. In addition, the Challenging Party may file a motion challenging a confidentiality designation at any time if there is good cause for doing so, including a challenge to the designation of a deposition transcript or any portions thereof. Any motion brought pursuant to this provision must be accompanied by a competent declaration affirming that the movant has complied with the meet and confer requirements imposed by the preceding paragraph.

The burden of persuasion in any such challenge proceeding shall be on the Designating Party. Frivolous challenges and those made for an improper purpose (e.g., to harass or impose unnecessary expenses and burdens on other parties) may expose the Challenging Party to sanctions. Unless the Designating Party has waived the confidentiality designation by failing to file a motion to retain confidentiality as described above, all parties shall continue to afford the material in question the level of protection to which it is entitled under the Producing Party's designation until the court rules on the challenge.

7. ACCESS TO AND USE OF PROTECTED MATERIAL

7.1 Basic Principles. A Receiving Party may use Protected Material that is disclosed or produced by another Party or by a Non-Party in connection with this case only for prosecuting, defending, or attempting to settle this litigation. Such Protected Material may be disclosed only to the categories of persons and under the conditions described in this Order. When the litigation has been terminated, a Receiving Party must comply with the provisions of section 15 below (FINAL DISPOSITION).

Protected Material must be stored and maintained by a Receiving Party at a location and in a secure manner that ensures that access is limited to the persons authorized under this Order.

7.2 Disclosure of "CONFIDENTIAL" Information or Items. Unless otherwise ordered by the court or permitted in writing by the Designating Party, a Receiving Party may disclose any information or item designated "CONFIDENTIAL" only to:

(a) the Receiving Party's Outside Counsel of Record in this action, as well as employees of said Outside Counsel of Record to whom it is reasonably necessary to disclose the information for this litigation and who have signed the "Acknowledgment and Agreement to Be Bound" that is attached hereto as Exhibit A;

(b) the officers, directors, and employees (including House Counsel) of the Receiving Party to whom disclosure is reasonably necessary for this litigation and who have signed the "Acknowledgment and Agreement to Be Bound" (Exhibit A);

(c) Experts (as defined in this Order) of the Receiving Party to whom disclosure is reasonably necessary for this litigation and who have signed the "Acknowledgment and Agreement to Be Bound" (Exhibit A);

(d) the court and its personnel;

(e) court reporters and their staff, professional jury or trial consultants, and Professional Vendors to whom disclosure is reasonably necessary for this litigation and who have signed the "Acknowledgment and Agreement to Be Bound" (Exhibit A);

(f) during their depositions, witnesses in the action to whom disclosure is reasonably necessary and who have signed the "Acknowledgment and Agreement to Be Bound" (Exhibit A), unless otherwise agreed by the Designating Party or ordered by the court. Pages of transcribed deposition testimony or exhibits to depositions that reveal Protected Material must be separately bound by the court reporter and may not be disclosed to anyone except as permitted under this Protective Order.

(g) the author or recipient of a document containing the information or a custodian or other person who otherwise possessed or knew the information.

7.3 Disclosure of "HIGHLY CONFIDENTIAL – ATTORNEYS' EYES ONLY" and "HIGHLY CONFIDENTIAL – SOURCE CODE" Information or Items. Unless otherwise ordered by the court or permitted in writing by the Designating Party, a Receiving Party may disclose any information or item designated "HIGHLY CONFIDENTIAL – ATTORNEYS' EYES ONLY" or "HIGHLY CONFIDENTIAL – SOURCE CODE" only to:

(a) the Receiving Party's Outside Counsel of Record in this action, as well as employees of said Outside Counsel of Record to whom it is reasonably necessary to disclose the information for this litigation and who have signed the "Acknowledgment and Agreement to Be Bound" that is attached hereto as Exhibit A;

(b) Designated House Counsel of the Receiving Party (1) who has no involvement in competitive decision-making, (2) to whom disclosure is reasonably necessary for this litigation, (3) who has signed the "Acknowledgment and Agreement to Be Bound" (Exhibit A), and (4) as to whom the procedures set forth in paragraph 7.4(a)(1), below, have been followed;[13]

(c) Experts of the Receiving Party (1) to whom disclosure is reasonably necessary for this litigation, (2) who have signed the "Acknowledgment and Agreement to Be Bound" (Exhibit A), and (3) as to whom the procedures set forth in paragraph 7.4(a)(2), below, have been followed;

(d) the court and its personnel;

(e) court reporters and their staff, professional jury or trial consultants, and Professional Vendors to whom disclosure is reasonably necessary for this litigation and who have signed the "Acknowledgment and Agreement to Be Bound" (Exhibit A); and

(f) the author or recipient of a document containing the information or a custodian or other person who otherwise possessed or knew the information.

7.4 Procedures for Approving or Objecting to Disclosure of "HIGHLY CONFIDENTIAL – ATTORNEYS' EYES ONLY" or "HIGHLY CONFIDENTIAL – SOURCE CODE" Information or Items to Designated House Counsel or Experts.

(a)(1) Unless otherwise ordered by the court or agreed to in writing by the Designating Party, a Party that seeks to disclose to Designated House Counsel any information or item that has been designated "HIGHLY CONFIDENTIAL – ATTORNEYS' EYES ONLY" pursuant to paragraph 7.3(b) first must make a written request to the Designating Party that (1) sets forth the full name of the Designated House Counsel and the city and state of his or her residence and (2) describes the Designated House Counsel's current and reasonably foreseeable future primary job duties and responsibilities in sufficient detail to determine if House Counsel is involved, or may become involved, in any competitive decision-making.

(a)(2) Unless otherwise ordered by the court or agreed to in writing by the Designating Party, a Party that seeks to disclose to an Expert (as defined in this Order) any information or item that has been designated "HIGHLY CONFIDENTIAL – ATTORNEYS' EYES ONLY" or "HIGHLY CONFIDENTIAL – SOURCE CODE" pursuant to paragraph 7.3(c) first must make a written request to the Designating

13. This Order contemplates that Designated House Counsel shall not have access to any information or items designated "HIGHLY CONFIDENTIAL – SOURCE CODE."

Party that (1) identifies the general categories of "HIGHLY CONFIDENTIAL – ATTORNEYS' EYES ONLY" or "HIGHLY CONFIDENTIAL – SOURCE CODE" information that the Receiving Party seeks permission to disclose to the Expert, (2) sets forth the full name of the Expert and the city and state of his or her primary residence, (3) attaches a copy of the Expert's current resume, (4) identifies the Expert's current employer(s), (5) identifies each person or entity from whom the Expert has received compensation or funding for work in his or her areas of expertise or to whom the expert has provided professional services, including in connection with a litigation, at any time during the preceding five years,[14] and (6) identifies (by name and number of the case, filing date, and location of court) any litigation in connection with which the Expert has offered expert testimony, including through a declaration, report, or testimony at a deposition or trial, during the preceding five years.

(b) A Party that makes a request and provides the information specified in the preceding respective paragraphs may disclose the subject Protected Material to the identified Designated House Counsel or Expert unless, within 14 days of delivering the request, the Party receives a written objection from the Designating Party. Any such objection must set forth in detail the grounds on which it is based.

(c) A Party that receives a timely written objection must meet and confer with the Designating Party (through direct voice to voice dialogue) to try to resolve the matter by agreement within seven days of the written objection. If no agreement is reached, the Party seeking to make the disclosure to Designated House Counsel or the Expert may file a motion as provided in Civil Local Rule 7 (and in compliance with Civil Local Rule 79-5, if applicable) seeking permission from the court to do so. Any such motion must describe the circumstances with specificity, set forth in detail the reasons why disclosure to Designated House Counsel or the Expert is reasonably necessary, assess the risk of harm that the disclosure would entail, and suggest any additional means that could be used to reduce that risk. In addition, any such motion must be accompanied by a competent declaration describing the parties' efforts to resolve the matter by agreement (i.e., the extent and the content of the meet and confer discussions) and setting forth the reasons advanced by the Designating Party for its refusal to approve the disclosure.

---

14. If the Expert believes any of this information is subject to a confidentiality obligation to a third-party, then the Expert should provide whatever information the Expert believes can be disclosed without violating any confidentiality agreements, and the Party seeking to disclose to the Expert shall be available to meet and confer with the Designating Party regarding any such engagement.

In any such proceeding, the Party opposing disclosure to Designated House Counsel or the Expert shall bear the burden of proving that the risk of harm that the disclosure would entail (under the safeguards proposed) outweighs the Receiving Party's need to disclose the Protected Material to its Designated House Counsel or Expert.

8. PROSECUTION BAR

Absent written consent from the Producing Party, any individual who receives access to "HIGHLY CONFIDENTIAL - ATTORNEYS' EYES ONLY" or "HIGHLY CONFIDENTIAL - SOURCE CODE" information shall not be involved in the prosecution of patents or patent applications relating to the subject matter of this action, including without limitation the patents asserted in this action and any patent or application claiming priority to or otherwise related to the patents asserted in this action, before any foreign or domestic agency, including the United States Patent and Trademark Office ("the Patent Office"). For purposes of this paragraph, "prosecution" includes directly or indirectly drafting, amending, advising, or otherwise affecting the scope or maintenance of patent claims.[15] To avoid any doubt, "prosecution" as used in this paragraph does not include representing a party challenging a patent before a domestic or foreign agency (including, but not limited to, a reissue protest, *ex parte* reexamination or *inter partes* reexamination). This Prosecution Bar shall begin when access to "HIGHLY CONFIDENTIAL - ATTORNEYS' EYES ONLY" or "HIGHLY CONFIDENTIAL - SOURCE CODE" information is first received by the affected individual and shall end two (2) years after final termination of this action.

9. SOURCE CODE

(a) To the extent production of source code becomes necessary in this case, a Producing Party may designate source code as "HIGHLY CONFIDENTIAL - SOURCE CODE" if it comprises or includes confidential, proprietary or trade secret source code.

(b) Protected Material designated as "HIGHLY CONFIDENTIAL - SOURCE CODE" shall be subject to all of the protections afforded to "HIGHLY CONFIDENTIAL - ATTORNEYS' EYES ONLY" information, including the Prosecution Bar set forth in Paragraph 8, and may be disclosed only to the individuals to whom "HIGHLY CONFIDENTIAL - ATTORNEYS' EYES ONLY" information may be disclosed,

---

15. Prosecution includes, for example, original prosecution, reissue and reexamination proceedings.

as set forth in Paragraphs 7.3 and 7.4, with the exception of Designated House Counsel.

(c) Any source code produced in discovery shall be made available for inspection, in a format allowing it to be reasonably reviewed and searched, during normal business hours or at other mutually agreeable times, at an office of the Producing Party's counsel or another mutually agreed upon location. The source code shall be made available for inspection on a secured computer in a secured room without Internet access or network access to other computers, and the Receiving Party shall not copy, remove, or otherwise transfer any portion of the source code onto any recordable media or recordable device. The Producing Party may visually monitor the activities of the Receiving Party's representatives during any source code review, but only to ensure that there is no unauthorized recording, copying, or transmission of the source code.

(d) The Receiving Party may request paper copies of limited portions of source code that are reasonably necessary for the preparation of court filings, pleadings, expert reports, or other papers, or for deposition or trial, but shall not request paper copies for the purpose of reviewing the source code other than electronically as set forth in paragraph (c) in the first instance. The Producing Party shall provide all such source code in paper form, including bates numbers and the label "HIGHLY CONFIDENTIAL – SOURCE CODE." The Producing Party may challenge the amount of source code requested in hard copy form pursuant to the dispute resolution procedure and timeframes set forth in Paragraph 6 whereby the Producing Party is the "Challenging Party" and the Receiving Party is the "Designating Party" for purposes of dispute resolution.

(e) The Receiving Party shall maintain a record of any individual who has inspected any portion of the source code in electronic or paper form. The Receiving Party shall maintain all paper copies of any printed portions of the source code in a secured, locked area. The Receiving Party shall not create any electronic or other images of the paper copies and shall not convert any of the information contained in the paper copies into any electronic format. The Receiving Party shall only make additional paper copies if such additional copies are (1) necessary to prepare court filings, pleadings, or other papers (including a testifying expert's expert report), (2) necessary for deposition, or (3) otherwise necessary for the preparation of its case. Any paper copies used during a deposition shall be retrieved by the Producing Party at the end of each day and must not be given to or left with a court reporter or any other unauthorized individual.

10. PROTECTED MATERIAL SUBPOENAED OR ORDERED PRODUCED IN OTHER LITIGATION

If a Party is served with a subpoena or a court order issued in other litigation that compels disclosure of any information or items designated in this action as "CONFIDENTIAL," "HIGHLY CONFIDENTIAL - ATTORNEYS' EYES ONLY," or "HIGHLY CONFIDENTIAL - SOURCE CODE," that Party must:

(a) promptly notify in writing the Designating Party. Such notification shall include a copy of the subpoena or court order;

(b) promptly notify in writing the party who caused the subpoena or order to issue in the other litigation that some or all of the material covered by the subpoena or order is subject to this Protective Order. Such notification shall include a copy of this Protective Order; and

(c) cooperate with respect to all reasonable procedures sought to be pursued by the Designating Party whose Protected Material may be affected.[16]

If the Designating Party timely seeks a protective order, the Party served with the subpoena or court order shall not produce any information designated in this action as "CONFIDENTIAL," "HIGHLY CONFIDENTIAL - ATTORNEYS' EYES ONLY." or "HIGHLY CONFIDENTIAL - SOURCE CODE" before a determination by the court from which the subpoena or order issued, unless the Party has obtained the Designating Party's permission. The Designating Party shall bear the burden and expense of seeking protection in that court of its confidential material - and nothing in these provisions should be construed as authorizing or encouraging a Receiving Party in this action to disobey a lawful directive from another court.

11. A NON-PARTY'S PROTECTED MATERIAL SOUGHT TO BE PRODUCED IN THIS LITIGATION

(a) The terms of this Order are applicable to information produced by a Non-Party in this action and designated as "CONFIDENTIAL," "HIGHLY CONFIDENTIAL - ATTORNEYS' EYES ONLY," or "HIGHLY CONFIDENTIAL - SOURCE CODE." Such information produced by Non-Parties in connection with this litigation is protected by the remedies and relief provided by this Order. Nothing in these provisions should be construed as prohibiting a Non-Party from seeking additional protections.

---

16. The purpose of imposing these duties is to alert the interested parties to the existence of this Protective Order and to afford the Designating Party in this case an opportunity to try to protect its confidentiality interests in the court from which the subpoena or order issued.

(b) In the event that a Party is required, by a valid discovery request, to produce a Non-Party's confidential information in its possession, and the Party is subject to an agreement with the Non-Party not to produce the Non-Party's confidential information, then the Party shall:

1. promptly notify in writing the Requesting Party and the Non-Party that some or all of the information requested is subject to a confidentiality agreement with a Non-Party;

2. promptly provide the Non-Party with a copy of the Protective Order in this litigation, the relevant discovery request(s), and a reasonably specific description of the information requested; and

3. make the information requested available for inspection by the Non-Party.

(c) If the Non-Party fails to object or seek a protective order from this court within 14 days of receiving the notice and accompanying information, the Receiving Party may produce the Non-Party's confidential information responsive to the discovery request. If the Non-Party timely seeks a protective order, the Receiving Party shall not produce any information in its possession or control that is subject to the confidentiality agreement with the Non-Party before a determination by the court.[17] Absent a court order to the contrary, the Non-Party shall bear the burden and expense of seeking protection in this court of its Protected Material.

12. UNAUTHORIZED DISCLOSURE OF PROTECTED MATERIAL

If a Receiving Party learns that, by inadvertence or otherwise, it has disclosed Protected Material to any person or in any circumstance not authorized under this Protective Order, the Receiving Party must immediately (a) notify in writing the Designating Party of the unauthorized disclosures, (b) use its best efforts to retrieve all unauthorized copies of the Protected Material, (c) inform the person or persons to whom unauthorized disclosures were made of all the terms of this Order, and (d) request such person or persons to execute the "Acknowledgment and Agreement to Be Bound" that is attached hereto as Exhibit A.

---

17. The purpose of this provision is to alert the interested parties to the existence of confidentiality rights of a Non-Party and to afford the Non-Party an opportunity to protect its confidentiality interests in this court.

13. INADVERTENT PRODUCTION OF PRIVILEGED OR OTHERWISE PROTECTED MATERIAL

When a Producing Party gives notice to Receiving Parties that certain inadvertently produced material is subject to a claim of privilege or other protection, the obligations of the Receiving Parties are those set forth in Federal Rule of Civil Procedure 26(b)(5)(B). This provision is not intended to modify whatever procedure may be established in an e-discovery order that provides for production without prior privilege review. Pursuant to Federal Rule of Evidence 502(d) and (e), insofar as the parties reach an agreement on the effect of disclosure of a communication or information covered by the attorney-client privilege or work product protection, the parties may incorporate their agreement in a stipulated protective order submitted to the court.

14. MISCELLANEOUS

14.1 Right to Further Relief. Nothing in this Order abridges the right of any person to seek its modification by the court in the future.

14.2 Right to Assert Other Objections. No Party waives any right it otherwise would have to object to disclosing or producing any information or item on any ground not addressed in this Protective Order. Similarly, no Party waives any right to object on any ground to use in evidence of any of the material covered by this Protective Order.

14.3 Export Control. Disclosure of Protected Material shall be subject to all applicable laws and regulations relating to the export of technical data contained in such Protected Material, including the release of such technical data to foreign persons or nationals in the United States or elsewhere. The Producing Party shall be responsible for identifying any such controlled technical data, and the Receiving Party shall take measures necessary to ensure compliance.

14.4 Filing Protected Material. Without written permission from the Designating Party or a court order secured after appropriate notice to all interested persons, a Party may not file in the public record in this action any Protected Material. A Party that seeks to file under seal any Protected Material must comply with Civil Local Rule 79-5. Protected Material may only be filed under seal pursuant to a court order authorizing the sealing of the specific Protected Material at issue. Pursuant to Civil Local Rule 79-5, a sealing order will issue only upon a request establishing that the Protected Material at issue is privileged, protectable as a trade secret, or otherwise entitled to protection under the law. If a Receiving Party's request to file Protected Material under seal pursuant to Civil Local Rule 79-5(e) is denied by the court, then the Receiving Party may file the Protected Material in the public record pursuant to Civil Local Rule 79-5(e)(2) unless otherwise instructed by the court.

15. FINAL DISPOSITION

Within 60 days after the final disposition of this action, as defined in paragraph 4, each Receiving Party must return all Protected Material to the Producing Party or destroy such material. As used in this subdivision, "all Protected Material" includes all copies, abstracts, compilations, summaries, and any other format reproducing or capturing any of the Protected Material. Whether the Protected Material is returned or destroyed, the Receiving Party must submit a written certification to the Producing Party (and, if not the same person or entity, to the Designating Party) by the 60 day deadline that (1) identifies (by category, where appropriate) all the Protected Material that was returned or destroyed and (2) affirms that the Receiving Party has not retained any copies, abstracts, compilations, summaries or any other format reproducing or capturing any of the Protected Material. Notwithstanding this provision, Counsel are entitled to retain an archival copy of all pleadings, motion papers, trial, deposition, and hearing transcripts, legal memoranda, correspondence, deposition and trial exhibits, expert reports, attorney work product, and consultant and expert work product, even if such materials contain Protected Material. Any such archival copies that contain or constitute Protected Material remain subject to this Protective Order as set forth in Section 4 (DURATION).

IT IS SO ORDERED.

DATED: ______________________

____

[Name of Judge]

United States District/Magistrate Judge

EXHIBIT A
ACKNOWLEDGMENT AND AGREEMENT TO BE BOUND

I, ___________________________ [print or type full name], of _______________ [print or type full address], declare under penalty of perjury that I have read in its entirety and understand the Protective Order that was issued by the United States District Court for the Northern District of California on _______ [date] in the case of ___________ **[insert formal name of the case and the number and initials assigned to it by the court]**. I agree to comply with and to be bound by all the terms of this Protective Order, and I understand and acknowledge that failure to so comply could expose me to sanctions and punishment in the nature of contempt. I solemnly promise that I will not disclose in any manner any information or item that is subject to this Protective Order to any person or entity except in strict compliance with the provisions of this Order.

I further agree to submit to the jurisdiction of the United States District Court for the Northern District of California for the purpose of enforcing the terms of this Protective Order, even if such enforcement proceedings occur after termination of this action.

I hereby appoint ___________________________ [print or type full name] of ____ [print or type full address and telephone number] as my California agent for service of process in connection with this action or any proceedings related to enforcement of this Protective Order.

Date: ___________________________________

City and State where sworn and signed: ___________________________________

Printed name: ________________________________
[printed name]

Signature: ___________________________________
[signature]

Appendix 2.4b
Northern District of California, Stipulated Protective Order for Litigation Involving Patents, Highly Sensitive Confidential Information, and/or Trade Secrets

UNITED STATES DISTRICT COURT
NORTHERN DISTRICT OF CALIFORNIA

Plaintiff, v. Defendant.	Case No. C STIPULATED PROTECTIVE ORDER FOR LITIGATION INVOLVING PATENTS, HIGHLY SENSITIVE CONFIDENTIAL INFORMATION AND/OR TRADE SECRETS

1. PURPOSES AND LIMITATIONS

Disclosure and discovery activity in this action are likely to involve production of confidential, proprietary, or private information for which special protection from public disclosure and from use for any purpose other than prosecuting this litigation may be warranted. Accordingly, the parties hereby stipulate to and petition the court to enter the following Stipulated Protective Order. The parties acknowledge that this Order does not confer blanket protections on all disclosures or responses to discovery and that the protection it affords from public disclosure and use extends only to the limited information or items that are entitled to confidential treatment under the applicable legal principles. The parties further acknowledge, as set forth in Section 14.4, below, that this Stipulated Protective Order does not entitle them to file confidential information under seal; Civil Local Rule 79-5 sets forth the procedures that must be followed and the standards that will be applied when a party seeks permission from the court to file material under seal.

2. DEFINITIONS

2.1 Challenging Party: a Party or Non-Party that challenges the designation of information or items under this Order.

2.2 "CONFIDENTIAL" Information or Items: information (regardless of how it is generated, stored or maintained) or tangible things that qualify for protection under Federal Rule of Civil Procedure 26(c).

2.3 Counsel (without qualifier): Outside Counsel of Record and House Counsel (as well as their support staff).

[2.4 *Optional*: Designated House Counsel: House Counsel who seek access to "HIGHLY CONFIDENTIAL – ATTORNEYS' EYES ONLY" information in this matter.]

2.5 Designating Party: a Party or Non-Party that designates information or items that it produces in disclosures or in responses to discovery as "CONFIDENTIAL" or "HIGHLY CONFIDENTIAL – ATTORNEYS' EYES ONLY" [*Optional*: or "HIGHLY CONFIDENTIAL – SOURCE CODE"].

2.6 Disclosure or Discovery Material: all items or information, regardless of the medium or manner in which it is generated, stored, or maintained (including, among other things, testimony, transcripts, and tangible things), that are produced or generated in disclosures or responses to discovery in this matter.

2.7 Expert: a person with specialized knowledge or experience in a matter pertinent to the litigation who (1) has been retained by a Party or its counsel to serve as an expert witness or as a consultant in this action, (2) is not a past or current employee of a Party or of a Party's competitor, and (3) at the time of retention, is not anticipated to become an employee of a Party or of a Party's competitor.

2.8 "HIGHLY CONFIDENTIAL – ATTORNEYS' EYES ONLY" Information or Items: extremely sensitive "Confidential Information or Items," disclosure of which to another Party or Non-Party would create a substantial risk of serious harm that could not be avoided by less restrictive means.

[2.9 *Optional*: "HIGHLY CONFIDENTIAL – SOURCE CODE" Information or Items: extremely sensitive "Confidential Information or Items" representing computer code and associated comments and revision histories, formulas, engineering specifications, or schematics that define or otherwise describe in detail the algorithms or structure of software or hardware designs, disclosure of which to another Party or Non-Party would create a substantial risk of serious harm that could not be avoided by less restrictive means.]

2.10 House Counsel: attorneys who are employees of a party to this action. House Counsel does not include Outside Counsel of Record or any other outside counsel.

2.11 Non-Party: any natural person, partnership, corporation, association, or other legal entity not named as a Party to this action.

2.12 Outside Counsel of Record: attorneys who are not employees of a party to this action but are retained to represent or advise a party to this action and have appeared in this action on behalf of that party or are affiliated with a law firm which has appeared on behalf of that party.

2.13 Party: any party to this action, including all of its officers, directors, employees, consultants, retained experts, and Outside Counsel of Record (and their support staffs).

2.14 Producing Party: a Party or Non-Party that produces Disclosure or Discovery Material in this action.

2.15 Professional Vendors: persons or entities that provide litigation support services (e.g., photocopying, videotaping, translating, preparing exhibits or demonstrations, and organizing, storing, or retrieving data in any form or medium) and their employees and subcontractors.

2.16 Protected Material: any Disclosure or Discovery Material that is designated as "CONFIDENTIAL," or as "HIGHLY CONFIDENTIAL – ATTORNEYS' EYES ONLY." [*Optional*: or as "HIGHLY CONFIDENTIAL – SOURCE CODE."]

2.17 Receiving Party: a Party that receives Disclosure or Discovery Material from a Producing Party.

3. SCOPE

The protections conferred by this Stipulation and Order cover not only Protected Material (as defined above), but also (1) any information copied or extracted from Protected Material; (2) all copies, excerpts, summaries, or compilations of Protected Material; and (3) any testimony, conversations, or presentations by Parties or their Counsel that might reveal Protected Material. However, the protections conferred by this Stipulation and Order do not cover the following information: (a) any information that is in the public domain at the time of disclosure to a Receiving Party or becomes part of the public domain after its disclosure to a Receiving Party as a result of publication not involving a violation of this Order, including becoming part of the public record through trial or otherwise; and (b) any information known to the Receiving Party prior to the disclosure or obtained by the Receiving Party after the disclosure from a source who obtained the information lawfully and under no obligation of confidentiality to the Designating Party. Any use of Protected Material at trial shall be governed by a separate agreement or order.

4. DURATION

Even after final disposition of this litigation, the confidentiality obligations imposed by this Order shall remain in effect until a Designating Party agrees otherwise in writing or a court order otherwise directs. Final disposition shall be deemed to be the later of (1) dismissal of all claims and defenses in this action, with or without prejudice; and (2) final judgment herein after the completion and exhaustion of all appeals, rehearings, remands, trials, or reviews of this action, including the time limits for filing any motions or applications for extension of time pursuant to applicable law.

5. DESIGNATING PROTECTED MATERIAL

5.1 Exercise of Restraint and Care in Designating Material for Protection. Each Party or Non-Party that designates information or items for protection under this Order must take care to limit any such designation to specific material that qualifies under the appropriate standards. To the extent it is practical to do so, the Designating Party must designate for protection only those parts of material, documents, items, or oral or written communications that qualify – so that other portions of the material, documents, items, or communications for which protection is not warranted are not swept unjustifiably within the ambit of this Order.

Mass, indiscriminate, or routinized designations are prohibited. Designations that are shown to be clearly unjustified or that have been made for an improper purpose (e.g., to unnecessarily encumber or retard the case development process or to impose unnecessary expenses and burdens on other parties) expose the Designating Party to sanctions.

If it comes to a Designating Party's attention that information or items that it designated for protection do not qualify for protection at all or do not qualify for the level of protection initially asserted, that Designating Party must promptly notify all other parties that it is withdrawing the mistaken designation.

5.2 Manner and Timing of Designations. Except as otherwise provided in this Order (see, e.g., second paragraph of section 5.2(a) below), or as otherwise stipulated or ordered, Disclosure or Discovery

Material that qualifies for protection under this Order must be clearly so designated before the material is disclosed or produced.

Designation in conformity with this Order requires:

(a) for information in documentary form (e.g., paper or electronic documents, but excluding transcripts of depositions or other pretrial or trial proceedings), that the Producing Party affix the legend "CONFIDENTIAL" or "HIGHLY CONFIDENTIAL – ATTORNEYS' EYES ONLY" [*Optional*: or "HIGHLY CONFIDENTIAL – SOURCE CODE"] to each page that contains protected material. If only a portion or portions of the material on a page qualifies for protection, the Producing Party also must clearly identify the protected portion(s) (e.g., by making appropriate markings in the margins) and must specify, for each portion, the level of protection being asserted.

A Party or Non-Party that makes original documents or materials available for inspection need not designate them for protection until after the inspecting Party has indicated which material it would like copied and produced. During the inspection and before the designation, all of the material made available for inspection shall be deemed "HIGHLY CONFIDENTIAL – ATTORNEYS' EYES ONLY." After the inspecting Party has identified the documents it wants copied and produced, the

Producing Party must determine which documents, or portions thereof, qualify for protection under this Order. Then, before producing the specified documents, the Producing Party must affix the appropriate legend ("CONFIDENTIAL" or "HIGHLY CONFIDENTIAL – ATTORNEYS' EYES ONLY" [*Optional:* or "HIGHLY CONFIDENTIAL – SOURCE CODE]) to each page that contains Protected Material. If only a portion or portions of the material on a page qualifies for protection, the Producing Party also must clearly identify the protected portion(s) (e.g., by making appropriate markings in the margins) and must specify, for each portion, the level of protection being asserted.

(b) for testimony given in deposition or in other pretrial or trial proceedings, that the Designating Party identify on the record, before the close of the deposition, hearing, or other proceeding, all protected testimony and specify the level of protection being asserted. When it is impractical to identify separately each portion of testimony that is entitled to protection and it appears that substantial portions of the testimony may qualify for protection, the Designating Party may invoke on the record (before the deposition, hearing, or other proceeding is concluded) a right to have up to 21 days to identify the specific portions of the testimony as to which protection is sought and to specify the level of protection being asserted. Only those portions of the testimony that are appropriately designated for protection within the 21 days shall be covered by the provisions of this Stipulated Protective Order. Alternatively, a Designating Party may specify, at the deposition or up to 21 days afterwards if that period is properly invoked, that the entire transcript shall be treated as "CONFIDENTIAL" or "HIGHLY CONFIDENTIAL – ATTORNEYS' EYES ONLY."

Parties shall give the other parties notice if they reasonably expect a deposition, hearing or other proceeding to include Protected Material so that the other parties can ensure that only authorized individuals who have signed the "Acknowledgment and Agreement to Be Bound" (Exhibit A) are present at those proceedings. The use of a document as an exhibit at a deposition shall not in any way affect its designation as "CONFIDENTIAL" or "HIGHLY CONFIDENTIAL – ATTORNEYS' EYES ONLY."

Transcripts containing Protected Material shall have an obvious legend on the title page that the transcript contains Protected Material, and the title page shall be followed by a list of all pages (including line numbers as appropriate) that have been designated as Protected Material and the level of protection being asserted by the Designating Party. The Designating Party shall inform the court reporter of these requirements. Any transcript that is prepared before the expiration of a 21-day period for designation shall be treated during that period as if it had been designated "HIGHLY CONFIDENTIAL – ATTORNEYS' EYES ONLY" in its entirety unless otherwise agreed. After the expiration of that period, the transcript shall be treated only as actually designated.

(c) for information produced in some form other than documentary and for any other tangible items, that the Producing Party affix in a prominent place on the exterior of the container or containers in which the information or item is stored the legend "CONFIDENTIAL" or "HIGHLY CONFIDENTIAL – ATTORNEYS' EYES ONLY" [*Optional*: or "HIGHLY CONFIDENTIAL – SOURCE CODE"]. If only a portion or portions of the information or item warrant protection, the Producing Party, to the extent practicable, shall identify the protected portion(s) and specify the level of protection being asserted.

5.3 Inadvertent Failures to Designate. If timely corrected, an inadvertent failure to designate qualified information or items does not, standing alone, waive the Designating Party's right to secure protection under this Order for such material. Upon timely correction of a designation, the Receiving Party must make reasonable efforts to assure that the material is treated in accordance with the provisions of this Order.

6. CHALLENGING CONFIDENTIALITY DESIGNATIONS

6.1 Timing of Challenges. Any Party or Non-Party may challenge a designation of confidentiality at any time. Unless a prompt challenge to a Designating Party's confidentiality designation is necessary to avoid foreseeable, substantial unfairness, unnecessary economic burdens, or a significant disruption or delay of the litigation, a Party does not waive its right to challenge a confidentiality designation by electing not to mount a challenge promptly after the original designation is disclosed.

6.2 Meet and Confer. The Challenging Party shall initiate the dispute resolution process by providing written notice of each designation it is challenging and describing the basis for each challenge. To avoid ambiguity as to whether a challenge has been made, the written notice must recite that the challenge to confidentiality is being made in accordance with this specific paragraph of the Protective Order. The parties shall attempt to resolve each challenge in good faith and must begin the process by conferring directly (in voice to voice dialogue; other forms of communication are not sufficient) within 14 days of the date of service of notice. In conferring, the Challenging Party must explain the basis for its belief that the confidentiality designation was not proper and must give the Designating Party an opportunity to review the designated material, to reconsider the circumstances, and, if no change in designation is offered, to explain the basis for the chosen designation. A Challenging Party may proceed to the next stage of the challenge process only if it has engaged in this meet and confer process first or establishes that the Designating Party is unwilling to participate in the meet and confer process in a timely manner.

6.3 Judicial Intervention. If the Parties cannot resolve a challenge without court intervention, the Designating Party shall file and serve a motion to retain confidentiality under Civil Local Rule 7 (and in compliance with Civil Local Rule 79-5, if applicable) within 21 days of the initial notice of challenge or within 14 days of the parties agreeing that the meet and confer process will not resolve their dispute, whichever is earlier.[18] Each such motion must be accompanied by a competent declaration affirming that the movant has complied with the meet and confer requirements imposed in the preceding paragraph. Failure by the Designating Party to make such a motion including the required declaration within 21 days (or 14 days, if applicable) shall automatically waive the confidentiality designation for each challenged designation. In addition, the Challenging Party may file a motion challenging a confidentiality designation at any time if there is good cause for doing so, including a challenge to the designation of a deposition transcript or any portions thereof. Any motion brought pursuant to this provision must be accompanied by a competent declaration affirming that the movant has complied with the meet and confer requirements imposed by the preceding paragraph.

The burden of persuasion in any such challenge proceeding shall be on the Designating Party. Frivolous challenges and those made for an improper purpose (e.g., to harass or impose unnecessary expenses and burdens on other parties) may expose the Challenging Party to sanctions. Unless the Designating Party has waived the confidentiality designation by failing to file a motion to retain confidentiality as described above, all parties shall continue to afford the material in question the level of protection to which it is entitled under the Producing Party's designation until the court rules on the challenge.

7. <u>ACCESS TO AND USE OF PROTECTED MATERIAL</u>

7.1 <u>Basic Principles</u>. A Receiving Party may use Protected Material that is disclosed or produced by another Party or by a Non-Party in connection with this case only for prosecuting, defending, or attempting to settle this litigation. Such Protected Material may be disclosed only to the categories of persons and under the conditions described in this Order. When the litigation has been terminated, a Receiving Party must comply with the provisions of section 15 below (FINAL DISPOSITION).

Protected Material must be stored and maintained by a Receiving Party at a location and in a secure manner[19] that ensures that access is limited to the persons authorized under this Order.

7.2 <u>Disclosure of "CONFIDENTIAL" Information or Items</u>. Unless otherwise ordered by the court or permitted in writing by the Designating Party, a Receiving Party may disclose any information or item designated "CONFIDENTIAL" only to:

---

18. Alternative: It may be appropriate in certain circumstances for the parties to agree to shift the burden to move on the Challenging Party after a certain number of challenges are made to avoid an abuse of the process. The burden of persuasion would remain on the Designating Party.

19. It may be appropriate under certain circumstances to require the Receiving Party to store any electronic Protected Material in password-protected form.

(a) the Receiving Party's Outside Counsel of Record in this action, as well as employees of said Outside Counsel of Record to whom it is reasonably necessary to disclose the information for this litigation and who have signed the "Acknowledgment and Agreement to Be Bound" that is attached hereto as Exhibit A;

(b) the officers, directors, and employees (including House Counsel) of the Receiving Party to whom disclosure is reasonably necessary for this litigation and who have signed the "Acknowledgment and Agreement to Be Bound" (Exhibit A);

(c) Experts (as defined in this Order) of the Receiving Party to whom disclosure is reasonably necessary for this litigation and who have signed the "Acknowledgment and Agreement to Be Bound" (Exhibit A);

(d) the court and its personnel;

(e) court reporters and their staff, professional jury or trial consultants, and Professional Vendors to whom disclosure is reasonably necessary for this litigation and who have signed the "Acknowledgment and Agreement to Be Bound" (Exhibit A);

(f) during their depositions, witnesses in the action to whom disclosure is reasonably necessary and who have signed the "Acknowledgment and Agreement to Be Bound" (Exhibit A), <u>unless otherwise agreed by the Designating Party or ordered by the court</u>. Pages of transcribed deposition testimony or exhibits to depositions that reveal Protected Material must be separately bound by the court reporter and may not be disclosed to anyone except as permitted under this Stipulated Protective Order.

(g) the author or recipient of a document containing the information or a custodian or other person who otherwise possessed or knew the information.

7.3 <u>Disclosure of "HIGHLY CONFIDENTIAL – ATTORNEYS' EYES ONLY"</u> [*Optional*: and "HIGHLY CONFIDENTIAL – SOURCE CODE"] <u>Information or Items</u>. Unless otherwise ordered by the court or permitted in writing by the Designating Party, a Receiving Party may disclose any information or item designated "HIGHLY CONFIDENTIAL – ATTORNEYS' EYES ONLY" [*Optional*: or "HIGHLY CONFIDENTIAL – SOURCE CODE"] only to:

(a) the Receiving Party's Outside Counsel of Record in this action, as well as employees of said Outside Counsel of Record to whom it is reasonably necessary to disclose the information for this litigation and who have signed the "Acknowledgment and Agreement to Be Bound" that is attached hereto as Exhibit A;

[(b) *Optional as deemed appropriate in case-specific circumstances:* Designated House Counsel of the Receiving Party[20] (1) who has no involvement in competitive decision-making, (2) to whom disclosure is reasonably necessary for this litigation, (3) who has signed the "Acknowledgment and Agreement to Be Bound" (Exhibit A), and (4) as to whom the procedures set forth in paragraph 7.4(a)(1), below, have been followed];[21]

(c) Experts of the Receiving Party (1) to whom disclosure is reasonably necessary for this litigation, (2) who have signed the "Acknowledgment and Agreement to Be Bound" (Exhibit A), and (3) as to whom the procedures set forth in paragraph 7.4(a)(2), below, have been followed];

(d) the court and its personnel;

(e) court reporters and their staff, professional jury or trial consultants,[22] and Professional Vendors to whom disclosure is reasonably necessary for this litigation and who have signed the "Acknowledgment and Agreement to Be Bound" (Exhibit A); and

(f) the author or recipient of a document containing the information or a custodian or other person who otherwise possessed or knew the information.

7.4 Procedures for Approving or Objecting to Disclosure of "HIGHLY CONFIDENTIAL – ATTORNEYS' EYES ONLY" [*Optional*: or "HIGHLY CONFIDENTIAL – SOURCE CODE"] Information or Items to Designated House Counsel[23] or Experts.[24]

---

20. It may be appropriate under certain circumstances to limit the number of Designated House Counsel who may access "HIGHLY CONFIDENTIAL – ATTORNEYS' EYES ONLY" information under this provision.

21. This Order contemplates that Designated House Counsel shall not have access to any information or items designated "HIGHLY CONFIDENTIAL – SOURCE CODE." It may also be appropriate under certain circumstances to limit how Designated House Counsel may access "HIGHLY CONFIDENTIAL – ATTORNEYS' EYES ONLY" information. For example, Designated House Counsel may be limited to viewing "HIGHLY CONFIDENTIAL – ATTORNEYS' EYES ONLY" information only if it is filed with the court under seal, or in the presence of Outside Counsel of Record at their offices.

22. *Alternative:* The parties may wish to allow disclosure of information not only to professional jury or trial consultants, but also to mock jurors, to further trial preparation. In that situation, the parties may wish to draft a simplified, precisely tailored Undertaking for mock jurors to sign.

23. *Alternative*: The parties may exchange names of a certain number of Designated House Counsel instead of following this procedure.

24. *Alternative:* "CONFIDENTIAL" or "HIGHLY CONFIDENTIAL – ATTORNEYS' EYES ONLY" information or items may be disclosed to an Expert without disclosure of the

(a)(1) Unless otherwise ordered by the court or agreed to in writing by the Designating Party, a Party that seeks to disclose to Designated House Counsel any information or item that has been designated "HIGHLY CONFIDENTIAL - ATTORNEYS' EYES ONLY" pursuant to paragraph 7.3(b) first must make a written request to the Designating Party that (1) sets forth the full name of the Designated House Counsel and the city and state of his or her residence, and (2) describes the Designated House Counsel's current and reasonably foreseeable future primary job duties and responsibilities in sufficient detail to determine if House Counsel is involved, or may become involved, in any competitive decision-making.[25]

(a)(2) Unless otherwise ordered by the court or agreed to in writing by the Designating Party, a Party that seeks to disclose to an Expert (as defined in this Order) any information or item that has been designated "HIGHLY CONFIDENTIAL - ATTORNEYS' EYES ONLY" [*Optional*: or "HIGHLY CONFIDENTIAL - SOURCE CODE"] pursuant to paragraph 7.3(c) first must make a written request to the Designating Party that (1) identifies the general categories of "HIGHLY CONFIDENTIAL - ATTORNEYS' EYES ONLY" [*Optional*: or "HIGHLY CONFIDENTIAL - SOURCE CODE"] information that the Receiving Party seeks permission to disclose to the Expert, (2) sets forth the full name of the Expert and the city and state of his or her primary residence, (3) attaches a copy of the Expert's current resume, (4) identifies the Expert's current employer(s), (5) identifies each person or entity from whom the Expert has received compensation or funding for work in his or her areas of expertise or to whom the expert has provided professional services, including in connection with a litigation, at any time during the preceding five years,[26] and (6) identifies (by name and number of the case, filing date, and location of court) any litigation in connection with which the Expert has offered expert testimony, including through a declaration, report, or testimony at a deposition or trial, during the preceding five years.[27]

---

identity of the Expert as long as the Expert is not a current officer, director, or employee of a competitor of a Party or anticipated to become one.

25. It may be appropriate in certain circumstances to require any Designated House Counsel who receives "HIGHLY CONFIDENTIAL - ATTORNEYS' EYES ONLY" information pursuant to this Order to disclose any relevant changes in job duties or responsibilities prior to final disposition of the litigation to allow the Designating Party to evaluate any later-arising competitive decision-making responsibilities.

26. If the Expert believes any of this information is subject to a confidentiality obligation to a third-party, then the Expert should provide whatever information the Expert believes can be disclosed without violating any confidentiality agreements, and the Party seeking to disclose to the Expert shall be available to meet and confer with the Designating Party regarding any such engagement.

27. It may be appropriate in certain circumstances to restrict the Expert from undertaking certain limited work prior to the termination of the litigation that could

(b) A Party that makes a request and provides the information specified in the preceding respective paragraphs may disclose the subject Protected Material to the identified Designated House Counsel or Expert unless, within 14 days of delivering the request, the Party receives a written objection from the Designating Party. Any such objection must set forth in detail the grounds on which it is based.

(c) A Party that receives a timely written objection must meet and confer with the Designating Party (through direct voice to voice dialogue) to try to resolve the matter by agreement within seven days of the written objection. If no agreement is reached, the Party seeking to make the disclosure to Designated House Counsel or the Expert may file a motion as provided in Civil Local Rule 7 (and in compliance with Civil Local Rule 79-5, if applicable) seeking permission from the court to do so. Any such motion must describe the circumstances with specificity, set forth in detail the reasons why the disclosure to Designated House Counsel or the Expert is reasonably necessary, assess the risk of harm that the disclosure would entail, and suggest any additional means that could be used to reduce that risk. In addition, any such motion must be accompanied by a competent declaration describing the parties' efforts to resolve the matter by agreement (i.e., the extent and the content of the meet and confer discussions) and setting forth the reasons advanced by the Designating Party for its refusal to approve the disclosure.

In any such proceeding, the Party opposing disclosure to Designated House Counsel or the Expert shall bear the burden of proving that the risk of harm that the disclosure would entail (under the safeguards proposed) outweighs the Receiving Party's need to disclose the Protected Material to its Designated House Counsel or Expert.

8. PROSECUTION BAR [*Optional*]

Absent written consent from the Producing Party, any individual who receives access to "HIGHLY CONFIDENTIAL – ATTORNEYS' EYES ONLY" [*Optional*: or "HIGHLY CONFIDENTIAL – SOURCE CODE"] information shall not be involved in the prosecution of patents or patent applications relating to [insert subject matter of the invention and of highly confidential technical information to be produced], including without limitation the patents asserted in this action and any patent or application claiming priority to or otherwise related to the patents asserted in this action, before any foreign or domestic agency, including the United States Patent and Trademark Office ("the Patent Office").[28] For purposes of this paragraph, "pros-

---

foreseeably result in an improper use of the Designating Party's "HIGHLY CONFIDENTIAL – ATTORNEYS' EYES ONLY" information.

28. It may be appropriate under certain circumstances to require Outside and House Counsel who receive access to "HIGHLY CONFIDENTIAL – ATTORNEYS' EYES ONLY" information to implement an "Ethical Wall."

ecution" includes directly or indirectly drafting, amending, advising, or otherwise affecting the scope or maintenance of patent claims.[29] To avoid any doubt, "prosecution" as used in this paragraph does not include representing a party challenging a patent before a domestic or foreign agency (including, but not limited to, a reissue protest, *ex parte* reexamination or *inter partes* reexamination). This Prosecution Bar shall begin when access to "HIGHLY CONFIDENTIAL – ATTORNEYS' EYES ONLY" [*Optional*: or "HIGHLY CONFIDENTIAL – SOURCE CODE"] information is first received by the affected individual and shall end two (2) years after final termination of this action.[30]

9. SOURCE CODE [*Optional*]

(a) To the extent production of source code becomes necessary in this case, a Producing Party may designate source code as "HIGHLY CONFIDENTIAL - SOURCE CODE" if it comprises or includes confidential, proprietary or trade secret source code.

(b) Protected Material designated as "HIGHLY CONFIDENTIAL – SOURCE CODE" shall be subject to all of the protections afforded to "HIGHLY CONFIDENTIAL – ATTORNEYS' EYES ONLY" information [*Optional*: including the Prosecution Bar set forth in Paragraph 8], and may be disclosed only to the individuals to whom "HIGHLY CONFIDENTIAL – ATTORNEYS' EYES ONLY" information may be disclosed, as set forth in Paragraphs 7.3 and 7.4, with the exception of Designated House Counsel.[31]

(c) Any source code produced in discovery shall be made available for inspection, in a format allowing it to be reasonably reviewed and searched, during normal business hours or at other mutually agreeable times, at an office of the Producing Party's counsel or another mutually agreed upon location.[32] The source code shall be made

29. Prosecution includes, for example, original prosecution, reissue and reexamination proceedings.

30. *Alternative:* It may be appropriate for the Prosecution Bar to apply only to individuals who receive access to another party's "HIGHLY CONFIDENTIAL – ATTORNEYS' EYES ONLY" technical or source code information pursuant to this Order, such as under circumstances where one or more parties is not expected to produce "HIGHLY CONFIDENTIAL – ATTORNEYS' EYES ONLY" information that is technical in nature or "HIGHLY CONFIDENTIAL – SOURCE CODE" information,

31. It may be appropriate under certain circumstances to allow House Counsel access to derivative materials including "HIGHLY CONFIDENTIAL - SOURCE CODE" information, such as exhibits to motions or expert reports,

32. *Alternative*: Any source code produced in discovery shall be made available for inspection in a format through which it could be reasonably reviewed and searched during normal business hours or other mutually agreeable times at a location that is reasonably convenient for the Receiving Party and any experts to whom the source code may be

available for inspection on a secured computer in a secured room without Internet access or network access to other computers, and the Receiving Party shall not copy, remove, or otherwise transfer any portion of the source code onto any recordable media or recordable device. The Producing Party may visually monitor the activities of the Receiving Party's representatives during any source code review, but only to ensure that there is no unauthorized recording, copying, or transmission of the source code.[33]

(d) The Receiving Party may request paper copies of limited portions of source code that are reasonably necessary for the preparation of court filings, pleadings, expert reports, or other papers, or for deposition or trial, but shall not request paper copies for the purposes of reviewing the source code other than electronically as set forth in paragraph (c) in the first instance. The Producing Party shall provide all such source code in paper form including bates numbers and the label "HIGHLY CONFIDENTIAL - SOURCE CODE." The Producing Party may challenge the amount of source code requested in hard copy form pursuant to the dispute resolution procedure and timeframes set forth in Paragraph 6 whereby the Producing Party is the "Challenging Party" and the Receiving Party is the "Designating Party" for purposes of dispute resolution.

(e) The Receiving Party shall maintain a record of any individual who has inspected any portion of the source code in electronic or paper form. The Receiving Party shall maintain all paper copies of any printed portions of the source code in a secured, locked area. The Receiving Party shall not create any electronic or other images of the paper copies and shall not convert any of the information contained in the paper copies into any electronic format. The Receiving Party shall only make additional paper copies if such additional copies are (1) necessary to prepare court filings, pleadings, or other papers (including a testifying expert's expert report), (2) necessary for deposition, or (3) otherwise necessary for the preparation of its case. Any paper copies used during a deposition shall be retrieved by the Producing Party at the end of each day and must not be given to or left with a court reporter or any other unauthorized individual.[34]

---

disclosed. This alternative may be appropriate if the Producing Party and/or its counsel are located in a different jurisdiction than counsel and/or experts for the Receiving Party.

33. It may be appropriate under certain circumstances to require the Receiving Party to keep a paper log indicating the names of any individuals inspecting the source code and dates and times of inspection, and the names of any individuals to whom paper copies of portions of source code are provided.

34. The nature of the source code at issue in a particular case may warrant additional protections or restrictions, For example, it may be appropriate under certain circumstances to require the Receiving Party to provide notice to the Producing Party before including "HIGHLY CONFIDENTIAL - SOURCE CODE" information in a court filing, pleading, or expert report.

10. PROTECTED MATERIAL SUBPOENAED OR ORDERED PRODUCED IN OTHER LITIGATION

If a Party is served with a subpoena or a court order issued in other litigation that compels disclosure of any information or items designated in this action as "CONFIDENTIAL" or "HIGHLY CONFIDENTIAL – ATTORNEYS' EYES ONLY" [*Optional*: or "HIGHLY CONFIDENTIAL – SOURCE CODE"] that Party must:

(a) promptly notify in writing the Designating Party. Such notification shall include a copy of the subpoena or court order;

(b) promptly notify in writing the party who caused the subpoena or order to issue in the other litigation that some or all of the material covered by the subpoena or order is subject to this Protective Order. Such notification shall include a copy of this Stipulated Protective Order; and

(c) cooperate with respect to all reasonable procedures sought to be pursued by the Designating Party whose Protected Material may be affected.[35]

If the Designating Party timely seeks a protective order, the Party served with the subpoena or court order shall not produce any information designated in this action as "CONFIDENTIAL" or "HIGHLY CONFIDENTIAL – ATTORNEYS' EYES ONLY" [*Optional*: or "HIGHLY CONFIDENTIAL – SOURCE CODE"] before a determination by the court from which the subpoena or order issued, unless the Party has obtained the Designating Party's permission. The Designating Party shall bear the burden and expense of seeking protection in that court of its confidential material – and nothing in these provisions should be construed as authorizing or encouraging a Receiving Party in this action to disobey a lawful directive from another court.

11. A NON-PARTY'S PROTECTED MATERIAL SOUGHT TO BE PRODUCED IN THIS LITIGATION

(a) The terms of this Order are applicable to information produced by a Non-Party in this action and designated as "CONFIDENTIAL" or "HIGHLY CONFIDENTIAL – ATTORNEYS' EYES ONLY" [*Optional:* or "HIGHLY CONFIDENTIAL – SOURCE CODE"]. Such information produced by Non-Parties in connection with this litigation is protected by the remedies and relief provided by this Order. Nothing in these provisions should be construed as prohibiting a Non-Party from seeking additional protections.

(b) In the event that a Party is required, by a valid discovery request, to produce a Non-Party's confidential information in its possession, and the Party is subject to

35. The purpose of imposing these duties is to alert the interested parties to the existence of this Protective Order and to afford the Designating Party in this case an opportunity to try to protect its confidentiality interests in the court from which the subpoena or order issued.

an agreement with the Non-Party not to produce the Non-Party's confidential information, then the Party shall:

1. promptly notify in writing the Requesting Party and the Non-Party that some or all of the information requested is subject to a confidentiality agreement with a Non-Party;

2. promptly provide the Non-Party with a copy of the Stipulated Protective Order in this litigation, the relevant discovery request(s), and a reasonably specific description of the information requested; and

3. make the information requested available for inspection by the Non-Party.

(c) If the Non-Party fails to object or seek a protective order from this court within 14 days of receiving the notice and accompanying information, the Receiving Party may produce the Non-Party's confidential information responsive to the discovery request. If the Non-Party timely seeks a protective order, the Receiving Party shall not produce any information in its possession or control that is subject to the confidentiality agreement with the Non-Party before a determination by the court.[36] Absent a court order to the contrary, the Non-Party shall bear the burden and expense of seeking protection in this court of its Protected Material.

12. UNAUTHORIZED DISCLOSURE OF PROTECTED MATERIAL

If a Receiving Party learns that, by inadvertence or otherwise, it has disclosed Protected Material to any person or in any circumstance not authorized under this Stipulated Protective Order, the Receiving Party must immediately (a) notify in writing the Designating Party of the unauthorized disclosures, (b) use its best efforts to retrieve all unauthorized copies of the Protected Material, (c) inform the person or persons to whom unauthorized disclosures were made of all the terms of this Order, and (d) request such person or persons to execute the "Acknowledgment and Agreement to Be Bound" that is attached hereto as Exhibit A.

13. INADVERTENT PRODUCTION OF PRIVILEGED OR OTHERWISE PROTECTED MATERIAL

When a Producing Party gives notice to Receiving Parties that certain inadvertently produced material is subject to a claim of privilege or other protection, the obligations of the Receiving Parties are those set forth in Federal Rule of Civil Procedure 26(b)(5)(B).[37] This provision is not intended to modify whatever procedure

36. The purpose of this provision is to alert the interested parties to the existence of confidentiality rights of a Non-Party and to afford the Non-Party an opportunity to protect its confidentiality interests in this court.

37. *Alternative*: The parties may agree that the recipient of an inadvertent production may not "sequester" or in any way use the document(s) pending resolution of a challenge to

may be established in an e-discovery order that provides for production without prior privilege review. Pursuant to Federal Rule of Evidence 502(d) and (e), insofar as the parties reach an agreement on the effect of disclosure of a communication or information covered by the attorney-client privilege or work product protection, the parties may incorporate their agreement in the stipulated protective order submitted to the court.

14. MISCELLANEOUS

14.1 Right to Further Relief. Nothing in this Order abridges the right of any person to seek its modification by the court in the future.

14.2 Right to Assert Other Objections. By stipulating to the entry of this Protective Order no Party waives any right it otherwise would have to object to disclosing or producing any information or item on any ground not addressed in this Stipulated Protective Order. Similarly, no Party waives any right to object on any ground to use in evidence of any of the material covered by this Protective Order.

[14.3 *Optional:* Export Control. Disclosure of Protected Material shall be subject to all applicable laws and regulations relating to the export of technical data contained in such Protected Material, including the release of such technical data to foreign persons or nationals in the United States or elsewhere. The Producing Party shall be responsible for identifying any such controlled technical data, and the Receiving Party shall take measures necessary to ensure compliance.]

14.4 Filing Protected Material. Without written permission from the Designating Party or a court order secured after appropriate notice to all interested persons, a Party may not file in the public record in this action any Protected Material. A Party that seeks to file under seal any Protected Material must comply with Civil Local Rule 79-5. Protected Material may only be filed under seal pursuant to a court order authorizing the sealing of the specific Protected Material at issue. Pursuant to Civil Local Rule 79-5, a sealing order will issue only upon a request establishing that the Protected Material at issue is privileged, protectable as a trade secret, or otherwise

---

the claim of privilege or other protection to the extent it would be otherwise allowed by Federal Rule of Civil Procedure 26(b)(5)(B) as amended in 2006. This could include a restriction against "presenting" the document(s) to the court to challenge the privilege claim as may otherwise be allowed under Rule 26(b)(5)(B) subject to ethical obligations.

An alternate provision could state: "If information is produced in discovery that is subject to a claim of privilege or of protection as trial-preparation material, the party making the claim may notify any party that received the information of the claim and the basis for it. After being notified, a party must promptly return or destroy the specified information and any copies it has and may not sequester, use or disclose the information until the claim is resolved. This includes a restriction against presenting the information to the court for a determination of the claim."

entitled to protection under the law. If a Receiving Party's request to file Protected Material under seal pursuant to Civil Local Rule 79-5(e) is denied by the court, then the Receiving Party may file the Protected Material in the public record pursuant to Civil Local Rule 79-5(e)(2) unless otherwise instructed by the court.

15. <u>FINAL DISPOSITION</u>

Within 60 days after the final disposition of this action, as defined in paragraph 4, each Receiving Party must return all Protected Material to the Producing Party or destroy such material. As used in this subdivision, "all Protected Material" includes all copies, abstracts, compilations, summaries, and any other format reproducing or capturing any of the Protected Material. Whether the Protected Material is returned or destroyed, the Receiving Party must submit a written certification to the Producing Party (and, if not the same person or entity, to the Designating Party) by the 60-day deadline that (1) identifies (by category, where appropriate) all the Protected Material that was returned or destroyed and (2) affirms that the Receiving Party has not retained any copies, abstracts, compilations, summaries or any other format reproducing or capturing any of the Protected Material. Notwithstanding this provision, Counsel are entitled to retain an archival copy of all pleadings, motion papers, trial, deposition, and hearing transcripts, legal memoranda, correspondence, deposition and trial exhibits, expert reports, attorney work product, and consultant and expert work product, even if such materials contain Protected Material. Any such archival copies that contain or constitute Protected Material remain subject to this Protective Order as set forth in Section 4 (DURATION).

IT IS SO STIPULATED, THROUGH COUNSEL OF RECORD.

DATED: ____________________ ____________________________________

Attorneys for Plaintiff

DATED: ____________________ ____________________________________

Attorneys for Defendant

PURSUANT TO STIPULATION, IT IS SO ORDERED.

DATED: ____________________ ____________________________________

[Name of Judge]

United States District/Magistrate Judge

EXHIBIT A

ACKNOWLEDGMENT AND AGREEMENT TO BE BOUND

I, ______________________________ [print or type full name], of ________________ [print or type full address], declare under penalty of perjury that I have read in its entirety and understand the Stipulated Protective Order that was issued by the United States District Court for the Northern District of California on [date] in the case of ___________ **[insert formal name of the case and the number and initials assigned to it by the court]**. I agree to comply with and to be bound by all the terms of this Stipulated Protective Order and I understand and acknowledge that failure to so comply could expose me to sanctions and punishment in the nature of contempt. I solemnly promise that I will not disclose in any manner any information or item that is subject to this Stipulated Protective Order to any person or entity except in strict compliance with the provisions of this Order.

I further agree to submit to the jurisdiction of the United States District Court for the Northern District of California for the purpose of enforcing the terms of this Stipulated Protective Order, even if such enforcement proceedings occur after termination of this action.

I hereby appoint __________________________ [print or type full name] of ____________________________________ [print or type full address and telephone number] as my California agent for service of process in connection with this action or any proceedings related to enforcement of this Stipulated Protective Order.

Date: ________________________________

City and State where sworn and signed: ___________________________

Printed name: ______________________________

[printed name]

Signature: __________________________________

[signature]

Appendix 2.4c
Model Protective Order from the Northern District of Illinois

IN THE UNITED STATES DISTRICT COURT FOR THE NORTHERN DISTRICT OF ILLINOIS EASTERN DIVISION

______________________,	)	
Plaintiff[s],	)	
	)	
	)	
vs.	)	Case No. ______
	)	
______________________,	)	
Defendant[s].	)	

PROTECTIVE ORDER

The Court enters the following protective order pursuant to Federal Rule of Civil Procedure 26(c)(1).

1. Findings: The Court finds that the parties to this case may request or produce information involving trade secrets or confidential research and development or commercial information, the disclosure of which is likely to cause harm to the party producing such information.

2. Definitions:

a. "Party" means a named party in this case. "Person" means an individual or an entity. "Producer" means a person who produces information via the discovery process in this case. "Recipient" means a person who receives information via the discovery process in this case.

b. "Confidential" information is information concerning a person's business operations, processes, and technical and development information within the scope of Rule 26(c)(1)(G), the disclosure of which is likely to harm that person's competitive position, or the disclosure of which would contravene an obligation of confidentiality to a third person or to a Court.

c. "Highly Confidential" information is information within the scope of Rule 26(c)(1)(G) that is current or future business or technical trade secrets and plans more sensitive or strategic than Confidential information, the disclosure of which is likely to significantly harm that person's competitive position, or the disclosure of which would contravene an obligation of confidentiality to a third person or to a Court.

d. Information is not Confidential or Highly Confidential if it is disclosed in a printed publication, is known to the public, was known to the recipient without obligation of confidentiality before the producer disclosed it, or is or becomes known to the recipient by means not constituting a breach of this Order. Information is likewise not Confidential or Highly Confidential if a person lawfully obtained it independently of this litigation.

3. Designation of information as Confidential or Highly Confidential:

a. A person's designation of information as Confidential or Highly Confidential means that the person believes in good faith, upon reasonable inquiry, that the information qualifies as such.

b. A person designates information in a document or thing as Confidential or Highly Confidential by clearly and prominently marking it on its face as "CONFIDENTIAL" or "HIGHLY CONFIDENTIAL." A producer may make documents or things containing Confidential or Highly Confidential information available for inspection and copying without marking them as confidential without forfeiting a claim of confidentiality, so long as the producer causes copies of the documents or things to be marked as Confidential or Highly Confidential before providing them to the recipient.

c. A person designates information in deposition testimony as Confidential or Highly Confidential by stating on the record at the deposition that the information is Confidential or Highly Confidential or by advising the opposing party and the stenographer and videographer in writing, within fourteen days after receipt of the deposition transcript, that the information is Confidential or Highly Confidential.

d. A person's failure to designate a document, thing, or testimony as Confidential or Highly Confidential does not constitute forfeiture of a claim of confidentiality as to any other document, thing, or testimony.

e. A person who has designated information as Confidential or Highly Confidential may withdraw the designation by written notification to all parties in the case.

f. If a party disputes a producer's designation of information as Confidential or Highly Confidential, the party shall notify the producer in writing of the basis for the dispute, identifying the specific document[s] or thing[s] as to which the designation is disputed and proposing a new designation for such materials. The party and the producer shall then meet and confer to attempt to resolve the dispute without involvement of the Court. If they cannot resolve the dispute, the proposed new designation shall be applied fourteen (14) days after notice of the dispute unless within that fourteen day period the producer files a motion with the Court to maintain the producer's designation. The producer bears the burden of proving that the information is properly designated as Confidential or Highly Confidential. The information shall remain subject to the producer's Confidential or Highly Confidential designation until the Court rules on the dispute. A party's failure to contest a designation of information as Confidential or Highly Confidential is not an admission that the information was properly designated as such.

4. Use and disclosure of Confidential [or Highly Confidential] information:

a. Confidential and Highly Confidential information may be used exclusively for purposes of this litigation, subject to the restrictions of this order.

b. Absent written permission from the producer or further order by the Court, the recipient may not disclose Confidential information to any person other than the following: (i) a party's outside counsel of record, including necessary paralegal, secretarial and clerical personnel assisting such counsel; (ii) a party's in-house counsel; (iii) a party's officers and employees directly involved in this case whose access to the information is reasonably required to supervise, manage, or participate in this case; (iv) a stenographer and videographer recording testimony concerning the information; (v) subject to the provisions of paragraph 4(d) of this order, experts and consultants and their staff whom a party employs for purposes of this litigation only; and (vi) the Court and personnel assisting the Court.

c. Absent written permission from the producer or further order by the Court, the recipient may not disclose Highly Confidential information to any person other than those identified in paragraph 4(b)(i), (iv), (v), and (vi).

d. A party may not disclose Confidential or Highly Confidential information to an expert or consultant pursuant to paragraph 4(b) or 4(c) of this order until after the expert or consultant has signed an undertaking in the form of Appendix 1 to this Order. The party obtaining the undertaking must serve it on all other parties within ten days after its execution. At least ten days before the first disclosure of Confidential or Highly Confidential information to an expert or consultant (or member of their staff), the party proposing to make the disclosure must serve the producer with a written identification of the expert or consultant and a copy of his or her curriculum vitae. If the producer has good cause to object to the disclosure (which does not include challenging the qualifications of the expert or consultant), it must serve the party proposing to make the disclosure with a written objection within ten days after service of the identification. Unless the parties resolve the dispute within ten days after service of the objection, the producer must move the Court promptly for a ruling, and the Confidential or Highly Confidential information may not be disclosed to the expert or consultant without the Court's approval.

e. Notwithstanding paragraph 4(a) and (b), a party may disclose Confidential or Highly Confidential information to: (i) any employee or author of the producer; (ii) any person, no longer affiliated with the producer, who authored the information in whole or in part; and (iii) any person who received the information before this case was filed.

f. A party who wishes to disclose Confidential or Highly Confidential information to a person not authorized under paragraph 4(b) or 4(c) must first make a reasonable attempt to obtain the producer's permission. If the party is unable to obtain permission, it may move the Court to obtain permission.

5. <u>Copies</u>: A party producing documents as part of discovery must, upon request, furnish the requesting party with one copy of the documents it requests, at the requesting party's expense. Before copying, the parties must agree upon the rate at which the requesting party will be charged for copying.

6. <u>Inadvertent Disclosure</u>: Inadvertent disclosures of material protected by the attorney-client privilege or the work product doctrine shall be handled in accordance with Federal Rule of Evidence 502.

7. Filing with the Court:

a. This protective order does not, by itself, authorize the filing of any document under seal. No document may be filed under seal without prior leave of court. A party wishing to file under seal a document containing Confidential or Highly Confidential information must move the Court, consistent with Local Rule 26.2(b) and prior to the due date for the document, for permission to file the document under seal. If a party obtains permission to file a document under seal, it must also (unless excused by the Court) file a public-record version that excludes any Confidential or Highly Confidential information.

b. If a party wishes to file in the public record a document that another producer has designated as Confidential or Highly Confidential, the party must advise the producer of the document no later than five business days before the document is due to be filed, so that the producer may move the Court to require the document to be filed under seal.

c. Pursuant to Local Rule 5.8, any document filed under seal must be accompanied by a cover sheet disclosing (i) the caption of the case, including the case number; (ii) the title "Restricted Document Pursuant to Local Rule 26.2;" (iii) a statement that the document is filed as restricted in accordance with a court order and the date of the order; and (iv) the signature of the attorney of record filing the document.

8. Document Disposal: Upon the conclusion of this case, each party must return to the producer all documents and copies of documents containing the producer's Confidential [or Highly Confidential] information, and must destroy all notes, memoranda, or other materials derived from or in any way revealing confidential or highly confidential information. Alternatively, if the producer agrees, the party may destroy all documents and copies of documents containing the producer's Confidential or Highly Confidential information. The party returning and/or destroying the producer's Confidential and Highly Confidential information must promptly certify in writing its compliance with the requirements of this paragraph. Notwithstanding the requirements of this paragraph, a party and its counsel may retain one complete set of all documents filed with the Court, remaining subject to all requirements of this order.

9. Originals: A legible photocopy of a document may be used as the "original" for all purposes in this action. The actual "original," in whatever form the producing party has it, must be made available to any other party within ten days after a written request.

10. Survival of obligations: This order's obligations regarding Confidential and Highly Confidential information survive the conclusion of this case.

Appendix 1

IN THE UNITED STATES DISTRICT COURT FOR THE NORTHERN DISTRICT OF ILLINOIS EASTERN DIVISION

______________________,	)	
Plaintiff[s],	)	
	)	
vs.	)	Case No. _____
	)	
______________________,	)	
Defendant[s].	)	

UNDERTAKING OF *[insert name]*

I, [insert person's name], state the following under penalties of perjury as provided by law:

I have been retained by [insert party's name] as an expert or consultant in connection with this case. I will be receiving Confidential [and Highly Confidential] information that is covered by the Court's protective order dated [fill in date]. I have read the Court's protective order and understand that the Confidential [and Highly Confidential] information is provided pursuant to the terms and conditions in that order.

I agree to be bound by the Court's protective order. I agree to use the Confidential [and Highly Confidential] information solely for purposes of this case. I understand that neither the Confidential [and Highly Confidential] information nor any notes concerning that information may be disclosed to anyone that is not bound by the Court's protective order. I agree to return the Confidential [and Highly Confidential] information and any notes concerning that information to the attorney for [insert name of retaining party] or to destroy the information and any notes at that attorney's request.

I submit to the jurisdiction of the Court that issued the protective order for purposes of enforcing that order. I give up any objections I might have to that Court's jurisdiction over me or to the propriety of venue in that Court.

[signature] Subscribed and sworn to ______________________________

before me this _____ day of __________ 20___.

____

Notary Public

Appendix 2.4d
Stipulation for Protective Order from the District of Minnesota

FORM 5 STIPULATION FOR PROTECTIVE ORDER

IN THE UNITED STATES DISTRICT COURT
FOR THE DISTRICT OF MINNESOTA

	)	
[NAME OF PARTY],	)	
Plaintiff,	)	Case No. ________
	)	
v.	)	
	)	STIPULATION FOR
[NAME OF PARTY],	)	PROTECTIVE ORDER
Defendant.	)	

Upon stipulation of the parties for an order pursuant to Fed. R. Civ. P. 26(c) that trade secret or other confidential information be disclosed only in designated ways:

1. As used in the Protective Order, these terms have the following meanings:

"Attorneys" means counsel of record;

"Confidential" documents are documents designated pursuant to paragraph 2;

"Confidential - Attorneys' Eyes Only" documents are the subset of Confidential documents designated pursuant to paragraph 5;

"Documents" are all materials within the scope of Fed. R. Civ. P. 34;

"Written Assurance" means an executed document in the form attached as Exhibit A.

2. By identifying a document "Confidential", a party may designate any document, including interrogatory responses, other discovery responses, or transcripts, that it in good faith contends to constitute or contain trade secret or other confidential information.

3. All Confidential documents, along with the information contained in the documents, shall be used solely for the purpose of this action, and no person receiving such documents shall, directly or indirectly, transfer, disclose, or communicate in any way the contents of the documents to any person other than those specified in paragraph 4. Prohibited purposes include, but are not limited to, use for competitive purposes or the prosecution of additional intellectual property rights.

4. Access to any Confidential document shall be limited to:

(a) the Court and its officers;

(b) Attorneys and their office associates, legal assistants, and stenographic and clerical employees;

(c) persons shown on the face of the document to have authored or received it;

(d) court reporters retained to transcribe testimony;

[Optional: (e) these inside counsel: [names];]

[Optional: (f) these employees of the parties: [names];]

(g) outside independent persons (i.e., persons not currently or formerly employed by, consulting with, or otherwise associated with any party) who are retained by a party or its attorneys to furnish technical or expert services, or to provide assistance as mock jurors or focus group members or the like, and/or to give testimony in this action.

5. The parties shall have the right to further designate Confidential documents or portions of documents [optional: in the areas of [identify]] as "Confidential - Attorneys' Eyes Only". Disclosure of such information shall be limited to the persons designated in paragraphs 4(a), (b), (c), (d), (e), and (g).

6. Third parties producing documents in the course of this action may also designate documents as "Confidential" or "Confidential - Attorneys' Eyes Only", subject to the same protections and constraints as the parties to the action. A copy of the Protective Order shall be served along with any subpoena served in connection with this action. All documents produced by such third parties shall be treated as "Confidential - Attorneys' Eyes Only" for a period of 14 days from the date of their production, and during that period any party may designate such documents as "Confidential" or "Confidential - Attorneys' Eyes Only" pursuant to the terms of the Protective Order.

7. Each person appropriately designated pursuant to paragraph 4(g) to receive Confidential information shall execute a "Written Assurance" in the form attached as Exhibit A. Opposing counsel shall be notified at least 14 days prior to disclosure to any such person who is known to be an employee or agent of, or consultant to, any competitor of the party whose designated documents are sought to be disclosed. Such notice shall provide a reasonable description of the outside independent person to whom disclosure is sought sufficient to permit objection to be made. If a party objects in writing to such disclosure within 14 days after receipt of notice, no disclosure shall be made until the party seeking disclosure obtains the prior approval of the Court or the objecting party.

8. All depositions or portions of depositions taken in this action that contain trade secret or other confidential information may be designated "Confidential" or "Confidential - Attorneys' Eyes Only" and thereby obtain the protections accorded other "Confidential" or "Confidential - Attorneys' Eyes Only" documents. Confidentiality designations for depositions shall be made either on the record or by written notice to the other party within 14 days of receipt of the transcript. Unless otherwise agreed, depositions shall be treated as "Confidential - Attorneys' Eyes Only" during the 14-day period following receipt of the transcript. The deposition of any witness (or any portion of such deposition) that encompasses Confidential information shall be taken only in the presence of persons who are qualified to have access to such information.

9. Any party who inadvertently fails to identify documents as "Confidential" or "Confidential - Attorneys' Eyes Only" shall have 14 days from the discovery of its oversight to correct its failure. Such failure shall be corrected by providing written notice of the error and substituted copies of the inadvertently produced documents. Any party receiving such inadvertently unmarked documents shall make reasonable efforts to retrieve documents distributed to persons not entitled to receive documents with the corrected designation.

10. Any party who inadvertently discloses documents that are privileged or otherwise immune from discovery shall, promptly upon discovery of such inadvertent disclosure, so advise the receiving party and request that the documents be returned. The receiving party shall return such inadvertently produced documents, including all copies, within 14 days of receiving such a written request. The party returning such inadvertently produced documents may thereafter seek re-production of any such documents pursuant to applicable law.

11. If a party files a document containing Confidential information with the Court, it shall do so in compliance with the Electronic Case Filing Procedures for the District of Minnesota. Prior to disclosure at trial or a hearing of materials or information designated "Confidential" or "Confidential - Attorneys' Eyes Only", the parties may seek further protections against public disclosure from the Court.

12. Any party may request a change in the designation of any information designated "Confidential" and/or "Confidential - Attorneys' Eyes Only". Any such document shall be treated as designated until the change is completed. If the requested change in designation is not agreed to, the party seeking the change may move the Court for appropriate relief, providing notice to any third party whose designation of produced documents as "Confidential" and/or "Confidential - Attorneys' Eyes Only" in the action may be affected. The party asserting that the material is Confidential shall have the burden of proving that the information in question is within the scope of protection afforded by Fed. R. Civ. P. 26(c).

13. Within 60 days of the termination of this action, including any appeals, each party shall either destroy or return to the opposing party all documents designated by the opposing party as "Confidential", and all copies of such documents, and shall destroy all extracts and/or data taken from such documents. Each party shall provide a certification as to such return or destruction as within the 60-day period. Attorneys shall be entitled to retain, however, a set of all documents filed with the Court and all correspondence generated in connection with the action.

14. Any party may apply to the Court for a modification of the Protective Order, and nothing in the Protective Order shall be construed to prevent a party from seeking such further provisions enhancing or limiting confidentiality as may be appropriate.

15. No action taken in accordance with the Protective Order shall be construed as a waiver of any claim or defense in the action or of any position as to discoverability or admissibility of evidence.

16. The obligations imposed by the Protective Order shall survive the termination of this action. Within 60 days following the expiration of the last period for appeal from any order issued in connection with this action, the parties shall remove any materials designated "Confidential" from the office of the Clerk of Court. Following that 60-day period, the Clerk of Court shall destroy all "Confidential" materials.

Stipulated to:

Date: ____________________ By: ____________________

Date: ____________________ By: ____________________

EXHIBIT A

WRITTEN ASSURANCE

______________________________ declares that:

I reside at ______________________________ in the city of ________________,

county ________________, state of ________________________ ;

I am currently employed by __________________________________ located at ________________________ and my current job title is ______________________.

I have read and believe I understand the terms of the Protective Order dated ________ , filed in Civil Action No. ________, pending in the United States District Court for the District of Minnesota. I agree to comply with and be bound by the provisions of the Protective Order. I understand that any violation of the Protective Order may subject me to sanctions by the Court.

I shall not divulge any documents, or copies of documents, designated "Confidential" or "Confidential - Attorneys' Eyes Only" obtained pursuant to such Protective Order, or the contents of such documents, to any person other than those specifically authorized by the Protective Order. I shall not copy or use such documents except for the purposes of this action and pursuant to the terms of the Protective Order.

As soon as practical, but no later than 30 days after final termination of this action, I shall return to the attorney from whom I have received them, any documents in my possession designated "Confidential" or "Confidential - Attorneys' Eyes Only", and all copies, excerpts, summaries, notes, digests, abstracts, and indices relating to such documents.

I submit myself to the jurisdiction of the United States District Court for the District of Minnesota for the purpose of enforcing or otherwise providing relief relating to the Protective Order.

I declare under penalty of perjury that the foregoing is true and correct.

Executed on ____________________ ________________________________

(Date) (Signature)

Appendix 2.4e
Default Standard for Access to Source Code from the District of Delaware

Absent agreement among the parties, the following procedures shall apply to ensure secure access to source code:

1. A single electronic copy of source code or executable code shall be made available for inspection on a stand-alone computer.

2. The stand-alone computer shall be password protected and supplied by the source code provider.

3. The stand-alone computer shall be located with an independent escrow agent, with the costs of such to be shared by the parties. If the parties cannot agree on such an agent, each party shall submit to the court the name and qualifications of their proposed agents for the court to choose.

4. Access to the stand-alone computer shall be permitted, after notice to the provider and an opportunity to object, to two (2) outside counsel representing the requesting party and two (2) experts retained by the requesting party, all of whom have been approved under the protective order in place. No one from the provider shall have further access to the computer during the remainder of discovery.

5. Source code may not be printed or copied without the agreement of the producing party or further order of the court.

6. The source code provider shall provide a manifest of the contents of the stand-alone computer. This manifest, which will be supplied in both printed and electronic form, will list the name, location, and MD5 checksum of every source and executable file escrowed on the computer.

7. The stand-alone computer shall include software utilities which will allow counsel and experts to view, search, and analyze the source code. At a minimum, these utilities must provide the ability to (a) view, search, and line-number any source file, (b) search for a given pattern of text through a number of files, (c) compare two files and display their differences, and (d) compute the MD5 checksum of a file.

8. If the court determines that the issue of missing files needs to be addressed, the source code provider will include on the stand-alone computer the build scripts, compilers, assemblers, and other utilities necessary to rebuild the application from source code, along with instructions for their use.

Appendix 2.5a
Mediation Evaluation Form for Attorneys, Northern District of Illinois

U.S. DISTRICT COURT
NORTHERN DISTRICT OF ILLINOIS (WESTERN DIVISION)
MEDIATION EVALUATION FORM

– For Attorneys –

Please promptly fill out this form after the mediation conference and return it to the ADR Administrator via fax at ___________. No case identification will be associated with these responses for purposes other than program evaluation.

Name of Mediator: ____

Case Number: ____

Date of Mediation: __________________ Type of Case: ______________

Outcome: [ ] settled [ ] partially settled [ ] not settled [ ] continued for further mediation

Number of mediation sessions held: __________

Number of hours spent in mediation: ________

Are you the [ ] defendant's attorney [ ] plaintiff's attorney

Number of cases in which you have participated in mediation prior to this one: ___

1. On a scale of 1 – 5 (1 = strongly disagree, 2 = disagree, 3 = neither agree nor disagree, 4 = agree, 5 = strongly agree), please respond to the following:

		SD	D	N	A	SA
a	The mediator was well-prepared for the mediation:	1	2	3	4	5
b	My client(s) and I understood the mediation process after it was explained:	1	2	3	4	5
c	The mediator helped the parties to generate options:	1	2	3	4	5
d	The mediator effectively moved the parties toward settlement:	1	2	3	4	5
e	The mediator was knowledgeable about the law in this case:	1	2	3	4	5
f	The mediation helped narrow or clarify the issues involved in this case	1	2	3	4	5
g	Overall, I am satisfied with the mediation process:	1	2	3	4	5
h	The process was fair to all parties:	1	2	3	4	5
i	Overall, I am satisfied with what was accomplished in the mediation:	1	2	3	4	5
j	Overall, I am satisfied with the agreement (if reached):	1	2	3	4	5

2. Overall, how helpful or detrimental was the mediation in the resolution of this case?

1. [ ] Very helpful
2. [ ] Somewhat helpful
3. [ ] It had little impact on the case
4. [ ] Somewhat detrimental
5. [ ] Very detrimental

3. The overall length of mediation was: [ ] too long [ ] too short [ ] about right

4. Did the mediator appear to have a bias for the [ ] Plaintiff? [ ] Defendant? [ ] No Bias

5. Do you think the assignment of this case to mediation:

[ ] Facilitated (or will facilitate) its early resolution
[ ] Will increase time to resolution
[ ] Will have no impact on time to resolution

6. Do you think the assignment of this case to mediation:

[ ] Has reduced (or will reduce) litigation costs to your client
[ ] Will increase litigation costs to your client
[ ] Will have no effect on costs to your client

7. If the case did not settle, why not?

____

____

8. Would you be willing to use mediation again? [ ] Yes [ ] No

Why or why not?

____

____

9. Would you be willing to use this mediator again? [ ] Yes [ ] No

Why or why not?

____

____

10. Comments on the mediator or the mediation process:

____

____

Appendix 2.5b Mediation Evaluation Form for Mediators, Northern District of Illinois

U.S. DISTRICT COURT
NORTHERN DISTRICT OF ILLINOIS (WESTERN DIVISION)
MEDIATION EVALUATION FORM

– For Mediators –

Please fill out this form and return it to the ADR Administrator via fax at _________ within 10 days of the mediation session. No case identification will be associated with these responses for purposes other than program evaluation.

Name: ____

Case Number: ____

Date of Mediation: _______________ Type of Case: ____________________

Outcome: [ ] settled [ ] partially settled [ ] not settled [ ] continued for further mediation

Number of cases for which you have acted as mediator prior to this one: ______

1. On a scale of 1 – 5 (1 = strongly disagree, 2 = disagree, 3 = neither agree nor disagree, 4 = agree, 5 = strongly agree), please respond to the following:

		SD	D	N	A	SA
a	This case was appropriate for mediation:	1	2	3	4	5
b	This case was referred to mediation at the appropriate time:	1	2	3	4	5
c	The lawyers were prepared for the mediation:	1	2	3	4	5
d	The litigants were prepared for the mediation:	1	2	3	4	5
e	The litigants were actively involved in the mediation:	1	2	3	4	5
f	The mediation helped narrow or clarify the issues involved in this case:	1	2	3	4	5
g	I have expertise in this type of dispute:	1	2	3	4	5
h	Overall, I am satisfied with what was accomplished in the mediation:	1	2	3	4	5

2. Overall, how helpful or detrimental was the mediation in the resolution of this case?

1. [ ] Very helpful
2. [ ] Somewhat helpful
3. [ ] It had little impact on the case
4. [ ] Somewhat detrimental
5. [ ] Very detrimental

3. The overall length of mediation was: [ ] too long [ ] too short [ ] about right

4. Do you think the assignment of this case to mediation:

[ ] Helped the case resolve more quickly

[ ] Will increase the time it takes to resolve the case

[ ] Will have no effect on the time it takes to resolve the case

5. Do you think the assignment of this case to mediation:

[ ] Has *reduced* (or will reduce) litigation costs to the parties

[ ] Will *increase* litigation costs to the parties

[ ] Will have *no effect* on costs to the parties

6. If the case did not settle, why not?

____

____

____

7. Please check the actions you undertook in the mediation:

[ ] Focused on legally relevant issues

[ ] Gave primacy to parties' needs & interests

[ ] Focused on the evidence of the case

[ ] Focused on parties' perception of case

[ ] Gave an advisory opinion of the likely outcome

[ ] Helped parties determine strengths & weaknesses of case

[ ] Provided parties with particular settlement options

[ ] Helped parties generate own proposal or range

8. Comments on the program:

Appendix 2.5c
Mediation Evaluation Form for Parties, Northern District of Illinois

U.S. DISTRICT COURT
NORTHERN DISTRICT OF ILLINOIS (WESTERN DIVISION)
MEDIATION EVALUATION FORM

– For Parties –

Please promptly fill out this form after the mediation conference and return it to the ADR Administrator via fax at __________. No case identification will be associated with these responses for purposes other than program evaluation.

Name of Mediator: ______________________________

Case Number: ______________________________

Date of Mediation: ________________ Type of Case: ________________

Outcome: [ ] settled [ ] partially settled [ ] not settled [ ] continued for further mediation

Number of mediation sessions held: ___ Number of hours spent in mediation: ___

Are you the [ ] defendant [ ] plaintiff

Number of cases in which you have participated in mediation prior to this one: ____

1. On a scale of 1 – 5 (1 = strongly disagree, 2 = disagree, 3 = neither agree nor disagree, 4 = agree, 5 = strongly agree), please respond to the following:

		SD	D	N	A	SA
a	The mediator was well-prepared for the mediation:	1	2	3	4	5
b	I understood the mediation process:	1	2	3	4	5
c	The mediator allowed me to fully present my case:	1	2	3	4	5
d	The mediator carefully listened to my side of the case:	1	2	3	4	5
e	The mediator helped me to generate options for settling the dispute:	1	2	3	4	5
f	The mediation asked appropriate questions to determine the facts of the case:	1	2	3	4	5
g	Overall, I am satisfied with the mediation process:	1	2	3	4	5
h	The process was fair to all parties:	1	2	3	4	5
i	Overall, I am satisfied with what was accomplished in the mediation:	1	2	3	4	5
j	Overall, I am satisfied with the agreement (if reached):	1	2	3	4	5

2. Overall, how helpful or detrimental was the mediation in the resolution of this case?

1. [ ] Very detrimental;
2. [ ] Somewhat detrimental;
3. [ ] It had little impact on the case;
4. [ ] Somewhat helpful;
5. [ ] Very helpful

3. The overall length of mediation was: [ ] too long [ ] too short [ ] about right

4. Did the mediator appear to have a bias for the [ ] Plaintiff? [ ] Defendant? [ ] No Bias

5. Do you think the assignment of this case to mediation:

[ ] Facilitated (or will facilitate) its early resolution
[ ] Will increase time to resolution
[ ] Will have no impact on time to resolution

6. Do you think the assignment of this case to mediation:

[ ] Has reduced (or will reduce) litigation costs
[ ] Will increase litigation costs
[ ] Will have no effect on costs

7. If the case did not settle, why not?

____

____

8. Would you be willing to use mediation again? [ ] Yes [ ] No

Why or why not?

____

____

9. Would you be willing to use this mediator again? [ ] Yes [ ] No

Why or why not?

____

____

10. Comments on the mediator or the mediation process:

____

____

____

Chapter 3
Preliminary Injunction

3.1 Introduction

The patent right—the right to exclude others from practicing the patented technology—has historically been protected by injunctive relief. Courts traditionally viewed patent rights like other property interests and routinely protected them through a "property" rule—barring transgressors from using the "property." *See* Guido Calabresi & A. Douglas Melamed, *Property Rules, Liability Rules, and Inalienability: One View of the Cathedral*, 85 Harv. L. Rev. 1089 (1972); *cf.* § 261 (declaring "patents shall have the attributes of personal property"); *Festo Corp. v. Shoketsu Kinzoku Kogyo Kabishiki Co.*, 535 U.S. 722, 720, 739 (2002) (a patent "is a property right"; patent rights constitute "the legitimate expectations of inventors in their property"); *Fla. Prepaid Postsecondary Educ. Expense Bd. v. Coll. Savings Bank*, 527 U.S. 627, 642 (1999) ("Patents . . . have long been considered a species of property.").

The principle that injunctive remedies should protect property interests traces to Blackstone's classic, although exaggerated, definition of property as "that sole and despotic dominion which one man claims and exercises over the external things of the world, in total exclusion of the right of any other individual in the universe"; "postpon[ing] even public necessity to the sacred and inviolable rights of private property." 2 William Blackstone, Commentaries on the Laws of England 2 (1775). From this idea, courts have traditionally presumed that compensation cannot rectify property-based harms. Moreover, in the traditional trespass scenario, ejecting the transgressor and preventing future transgressions will often make good sense, although even there the rigidity of the classic "property rule" has been loosened. *See, e.g.*, *Raab v. Casper*, 51 Cal. App. 3d 866 (1975) (discussing the California Civil Code provision affording jurists equitable discretion in encroachment cases).

For much of the patent system's history, extrapolating relatively absolute property remedial rules to the protection of patented inventions functioned reasonably well. Although the harm from patent infringement might not always have been irreparable, barring future infringement was relatively easy to administer and did not obviously stand in the way of progress. Thus, in nearly every patent case up until 2006, a victorious patent owner could count on and obtain a permanent injunction. By contrast, preliminary injunctions required a balancing analysis because validity, infringement, and enforceability had not yet been conclusively established. Thus, the choice to pursue preliminary injunctive relief turned on assessing the costs and benefits of seeking expedited review of the case, and the attendant higher burden.

The rise of software and business method patents, as well as the emergence of nonpracticing, patent monetization entities, have strained the traditional view of patents as property interests that deserve near-automatic injunctive relief. *See* Peter S. Menell, *Governance of Intellectual Resources and Disintegration of Intellectual Property in the Digital Age*, 26 Berkeley Tech. L.J. 1523 (2011). Moreover, markets for many high-technology products could be severely disrupted by the potential for mandatory injunctions for patented components of a complex product.

Several of these issues came to the fore in litigation over a patent claiming the "buy it now" feature of an online purchasing system. *See eBay, Inc. v. MercExchange, LLC*, 547 U.S. 388 (2006). In rejecting the Federal Circuit's presumption that permanent injunctions should issue after findings of infringement in the absence of "extraordinary circumstances," the Supreme Court held that the traditional four-factor balancing test that courts of equity employed should apply with equal force in patent cases. *Id.* at 391–94; *but see* Mark P. Gergen, John M. Golden & Henry E. Smith, *The Supreme Court's Accidental Revolution? The Test for Permanent Injunctions*, 112 Colum. L. Rev. 203 (2012) (showing that the Supreme Court's *eBay* decision abrogated long-standing remedial standards for permanent injunctions). In so declaring, the Supreme Court opened a new chapter in patent remedies. District courts now enjoy substantial discretion in considering and crafting injunctive relief.

Whereas courts awarded permanent injunctions in nearly all patent cases in which the patent owner prevailed prior to 2006, the grant rate has dropped to 70–75% since the *eBay* decision. *See* Christopher B. Seaman, *Property Rules vs. Liability Rules in Patent Litigation after* eBay: *An Empirical Study*, 101 Iowa L. Rev. (forthcoming 2016). Permanent injunctions are still relatively routine in life sciences patent cases. They are far less common in the software field, where courts have granted approximately 50% of permanent injunction requests. Operating companies obtain permanent injunctions in about 80% of the cases in which they win, whereas non-practicing entities have obtained permanent injunctions in only 16% of their victories since *eBay*. Similarly, competitors obtain permanent injunctions against rivals in 82% of cases in which they prevail, whereas noncompetitors obtain injunctive relief in just over 20% of the cases where they win.

The equitable framework articulated for awarding permanent injunctions in the *eBay* case derives from traditional standards for *preliminary* injunctions. *See* Gergen, Golden & Smith, 112 Colum. L. Rev. at 208; David I. Levine, David J. Jung & Tracy A. Thomas, Remedies: Public and Private 100 (5th ed. 2009). Not surprisingly, courts look to the *eBay* framework in analyzing preliminary injunction motions. *See* Kirti Gupta & Jay P. Kesan, *Studying the Impact of* eBay *on Injunctive Relief in Patent Cases* (draft July 10, 2015) (finding that that the *eBay* decision has dramatically reduced both the level at which injunctive relief is sought in patent cases and the rate at which it is granted, particularly for preliminary injunctions).

As reflected in Figure 3.1, the total number of preliminary injunction motions on a nationwide basis has been falling since the turn of the millennium. The grant rate has also declined since 2003.

Figure 3.1
Preliminary Injunctions in Patent Cases

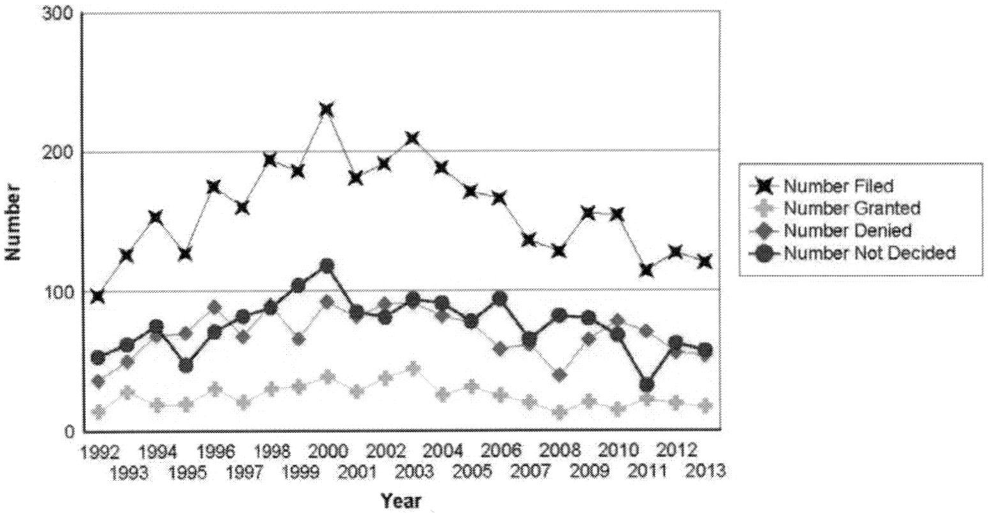

Source: LegalMetric (2015)

3.1.1 The Special Circumstances of the Preliminary Injunction Application in Patent Cases

Preliminary injunction applications in patent matters present special challenges. As in other cases, a party seeking a preliminary injunction in a patent case must demonstrate a likelihood of success on the merits and ongoing irreparable harm. Unlike in other types of cases, this showing in a patent case typically calls for analysis of nearly every substantive issue that ultimately will be presented at trial. To address the merits, the court must at least preliminarily construe patent claim terms. Invalidity, infringement, and enforceability must be addressed based on those constructions. To address harm, the parties often present complicated market analyses. These issues typically require both fact and expert discovery, undertaken on a compressed preliminary injunction schedule. Preliminary injunction applications can, therefore, place a tremendous strain on the court and the parties.

3.1.2 Opportunities Presented by Preliminary Injunction Applications in Patent Cases

While there is no question that a preliminary injunction application places a weighty burden on a court's limited resources, it also presents opportunities for prioritizing case management. Aggressive use of expedited discovery strategies enhances these opportunities. *See* § 3.4. Effectively managing the parties' expedited discovery demands can put the court in a good position to promote early settlement, summary judgment, and possibly a consolidated trial under Rule 65(a)(2).

Settlement. Because they have identified key claim terms and developed their best arguments for infringement and invalidity, the parties will exit the preliminary injunction process with a better understanding of the relative strengths of their cases. The court will be familiar with the technology and will have heard at least some of the fundamental arguments and counterarguments in the case. This is a propitious time to consider settlement. *See* § 2.7 (concerning settlement generally). The court may ask the parties to engage in settlement talks and/or mediation either immediately before or immediately after it rules on the preliminary injunction motion.

Early summary judgment or Federal Rule of Civil Procedure 65(a)(2) trial. The preliminary injunction process may reveal one or more case-dispositive issues. For example, the plaintiff may present a clear-cut case of infringement or the defendant may raise a particularly strong invalidity argument. If it appears from a party's submission that there exists a clear, potentially case-dispositive issue, the court can use the preliminary injunction process to expedite discovery on the issue and order an early summary judgment motion or expedited trial on the merits under Federal Rule of Civil Procedure 65(a)(2). *See generally* § 3.6.

3.1.3 Frequency of Preliminary Injunction Applications in Patent Cases

The frequency with which patentees have sought preliminary injunctions has ebbed and flowed with changes in legal standards and economic conditions over the years. Before the creation of the Federal Circuit in 1982, preliminary injunctions were rarely granted because courts typically required a prior judicial determination of patent validity, and considered damages after trial adequate to compensate for infringement. This made the irreparable-harm prong particularly difficult to establish.

Shortly after its establishment, the Federal Circuit ushered in a new era, emphasizing that "the very nature of the patent right is the right to exclude others.... A court should not be reluctant to use its equity powers once a party has so clearly established his patent rights." *Smith Int'l v. Hughes Tool Co.*, 718 F.2d 1573, 1581 (Fed. Cir. 1983). The court ruled that "where validity and continuing infringement have been clearly established . . . immediate irreparable harm is presumed." *Id.* (footnote omitted). Over time, however, the Federal Circuit raised the bar for plaintiffs, giving greater weight to the classical view of a preliminary injunction as "a drastic and extraordinary remedy that is not to be routinely granted." *Intel Corp. v. ULSI Sys. Tech., Inc.*, 995 F.2d 1566, 1568 (Fed. Cir. 1993); *see also Amazon.com, Inc. v. Barnesandnoble.com, Inc.*, 239 F.3d 1343, 1366 (Fed. Cir. 2001) (overturning grant of a preliminary injunction where the defendant "raised substantial questions" as to the patent's validity). In 2006, the Supreme Court reinforced this more searching and cautious perspective when it held that courts in patent cases must weigh all of the factors in any injunction analysis—likelihood of success on the merits, irreparable harm, balance of hardships, and public interest. *eBay*, 547 U.S. at 391–92. As reflected in Figure 3.1, the *eBay* decision likely has perpetuated the downward trend in preliminary injunction motions that began in 2000.

Nevertheless, preliminary injunctions remain an important option in some patent cases, particularly those involving dynamic, fast-paced, highly competitive markets where plaintiffs believe they will lose the benefit of their patent rights absent a preliminary injunction. Furthermore, the Federal Circuit's en banc *In re Seagate Tech., LLC*, 497 F.3d 1360 (Fed. Cir. 2007), decision may encourage preliminary injunction applications where the alleged infringement begins on or about the date that the plaintiff filed the infringement suit.[1] In *Seagate*, the Federal Circuit explained that "[a] patentee who does not attempt to stop an accused infringer's activities [by seeking a preliminary injunction] should not be allowed to accrue enhanced damages based solely on the infringer's post-filing conduct." *Id.* at 1374. It is unclear how this portion of *Seagate*'s analysis will apply in light of the Supreme Court's decision in *Halo Electronics, Inc., v. Pulse Electronics, Inc.*, Nos. 14-1513 and 14-1520 (June 3, 2016) (*see* § 9.2.2), but because *Halo* continues to consider willfulness an important factor in an enhanced damages determination, that a plaintiff did not seek a preliminary injunction likely will continue to be an important consideration is some cases.

Under the *Seagate* test, in most cases in which a plaintiff seeks only prospective damages (i.e., where both the conduct giving rise to alleged damages and the conduct giving rise to the alleged willfulness occurred after the complaint was filed), the plaintiff must seek a preliminary injunction to have a reasonable chance of recovering enhanced damages for willful infringement. Where the conduct allegedly giving rise to willfulness includes prefiling conduct, however, *Seagate* does not suggest the plaintiff should move for a preliminary injunction as a predicate to obtaining enhanced damages. The Federal Circuit in *Seagate* explained that "if a patentee attempts to secure injunctive relief but fails, it is likely the infringement did not rise to the level of recklessness [that is necessary for a willfulness finding]." *Id.* The court reasoned that "[a] substantial question about invalidity or infringement is likely sufficient not only to avoid a preliminary injunction, but also a charge of willfulness based on post-filing conduct." *Id.* Thus, a party that seeks but fails to win a preliminary injunction for reasons relating to the patent's validity or infringement may have done significant harm to its case for enhanced postfiling damages.

There is one notable exception: "in some cases a patentee may be denied a preliminary injunction despite establishing a likelihood of success on the merits, such as when the remaining factors are considered and balanced. In that event, whether a willfulness claim based on conduct occurring solely after litigation began is sustainable will depend on the facts of each case." *Id.* at 1374; *see also Aqua Shield v. Inter Pool Cover Team*, 774 F.3d 766, 773–75 (Fed. Cir. 2014) (denial of preliminary injunction for reasons other than validity or infringement does not preclude finding of willfulness).

---

1. Patent litigation is often filed shortly after a patent issues or a new product is introduced. In such cases, damages typically are based solely on postfiling conduct.

3.1.4 Governing Legal Standards: § 283, Federal Circuit Law, and Federal Rule of Civil Procedure 65

District courts have discretion to grant injunctions to prevent the violation of patent rights. Section 283 provides that courts "may grant injunctions in accordance with the principles of equity to prevent the violation of any right secured by patent, on such terms as the court deems reasonable." To evaluate a preliminary injunction application, the court uses the traditional four-factor test: the court weighs the applicant's likelihood of success on the merits, irreparable harm to the applicant, the balance of harm between the parties, and the public interest. *See eBay*, 547 U.S. at 391–92. This standard is essentially the same as that for a permanent injunction (*see* § 9.2.1), except that the applicant must prove a likelihood of success on the merits rather than actual success. *Apple Inc. v. Samsung Elecs. Co.* (*Apple III*), 735 F.3d 1352, 1381 (Fed. Cir. 2013) (a permanent injunction case). Courts therefore often look to permanent injunction cases for guidance in evaluating the relevant factors.

Federal Rule of Civil Procedure 65 sets forth the procedures governing preliminary injunction motions. Federal Circuit law governs the analysis. While "the grant of a preliminary injunction [is] a matter of procedural law not unique to the exclusive jurisdiction of the Federal Circuit, and on appellate review . . . procedural law of the regional circuit in which the case was brought [applies]," Federal Circuit law governs the decision as to whether to grant a preliminary injunction. *Mikohn Gaming Corp. v. Acres Gaming, Inc.*, 165 F.3d 891, 894 (Fed. Cir. 1998). "Because the issuance of an injunction . . . enjoins 'the violation of any right secured by a patent, on such terms as the court deems reasonable,' a preliminary injunction . . . , although a procedural matter, involves substantive matters unique to patent law and, therefore, is governed by the law of [the Federal Circuit].'" *Revision Military, Inc. v. Balboa Mfg. Co.*, 700 F.3d 524, 525 (Fed. Cir. 2012) (quoting *Hybritech Inc. v. Abbott Labs.*, 849 F.2d 1446, 1451 n.12 (Fed. Cir. 1988).

While the district court can grant or deny the injunction at its discretion, the grant or denial must be supported by findings of fact that explicitly address the equitable factors weighed in the decision process. *See* Fed. R. Civ. P. 52(a); *Pretty Punch Shoppettes, Inc. v. Hauk*, 844 F.2d 782, 784 (Fed. Cir. 1988). The trial court must provide sufficient factual findings to enable meaningful review of the merits of its order. *Nutrition 21 v. United States*, 930 F.2d 867, 869 (Fed. Cir. 1991) ("Sufficient factual findings on the material issues are necessary to allow [the Federal Circuit] to have a basis for meaningful review. Otherwise, [the Federal Circuit] has no basis for evaluating what facts entered into the district court's analysis or whether the district court's reasoning comports with the applicable legal standard.") (citations omitted); *Oakley, Inc. v. Int'l Tropic-Cal, Inc.*, 923 F.2d 167, 168 (Fed. Cir. 1991) (vacating preliminary injunction where "the court's findings . . . [were] so limited and conclusory that meaningful appellate review [was] not possible").

"[A] district court must consider all four factors before *granting* a preliminary injunction to determine whether the moving party has carried its burden of establishing each of the four." *Reebok Int'l Ltd. v. J. Baker, Inc.*, 32 F.3d 1552, 1556 (Fed. Cir. 1994). This requirement does not, however, extend to the denial of a preliminary injunction, which may be based on a party's failure to make a showing on any one of the four factors, particularly, the first two—likelihood of success on the merits and irreparable harm. *See, e.g.*, *Guttman, Inc. v. Kopykake Enters.*, 302 F.3d 1352, 1356 (Fed. Cir. 2002); *Polymer Techs., Inc. v. Bridwell*, 103 F.3d 970, 973–74 (Fed. Cir. 1996) ("[A] trial court need not make findings concerning the third or fourth factors if the moving party fails to establish either of the first two factors.").

3.1.5 Tension Between Right to Exclude and Equitable Considerations

Due to the evolution of the legal standards governing preliminary injunction determinations as well as philosophical differences among Federal Circuit jurists, litigants will be able to cite apparently conflicting authority regarding the proper standard. As traced above, *see* § 3.1.3, the Federal Circuit initially emphasized the role of equity to protect the right to exclude, erecting a rebuttable presumption of irreparable harm once validity and continuing infringement were established. *Smith Int'l*, 718 F.2d 1573. Over time, the Federal Circuit has shifted away from that standard, although it still echoes in decisions. *See, e.g.*, *Presidio Components, Inc. v. Am. Tech. Ceramics Corp.*, 702 F.3d 1351, 1363 (Fed. Cir. 2012) ("This analysis proceeds under the 'long tradition of equity practice' granting 'injunctive relief upon a finding of infringement in the vast majority of patent cases'" (quoting *eBay*, 547 U.S. at 395 (Roberts, C.J., concurring))). As these Federal Circuit cases recognize, however, the Supreme Court's decision in *eBay* firmly establishes the need for courts to balance all of the equitable considerations carefully. 547 U.S. at 391–92.

3.1.6 Meaning of Status Quo

As in other cases, "[t]he purpose of a preliminary injunction is to preserve the relative positions of the parties until a trial on the merits can be held." *Univ. of Tex. v. Camenisch*, 451 U.S. 390, 395 (1981). A preliminary injunction preserves the status quo if it prevents future infringement, but does not undertake to assess the pecuniary or other consequences of past infringement. *Atlas Powder Co. v. Ireco Chems.*, 773 F.2d 1230, 1232 (Fed. Cir. 1985). Thus, an accused infringer cannot avoid a preliminary injunction merely by arguing that, because it is presently practicing the disputed technology, preserving the status quo requires that it be allowed to continue the practice. *Id.* Balancing the harms considers the accused infringer's dependence on allegedly infringing activity. *Id.*; *Circle R, Inc. v. Smithco Mfg.*, 919 F. Supp. 1272, 1303 (N.D. Iowa 1996). However, "the status quo catchword does not necessarily allow [an accused infringer] to continue such dependence, apart from other factors .... '[S]tatus quo' is not a talisman to dispose of the question by itself." *Atlas Powder*, 773 F.2d at 1232; *see also Windsurfing Int'l, Inc. v. AMF, Inc.*, 782 F.2d 995, 1003 n.12 (Fed. Cir. 1986) (considering a *permanent* injunction). *But see Archive Corp. v. Cipher Data Prods., Inc.*, CIV A Nos. SACV88296AHSRWRX, SACV88472AHSRRS, 1988 WL 168533, 1988 U.S. Dist. LEXIS 17190, at *18 (C.D. Cal. Dec. 22, 1988) ("Because [the defendant] has been manufacturing [and selling] the accused [products] long prior to the issuance of [the asserted] patent, [a preliminary] injunction could not preserve the status quo and would conversely create new market conditions.").[2]

3.2 Standards and Burdens

3.2.1 Discretion of Trial Court

The grant or denial of a preliminary injunction is within the sound discretion of the district court. *See Abbott Labs. v. Andrx Pharm., Inc.*, 452 F.3d 1331, 1334 (Fed. Cir. 2006). Abuse of discretion in granting or denying a preliminary injunction requires a "showing that the court made a clear error of judgment in weighing relevant factors or exercised its discretion based upon an error of law or clearly erroneous factual findings." *Id.* at 1335 (quoting *Polymer Techs.*, 103 F.3d at 973).

Findings of fact are reviewed for clear error. However, "[t]o the extent that a district court's decision to grant a preliminary injunction hinges on questions of law, [appellate] review is de novo." *Mylan Pharm., Inc. v. Thompson*, 268 F.3d 1323, 1329 (Fed. Cir. 2001).

3.2.2 Factors to Be Considered

The traditional equitable considerations apply to the analysis of injunctions in patent cases. *eBay*, 547 U.S. 388. Courts must apply Federal Circuit law to assess these considerations. *Mikohn*, 165 F.3d at 894.

The factors—likelihood of success on the merits, irreparable harm, balance of hardship, and public interest—"taken individually, are not dispositive; rather, the district court must weigh and measure each factor against the other factors and against the form and magnitude of the relief requested." *Hybritech*, 849 F.2d at 1451. However, the factors do not all carry equal weight; the first two factors effectively set up a threshold showing that the patent holder must meet before the other factors are weighed. *See Amazon.com*, 239 F.3d at 1350 ("[A] movant cannot be granted a preliminary injunction unless it establishes *both* of the first two factors, *i.e.*, likelihood of success on the merits and irreparable harm.").

---

2. The facts of a given case may temper a court's response to a defendant's decision to build a business on an infringing product. Shutting down a defendant's business through a preliminary injunction likely would require an unusually strong showing on the merits, the absence of which could dictate that a defendant should have the opportunity of a trial, before seeing its business destroyed. *See Ill. Tool Works, Inc. v. Grip-Pak, Inc.*, 906 F.2d 679, 683–84 (Fed. Cir. 1990) (observing that the result in *Windsurfing* did not support a preliminary injunction where the defendant would not be allowed its day in court).

3.2.2.1 Reasonable Likelihood of Success on the Merits

To satisfy the first equitable factor, the moving party must demonstrate that, "in light of the presumptions and burdens that will inhere at trial on the merits, [the movant] will likely prove that [the accused infringer's] product infringes the [asserted] patent and that it will withstand [the accused infringer's] challenges to the validity and enforceability of the . . . patent." *Sanofi-Synthelabo v. Apotex, Inc.*, 470 F.3d 1368, 1374 (Fed. Cir. 2006) (internal citations omitted); *see also Trebro Mfg., Inc. v. Firefly Equip., LLC*, 748 F.3d 1159 (Fed. Cir. 2014); *AstraZeneca LP v. Apotex, Inc.*, 633 F.3d 1042, 1050 (Fed. Cir. 2010); *Amazon.com*, 239 F.3d at 1350 (Fed. Cir. 2001).

3.2.2.1.1 Claim Construction and Infringement

Likelihood of success in proving infringement and defending validity "depends fundamentally on the meaning of the asserted claim and its relationship to the accused product or process. Therefore, a correct claim construction is almost always a prerequisite for imposition of a preliminary injunction." *Chamberlain Grp., Inc. v. Lear Corp.*, 516 F.3d 1331, 1339–40 (Fed. Cir. 2008). However, claim constructions determined during the preliminary injunction stage are always subject to later revision and do not stand as law of the case for purposes of subsequent proceedings. *See* § 5.3.2.4.1; *Guttman*, 302 F.3d at 1361 (explaining that "district courts may engage in a rolling claim construction" when beginning at the preliminary injunction stage); *Purdue Pharma L.P. v. Boehringer Ingelheim GmbH*, 237 F.3d 1359, 1363 (Fed. Cir. 2001) ("[F]indings of fact and conclusions of law at the preliminary injunction stage are subject to change.").

3.2.2.1.2 Invalidity

The patentee seeking a preliminary injunction is expected to make a clear showing it is entitled to relief, including the absence of any substantial question as to the validity of the asserted patent claim(s). *Trebro Mfg.*, 748 F.3d at 1166–67. In addition to evidence rebutting any invalidity claim by the defendant, evidence that supports such a showing includes the patent previously withstanding a validity challenge or industry acquiescence to the patent's validity by licensing. *Id.* Similarly, where a defendant asserts that a patent is unenforceable (e.g., resulting from inequitable conduct), the patentee must show that the defense "lacks substantial merit." *Purdue Pharma*, 237 F.3d at 1366.

As a practical matter, the opposing party bears the burden of persuasion. The opposing party "must show a substantial question of invalidity to avoid a showing of likelihood of success." *Erico Int'l Corp. v. Vutec Corp.*, 516 F.3d 1350, 1354 (Fed. Cir. 2008); *see Sciele Pharma Inc. v. Lupin Ltd.*, 684 F.3d 1253, 1359 (Fed. Cir. 2012). Note, however, that "an accused infringer may avoid a preliminary injunction by showing only a *substantial question* as to invalidity, as opposed to the higher clear and convincing standard required to prevail on the merits." *In re Seagate Tech.*, 497 F.3d at 1374 (emphasis added) (citing *Amazon.com*, 239 F.3d at 1359). Stated another way, "[v]ulnerability is the issue at the preliminary injunction stage, while validity is the issue at trial. The showing of a substantial question as to invalidity thus requires less proof than the clear and convincing showing necessary to establish invalidity itself." *Amazon.com*, 239 F.3d at 1359.

3.2.2.2 Irreparable Harm if the Preliminary Injunction Is Not Granted

3.2.2.2.1 Presumption

Following the Supreme Court's decision in *eBay*, the Federal Circuit overturned its prior rule that patent owners who demonstrate a likelihood of success on the merits enjoy a presumption of irreparable injury. *Robert Bosch LLC v. Pylon Mfg. Corp.*, 659 F.3d 1142, 1148–49 (Fed. Cir. 2011). Nevertheless, in evaluating irreparable harm, the court should consider a patent holder's right to exclude infringers. *Id.*

3.2.2.2.2 Evidentiary Factors

Table 3.1 summarizes how Federal Circuit cases since *eBay* have applied the irreparable harm factor in common fact patterns. For multifeatured products, these factors are applied in light of the nexus requirement described in § 3.2.2.2.4.

Table 3.1
Post-*eBay* Application of Irreparable Harm

Facts Supporting Irreparable Harm	Facts Against Irreparable Harm
• Infringer is competitor ○ Two- or few-player market[1,8] ○ Potential loss of market share and customers[1,3,7] ○ Potential loss to patent owner of follow-on purchases[1] ○ Price erosion[3,5,6] ○ Harm to goodwill, brand recognition[3,4,6] ○ Harm to reputation[3] ○ Workforce reduction resulting from competition[4,6,7] • That customers are unlikely to switch in the future, and therefore infringement causes long-term loss[1]	• Delay in seeking relief[1] • Availability of calculable award of money damages to patent holder that includes compensation based on future sales of infringing product[1] • Lack of causal nexus between alleged irreparable harm and infringement[2]

1. *Apple, Inc. v. Samsung Elecs. Co. (Apple I)*, 678 F.3d 1314 (Fed. Cir. 2012) (including concurrence).
2. *Apple, Inc. v. Samsung Elecs. Co. (Apple II)*, 695 F.3d 1370 (Fed. Cir. 2012).
3. *Aria Diagnostics, Inc. v. Sequenom, Inc.*, 726 F.3d 1296 (Fed. Cir. 2013).
4. *AstraZeneca LP v. Apotex, Inc.*, 633 F.3d 1042 (Fed. Cir. 2010).
5. *Celsis In Vitro, Inc. v. CellzDirect, Inc.*, 664 F.3d 922, 930 (Fed. Cir. 2012).
6. *Sanofi-Synthelabo v. Apotex, Inc.*, 470 F.3d 1368 (Fed. Cir. 2006).
7. *Trebro Mfg., Inc. v. Firefly Equip., LLC*, 748 F.3d 1159 (Fed. Cir. 2014).
8. *Robert Bosch LLC v. Pylon Mfg. Corp.*, 659 F.3d 1142, 1151 (Fed. Cir. 2011).

When the parties are direct competitors, irreparable harm is more likely. *Robert Bosch LLC*, 659 F.3d at 1152–54. Even when the usual economic consequences of competition—price and market erosion—likely would be calculable and thus "reparable" through a damages award, this is not a sufficient reason to deny a preliminary injunction. *Aria Diagnostics, Inc. v. Sequenom, Inc.*, 726 F.3d 1296, 1304 (Fed. Cir. 2013) (vacating denial of preliminary injunction); *see also Trebro Mfg.*, 748 F.3d at 1170–71 (Fed. Cir. 2014) (same). In a competitive situation, that the patent holder does not practice its patent also is not necessarily a reason to deny a preliminary injunction. *Trebro Mfg.*, 748 F.3d at 1171.

While the facts may warrant a preliminary injunction, in some instances, it should be narrowly tailored to minimize irreparable harm while still allowing the accused infringer some commercialization. *See, e.g., P.N.A. Constr. Techs. v. McTech Grp., Inc.*, 414 F. Supp. 2d 1228, 1244 (N.D. Ga. 2006) ("[T]he Court believes preliminary injunctive relief tailored to the unique facts here best serves the law and the parties. Specifically, the Court is not inclined to consider granting a comprehensive injunction, especially one that would prohibit Defendants from performing contracts into which it already has entered. The risk to Plaintiff's patent rights derives, in the Court's view, from continuing sales, and if a preliminary injunction is entered, it ought to apply only to new contracts.").

Irreparable harm may be rebutted by showing that the patent holder delayed in bringing its infringement action. *See Apple, Inc. v. Samsung Elecs. Co.*, 678 F.3d 1314, 1325–26 (Fed. Cir. 2012); *Pfizer, Inc. v. Teva Pharms., USA, Inc.*, 429 F.3d 1364, 1381 (Fed. Cir. 2005). *But see High Tech Med. Instr., Inc. v. New Image Indus., Inc.*, 49 F.3d 1551 (Fed. Cir. 1995) ("[T]he period of delay may not have been enough, standing alone, to demonstrate the absence of irreparable harm."). Likewise, if future infringement is unlikely or the patent holder has licensed the patent to others, irreparable injury may be more difficult to establish. *See Pfizer, Inc.*, 429 F.3d at 1381; *Novo Nordisk A/S v. Sanofi-Aventis U.S. LLC*, Civ. Action No. 07-3206 (MLC), 2008 WL 6098829, 2008 U.S. Dist. LEXIS 12342, 21–22 (D.N.J. Feb. 19, 2008) (*aff'd, Novo Nordisk A/S v. Sanofi-Aventis U.S. LLC*, 290 F. App'x 334 (Fed. Cir. July 30, 2008) (unpublished)). In considering a patent holder's past licensing, however, a court must consider relevant differences between past situations in which licenses were granted and the current alleged infringement. *Apple III*, 735 F.3d at 1370 (Fed. Cir. 2013); *see also eBay*, 547 U.S. at 393.

Irreparable harm, however, is not necessarily rebutted by showing that other competitors also infringe the patent (*Aria Diagnostics*, 726 F.3d at 1305; *Robert Bosch LLC*, 659 F.3d at 1150–52; *Pfizer, Inc.*, 429 F.3d at 1381), the patented product is not "core" to the patent holder's business (*Robert Bosch LLC*, 659 F.3d at 1150–52), or the alleged infringer can pay any damages award (*Apple III*, 735 F.3d at 1369). Nor is it rebutted by the potential that damages and market recovery *might* ameliorate the harm resulting from price and market erosion (*Aria Diagnostics*, 726 F.3d at 1304) or that damages from market erosion *might* be estimable (*Trebro Mfg.*, 749 F.3d at 1170 (Fed. Cir. 2014)).

3.2.2.2.3 Nonpracticing Entities

Where a patentee does not practice the invention or otherwise commercially exploit it and is not a competitor of the alleged infringer, irreparable harm is more difficult to demonstrate. *See High Tech Med. Instruments*, 49 F.3d at 1556 ("Although a patentee's failure to practice an invention does not necessarily defeat the patentee's claim of irreparable harm, the lack of commercial activity by the patentee is a significant factor in the calculus."). That the patentee neither competes with the alleged infringer nor practices the invention is a factor that concerns trial courts. *See, e.g.*, *Paice LLC v. Toyota Motor Corp.*, 2006 WL 2385139, 2006 U.S. Dist. LEXIS 61600 (E.D. Tex. Aug. 16, 2006), *aff'd in part and vacated*, 504 F.3d 1293, 1303 (Fed. Cir. 2007) (holding that "because Plaintiff does not compete for market share . . . concerns regarding loss of brand name recognition and market share similarly are not implicated").

Nevertheless, a nonpracticing entity is not barred from obtaining a preliminary injunction:

> [S]ome patent holders, such as university researchers or self-made inventors, might reasonably prefer to license their patents, rather than undertake efforts to secure the financing necessary to bring their work to market themselves. Such patent holders may be able to satisfy the traditional four-factor test, and we see no basis for categorically denying them the opportunity to do so.

eBay, 547 U.S. at 392. Relying on this portion of the *eBay* opinion, the district court in *Commonwealth Scientific and Industrial Research Organisation (CSIRO) v. Buffalo Technology Inc.*, 492 F. Supp. 2d 600 (E.D. Tex. 2007), granted a permanent injunction to a nonpracticing entity. CSIRO is the principal scientific research organization of the Australian government, similar to the United States' National Science Foundation and National Institutes of Health. It "relies heavily on the ability to license its intellectual property to finance its research and development." *Id.* at 604. The trial court held that, even though CSIRO did not commercialize its patent itself and instead sought licensing revenue, the harm CSIRO suffered was not merely financial: Buffalo's infringement meant that CSIRO's "reputation as a research institution has been impugned just as another company's brand recognition or good will may be damaged." *Id.* at 605.

In discussions of the subject of nonpracticing entities (and sometimes in briefs), the pejorative term "patent troll" is often used to conjure an image of opportunistic misuse of the patent system. The label is as analytically unhelpful as it is attention-grabbing, which is why it is not generally found in judicial opinions. It is not necessary for a court to determine whether a patent owner is a "troll" to determine where the equities lie. Instead, as *Paice* and *CSIRO* show, the issue is whether the infringement causes irreparable harm to the patentee. Under some circumstances, a nonpracticing patentee may suffer irreparable harm from ongoing infringement, *CSIRO*, 492 F. Supp. 2d at 607–08, but under other circumstances it may not, *Paice*, 504 F.3d at 1303.

3.2.2.2.4 Nexus Requirement

Not all patents encompass all or major portions of a product. When a patent encompasses just one or a small number of features, the patentee must show a causal nexus between irreparable harm resulting from the sale and an infringing feature to prove irreparable harm. *Apple, Inc. v. Samsung Elecs. Co.* (*Apple II*), 695 F.3d 1370, 1374–75 (Fed. Cir. 2012); *Apple, Inc. v. Samsung Elecs. Co.* (*Apple I*), 678 F.3d 1314, 1324 (Fed. Cir. 2012). This is not a true or false determination that showing any nexus satisfies. Instead, it requires a determination of the extent to which the irreparable harm that results from the sale of the accused product can be ascribed to the infringing feature. *Apple II*, 695 F.3d at 1375. The required showing is usually made by proof that the infringing feature drives consumer demand for the accused product. *Id.* The forces driving consumers' purchase of the product can be proven in various ways, including evidence that the infringing feature is, if not the sole driver of consumer demand, one of several that influence consumer purchases; that inclusion of the infringing feature makes the product significantly more desirable; or that consumers would pay significantly more for a product if it contains the feature. *Id.* at 1364–65, 1367. If most customers buy the infringing product for other reasons, however, the infringement is not deemed to result in irreparable harm. *Id.* at 1375. It is not enough to show only that removal of the infringing feature would render the product inoperative or worthless, because such a test could be satisfied by many features that are necessary for a product to operate properly, but nevertheless have little or no impact on a consumer's buying decision. *Id.* at 1376. In situations where multiple product features infringe the patentee's patents, it is their cumulative impact on consumer buying decisions that should be considered. *Apple III*, 735 F.3d at 1364.

3.2.2.3 Balance of Hardships

The grant of a preliminary injunction in a patent case often results in the defendant having to remove a product from the market, or at least drastically modify it, pending trial. Furthermore, given the extended duration of many patent cases, the defendant may face months or even years before the product can be reintroduced (assuming the defendant prevails). As a result, the hardship on the defendant can be drastic. That is why the patentee must post a bond to get a TRO or preliminary injunction. *See* § 3.7. On the other hand, a patent holder enjoys a right that can only be exploited for a limited time. Denial of that right for the months or years of a patent case can lead to hardship in the form of price erosion, loss of reputation, loss of market share, and lost opportunity to lead or even dominate a market the patent holder ought rightfully to lead (assuming the patent holder prevails). In *Illinois Tool Works*, the Federal Circuit considered these opposing hardships and explained:

> The hardship on a preliminarily enjoined manufacturer who must withdraw its product from the market before trial can be devastating. On the other hand, the hardship on a patentee denied an injunction after showing a strong likelihood of success on validity and infringement consists in a frequently and equally serious delay in the exercise of his limited-in-time property right to exclude. Neither hardship can be controlling in all cases. Because the court must balance the hardships, at least

> in part in light of its estimate of what is likely to happen at trial, it must consider the movant's showing of likelihood of success. Yet, a court must remain free to deny a preliminary injunction, whatever be the showing of likelihood of success, when equity in the light of all the factors so requires.

Ill. Tool Works, Inc. v. Grip-Pak, Inc., 906 F.2d 679, 683 (Fed. Cir. 1990). Courts facing the prospect of such dire consequences to one party or the other, therefore, must engage in a sensitive analysis of the unique facts of each case.

A party's considered business decision to take a calculated risk of infringement cannot, however, alone form the basis of a finding of harm to justify denying injunctive relief. *See Aria Diagnostics*, 726 F.3d at 1305 (harm to infringer must be balanced against harm to patentee's "R&D and investment in the technology, undermining work and money spent developing, validating, and commercializing any covered product"); *Sanofi-Synthelabo, Inc.*, 470 F.3d at 1383 ("The court did not clearly err in finding that Apotex's harms were 'almost entirely preventable' and were the result of its own calculated risk to launch its product pre-judgment."). Thus, for example, a party that elected to launch an accused product during patent litigation could not avoid a preliminary injunction by complaining that the harm incurred in having to cease manufacture and sale of the product outweighed the patent holder's harm in facing irreversible price erosion. *Sanofi-Synthelabo*, 470 F.3d at 1382–83.

3.2.2.4 Impact on the Public Interest

Although the public has an abstract interest in protecting rights secured by valid patents, the focus of the district court's public-interest analysis should be whether the public has some critical interest in the specific case that would be injured by the grant or denial of preliminary relief. *See Hybritech*, 849 F.2d 1446, 1458 (Fed. Cir. 1988). Thus, the public interest in enforcement of valid patents, taken alone, does not skew this factor toward the patent holder. *See id.* However, a specific public concern can weigh heavily in the analysis, particularly in an industry, such as pharmaceuticals, where development costs can be especially high and the public interest in effective new products is also high. *See Sanofi-Synthelabo*, 470 F.3d at 1383–84 (finding that district court did not clearly err in concluding that the significant public interest in encouraging investment in development and protecting the exclusionary rights conveyed in valid patents tipped the scale in favor of pharmaceutical patent holder).

In some cases, the public interest could weigh heavily enough that a court might deny an injunction even where the patent holder makes a reasonable showing on likelihood of success and irreparable harm. For example, "[i]f a patentee's failure to practice a patented invention frustrates an important public need for the invention, a court need not enjoin infringement of the patent. Accordingly, courts have in rare instances exercised their discretion to deny injunctive relief in order to protect the public interest." *Rite-Hite Corp. v. Kelley Co.*, 56 F.3d 1538, 1547 (Fed. Cir. 1995) (citations omitted). In *z4 Technologies*, the district court found that the public interest weighed against enjoining ongoing infringement. *See z4 Techs. Inc. v. Microsoft Corp.*, 434 F. Supp. 2d 437, 439 (E.D. Tex. 2006). The case involved product activation software that was used by every genuine purchaser of Microsoft's popular Windows XP and Office products. *See id.* at 439. Although the jury found willful infringement, the district court declined to order Microsoft to redesign its software or turn off its product activation servers. The court was "unaware of any negative effects that might befall the public in the absence of an injunction," that "it is likely that any minor disruption to the distribution of the products in question could occur and would have an effect on the public due to the public's undisputed and enormous reliance on these products" and "[a]lthough these negative effects are somewhat speculative, such potential negative effects on the public weigh, even if only slightly, against granting an injunction." *Id.* at 443–44. Similarly, when a multifeatured product is involved, the court should consider the prospect that an injunction would deprive customers of access to a large number of desired, noninfringing features. *eBay*, 547 U.S. at 396–97 (Kennedy, J., concurring); *Apple III*, 735 F.3d at 1372–73.

3.2.2.5 Burdens of Proof and Persuasion

The patent holder has the burden of proof to demonstrate the predicates for a preliminary injunction. *See Abbott Labs.*, 452 F.3d at 1334 (Fed. Cir. 2006). This includes the burden of showing that the asserted patents likely are infringed and the absence of any substantial question that the asserted patent claims are valid (*Trebro Mfg.*, 748 F.3d at 1166–67 (Fed. Cir. 2014)), or that the patent is enforceable (*Purdue Pharma*, 237 F.3d at 1366). The validity and enforceability determinations should be made in light of the presumption of patent validity and that the accused infringer has the ultimate burden of proof on these issues at trial. *See, e.g.*, *Sciele Pharma.*, 684 F.3d 1253, 1259 (Fed. Cir. 2012); *Amazon.com*, 239 F.3d at 1350.

The patentee may make its showing of patent validity and enforceability based on the patent's prosecution history, prior litigation involving the patent, or other evidence such as industry having "acquiesced in" the patent's validity (e.g., competitors having paid royalties to license it). *See Amazon.com*, 239 F.3d at 1359; *Eyeticket Corp. v. Unisys Corp.*, 155 F. Supp. 2d 527, 542–43 (E.D. Va. 2001) (citing *H.H. Robertson, Co. v. United Steel Deck, Inc.*, 820 F.2d 384, 388–89 (Fed. Cir. 1987)).

Once the patent holder makes its showing, the accused infringer must come forward with evidence that raises a "substantial question" of invalidity. *Amazon.com*, 239 F.3d at 1358. However, validity challenges can defeat a preliminary injunction application "on evidence that would not suffice to support a judgment of invalidity at trial." *Id.* at 1358–59. At the preliminary injunction stage, the defendant need not meet the "clear and convincing" burden of proof it must meet to prevail on invalidity or unenforceability at trial. *Id.* ("Vulnerability is the issue at the preliminary injunction stage, while validity is the issue at trial. The showing of a substantial question as to invalidity thus requires less proof than the clear and convincing showing necessary to establish invalidity itself.").

3.2.2.6 Effect of PTAB Review Proceedings

Where a patentee moves for a preliminary injunction with regard to a patent that is subject to pending AIA Review, reexamination, or interference proceedings at the USPTO, the question arises whether those proceedings constitute evidence of substantial doubt as to the validity of the patent.

As discussed in § 14.2.5.6.1, the USPTO grants reexamination requests when it determines that a "substantial new question of patentability" has been raised. § 303. In contrast, the USPTO grants an inter partes review (IPR) request when the petitioner has demonstrated a reasonable likelihood that at least one challenged claim is unpatentable, § 314, and the petitioner must show a claim is more likely than not unpatentable for the USPTO to institute covered business method review (CBMR) or postgrant review (PGR). § 324; § 14.2.5.7.

3.2.2.6.1 Grant of Ex Parte Reexamination

In the context of reexamination, the Federal Circuit has stated that "validity challenges during preliminary injunction proceedings can be successful, that is, they may raise substantial questions of invalidity, on evidence that would not suffice to support a judgment of invalidity at trial." *Amazon.com*, 239 F.3d at 1358. This suggests that the USPTO's grant of a reexamination request supports an accused infringer's invalidity argument at the preliminary injunction stage. *See Pergo, Inc. v. Faus Grp., Inc.*, 401 F. Supp. 2d 515, 524 (E.D.N.C. 2005) ("[W]hile the grant of a motion for reexamination is not conclusive as to the issue of validity, it is probative to the issue of whether defendants have raised a substantial question of validity."); *DUSA Pharm., Inc. v. River's Edge Pharm.*, No. 06-1843(SRC), 2007 WL 748448, 2007 U.S. Dist. LEXIS 16005, at *9 (D.N.J. Mar. 7, 2007) (reaching a similar conclusion). Of course, extending the grant of a reexamination request to support the denial of a preliminary injunction requires the assumption that a "substantial new question of patentability" has the same meaning as a substantial question about the merits of a patent holder's case. In applying *Seagate* to a willfulness analysis, one district court made this assumption: "To the extent the Court accepts the USPTO's determinations that there are substantial questions of validity, the Court grants partial summary judgment of no willful infringement with respect to post-filing conduct." *Lucent Techs., Inc. v. Gateway, Inc.*, Nos. 07-CV-2000-H (CAB), 02-CV-2060-B (CAB), 03-CV-0699-B (CAB), 03-CV-1108-B (CAB), 2007 WL 6955272, 2007 U.S. Dist. LEXIS 95934, at *18–19 (S.D. Cal. Oct. 30, 2007) (reasoning that, because there was a substantial question, there could have been no willful infringement).

On the other hand, in the context of a willfulness inquiry, the Federal Circuit has stated that "the grant by the examiner of a request for reexamination is not probative of unpatentability. The grant of a request for reexamination, although surely evidence that the criterion for reexamination has been met . . . does not establish a *likelihood* of patent invalidity." *Hoechst Celanese Corp. v. BP Chems. Ltd.*, 78 F.3d 1575, 1584 (Fed. Cir. 1996) (emphasis added). Accordingly, while a court should consider the arguments raised in a request for reexamination, and should probe the patent holders' counterarguments to assess their persuasiveness, the reexamination grant itself likely is not enough to warrant denial of a preliminary injunction. *Cf. DUSA Pharm.*, 2007 WL 748448, 2007 U.S. Dist. LEXIS 16005, at *10 (D.N.J. Mar. 6, 2007) (granting motion to dissolve preliminary injunction where patent holder "ha[d] not shown that the validity question raised by the reexamination order and the Office Action lacks substantial merit").

3.2.2.6.2 Institution of Inter Partes Review, Covered Business Method Review, or Postgrant Review

While few courts have addressed what effect the institution of an AIA review has in the preliminary injunction analysis, the higher burdens for institution relative to reexamination seem to favor an accused infringer's invalidity argument. IPR's "reasonable likelihood" standard was intended to force the petitioner to make a stronger showing of unpatentability compared to the "substantial question" patentability standard used for reexamination. And the "more likely than not" standard for CBMR and PGR was intended to be an even higher burden.

This has proven to be the case. In the last two years, the PTAB has instituted 75% of IPR requests and 73% of CBMR requests, both much lower than the historical 93% of requests granted for reexamination. *See* http://www.uspto.gov/sites/default/files/documents/041615_aia_stat_graph.pdf; http://www.uspto.gov/patents/stats/inter_parte_historical_stats_roll_up_EOY2013.pdf. Although this would seem to provide more support for an accused infringer's invalidity argument at the preliminary injunction stage, few courts have grappled with this issue. The court in *Power Survey, LLC v. Premier Utility Services, LLC*, No. 13-5670, 2015 WL 687716, 2015 U.S. Dist. LEXIS 19139, at *6 (D.N.J. Feb. 18, 2015), for example, denied the defendant's motion to reconsider a preliminary injunction order after the PTAB subsequently granted the defendant's IPR petition requesting review of all claims of the patent. The court explained that during the preliminary injunction hearing, the defendant disclaimed reliance on the prior art the PTAB used to institute review. *Id.* at *4–5. The court noted that a "strategic decision to present different evidence in federal court than in an administrative court does not entitle a party to reconsideration simply because the administrative court later initiated review based on alleged facts and argument—including argument explicitly disclaimed before this Court." *Id.* at *6.

3.2.2.6.3 PTAB Cancellation of Rejection of Claims

Where the reexamination proceeding has progressed beyond a grant, and some or all patent claims have been rejected by the PTO, such evidence should weigh in the court's analysis—although it is not dispositive of the likelihood of the patent's withstanding a validity challenge. *See Tap Pharm. Prods. v. Atrix Labs., Inc.*, No. 03 C 7822, 2004 WL 2034073, 2004 U.S. Dist. LEXIS 17118, at *8 (N.D. Ill. Aug. 26, 2004) ("Since the PTO's [reexamination] proceeding has only passed its first stages, I have had difficulty determining what bearing the PTO's preliminary invalidation of the '721 patent should have in these proceedings. At the very minimum, however, the PTO's invalidation raises a substantial question about the patent's validity and is, therefore, fatal to a motion for a preliminary injunction."). A similar analysis should apply to claims canceled in IPR, CBMR, or PGR proceedings.

Note that infringement and validity are determined on a claim-by-claim basis. It is important that the court evaluate each claim that is asserted as the basis for preliminary relief.

3.3 Temporary/Ex Parte Orders

3.3.1 Generally

As in any other case, a temporary restraining order [TRO] "is available under FRCP 65 to a [patent] litigant facing a threat of irreparable harm before a preliminary injunction hearing can be held." *Fairchild Semiconductor Corp. v. Third Dimension (3D) Semiconductor, Inc.*, 564 F. Supp. 2d 63, 66 (D. Me. 2008) (citing Charles Alan Wright & Arthur R. Miller, Federal Practice and Procedure § 2951 (3d ed. 2008)). The Supreme Court has explained that "*ex parte* temporary restraining orders are no doubt necessary in certain circumstances, but under federal law they should be restricted to serving their underlying purpose of preserving the status quo and preventing irreparable harm just so long as is necessary to hold a hearing, and no longer." *Granny Goose Foods, Inc. v. Bhd. of Teamsters Local 70*, 415 U.S. 423, 439 (1974) (citation omitted). Entering a TRO enjoining the practice of a given technology can have extreme consequences, including the complete shutdown of a competitor's business. Further, the factual and legal complexity of patent cases makes it difficult—if not impossible—for a court to make the sort of hair-trigger decisions necessary to grant a TRO application. These considerations render the Supreme Court's cautionary guidance in *Granny Goose* even more forceful in a patent case.

Consequently, as a practical matter, TROs are exceedingly rare in patent cases. With the possible exception of blatant copying of technology in a patent that has previously withstood legal challenge, TROs are almost never granted in the face of competition between legitimate businesses. Likewise, as it is most difficult for a non-practicing entity to prove irreparable harm in the time frame associated with a TRO, TROs in such cases should be similarly rare.

In evaluating an ex parte TRO application a court assesses the same four factors as for a preliminary injunction: likelihood of success on the merits, irreparable harm, balance of hardships, and public interest. A TRO may be granted only on a clear showing of *immediate* irreparable injury. Fed. R. Civ. P. 65(b)(1)(A); *Rhino Ass'n, L.P. v. Berg Mfg. and Sales Corp.*, Civil Action No. 1:04-CV-1611, Order Granting Temporary Restraining Order (Docket No. 44) (M.D. Pa. July 1, 2005) (granting a TRO where "continuing manufacture and sale of the infringing products present a *serious and immediate risk* to plaintiff of loss of good will in its customer base and of cascading and undefinable loss of revenues due to resales of the infringing products") (emphasis added). In a patent case, assessment of the merits of a TRO application will typically touch on factual and expert discovery in most, if not all, aspects of the case. The time required to address the application, therefore, often dictates that it be evaluated in the context of a later preliminary injunction hearing. *See,* *e.g.*, *Robotic Vision Sys. v. View Eng'g*, No. CV 95-7441 LGB (AJWx), 1996 WL 383900, 1996 U.S. Dist. LEXIS 11917, at *2–3 (C.D. Cal. Mar. 1, 1996), *rev'd in part, vacated in part by Robotic Vision Sys., Inc. v. View Eng'g*, 112 F.3d 1163 (Fed. Cir. 1997).

While a preliminary injunction may be issued only on notice to the adverse party, a TRO may issue without such notice. Fed. R. Civ. P. 65(a)(1), 65(b)(1). Nonetheless, where an adverse party has adequate notice of an application for a TRO, such that a meaningful adversarial hearing on the issues may be held, the court may treat an application for TRO as a motion for preliminary injunction. *See CVI/Beta Ventures v. Custom Optical Frames*, 859 F. Supp. 945, 948 (D. Md. 1994) (citing Charles Alan Wright & Arthur R. Miller, Federal Practice and Procedure, § 2951 (1973)).

3.3.2 Procedure

Courts have discretion to handle the attendant hearing, scheduling, and expedited discovery associated with TRO applications in a manner that best suits the circumstances of an individual case. The court may grant or deny the ex parte application without a hearing. Alternatively, the court may decline to rule on the TRO application until the adverse party has had an opportunity to respond. *See Chem-Tainer Indus. v. Wilkin*, No. CV 97-0829LGB(EX), 1997 WL 715014, 1997 U.S. Dist. LEXIS 17241, at *3 (C.D. Cal. Feb. 24, 1997) ("The Court declined to rule on the TRO application. Instead, the Court set a hearing . . . and ordered Chem-Tainer's counsel to serve the papers on Defendant that same day . . . and to inform Defendant of the hearing and that any opposition was due . . ."). The court may also decide to combine the hearings and discovery for the TRO with a pending preliminary injunction application. *Robotic Vision Sys. v. View Eng'g*, 1996 WL 383900, 1996 U.S. Dist. LEXIS 11917, at *2–3 (C.D. Cal. Mar. 1, 1996) *rev'd on other grounds*, 112 F.3d 1163 (Fed. Cir. 1997).

In determining the proper procedure, courts balance the heavy burden on the parties—often the required expedited discovery will require double and triple tracking of depositions—against the necessity for quick resolution of the applications. As discussed further below, assessing the merits of a TRO or preliminary injunction application could conceivably require discovery into nearly every aspect of the case. At a minimum, plaintiffs will likely seek documents and deposition testimony regarding the structure and function of accused products (relevant to infringement allegations) and market and financial data (relative to irreparable harm). Defendants will seek discovery relating to the plaintiff's patents, including their prosecution, and possibly the sale of plaintiff's products covered by the patents (relevant to invalidity and potential on-sale bar allegations). Defendants may also seek financial data relevant to the amount of bond necessary should a preliminary injunction issue. Both parties may offer experts for both claim construction (if claim terms have particular meaning in the industry) and infringement.

Thus, from a practical standpoint, for a court to consider a TRO application, the parties must focus the issues to permit an expeditious resolution of the TRO application. Even if the issues are focused, factual complexity almost always precludes meaningful TRO relief. Therefore, the TRO application usually is best treated as a preliminary injunction application. Depending on information developed in initial discovery and on the actions of the parties, the court may modify the discovery, briefing, and hearing schedules. *See CVI/Beta Ventures*, 859 F. Supp. at 946–48 (describing the court's evolving approach to discovery and hearing related to a TRO application, in which the court ultimately treated the request as a preliminary injunction application because the defendant was determined to have notice and opportunity to respond). At all times, the objective under Federal Rule of Civil Procedure 65(b) should be to preserve the status quo, protect the rights of the patent holder, and "ensure that parties subject to [TROs] are given an opportunity to present their case as soon as possible." *Id.* (granting preliminary injunction, but ordering a hearing for reconsideration after further discovery was completed).

3.4 Discovery

Discovery relating to a preliminary injunction application can touch on nearly every substantive issue in a patent case. Claim construction is usually required, which in turn may require expert discovery if certain terms have special meaning in the art. The plaintiff may require fact and expert testimony as to the defendant's products, including their development, structure, and operation. The plaintiff's irreparable harm allegations may require fact and expert discovery as to market conditions and the defendant's financial condition. The defendant's invalidity and unenforceability allegations may require discovery into the prosecution of the plaintiff's patents (especially where the defendant asserts inequitable conduct) and sales by the plaintiff of products covered by the patent as relevant to a potential on-sale bar argument. The defendants might also seek financial data relevant to the amount of bond necessary should a TRO or preliminary injunction issue.

The initial challenge for a court confronting a preliminary injunction application in a patent case is balancing the need to resolve the application based on a reasonably full record against the twin considerations that a preliminary injunction proceeding needs to be resolved expeditiously and that the parties need to conduct their business in the interim. Where a preliminary injunction application is filed prior to the initiation of discovery, expedited discovery may be ordered upon motion or stipulation. *See Semitool, Inc. v. Tokyo Elec. Am.*, 208 F.R.D. 273, 276 (N.D. Cal. 2002) (explaining that "good cause [for expedited discovery] may be found where the need for expedited discovery, in consideration of the administration of justice, outweighs the prejudice to the responding party. It should be noted that courts have recognized that good cause is frequently found in cases involving claims of infringement;" granting motion where plaintiff sought narrowly defined "core" discovery but denying motion as to third-party expedited discovery); Fed. R. Civ. P. 26(d).

The parties should be encouraged to confer and stipulate with respect to a discovery and hearing schedule to the extent feasible. In finalizing the schedule, courts consider whether the parties have already engaged in discovery in the instant litigation or a related matter, the complexity of the technology, any delay by the plaintiff in bringing its preliminary injunction application (which weighs against aggressive expediting), *see Power Integrations, Inc. v. BCD Semiconductor Corp.*, C.A. No. 07-633-JJF-LPS, 2008 WL 496446, 2008 U.S. Dist. LEXIS 16021, at *3–4 (D. Del. Feb. 11, 2008), the necessity for expert discovery, and other considerations unique to the case. Depending on the facts, discovery and hearing may be set on a shortened schedule or may need to be delayed for weeks or even months. *Compare Power Integrations*, 2008 WL 496446, 2008 U.S. Dist. LEXIS 16021, at *3–4 (finding expedited discovery appropriate and setting time to preliminary injunction hearing of eighty-five days) *with Furminator, Inc. v. Ontel Prods. Corp.*, 246 F.R.D. 579, 581 (E.D. Mo. 2007) (granting plaintiff's request for expedited discovery and setting the hearing for February 14, after plaintiff filed motion on January 24).

The general strategies for patent case management apply here, but with even greater force. Courts should use every means to encourage the parties to focus the issues and should keep a watchful eye for signs that the parties are using litigation tactics as a business lever: attempting to gain access to a competitor's confidential business information, disrupting a competitor's business with burdensome discovery, or driving a competitor out of business by running up litigation bills—a particular concern where one or both parties is a small or new company.[3] For purposes of the preliminary injunction, the court should, therefore, consider strictly limiting:

1. the number of patent claims and prior art references that may be asserted
2. the number of claim terms that will be construed
3. the number of depositions that may be taken (Consider allowing each side to take one 30(b)(6) deposition—on the accused product and on the prosecution of the patents—without precluding later 30(b)(6) depositions. *See, e.g.*, *Eyeticket Corp.*, 155 F. Supp. 2d at 530 (E.D. Va. 2001) (allowing limited expedited discovery in which each party was permitted to depose two key witnesses prior to the preliminary injunction hearing).)
4. the number and nature of document requests (This is an area particularly subject to abuse.)
5. the issues to be considered (To the extent appropriate, screen out financial argument. Sales and profits likely need not be discovered absent a party's convincing showing that lost sales could not be remedied in damages. If financial discovery is necessary to determine a proper bond amount, consider bifurcating this issue pending a decision on the application. Also, consider whether the preliminary injunction briefing and argument need to address the doctrine of equivalents. (Where prosecution history has limited a patent's scope on a key claim term, a patent holder could face a very high bar in showing likelihood of success on the merits of a doctrine of equivalents argument.))

---

3. Note that because much of the business information in a patent case is highly confidential, it will likely be necessary for the court to enter a protective order before PI discovery can go forward. On protective orders generally, see § 4.2.5.

3.5 Hearing

3.5.1 Whether to Conduct a Hearing

As with other aspects of case management, a court has considerable discretion as to the handling of a hearing for a TRO or preliminary injunction application. Under Federal Rule of Civil Procedure 65, a court need not have a hearing on a TRO application. Rule 65 is not explicit about whether the court must have a hearing to consider a preliminary injunction. However, as a practical matter given the complexity of patent TRO and preliminary injunction applications, courts generally hear arguments, which is the better practice.

A hearing offers the opportunity to move the case forward significantly. Evidence received on a preliminary injunction motion that would be admissible at trial "becomes part of the trial record and need not be repeated at trial." Fed. R. Civ. P. 65(a)(2). Note, however, that, to the extent a party has preserved the right to jury trial, the evidence may have to be repeated to the jury if the matter goes to trial. *See* Fed. R. Civ. P. 65(a)(2) Advisory Committee's Note ("[T]he jury will have to hear all the evidence bearing on its verdict, even if some part of the evidence has already been heard by the judge alone on the application for the preliminary injunction.").

As discussed further in § 3.6, the court may dispose of certain issues by advancing their trial on the merits. *See id.*

3.5.2 Notice and Scheduling

"The court may issue a preliminary injunction only on notice to the adverse party." Fed. R. Civ. P. 65(a)(1). Notice must be effective as to all parties that will be bound by the order. Fed. R. Civ. P. 65(d) ("[An order granting an injunction] is binding upon the parties to the action, their officers, agents, servants, employees, and attorneys, and upon those persons in active concert or participation with them who receive actual notice of the order by personal service or otherwise."); *see also Dentsply Int'l, Inc. v. Kerr Mfg. Co.*, 42 F. Supp. 2d 385, 394–400 (D. Del. 1999) (analyzing whether nonparty was bound by injunction and concluding that nonparty was in privity with party and was therefore bound).

If expedited discovery relating to the preliminary injunction application is an issue, the preliminary injunction hearing may be set following a conference with the parties during which the court should explore the discovery that will be necessary to address the merits of the application. *See* § 3.4 (discussing strategies for focusing this discovery). Discovery for preliminary injunction applications is necessarily expedited and can be quite burdensome. Nevertheless, as discussed in § 3.4, it is not uncommon for this discovery to take several weeks or longer because of the breadth of fact and expert discovery that may be required for a preliminary injunction application in a new patent case.

3.5.3 Evidentiary Showing—What to Expect

As discussed above, the analysis of a preliminary injunction application can touch on nearly every aspect of a patent case. Evidence that will likely be brought to the court during the preliminary injunction process includes:

- *Claim construction:* fact evidence as to the prosecution of the patent and any limitations imposed on claim meaning and/or available equivalents; expert testimony as to special meanings of claim terms in the industry.
- *Infringement:* fact and expert evidence as to structure and operation of accused products and comparison of accused products to patent claim terms.
- *Validity/enforceability:* fact and expert evidence as to allegedly invalidating prior art references; fact evidence as to alleged inequitable conduct or other unenforceability defenses.
- *Irreparable harm:* fact and expert evidence as to market conditions and growth projections, status of the parties in the industry (e.g., market leader, new entrant to market, etc.), special circumstances (e.g., approaching holiday sales or changes in the market brought on by legislation or regulatory action).
- *Other:* evidence relating to public interest, such as the public's need for an accused medical device or pharmaceutical; evidence relating to the proper bond amount.

3.6 Rule 65 Trial

As can be seen from the above, the bulk of the substance of a patent case will be in play in deciding a preliminary injunction motion. Depending on the facts of a given case, one or more issues may be ripe for final disposition, even at this early stage.

For example, a defendant may argue that its product is noninfringing because it is clear that a particular claim element is not in its revised product and that plaintiff is using patent litigation as a tactic to disrupt or destroy defendant's business. In such a case, Rule 65 presents the court and the litigation "victim" with an opportunity in the form of an early trial on the merits, through consolidation with the preliminary injunction hearing. *See* Fed. R. Civ. P. 65(a)(2). Likewise, where a prior art reference or inequitable conduct allegation appears convincingly to render a patent invalid or unenforceable, a Rule 65 trial may be warranted.

While an early trial may require front loading of casework by both the parties and the court, the benefits can be substantial. First, while the result of a preliminary injunction motion provides the parties early notice of the relative strengths of their cases, a Rule 65 trial crystallizes the parties' positions with respect to the issues it resolves—and these issues tend to be pivotal. The plaintiff who loses on infringement on its "best" claim, or the defendant who loses on its "best shot" invalidating prior art-reference will have strong reasons to reassess whether pressing forward with the litigation is wise, or whether settlement and/or dismissal of the case makes better business sense. Second, the court's offer of a Rule 65 trial gives an opportunity to force the hand of litigants that are misusing the litigation process. Foot-dragging by a plaintiff that claims an infringement case is simple and straightforward may be a sign of misleading representations or pursuit of ulterior motives. Finally, the evidence presented during the trial becomes part of the record of the case. Nonetheless, the evidence may have to be repeated to the jury if the matter goes to trial. *See* Fed. R. Civ. P. 65(a)(2) Advisory Committee's Note; § 3.5.1.

A district court may order advancement of trial and consolidation with a preliminary injunction hearing on its own motion. Fed. R. Civ. P. 65(a)(2). Of course, the decision to do so must be tempered by due process considerations. *See, e.g.*, *Pughsley v. 3750 Lake Shore Drive Coop. Bldg.*, 463 F.2d 1055, 1057 (7th Cir. 1972). Parties "should be given a clear opportunity to object, or to suggest special procedures, if a consolidation is to be ordered." *Id.*

The answers to the following questions may help the district court and the parties determine whether to proceed with the preliminary injunction motion or an expedited trial on the merits:

1. What is the urgency that requires a prompt hearing?
2. Can complete relief be provided if the case proceeds to an expedited trial on the merits?
3. Will the plaintiff be able to post an injunction bond?
4. Can a standstill agreement be worked out between the parties, with or without a bond?
5. How long will it take the parties to be ready for a trial on the merits?
6. How long will it take the parties to be ready for a preliminary injunction hearing?
7. Can the parties afford the possibility of two rounds of discovery, two trials, and two appeals?
8. Will there be a jury demand?
9. Does it make sense to bifurcate liability from the damages remedy?
10. How much time will a trial on the merits take compared to a hearing on the preliminary injunction?

Morton Denlow, *The Motion for a Preliminary Injunction: Time for a Uniform Federal Standard*, 22 Rev. Litig. 495, 536 (2003).[4]

3.7 Bond

> No restraining order or preliminary injunction shall issue except upon the giving of security by the applicant, in such sum as the court deems proper, for the payment of such costs and damages as may be incurred or suffered by any party who is found to have been wrongfully enjoined or restrained.

Fed. R. Civ. P. 65(c). Because the amount of the security bond is a procedural issue not unique to patent law, the amount is determined according to the law of the dis-

4. The author was, at the time that he wrote this article, a U.S. magistrate judge for the Northern District of Illinois.

trict court's regional circuit. *See Int'l Game Tech. v. WMS Gaming Inc.*, No. 98-1361, 1999 U.S. App. LEXIS 22971217 F.3d 850, at *4 n.1 (Fed. Cir. Sept. 3, 1999) (unpublished opinion; decision without published opinion at 217 F.3d 850 (Fed. Cir. Sept. 3, 1999)).

The amount of a bond rests within the sound discretion of a trial court. *See Sanofi-Synthelabo*, 470 F.3d at 1384–85 (citing *Doctor's Assocs., Inc. v. Distajo*, 107 F.3d 126, 136 (2d Cir. 1997)).

A court may exercise discretion in the procedure it follows for argument and decision on a bond amount. Briefing and argument may be made along with briefing on the merits or may be postponed until after the decision on the injunction. *See, e.g., Eisai Co. v. Teva Pharms. USA, Inc.*, Civ. Nos. 05-5727 (HAA)(ES), 07-5489 (HAA)(ES), 2008 WL 1722098, 2008 U.S. Dist. LEXIS 33747 at *38 (D.N.J. Mar. 28, 2008) ("[T]he Court will require Eisai to post security in an amount sufficient to compensate Teva should the injunction later be found to be unjustified. Therefore, the parties shall submit evidence concerning the proper amount of bond."); *Warrior Sports, Inc. v. STX, L.L.C.*, 2008 WL 783768, 2008 U.S. Dist. LEXIS 21387 at *1 (E.D. Mich. Mar. 19, 2008) ("[T]he Court grants the Motion, but in order to determine the appropriate amount of bond, holds it in abeyance pending receipt of Defendant's estimated lost profits."). Of course, if briefing on this issue is postponed, it should be required within a reasonably short time after an injunction is ordered, because the injunction cannot take effect until the bond is posted. *See Warrior Sports*, 2008 U.S. Dist. LEXIS 21387, at *37 (ordering submittal of lost-profits estimate five days after order granting injunction); *Eisai*, 2008 U.S. Dist. LEXIS 33747, at *38 (presenting evidence on bond amount within two weeks after an order granting injunction).

Discovery relating to bond amount is often intertwined with discovery relating to irreparable harm. However, the quantitative data necessary to evaluate the proper bond amount may require more in-depth discovery of financial documents than the irreparable harm analysis would require.

3.8 Order

3.8.1 Specificity

To withstand appeal, a court's order must comply with Rule 65's requirements which expressly address the factors considered in granting or denying the injunction. Fed. R. Civ. P. 65(d)(1)(A). It must also specifically describe the infringing actions enjoined, with reference to particular products. *See* Fed. R. Civ. P. 65(d)(1)(C). While a denial may be based on a finding that the movant has failed to demonstrate likelihood of success on the merits or irreparable harm, *see, e.g., Novo Nordisk*, 2008 WL 6098829, 2008 U.S. Dist. LEXIS 12342, a grant must be based on an assessment of both of these factors as well as the balance of harms and public interest. The structure of an order granting a preliminary injunction should systematically address each of these issues, providing the court's reasoning and conclusion. The order should also address the technology at issue as well as the scope of the injunction and the amount of the bond. The preliminary injunction order in *Oakley, Inc. v. Sunglass*

Hut Int'l, No. SA CV 01-1065 AHS, 2001 WL 1683252, 2001 U.S. Dist. LEXIS 23572 (C.D. Cal. Dec. 7, 2001) (*aff'd, Oakley, Inc. v. Sunglass Hut Int'l*, 316 F.3d 1331, 1346 (Fed. Cir. 2003)), suggesting the following general outline, is an example of such a well-drafted order:

(1) Introductory material. Describe the parties, patents, and technology at issue. *See id.* at *6–10.

(2) Claim construction. Perform preliminary construction of key claim terms. *See id.* at *11–12. Recall that the court's construction for preliminary injunction purposes can be revisited.

(3) Likelihood of Success on the Merits:

  a. Infringement—analyze whether the accused devices have every element of any asserted claim under the court's construction. *See id.* at *10–14.

  b. Validity—analyze asserted invalidity contentions. *See id.* at *15–29.

  c. Enforceability—analyze asserted inequitable conduct arguments and/or other unenforceability arguments. *See id.* at *30–31.

  d. Conclusion—decide whether the movant has shown it will likely prevail in showing infringement and in countering opponent's invalidity and/or unenforceability arguments. *See id.* at *31.

(4) Irreparable Harm. *See id.* at *31–34. Note that the district court in *Oakley* recited a presumption of irreparable harm but also analyzed actual harm. As explained above (*see* § 3.2.2.2.1) *Robert Bosch LLC*, 659 F.3d at 1148–49, made clear irreparable harm no longer is presumed. Therefore, it is necessary for the order to analyze actual harm.

(5) Balance of Harms. *See id.* at *34.

(6) Public Interest. *See id.* at *34–35.

(7) Scope of Injunction. *Id.* at *3. Note that, while the court's description of the acts enjoined was somewhat cursory, the Federal Circuit affirmed, explaining that the enjoined party demonstrated its understanding of the enjoined acts by way of its actions in response to the similarly worded TRO. *Oakley*, 316 F.3d at 1346.

(8) Amount of Bond. *See id.* at **35–36.

A template for drafting an order granting a preliminary injunction is provided in Appendix 3.1.

Depending on the facts of the case, the court may also need to address the persons bound by the order. (*See* § 3.8.2.) As can be seen from this outline, a well-drafted order granting a preliminary injunction can be a complicated and lengthy document that is time-consuming and challenging to prepare. This is one more reason to apply the strategies described above, *see* § 3.4, to encourage the parties to narrow and focus the issues.

3.8.2 Parties Affected

A court's preliminary injunction can bind "only the following who receive actual notice . . . (A) the parties; (B) the parties' officers, agents, servants, employees, and attorney; and (C) other persons who are in active concert or participation with anyone described in [parts (A) or (B)]." Fed. R. Civ. P. 65(d)(2). In applying Rule 65(d), the Federal Circuit has emphasized that "a court may not enter an injunction against a person who has not been made a party to the case before it." *Additive Controls & Measurement Sys., Inc. v. Flowdata, Inc.*, 96 F.3d 1390, 1394 (Fed. Cir. 1996).

A court is not, however, powerless against nonparties that act to frustrate a preliminary injunction. "[T]hose who act in concert with an enjoined party may be held in contempt, but only for assisting the enjoined party in violating the injunction." *Id.* (citing *Spindelfabrik Suessen-Schurr v. Schubert & Salzer Maschinenfabrik Aktiengesellschaft*, 903 F.2d 1568, 1580–81 (Fed. Cir. 1990)); Fed. R. Civ. P. 65(d)(2)(C). As the Federal Circuit explained in a second *Additive Controls* case, "[n]on-parties may be held in contempt . . . if they either abet the defendant, or are legally identified with him." *Additive Controls*, 154 F.3d at 1351 (considering whether a resigned corporate officer was "legally identified" with a corporation and listing factors that might influence the fact-specific inquiry) (quoting *Alemite Mfg. Co. v. Staff*, 42 F.2d 832, 833 (2d Cir. 1930)); *see also Power-One, Inc. v. Artesyn Techs., Inc.*, Civ. Action No. 2:05-CV-463, 2008 WL 1746636, 2008 U.S. Dist. LEXIS 30338, at *10–11 (E.D. Tex. Apr. 11, 2008) (concluding that certain nonparties could not be named in an injunction, as they had not appeared before the court to have their rights adjudicated, but crafting an injunction that encompassed "successors in interest" to or persons "in active concert" with the named parties). While a party need not intend to violate an injunction to be found in contempt, nonparties may be found in contempt only if they are aware of the injunction and know that their acts, made in concert with an enjoined party, violate the injunction. *Additive Controls*, 154 F.3d at 1353. That is, the nonparty must know both that the acts are proscribed and that the person(s) with whom they are acting are subject to the injunction. *Id.* at 1353–54.

3.8.3 Modification

Modification of a preliminary injunction in a patent case may be necessary to address new facts or circumstances. For example, an enjoined accused infringer may place a new product on the market through which it has attempted, but failed, to design around a patent-in-suit. In such a case, the court may modify its preliminary injunction to include the manufacture and sale of the new product in the scope of enjoined actions. *See SEB S.A. v. Montgomery Ward & Co.*, 137 F. Supp. 2d 285, 287 (S.D.N.Y. 2001) ("Finding that the modified fryer infringes the '312 Patent by equivalences, this Court grants SEB further injunction relief . . . ."). Consideration of the motion for modification requires analysis of the same factors as are required for the initial grant of the preliminary injunction. *See id.* at 287–91. The objective in modifying the injunction should be to maintain the status quo. *See id.* ("Enjoining the sale of the modified fryer will restore the status quo.") (citing *Atlas Powder*, 773 F.2d at

1231). Courts may also modify preliminary injunction orders to encompass additional, potentially infringing products that come to light during discovery, include newly issued patents, or remove expired patents.

3.9 Appellate Review

A district court's decision on a motion for preliminary injunction is usually immediately appealable, whether it has decided to grant or deny the injunction. 28 U.S.C. § 1292(a)(1).[5] As an abstract principle, the grant or denial of a preliminary injunction is a procedural issue that is not unique to the exclusive jurisdiction of the Federal Circuit. *Tex. Instruments, Inc. v. Tessera, Inc.*, 231 F.3d 1325, 1327 (Fed. Cir. 2000). When reviewing "procedural matters not unique to the areas that are exclusively assigned to the Federal Circuit," the Federal Circuit generally applies the procedural law of the regional circuit where the case originated. *Id.* (quoting *Nat'l Presto Indus., Inc. v. W. Bend Co.*, 76 F.3d 1185, 1188 n.2 (Fed. Cir. 1996)). However, Federal Circuit precedent applies "to uniformly deal with procedural matters arising from substantive issues in areas of law within the unique jurisdiction of this circuit"—such as the grant or denial of a preliminary injunction in a patent case. *Id.*

"A decision to grant or deny a preliminary injunction pursuant to 35 U.S.C. § 283 is within the sound discretion of the district court," reviewed for abuse of discretion. *Sanofi-Synthelabo*, 470 F.3d 1368, 1374 (Fed. Cir. 2006). "[A] decision granting a preliminary injunction will be overturned on appeal only if it is established 'that the court made a clear error of judgment in weighing relevant factors or exercised its discretion based upon an error of law or clearly erroneous factual findings.'" *Id.* (quoting *Genentech, Inc. v. Novo Nordisk A/S*, 108 F.3d 1361, 1364 (Fed. Cir. 1997)). However, to the extent a district court's decision is based upon an issue of law, that issue is reviewed de novo. *Id.* Such issues include preliminary claim constructions and obviousness determinations. *Oakley*, 316 F.3d at 1339.

3.9.1 Writ Review

Instead of appealing, a party may seek a writ of mandamus from the Federal Circuit ordering imposition or dissolution of a preliminary injunction. "The remedy of mandamus is available only in extraordinary situations to correct a clear abuse of discretion or usurpation of judicial power. A party seeking a writ bears the burden of proving that it has no other means of attaining the relief desired, and that the right to issuance of the writ is clear and indisputable." *Razor USA LLC v. ASA Prods., Inc.*, Nos. 01-1080, 636, 637, 638, 2000 WL 1819400, 2000 U.S. App. LEXIS 33182, at *4–5 (Fed. Cir. Nov. 22, 2000) (unpublished opinion) (citations omitted). Accordingly, a party dissatisfied with the outcome of a motion for preliminary injunction should

5. A decision to grant or deny a TRO is not usually appealable. Fed. R. Civ. P. 65; *Nikken USA, Inc. v. Robinson-May, Inc.*, 1999 WL 1046620, 1999 U.S. App. LEXIS 31925 (Fed. Cir. Oct. 25, 1999) (unpublished case).

first seek to stay the result and file a notice of appeal. *In re Lumenis, Inc.*, 89 F. App'x 255, 256 (Fed. Cir. 2004) ("The proper procedure for seeking to stay or vacate an injunction is to file a notice of appeal and a motion in the district court for a stay of the injunction, pending appeal.") (unpublished opinion).

3.9.2 Stays

A party subjected to a preliminary injunction may ask the district court to stay the injunction pending appeal. *See Razor USA LLC*, 2000 U.S. App. LEXIS 33182, at *4–5 (Fed. Cir. Nov. 22, 2000) (unpublished opinion). "While an appeal is pending . . . from an order . . . that grants, dissolves or denies an injunction, the court may suspend, [or] modify" the injunction. Fed. R. Civ. P. 62(c). Whether to issue a stay of enforcement of a preliminary injunction is within the sound discretion of the district court. *Abbott Labs. v. Sandoz, Inc.*, 500 F. Supp. 2d 846, 849 (N.D. Ill. 2007) (citing Fed. R. Civ. P. 62(c)).

"To obtain a stay, pending appeal, a movant must establish a strong likelihood of success on the merits [of the appeal] or, failing that, nonetheless demonstrate a substantial case on the merits provided that the harm factors militate in its favor." *Eon-Net, L.P. v. Flagstar Bancorp, Inc.*, 222 F. App'x 970, 971–72 (Fed. Cir. 2007) (citing *Hilton v. Braunskill*, 481 U.S. 770, 778 (1987)). In deciding whether to grant a stay, pending appeal, the court weighs four factors: "(1) whether the stay applicant has made a strong showing that he is likely to succeed on the merits; (2) whether the applicant will be irreparably injured absent a stay; (3) whether issuance of the stay will substantially injure the other parties interested in the proceeding; and (4) where the public interest lies." *Standard Havens Prods., Inc. v. Gencor Indus., Inc.*, 897 F.2d 511, 512 (Fed. Cir. 1990) (quoting *Hilton*, 481 U.S. at 776).

As with preliminary injunction determinations, courts apply a flexible approach: "the more likely the plaintiff is to win, the less heavily need the balance of harms weigh in his favor; the less likely he is to win, the more need it weigh in his favor." *Id.* (quoting *Roland Mach. Co. v. Dresser Indus., Inc.*, 749 F.2d 380, 387–88 (7th Cir. 1984)). "Thus, the four factors can effectively be merged and a sliding scale approach is utilized, which states: 'in considering whether to grant a stay pending appeal, this court assesses movant's chances for success on appeal and weighs the equities as they affect the parties and the public.'" *Honeywell Int'l, Inc. v. Universal Avionics Sys. Corp.*, 397 F. Supp. 2d 537, 548 (D. Del. 2005) (quoting *Standard Havens*, 897 F.2d at 513); *see also E. I. du Pont de Nemours & Co. v. Phillips Petroleum Co.*, 835 F.2d 277, 278 (Fed. Cir. 1987).

For a district court that has weighed the equitable factors and issued a preliminary injunction, it may seem unlikely that a consideration of quite similar factors could lead to a decision to stay the injunction. Changed legal or factual circumstances can, of course, change the calculus. For example, in *Standard Havens*, the Federal Circuit stayed an injunction in part because, after the trial court had entered the injunction, the Patent Office rejected all the infringed patent claims in a director-initiated reexamination. 897 F.2d at 514. Other examples could include actual or imminent substantial changes in governing patent law, such as the Supreme Court or the Federal Circuit en banc deciding to take up the "next" *KSR*, *eBay*, or *Bilski* case.

3.10 Enforcement

A party subject to an injunction will often attempt to modify its product to avoid the patent, that is, to "design around" the patent. Parties may dispute whether the redesigned product still infringes. In such cases, the patent holder will often return to the court, seeking a finding that the infringer is in contempt for having violated the injunction and an order enjoining production and sale of the redesigned product. "[A] judgment of contempt against an enjoined party for violation of an injunction against patent infringement by the making, using or selling of a modified device [requires] a finding that the modified device falls within the admitted or adjudicated scope of the claims and is, therefore, an infringement." *KSM Fastening Sys., Inc. v. H.A. Jones Co.*, 776 F.2d 1522, 1530 (Fed. Cir. 1985). Accordingly,

> [b]efore entering a finding of contempt of an injunction in a patent infringement case, a district court must address two separate questions. The first is whether a contempt hearing is an appropriate forum in which to determine whether a redesigned device infringes, or whether the issue of infringement should be resolved in a separate infringement action. That decision turns on a comparison between the original infringing product and the redesigned device. If the differences are such that "substantial open issues" of infringement are raised by the new device, then contempt proceedings are inappropriate. If contempt proceedings are appropriate, the second question the district court must resolve is whether the new accused device infringes the claims of the patent. Within those general constraints, the district court has broad discretion to determine how best to enforce its injunctive decrees.

Additive Controls, 154 F.3d at 1349 (citing *KSM*, 776 F.2d at 1530–32) (internal citations omitted).

Because expert testimony is often required to resolve the question of whether a redesign (or "workaround") still infringes, the Federal Circuit has advised that contempt proceedings are usually inappropriate to address the adequacy of the design-around effort. *Id.* at 1349–50 ("[O]ur case law suggests that the need for expert testimony counsels against the use of contempt proceedings to try infringement . . ."); *see also KSM*, 776 F.2d at 1530 ("[P]roceedings by way of contempt should not go forward if there is more than a 'colorable difference' in the accused and adjudged devices."). However, some cases are not so close. Where a redesign is found to be a "mere colorable variation" that raises "no substantial open question of infringement," a contempt proceeding may be adequate. *Additive Controls*, 154 F.3d at 1349 (affirming district court's resolution of redesign dispute through contempt proceeding and explaining that "the district court satisfied the procedural requirements of *KSM* by separately analyzing the questions whether contempt proceedings were appropriate and whether the redesigned device infringed the patent").

Appendix 3.1
Template for Order Granting a Preliminary Injunction

A. Introduction and Background

Describe the parties, patents and technology at issue. Include relevant excerpts from the patents in suit.

B. Claim Construction

Perform preliminary construction of key claim terms. Include any intrinsic or extrinsic evidence relied on for the preliminary construction.

C. Likelihood of Success on the Merits

1. Infringement

Analyze whether the accused devices have every element of any asserted claim under the court's construction.

2. Validity

Analyze asserted invalidity contentions.

3. Enforceability

Analyze asserted inequitable conduct arguments and/or other unenforceability arguments.

4. Conclusion

Decide whether movant has shown it will likely prevail in showing infringement and in countering opponent's invalidity and/or unenforceability arguments.

D. Irreparable Harm

Given that the status of the presumption of irreparable harm is presently uncertain, a court's order granting a preliminary injunction should include analysis of this factor beyond a recitation of the presumption.

E. Balance of Harms

F. Public Interest

G. Scope of Injunction

H. Amount of Bond

Chapter 4
Discovery

Discovery in patent cases can be exhaustive and exhausting for a variety of structural reasons. First, patent claims and defenses are commonly broad, justifying deep inquiry into product development and financial records. This aspect is only magnified by the emerging emphasis on electronic discovery. Not surprisingly, many technology companies make extensive use of digital technology. Second, patent litigation comes freighted with special issues such as willfulness and inequitable conduct, where concerns over privilege and work product complicate these already difficult matters. Third, the potentially consequential but unpredictable outcomes—large damage awards, the possibility of an injunction—lead counsel to demand every piece of data and sometimes avoid compromise in discovery disputes.

Discovery in patent cases should be managed carefully to promote effective dispute resolution. This chapter reviews the typical categories of information sought, explains the forces underlying discovery controversies, and notes recent developments in and approaches to electronic discovery. We examine the most common points of dispute and analyze ways of resolving them. We conclude by discussing the most common discovery motions, with particular emphasis on the court's range of discretion and suggested best practices for resolving disagreements.

4.1 Controlling Law and Standard of Review

Where issues of patent law control disposition of a discovery dispute, Federal Circuit law will apply. *Midwest Indus., Inc. v. Karavan Trailers, Inc.*, 175 F.3d 1356 (Fed. Cir. 1999). But in the vast majority of discovery matters, courts should rely on the decisions of their regional circuit interpreting the Federal Rules of Civil Procedure. As in other types of federal civil litigation, discovery rulings are reviewed under an abuse-of-discretion standard.

4.2 Scope of Patent Discovery

Issues unique to patent cases will drive much of the discovery effort. For example, a patentee will typically seek information about development of the accused product or process, marketing and sales by the defendant, including cost and profit margins, and license fees paid by the defendant for comparable technology rights. These categories typically include highly confidential commercial and technical information, kept as trade secrets by the litigants and third parties. The sensitive nature of the information can lead to discovery disputes. Moreover, because patentees usually seek to prove that infringement was willful, they will inquire into defendants' knowledge of the patents, efforts to "design around" them, and opinions of counsel about infringement (if the defendants decide to assert advice of counsel as a defense to a willfulness charge; *see* §§ 4.6.7–4.6.9).

An accused infringer in turn will focus on trying to invalidate the patent, gathering information about conception and reduction to practice of the invention, and prefiling offers for sale. Inequitable-conduct claims motivate inquiry into the record of prosecution of the patent. Finally, in the search for prior art, the defense may pursue discovery from third parties, often located in other districts or countries.

Thus patent litigation discovery tends to be broad and demanding, touches highly sensitive information, and is extremely expensive. This can lead to highly contentious, unproductive friction between counsel. To assist courts in de-escalating these tensions, we provide some general suggestions for management of the basic discovery tools in patent litigation.

4.2.1 Proportionality

The 2015 amendments to the Federal Rules of Civil Procedure provide courts with new standards and new tools to apply to discovery disputes. The U.S. Supreme Court adopted a number of amendments, including one to Rule 26(b) that limits the scope of discovery to "any nonprivileged matter that is relevant to any party's claim or defense and proportional to the needs of the case . . . ." The "proportionality" requirement is expected to better focus courts and litigants on the expected contribution of discovery to the resolution of the case. For the same reason, the amendment deletes the sentence in Rule 26(b)(1) that states, "Relevant information need not be admissible at the trial if the discovery appears reasonably calculated to lead to the discovery of admissible evidence," and replaces it with "Information within this scope of discovery need not be admissible in evidence to be discoverable." Although the original intent of the "reasonably calculated" sentence was not to expand the scope of discovery beyond relevance, the amendment addresses the concern that it has been incorrectly used to do so.

In the note accompanying the amendment to Rule 26, the Federal Rules Advisory Committee reiterated that the parties and the district court "have a collective responsibility to consider the proportionality of all discovery and consider it in resolving discovery disputes." The amendment serves to return the proportionality calculation to Rule 26(b)(1) by moving it from present Rule 26(b)(2)(C)(iii), slightly rearranged and with one addition. This reinforces the parties' obligation under Rule 26(g) to consider these factors in making discovery requests, responses, or objections. The committee emphasized that the changes are not intended to permit a party opposing discovery to simply make a boilerplate objection that the discovery is not proportional. Because one factor to be considered in determining proportionality is the amount in controversy, district courts can benefit from a reasoned conversation with the parties about the nature and scope of the case, the amount of any damages sought, and how the case compares to other patent cases, with as much specificity as is possible. This discussion can then provide a useful baseline to judge proportionality as the case progresses, with the understanding that developments in the case or information obtained in discovery may warrant revision of what further discovery is considered "proportional." At the same time, as the committee noted, the monetary stakes are only one factor to be considered, as are the resources of the parties. District courts must apply the standards in an even-handed manner to prevent the use of discovery to wage a war of attrition or as a device of coercion.

Effective judicial management of discovery disputes is a key component of the amended rules. Not every party may have all the necessary information needed to assess the proportionality factors. To the extent possible, district courts should encourage and enforce the frank exchange of information about relevant information and the burden and expense of providing it. The initial case-management conference, following the parties' Rule 26(f) conference, is key to ensuring that discovery is on the right path. Sincere and realistic participation in discovery management by both parties and courts will help achieve the "just, speedy, and inexpensive determination" of litigation.

4.2.2 Initial Disclosures

Rule 26 disclosures present few issues unique to patent cases. At the resulting Rule 16(b) conference, competing proposals may be made regarding the number of interrogatories and depositions. Keep in mind that patent cases in general require more extensive use of discovery tools. For example, it is the unusual patent case that results in fewer than ten depositions.

As noted in Chapter 2, many districts have enacted special local rules for patent cases that require early disclosure of infringement contentions by the patentee, and of invalidity contentions by the defendant. This approach, which can be tailored for particular cases, has the advantage of collapsing into one procedure a major aspect of the "after you; no, after you" discovery impasse that otherwise occurs in patent litigation. That is not to say that requiring exchange of contentions is a panacea; the parties frequently contest the specificity of the other side's disclosure, for example. But it focuses the parties on the core issues, in particular on preparation for claim construction.

Rule 26(a)(1)(C) requires disclosure of a computation of any category of damages claimed, the documents or other evidence supporting the computation, and materials bearing on the nature and extent of injuries suffered. However, in patent cases, a plaintiff will rarely have access to this information in advance of discovery. As discussed in § 14.4.3.2, patent damages are based on profits lost by the patentee or, at a minimum, the reasonable royalty that the infringer would have paid to license the patented technology, both of which depend on the sales and offers made by the accused infringer. Thus, much of the evidence as to the patentee's damages resides in the hands of the accused infringer. Accordingly, initial disclosures as to damages typically only describe the types of damages sought (rather than providing a rough computation of the amount of damages sought) and necessarily defer disclosure of documents and other evidence to a date after discovery has been completed. In the past, such minimal disclosures were not normally considered to be deficient.

Recently, however, courts have begun requiring the parties to provide more specificity earlier in the case. As discussed more fully in § 2.6.6, an early disclosure of damages theories can, among other things, help promote settlement and can flag potential legal issues that may prompt early *Daubert* motions and early motions for summary judgment. Furthermore, the identification of specific damages theories early in the case may help identify areas for discovery. *See, e.g.*, §§ 2.6.6, 4.6.10. Such early disclosures are increasingly important as developing patent damages standards have led in recent years to an increase in the volume of challenges to damages theories and evidence that are raised, invariably, right before trial. Of course, requiring the patentee to provide an early damages disclosure is likely to be effective only if the accused infringer provides an even earlier disclosure of information about its business. This ensures that the patentee's disclosure can take into account information held only by the accused infringer. By requiring parties to exchange damages contentions, and perhaps by taking other measures, such as a shortened damages-related discovery period aimed at accelerating timelines for damages-related issues, courts can frontload more of these disputes and thereby provide themselves with a wider range of practical options for resolving them. Moreover, an early damages estimate can help courts weigh the proportionality factors that pertain to discovery.

4.2.3 Requests for Production of Documents

Reflecting the broad scope of activities relevant to patent cases, it is common for litigants to propound 100 or more document requests. Document requests typically reach into nearly every facet of a party's business, including product research and development, customer service and support, sales, marketing, accounting, and legal affairs. Indeed, for a smaller company that offers a single product line accused of infringing a patent, the document requests may well encompass the vast majority of records ever created in the course of the company's business. The documents must be collected in hard copy form from custodians in nearly every department and in electronic form from both the company's active computer files and all readily accessible archives.

The costs of document production include legal fees for collecting and processing the documents. The documents must be reviewed for privilege and to provide confidentiality designations to protect the party's trade secrets and other confidential information. These fees can rapidly escalate into the millions of dollars for medium to large companies.

Document production also disrupts businesses. It may take several months for counsel working with document custodians and literally hundreds of temporary-employee document reviewers to identify and produce responsive documents. Hard-copy documents must then be removed from the custodians for a period of time for copying. Electronic documents in the company's active computer system may be more readily copied once they are identified, but the effort to pinpoint the relevant documents and copy them distracts the company's information technology (IT) personnel from their ordinary duties. Documents in a company's archives require substantially more time from IT personnel. Identification of responsive documents first requires retrieval of archival tapes or drives, loading the drives, possibly reading the drives using obsolete software, and often searching for responsive documents in file systems created by personnel no longer at the company. In addition, companies often have stores of electronic information that are not centrally maintained—laptop hard drives, for example—that may be difficult to locate or may have been lost before litigation began. An inventor's laptop may have been provisioned to another employee when the inventor upgraded to a new machine; yet relevant data may still exist on a currently unused portion of the laptop's hard drive, unknown to anyone. It can be expensive in absolute terms to find and produce such data, and the ultimate value of the data to the litigation may not justify that cost. The difference in patent litigants' cost/benefit positions often spurs discovery disputes.

In addition, patent litigation often requires the production of technical information that is highly sensitive and difficult to reproduce for production. Some technical information, such as semiconductor schematics, can only be reviewed in native format using proprietary software that is itself valuable and sensitive. Such information may need to be reviewed on-site on the producing parties' computers. Computer source code is also highly sensitive[1] and may need to be reviewed in native format. Often it is produced on a stand-alone computer, unconnected to the Internet and in a secure location, and with limitations imposed on the number of pages that may be printed.

Financial information related to damages is also viewed as highly sensitive and can be difficult to produce. Often in lieu of the underlying financial documents (such as numerous invoices), companies produce reports from their financial databases. They must agree on which categories of information will be produced from these databases or come to terms with the fact that some categories of information cannot be generated by such systems.

Third-party confidential documents, such as patent licenses, are also usually relevant to the damages case, and third-party technical documents can be relevant to the liability case (for example, if a third party makes the accused chip). The production of these documents often requires permission from third parties, the negotiation of protective orders, or even compulsory process and motions practice.

In short, document production can be extremely painful and costly for patent litigants. Document requests in patent cases usually generate multiple motions to compel and/or motions for protective orders. Courts can facilitate more effective document collection and production processes by:

- Reviewing the parties' electronic discovery plan at the case-management conference, as required by Rule 26.
- Requiring the parties to meet and confer to narrow document requests and to document their efforts in any motion to compel.
- Requiring the parties to file a letter brief seeking permission to file a motion to compel or requiring a pre-motion telephonic conference with the Court or with a magistrate or special master prior to the filing of a motion to compel.
- Placing a limitation on the number of document requests permitted per side.

4.2.3.1 Nonparty Subpoena Requests

Nonparty subpoenas are routinely served as part of patent litigation. Federal Rule of Civil Procedure 45 governs nonparty discovery. This rule protects against the disclosure of privileged or other protected matter and the imposition of undue burdens. However, nonparties must otherwise comply with subpoenas, which can involve significant time and expense. Even challenging a subpoena can require considerable effort.

One remedy for nonparties in such situations is cost-shifting. In cases where the court believes the subpoena imposes significant expense on the nonparty, it may

1. Software companies typically distribute their computer programs solely in machine-readable object code (binary) format, while keeping the human-readable source code proprietary. Typcially, the great difficulty of decompiling object code into source code enables the source code form of computer programs to qualify as a trade secret. Control of access to source code can be of tremendous strategic importance to software companies.

shift enough of the cost to the party seeking discovery so that the net cost to the nonparty is "nonsignificant." *See, e.g.*, *Legal Voice v. Stormans Inc.*, 738 F.3d 1178 (9th Cir. 2013); *Linder v. Calero-Portocarrero*, 251 F.3d 178 (D.C. Cir. 2001). Whether or not a cost or fee is "significant" is a discretionary matter for the district court, but at least one district court has ruled that attorneys' fees may be considered as a cost of compliance. Order Regarding Callwave and Location Labs' Joint Discovery Dispute Letter at ECF No. 32, *Callwave Commc'n v. Wavemarket Inc.*, No. 35, C 14-80112 JSW (LB) (N.D. Cal. Aug. 29, 2014).

4.2.4 Interrogatories

The Federal Rules of Civil Procedure have a default limit of twenty-five interrogatories per party. In their joint case-management statement, parties often make a joint request for additional interrogatories. These requests should typically be granted as the scope of subject matter in patent litigation is quite broad. Because patent litigation often includes multiple plaintiffs and defendants, however, courts should consider imposing an interrogatory limit per side, rather than per party.

The case-focusing benefit of interrogatories can often be swamped by premature use of contention interrogatories that waste the parties' efforts before meaningful responses can be developed based on completion of fact and expert discovery. *See, e.g.*, *In re Convergent Techs. Sec. Litig.*, 108 F.R.D. 328, 337 (N.D. Cal. 1985) (observing that "there is substantial reason to believe that the *early* knee-jerk filing of sets of contention interrogatories that systematically track all the allegations in an opposing party's pleadings is a serious form of discovery abuse. Such comprehensive sets of contention interrogatories can be almost mindlessly generated, can be used to impose great burdens on opponents, and can generate a great deal of counterproductive friction between parties and counsel."). Conversely, however, appropriately timed contention interrogatories (i.e., after a meaningful opportunity for discovery) can help streamline discovery and flag potential disputes early enough to seek judicial resolution well before trial. This is particularly true in districts that have not adopted patent local rules requiring exchanges of infringement and invalidity contentions. In addition, contention interrogatories provide another vehicle for courts to require parties to disclose their damages theories early enough in the case that fundamental disputes about the viability or legality of damages theories are not relegated to the eve of trial (i.e., during fact discovery)—provided, of course, that responses are not required so early that the answering party has not yet obtained damages-related fact discovery from the opposing party. As discussed further below, requiring complete answers to contention interrogatories should typically be postponed until the late stages of fact discovery. Courts should also be mindful of the fact that some "contentions" are a matter of expert opinion (e.g., what figure constitutes a "reasonable" royalty, in contrast to an established royalty), and should consider giving the parties leave to supplement their contention interrogatory responses at a date after the completion of expert discovery. A court can prevent the all-too-common disputes as to when contention interrogatories should be answered by setting a date (or a series of dates) in the case-management order for the exchange of responses to these interrogatories, such as a date for initial responses and a date after close of fact discovery for final responses. Section 4.6.3 discusses motion practice relating to contention interrogatories.

4.2.5 Depositions

Federal Rule of Civil Procedure 30(a)(2)(A) limits to ten the number of depositions that may be taken by a party without leave of court. Again, however, as a result of the breadth of discovery in patent cases, and in spite of the more extensive mandatory disclosure requirements imposed by patent local rules, litigants often seek to take in excess of twenty depositions to develop their case, and may legitimately need more than the presumptive ten depositions allowed under Rule 30. The court should strongly encourage the parties to reach mutual agreement in their Rule 26(f) proposed discovery plan regarding the number of depositions or cumulative hours that will be allowed without court order. Absent agreement, a limit should be set to promote the parties' efficient use of the depositions. A limit of fifteen to twenty depositions per side, or about 100 hours, typically provides the parties with plenty of opportunity to cover the major issues in a case. Many judges set significantly lower presumptive limits (e.g., 40 hours per side), allowing the parties to petition for more time where justified. The most common practice is to apply these limits to fact discovery, since expert depositions tend to be self-regulating and do not involve inconvenience to the parties themselves.

The one-person/one-day limitation of Rule 30(d)(1) should presumptively apply in the absence of a showing of real need for more time (e.g., if an inventor also has a role in the business). The 30(b)(6) depositions of parties in patent litigation are, however, often critical to the case. Typically, these depositions can encompass highly technical and/or detailed information spanning the course of years or even decades. It is often effective to allow 30(b)(6) depositions to continue for more than a single day. However, to prevent runaway 30(b)(6) depositions, the court can also require that each day of 30(b)(6) deposition counts as a separate deposition for purposes of the per-side deposition limit. Alternatively, a limit on the total number of deposition hours also helps avoid disputes over how many "depositions" a 30(b)(6) deposition counts as, when it encompasses more than one topic.

Often, in noticing a 30(b)(6) deposition, a party will seek testimony on its opponent's contentions on issues of infringement and invalidity. Courts split on whether such information can be gathered by deposition or is best left to interrogatory responses. *Compare B & H Mfg., Inc. v. Foster-Forbes Glass Co.*, 143 F.R.D. 664 (N.D. Ind. 1992), *with McCormick-Morgan, Inc. v. Teledyne Indus., Inc.*, 765 F. Supp. 611 (N.D. Cal. 1991). Given that a party's contentions on infringement and invalidity issues are often in flux until after claim construction and expert discovery, objections to depositions on these issues are usually well founded. The better course of action is to address a party's contentions through interrogatory responses while limiting deposition testimony to factual matters underlying a party's contentions.

4.2.6 Protective Orders—Handling of Confidential Documents

As noted in § 2.1.2, most patent cases involve important trade secrets requiring the early entry of a protective order. As we explored there, many districts have developed default protective orders that go into effect immediately upon the filing of a patent case or soon thereafter upon a motion of a party. These rules enable the discovery process to begin promptly.

The default protective orders contained in Appendix 2.2 provide a range of balanced alternatives for protecting trade secrets while enabling discovery to proceed. Most sophisticated parties will typically want to customize the protective order and will generally agree relatively quickly on an order best tailored to their particular circumstances. The expectation that the court will enter a default protective order often facilitates consensus among the parties.

The following sections address common disputes that arise with respect to protective orders: (1) overdesignation of confidential documents, (2) claw-back provisions, and (3) prosecution bars.

4.2.6.1 Overdesignation of Confidential Documents

Disputes can arise over restrictions on access by particular party representatives. For example, one party may wish to have certain technical information available to an employed engineer or scientist and to provide financial data to one of its financial officers. Exercising discretion in these disputes will require the court to weigh several considerations, such as the current sensitivity of the data, the difficulty of detecting any misuse, and the level of direct competition that might be put at risk. In addition, the court may want to consider practical issues such as the number of non-lawyers that are proposed to have access and the administrative challenge of keeping track of who has had access to what information.

On the other hand, parties often overdesignate confidential information—that is, documents that do not require protection are designated as confidential or highly confidential. This sometimes occurs because the producing party faces a significant challenge in reviewing hundreds of thousands of pages of documents not just for privilege but also for making judgment calls on the level of appropriate access. In an effort to be cost-effective and efficient, parties often "block designate" files from a particular source as highly confidential. For example, documents collected from a lead research engineer's file labeled "Strategy for Development of New XYZ Product" might reasonably be assumed to be of a highly confidential nature and might be block designated as such. Inevitably, however, this will result in some overdesignation, such as for published articles included in the files or e-mails setting up meetings. In such cases, de-designation of specific documents upon reasonable request of the receiving party is the best and simplest solution.

In cases where designation disputes arise, parties should be strongly encouraged to resolve them without court intervention. Requiring a motion to focus on particular documents is one way to prompt parties to reach their own solution. It is the rare document that absolutely must be provided to an executive of a party's adversary (not just outside counsel) for that executive to make a decision about settlement, and yet would cause irreparable harm to the producing party if its adversary's executive had access to it. If parties are required to justify their positions on a document-by-document basis, one side or the other will often see that the dispute does not warrant court intervention. If the parties persist, referral to a special master or magistrate judge, depending on local practice, may be appropriate. In extreme cases, a party's overzealous confidentiality designations may warrant sanctions. *See In re Violation of Rule 28(d)*, 635 F.3d 1352, 1355–56 (Fed. Cir. 2011) (sanctioning parties, in briefing before the Federal Circuit, for having designated as confidential case citations, legal arguments, and quotations from publicly available opinions; noting public policy of access to court proceedings). The heavy burden of considering motions to seal has led some judges in the Northern District of California to be skeptical of such requests. *See, e.g.*, Order Denying Administrative Motion to File Under Seal, *Innovative Automation LLC v. Kaleidescape, Inc.*, No. 3:13-CV-05651 (N.D. Cal. Oct. 17, 2014); Order Re: Motion to Seal, *Apple Inc. v. Samsung Elecs. Co., Ltd.*, No. 5:11-CV-01846 (N.D. Cal. Nov. 18, 2014).

4.2.6.2 Claw-Back Provisions for Privileged Documents

Another common consequence of the voluminous document discovery in patent litigation is inadvertent production of documents protected by attorney–client privilege and/or work-product doctrine. Such inadvertent production may occur despite diligent efforts by a party to prevent it. For example, large teams of attorneys, including contract attorneys unfamiliar with the actors in a case, may be used to complete document processing quickly. In such cases, a document may be inadvertently produced because the attorney reviewing it did not understand that it was generated by or at the direction of a party's counsel.

Federal Rule of Civil Procedure 26(b)(5)(B) addresses this situation. A party that believes it has unintentionally produced privileged information may give notice to the receiving party, who must then "promptly return, sequester, or destroy the specified information and any copies it has" and "take reasonable steps to retrieve" any information it has already distributed or disclosed to others. Fed. R. Civ. P. 26(b)(5)(B). Until the claim of inadvertent production is resolved, the producing party is required to preserve the information and the receiving party may not use or disclose it.

Courts should consider including in their protective orders a so-called claw-back provision, which provides some procedural structure to the substantive command of Rule 26. Such provisions often require that a receiving party promptly return or destroy, rather than sequester, allegedly inadvertently produced privileged documents. If a receiving party disputes the privileged nature of the document, it may then make a motion to compel its production.

Of course, Rule 26(b)(5)(B) does not change the substantive law that determines whether privilege was waived by the production. *See* Fed. R. Civ. P. 26(b)(5) (2006 advisory committee notes). The principles by which courts decide questions of inadvertent waiver may vary from circuit to circuit. *Compare United States ex. rel. Bagley v. TRW, Inc.*, 204 F.R.D. 170, 177 (C.D. Cal. 2001), *with Helman v. Murry's Steaks, Inc.*, 728 F. Supp. 1099, 1104 (D. Del. 1990). But the Advisory Committee reminds courts that they may include parties' agreements regarding issues of privilege and waiver in an order under Rule 16(b)(6), and that such agreements and orders may be considered when deciding whether a waiver has occurred in a particular instance. Fed. R. Civ. P. 26(b)(5) (2006 advisory committee notes). The factual inquiry underlying the cause of the inadvertent disclosure of privileged material can include the amount of time and circumstances under which the electronic production was reviewed. *See, e.g., First Tech. Capital, Inc. v. JPMorgan Chase Bank, N.A.*, 2013 WL 7800409, 2013 U.S. Dist. LEXIS 185763 (E.D. Ky. Dec. 10, 2013) (finding waiver where counsel's review process employed "essentially no care" in protecting the privileged documents because each document had received only 9.84 seconds of review and had not been tracked using a privilege log).

Another less utilized mechanism, Federal Rule of Evidence 502(d), protects against the waiver of privilege for inadvertently disclosed documents. Although FRE 502(b) provides some protection by considering whether the conduct that resulted in disclosure was "reasonable," a Rule 502(d) claw-back agreement entered as an order of the court can replace the Rule 502(b) "reasonableness" standard and protect from waiver of privilege. *See Great-West Life & Annuity Ins. Co. v. Am. Econ. Ins. Co.*, 2013 WL 5332410, 2013 U.S. Dist. LEXIS 135750 (D. Nev. Sept. 23, 2013) (upholding a Rule 502(d) claw-back agreement).

4.2.6.3 Prosecution Bars

Sometimes a party's litigation counsel also represented—and continues to represent—that party in preparing and prosecuting patent applications in the U.S. Patent and Trademark Office (USPTO). In such cases, a protective order that restricts access to sensitive documents to "litigation counsel" offers faint protection to the other party, whose sensitive information might be used—unintentionally—to the competitor's advantage in prosecuting ongoing patent applications. To address this concern, courts often include in the protective order a "prosecution bar" that prohibits any attorney who has viewed a party's confidential information from preparing or prosecuting patent applications that use or otherwise benefit from the attorney's having viewed the information. Moreover, courts frequently bar any attorney who has viewed a party's confidential information from prosecuting applications that are related to the same technological subject matter of the patent dispute for a period of years. Many courts often extend prosecution bars to cover any person (not only attorneys) to whom highly confidential information is disclosed, which impacts experts as well as attorneys. Section 4.6.9 discusses motion practice relating to prosecution bars.

The Federal Circuit addressed the standard that lower courts should apply in determining when an unacceptable risk of inadvertent disclosure of highly confidential information arises in *In re Deutsche Bank*, 605 F.3d 1373 (Fed. Cir. 2010). The court drew on the guiding principles of prosecution bars enunciated in *U.S. Steel Corp. v. United States*, 730 F.2d 1465 (Fed. Cir. 1984).

In re Deutsche Bank considered whether a trial counsel who also routinely prosecuted patent applications for his client should be exempted from a prosecution bar. The lower court permitted the lead trial counsel to view highly confidential documents and exempted him from the prosecution bar. The Federal Circuit held that the parties must make specific showings regarding the scope of the bar and any exceptions to be made to the bar. The party seeking imposition of the bar must show a nexus between the scope of the bar and the risk of inadvertent disclosure. The party seeking an exemption from the bar must show on a counsel-by-counsel basis: (1) that counsel's representation of the client in matters before the USPTO does not, and is not, likely to implicate competitive decision making related to the subject matter of the litigation, so as to give rise to a risk of inadvertent use of confidential information learned in litigation, and (2) that the potential injury to the moving party from restrictions imposed on its choice of litigation and prosecution counsel outweighs the potential injury to the opposing party caused by such inadvertent use. *Id.* at 1381.

Several courts refusing to extend prosecution bars to prosecution activities during reexamination proceedings have reasoned that reexamination does not pose the same risks as other types of prosecution because patent claims may only be narrowed during reexamination. *See, e.g.*, *Document Generation Corp. v. Allscripts, LLC*, 2009 WL 1766096, 2009 U.S. Dist. LEXIS 52874 (E.D. Tex. June 23, 2009); *Kenexa Brassring Inc. v. Taleo Corp.*, 2009 WL 393782, U.S. Dist. LEXIS 12002 (D. Del. Feb. 18, 2009). These decisions may not reflect the realities of some reexamination practices. Although patent claims may not be broadened during reexamination proceedings, an attorney with knowledge of a competitor's highly sensitive information can potentially use that information (perhaps inadvertently) to fashion the narrower claims in a way to avoid key prior art while capturing a competitor's product (or future product). Thus, as this example illustrates, reexamination proceedings are not immune from the pitfalls of competitive decision making inherent in patent prosecution. In light of the Federal Circuit's *In re Deutsche Bank* ruling, a more thorough approach for determining whether reexamination activities should be included in a prosecution bar would be to apply the standard set forth by the Federal Circuit for each attorney who might participate in the reexamination activity.

4.2.6.3.1 Prosecution Bars and PTAB Review

The postgrant review procedures introduced by the America Invents Act (AIA), *see* §§ 14.2.5.7–14.2.5.8, have been enthusiastically embraced by many attorneys in the patent bar as an alternative (and in many cases an accompanying action) to patent litigation. *See* § 2.2.6.4. These procedures are seen by some alleged infringers as a favorable alternative to patent litigation because they are significantly less expensive and are required by statute to be completed within a year of institution. From the petitioner's point of view, these procedures are also advantageous because of the lower burden of proof for invalidity and the broader claim-construction standard ("broadest reasonable interpretation") applied in the Patent Trial and Appeal Board

(PTAB) proceeding. Furthermore, as a result of the short time to determination, courts have been more inclined to stay cases in their early phases in light of an instituted inter partes review (IPR) or covered business method (CBM) petition. *See* § 2.2.6.4. While IPR and CBM procedures permit for certain discovery, it is significantly less than that in district court litigation. The discovery is largely limited to expert examinations, and any additional discovery must be requested and must be "in the interests of justice." *See, e.g., Garmin Int'l, Inc. v. Cuozzo Techs. LLC*, Case IPR2012-00001, 2013 Pat. App. LEXIS 2445, 2013 WL 2023626, at *5 (P.T.A.B. Mar. 5, 2013) (denying a motion for additional discovery, listing as relevant factors that the requested discovery must: (1) rise above more than a possibility and mere allegation of something useful, (2) is clear and understandable, (3) is not overly burdensome, (4) cannot be equivalently obtained by other means, and (5) is not directed to the opposing party's litigation positions and bases for their positions).

Claim amendment during IPR is also markedly different than amendment during regular prosecution or ex parte reexamination practice. First, common claim amendment practices permitted in ex parte prosecution, such as automatic claim amendment and ability to broaden claims, are not permitted in IPR proceedings. Additionally, the patent owner bears the burden of showing that any proposed new or amended claims are patentable. *See Idle Free Sys., Inc. v. Bergstrom Inc.*, IPR 2012-00027, Paper No. 66 (P.T.A.B. Jan. 7, 2014) (reasoning that the IPR is an adjudicative rather than an examining proceeding, and the board does not "examine" patent claims in the same way as a patent examiner does during patent prosecution). These limitations likely explain why most proposed amendments have not been accepted by the PTAB panels. The PTAB's opinion in *International Flavors & Fragrances, Inc. v. U.S. Agriculture*, IPR2013-00124 (P.T.A.B. May 20, 2014), marked the first time it had granted a motion to amend since the enactment of the AIA, although the USPTO has indicated that it intended to liberalize its amendment practice. Michelle K. Lee, *Director's Forum: PTAB's Quick-Fixes for AIA Rules Are to Be Implemented Immediately*, USPTO Director's Forum (Mar. 27, 2015, 10:18 AM), http://www.uspto.gov/blog/director/entry/ptab_s_quick_fixes_for.

As a result of the differences between IPR practice and the former reexamination practice, courts have been less likely to bar attorneys who have had access to designated material from participating in PTAB proceedings. *See, e.g., Endo Pharm. Inc. v. Actavis Inc.*, 2014 U.S. Dist. LEXIS 112642, 2014 WL 3950900 (S.D.N.Y. Aug. 13, 2014); *see also* Oral Order, *M/A-COM Tech. Solutions Holdings Inc. v. Laird Techs. Inc.*, C.A. No. 14-181-LPS (D. Del. July 31, 2014). That could change if the PTAB substantially loosens its rules regarding claim amendments during postgrant review proceedings.

4.2.7 Foreign Discovery Issues

It is becoming increasingly common for foreign discovery issues to arise in patent litigation. In part this is because of globalization—not only manufacturing but also research and development are now increasingly performed abroad—and in part this is because the American patent system is perceived to offer advantages that other jurisdictions do not, including strong protection for intellectual property and the availability of broad discovery. Foreign patentees may prefer resolving intellectual property disputes in the United States, even when the dispute is with a foreign defendant. They may believe they can get more effective relief in the United States due to the large size of the American market as well as the perceived strength of available remedies.

Of course, when a foreign entity is a party to the litigation, discovery may be had through Federal Rules of Civil Procedure 33–36, just as with any other party. But frequently the party will be a subsidiary of a foreign entity that is not a party, perhaps because of jurisdictional issues. The issue then arises of whether the documents, information, and witnesses of the foreign parent are within the "possession, custody, and control" of the subsidiary. Under the "control" prong, courts may find that documents in the possession of a foreign parent, subsidiary, or affiliate company are in the "control" of the party. For example, a party has been found to "control" the documents at issue when it can ordinarily obtain them in the usual course of its business from the foreign entity. *See, e.g., Alcan Int'l Ltd. v. S.A. Day Mfg. Co., Inc.*, 176 F.R.D. 75, 79 (W.D.N.Y. 1996); *Afros S.P.A. v. Krauss-Maffei Corp.*, 113 F.R.D. 127, 129–32 (D. Del. 1986).

If a foreign entity is not a party, discovery may still be sought through a letter rogatory, or a letter of request to a foreign or international tribunal, under 28 U.S.C. § 1781. International treaties, such as the Hague Convention on Taking of Evidence Abroad in Civil or Commercial Matters, or the Inter-American Convention on Letters Rogatory, provide a procedure whereby the district court can request the assistance of a foreign tribunal. Not every country is a treaty signatory, and many signatory countries have taken advantage of the ability to "opt out" of requirements to provide certain types of discovery. Article 23 of the Hague Convention permits signatory countries to make a declaration or a reservation that they "will not execute Letters of Request issued for the purpose of obtaining pre-trial discovery of documents as known in Common Law countries."

The Federal Rules and treaties such as the Hague Convention are not mutually exclusive, but courts should be mindful of principles of international comity and take a supervisory role in foreign discovery disputes. *See Société Nationale Industrielle Aerospatiale v. United States Dist. Ct.*, 482 U.S. 522, 546 (1987). Some countries (e.g., the United Kingdom, Canada, and France) have enacted "blocking" statutes, which prohibit compliance with foreign discovery orders for the production of evidence located within the blocking state's territory. Blocking statutes often include a penal sanction for violations. Nevertheless, "[i]t is well settled that [foreign "blocking"] statutes do not deprive an American court of the power to order a party subject to its jurisdiction to produce evidence even though the act of production may violate that statute." *Id.* at 544 n.29. Accordingly, in considering whether to compel discovery, courts must balance a variety of factors, including whether compliance with the request would undermine important interests of the state where the information is located. *Id.* at 544 n.28.

4.3 Claim Construction and Discovery

Since claim construction is considered an issue of law and is focused on the fixed, textual language of the patent in suit, one might reasonably ask what discovery can possibly have to do with it. There are two principal answers. First, as the Supreme Court pointed out in the *Markman* decision, claim construction mixes law with fact, the latter consisting of the perspective of one of ordinary skill in the art. To decide how such a person would view the claims in light of the intrinsic evidence, the court has to determine the point of view of that person. Discovery can aid in that process. For example, depositions of inventors—whose views on what claim terms mean are of attenuated relevance—may be quite helpful to the process of claim construction by illuminating relevant aspects of the prosecution history or by describing the technology or the state of the art. *Voice Techs. Grp., Inc. v. VMC Sys., Inc.*, 164 F.3d 605, 615 (Fed. Cir. 1999).

Second, discovery can reveal the parties' contentions regarding infringement and validity, informing the choice of claim terms requiring construction. This is important as a practical matter, since many patents contain dozens of claims with hundreds of words or phrases that could potentially be candidates for interpretation. By allowing the parties to conduct sufficient discovery to understand what products are accused of infringement (and why) and what prior art might be asserted against the patent, the court can effectively reduce the number of disputed claim terms that would otherwise be presented for interpretation.

In light of the special utility of this early discovery, courts might consider allowing the parties to phase their discovery efforts—for example, by allowing the defendant to take a preliminary deposition of the inventor in aid of claim construction, reserving additional time for other issues.

4.4 Electronic Discovery

A significant portion of discovery in patent litigation is electronic discovery. Although electronic discovery in patent litigation presents similar issues as electronic discovery in other complex litigation, certain unique challenges arise more frequently in patent cases.

4.4.1 Overview of Electronic Discovery

In 2006, the Federal Rules of Civil Procedure were amended to provide rules for discovery of electronically stored information (ESI). These amendments modified Rules 16, 26, 33, 34, 37, and 45 in an effort to clarify the law on electronic discovery. Although a complete analysis of all the rules relating to electronic discovery is beyond the scope of this section, it is beneficial to review some of the major features of electronic discovery.

The Federal Rules require consideration of electronic discovery at the beginning of a case. Pursuant to Federal Rule of Civil Procedure 26(f)(2), the parties must "discuss any issues about preserving discoverable information; and develop a proposed discovery plan." The discovery plan produced under Rule 26 must address "any issues about disclosure or discovery of electronically stored information, including the form or forms in which it should be produced." Fed. R. Civ. P. 26(f)(3)(C). Additionally, each party's initial disclosures under Rule 26(a) must identify any ESI that it intends to use to support its case.

The nature of ESI is such that some types of documents are more accessible than others. The *Zubulake* decision outlines five categories of discoverable electronic data in order of decreasing accessibility: (1) active, online data, (2) near-line data, (3) offline storage and archives, (4) backup tapes, and (5) erased, fragmented, or damaged data. *Zubulake v. UBS Warburg, LLC*, 217 F.R.D. 309 (S.D.N.Y. 2003). Inasmuch as the last two categories contain "inaccessible" data, classification of data can be important in cost-shifting analysis. Under the Federal Rules, ESI is presumptively not discoverable if it comes from a source that is "not reasonably accessible because of undue burden or cost." To raise the presumption, the responding party to a discovery request must identify the sources that are "not reasonably accessible" that it will not search or produce. In response, the requesting party may challenge the designation by moving to compel, whereupon the burden shifts to the responding party to show that the information is not reasonably accessible. The court may then hold that the information is not reasonably accessible and so is presumptively not discoverable. Even if the requesting party shows "good cause" to obtain production, the court may specify conditions on the production, such as cost-shifting.

The Seventh Circuit has adopted a pilot program for electronic discovery that, among other things, provides greater specificity on what categories of ESI are discoverable. Under this program, "deleted," "slack," "fragmented," and "unallocated" data on hard drives, random access memory (RAM), online access data, and data in metadata fields that are frequently updated automatically is generally deemed not accessible. Additionally, other forms of ESI whose preservation requires extraordinary affirmative measures that are not utilized in the ordinary course of business are not accessible. *See Discovery Pilot: Seventh Circuit Electronic Discovery Pilot Program, available at* http://www.discoverypilot.com/.

The International Trade Commission (ITC) also recently adopted amendments to its rules of procedure (19 C.F.R. § 210.27 (2014)) to "reduce expensive, inefficient, unjustified, or unnecessary discovery practices." The amendments allow a party to object to an e-discovery request when the requested data is "not reasonably accessible because of undue burden or cost" and give discretion to administrative law judges to limit duplicative or unduly expensive discovery.

Spoliation is more complicated in the context of electronic discovery. Freezing corporate documents in the electronic age is difficult, if not impossible, and documents are often destroyed automatically by computer systems rather than at the instruction of a human being. Computer data is in an almost constant state of fluctuation, being altered, overwritten, and otherwise changed. Attempting to arrest this process could prove disastrous for many systems and/or result in enormous costs to the preserving party. Recognizing this fact, Rule 37 states that "Absent exceptional circumstances, a court may not impose sanctions under these rules on a party for failing to provide electronically stored information lost as a result of the routine, good-faith operation of an electronic information system." This provision, while providing a safe harbor, does require good faith on the part of litigants. Thus, routine operations of data deletion may not be coopted to intentionally deprive the opposing party of documents believed to be relevant to the litigation and, in some circumstances, may need to be suspended during the litigation. The amendments to Federal Rule of Civil Procedure 37(e), which became effective on December 1, 2015, alter this standard. The amended rule authorizes sanctions for failures to preserve information if they caused substantial prejudice in the litigation and were a result of "willful or bad faith" conduct, or if they "irreparably deprived" a party of a "meaningful" ability to present or defend against claims in the litigation.

Furthermore, sanctions for spoliation in the context of electronic discovery are fraught with uncertainty. Indeed, although in theory the duty to preserve evidence begins when litigation is "pending or reasonably foreseeable," in practice the standard is not so uniform, nor is there a uniform standard governing the scope of that duty, what conduct justifies sanctions, or the nature and severity of appropriate sanctions. In *Victor Stanley, Inc. v. Creative Pipe, Inc.*, 269 F.R.D. 497, 542 (D. Md. 2010), the court provided a comprehensive table showing how each circuit handles these questions. *Id.* at 542. A copy of this table is included as Appendix 4.1.

4.4.2 Electronic Discovery in Patent Cases

In principle, patent cases present the same electronic discovery issues as do other types of litigation. Document requests in patent cases typically call for enormous and costly exchanges of documents. This is not different from antitrust or employment discrimination litigation. But in practice, some factual situations in patent cases pose distinctive challenges.

First, in a patent case, relevant documents can often be much older than they are in other cases. Damages for past infringement can be sought even after a patent has expired—in such a case, documentation of the invention's conception and reduction to practice can be more than twenty years old. Determination of a reasonable royalty is done at the time of first infringement, which likewise can reach back more than six years. Thus, patent discovery is directed to a potentially larger and older set of documents, which can dramatically increase the complexity and costs.

Second, because they are often technology companies, parties in patent cases tend to have adopted new communication techniques earlier than others. As a result, they can have a greater percentage of critical records that are electronic instead of paper. Moreover, because technology companies tend to have begun using electronic communication programs earlier than others, the communication programs of parties in patent cases have been through more product cycles on average, resulting in more documents being lost or inaccessible. In general, the corporate e-mail systems that were used in the mid-1990s are no longer in use, and resurrecting those systems to recover data can be prohibitively expensive. And an inventor's computer may have been replaced or upgraded several times, losing some information each time.

Third, patent cases tend to involve a much higher burden of discovery than other cases. Patent cases typically involve high stakes, with companies risking entire product lines or the company itself. Discovery for patent cases can implicate the entire operations of companies, including design, manufacturing, marketing, sales, and more. Thus, the cost to comply with discovery requests can be quite high. This is especially salient in cases where patent holding companies that make no products ("nonpracticing entities") bring suit against companies making an allegedly infringing product. In these cases, the heavy burden of discovery is borne almost exclusively by the defendant, and this asymmetry allows the plaintiff to use discovery as a tool to coerce a favorable settlement.

Because of the high costs and unique burdens of e-discovery in patent cases, the Federal Circuit Advisory Council convened an e-discovery committee. In November 2011, the council adopted the committee's recommended *Model Order Regarding e-Discovery in Patent Cases*, reproduced here at Appendix 4.2. The order attempts to streamline e-discovery and provides for a tiered approach under which parties exchange core documentation regarding the at-issue technology before producing any e-mails. Further, the model order limits e-mail-production requests to five custodians and five search terms. Litigants around the country have often proposed the order to district courts. In March 2012, the Eastern District of Texas promulgated a model e-discovery order that sets guidelines for the collection and production of electronic data in patent cases and, for example, limits production of e-mail to eight custodians per party based on fifteen search terms per custodian, absent a court order. *See* E.D. Tex. Local Rules, Appendix P. Other district courts have also promulgated their own model e-discovery orders, such as the Western District of New York's "Model Order Regarding e-Discovery in Patent Cases," the District of Delaware's "Default Standard for Discovery, Including Discovery of Electronically Stored Information (ESI)," and the Northern District of California's "Guidelines for the Discovery of Electronically Stored Information" (available in Appendix 4.3). The Northern District of California's guidelines encourage the parties to meet at the beginning of the case to discuss the preservation, search, and production of electronically stored information. The District of Delaware's standard promulgates particular timing requirements for e-discovery, formats for producing data, and custodian limitations. In line with these developments, the Federal Judicial Center also added a new section on civil case management (including how to address e-discovery issues) in its sixth edition of the *Benchbook for U.S. District Court Judges* (Federal Judicial Center, 6th ed. 2013). Given the current attention to reducing the cost and complexity of electronic discovery in patent cases, it is likely that other districts will promulgate similar standards for cabining electronic discovery in the years to come.

Although there is much wisdom in this effort to reduce the costs of e-discovery, there is no one-size-fits-all solution, and greater experience in managing the scope of electronic discovery will likely result in further evolution and explication of the various guidelines. For example, in many cases, the most expensive ESI to collect is not e-mail, which is often stored on relatively accessible central servers, but the rather contents of the computer hard drives of individual users, which must be copied or "imaged" one by one to collect and produce the users' working documents. Parties could look to their Federal Rule of Civil Procedure 26(a) initial disclosures to determine whose computers should be imaged. As another example, courts are likely to face situations in which a witness whose electronic documents were not gathered for a party's production (i.e., the witness was not one of the designated custodians) is called by that party to testify at trial. Courts can adopt a general rule, for example, requiring that the witness's documents be produced in every case (as the Eastern District of Texas requires), or address the situation when it arises to allow for a response tailored to the particular circumstances. Either way, courts will have to balance the equities carefully to ensure that parties have a fair opportunity to obtain discovery, but also that the exceptions to e-discovery management do not swallow the rule.

As technology improves, new search techniques based on a document's relationship to other documents (such as having senders or recipients in common, being close in time, being stored in the same location, and the like) are beginning to supplant "search terms" that only select documents based on the presence of particular key words in a document. However e-discovery is done, parties can be encouraged to work together to test their searches to ensure that they are likely to discover relevant information. This can involve an iterative meet-and-confer process between the parties, whereby the party seeking documents proposes a set of search terms, which are then tested by the producing party to determine whether the terms result in an unwieldy number of documents being produced, such that the terms should be renegotiated.

Parties can also turn to the court to resolve these issues. District courts have provided specific guidance on the search methods and terms that parties use during discovery. Some courts have compelled parties to disclose the search terms and custodians they use to find responsive documents. Some courts have ruled on the actual search terms that parties should use, while other courts order the parties to reach a compromise on their own. Courts are also beginning to discuss the issue of whether predictive coding (automated review of electronic documents through linguistic analysis) may appropriately replace manual review and keyword searches. The first federal case permitting computer-assisted review of ESI by predictive coding is *Da Silva Moore v. Publicis Groupe*, 287 F.R.D. 182, 184 n.2 (S.D.N.Y. 2012). The *Da Silva Moore* court permitted the use of predictive coding after considering the amount of material at issue (over three million documents), the superiority of computer-assisted review in that case, and the fact that the parties agreed to computer-assisted review. Another court allowed a party to employ predictive coding to review over two million documents originally reviewed through the use of search terms. *See Bridgestone Ams., Inc. v. Int'l Bus. Machs. Corp.*, No. 3:13-1196, 2014 U.S. Dist. LEXIS 142525, 2014 WL 4923014 (M.D. Tenn. July 22, 2014). Ultimately, because courts generally depend on the parties for the information needed to decide e-discovery-related disputes, courts must impress upon the parties and their counsel the need to educate themselves about their electronically stored information, so that they can effectively carry out their obligations under Federal Rule of Civil Procedure 26(f)(3)(C), resolve issues without judicial intervention to the greatest extent possible, and be prepared to provide the necessary context for the court to decide any contested issues.

4.4.2.1 Spoliation in Patent Cases

Given the broad potential scope of electronic discovery in patent cases, spoliation issues—or at least accusations—often arise. Parties may find it difficult to understand what documents they have; few have a central repository where all records, especially the oldest, may be found. It can be difficult for a party to produce "all" documents responsive to a discovery request. Increasingly, problems in electronic document production lead to spoliation motions by the party seeking discovery. A thorough understanding of the litigants' technological challenges is key to determining whether spoliation has occurred. The absence of certain documents from a production may be the result of document destruction policies carried out in good faith, poor document collection practices, or intentional spoliation—the results all look the same at first glance. For example, there is a difference, of course, between searching diligently for electronic records and not finding those that no longer exist, and searching only the most immediately accessible locations and ignoring the rest.

The amendments to Federal Rule of Civil Procedure 37(e), which became effective on December 1, 2015, authorize sanctions for failures to preserve information if these failures caused substantial prejudice in the litigation and were a result of "willful or bad faith" conduct, or if the failures to preserve "irreparably deprived" a party of a "meaningful" ability to present or defend against claims in the litigation.

Spoliation turns on the duty to preserve records. "A party can only be sanctioned for destroying evidence if it had a duty to preserve it." *Zubulake v. UBS Warburg LLC*, 220 F.R.D. 212, 216 (S.D.N.Y. 2003). The duty to preserve evidence begins when litigation is "pending or reasonably foreseeable." *Silvestri v. Gen. Motors Corp.*, 271 F.3d 583, 590 (4th Cir. 2001). The Federal Circuit held in *Micron Tech., Inc. v. Rambus Inc.*, 645 F.3d 1311 (Fed. Cir. 2011) that Rambus engaged in spoliation of evidence because it continued to destroy documents after litigation became "reasonably foreseeable." *Id.* at 1320–26. The court observed that "[w]hen litigation is 'reasonably foreseeable' is a flexible fact-specific standard that allows a district court to exercise the discretion necessary to confront the myriad factual situations inherent in the spoliation inquiry. *Fujitsu Ltd. v. Fed. Express Corp.*, 247 F.3d 423, 436 (2d Cir. 2001). This standard does not trigger the duty to preserve documents from the mere existence of a potential claim or the distant possibility of litigation. *See, e.g., Trask-Morton v. Motel 6 Operating L.P.*, 534 F.3d 672, 681–82 (7th Cir. 2008). However, it is not so inflexible as to require that litigation be 'imminent, or probable without significant contingencies . . . .'" *Id.* at 1320; *see also Hynix Semiconductor Inc. v. Rambus Inc.*, 645 F.3d 1336 (Fed. Cir. 2011).

After the duty to preserve is triggered, prejudice occurs when a spoliating party intentionally destroys evidence, although the destruction might not be prejudicial if the evidence is not relevant or is cumulative to other, surviving evidence. *See Sekisui Am. Corp. v. Hart*, No. 12 Civ. 3479 (SAS) (FM), 2013 WL 4116322 (S.D.N.Y. Aug. 15, 2013). One consideration is whether counsel for the litigant adequately and reasonably consulted with their client about the preservation of ESI. One court imposed sanctions on a party's counsel who did not "examine critically" the client's representations about document availability and instead assumed that a third-party service provider would preserve the data. *See Brown v. Tellermate Holdings*, No. 2:11-cv-

1122, 2014 U.S. Dist. LEXIS 90123, 2014 WL 2987051 (S.D. Ohio July 1, 2014). In *Procaps S.A. v. Patheon, Inc.*, No. 12-24356-CIV, 2014 U.S. Dist. LEXIS 35225, 2014 WL 1047748 (S.D. Fla. Mar. 18, 2014), the court found ESI searches inadequate because counsel did not meet with IT or ESI personnel or other relevant individuals to discuss document collection and did not assist custodians in the document collection process. On the other hand, automatically deleting e-mails per a routine company deletion policy does not necessarily rise to the level of spoliation. *See In re Pradaxa (Dabigatran Etexilate) Prods. Liab. Litig.*, MDL No. 2385, 3:12-md-02385-DRH-SCW, 2013 U.S. Dist. LEXIS 137235, 2013 WL 5377164 (S.D. Ill. Sept. 25, 2013); *AMC Tech., LLC v. Cisco Sys., Inc.*, No. 11-3403 PSG, 2013 U.S. Dist. LEXIS 101372, 2013 WL 3733390 (N.D. Cal. July 15, 2013).

4.4.3 Issues with Specific File Types in Electronic Discovery

Disputes can arise regarding the decipherability of electronic files. Some file types may be proprietary to one party or require a program that the other party does not have (e.g., source code or semiconductor schematics). Although Rule 34(b) requires that documents be produced in a "reasonably usable form," there is little guidance as to what satisfies this requirement. Under the Seventh Circuit Pilot e-Discovery Program, discussed in § 4.4.1, the parties must make a good-faith effort to agree on a production format at the Rule 26(f) conference. If they are unable to resolve a production-format issue, that issue should be raised before the court. Under this program, the requesting party is responsible for the incremental cost of creating its copy of the requested information, and the parties are encouraged to discuss cost sharing for optical character recognition (OCR) or other upgrades of non-text-searchable electronic images. The Seventh Circuit program thus conforms to the existing case law that requires balancing the need of one party for the data in its requested form versus the hardship to the other to produce it. *See, e.g., Zubulake v. UBS Warburg LLC*, 217 F.R.D. 309 (S.D.N.Y. 2003).

The District of Delaware has also adopted default standards for handling electronic discovery. *See Default Standard for Discovery, Including Discovery of Electronically Stored Information ("ESI")*, District of Delaware, *available at* http://www.ded.uscourts.gov/sites/default/files/Chambers/SLR/Misc/EDiscov.pdf (reprinted in Appendix 4.3). Like the Seventh Circuit program, Delaware's standard includes a Rule 26(f) conference. *Id.* At the conference, the parties must discuss "issues, claims and defenses . . . that define the scope of discovery," "technical information," and "the categories of ESI that should be preserved." *Id.* The Delaware standard also provides that parties produce ESI and non-ESI as "text searchable image files (e.g., PDF or TIFF)," but must produce in native (or original) file format any "files not easily converted to image format, such as Excel and Access files." In either case, parties must preserve the integrity of the underlying ESI (i.e., its formatting and metadata).

Source code is computer program information in a format that humans can read (before the code is "compiled" into a format a computer can read), and it poses unique discovery challenges. A thorough discussion of electronically stored information in many patent cases should address conditions for the production of source code. Given the highly sensitive nature of source code and the lengths to which companies go to protect it during the normal course of business, parties commonly negotiate a more restrained production of source code than for other highly confidential documents. An example of additional security measures that may be appropriate for the production of source code is producing source code on a standalone (non-networked computer) for review in a secure facility. *See SKF Condition Monitoring, Inc. v. Invensys Sys. Inc.*, 07-CV-1116 BTM (NLS), 2010 U.S. Dist. LEXIS 35130, 2010 WL 3463686 (S.D. Cal. Apr. 9, 2010); *Leader Techs. Inc. v. Facebook Inc.*, Civ. No. 08-862-JJF-LPS, 2009 WL 3021168, 2009 U.S. Dist. LEXIS 93807 (D. Del. Sept. 4, 2009); District of Delaware, *Default Standard for Access to Source Code, available at* http://www.ded.uscourts.gov/sites/default/files/Chambers/SLR/Misc/DefStdAccess.pdf (last visited Apr. 27, 2015) (available in Appendix 2.4). For example, the District of Delaware's *Default Standard for Access to Source Code*, which applies absent agreement of the parties, provides for the production of source code on a stand-alone computer to which two outside counsel and two experts may have access.

The proliferation of mobile electronic devices and cloud-storage capability has expanded the discovery domain. Recent decisions highlight the importance of preserving dynamic forms of evidence, including those stored on mobile devices (e.g., text messages and mobile device data), social media networks, and cloud-computing platforms. In one case, a court-appointed electronic discovery special master recommended sanctions against a defendant who had systematically destroyed ESI, including text messages and other mobile data. *See Small v. Univ. Med. Ctr. of S. Nevada*, Case No. 2:13-cv-00298-APG-PAL, 2014 WL 4079507, 2014 U.S. Dist. LEXIS 114406 (D. Nev. Aug. 18, 2014). Similarly, in another case, a U.S. magistrate judge imposed sanctions on defendants for their unwillingness and inability to produce information stored on cloud-computing platforms. *Brown v. Tellermate*, 2014 U.S. Dist. LEXIS 90123, 2014 WL 2987051. In *Barrette Outdoor Living v. Michigan Resin Representatives, LLC*, No. 11-13335, 2013 U.S. Dist. LEXIS 60309, 2013 WL 1800356 (E.D. Mich. Apr. 29, 2013), the court sanctioned one of the plaintiff's former employees who had disposed of his mobile phone. These decisions show that courts are becoming increasingly sensitive to the need for preserving electronic data in a variety of forms and media.

The new federal rules dealing with ESI guide courts and parties in dealing with costly electronic discovery issues in patent cases. Several courts provide more specific guidance in the form of default orders. *See, e.g.*, District of Delaware *Default Standard for Discovery, Including Discovery of Electronically Stored Information ("ESI"), available at* http://www.ded.uscourts.gov/sites/default/files/Chambers/SLR/Misc/EDiscov.pdf; District of Kansas, *Guidelines for Cases Involving Electronically Stored Information [ESI], available at* http://www.ksd.uscourts.gov/guidelines-for-esi/ (both reprinted in Appendix 4.3). In practice, default orders tend to encourage parties to agree to any necessary, case-specific electronic discovery procedures. The Sedona Conference is also a good resource, providing electronic discovery principles courts and litigants have relied upon. *See* The Sedona Conference, Publications, *available at* http://www.thesedonaconference.org/publications (last visited May 5, 2016).

4.5 Management of Discovery Disputes

Given the high stakes of patent litigation, lawyers frequently get mired in contentious discovery battles. Effective case management requires that the court discourage this tendency, reserving intervention only for those disputes that matter and that remain unresolved after good faith negotiations between the parties. One way to accomplish this objective is to encourage self-regulation by keeping calendar dates firm so as to avoid the kind of foot-dragging that can occur if extensions of time are easily available. Many judges issue special warnings to counsel in patent cases, threatening to call in principals of the parties if discovery becomes too contentious. Some courts set a presumptive limit on the number of discovery motions that will be heard (e.g., three), after which a discovery special master will be appointed. An increasingly common procedure requires the parties to submit a letter (not to exceed two to four pages) in advance of a telephone conference, asking for permission to file a motion; typically the issues are resolved on the conference call.

Courts can also streamline discovery disputes through speedier and more efficient case-management procedures. In 2014, the Eastern District of Texas created a second set of case-management procedures for patent cases ("Track B") that can be enforced through party agreement or applied *sua sponte* by the court. Track B provides for a quicker schedule, earlier disclosure of infringement contentions, licenses, and settlement agreements, immediate limited discovery, and an early, good-faith damages estimate. Along the same lines, some judges in the Southern District of New York are imposing case-management orders that expedite the docket by, for example, requiring discovery to be completed within 120 days of the initial pretrial conference and expert discovery to be completed twenty-five days following fact discovery. *See, e.g.*, Hon. Vernon Broderick, Case Management Plan and Scheduling Order §§ 7, 12, *available at* http://www.nysd.uscourts.gov/cases/show.php?db=judge_info&id=982; Hon. Valerie Caproni, Civil Case Management Plan and Scheduling Order § 5(a), *available at* http://www.nysd.uscourts.gov/cases/show.php?db=judge_info&id=1035; Hon. Katherine Forrest, Scheduling Order, *available at* http://www.nysd.uscourts.gov/cases/show.php?db=judge_info&id=980 (fact discovery to close within 120 days of initial pretrial conference, expert discovery complete within twenty-five days of close of fact discovery); Hon. Jed Rakoff, Individual Rules of Practice § 3(b), *available at* http://www.nysd.uscourts.gov/cases/show.php?db=judge_info&id=832 ("At the initial conference, the Court will issue a binding Case Management Order that, in most cases, will require the case to be ready for trial within five months of the date thereof.").

In general, courts should emphasize to counsel the importance of the meet-and-confer process. If necessary, courts can order additional procedural requirements to help adversaries keep lines of communication open. For example, courts can require that parties schedule regular teleconferences (e.g., every two weeks) during fact discovery to discuss and resolve accumulated discovery issues. Courts can require in-person meetings where necessary, followed by the submission of a joint letter brief presenting the dispute to the court. Some courts have required an in-person meet-and-confer between lead trial counsel. An onerous requirement, however, risks abuse by litigants who refuse to provide any discovery until the requirement is satisfied.

The most important consideration is that counsel must meet and confer in good faith, and not just as a perfunctory matter. One recurring problem arises when a party is overly demanding and refuses to compromise during the meet-and-confer process. At least one court quashed a subpoena when a party refused to accept a reasonable offer during the meet-and-confer, but then later tried to accept it. *See Boston Sci. Corp. v. Lee*, No. 5-14-mc-80188-BLF-PSG, 2014 U.S. Dist. LEXIS 107584, 2014 WL 3851157 (N.D. Cal. Aug. 4, 2014). The court reasoned that to allow the party to resume a fallback position it had rejected during the meet-and-confer process "would make a mockery of both parties' obligation to meet and confer in good faith from the start. The time to tap flexibility and creativity is during meet and confer, not after." *Id.* Where the court deems it necessary to impose sanctions, experience shows that progressive penalties (from mild to severe, including issue and evidence preclusion or default) are effective at controlling discovery abuses in patent cases.

Referrals of discovery management to magistrate judges are commonplace in many courts and districts. The advantage of referring discovery issues is that it frees the district judge for other work, while keeping responsibility for discovery helps the district judge remain aware of the case and coordinate discovery and scheduling issues. Moreover, there is a certain *in terrorem* effect at work when the district court hears discovery disputes. Litigants may be less likely to raise as many disputes and will likely be more conciliatory if the judge deciding the case has a greater opportunity to assess whether counsel are being unreasonable. Where referral is the common practice, experienced counsel soon learn the tendencies of the magistrate judges on particular issues, resulting in fewer motions. If this doesn't happen, or if the case otherwise appears likely to generate a disproportionate level of discovery controversy, courts can require the parties to engage a special master under Rule 53. When the special master possesses substantial experience with patent litigation, the resulting process, although sometimes costly, can be substantially more efficient and effective.

4.6 Common Discovery Motions

What follows is a list of the most common discovery motions that raise patent-specific issues, with recommended approaches.

4.6.1 Discovery Regarding Patentee's Prefiling Investigation

The accused infringer may challenge the basis for the patentee's having filed suit. Normally this would happen in the context of a Rule 11 motion. The Federal Circuit has laid out guidelines for patent cases describing a minimum investigation, including preparation of a claim chart that matches elements of the patent claims to the accused product. *See Antonious v. Spalding & Evenflo Cos., Inc.*, 275 F.3d 1066,

1073–74 (Fed. Cir. 2002); *View Eng'g, Inc. v. Robotic Vision Sys., Inc.*, 208 F.3d 981, 986 (Fed. Cir. 2000). Generally speaking, the requirements for a prefiling investigation are much more stringent than the Rule 8 notice-pleading standard. *See McZeal v. Sprint Nextel Corp.*, 501 F.3d 1354, 1356–57 (Fed. Cir. 2007); *see also id.* at 1359–60 (Dyk, J., dissenting in part). The patentee may submit its records of investigation for *in camera* review to meet the challenge while still preserving work-product protection. *See, e.g.*, *Centillion Data Sys., LLC v. Convergys Corp.*, No. 104CV0073LJM-WTL, 2006 WL 20777, 2006 U.S. Dist. LEXIS 846, at *3 n.1 (S.D. Ind. Jan. 4, 2006); *see also* Fed. R. Civ. P. 11 advisory committee notes (1983 Amendment).

The issue occasionally arises outside of the Rule 11 context, where a dispute over infringement contentions, for example, leads a defendant to request discovery of the patentee's prefiling investigation. In the absence of a waiver, the best practice is to deny such discovery. However, the patentee should be required early in the proceeding, either through traditional contention discovery or as a result of patent local rules, to describe its infringement position, without revealing what it did to analyze the accused product before filing. *See, e.g.*, *O2 Micro Int'l, Ltd. v. Monolithic Power Sys., Inc.*, 467 F.3d 1355, 1365–66 (Fed. Cir. 2006); *Nova Measuring Instruments Ltd. v. Nanometrics, Inc.*, 417 F. Supp. 2d 1121, 1123 (N.D. Cal. 2006).

4.6.2 Production of Information About Products

The patentee may make an early request for production of the accused product by inspection, samples, or, in the case of software, for example, copies. The defendant can resist on the grounds that the information is a trade secret and that the patentee should already have met its obligations under Rule 11 to investigate and compare the patent claims to the accused product. This position, however, assumes that the product could have been available to the patentee outside of the discovery process. Some products, such as software or processes, cannot reasonably be obtained before filing litigation, and the patentee must rely on indirect evidence such as marketing materials in making its analysis. *See, e.g.*, *Intamin Ltd. v. Magnetar Techs. Corp.*, 483 F.3d 1328, 1338 (Fed. Cir. 2007). In that event, best practice dictates that the product or copies be made available to the patentee in discovery subject to the terms of a protective order to maintain confidentiality.

Each side in patent litigation may seek information about the other's products, including future or "unannounced" products still in development. Information about the accused infringer's future products is relevant for the patentee because it wants protection against future infringement and because pending changes in the accused products can be probative of willfulness. An accused infringer's inquiry into the patentee's products is also legitimate because the use by the patentee of its claimed invention can bear on damages. For example, the patentee may have been required to mark its products in order to obtain damages. This inquiry is also relevant to whether the patentee is entitled to lost profits. Finally, the patentee's use of its invention can evidence whether the patented invention enjoys or lacks commercial success, which is relevant to nonobviousness and can be relevant to reasonable royalty damages. As with early production relating to the accused product, the best approach is to allow discovery, subject to orders that maintain security of the confidential data.

4.6.3 Contentions About Infringement, Invalidity, and Unenforceability

In courts without patent local rules, early discovery disputes are likely to focus on contentions, as the accused infringer presses the patentee to articulate its infringement theories while the patentee tries to force the accused infringer to explain its noninfringement and invalidity theories. Indeed, the frequency of such disputes motivated the adoption of patent local rules in many patent-intensive districts. The key to solving this problem lies in understanding the parties' respective burdens and how positions naturally evolve in patent litigation.

As noted in § 4.6.1, patentees are expected to comply with their Rule 11 obligations by carefully comparing the patent claims to the accused product. Therefore, one would assume that any patentee would have a reasonably precise sense of its infringement theory at the outset. However, there are two major issues that can make that expectation unrealistic. First, the patentee might not have been able to get access to the necessary information because it is hidden from view (for example, source code); the product is unavailable (for example, because of tightly controlled distribution); or the target is a process that is only used behind closed doors. In these circumstances, a patentee has to make an educated guess about infringement from the information that is publicly available and rely on early discovery to illuminate the details. Second, because the claim-construction process lies ahead, the patentee will be reluctant to commit to a position that depends on particular interpretations of the claim language.

The defendant is in a comparable situation at the outset of the case since it needs to know what the claims mean before it can have a clear view of why it does not infringe. In the same vein, the defendant's invalidity contentions, in particular defenses like inadequate written description (§ 112(a)), may depend on the outcome of claim construction. Moreover, invalidity contentions relating to §§ 102 and 103 often require time for investigation of the prior art and discovery of the plaintiff's invention and sales records.

Best practice in this environment requires a combination of flexibility (to accommodate the reasonable constraints faced by each party) and pressure (to force movement and expressions of position that can later be refined). Frequently district courts have imposed a process that draws from the experience of patent local rules, setting a schedule for preliminary contentions, followed by a more committed position following issuance of a claim-construction order.

Unenforceability (inequitable conduct) raises a separate, but related, concern. Because this defense basically asserts fraud on the USPTO, the particularity requirements of Rule 9 require that the accused infringer be specific about the underlying basis for the charge. *See Therasense, Inc. v. Becton, Dickinson & Co.*, 649 F.3d 1276 (Fed. Cir. 2011) (en banc). However, as in other kinds of fraud, the detailed facts, especially those related to materiality and intent, often require substantial discovery before the proponent can be expected to provide a full explanation of the charge.

As noted in §§ 2.6.4, 4.2.2, and 4.2.3, courts should find opportunities to encourage or require parties to disclose their damages contentions and supporting evidence during the fact discovery period. Requiring parties to provide fulsome responses to contention interrogatories concerning damages (and not to simply incorporate by reference expert reports that have not yet been served, as is customary) can prod such disclosures, provided that the responding party has had a meaningful opportunity to take damages-related discovery.

4.6.4 Bifurcation or Stay of Discovery Pending Reexamination of Patent

As described in §§ 2.2.6.4 and 14.2.5.6, anyone can request that the USPTO institute a reexamination proceeding to take a second look at the validity of a patent. Such requests are increasingly common in general and occur more often in the shadow of patent litigation. Often such requests are attended by a motion to the district court to stay discovery or even the entire litigation pending the outcome of the USPTO proceedings. Section 2.2.6.4 explores the general standard for granting a stay of the litigation.

Even when a district court is not inclined to stay the entire litigation, courts are often asked to stay discovery pending reexamination. Where there would be substantial overlap in that discovery with what may still be going on in the case following invalidation of the reexamined claims, it may well be more efficient and equitable to allow some discovery to proceed. A partial stay of discovery in a patent case, however, is difficult to enforce because there are typically no bright-line borders for relevance among different issues in any given case. What may appear as a timesaving hold on some issues may actually result in more time spent resolving disputes over the boundaries of the discovery stay.

4.6.5 Bifurcation or Stay of Discovery Pending Early Dispositive Motion

Sometimes a case presents obvious issues for early termination, and in patent cases this could arise from a jurisdictional challenge (e.g., personal jurisdiction, ownership), *see, e.g.*, *Mullally v. Jones*, No. 2:05CV00154-BES-GWF, 2007 WL 1213704, 2007 U.S. Dist. LEXIS 30283, at *6–7 (D. Nev. Apr. 24, 2007), or from a challenge to infringement that depends entirely on a specific question of claim construction, *see, e.g.*, *Cornell Research Found., Inc. v. Hewlett Packard Co.*, 223 F.R.D. 55, 58 (N.D.N.Y. 2003). In these situations, it may be appropriate to limit discovery to the single issue to enable the parties to prepare a dispositive motion. *See* §§ 6.1.3, 6.1.3.4 (discussing dual-track summary judgment framework). Although some questions may arise about whether specific discovery is within the bounds set by the court, the amount of time necessary to resolve that controversy is generally more than offset by the potential savings through early termination.

4.6.6 Bifurcation or Stay of Discovery on Issues Bifurcated for Trial

District courts sometimes bifurcate issues for trial in patent cases. Most common is a counterclaim for antitrust based on an allegation that the patent complaint is a sham, *see In re Innotron Diagnostics*, 800 F.2d 1077 (Fed. Cir. 1986), the defense of inequitable conduct, *Gardco Mfg., Inc. v. Herst Lighting Co.*, 820 F.2d 1209 (Fed. Cir. 1987), and a plaintiff's assertion of willfulness, *see Medpointe Healthcare, Inc. v. Hi-Tech Pharmacal Co., Inc.*, Civ. Action Nos. 03-5550 (MLC), 04-1686 (MLC), 2007 WL 188285, 2007 U.S. Dist. LEXIS 4652, at *17 (D.N.J. Jan. 22, 2007). We address the risks and potential rewards of this discretionary decision to divide up the trial in § 8.1.1.

Having made or entertained trial bifurcation, courts will also need to consider whether discovery should go forward on the bifurcated issue. Here, unless a primary driver of the decision to bifurcate is to save time and other complications in discovery (as is often true in bifurcating willfulness, for example), often the best practice is to presume that discovery should go forward on all issues. *See, e.g., Ecrix Corp. v. Exabyte Corp.*, 191 F.R.D. 611, 614 (D. Colo. 2000). In this way, the parties will be prepared to proceed immediately with trial on the bifurcated issue if it becomes relevant, the court will be spared the difficulty of drawing lines about what is relevant for discovery, and the parties will be fully informed on all the issues for purposes of settlement discussions. On the other hand, when an essential element of a claim is related to the outcome of another claim in the suit, as in a sham-litigation antitrust counterclaim, it might make more sense to stay the one claim in its entirety (including discovery) until the underlying claim is adjudicated. *See Prof. Real Estate Investors, Inc. v. Columbia Pictures, Inc.*, 508 U.S. 49, 60 (1993) (affirming grant of summary judgment against antitrust counterclaim, though further discovery into anticompetitive intent had been denied by the district court) (holding that "[o]nly if challenged litigation is objectively meritless may a court examine the litigant's subjective motivation"). After all, a "winning lawsuit is by definition a reasonable effort at petitioning for redress and therefore not a sham." *Id.* at 60 n.5.

4.6.7 Privilege Waiver Based on Defendant's Election to Rely on Advice of Counsel

The Federal Circuit's decision in *In re Seagate Tech. LLC*, 497 F.3d 1360 (Fed. Cir. 2007) (en banc) reduced motion practice regarding privilege waiver scope in holding that disclosing an opinion of counsel to support an advice-of-counsel defense does not extend the waiver to trial counsel. *Id.* at 1372–75. The same rationale applies to the work-product doctrine as well, protecting from discovery the sometimes voluminous and provocative thoughts and strategies of litigation counsel. *Id.* at 1375–76. The Federal Circuit left unanswered the question of what to do when opinion counsel and trial counsel are from the same firm, or even the same person.

4.6.8 Discovery from Patent Prosecution Counsel

A claim of patent infringement by itself does not usually require taking discovery from the lawyer who prosecuted the application. Whatever happened in prosecution is a matter of record, and claim-construction issues are decided based on that "intrinsic" record. *See* § 5.2.2. For example, if the defendant asserts that a statement by the patentee to the USPTO should be considered as a "disclaimer" of claim scope, normally the court would not hear testimony from the patent lawyer to explain what was said or why it was said. Therefore, while inventor testimony is almost always taken during discovery, the same is not true of the patent lawyer.

That is not to say, however, that patent prosecutors are never or even seldom deposed. In some cases, the defense of unenforceability will be asserted based on allegations of inequitable conduct in the procurement of the patent. Most often this consists of a failure to disclose certain prior art, but it can also involve mischaracterization of the art that was submitted or other misstatements made to the USPTO. In those cases, the patent attorney is almost always deposed.

As in other areas of the law, attorney testimony raises issues of work-product protection and privilege. In the patent prosecution context, the general rule is that the attorney–client privilege applies to communications between the inventor and the prosecuting attorney but there is no protection against discovery of communications, whether written or oral, between the patent prosecutor and the USPTO. *See In re Spalding Sports Worldwide, Inc.*, 203 F.3d 800 (Fed. Cir. 2000); *Winbond Elecs. Corp. v. ITC*, 262 F.3d 1363, 1376 (Fed. Cir. 2001). Courts generally find that work performed by an attorney to prepare and prosecute a patent application does not fall within the parameters of the work-product protection because it is usually part of a nonadversarial, ex parte proceeding. *See, e.g., In re Minebea Co.*, 143 F.R.D. 494, 499 (S.D.N.Y. 1992). Accordingly, work done to that end is not usually "in anticipation of" or "concerning" litigation. Discovery disputes in this context often test the application of this rule. *See, e.g., Rowe Int'l Corp. v. Ecast, Inc.*, 241 F.R.D. 296, 300–01 (N.D. Ill. 2007); *Bd. of Trs. of the Leland Stanford Junior Univ. v. Roche Molecular Sys., Inc.*, 237 F.R.D. 618, 623–25 (N.D. Cal. 2006). Indeed, the work-product doctrine can protect work performed to prosecute a patent application if it was *also* performed in anticipation of or concerning litigation. *Minebea*, 143 F.R.D. at 499.

In practice, discovery taken from patent prosecutors may not be very helpful, either because memories have lapsed with the passage of time or the prosecutor purged all nonessential papers (such as drafts) once the patent issued. This file management practice is relatively common, but it is inconsistent with a later assertion of work-product protection. If litigation was anticipated, a patent prosecutor was duty-bound to preserve potential evidence, and nothing should have been discarded.

Occasionally the lawyer who prosecuted the patent application also serves as counsel of record in the litigation. Here, the lawyer's choice to act as both advocate and witness is necessarily awkward, but the authority that bars taking deposition of trial counsel will usually not apply. *See, e.g., Plymouth Indus., LLC v. Sioux Steel Co.*, No. 8:05CV196, 8:05CV469, 2006 WL 695458, 2006 U.S. Dist. LEXIS 14706, at *14–15 (D. Neb. Mar. 17, 2006); *Genal Strap, Inc. v. Dar*, No. CV2004-1691(SJ)(MDG), 2006 WL 525794, 2006 U.S. Dist. LEXIS 11474, at *6–10 (E.D.N.Y. Mar. 3, 2006);

aaiPharma, Inc. v. Kremers Urban Dev. Co., 361 F. Supp. 2d 770, 774–75 (N.D. Ill. 2005); *Alcon Labs., Inc. v. Pharmacia Corp.*, 225 F. Supp. 2d 340, 344 (S.D.N.Y. 2002); *Amicus Commc'ns, L.P. v. Hewlett-Packard Co.*, No. 99-0284 HHK/DAR, 1999 WL 33117227, 1999 U.S. Dist. LEXIS 20901, at *4–5 (D.D.C. Dec. 3, 1999); *Environ Prods. v. Total Containment, Inc.*, 41 U.S.P.Q.2d (BNA) 1302, at *11–14 (E.D. Pa. Aug. 21, 1996). In general, the prosecutor should receive no special dispensation from discovery merely because of the decision to also act as litigation counsel, but privilege and work-product protections will normally apply to communications made and information developed in the context of litigation rather than prosecution. To resolve such contextual issues, the court may have to examine relevant material in camera. *See Quantum Corp. v. Tandon Corp.*, 940 F.2d 642, 644 (Fed. Cir. 1991). Whether the prosecutor as litigator requires disqualification is a matter of the ethics rules of a particular jurisdiction. *See, e.g., Gen. Elec. Co. v. Industra Prods., Inc.*, 683 F. Supp. 1254, 1258 (N.D. Ind. 1988).

4.6.9 Access to Confidential Information by Patent Prosecution Counsel

In settling on the form of an umbrella protective order, a dispute may arise over whether a party's patent prosecution lawyers may appear as counsel of record in the litigation and, therefore, have access to attorneys-only information. The advantage to the requesting party is easy to understand: its patent attorneys already have experience with the technology and their participation on the litigation team will enhance efficiency. This perceived advantage, as well as the natural deference owed to a party's choice of counsel, must be weighed against the risk that such access might pose to the other side.

Much of the risk arises from the fact that a single patent can spawn a family of later patents on the same subject. These "continuation" applications seek to fashion better claims based on the same original disclosure. Indeed, it is common and acceptable for a patentee to draft later claims that precisely target the products of a competitor. *See Kingsdown Med. Consultants, Ltd. v. Hollister, Inc.*, 863 F.2d 867, 874 (Fed. Cir. 1988). But the fairness of that practice presumes that such claims are drafted based on *public* information. When a patent prosecutor gets access to attorneys-only information in litigation, this can open a door into the details of secret projects and provide an unfair advantage. Because of this concern, some courts have imposed a "prosecution bar" as part of the normal discovery protective order. *See* §§ 2.1.2, 4.2.5. In its most typical form, the provision bars any lawyer having access to designated information from participating in prosecution of patents in a particular subject during the pendency of the litigation and a year after its termination. If it appears that a prosecution bar is appropriate, the dispute may devolve to the subject-matter restriction, with the proponent of the bar arguing for a broad area, and the resisting party proposing only the particular patent family being prosecuted on behalf of that party. *See, e.g., Cummins-Allison Corp. v. Glory Ltd.*, No. 02 C 7008, 2003 WL 26620151, 2003 U.S. Dist. LEXIS 23653, at *31–33 (N.D. Ill. Dec. 31, 2003).

The decision on whether to impose a prosecution bar, and its conditions, should be informed by such factors as (1) the level of competition and sensitivity of the data, (2) the attorney's role in ongoing prosecution, (3) the size of the attorney's firm and effectiveness of any proposed ethical walls, (4) the availability of other counsel to handle the litigation, and (5) whether the attorney participated in prosecution of the patent in suit and therefore may be called as a witness. *See, e.g.*, *In re Deutsche Bank*, 605 F.3d 1373 (Fed. Cir. 2010) (granting writ of mandamus to vacate a protective order and remanding with instructions to apply the new standard regarding the scope of prosecution bars); *Commissariat a L'Energie Atomique v. Dell Comput. Corp.*, No. Civ.A. 03-484-KAJ, 2004 WL 406351, 2004 U.S. Dist. LEXIS 12782 (D. Del. Mar. 3, 2004); *Motorola, Inc. v. Interdigital Tech. Corp.*, No. Civ.A. 93-488-LON, 1994 WL 16189689, 1994 U.S. Dist. LEXIS 20714 (D. Del. Dec. 19, 1994); *see also U.S. Steel Corp. v. United States*, 730 F.2d 1465, 1468 (Fed. Cir. 1984).

This analysis has been challenging to apply with respect to PTAB proceedings. As discussed in §§ 2.1.2.1.3, 2.2.6.4, and 4.2.5.3, many courts carve PTAB review practice out of the definition of "prosecution" in prosecution bars in protective orders because the PTAB has been reluctant to permit claim amendments during its review proceedings. The liberalization of the PTAB's amendment practices could justify tightening prosecution bars to limit access by counsel involved in PTAB review.

4.6.10 License Agreements and Other Third-Party Confidential Information

Damage calculations in a patent case depend on assessment of a number of factors, including licenses entered into by either party for the relevant technology or for comparable intellectual property. *See* §§ 2.6.6, 14.4.3.2.1.4; *Georgia-Pacific Corp. v. United States Plywood Corp.*, 318 F. Supp. 1116 (S.D.N.Y. 1970). Many of these agreements are confidential and competitively sensitive, sometimes involving rights of third parties. Therefore, a common area of dispute is the discoverability of proprietary license agreements. The resisting party may argue that they are not sufficiently comparable to provide relevant information or that they interfere with obligations of confidentiality to a nonparty. A court's decision should be guided not only by resolving those arguments as factual predicates, but also by the terms of any protective order that might diminish the risk of harm from production. *See, e.g.*, *Rates Tech., Inc. v. Cablevision Sys. Corp.*, No. CV 05-3583 DRH WDW, 2006 WL 1026044, 2006 U.S. Dist. LEXIS 19668, at *5 (E.D.N.Y. Apr. 14, 2006); *Anchor Plastics Co. v. Dynex Indus. Plastics Corp.*, 184 U.S.P.Q. (BNA) 482 (D.N.J. 1974). Discovery is normally allowed and use at trial is decided later with a fuller record on relatedness.

Other common ways that third-party interests arise in patent litigation include product development, prior art, and users of an accused device. In the first category, third parties may have been involved, through a joint venture or other collaborative relationship, in the discovery of the claimed invention. The circumstances may lead to questions about ownership, standing, or other matters bearing on validity. In the second category are companies or individuals believed to have published or practiced the relevant technology before the patentee claims to have conceived of it. The third category comprises users of the accused product whose use of it (for example, combining it into a bigger product that itself infringes) may be relevant to proving contributory infringement or inducement, or demonstrating commercial success. All of these third parties could resist discovery because it is claimed to be unduly burdensome; and indeed their status as outsiders to the dispute is entitled to some consideration. *See, e.g.*, *Katz v. Batavia Marine & Sporting Supplies, Inc.*, 984 F.2d 422, 424 (Fed. Cir. 1993). Third parties can also object because the requested information is extremely sensitive and should not be made available to an arch-competitor. These objections, while legitimate, are usually addressed by the terms of a protective order that appropriately limits access and use of the information. However, sometimes the information, while relevant and protectable in the abstract, can be sought in ways that inappropriately threaten damage to customer relationships. In such circumstances, the court can issue a protective order requiring a heightened showing of need before the discovery goes forward. *See, e.g.*, *Joy Techs., Inc. v. Flakt, Inc.*, 722 F. Supp. 842 (D. Del. 1991).

4.6.10.1 Discovery Regarding Prior License and Settlement Negotiations

The increasing importance of prior license agreements in assessing reasonable royalty damages, *see* § 14.4.3.2.1.4; *Lucent Techs., Inc. v. Gateway, Inc.*, 580 F.3d 1301 (Fed. Cir. 2009), has focused attention on the discoverability of prior confidential license agreements and settlement negotiations. *See ResQNet.com, Inc. v. Lansa, Inc.*, 594 F.3d 860 (Fed. Cir. 2010); *Wordtech Sys. v. Integrated Network Sols., Inc.*, 609 F.3d 1308 (Fed. Cir. 2010); *IP Innovation L.L.C. v. Red Hat, Inc.*, Case No. 2:07-cv-447 (RRR), 705 F. Supp. 2d 687 (E.D. Tex. 2010) (Rader, C.J., circuit judge, sitting by designation). Under these cases, the damages inquiry at all times "must concentrate on compensation for the economic harm caused by infringement of the claimed inventions," and proof of damages must be tied carefully to "the claimed invention's footprint in the market place." *ResQNet.com*, 594 F.3d at 869. The key inquiry is whether the claims describe features that create market demand. The amount of damages must closely reflect the economic value of the patented feature in relation to the accused product. *See, e.g.*, *Lucent Techs.*, 580 F.3d at 1332–33.

Under these decisions, prior license agreements gain heightened importance. In many cases, one party would like to argue that a prior license is not a fair representation of the actual market value, but instead reflects an idiosyncratic negotiation. In these situations, parties will seek discovery regarding the negotiation that resulted in the license. *See Clear With Computers, LLC v. Hyundai Motor Am., Inc.*, 753 F. Supp. 2d 662 (E.D. Tex. 2010).

Despite these decisions, some parties have attempted to block discovery into negotiation documents by claiming that they are protected from disclosure by a so-called settlement privilege that encompasses not only internal documents of one party to the agreement or proposed agreement, but also documents exchanged between the parties. The Federal Circuit closed the door on this alleged privilege in *In re MSTG*, 675 F.3d 1337 (Fed. Cir. 2012). First, the court held that the determination about whether a settlement privilege bars discovery of negotiation documents, which have relevance to the determination of a reasonable royalty, is a matter of Federal Circuit, rather than regional circuit, law. *Id.* at 1341. Next, the court held that, as a matter of Federal Circuit law, "settlement negotiations related to reasonable royalty and damage calculations are not protected by a settlement negotiation privilege." *Id.* at 1348. In so holding, it observed that Federal Rule of Evidence 408, which was adopted with congressional approval, includes exceptions that contemplate the discovery of such materials (e.g., the rule permits use of settlement materials to impeach a witness's credibility). *Id.* at 1343–45. The court also observed that a "settlement privilege" has been recognized by no states and by only one regional circuit (the 6th Circuit). *Id.* at 1342. And a "new privilege" is not necessary to foster settlement, of course, because "disputes are routinely settled without the benefit of a settlement privilege." *Id.* at 1345. Finally, the court noted that, to prevent abuse of the discovery process, courts have the power to restrict the discoverability or use of information, such as by "limit[ing] discovery of material that is not itself admissible and that was not utilized by the opposing party" in appropriate circumstances. *Id.* at 1346–48.

The purported settlement privilege having been rejected outright, future attempts to shield discovery of negotiation materials in patent cases are most likely to focus on this last observation. Indeed, the court expressly "reserve[d] for another day the issue of what limits can appropriately be placed on discovery of settlement negotiations." *Id.* at 1347. One such area left untouched, at least explicitly, by *MSTG* is the discoverability or nondiscoverability of materials generated as part of a court-mandated mediation process. But, with respect to materials that were not generated as part of court-mandated mediation, even this language in *MSTG* seems unlikely to yield substantial protection in view of the recent Federal Circuit holdings permitting the use of settlement agreements in factoring damages. As one example, because a patentee's agreements concerning the patents-in-suit are themselves typically discoverable and admissible, its damages expert has little practical choice but to consider them—in this example, if he or she does not, he or she would have no ability to respond if the opposing party's damages expert relies upon them in rebutting the patentee's damages opinions. In this example, once such agreements are considered, discovery of negotiation documents concerning those agreements seems naturally to follow, if for no other reason than to enable the opposing party to determine whether the patentee's damages expert can be impeached. Of course, this is but one example of the myriad fact patterns from which a dispute of this nature could be presented to a district court, and, general observations about likely outcomes notwithstanding, courts should consider the specific facts of each such dispute carefully.

The *MSTG* decision also noted that other courts had "imposed heightened standards of discovery in order to protect confidential settlement discussions." *Id.* at 1347. The court did not specifically address whether such heightened standards would apply under Federal Circuit law, but expressly reserved this issue for another day. *Id.* An open question thus remains whether such heightened standards apply to settlement evidence under Federal Circuit law, and if so, under what circumstances they would apply. In 2012, the Federal Circuit took another step toward clarifying *ResQNet.com* and *MSTG*, observing that the admissibility of settlement-related evidence is generally disfavored under the Federal Rules of Evidence because of its inherent unreliability. *See LaserDynamics, Inc. v. Quanta Comput., Inc.*, 694 F.3d 51, 78 (Fed. Cir. 2012). The court noted, however, that the unique facts presented in *ResQNet.com* (where the only relevant evidence in the record was a settlement license) rendered it an outlier to this general rule. *Id.* at 77–78. It is also still unclear whether (and how) Federal Rule of Evidence 408 applies to patent-settlement-related evidence, and if so, how Rule 408 should properly interact with Article VII of the Federal Rules of Evidence.

Appendix 4.1
Table: Circuit Courts' Approach to Sanctions for Spoliation

Reprinted from *Victor Stanley, Inc. v. Creative Pipe, Inc.*, 269 F.R.D. 497, 542 (D. Md. 2010).

Sanctions for Spoliation

Circuit/ Case law	Scope of duty to preserve	Can conduct be culpable per se without consideration of reasonableness?	Culpability and prejudice requirements				What constitutes prejudice	Culpability and corresponding jury instructions
			for sanctions in general	for dispositive sanctions	for adverse inference instruction	for a rebuttable presumption of relevance		
First	It is a duty to preserve potentially relevant evidence a party owns or controls and also a duty to notify the opposing party of evidence in the hands of third parties. *Velez v. Marriott PR Mgmt., Inc.*, 590 F. Supp. 2d 235, 258 (D.P.R. 2008).	This specific issue has not been addressed.	"The measure of the appropriate sanctions will depend on the severity of the prejudice suffered." *Velez v. Marriott PR Mgmt., Inc.*, 590 F. Supp. 2d 235, 259 (D.P.R. 2008). "[C]arelessness is enough for a district court to consider imposing sanctions." *Driggin v. Am. Sec. Alarm Co.*, 141 F. Supp. 2d 113, 123 (D. Me. 2000).	"severe prejudice or egregious conduct" *Driggin v. Am. Sec. Alarm Co.*, 141 F. Supp. 2d 113, 123 (D. Me. 2000).	"does not require bad faith or comparable bad motive" *Trull v. Volkswagon of Am., Inc.*, 187 F.3d 88, 95 (1st Cir. 1999); *Oxley v. Penobscot County*, No. CV-09-21-JAW, 2010 WL 3154975 (D. Me. 2010).	Whether relevance can be presumed has not been addressed.	When spoliation substantially denies a party the ability to support or defend the claim. *Velez v. Marriott PR Mgmt., Inc.*, 590 F. Supp. 2d 235, 259 (D.P.R. 2008).	Intentional spoliation; permissive adverse inference if the jury finds that the spoliator knew of the lawsuit and the documents' relevance when it destroyed them. *Testa v. Wal-Mart Stores, Inc.*, 144 F.3d 173, 178 (1st Cir. 1998).

Circuit/ Case law	Scope of duty to preserve	Can conduct be culpable per se without consideration of reasonableness?	Culpability and prejudice requirements				What constitutes prejudice	Culpability and corresponding jury instructions
			for sanctions in general	for dispositive sanctions	for adverse inference instruction	for a rebuttable presumption of relevance		
Second	Documents that are potentially relevant to likely litigation "are considered to be under a party's control," such that the party has a duty to preserve them, "when that party has the right, authority, or practical ability to obtain the documents from a non-party to the action." *In re NTL, Inc. Sec. Litig.*, 244 F.R.D. 179, 195 (S.D.N.Y. 2007). The duty extends to key players. *Zubulake v. UBS Warburg LLC*, 220 F.R.D. 212, 217 (S.D.N.Y. 2003).	Yes; specific actions, such as the failure "to issue a written litigation hold," constitute gross negligence *per se*. *Pension Comm. of the Univ. of Montreal Pension Plan v. Banc of Am. Sec.*, 685 F. Supp. 2d 456, 471 (S.D.N.Y. 2010).	"[D]iscovery sanctions . . . may be imposed upon a party that has breached a discovery obligation not only through bad faith or gross negligence, but also through ordinary negligence." *Residential Funding Corp. v. DeGeorge Fin. Corp.*, 306 F.3d 99, 113 (2d Cir. 2002).	"'willfulness, bad faith, or fault on the part of the sanctioned party'" *Dahoda v. John Deere Co.*, 216 F. App'x 124, 125, 2007 WL 491846, at *1 (2d Cir. 2007) (quoting *West v. Goodyear Tire & Rubber Co.*, 167 F.3d 776, 779 (2d Cir. 1999)).	Gross negligence. *Pension Comm. of the Univ. of Montreal Pension Plan v. Banc of Am. Sec.*, 685 F. Supp. 2d 456, 478- 79 (S.D.N.Y. 2010). Negligence. *Residential Funding Corp. v. DeGeorge Fin. Corp.*, 306 F.3d 99, 108 (2d Cir. 2002). Intentional conduct. *In re Terrorist Bombings of U.S. Embassies in East Africa*, 552 F.3d 93, 148 (2d Cir. 2008).	Bad faith or gross negligence. *Pension Comm. of the Univ. of Montreal Pension Plan v. Banc of Am. Sec.*, 685 F. Supp. 2d 456, 467 (S.D.N.Y. 2010).	When spoliation substantially denies a party the ability to support or defend the claim. *Pension Comm. of the Univ. of Montreal Pension Plan v. Banc of Am. Sec.*, 685 F. Supp. 2d 456, 479 (S.D.N.Y. 2010).	Grossly negligent conduct; permissible inference of "the relevance of the missing documents and resulting prejudice to the . . . Defendants, subject to the plaintiffs' ability to rebut the presumption to the satisfaction of the trier of fact." *Pension Comm. of the Univ. of Montreal Pension Plan v. Banc of Am. Sec.*, 685 F. Supp. 2d 456, 478 (S.D.N.Y. 2010).

Circuit/ Case law	Scope of duty to preserve	Can conduct be culpable per se without consideration of reasonableness?	Culpability and prejudice requirements				What constitutes prejudice	Culpability and corresponding jury instructions
			for sanctions in general	for dispositive sanctions	for adverse inference instruction	for a rebuttable presumption of relevance		
Third	Potentially relevant evidence; "'it is essential that the evidence in question be within the party's control.'" *Canton v. Kmart Corp.*, No. 1:05-CV- 143, 2009 WL 2058908, at *2 (D.V.I. July 13, 2009) (quoting *Brewer v. Quaker State Oil Refining Corp.*, 72 F.3d 326, 334 (3d Cir. 1995)).	No; conduct is culpable if "party [with] notice that evidence is relevant to an action . . . either proceeds to destroy that evidence or allows it to be destroyed by failing to take *reasonable* precautions." *Canton v. Kmart Corp.*, No. 1:05-CV-143, 2009 WL 2058908, at *3 (D.V.I. July 13, 2009) (quoting *Mosaid Techs., Inc. v. Samsung Elecs. Co.*, 348 F. Supp. 2d 332, 338 (D.N.J. 2004)) (emphasis added).	Bad faith. *Bensel v. Allied Pilots Ass'n*, 263 F.R.D. 150, 152 (D.N.J. 2009).	The degree of fault is considered, and dispositive sanctions "should only be imposed in the most extraordinary of circumstances," *see Mosaid Techs., Inc. v. Samsung Elecs. Co.*, 348 F. Supp. 2d 332, 335 (D.N.J. 2004), but a minimum degree of culpability has not been identified.	Negligence. *Canton v. Kmart Corp.*, No. 1:05-CV-143, 2009 WL 2058908, at *2–3 (D.V.I. July 13, 2009). Intentional conduct. *Brewer v. Quaker State Oil Refining Corp.*, 72 F.3d 326, 334 (3d Cir. 1995).	Whether relevance can be presumed has not been addressed.	Spoliation of evidence that would have helped a party's case. *In re Hechinger Inv. Co. of Del., Inc.*, 489 F.3d 568, 579 (3d Cir. 2007).	Intentional spoliation; permissible inference. *Mosaid Techs., Inc. v. Samsung Elecs. Co.*, 348 F. Supp. 2d 332, 334 (D.N.J. 2004).

Circuit/ Case law	Scope of duty to preserve	Can conduct be culpable per se without consideration of reasonableness?	Culpability and prejudice requirements: for sanctions in general	Culpability and prejudice requirements: for dispositive sanctions	Culpability and prejudice requirements: for adverse inference instruction	Culpability and prejudice requirements: for a rebuttable presumption of relevance	What constitutes prejudice	Culpability and corresponding jury instructions
Fourth	Documents potentially relevant to likely litigation "are considered to be under a party's control," such that the party has a duty to preserve them, "when that party has 'the right, authority, or practical ability to obtain the documents from a non-party to the action.'" *Goodman v. Praxair Servs., Inc.*, 632 F. Supp. 2d 494, 515 (D. Md. 2009). Also a duty to notify the opposing party of evidence in the hands of third parties. *Silvestri v. Gen. Motors Corp.*, 271 F.3d 583, 590 (4th Cir. 2001). Duty extends to key players. *Goodman*, 632 F. Supp. 2d at 512.	The District of Maryland has quoted *Zubulake IV*, 220 F.R.D. at 220 ("Once the duty to preserve attaches, any destruction of documents is, at a minimum, negligent."). *See Sampson v. City of Cambridge*, No. WDQ-06-1819, 2008 WL 7514364, at *8 (D. Md. May 1, 2008); *Pandora Jewelry, LLC v. Chamilia, LLC*, No. CCB-06-3041, 2008 WL 4533902, at *9 (D. Md. Sept. 30, 2008) (finding defendant's conduct grossly negligent); *cf. Goodman*, 632 F. Supp. 2d at 522 (stating that defendant, "much like the defendants in *Sampson* and *Pandora*, was clearly negligent" because it failed to implement a litigation hold, but also explaining why such action was negligent).	"only a showing of fault, with the degree of fault impacting the severity of sanctions" *Sampson v. City of Cambridge*, 251 F.R.D. 172, 179 (D. Md. 2008) (using "fault" to describe conduct ranging from bad faith destruction to ordinary negligence).	The court must "be able to conclude either (1) that the spoliator's conduct was so egregious as to amount to a forfeiture of his claim, or (2) that the effect of the spoliator's conduct was so prejudicial that it substantially denied the defendant the ability to defend the claim." *Silvestri v. Gen. Motors Corp.*, 271 F.3d 583, 593 (4th Cir. 2001).	The court "must only find that spoliator acted willfully in the destruction of evidence." *Goodman v. Praxair Servs., Inc.*, 632 F. Supp. 2d 494, 519 (D. Md. 2009).	Willful behavior. *Sampson v. City of Cambridge*, 251 F.R.D. 172, 179 (D. Md. 2008).	When spoliation substantially denies a party the ability to support or defend the claim. *Goodman v. Praxair Servs., Inc.*, 632 F. Supp. 2d 494, 519 (D. Md. 2009); *Sampson v. City of Cambridge*, 251 F.R.D. 172, 180 (D. Md. 2008).	Willful spoliation; adverse jury instruction, but not the "series of fact-specific adverse jury instructions" that the plaintiff requested. *Goodman v. Praxair Servs., Inc.*, 632 F. Supp. 2d 494, 523 (D. Md. 2009).

Circuit/ Case law	Scope of duty to preserve	Can conduct be culpable per se without consideration of reasonableness?	Culpability and prejudice requirements				What constitutes prejudice	Culpability and corresponding jury instructions
			for sanctions in general	for dispositive sanctions	for adverse inference instruction	for a rebuttable presumption of relevance		
Fifth	Party with control over potentially relevant evidence has a duty to preserve it; scope includes evidence in possession of "employees likely to have relevant information, i.e., 'the key players.'" *Tango Transp., LLC v. Transp. Int'l Pool, Inc.*, No. 5:08-CV-0559, 2009 WL 3254882, at *3 (W.D. La. Oct. 8, 2009).	No: "Whether preservation or discovery conduct is acceptable in a case depends on what is reasonable, and that in turn depends on whether what was done- or not done- was proportional to that case and consistent with clearly established applicable standards." *Rimkus Consulting Grp., Inc. v. Cammarata*, 688 F. Supp. 2d 598, 613 (S.D. Tex. 2010).	"some degree of culpability" *Rimkus Consulting Grp., Inc. v. Cammarata*, 688 F. Supp. 2d 598, 613 (S.D. Tex. 2010).	Bad faith (and prejudice). *Rimkus Consulting Grp., Inc. v. Cammarata*, 688 F. Supp. 2d 598, 614 (S.D. Tex. 2010).	Bad faith. *Rimkus Consulting Grp., Inc. v. Cammarata*, 688 F. Supp. 2d 598, 617 (S.D. Tex. 2010).	"The Fifth Circuit has not explicitly addressed whether even bad-faith destruction of evidence allows a court to presume that the destroyed evidence was relevant or its loss prejudicial." *Rimkus Consulting Grp., Inc. v. Cammarata*, 688 F. Supp. 2d 598, 617–18 (S.D. Tex. 2010).	When spoliation substantially denies a party the ability to support or defend the claim. *Rimkus Consulting Grp., Inc. v. Cammarata*, 688 F. Supp. 2d 598, 613 (S.D. Tex. 2010).	Willful spoliation; jury instruction would "ask the jury to decide whether the defendants intentionally deleted e-mails and attachments to prevent their use in litigation." *Rimkus Consulting Grp., Inc. v. Cammarata*, 688 F. Supp. 2d 598, 620, 646 (S.D. Tex. 2010).

Circuit/ Case law	Scope of duty to preserve	Can conduct be culpable per se without consideration of reasonableness?	Culpability and prejudice requirements				What constitutes prejudice	Culpability and corresponding jury instructions
			for sanctions in general	for dispositive sanctions	for adverse inference instruction	for a rebuttable presumption of relevance		
Sixth	It is a duty to preserve potentially relevant evidence that a party owns or controls and to notify the opposing party of evidence in the hands of third parties. *Jain v. Memphis Shelby Airport Auth.*, No. 08-2119-STA-dkv, 2010 WL 711328, at *2 (W.D. Tenn. Feb. 25, 2010). Duty extends to key players *In re Nat'l Century Fin. Enters., Inc. Fin. Inv. Litig.*, No. 2:03-md- 1565, 2009 WL 2169174, at *11 (S.D. Ohio July 16, 2009).	This specific issue has not been addressed. In *BancorpSouth Bank v. Herter*, 643 F. Supp. 2d 1041, 1061 (W.D. Tenn. 2009), the court quoted *Zubulake IV*, 220 F.R.D. at 220 ("Once the duty to preserve attaches, any destruction of documents is, at a minimum, negligent."), but it also analyzed the defendant's conduct to make the finding that it was "more than negligent."	Bad faith (intentional) destruction, gross negligence, or ordinary negligence. *In re Global Technovations, Inc.*, 431 B.R. 739, 780 (Bankr. E.D. Mich. 2010) (equating intentional and bad faith conduct).	willfulness, bad faith, or fault *In re Global Technovations, Inc.*, 431 B.R. 739, 779 (Bankr. E.D. Mich. 2010) (using "fault" to describe conduct ranging from intentional conduct to ordinary negligence). Other cases in circuit define "fault" as "objectively unreasonable behavior." *E.g., BancorpSouth Bank v. Herter*, 643 F. Supp. 2d 1041, 1060 (W.D. Tenn. 2009); *Jain v. Memphis Shelby Airport Auth.*, No. 08-2119-STA-dkv, 2010 WL 711328, at *3 (W.D. Tenn. Feb. 25, 2010).	Bad faith. *In re Global Technovations, Inc.*, 431 B.R. 739, 782 (Bankr. E.D. Mich. 2010). Bad faith not required *Miller v. Home Depot USA, Inc.*, No. 3-08-0281, 2010 WL 373860, at *1 (M.D. Tenn. Jan. 28, 2010). Ordinary negligence *Jain v. Memphis Shelby Airport Auth.*, No. 08- 2119-STA-dkv, 2010 WL 711328, at *3 (W.D. Tenn. Feb. 25, 2010); *Forest Labs., Inc. v. Caraco Pharm. Labs., Ltd.*, No. 06- CV-13143, 2009 WL 998402, at *5– 6 (E.D. Mich. Apr. 14, 2009).	"The spoliating party bears the burden of establishing lack of prejudice to the opposing party, a burden the Sixth Circuit has described as 'an uphill battle.'" *Jain v. Memphis Shelby Airport Auth.*, No. 08-2119-STA- dkv, 2010 WL 711328, at *2 (W.D. Tenn. Feb. 25, 2010).	When spoliation substantially denies a party the ability to support or defend the claim. *Jain v. Memphis Shelby Airport Auth.*, No. 08-2119-STA-dkv, 2010 WL 711328, at *4 (W.D. Tenn. Feb. 25, 2010).	Unintentional conduct; permissible inference. *Jain v. Memphis Shelby Airport Auth.*, No. 08-2119-STA-dkv, 2010 WL 711328, at *4-5 (W.D. Tenn. Feb. 25, 2010).

Circuit/ Case law	Scope of duty to preserve	Can conduct be culpable per se without consideration of reasonableness?	Culpability and prejudice requirements				What constitutes prejudice	Culpability and corresponding jury instructions
			for sanctions in general	for dispositive sanctions	for adverse inference instruction	for a rebuttable presumption of relevance		
Seventh	Duty to preserve potentially relevant evidence party has control over *Jones v. Bremen High Sch. Dist. 228*, No. 08-C-3548, 2010 WL 2106640, at *5 (N.D. Ill. May 25, 2010).	No: Breach is failure to act reasonably under the circumstances. *Jones v. Bremen High Sch. Dist. 228*, No. 08-C- 3548, 2010 WL 2106640, at *6–7 (N.D. Ill. May 25, 2010). "The failure to institute a document retention policy, in the form of a litigation hold, is relevant to the court's consideration, but it is not *per se* evidence of sanctionable conduct." *Haynes v. Dart*, No. 08 C 4834, 2010 WL 140387, at *4 (N.D. Ill. Jan. 11, 2010).	Willfulness, bad faith, or fault. *Jones v. Bremen High Sch. Dist. 228*, No. 08-C-3548, 2010 WL 2106640, at *5 (N.D. Ill. May 25, 2010) (stating that fault is based on the reasonableness of the party's conduct). Bad faith. *BP Amoco Chemical Co. v. Flint Hills Resources, LLC*, No. 05 C 5, 2010 WL 1131660, at *24 (N.D. Ill. Mar. 25, 2010).	Willfulness, bad faith, or fault. *In re Kmart Corp.*, 371 B.R. 823, 840 (Bankr. N.D. Ill. 2007) (noting that fault, while based on reasonableness, is more than a "'slight error in judgment'") (citation omitted)	Bad faith. *Faas v. Sears, Roebuck & Co.*, 532 F.3d 633, 644 (7th Cir. 2008).	Unintentional conduct is insufficient for presumption of relevance. *In re Kmart Corp.*, 371 B.R. 823, 853-54 (Bankr. N.D. Ill. 2007).	When spoliation substantially denies a party the ability to support or defend the claim. *Krumwiede v. Brighton Assocs., L.L.C.*, No. 05-C-3003, 2006 WL 1308629, at *10 (N.D. Ill. May 8, 2006). When spoliation substantially denies a party the ability to support or defend the claim OR delays production of evidence. *Jones v. Bremen High Sch. Dist. 228*, No. 08-C-3548, 2010 WL 2106640, at *8–9 (N.D. Ill. May 25, 2010).	Grossly negligent conduct; jury instruction to inform the jury of the defendant's duty and breach thereof. *Jones v. Bremen High Sch. Dist. 228*, No. 08-C-3548, 2010 WL 2106640, at *10 (N.D. Ill. May 25, 2010).

Circuit/ Case law	Scope of duty to preserve	Can conduct be culpable per se without consideration of reasonableness?	Culpability and prejudice requirements				What constitutes prejudice	Culpability and corresponding jury instructions
			for sanctions in general	for dispositive sanctions	for adverse inference instruction	for a rebuttable presumption of relevance		
Eighth	Duty to preserve potentially relevant documents in party's possession. *Dillon v. Nissan Motor Co.*, 986 F.2d 263, 267 (8th Cir. 1993).	Courts in the Eighth Circuit have not found conduct culpable without analyzing the facts, although reasonableness is not discussed.	Bad faith. *Wright v. City of Salisbury*, No. 2:07CV0056 AGF, 2010 WL 126011, at *2 (E.D. Mo. Apr. 6, 2010).	Bad faith. *Johnson v. Avco Corp.*, No. 4:07CV 1695 CDP, 2010 WL 1329361, at *13 (E.D. Mo. 2010); *Menz v. New Holland N. Am., Inc.*, 440 F.3d 1002, 1006 (8th Cir. 2006).	Bad faith. *Greyhound Lines, Inc. v. Wade*, 485 F.3d 1032, 1035 (8th Cir. 2007); *Menz v. New Holland N. Am., Inc.*, 440 F.3d 1002, 1006 (8th Cir. 2006); *Stevenson v. Union Pac. RR*, 354 F.3d 739, 747 (8th Cir. 2004) (bad faith required if spoliation happens prelitigation). Bad faith is not required to sanction for "the ongoing destruction of records **during litigation** and discovery." *Stevenson*, 354 F.3d at 750; *MeccaTech, Inc. v. Kiser*, 2008 WL 6010937, at *8 (D. Neb. 2008) (same), *adopted in part*, No. 8:05CV570, 2009 WL 1152267 (D. Neb. Apr. 23, 2009).	This issue has not been addressed, but it has been stated that there is no presumption of irrelevance of intentionally destroyed documents. *Alexander v. Nat'l Farmers Org.*, 687 F.2d 1173, 1205 (8th Cir. 1982).	Destruction of evidence that "may have [been] helpful." *Dillon v. Nissan Motor Co.*, 986 F.2d 263, 268 (8th Cir. 1993). "irreparable injury to plaintiffs' claims" *Monsanto Co. v. Woods*, 250 F.R.D. 411, 414 (E.D. Mo. 2008).	"destruction was not 'willful' or malicious,'" but plaintiffs' counsel should have known to preserve the evidence; jury was instructed that "an adverse inference may be drawn from plaintiffs' failure to preserve the vehicle" *Bass v. Gen. Motors Corp.*, 929 F. Supp. 1287, 1290 (W.D. Mo. 1996), *aff'd on this ground*, 150 F.3d 842, 851 (8th Cir. 1998).

Circuit/ Case law	Scope of duty to preserve	Can conduct be culpable per se without consideration of reasonableness?	Culpability and prejudice requirements				What constitutes prejudice	Culpability and corresponding jury instructions
			for sanctions in general	for dispositive sanctions	for adverse inference instruction	for a rebuttable presumption of relevance		
Ninth	Duty to preserve potentially relevant evidence in party's possession *Leon v. IDX Systems Corp.*, 2004 WL 5571412, at *3 (W.D. Wash. 2004), *aff'd*, 464 F.3d 951 (9th Cir. 2006). Duty extends to key players. *Hous. Rights Ctr. v. Sterling*, 2005 WL 3320739, at *3 (C.D. Cal. Mar. 2, 2005).	In *Hous. Rights Ctr. v. Sterling*, 2005 WL 3320739, at *3 (C.D. Cal. Mar. 2, 2005), the court quoted *Zubulake IV*, 220 F.R.D. at 220 ("Once the duty to preserve attaches, any destruction of documents is, at a minimum, negligent."), and found that defendants' "[d]estruction of documents during ongoing litigation was, at a minimum, negligent."	Bad faith not required. *Dae Kon Kwon v. Costco Wholesale Corp.*, No. CIV. 08-360 JMSBMK, 2010 WL 571941, at *2 (D. Haw. 2010); *Carl Zeiss Vision Intern. GmbH v. Signet Armorlite, Inc.*, No. 07CV0894 DMS(POR), 2010 WL 743792, at *15 (S.D. Cal. Mar. 1, 2010), *amended on other grounds*, 2010 WL 1626071 (S.D. Cal. Apr. 21, 2010).	Willfulness, bad faith, or fault. *Dae Kon Kwon v. Costco Wholesale Corp.*, No. CIV. 08-360 JMSBMK, 2010 WL 571941, at *2 (D. Haw. 2010) (requiring that party "engaged deliberately in deceptive practices") "'[D]isobedient conduct not shown to be outside the control of the litigant' is all that is required to demonstrate willfulness, bad faith, or fault." *Henry v. Gill Indus.*, 983 F.2d 943, 948 (9th Cir. 1993).	Bad faith or gross negligence. *Karnazes v. County of San Mateo*, No. 09-0767 MMC (MEJ), 2010 WL 2672003, at *2 (N.D. Cal. July 2, 2010). Bad faith not required. *Otsuka v. Polo Ralph Lauren Corp.*, No. C 07- 02780 SI, 2010 WL 366653, at *3 (N.D. Cal. Jan. 25, 2010).	This issue has not been addressed.	When spoliation substantially denies a party the ability to support or defend the claim. *Henry v. Gill Indus.*, 983 F.2d 943, 948 (9th Cir. 1993).	The Court's research has not located a case in which the court granted an adverse inference instruction and stated what the instruction would be.

Circuit/ Case law	Scope of duty to preserve	Can conduct be culpable per se without consideration of reasonableness?	Culpability and prejudice requirements				What constitutes prejudice	Culpability and corresponding jury instructions
			for sanctions in general	for dispositive sanctions	for adverse inference instruction	for a rebuttable presumption of relevance		
Tenth	Duty extends to key players. *Pinstripe, Inc. v. Manpower, Inc.*, No. 07- CV-620- GKF- PJC, 2009 WL 2252131, at *1 (N.D. Okla. July 29, 2009). A party with possession of potentially relevant evidence has a duty to preserve it; even if the party relinquishes ownership or custody, it must contact the new custodian to preserve the evidence. *Jordan F. Miller Corp. v. Mid-Continent Aircraft Serv.*, 139 F.3d 912, 1998 WL 68879, at *5–6 (10th Cir. 1998).	No. *Procter & Gamble Co. v. Haugen*, 427 F.3d 727, 739 n.8 (10th Cir. 2005) (stating that district court must consider Rule 26(b)(2)[(C)](iii), which requires the court to limit discovery if "the burden or expense of the proposed discovery outweighs its likely benefit").	Bad faith not required. *Hatfield v. Wal-Mart Stores, Inc.*, 335 F. App'x 796, 804 (10th Cir. 2009). Negligence. *Pipes v. UPS, Inc.*, No. CIV.A.07-1762, 2009 WL 2214990, at *1 (W.D. La. July 22, 2009).	"willfulness, bad faith, or [some] fault" *Procter & Gamble Co. v. Haugen*, 427 F.3d 727, 738 (10th Cir. 2005) (using language originally in *Societe Internationale v. Rogers*, 357 U.S. 197, 212 (1958), which distinguished "fault" from a party's inability to act otherwise).	Bad faith. *Turner v. Pub. Serv. Co. of Colo.*, 563 F.3d 1136, 1149 (10th Cir. 2009). Neither bad faith nor intentionality required. *Hatfield v. Wal-Mart Stores, Inc.*, 335 F. App'x 796, 804 (10th Cir. 2009); *Schrieber v. Fed. Ex. Corp.*, No. 09- CV-128-JHP-PJC, 2010 WL 1078463 (N.D. Okla. Mar. 18, 2010).	Although this specific issue has not been addressed, the court declined to "create a presumption in favor of spoliation whenever a moving party can prove that records that might have contained relevant evidence have been destroyed" in *Crandall v. City & County of Denver, Colo.*, No. 05-CV-00242-MSK-MEH, 2006 WL 2683754, at *2 (D. Colo. Sept. 19, 2006).	Spoliation that impairs a party's ability to support a claim or defense. *Pinstripe, Inc. v. Manpower, Inc.*, No. 07-CV-620-GKF-PJC, 2009 WL 2252131, at *2 (N.D. Okla. July 29, 2009).	Bad faith; adverse inference instruction. *Smith v. Slifer Smith & Frampton/Vail Assocs. Real Estate, LLC*, No. CIVA 06CV02206-JLK, 2009 WL 482603, at *13 (D. Colo. Feb. 25, 2009).

Circuit/ Case law	Scope of duty to preserve	Can conduct be culpable per se without consideration of reasonableness?	Culpability and prejudice requirements				What constitutes prejudice	Culpability and corresponding jury instructions
			for sanctions in general	for dispositive sanctions	for adverse inference instruction	for a rebuttable presumption of relevance		
Eleventh	Duty to preserve potentially relevant evidence that party has "access to and control over" *Nat'l Grange Mut. Ins. Co. v. Hearth & Home, Inc.*, No. CIV.A. 2:06CV54WCO, 2006 WL 5157694 at *5 (N.D. Ga. Dec. 19, 2006).	Courts in the Eleventh Circuit have not found conduct culpable without analyzing the facts, although reasonableness is not discussed.	Bad faith. *Managed Care Solutions, Inc. v. Essent Healthcare, Inc.*, No. 09- 60351-CIV, 2010 WL 3368654, at *4 (S.D. Fla. Aug. 23, 2010). Degree of culpability is weighed against prejudice caused by spoliation. *Flury v. Daimler Chrysler Corp.*, 427 F.3d 939, 945 (11th Cir. 2005); *Brown v. Chertoff*, 563 F. Supp. 2d 1372, 1381 (S.D. Ga. 2008).	Bad faith. *Managed Care Solutions, Inc. v. Essent Healthcare, Inc.*, No. 09-60351-CIV, 2010 WL 3368654, at *12 (S.D. Fla. Aug. 23, 2010).	Bad faith. *Penalty Kick Mgmt. Ltd. v. Coca Cola Co.*, 318 F.3d 1284, 1294 (11th Cir. 2003); *Managed Care Solutions, Inc. v. Essent Healthcare, Inc.*, No. 09-60351- CIV, 2010 WL 3368654, at *13 (S.D. Fla. Aug. 23, 2010).	This issue has not been addressed.	Spoliation of evidence that was not just relevant but "crucial" to a claim or defense. *Managed Care Solutions, Inc. v. Essent Healthcare, Inc.*, No. 09-60351- CIV, 2010 WL 3368654, at *8 (S.D. Fla. Aug. 23, 2010).	Negligence; jury to be instructed that the destruction raises a rebuttable inference that the evidence supported plaintiff's claim. *Brown v. Chertoff*, 563 F. Supp. 2d 1372, 1381 (S.D. Ga. 2008) (but other courts in Eleventh Circuit will not order any sanctions without bad faith).

Circuit/ Case law	Scope of duty to preserve	Can conduct be culpable per se without consideration of reasonableness?	Culpability and prejudice requirements: for sanctions in general	Culpability and prejudice requirements: for dispositive sanctions	Culpability and prejudice requirements: for adverse inference instruction	Culpability and prejudice requirements: for a rebuttable presumption of relevance	What constitutes prejudice	Culpability and corresponding jury instructions
D.C.	Duty to preserve potentially relevant evidence "within the ability of the defendant to produce it." *Friends for All Children v. Lockheed Aircraft Corp.*, 587 F. Supp. 180, 189 (D.D.C.), *modified*, 593 F. Supp. 388 (D.D.C.), *aff'd*, 746 F.2d 816 (D.C. Cir. 1984).	Courts in the D.C. Circuit have not found conduct culpable without analyzing the facts, although reasonableness is not discussed.	Case law addresses specific sanctions, rather than sanctions generally.	Bad faith. *Shepherd v. Am. Broad Cos.*, 62 F.3d 1469, 1477 (D.C. Cir. 1995); *D'Onofrio v. SFX Sports Grp., Inc.*, No. 06-687 (JDB/JMF), 2010 WL 3324964, at *5 (D.D.C. Aug. 24, 2010).	Negligent or deliberate. *Mazloum v. D.C. Metro. Police Dep't*, 530 F. Supp. 2d 282, 292 (D.D.C. 2008); *More v. Snow*, 480 F. Supp. 2d 257, 274–75 (D.D.C. 2007); *D'Onofrio v. SFX Sports Grp., Inc.*, No. 06-687 (JDB/JMF), 2010 WL 3324964, at *10 (D.D.C. Aug. 24, 2010) (not for mere negligence unless "the interests in righting the evidentiary balance and in the deterring of others trumps the lacuna that a logician would detect in the logic of giving such an instruction").	This issue has not been addressed.	Case law states that the spoliated evidence must have been relevant, i.e., information that would have supported a claim or defense, but it does not address prejudice.	"[A]ny adverse inference instruction grounded in negligence would be considerably weaker in both language and probative force than an instruction regarding deliberate destruction." *Mazloum v. D.C. Metro. Police Dep't*, 530 F. Supp. 2d 282, 293 (D.D.C. 2008).

Circuit/ Case law	***Scope of duty to preserve***	***Can conduct be culpable per se without consideration of reasonableness?***	***Culpability and prejudice requirements***				***What constitutes prejudice***	***Culpability and corresponding jury instructions***
			for sanctions in general	***for dispositive sanctions***	***for adverse inference instruction***	***for a rebuttable presumption of relevance***		
Federal	"In reviewing sanction orders, [the Federal Circuit] applies the law of the regional circuit from which the case arose." *Monsanto Co. v. Ralph*, 382 F.3d 1374, 1380 (Fed. Cir. 2004). In *Consolidated Edison Co. of N.Y., Inc. v. United States*, 90 Fed. Cl. 228, 255 n.20 (Ct. Cl. 2009), the United States Court of Federal Claims observed that "the United States Court of Appeals for the Federal Circuit, has not definitively addressed whether a finding of bad faith is required before a court can find spoliation or impose an adverse inference or other sanction. Because many of the spoliation cases decided to date by the Federal Circuit have been patent cases in which the Federal Circuit applies the law of the relevant regional circuit, the Federal Circuit has not had the opportunity to announce a position binding on this court as to a possible 'bad faith' or other standard to trigger a spoliation of evidence sanction. Consequently, judges of the United States Court of Federal Claims have taken differing positions on the "bad faith" requirement. *Compare United Med. Supply Co. v. United States*, 77 Fed. Cl. 257, 268 (2007) ('[A]n injured party need not demonstrate bad faith in order for the court to impose, under its inherent authority, spoliation sanctions.'), *with Columbia First Bank, FSB v. United States*, 54 Fed. Cl. 693, 703 (2002) (noting findings of bad faith are required before the court can determine that there was spoliation)." (Citation omitted.)							

Appendix 4.2 Federal Circuit Model Order Regarding e-Discovery in Patent Cases[1]

AN E-DISCOVERY MODEL ORDER

INTRODUCTION

Since becoming a staple of American civil litigation, e-discovery has been the subject of extensive review, study, and commentary. *See The Sedona Principles: Best Practices, Recommendations & Principles for Addressing Electronic Document Production* (2d ed. June 2007). In view of the growing concern about e-discovery, the Federal Rules of Civil Procedure were amended in 2006 to address e-discovery more fully. Likewise, several district courts have adopted local e-discovery rules.[2]

Despite these amendments, e-discovery continues to present a broad spectrum of challenges, such as preservation obligations, production format, and the disproportionate cost of e-discovery.[3] Patent cases, in particular, tend to suffer from disproportionally high discovery expenses. *See* Emery G. Lee III & Thomas E. Willging, *Litigation Costs in Civil Cases: Multivariate Analysis* 8 (Federal Judicial Center 2010) ("Intellectual Property cases had costs almost 62% higher, all else equal, than the baseline 'Other' category."); *see also* Thomas E. Willging et al., *Discovery and Disclosure Practice, Problems, and Proposals for Change: A Case-Based National Survey of Counsel in Closed Federal Civil Cases*

---

1. Note that the E-Discovery model order included here was published by the Advisory Council for the Federal Circuit. The Federal Circuit itself has not sponsored or endorsed the Advisory Council's model orders. *See* http://www.cafc.uscourts.gov/the-court/advisory-council.html; http://www.cafc.uscourts.gov/images/model_orders.pdf.

2. District Courts in Delaware, Kansas and Maryland have adopted e-discovery local rules. The Seventh Circuit has adopted an e-discovery pilot program.

3. The following are the main cost areas for e-discovery:

Collection: Forensically sound (e.g., preserving the document date) collection can require a trained specialist. Costs will include vendor fees and/or licensing fees, and media related charges. Inactive data requires restoration and software licensing fees.

Processing: Requires use of licensed assessment or review tools (more than 1 tool are often used for this process). Expenses will include data and text extraction, de-duplication, imaging fees, project management time and potential hosting fees. Frequently includes narrowing or broadening the scope of collection based on results.

Review: Requires continued hosting and licensing fees. Project management time is necessary for database setup and management, additional keyword filtering/assessment and searching. If human review is involved, this is the largest area of cost.

Production: Requires any additional data and image conversion, text extraction and/or appropriate language OCR generation. Tech time will include dealing with problematic files (e.g., Excel). Also requires endorsement and control numbering. Costs will also be incurred for project management/tech time and media related charges.

Post Production: Project management and load time for importing productions into production review tool or index. Additional costs for associating native files to records.

38–39 (Federal Judicial Center 1997) (finding that patent cases "stood out for their high discovery expenses"). Such expenses are compounded when attorneys use discovery tools as tactical weapons, which hinders the "just, speedy, and inexpensive determination of every action and proceeding." Fed. R. Civ. P. 1.

In recent years, the exponential growth of and reliance on electronic documents and communications has exacerbated such discovery abuses. Excessive e-discovery, including disproportionate, overbroad email production requests, carry staggering time and production costs that have a debilitating effect on litigation. Routine requests seeking all categories of Electronically Stored Information often result in mass productions of marginally relevant and cumulative documents. Generally, the production burden of these expansive requests outweighs the minimal benefits of such broad disclosure.

Most discovery in patent litigation centers on what the patent states, how the accused products work, what the prior art discloses, and the proper calculation of damages. These topics are normally the most consequential in patent cases. Thus, far-reaching e-discovery, such as mass email searches, is often tangential to adjudicating these issues.

As technology and knowledge play an increasingly important role in our economy, the courts must not become an intolerably expensive way to resolve patent disputes. Specifically, litigation costs should not be permitted to unduly interfere with the availability of the court to those who seek to vindicate their patent rights—the enforcement of such rights is both an obligation of the legal system and important to innovation. Likewise, disproportionate expense should not be permitted to force those accused of infringement to acquiesce to nonmeritorious claims. This only serves as an unhealthy tax on legitimate commerce.

Fortunately, district courts have inherent power to control their dockets to further "economy of time and effort for itself, for counsel and for litigants." *Landis v. North Am. Co.*, 299 U.S. 248, 254 (1936). Our objective is thus narrow, but important. The accompanying Model Order Limiting E-Discovery in Patent Cases is intended to be a helpful starting point for district courts to use in requiring the responsible, targeted use of e-discovery in patent cases. The goal of this Model Order is to promote economic and judicial efficiency by streamlining e-discovery, particularly email production, and requiring litigants to focus on the proper purpose of discovery—the gathering of material information—rather than permitting unlimited fishing expeditions. It is further intended to encourage discussion and public commentary by judges, litigants, and other interested parties regarding e-discovery problems and potential solutions.

DISCUSSION OF THE MODEL ORDER

Hard-worn experience in patent cases and recent commentary teach that efforts to identify comprehensively the discovery issues or to produce all "relevant" documents at once at the outset of the case can result in the vastly overbroad production of e-discovery. Indeed, the practice of gathering huge amounts of information at the front of a case and running broad key searches as the issues emerge has come under increasing question. The *Judges' Guide to Cost-Effective E-Discovery* critiqued this practice sharply:

> Some argue that e-discovery is best accomplished by taking large amounts of data from clients and then applying keyword or other searches or filters. While, in some rare cases, this method might be the only option, it is also apt to be the most expensive. In fact, keyword searching against large volumes of data to find relevant information is a challenging, costly, and imperfect process.

Anne Kershaw & Joe Howie, *Judges' Guide to Cost-Effective E-Discovery* 4 (Federal Judicial Center 2010).

Hence, this Model Order requires a discovery process whereby the parties exchange core documentation concerning the patent, the accused product, the prior art, and the finances before making email production requests. Moreover, email production requests should be focused on a particular issue for which that type of discovery is warranted. Much as Federal Rule of Civil Procedure 30 presumptively limits cases to ten depositions and seven hours per deposition,[4] this Model Order presumptively limits the number of custodians and search terms for all email production requests. However, the parties may jointly agree to modify these limits or request court modification for good cause.

This is not to say a discovering party should be precluded from obtaining more e-discovery than agreed upon by the parties or allowed by the court. Rather, the discovering party shall bear all reasonable costs of discovery that exceeds these limits. This will help ensure that discovery requests are being made with a true eye on the balance between the value of the discovery and its cost.

A large source of e-discovery cost is the pre-production review of documents by attorneys or other human reviewers. Even with claw-back provisions, this pre-production review is often undertaken to avoid the disclosure of privileged or other sensitive documents to adversaries. Accordingly, this Model Order addresses concerns regarding waiver of attorney-client privilege and work product protection in order to minimize human pre-production review.

E-Discovery Committee
Chief Judge James Ware (N.D. Cal.)
Judge Virginia Kendall (N.D. Ill.)
Magistrate Judge Chad Everingham (E.D. Tex.)
Chief Judge Randall Rader (Fed. Cir.)
Tina Chappell
Richard "Chip" Lutton
Joe Re
Edward Reines
Steve Susman
John Whealan

---

4. Such limits have reformed deposition practice, making it more efficient. *See* Fed. R. Civ. P. 30(a), 1993 Advisory Committee Notes (explaining that Rule 30 limits the number of depositions a party may take in order to "to emphasize that counsel have a professional obligation to develop a mutual cost-effective plan for discovery in the case").

Addendum: Discovery Model Order

	)	
Plaintiff,	)	
v.	)	
	)	
Defendant.	)	Case No.
	)	

[MODEL] ORDER REGARDING E-DISCOVERY IN PATENT CASES

The Court ORDERS as follows:

1. This Order supplements all other discovery rules and orders. It streamlines Electronically Stored Information ("ESI") production to promote a "just, speedy, and inexpensive determination" of this action, as required by Federal Rule of Civil Procedure 1.

2. This Order may be modified for good cause. The parties shall jointly submit any proposed modifications within 30 days after the Federal Rule of Civil Procedure 16 conference. If the parties cannot resolve their disagreements regarding these modifications, the parties shall submit their competing proposals and a summary of their dispute.

3. Costs will be shifted for disproportionate ESI production requests pursuant to Federal Rule of Civil Procedure 26. Likewise, a party's nonresponsive or dilatory discovery tactics will be cost-shifting considerations.

4. A party's meaningful compliance with this Order and efforts to promote efficiency and reduce costs will be considered in cost-shifting determinations.

5. General ESI production requests under Federal Rules of Civil Procedure 34 and 45 shall not include metadata absent a showing of good cause. However, fields showing the date and time that the document was sent and received, as well as the complete distribution list, shall generally be included in the production.

6. General ESI production requests under Federal Rules of Civil Procedure 34 and 45 shall not include email or other forms of electronic correspondence (collectively "email"). To obtain email parties must propound specific email production requests.

7. Email production requests shall only be propounded for specific issues, rather than general discovery of a product or business.

8. Email production requests shall be phased to occur after the parties have exchanged initial disclosures and basic documentation about the patents, the prior art, the accused instrumentalities, and the relevant finances. While this provision does not require the production of such information, the Court encourages prompt and early production of this information to promote efficient and economical streamlining of the case.

9. Email production requests shall identify the custodian, search terms, and time frame. The parties shall cooperate to identify the proper custodians, proper search terms and proper timeframe.

10. Each requesting party shall limit its email production requests to a total of five custodians per producing party for all such requests. The parties may jointly agree to modify this limit without the Court's leave. The Court shall consider contested requests for up to five additional custodians per producing party, upon showing a distinct need based on the size, complexity, and issues of this specific case. Should a party serve email production requests for additional custodians beyond the limits agreed to by the parties or granted by the Court pursuant to this paragraph, the requesting party shall bear all reasonable costs caused by such additional discovery.

11. Each requesting party shall limit its email production requests to a total of five search terms per custodian per party. The parties may jointly agree to modify this limit without the Court's leave. The Court shall consider contested requests for up to five additional search terms per custodian, upon showing a distinct need based on the size, complexity, and issues of this specific case. The search terms shall be narrowly tailored to particular issues. Indiscriminate terms, such as the producing company's name or its product name, are inappropriate unless combined with narrowing search criteria that sufficiently reduce the risk of overproduction. A conjunctive combination of multiple words or phrases (*e.g.*, "computer" and "system") narrows the search and shall count as a single search term. A disjunctive combination of multiple words or phrases (*e.g.*, "computer" or "system") broadens the search, and thus each word or phrase shall count as a separate search term unless they are variants of the same word. Use of narrowing search criteria (*e.g.*, "and," "but not," "w/x") is encouraged to limit the production and shall be considered when determining whether to shift costs for disproportionate discovery. Should a party serve email production requests with search terms beyond the limits agreed to by the parties or granted by the Court pursuant to this paragraph, the requesting party shall bear all reasonable costs caused by such additional discovery.

12. The receiving party shall not use ESI that the producing party asserts is attorney-client privileged or work product protected to challenge the privilege or protection.

13. Pursuant to Federal Rule of Evidence 502(d), the inadvertent production of a privileged or work product protected ESI is not a waiver in the pending case or in any other federal or state proceeding.

14. The mere production of ESI in a litigation as part of a mass production shall not itself constitute a waiver for any purpose.

Appendix 4.3
Model Orders for e-Discovery

This Appendix includes guidelines and model orders from various districts, focused on the discovery process for ESI.

Northern District of California: Guidelines for the Discovery of Electronically Stored Information and Model Stipulation and Order Re: Discovery of Electronically Stored Information for Patent Litigation

District of Delaware: Default Standard for Discovery, Including Discovery of Electronically Stored Information ("ESI")

District of Kansas: Guidelines for Cases Involving Electronically Stored Information

Western District of New York: [Model] Order Regarding E-Discovery in Patent Cases

Eastern District of Texas: [Model] Order Regarding E-Discovery in Patent Cases

Northern District of California
United States District Court

Northern District of California Guidelines for the Discovery of Electronically Stored Information

GENERAL GUIDELINES

Guideline 1.01 (Purpose)

Discoverable information today is mainly electronic. The discovery of electronically stored information (ESI) provides many benefits such as the ability to search, organize, and target the ESI using the text and associated data. At the same time, the Court is aware that the discovery of ESI is a potential source of cost, burden, and delay.

These Guidelines should guide the parties as they engage in electronic discovery. The purpose of these Guidelines is to encourage reasonable electronic discovery with the goal of limiting the cost, burden and time spent, while ensuring that information subject to discovery is preserved and produced to allow for fair adjudication of the merits. At all times, the discovery of ESI should be handled consistently with Fed. R. Civ. P. 1 to "secure the just, speedy, and inexpensive determination of every action and proceeding."

These Guidelines also promote, when ripe, the early resolution of disputes regarding the discovery of ESI without Court intervention.

Guideline 1.02 (Cooperation)

The Court expects cooperation on issues relating to the preservation, collection, search, review, and production of ESI. The Court notes that an attorney's zealous representation of a client is not compromised by conducting discovery in a cooperative manner. Cooperation in reasonably limiting ESI discovery requests on the one hand, and in reasonably responding to ESI discovery requests on the other hand, tends to reduce litigation costs and delay. The Court emphasizes the particular importance of cooperative exchanges of information at the earliest possible stage of discovery, including during the parties' Fed. R. Civ. P. 26(f) conference.

Guideline 1.03 (Discovery Proportionality)

The proportionality standard set forth in Fed. R. Civ. P. 26(b)(2)(C) and 26(g)(1)(B)(iii) should be applied to the discovery plan and its elements, including the preservation, collection, search, review, and production of ESI. To assure reasonableness and proportionality in discovery, parties should consider factors that include the burden or expense of the proposed discovery compared to its likely benefit, the amount in controversy, the parties' resources, the importance of the issues at stake in the action, and the importance of the discovery in adjudicating the merits of the case.

To further the application of the proportionality standard, discovery requests for production of ESI and related responses should be reasonably targeted, clear, and as specific as practicable.

ESI DISCOVERY GUIDELINES

Guideline 2.01 (Preservation)

a) At the outset of a case, or sooner if feasible, counsel for the parties should discuss preservation. Such discussions should continue to occur periodically as the case and issues evolve.

b) In determining what ESI to preserve, parties should apply the proportionality standard referenced in Guideline 1.03. The parties should strive to define a scope of preservation that is proportionate and reasonable and not disproportionately broad, expensive, or burdensome.

c) Parties are not required to use preservation letters to notify an opposing party of the preservation obligation, but if a party does so, the Court discourages the use of overbroad preservation letters. Instead, if a party prepares a preservation letter, the letter should provide as much detail as possible, such as the names of parties, a description of claims, potential witnesses, the relevant time period, sources of ESI the party knows or believes are likely to contain relevant information, and any other information that might assist the responding party in determining what information to preserve.

d) If there is a dispute concerning the scope of a party's preservation efforts, the parties or their counsel should meet and confer and fully discuss the reasonableness and proportionality of the preservation. If the parties are unable to resolve a preservation issue, then the issue should be raised promptly with the Court.

e) The parties should discuss what ESI from sources that are not reasonably accessible will be preserved, but not searched, reviewed, or produced. As well as discussing ESI sources that are not reasonably accessible, the parties should consider identifying data from sources that (1) the parties believe could contain relevant information but (2) determine, under the proportionality factors, should not be preserved.

Guideline 2.02 (Rule 26(f) Meet and Confer)

At the required Rule 26(f) meet and confer conference, when a case involves electronic discovery, the topics that the parties should consider discussing include: 1) preservation; 2) systems that contain discoverable ESI; 3) search and production; 4) phasing of discovery; 5) protective orders; and 6) opportunities to reduce costs and increase efficiency. In order to be meaningful, the meet and confer should be as sufficiently detailed on these topics as is appropriate in light of the specific claims and defenses at issue in the case. Some or all of the following details may be useful to discuss, especially in cases where the discovery of ESI is likely to be a significant cost or burden:

a) The sources, scope and type of ESI that has been and will be preserved -- considering the needs of the case and other proportionality factors-- including date ranges, identity and number of potential custodians, and other details that help clarify the scope of preservation;

b) Any difficulties related to preservation;

c) Search and production of ESI, such as any planned methods to identify discoverable ESI and filter out ESI that is not subject to discovery, or whether ESI stored in a database can be produced by querying the database and producing discoverable information in a report or an exportable electronic file;

d) The phasing of discovery so that discovery occurs first from sources most likely to contain relevant and discoverable information and is postponed or avoided from sources less likely to contain relevant and discoverable information;

e) The potential need for a protective order and any procedures to which the parties might agree for handling inadvertent production of privileged information and other privilege waiver issues pursuant to Fed. R. Evid. 502(d) or (e), including a Rule 502(d) Order;

f) Opportunities to reduce costs and increase efficiency and speed, such as by conferring about the methods and technology used for searching ESI to help identify the relevant information and sampling methods to validate the search for relevant information, using agreements for truncated or limited privilege logs, or by sharing expenses like those related to litigation document repositories.

The Court encourages the parties to address any agreements or disagreements related to the above matters in the joint case management statement required by Civil Local Rule 16-9.

Guideline 2.03 (Cooperation and Informal Discovery Regarding ESI)

The Court strongly encourages an informal discussion about the discovery of ESI (rather than deposition) at the earliest reasonable stage of the discovery process. Counsel, or others knowledgeable about the parties' electronic systems, including how potentially relevant data is stored and retrieved, should be involved or made available as necessary. Such a discussion will help the parties be more efficient in framing and responding to ESI discovery issues, reduce costs, and assist the parties and the Court in the event of a dispute involving ESI issues.

Guideline 2.04 (Disputes Regarding ESI Issues)

Disputes regarding ESI that counsel for the parties are unable to resolve shall be presented to the Court at the earliest possible opportunity, such as at the initial Case Management Conference. If the Court determines that any counsel or party in a case has failed to cooperate and participate in good faith in the meet and confer process, the Court may require additional meet and confer discussions, if appropriate.

Guideline 2.05 (E-Discovery Liaison(s))

In most cases, the meet and confer process will be aided by participation of e-discovery liaisons as defined in this Guideline. If a dispute arises that involves the technical aspects of e-discovery, each party shall designate an e-discovery liaison who will be knowledgeable about and responsible for discussing their respective ESI. An e-discovery liaison will be, or have access to those who are, knowledgeable about the location, nature, accessibility, format, collection, searching, and production of ESI in the matter. Regardless of whether the e-discovery liaison is an attorney (in- house or outside counsel), an employee of the party, or a third party consultant, the e-discovery liaison should:

a) Be prepared to participate in e-discovery dispute resolution to limit the need for Court intervention;

b) Be knowledgeable about the party's e-discovery efforts;

c) Be familiar with, or gain knowledge about, the party's electronic systems and capabilities in order to explain those systems and answer related questions; and

d) Be familiar with, or gain knowledge about, the technical aspects of e-discovery in the matter, including electronic document storage, organization, and format issues, and relevant information retrieval technology, including search methodology.

EDUCATION GUIDELINES

Guideline 3.01 (Judicial Expectations of Counsel)

It is expected that counsel for the parties, including all counsel who have appeared, as well as all others responsible for making representations to the Court or opposing counsel (whether or not they make an appearance), will be familiar with the following in each litigation matter:

(a) The electronic discovery provisions of the Federal Rules of Civil Procedure, including Rules 26, 33, 34, 37, and 45, and Federal Rule of Evidence 502;

(b) The Advisory Committee Report on the 2006 Amendments to the Federal Rules of Civil Procedure, available at uscourts.gov/uscourts/RulesAndPolicies/rules/Reports/CV5-2005.pdf; and

(c) These Guidelines and this Court's *Checklist for Rule 26(f) Meet and Confer Regarding ESI and Stipulated E-Discovery Order for Standard Litigation.*

UNITED STATES DISTRICT COURT

NORTHERN DISTRICT OF CALIFORNIA

Plaintiff(s),	)	Case Number: C xx-xxxx
	)	[MODEL] STIPULATION & ORDER RE:
vs.	)	DISCOVERY OF ELECTRONICALLY
	)	STORED INFORMATION FOR
Defendant(s).	)	PATENT LITIGATION

Upon the stipulation of the parties, the Court ORDERS as follows:

1. This Order supplements all other discovery rules and orders. It streamlines Electronically Stored Information ("ESI") production to promote a "just, speedy, and inexpensive determination of this action, as required by Federal Rule of Civil Procedure 1."

2. This Order may be modified in the Court's discretion or by stipulation. The parties shall jointly submit any proposed modifications within 30 days after the Federal Rule of Civil Procedure 16 Conference.

3. As in all cases, costs may be shifted for disproportionate ESI production requests pursuant to Federal Rule of Civil Procedure 26. Likewise, a party's nonresponsive or dilatory discovery tactics are cost-shifting considerations.

4. A party's meaningful compliance with this Order and efforts to promote efficiency and reduce costs will be considered in cost-shifting determinations.

5. The parties are expected to comply with the District's E-Discovery Guidelines ("Guidelines") and are encouraged to employ the District's Model Stipulated Order Re: the Discovery of Electronically Stored Information and Checklist for Rule 26(f) Meet and Confer regarding Electronically Stored Information.

6. General ESI production requests under Federal Rules of Civil Procedure 34 and 45 shall not include email or other forms of electronic correspondence (collectively "email"). To obtain email parties must propound specific email production requests.

7. Email production requests shall only be propounded for specific issues, rather than general discovery of a product or business.

8. Email production requests shall be phased to occur after the parties have exchanged initial disclosures and basic documentation about the patents, the prior art, the accused instrumentalities, and the relevant finances. While this provision does not require the production of such information, the Court encourages prompt and early production of this information to promote efficient and economical streamlining of the case.

9. Email production requests shall identify the custodian, search terms, and time frame. The parties shall cooperate to identify the proper custodians, proper search terms and proper timeframe as set forth in the Guidelines.

10. Each requesting party shall limit its email production requests to a total of five custodians per producing party for all such requests. The parties may jointly agree to modify this limit without the Court's leave. The Court shall consider contested requests for additional custodians, upon showing a distinct need based on the size, complexity, and issues of this specific case. Cost-shifting may be considered as part of any such request.

11. Each requesting party shall limit its email production requests to a total of five search terms per custodian per party. The parties may jointly agree to modify this limit without the Court's leave. The Court shall consider contested requests for additional search terms per custodian, upon showing a distinct need based on the size, complexity, and issues of this specific case. The Court encourages the parties to confer on a process to test the efficacy of the search terms. The search terms shall be narrowly tailored to particular issues. Indiscriminate terms, such as the producing company's name or its product name, are inappropriate unless combined with narrowing search criteria that sufficiently reduce the risk of overproduction. A conjunctive combination of multiple words or phrases (*e.g.*, "computer" and "system") narrows the search and shall count as a single search term. A disjunctive combination of multiple words or phrases (*e.g.*, "computer" or "system") broadens the search, and thus each word or phrase shall count as a separate search term unless they are variants of the same word. Use of narrowing search criteria (*e.g.*, "and," "but not," "w/x") is encouraged to limit the production and shall be considered when determining whether to shift costs for disproportionate discovery. Should a party serve email production requests with search terms beyond the limits agreed to by the parties or granted by the Court pursuant to this paragraph, this shall be considered in determining whether any party shall bear all reasonable costs caused by such additional discovery.

12. Nothing in this Order prevents the parties from agreeing to use technology assisted review and other techniques insofar as their use improves the efficacy of discovery. Such topics should be discussed pursuant to the District's E-Discovery Guidelines.

IT IS SO STIPULATED, through Counsel of Record.

Dated: ______________________________

Counsel for Plaintiff

Dated: ______________________________

Counsel for Defendant

IT IS ORDERED that the foregoing Agreement is approved.

Dated: ______________________________

UNITED STATES DISTRICT/MAGISTRATE JUDGE

District of Delaware
United States District Court

DEFAULT STANDARD FOR DISCOVERY, INCLUDING DISCOVERY OF ELECTRONICALLY STORED INFORMATION ("ESI")

1. General Provisions

a. **Cooperation**. Parties are expected to reach agreements cooperatively on how to conduct discovery under Fed. R. Civ. P. 26-36. In the event that the parties are unable to agree on the parameters and/or timing of discovery, the following default standards shall apply until further order of the Court or the parties reach agreement.

b. **Proportionality**. Parties are expected to use reasonable, good faith and proportional efforts to preserve, identify and produce relevant information.[6] This includes identifying appropriate limits to discovery, including limits on custodians, identification of relevant subject matter, time periods for discovery and other parameters to limit and guide preservation and discovery issues.

c. **Preservation of Discoverable Information**. A party has a common law obligation to take reasonable and proportional steps to preserve discoverable information in the party's possession, custody or control.

(i) Absent a showing of good cause by the requesting party, the parties shall not be required to modify, on a going-forward basis, the procedures used by them in the ordinary course of business to back up and archive data; provided, however, that the parties shall preserve the non-duplicative discoverable information currently in their possession, custody or control.

(ii) Absent a showing of good cause by the requesting party, the categories of ESI identified in Schedule A attached hereto need not be preserved.

d. **Privilege**.

(i) The parties are to confer on the nature and scope of privilege logs for the case, including whether categories of information may be excluded from any logging requirements and whether alternatives to document-by-document logs can be exchanged.

(ii) With respect to information generated after the filing of the complaint, parties are not required to include any such information in privilege logs.

(iii) Activities undertaken in compliance with the duty to preserve information are protected from disclosure and discovery under Fed. R. Civ. P. 26(b)(3)(A) and (B).

(iv) Parties shall confer on an appropriate non-waiver order under Fed. R. Evid. 502. Until a non-waiver order is entered, information that con-

6. Information can originate in any form, including ESI and paper, and is not limited to information created or stored electronically.

tains privileged matter or attorney work product shall be immediately returned if such information appears on its face to have been inadvertently produced or if notice is provided within 30 days of inadvertent production.

2. Initial Discovery Conference.

a. **Timing**. Consistent with the guidelines that follow, the parties shall discuss the parameters of their anticipated discovery at the initial discovery conference (the "Initial Discovery Conference") pursuant to Fed. R. Civ. P. 26(f), which shall take place before the Fed. R. Civ. P. 16 scheduling conference ("Rule 16 Conference").

b. **Content**. The parties shall discuss the following:

(i) The issues, claims and defenses asserted in the case that define the scope of discovery.

(ii) The likely sources of potentially relevant information (i.e., the "discoverable information"), including witnesses, custodians and other data sources (e.g., paper files, email, databases, servers, etc.).

(iii) Technical information, including the exchange of production formats.

(iv) The existence and handling of privileged information.

(v) The categories of ESI that should be preserved.

3. Initial Disclosures. Within 30 days after the Rule 16 Conference, each party shall disclose:

a. **Custodians**. The 10 custodians most likely to have discoverable information in their possession, custody or control, from the most likely to the least likely. The custodians shall be identified by name, title, role in the instant dispute, and the subject matter of the information.

b. **Non-custodial data sources.**[7] A list of the non-custodial data sources that are most likely to contain non-duplicative discoverable information for preservation and production consideration, from the most likely to the least likely.

c. **Notice.** The parties shall identify any issues relating to:

(i) Any ESI (by type, date, custodian, electronic system or other criteria) that a party asserts is not reasonably accessible under Fed. R. Civ. P. 26(b)(2)(C)(i).

(ii) Third-party discovery under Fed. R. Civ. P. 45 and otherwise, including the timing and sequencing of such discovery.

(iii) Production of information subject to privacy protections, including information that may need to be produced from outside of the United States and subject to foreign laws.

---

7. That is, a system or container that stores ESI, but over which an individual custodian does not organize, manage, or maintain the ESI in the system or container (e.g., enterprise system or database).

Lack of proper notice of such issues may result in a party losing the ability to pursue or to protect such information.

4. Initial Discovery in Patent Litigation.[8]

a. Within 30 days after the Rule 16 Conference and for each defendant,[9] the plaintiff shall specifically identify the accused products[10] and the asserted patent(s) they allegedly infringe, and produce the file history for each asserted patent.

b. Within 30 days after receipt of the above, each defendant shall produce to the plaintiff the core technical documents related to the accused product(s), including but not limited to operation manuals, product literature, schematics, and specifications.

c. Within 30 days after receipt of the above, plaintiff shall produce to each defendant an initial claim chart relating each accused product to the asserted claims each product allegedly infringes.

d. Within 30 days after receipt of the above, each defendant shall produce to the plaintiff its initial invalidity contentions for each asserted claim, as well as the related invalidating references (e.g., publications, manuals and patents).

e. Absent a showing of good cause, follow-up discovery shall be limited to a term of 6 years before the filing of the complaint, except that discovery related to asserted prior art or the conception and reduction to practice of the inventions claimed in any patent-in-suit shall not be so limited.

5. Specific E-Discovery Issues.

a. **On-site inspection of electronic media**. Such an inspection shall not be permitted absent a demonstration by the requesting party of specific need and good cause.

b. **Search methodology**. If the producing party elects to use search terms to locate potentially responsive ESI, it shall disclose the search terms to the requesting party. Absent a showing of good cause, a requesting party may request no more than 10 additional terms to be used in connection with the electronic search. Focused terms, rather than overbroad terms (e.g., product and company names), shall be employed. The producing party shall search (i) the non-custodial data sources identified in accordance with paragraph 3(b); and (ii) emails and other ESI maintained by the custodians identified in accordance with paragraph 3(a).

c. **Format**. ESI and non-ESI shall be produced to the requesting party as text searchable image files (e.g., PDF or TIFF). When a text-searchable image file is produced, the producing party must preserve the integrity of the underlying ESI, i.e., the original formatting, the metadata (as noted below) and, where applicable,

---

8. As these disclosures are "initial," each party shall be permitted to supplement.

9. For ease of reference, "defendant" is used to identify the alleged infringer and "plaintiff" to identify the patentee.

10. For ease of reference, the word "product" encompasses accused methods and systems as well.

the revision history. The parties shall produce their information in the following format: single page TIFF images and associated multipage text files containing extracted text or OCR with Concordance and Opticon load files containing all requisite information including relevant metadata.

d. **Native files**. The only files that should be produced in native format are files not easily converted to image format, such as Excel and Access files.

e. **Metadata fields**. The parties are only obligated to provide the following metadata for all ESI produced, to the extent such metadata exists: Custodian, File Path, Email Subject, Conversation Index, From, To, CC, BCC, Date Sent, Time Sent, Date Received, Time Received, Filename, Author, Date Created, Date Modified, MD5 Hash, File Size, File Extension, Control Number Begin, Control Number End, Attachment Range, Attachment Begin, and Attachment End (or the equivalent thereof).

SCHEDULE A

1. Deleted, slack, fragmented, or other data only accessible by forensics.

2. Random access memory (RAM), temporary files, or other ephemeral data that are difficult to preserve without disabling the operating system.

3. On-line access data such as temporary internet files, history, cache, cookies, and the like.

4. Data in metadata fields that are frequently updated automatically, such as last-opened dates.

5. Back-up data that are substantially duplicative of data that are more accessible elsewhere.

6. Voice messages.

7. Instant messages that are not ordinarily printed or maintained in a server dedicated to instant messaging.

8. Electronic mail or pin-to-pin messages sent to or from mobile devices (e.g., iPhone and Blackberry devices), provided that a copy of such mail is routinely saved elsewhere.

9. Other electronic data stored on a mobile device, such as calendar or contact data or notes, provided that a copy of such information is routinely saved elsewhere.

10. Logs of calls made from mobile devices.

11. Server, system or network logs.

12. Electronic data temporarily stored by laboratory equipment or attached electronic equipment, provided that such data is not ordinarily preserved as part of a laboratory report.

13. Data remaining from systems no longer in use that is unintelligible on the systems in use.

THE UNITED STATES DISTRICT COURT FOR THE DISTRICT OF KANSAS

GUIDELINES FOR CASES INVOLVING ELECTRONICALLY STORED INFORMATION [ESI]

These guidelines are intended to facilitate compliance with the provisions of Fed. R. Civ. P. 1, 16, 26, 33, 34, 37, and 45 relating to the discovery of electronically stored information ("ESI") and the current applicable case law. In the case of any asserted conflict between these guidelines and either the referenced rules or applicable case law, the latter should control.

INTRODUCTION

1. **Purpose**
   The purpose of these guidelines is to facilitate the just, speedy, and inexpensive resolution of disputes involving ESI, and to promote, whenever possible, the resolution of disputes regarding the discovery of ESI without Court intervention. Parties should consider the proportionality principle inherent within the Federal Rules in using these guidelines. *See* Fed. R. Civ. P. 26(b)(2)(C)(iii) and 26(g)(1)(B)(iii).

2. **Principle of Cooperation**
   An attorney's representation of a client is improved by conducting discovery in a cooperative manner. The failure of counsel or the parties in litigation to cooperate in facilitating and reasonably limiting discovery requests and responses increases litigation costs and contributes to the risk of sanctions. For a more complete discussion of this principle, please review the Sedona Conference Cooperation Proclamation[1] endorsed by seven judges[2] from Kansas and "Cooperation — What Is It and Why Do It?" by David J. Waxse.[3]

1. http://www.thesedonaconference.org/dltForm?did=proclamation.pdf

2. Hon. Gerald J. Elliott, Johnson County District Court, Olathe, Hon. Kenneth Gale, U.S. District Court for the District of Kansas, Wichita, Hon. Karen M. Humphreys, U.S. District Court for the District of Kansas, Wichita, Hon. J. Thomas Marten, U.S. District Court for the District of Kansas, Wichita, Hon. James P. O'Hara, U.S. District Court for the District of Kansas, Kansas City, Hon. Gerald L. Rushfelt, U.S. District Court for the District of Kansas, Kansas City, Hon. K. Gary Sebelius, U.S. District Court for the District of Kansas, Topeka, Hon. David Waxse, U.S. District Court for the District of Kansas, Kansas City.

3. http://jolt.richmond.edu.v18i3/article8.pdf

4. https://thesedonaconference.org/publication/The%20Sedona%20Conference%C2%AE%20Glossary.

DEFINITIONS

3. **General**

   To avoid misunderstandings about terms, all parties should consult the most current edition of The Sedona Conference® Glossary [4] and "The Grossman-Cormack Glossary of Technology-Assisted Review.[5] In addition, references in these guidelines to counsel include parties who are not represented by counsel.

4. **Form of Production**

   Parties and counsel should recognize the distinction between format and media. Format, the internal structure of the data, suggests the software needed to create and open the file (i.e., an Excel spreadsheet, a Word document, a PDF file). Media refers to the hardware containing the file (i.e., a flash drive or disc). Electronic documents have an associated file structure defined by the original creating application. This file structure is referred to as the "native format" of the document.[6]

   Native format refers to the document's internal structure at the time of the creation. In general, a file maintained in native format includes any metadata embedded inside the document that would otherwise be lost by conversion to another format or hard copy. In contrast, a "static format," such as a .PDF or .TIF, creates an image of the document as it originally appeared in native format but usually without retaining any metadata. Counsel need to be clear as to what they want and what they are producing.

   Counsel should know the format of the file and, if counsel does not know how to read the file format, should consult with an expert as necessary to determine the software programs required to read the file format.

5. **Meta and Embedded Data**

   "Metadata" typically refers to information describing the history, tracking, or management of an electronic file. Some forms of metadata are maintained by the system to describe the file's author, dates of creation and modification, location on the drive, and filename. Other examples of metadata include spreadsheet formulas, database structures, and other details which, in a given context, could prove critical to understanding the information contained in the file. "Embedded data" typically refers to draft language, editorial comments, and other deleted or linked matter retained by computer programs.

5. Federal Courts Law Review, Vol. 7, Issue 1 (2013).

6. http://www.thesedonaconference.org/dltForm?did=glossary2010.pdf.

Metadata and embedded data may contain privileged or protected information. Litigants should be aware of metadata and embedded data when reviewing documents but should refrain from "scrubbing" either metadata or embedded data without cause or agreement of adverse parties.

PRIOR TO THE FILING OF LITIGATION

6. **Identification of Potential Parties and Issues**
When there is a reasonable anticipation of litigation or when litigation is imminent[7], efforts should be made to identify potential parties and their counsel to that litigation to facilitate early cooperation in the preservation and exchange of relevant electronically stored information. To comply with Fed. R. Civ. P. 26(b)(1) scope of discovery "regarding any nonprivileged matter that is relevant to any party's claim or defense," counsel should consider determining the issues that will likely arise in the litigation. They should also consider discussing with opposing counsel which issues are actually in dispute and which can be resolved by agreement. Agreement that an issue is not disputed can reduce discovery costs.

7. **Identification of Electronically Stored Information**
In anticipation of litigation, counsel should become knowledgeable about their client's information management systems and its operation, including how information is stored and retrieved. Counsel should also consider determining whether discoverable ESI is being stored by third parties for example in cloud storage facilities or social media. In addition, counsel should make a reasonable attempt to review their client's relevant and/or discoverable ESI to ascertain the contents, including backup, archival and legacy data (outdated formats or media).

8. **Preservation**
In general, electronic files are usually preserved in native format with metadata intact. Every party either reasonably anticipating litigation or believing litigation is imminent[8] must take reasonable and proportionate steps to preserve relevant and discoverable ESI within its possession, custody or control.[9] Determining which steps are reasonable and proportionate in particular litigation is a fact specific inquiry that will vary from case to case. The parties and

7. The Tenth Circuit has not yet addressed the relevant standard on when parties should take action regarding ESI prior to litigation being initiated but has said action should have been taken when litigation is "imminent" in the general litigation context. Judges in the District of Kansas have used both that standard and the standard of when litigation is "reasonably anticipated" in the context of litigation involving ESI.

8. *Ibid* p.2.

9 Counsel should become aware of the current 10th Circuit law defining "possession, custody and control."

counsel should address preservation issues immediately, and should continue to address them as the case progresses and their understanding of the issues and the facts improves. If opposing parties and counsel can be identified, efforts should be made to reach agreement on preservation issues. The parties and counsel should consider the following:

(a) The categories of potentially discoverable information to be segregated and preserved;

(b) The "key persons" and likely witnesses and persons with knowledge regarding relevant events;

(c) The relevant time period for the litigation hold;

(d) The nature of specific types of ESI, including email and attachments, word processing documents, spreadsheets, graphics and presentation documents, images, text files, hard drives, databases, instant messages, transaction logs, audio and video files, voicemail, Internet data, computer logs, text messages, or backup materials, and native files, and how it should be preserved.

(e) Data maintained by third parties, including data stored in social media and cloud servers. Because of the dynamic nature of social media, preservation of this data may require the use of additional tools and expertise.

INITIATION OF LITIGATION

9. **Narrowing the Issues**
After litigation has begun, counsel should attempt to narrow the issues early in the litigation process by review of the pleadings and consultation with opposing counsel. Through discussion, counsel should identify the material factual issues that will require discovery. Counsel should engage with opposing counsel in a respectful, reasonable, and good faith manner, with due regard to the mandate of Rule 1 that the rules "should be construed and administered to secure the just, speedy, and inexpensive determination of every action and proceeding." In addition, counsel should comply with their professional and ethical obligations including candor to the court and opposing counsel. Note that the issues discussed will need to be revisited throughout the litigation.

10. **E-Discovery Liaison**
To promote communication and cooperation between the parties, each party to a case with significant e-discovery issues may designate an e-discovery liaison for purposes of assisting counsel, meeting, conferring, and attending court hearings on the subject. Regardless of whether the liaison is an attorney (in-house or outside counsel), a third party consultant, or an employee of the party, he or she should be:

- Familiar with the party's electronic information systems and capabilities in order to explain these systems and answer relevant questions.
- Knowledgeable about the technical aspects of e-discovery, including the storage, organization, and format issues relating to electronically stored information.
- Prepared to participate in e-discovery dispute resolutions.

The attorneys of record are responsible for compliance with e-discovery requests and, if necessary, for obtaining a protective order to maintain confidentiality while facilitating open communication and the sharing of technical information. However, the liaison should be responsible for organizing each party's e-discovery efforts to insure consistency and thoroughness and, generally, to facilitate the e-discovery process.

AT THE RULE 26(f) CONFERENCES

11. **General**

At the Rule 26(f) conference or prior to the conference if possible, a party seeking discovery of ESI should notify the opposing party of that fact immediately, and, if known at that time, should identify as clearly as possible the categories of information that may be sought. Parties and counsel are reminded that, under Fed. R. Civ. P. 34, if the requesting party has not designated a form of production in its request, or if the responding party objects to the designated form, then the responding party must state in its written response the form it intends to use for producing ESI. In cases with substantial ESI issues, counsel should assume that this discussion will be an ongoing process and not a onetime meeting.[10]

12. **Reasonably Accessible Information and Costs**

a. The volume of, and ability to search, ESI means that most parties' discovery needs will be satisfied from reasonably accessible sources. Counsel should attempt to determine if any responsive ESI is not reasonably accessible, i.e., information that is only accessible by incurring undue burdens or costs. If the responding party is not searching or does not plan to search sources containing potentially responsive information, it should identify the category or type of

10. For a more detailed description of matters that may need to be discussed, see Craig Ball, *Ask and Answer to Right Questions in EDD,* LAW TECHNOLOGY NEWS, Jan. 4, 2008, accessed on Feb. 1, 2008 at http://www.law.com/jsp/ihc/PubArticleIHC.jsp?id=1199441131702# and reprinted in these Guidelines with permission at Appendix 1.

such information. If the requesting party intends to seek discovery of ESI from sources identified as not reasonably accessible, the parties should discuss: (1) the burden and cost of accessing and retrieving the information, (2) the needs that may establish good cause for requiring production of all or part of the information, even if the information sought is not reasonably accessible, and (3) conditions on obtaining and producing this information such as scope, time, and allocation of cost.

b. Absent a contrary showing of good cause, *e.g.*, Fed. R. Civ. P. 26(b)(2)(c), the parties should generally presume that the producing party will bear all costs for reasonably accessible ESI. The parties should generally presume that there will be cost sharing or cost shifting for ESI that is not reasonably accessible.

13. **Creation of a Shared Database and Use of One Search Protocol**
In appropriate cases counsel may want to attempt to agree on the construction of a shared database, accessible and searchable by both parties. In such cases, they should consider both hiring a neutral vendor and/or using one search protocol with a goal of minimizing the costs of discovery for both sides.[11]

14. **Removing Duplicated Data and De-NISTing**
Counsel should discuss the elimination of duplicative ESI and whether such elimination will occur only within each particular custodian's data set or whether it will occur across all custodians, also known as vertical and horizontal views of ESI.

In addition, counsel should discuss the de-NISTing of files which is the use of an automated filter program that screens files against the NIST list of computer file types to separate those generated by a system and those generated by a user. [NIST (National Institute of Standards and Technology) is a federal agency that works with industry to develop technology measurements and standards.] NIST developed a hash database of computer files to identify files that are system generated and generally accepted to have no substantive value in most cases.[12]

15. **Search Methodologies**
If counsel intend to employ technology assisted review[13] (TAR) to locate relevant ESI and privileged information, counsel should attempt to reach agree

11. Vice Chancellor Travis Laster ordered counsel to use the same search protocol in *EORHB, Inc. v. HOA Holdings, LLC*, C.A. No. 7409-VCL (Del. Ch. Oct. 15, 2012). He later modified his order. See 2013 WL 1960621 (Del. Ch. May 6, 2013).

12. http://www.thesedonaconference.org/dltForm?did=glossary2010.pdf

13. "The Grossman-Cormack Glossary of Technology-Assisted Review.

ment about the method of searching or the search protocol. TAR is a process for prioritizing or coding a collection of documents using a computerized system that harnesses human judgments of one or more subject matter expert(s) on a smaller set of documents and then extrapolates those judgments to the remaining document collection.[14]

If word searches are to be used, the words, terms, and phrases to be searched should be determined with the assistance of the respective e-discovery liaisons, who are charged with familiarity with the parties' respective systems. In addition, any attempt to use word searches should be based on words that have been tested against a randomly selected sample of the data being searched.

Counsel also should attempt to reach agreement as to the timing and conditions of any searches which may become necessary in the normal course of discovery. To minimize the expense, counsel may consider limiting the scope of the electronic search (e.g., time frames, fields, document types) and sampling techniques to make the search more effective.

16. **E-Mail**

Counsel should attempt to agree on the scope of e-mail discovery and e-mail search protocol. The scope of e-mail discovery may require determining whether the unit for production should focus on the immediately relevant e-mail or the entire string that contains the relevant e-mail.

In addition, counsel should focus on the privilege log ramifications of selecting a particular unit of production.[15]

17. **Deleted Information**

Counsel should attempt to agree on whether responsive deleted information still exists, the extent to which restoration of deleted information is needed, and who will bear the costs of restoration.

14. There is no current agreement on what to call the searches that are performed with the assistance of technology. Some currently used other terms include: (CAR) computer assisted review, predictive coding, concept search, contextual search, boolean search, fuzzy search and others.

15. *In re* Universal Service Fund Telephone Billing Practices Litigation, 232 F.R.D. 669, 674 (D. Kan. 2005).

18. **Meta and Embedded Data**
Counsel should discuss whether "embedded data" and "metadata" exist, whether it will be requested or should be produced, and how to handle determinations regarding privilege or protection of trial preparation materials.

19. **Data Possessed by Third Parties**
Counsel should attempt to agree on an approach to ESI stored by third parties. This includes files stored on a cloud server or social networking data on services like Facebook, Twitter, and MySpace.

20. **Format and Media**
The parties have discretion to determine production format and should cooperate in good faith to promote efficiencies. Reasonable requests for production of particular documents in native format with metadata intact should be considered.

21. **Identifying Information**
Because identifying information may not be placed on ESI as easily as bates stamping paper documents, methods of identifying pages or segments of ESI produced in discovery should be discussed.[16] Counsel are encouraged to discuss the use of either a digital notary, hash value indices or other similar methods for producing native files.

22. **Priorities and Sequencing**
Counsel should attempt to reach an agreement on the sequence of processing data for review and production. Some criteria to consider include ease of access or collection, sources of data, date ranges, file types, and keyword matches. Counsel should attempt to reach an agreement regarding what will happen in the event of inadvertent disclosure of privileged or trial preparation materials.[17] If the disclosing party inadvertently produces privileged or trial preparation materials, it must notify the requesting party of such disclosure. After the requesting party is notified, it must return, sequester, or destroy all information and copies and may not use or disclose this information until the claim of privilege or protection as trial preparation materials is resolved.

16. For a viable electronic alternative to bates stamps, see Ralph C. Losey, *HASH: The New Bates Stamp*, 12 J. Tech. L. & Pol'y 1 (2007).

17. In addition counsel should comply with current rules and case law on the requirement of creating privilege logs.

23. Privilege

A. To accelerate the discovery process, the parties may establish a "clawback agreement," whereby materials that are disclosed without intent to waive privilege or protection are not waived and are returned to the responding party, so long as the responding party identifies the materials mistakenly produced. Counsel should be aware of the requirements of Federal Rule of Evidence 502(d) to protect against waivers of privilege in other settings.

B. The parties may agree to provide a "quick peek," whereby the responding party provides certain requested materials for initial examination without waiving any privilege or protection.

Other voluntary agreements should be considered as appropriate. Counsel should be aware that there is an issue of whether such agreements bind third parties who are not parties to the agreements. The Court may enter a clawback arrangement for good cause even if there is no agreement. In that case, third parties may be bound but only pursuant to the court order.[18]

DISCOVERY PROCESS

24. Timing

Counsel should attempt to agree on the timing and sequencing of e-discovery. In general, e-discovery should proceed in the following order.

(a) Mandatory Disclosure

Disclosures pursuant to Fed. R. Civ. P. 26(a)(1) must include any ESI that the disclosing party may use to support its claims or defenses (unless used solely for impeachment). To determine what information must be disclosed pursuant to this rule, counsel should review, with their clients, the client's ESI files, including current, back-up, archival, and legacy computer files. Counsel should be aware that documents in paper form may have been generated by the client's information system; thus, there may be ESI related to that paper document. If any party intends to disclose ESI, counsel should identify those individuals with knowledge of their client's electronic information systems who can facilitate the location and identification of discoverable ESI prior to the Fed. R. Civ. P. 26(f) conference.

18. See *Rajala v. McGuire Woods, LLP*, No. 08-2638-CM-DJW, 2010 WL 2949582 (D. Kan. July 22, 2010).

(b) Search of Reasonably Accessible Information

After receiving requests for production under Fed. R. Civ. P. 34, the parties shall search their electronically stored information, other than that identified as not reasonably accessible due to undue burden and/or substantial cost, and produce responsive information in accordance with Fed. R. Civ. P. 26(b).

(c) Search of Unreasonably Accessible Information

Electronic searches of information identified as not reasonably accessible should not be conducted until the initial search has been completed and then only by agreement of the parties or pursuant to a court order. Requests for electronically stored information that is not reasonably accessible must be narrowly focused with good cause supporting the request. See Fed. R. Civ. P. 26(b)(2), Advisory Committee Notes, December 2006 Amendment (good cause factors).

(d) Requests for On-Site Inspections

Requests for on-site inspections of electronic media under Fed. R. Civ. P. 34(b) should be reviewed to determine if good cause and specific need have been demonstrated.

25. **Discovery Concerning Preservation and Collection Efforts**
Discovery concerning the preservation and collection efforts of another party, if used unadvisedly, can contribute to unnecessary expense and delay and may inappropriately implicate work product and attorney-client privileged matter. Routine discovery into such matters is therefore strongly discouraged and may be in violation of Fed. R. Civ. P. 26(g)'s requirement that discovery be "neither unreasonable nor unduly burdensome or expensive". Prior to initiating any such discovery, counsel shall confer with counsel for the party from whom the information is sought concerning: (i) the specific need for such discovery, including its relevance to issues likely to arise in the litigation; and (ii) the suitability of alternative means for obtaining the information. Discovery into such matters may be compelled only on a showing of good cause considering at least the aforementioned factors. Nothing herein exempts deponents on merits issues from answering questions concerning the preservation and collection of their documents, ESI, and tangible things.

26. **Duty to Meet and Confer When Requesting ESI from Nonparties (Fed. R. Civ. P. 45)**
Counsel issuing requests for ESI from nonparties should attempt to informally meet and confer with the non-party (or counsel, if represented). During this

meeting, counsel should discuss the same issues regarding ESI requests that they would with opposing counsel as set forth in Paragraph 11 above.

July 18, 2013

APPENDIX 1

Ask and Answer the Right Questions in EDD

Craig Ball, *Law Technology News* (Jan. 4, 2008)

Sometimes it's more important to ask the right questions than to know the right answers, especially when it comes to nailing down sources of electronically stored information, preservation efforts and plans for production in the FRCP Rule 26(f) conference, the so-called "meet and confer."

The federal bench is deadly serious about meet and confers, and heavy boots have begun to meet recalcitrant behinds when Rule 26(f) encounters are perfunctory, drive-by events. Enlightened judges see that meet and confers must evolve into candid, constructive mind melds if we are to take some of the sting and "gotcha" out of e-discovery. Meet and confer requires intense preparation built on a broad and deep gathering of detailed information about systems, applications, users, issues and actions. An hour or two of hard work should lie behind every minute of a Rule 26(f) conference. Forget "winging it" on charm or bluster and forget "We'll get back to you on that."

Here are 50 questions of the sort I think should be hashed out in a Rule 26(f) conference. If you think asking them is challenging, think about what's required to deliver answers you can certify in court. It's going to take considerable arm-twisting by the courts to get lawyers and clients to do this much homework and master a new vocabulary, but, there is no other way.

These 50 aren't all the right questions for you to pose to your opponent, but there's a good chance many of them are . . . and a likelihood you'll be in the hot seat facing them, too.

1. What are the issues in the case?
2. Who are the key players in the case?
3. Who are the persons most knowledgeable about ESI systems?
4. What events and intervals are relevant?
5. When did preservation duties and privileges attach?
6. What data are at greatest risk of alteration or destruction?
7. Are systems slated for replacement or disposal?
8. What steps have been or will be taken to preserve ESI?
9. What third parties hold information that must be preserved, and who will notify them?
10. What data require forensically sound preservation?
11. Are there unique chain-of-custody needs to be met?
12. What metadata are relevant, and how will it be preserved, extracted and produced?
13. What are the data retention policies and practices?
14. What are the backup practices, and what tape archives exist?
15. Are there legacy systems to be addressed?
16. How will the parties handle voice mail, instant messaging and other challenging ESI?

17. Is there a preservation duty going forward, and how will it be met?
18. Is a preservation or protective order needed?
19. What e-mail applications are used currently and in the relevant past?
20. Are personal e-mail accounts and computer systems involved?
21. What principal applications are used in the business, now and in the past?
22. What electronic formats are common, and in what anticipated volumes?
23. Is there a document or messaging archival system?
24. What relevant databases exist?
25. Will paper documents be scanned, and if so, at what resolution and with what OCR and metadata?
26. What search techniques will be used to identify responsive or privileged ESI?
27. If keyword searching is contemplated, can the parties agree on keywords?
28. Can supplementary keyword searches be pursued?
29. How will the contents of databases be discovered? Queries? Export? Copies? Access?
30. How will de-duplication be handled, and will data be re-populated for production?
31. What forms of production are offered or sought?
32. Will single- or multipage .tiffs, PDFs or other image formats be produced?
33. Will load files accompany document images, and how will they be populated?
34. How will the parties approach file naming, unique identification and Bates numbering?
35. Will there be a need for native file production? Quasi-native production?
36. On what media will ESI be delivered? Optical disks? External drives? FTP?
37. How will we handle inadvertent production of privileged ESI?
38. How will we protect trade secrets and other confidential information in the ESI?
39. Do regulatory prohibitions on disclosure, foreign privacy laws or export restrictions apply?
40. How do we resolve questions about printouts before their use in deposition or at trial?
41. How will we handle authentication of native ESI used in deposition or trial?
42. What ESI will be claimed as not reasonably accessible, and on what bases?
43. Who will serve as liaisons or coordinators for each side on ESI issues?
44. Will technical assistants be permitted to communicate directly?
45. Is there a need for an e-discovery special master?
46. Can any costs be shared or shifted by agreement?
47. Can cost savings be realized using shared vendors, repositories or neutral experts?
48. How much time is required to identify, collect, process, review, redact and produce ESI?
49. How can production be structured to accommodate depositions and deadlines?
50. When is the next Rule 26(f) conference (because we need to do this more than once)?

APPENDIX B

UNITED STATES DISTRICT COURT
WESTERN DISTRICT OF NEW YORK

Plaintiff,
v. Civil Action No. ________
Defendant.

[MODEL] ORDER REGARDING E-DISCOVERY IN PATENT CASES

The Court ORDERS as follows:

1. This Order supplements all other discovery rules and orders. It streamlines Electronically Stored Information ("ESI") production to promote a "just, speedy, and inexpensive determination" of this action, as required by Federal Rule of Civil Procedure 1.

2. This Order may be modified in the Court's discretion or by agreement of the parties. The parties shall jointly submit any proposed modifications within 30 days after the Federal Rule of Civil Procedure 16 conference. If the parties cannot resolve their disagreements regarding these modifications, the parties shall submit their competing proposals and a summary of their dispute.

3. Costs will be shifted for disproportionate ESI production requests pursuant to Federal Rule of Civil Procedure 26. Likewise, a party's nonresponsive or dilatory discovery tactics will be cost-shifting considerations.

4. A party's meaningful compliance with this Order and efforts to promote efficiency and reduce costs will be considered in cost-shifting determinations.

5. Absent a showing of good cause, general ESI production requests under Federal Rules of Civil Procedure 34 and 45, or compliance with disclosure requirements of the Local Patent Rules, shall not include metadata. However, fields showing the date and time that the document was sent and received, as well as the complete distribution list, shall generally be included in the production if such fields exist.

6. General ESI production requests under Federal Rules of Civil Procedure 34 and 45, or compliance with disclosure requirements of the Local Patent Rules, shall not include email or other forms of electronic correspondence (collectively "email"). To obtain email parties must propound specific email production requests.

7. Email production requests shall only be propounded for specific issues, rather than general discovery of a product or business.

8. Email production requests shall be phased to occur after the parties have exchanged initial disclosures, infringement contentions and accompanying documents pursuant to the Local Patent Rules, and invalidity contentions and accompanying documents pursuant to the Local Patent Rules.

9. Email production requests shall identify the custodian, search terms, and time frame. The parties shall cooperate to identify the proper custodians, proper search terms and proper timeframe.

10. Each requesting party shall limit its email production requests to a total of five custodians per producing party for all such requests. The parties may jointly agree to modify this limit without the Court's leave. The Court shall consider contested requests for up to five additional custodians per producing party, upon showing a distinct need based on the size, complexity, and issues of this specific case. Should a party serve email production requests for additional custodians beyond the limits agreed to by the parties or granted by the Court pursuant to this paragraph, the requesting party shall bear all reasonable costs caused by such additional discovery.

11. Each requesting party shall limit its email production requests to a total of five search terms per custodian per party. The parties may jointly agree to modify this limit without the Court's leave. The Court shall consider contested requests for up to five additional search terms per custodian, upon showing a distinct need based on the size, complexity, and issues of this specific case. The search terms shall be narrowly tailored to particular issues. Indiscriminate terms, such as the producing company's name or its product name, are inappropriate unless combined with narrowing search criteria that sufficiently reduce the risk of overproduction. A conjunctive combination of multiple words or phrases *(e.g.,* "computer" and "system") narrows the search and shall count as a single search term. A disjunctive combination of multiple words or phrases *(e.g.,* "computer" or "system") broadens the search, and thus each word or phrase shall count as a separate search term unless they are variants of the same word. Use of narrowing search criteria *(e.g.,* "and," "but not," "w/x") is encouraged to limit the production and shall be considered when determining whether to shift costs for disproportionate discovery. Should a party serve email production requests with search terms beyond the limits agreed to by the parties or granted by the Court pursuant to this paragraph, the requesting party shall bear all reasonable costs caused by such additional discovery.

12. The receiving party shall not use ESI that the producing party asserts is attorney-client privileged or work product protected to challenge the privilege or protection.

13. Pursuant to Federal Rule of Evidence 502(d), the inadvertent production of a privileged or work product protected ESI is not a waiver in the pending case or in any other federal or state proceeding.

14. The mere production of ESI in a litigation as part of a mass production shall not itself constitute a waiver for any purpose.

15. Except as expressly stated herein, nothing is this Order affects the parties' discovery obligation under the Federal or Local Rules.

DISTRICT COURT
EASTERN DISTRICT OF TEXAS

____________ DIVISION

Plaintiff,	§	
	§	
v.	§	Case No.
	§	
Defendant.	§	

[MODEL] ORDER REGARDING E-DISCOVERY IN PATENT CASES

The Court ORDERS as follows:

1. This order supplements all other discovery rules and orders. It streamlines Electronically Stored Information ("ESI") production to promote a "just, speedy, and inexpensive determination" of this action, as required by Federal Rule of Civil Procedure 1.

2. This order may be modified in the court's discretion or by agreement of the parties. The parties shall jointly submit any proposed modifications within 30 days after the Federal Rule of Civil Procedure 16 conference. If the parties cannot resolve their disagreements regarding these modifications, the parties shall submit their competing proposals and a summary of their dispute.

3. A party's meaningful compliance with this order and efforts to promote efficiency and reduce costs will be considered in cost-shifting determinations.

4. Absent a showing of good cause, general ESI production requests under Federal Rules of Civil Procedure 34 and 45, or compliance with a mandatory disclosure requirement of this Court, shall not include metadata. However, fields showing the date and time that the document was sent and received, as well as the complete distribution list, shall generally be included in the production if such fields exist.

5. Absent agreement of the parties or further order of this court, the following parameters shall apply to ESI production:

A. **General Document Image Format**. Each electronic document shall be produced in single-page Tagged Image File Format ("TIFF") format. TIFF files shall be single page and shall be named with a unique production number followed by the appropriate file extension. Load files shall be provided to indicate the location and unitization of the TIFF files. If a document is more than one page, the unitization of the document and any attachments and/or affixed notes shall be maintained as they existed in the original document.

B. **Text-Searchable Documents**. No party has an obligation to make its production text- searchable; however, if a party's documents already exist in text-searchable format independent of this litigation, or are converted to text-searchable format for use in this litigation, including for use by the producing party's counsel, then such documents shall be produced in the same text-searchable format at no cost to the receiving party.

C. **Footer**. Each document image shall contain a footer with a sequentially ascending production number.

D. **Native Files**. A party that receives a document produced in a format specified above may make a reasonable request to receive the document in its native format, and upon receipt of such a request, the producing party shall produce the document in its native format.

E. **No Backup Restoration Required.** Absent a showing of good cause, no party need restore any form of media upon which backup data is maintained in a party's normal discovery obligations in the present case.

F. **Voicemail and Mobile Devices.** Absent a showing of good cause, voicemails, PDAs and mobile phones are deemed not reasonably accessible and need not be collected and preserved.

6. General ESI production requests under Federal Rules of Civil Procedure 34 and 45, or compliance with a mandatory disclosure order of this court, shall not include e-mail or other forms of electronic correspondence (collectively "e-mail"). To obtain e-mail parties must propound specific e-mail production requests.

7. E-mail production requests shall be phased to occur timely after the parties have exchanged initial disclosures, a specific listing of likely e-mail custodians, a specific identification of the fifteen most significant listed e-mail custodians in view of the pleaded claims and defenses,[*] infringement contentions and accompanying documents pursuant to P.R. 3-1 and 3-2, invalidity contentions and accompanying documents pursuant to P.R. 3-3 and 3-4, and preliminary information relevant to damages. The exchange of this information shall occur at the time required under the Federal Rules of Civil Procedure, Local Rules, or by order of the court. Each requesting party may also propound up to five written discovery requests and take one deposition per producing party to identify the proper custodians, proper search terms, and proper time frame for e-mail production requests. The court may allow additional discovery upon a showing of good cause.

8. E-mail production requests shall identify the custodian, search terms, and time frame. The parties shall cooperate to identify the proper custodians, proper search terms, and proper time frame. Each requesting party shall limit its e-mail production requests to a total of eight custodians per producing party for all such requests. The parties may jointly agree to modify this limit without the court's leave. The court shall consider contested requests for additional or fewer custodians per producing party, upon showing a distinct need based on the size, complexity, and issues of this specific case.

---

* A "specific identification" requires a short description of why the custodian is believed to be significant.

9. Each requesting party shall limit its e-mail production requests to a total of ten search terms per custodian per party. The parties may jointly agree to modify this limit without the court's leave. The court shall consider contested requests for additional or fewer search terms per custodian, upon showing a distinct need based on the size, complexity, and issues of this specific case. The search terms shall be narrowly tailored to particular issues. Indiscriminate terms, such as the producing company's name or its product name, are inappropriate unless combined with narrowing search criteria that sufficiently reduce the risk of overproduction. A conjunctive combination of multiple words or phrases (e.g., "computer" and "system") narrows the search and shall count as a single search term. A disjunctive combination of multiple words or phrases (e.g., "computer" or "system") broadens the search, and thus each word or phrase shall count as a separate search term unless they are variants of the same word. Use of narrowing search criteria (e.g., "and," "but not," "w/x") is encouraged to limit the production and shall be considered when determining whether to shift costs for disproportionate discovery.

10. Pursuant to Federal Rule of Evidence 502(d), the inadvertent production of a privileged or work product protected ESI is not a waiver in the pending case or in any other federal or state proceeding.

11. The mere production of ESI in a litigation as part of a mass production shall not itself constitute a waiver for any purpose.

12. Except as expressly stated, nothing in this order affects the parties' discovery obligations under the Federal or Local Rules.

- current as of March 19, 2014 (General Order 14-6)

Chapter 5
Claim Construction

The construction of patent claims plays a critical role in nearly every patent case. It is central to the evaluation of infringement and validity, and can affect or determine the outcome of other significant issues such as unenforceability, enablement, and remedies. The process by which courts interpret patent claims represents one of the most distinctive aspects of patent litigation. This chapter explores the procedural and substantive aspects of claim construction.

It will be useful to have some historical and jurisprudential context for claim construction before delving into the details. *See generally* J. Jonas Anderson & Peter S. Menell, *Informal Deference: A Historical, Empirical, and Normative Analysis of Patent Claim Construction*, 108 Nw. U. L. Rev. 1 (2014). As the use of juries in patent cases has grown since 1980, whether the judge or the jury should construe the terms of patent claims has emerged as a pressing issue. Until 1996, it was common for courts to charge juries with claim construction. Resolving the scope of patent claims in this manner, however, significantly increased the complexity and uncertainty of trials. The question of who should determine the meaning of patent claims came before the Supreme Court in the seminal case of *Markman v. Westview Instruments*, 517 U.S. 370 (1996), resulting in the term "*Markman* hearing."

Markman sued Westview Instruments for infringement of its patent on a system for tracking articles of clothing in a dry-cleaning operation. After a jury found infringement, Westview Instruments moved for judgment as a matter of law on the ground that the patent and its prosecution history made it clear that the patent claims at issue did not extend to Westview's accused device. The trial court granted the motion based on its examination of the relevant documentation. On appeal, the patentee asserted that the trial court's judgment violated its Seventh Amendment right to a jury trial on claim construction. Markman stressed that it had introduced expert testimony on the issue. Based largely on functional considerations, the Supreme Court held that claim construction is a matter for the court and hence beyond the province of the jury. The Court emphasized that judges are better equipped than juries to construe the meaning of patent claim terms, given their training and experience interpreting written instruments (such as contracts and statutes). Even though cases may arise in which the credibility of competing experts affects the determination of claim meaning, "in the main" the Court anticipated that claim-construction determinations will be "subsumed within the necessarily sophisticated analysis of the whole document, required by the standard construction rule that a term can be defined only in a way that comports with the instrument as a whole." *Id.* at 389. The Court also emphasized that judges are better able to promote uniformity and certainty in claim construction.

Notwithstanding clear indications in the Supreme Court's *Markman* opinion that the Court did not consider claim construction to be a pure question of law, *see id.* at 378 (characterizing claim construction as a "mongrel [or mixed fact/law] practice"), a sharply divided Federal Circuit adhered to its view that claim construction is a pure question of law subject to de novo review and downplayed the Supreme Court's more limited characterization of claim construction as simply an "issue for the judge, not the jury." *See Cybor Corp. v. FAS Techs., Inc.*, 138 F.3d 1448 (Fed. Cir. 1998) (en banc). Over the next eighteen years, the Federal Circuit struggled with this issue, with several members continuing to question *Cybor*'s view that claim construction is a pure question of law. *See, e.g., Lighting Ballast Control LLC v. Philips Elecs. N. Am. Corp.*, 744 F.3d 1272, 1297 (Fed. Cir. 2014) (en banc) (O'Malley, J., dissenting); *Amgen Inc. v. Hoechst Marion Roussel, Inc.*, 469 F.3d 1039, 1040 (Fed. Cir. 2006) (Michel, C.J., joined by Rader, J., dissenting from denial of rehearing en banc). The Supreme Court resolved the controversy in 2015, holding that patent claim construction can entail factfinding. It restored the fundamental juridical principle—reflected in Federal Rule of Civil Procedure 52(a)(6)—that the Federal Circuit, like other appellate courts, must "give due regard to the trial court's opportunity to judge the witnesses' credibility" and defer to the trial court's factual determinations unless "clearly erroneous." *See Teva Pharms. USA, Inc. v. Sandoz, Inc.*, 135 S. Ct. 831, 834 (2015).

Building on its *Markman* framework, the Supreme Court's *Teva* decision endorses a hybrid standard of appellate review that is balanced, structurally sound, and legally appropriate. Under this hybrid standard, the factual determinations underlying claim-construction rulings are subject to the "clearly erroneous" (or "abuse of discretion") standard of review, while the Federal Circuit exercises de novo review over the ultimate claim-construction decision. In this manner, district judges can use their distinctive vantage point and evidentiary tools to ferret out factual underpinnings while the Federal Circuit can operate as a check on fidelity to the patent instrument. Therefore, even though the Federal Circuit retains de novo review of whether a trial court's construction of a patent claim comports with the intrinsic evidence—the patent document and prosecution history—the appellate court must nonetheless sustain the trial court's subsidiary factual findings unless clearly erroneous. Thus, where the intrinsic evidence does not resolve the meaning of a disputed patent claim term, the district court's resolution, if adequately grounded in extrinsic evidence, will control. *See* J. Jonas Anderson & Peter S. Menell, *Restoring the Fact/Law Distinction in Patent Claim Construction*, 109 Nw. U. L. Rev. Online 187 (2015).

This chapter begins with the procedural matters relating to claim construction and then presents the framework and substantive rules governing claim interpretation.

5.1 Timing and Procedure

In the years since *Markman*, courts have experimented with different approaches to the claim-construction process. This section presents and discusses the main lessons for:

- determining when to hold the *Markman* hearing
- streamlining the pre-*Markman* process
- the use of tutorials, experts, and advisors in claim construction
- identifying subsidiary factual questions on which extrinsic evidence and evidentiary hearings could be useful
- conducting a *Markman* hearing efficiently and effectively;
- rendering a *Markman* ruling
- integrating the *Markman* ruling into a trial

We identify issues that commonly arise in the claim-construction process (from the commencement of the case through trial), explain the pros and cons of different approaches to these issues, characterize best practices, and suggest tools to address specific situations.

5.1.1 Timing of *Markman* Hearings

Perhaps the most important case-management decision relating to the *Markman* process is its timing. Nearly twenty years of practice provide a guide to when to hold the *Markman* hearing. It has also shown the importance of flexibility to accommodate the demands of different types of cases.

Early *Markman* hearings (i.e., within about five months of the case-management conference) can be appropriate in some contexts. In cases that present a well-crystallized question of claim construction that can resolve liability without extensive discovery, an early *Markman* hearing can be advantageous. Providing parties with an early ruling on key claim-construction issues can promote settlement and avoid the cost and burden of lengthy discovery. However, in practice, several disadvantages often outweigh these advantages. Knowing what issues to present at a *Markman* hearing frequently requires significant discovery into the nature of the accused device and of the prior art. Thus, a court will often have to revisit an early *Markman* ruling when new issues emerge.

A majority of courts have found that the most opportune time to hold the *Markman* hearing is midway through, or before the close of, fact discovery, and prior to expert discovery. This timing affords the parties sufficient discovery in advance of the claim-construction hearing to gain an understanding of the liability issues and accurately identify the terms needing construction. It also leaves time for the parties to finish fact discovery and to focus expert discovery after the court has issued its claim-construction ruling. This timing also avoids requiring an expert to base her opinion on alternative claim constructions or to do a new report if the court does not adopt either party's construction and devises its own. *See, e.g.*, *Magarl, L.L.C. v. Crane Co.*, 2004 U.S. Dist. LEXIS 24283, at *44, 2004 WL 2750252 (S.D. Ind. 2004) (encouraging holding *Markman* hearings in advance of summary judgment briefing, because a "claim construction which precedes summary judgment could avoid unnecessary alternative briefing and evidentiary submissions, including expert witness testimony addressed to or based on rejected claim constructions").

If, however, a particular claim construction will be case or claim dispositive, the court should hold a joint claim-construction/summary judgment hearing on case-dispositive terms. Although this may require that the experts address several possible claim constructions, the benefits of efficiency and cost savings outweigh the additional burden. *See* §§ 6.1.2–6.1.3.4.

Some courts have deferred *Markman* hearings until the completion of expert discovery. They resolved claim-construction disputes in conjunction with summary motions made shortly before trial, or at trial, when jury instructions are settled. Although there may be some advantages to holding a *Markman* hearing at or near the end of a case, this approach has many drawbacks in practice. Holding a late *Markman* hearing may upset the experts' positions, inject new issues into the case, especially where the court devises its own construction that does not square with that of either party, or it may deprive litigants of enough time to settle the case before trial.

5.1.2 Pre-*Markman* Procedures

To promote efficient and effective *Markman* hearings, a court will want to address the procedures and ground rules at a relatively early stage in case management. As discussed in Chapter 2, patent local rules place particular emphasis on timely and orderly identification of disputed claim terms. We begin this section with further discussion of best practices to bring those disputes and the parties' arguments to the surface prior to the *Markman* hearing. Depending on the complexity of the technology at issue, it is often useful to plan for technology tutorials in conjunction with the *Markman* proceeding. We discuss several practical issues relating to the timing, form, and conduct of such tutorials and the use of court-appointed experts to assist in claim construction.

5.1.2.1 Mandatory Disclosure of Positions

The primary goals of the procedures before a *Markman* hearing are to: (1) ensure that the parties' claim-construction positions are squarely joined, which reduces false and hidden disputes; and (2) resolve any disputes about how the *Markman* hearing should be conducted so the hearing is efficient, helpful to the court, and without procedural disarray.

The following steps have proven especially effective in accomplishing these objectives.

5.1.2.1.1 Early Disclosure of Infringement and Invalidity Contentions

Requiring disclosure of infringement contentions at the start of the case is a proven way to focus at least some of the disputes at issue for the *Markman* hearing. Early disclosure of infringement contentions is a feature of the patent local rules discussed in Chapter 2. *See* Appendix D (listing jurisdictions with patent local rules). In jurisdictions that have not adopted patent local rules, courts are free to build these disclosure requirements into their scheduling orders. These infringement contentions require the patentee to specify, among other things, each claim of each patent in suit that is allegedly infringed; each instrumentality that allegedly infringes each asserted claim; and a claim chart detailing where each element of an asserted claim is found in each accused instrumentality. *See, e.g.*, N.D. Cal. Patent L.R. 3-1; E.D. Tex. Patent L.R. 3-1.

With its infringement contentions, the party must produce, among other things, all documents evidencing the conception and reduction to practice of each asserted claim, along with documents sufficient to show the disclosure of the claimed inventions to others prior to filing of the patent application. Similarly, the court can help focus *Markman* issues by requiring that the alleged infringer disclose invalidity contentions after receipt of the infringement contentions. This requires the alleged infringer to specify, among other things, the identity of each item of prior art that allegedly anticipates each asserted claim or renders it obvious, and any grounds for invalidity due to indefiniteness, enablement, or written description. *See* § 112. With its invalidity contentions, the accused infringer must produce all prior art not already of record, as well as documents sufficient to show the operation of the accused devices.

These disclosures force parties to crystallize their theories early in the case and thereby identify matters that the *Markman* hearing must resolve. They also help streamline discovery by mandating the disclosures that are core to patent cases, thus reducing the need for interrogatories, document requests, and contention depositions. Early infringement contentions can, however, lead to unnecessary discovery disputes because they can occur before parties fully understand their positions.

5.1.2.1.2 Disclosure of Claims to Construe and Proposed Constructions

A widespread problem in patent cases is that the parties' *Markman* briefing might not effectively join the issues that the *Markman* hearing must resolve, or might not confront claim-construction issues that the parties will ultimately litigate at trial. To avoid this problem, the court should set a meet-and-confer schedule in its scheduling order to require parties to identify terms that need construction. These procedures help ensure that the issues for the *Markman* hearing are specified in advance of the briefing cycle, as opposed to briefing revealing issues for the first time. Ordering a meet-and-confer process also helps ensure that the parties' briefing does not wastefully address false or merely hypothetical disputes. Ordering parties to disclose their claim-construction positions also discourages "hidden" disputes that may otherwise arise at trial. This structured meet-and-confer process is part of the patent local rules of the Northern District of California, the Eastern District of Texas, and a growing number of district courts. It is required within ten days of service of the invalidity contentions. *See, e.g.*, N.D. Cal. Patent L.R. 4-1 to 4-3; E.D. Tex. P.R. 4-1 to 4-3.

As part of this process, the court's scheduling order should set a date for the parties to exchange proposed constructions of the identified terms. Setting this date approximately twenty days after exchanging lists of terms is appropriate. As part of this disclosure, some jurisdictions also require that the parties disclose their supporting evidence, including whether they will rely on expert witnesses. This disclosure of extrinsic evidence is particularly important to provide a baseline understanding of what aspects of the claim-construction process will involve district court fact-finding in accordance with *Teva Pharmaceuticals USA, Inc. v. Sandoz*, 135 S. Ct. 831 (2014).

5.1.2.1.3 Mechanisms for Limiting the Number of Claim Terms to Construe

Cases commonly involve multiple patents, dozens or even hundreds of claims, and multitudes of claim terms that may need construction. If left unmanaged, the sheer complexity of this tangle of terms can overwhelm the merits of a lawsuit. Courts should exercise their inherent case-management authority to limit the number of claims and claim terms at issue, as appropriate. *See* §§ 2.1.3.1 (patent and claim winnowing); 2.1.3.2.1 (claim-term winnowing).

At the *Markman* phase, courts have wide discretion to limit the number of claim terms at issue. Restricting the scope of the *Markman* hearing focuses the parties' and the court's attention on the key issues, which may dispose of the case. It also facilitates more prompt and well-reasoned ruling on the central matters in the case. Courts have experimented widely with various approaches to managing the scope of *Markman* hearings. A substantial body of experience has shown that allowing the parties wide discretion to brief all claim terms that are potentially at issue invites false or inconsequential disputes, particularly because parties reflexively seek to avoid the risk of a waiver finding if they refrain from raising peripheral disputes.

To focus patent litigation on the most salient issues, a growing number of courts have established a presumptive limit on the number of claim terms—typically ten—that will be presented at the *Markman* hearing. The Northern District of California revised its patent local rules to require the parties to jointly identify ten terms "likely to be most significant to resolving the parties' dispute, including those terms for which construction may be case or claim dispositive." *See* N.D. Cal. Patent L.R. 1-2; *see also* N.D. Ill. LPR 4.1(b) (requiring parties to limit terms submitted for construction to ten, absent a showing of good cause). The default ten-term limit can be adjusted upward or downward depending on the circumstances of the case.

There are several factors that may influence whether to increase the number of terms to be construed, such as the number of patents in dispute and the extent to which means-plus-function (§ 112(f)) claim terms are present. Ten can be high for single-patent cases, but low for multipatent cases. *See* N.D. Ill. LPR 4.1(b) (noting that the "assertion of multiple nonrelated patents shall, in an appropriate case, constitute good cause"). Means-plus-function claims generally must be construed to identify the corresponding structure in the specification. Hence, where multiple such claims are present, courts may need to adjust the term ceiling upward.

The parties are generally required to meet and confer to identify the ten most significant terms in dispute. In addition to any terms that the parties mutually agree are the most significant, the parties are allocated half of the remaining ten terms. With this allocation, they can identify additional terms for the *Markman* hearing to construe. *See* N.D. Ill. LPR 4.1(b) (stating that "[i]f the parties are unable to agree upon ten terms, then five shall be allocated to all plaintiffs and five to all defendants").

The ten-term limit does not fix the total number of terms that can be construed before trial. Parties can seek to construe additional terms at later phases in the case. *See, e.g., Apple, Inc. v. Samsung Elecs. Co.*, 932 F. Supp. 2d 1076, 1079 (N.D. Cal. 2013) (finding no waiver of right to construe term that was not included in the initial ten-term proceedings, where party disclosed its intent to contest additional terms). However, for purposes of the principal *Markman* hearing, this channeling of the most significant terms allows courts to resolve the key disputes efficiently.

The ten-term default rule has generally worked well. It has focused the parties on the terms that are most likely to be outcome determinative. *See* N.D. Ill. LPR 4.1 (requiring the parties to certify whether a term identified for construction is potentially outcome-determinative); *id.* (Comment) (noting that the ten-term limit is intended to require the parties to focus upon outcome-determinative or otherwise significant disputes"). Courts have adopted variants to suit the needs of particular cases. *See, e.g., In re MyKey Tech. Inc. Patent Litig.*, 2014 U.S. Dist. LEXIS 83147, 2014 WL 2740733 (C.D. Cal. 2014) (in an MDL proceeding combining six lawsuits, the court construed up to ten terms per patent among the three patents).

Courts should be sensitive to the gamesmanship that can arise in selecting the ten terms. Often, one party will be less interested in having terms construed than the other party. It may list terms of little consequence to the case, thereby effectively "burning" half of the terms that the court will hear. Typically, the defendant is the party with a greater interest in having claims construed, and it may be prejudicial to the defendant to limit its ability to only have ten claim terms construed (particularly where the plaintiff has asserted a large number of claims). For this reason, equal division of the ten-term limit can be overly rigid, especially where the parties disagree on which are the most salient disputed claim terms. By insisting that parties explain why they seek construction of the terms they propose, as discussed in § 5.1.2.1.4, courts can reduce the potential for this type of abuse. Furthermore, a claim phrase can reappear in different claims with slightly different wording, giving rise to the argument that each particular instance of the term must be counted against the ten-term limit. Because the same underlying factors will typically drive the proper construction of similarly worded terms (although they might not be exactly the same), courts should accommodate reasonable requests to group similarly worded terms together in counting toward the ten-term limit.

Other mechanisms to manage the scope of *Markman* proceedings include page limits on briefing and time restrictions at the *Markman* hearing. Parties will naturally allocate limited presentation times (written or oral) to the key disputes, and limits on briefing or oral argument will help streamline the *Markman* proceedings. However, when parties feel that they could face a waiver situation if all disputed terms are not addressed at the *Markman* proceedings, they will tend to cram additional arguments into the written or oral presentations. Ultimately, this is a less helpful mechanism than limiting the number of terms that the court will address in the main *Markman* proceeding.

Courts risk upsetting trial dates and can invite reversal if they overly constrain or defer the *Markman* process. Ultimately, the court must rule on all material claim-construction disputes in cases that go to trial. *See O2 Micro Int'l Ltd. v. Beyond Innovation Tech. Co.*, 521 F.3d 1351, 1360–61 (Fed. Cir. 2008). It is legal error, however, for the court to allow the parties to argue competing claim-construction positions to the jury and, as discussed in § 5.1.4.3, the court may properly resolve the claim-construction dispute with reference to a "plain meaning" construction. *See CytoLogix Corp. v. Ventana Med. Sys., Inc.*, 424 F.3d 1168, 1172 (Fed. Cir. 2005) ("[B]y agreement the parties also presented expert witnesses who testified before the jury regarding claim construction, and counsel argued conflicting claim constructions to the jury. This was improper, and the district court should have refused to allow such testimony despite the agreement of the parties."); *Every Penny Counts, Inc. v. Am. Express Co.*, 563 F.3d 1378, 1383 (Fed. Cir. 2009) ("[T]he court's obligation is to ensure that questions of the scope of the patent claims are not left to the jury. To fulfill this obligation, the court must see to it that disputes concerning the scope of the patent claims are fully resolved.") (internal citation omitted); *Medien Patent Verwaltung AG v. Warner Bros. Entm't*, 2014 U.S. Dist. LEXIS 12360, *31, 2014 WL 333470, *11 (S.D.N.Y. Jan. 29, 2014) ("Only the Court can resolve what is obviously a dispute about the meaning of the claim language, and the fact that the dispute is raised late in the day does not relieve me of that burden."); *Wi-Lan, Inc. v. Apple Inc.*, 811 F.3d 455, 464–66 (Fed. Cir. 2016) (reversing JMOL that was premised on new claim-construction issue not previously raised before the jury). The more that outstanding claim-construction issues are deferred until the late phases of litigation or are not resolved until trial, the greater the likelihood of legal error and surprises at trial. Resolving the material claim-construction disputes well in advance of trial will prevent procedural aberrations from distracting from or distorting the merits of a case and minimize the risk of reversal and the need for retrial.

5.1.2.1.3.1 Severance Versus Postponement

Courts faced with a case involving many patents and patent claims, frequently with diverse technologies, have struggled to find ways to reduce the case to a manageable size that the court and a jury can handle in one trial.

District courts typically have addressed this issue in the context of multipatent disputes in two ways: (1) allowing the parties to select a limited subset of patents to be tried in the first instance and severing the remaining patents for a subsequent trial if needed, or requiring the plaintiff to winnow the number of patents and/or claims asserted, in the interests of avoiding duplicative litigation; and (2) limiting the total number of disputed claim terms to be construed, and hoping that those terms will resolve the dispute.

With regard to the first approach, the Federal Circuit has ruled that the district court's case-management prerogatives can trump a patentee's alleged right to try all of the patent claims it asserts, even when the additional claims would have been tried in a severed action. In a particularly large, multidistrict litigation involving twenty-five separate actions, with 1,975 asserted claims from thirty-one patents, against fifty groups of related defendants, the district court substantially pared the number of claims that the patentee could try. *See In re Katz Interactive Call Processing Patent Litig.*, 639 F.3d 1303 (Fed. Cir. 2011). The court ordered the patentee to limit its claims to sixty-four (including no more than forty claims per defendant group, to be narrowed to sixteen claims per group after discovery). Further, it included a proviso that the patentee could add new claims if they "raise[d] issues of infringement/validity that [were] not duplicative" of previously selected claims. *Id.* at 1309. The patentee then moved to sever and stay the litigation as to the unselected claims, reasoning that, absent a severance, the litigation would have a preclusive effect on the unselected claims. The district court refused to sever, and the Federal Circuit affirmed, finding no violation of the patentee's right to due process. Particularly important in the court's ruling was that the patentee had failed to state why the unselected claims were not duplicative of those already set for trial. The Federal Circuit's approval of the district court's approach cautioned that if the court had not allowed the patentee to show why the unselected claims presented unique issues, the refusal to sever those claims would have been reversed. *Id.* at 1312–13. Understandably for patentees, showing why the subset of claims to be tried is insufficient could reveal potential weaknesses, possibly explaining why it was not done in *Katz*.

Subsequent courts have reaffirmed *Katz*'s principle that a district court can impose limits on the number of claims that a patentee may try, so long as the court provides for a "safety valve" that permits later trial on claims that present unique issues on liability or damages. *See, e.g., Masimo Corp. v. Philips Elecs. N. Am. Corp.*, 918 F. Supp. 2d 277, 284 (D. Del. 2013) (limiting the patentee to thirty claims for trial, and limiting claim construction to twenty terms, but allowing expansion upon a showing of good cause); *Joao Control and Monitoring Sys., LLC v. Ford Motor Co.*, Nos. 13-CV-13615, 13-CV-13957, 2014 U.S. Dist. LEXIS 2966, 2014 WL 106926 (E.D. Mich. Jan. 10, 2014) (limiting the plaintiff to three asserted claims per each of three patents and allowing modification for good cause).

Whereas patent and patent claim winnowing has been applied in a relatively small, but growing, subset of especially complex cases, the second approach—limiting the number of claim terms to be construed—has become routine in many districts. Winnowing the number of claim terms construed risks that the chosen terms will not resolve the dispute, which leaves the court with two unattractive options: either doing claim construction hurriedly at the end of the pretrial schedule, which disrupts expert reports, summary judgment, and other pretrial scheduling, or postponing the trial for another round of claim construction. The Federal Circuit has made clear that the district court may not proceed to trial without resolving all remaining claim-construction disputes. *See O2 Micro Int'l*, 521 F.3d at 1360–63. To preclude improper invitation of jurors to define terms, the Federal Circuit has permitted courts to modify and further construe terms at trial. *See, e.g.*, *Pressure Prods. Med. Supplies, Inc. v. Greatbatch Ltd.*, 599 F.3d 1308, 1316 (Fed. Cir. 2010) ("As this court has recognized, 'district courts may engage in a rolling claim construction, which the court revisits and alters its interpretation of the claim terms as its understanding of the technology evolves.'"). In general, courts have gravitated toward the severance and stay option and have found that the subsequent trials are not needed. Some courts limit the number of asserted patent claims prior to claim construction, with a further limitation imposed after claim construction, and yet a further limitation before trial. This step-wise approach allows the plaintiff to refine its theories as the case progress through discovery, claim construction, and dispositive motions.

5.1.2.1.4 Recommended Approach: Mandatory Disclosure of Impact of Proposed Constructions

Requiring parties to state the intended ramifications of their proposed constructions on the merits of the case is an especially useful case-management tool. Many infringement and invalidity disputes hinge on legal questions of claim interpretation and can be resolved on summary judgment. The Northern District of California requires parties to specify in their joint claim-construction statement any term whose construction will be case or claim dispositive to provide context to the claim-construction disputes. *See* N.D. Cal. Patent L.R. 4-3(c).

As outlined in § 6.1.2, courts should integrate the summary judgment process with claim construction by providing a framework for parties to specify how claim-construction rulings would affect summary judgment. Chapter 6 outlines a dual-track summary judgment process, whereby claim-construction-driven motions are resolved in connection with the *Markman* process, and remaining motions are resolved at a separate stage in the case.

This integrated approach requires the parties to state the reasons for seeking construction of any terms that are litigated in the *Markman* process, regardless of whether they are asserted for summary judgment purposes. It affords courts the context for making important rulings in the *Markman* process and also provides a useful tool for reducing disputes. In practice, parties often cannot articulate why their definition differs materially from their opponent's, but they may nonetheless adhere to it. Left unresolved, these less-than-meaningful discrepancies in wording can result in wasteful briefing and unnecessary consumption of the court's time. Requiring disclosure of *why* these terms need to be construed often reveals false disputes. Where there is not a meaningful dispute underlying a party's request for a construction, courts are well within their authority to decline construing that term. *See Vivid Techs., Inc. v. Am. Sci. & Eng'g, Inc.*, 200 F.3d 795, 803 (Fed. Cir. 1999) ("AS&E is correct that although the claims are construed objectively and without reference to the accused device, only those terms need be construed that are in controversy, and only to the extent necessary to resolve the controversy.").

Terms that are to be construed for summary judgment purposes should be specifically identified, along with a statement of which party (or both) would seek summary judgment on the basis of that term and why. As an example of the recommended form of disclosure, Table 5.1 illustrates a sample claim chart showing a term to be construed ("steering wheel"), along with the defendant's reasons for seeking summary judgment.

Table 5.1
Claim Construction Chart

Claim Term	Plaintiff's Construction	Ramifications	Defendant's Construction	Ramifications
"steering wheel"	any device for directing a vehicle		a circular device for directing a vehicle	Noninfringement: Accused device lacks a circular steering device, so summary judgment of no infringement is proper. Invalidity: ABC reference anticipates the claims as a matter of law so the patent [or specific claim] is invalid and summary judgment should be granted.

Appendix 5.1 contains a model order for requiring parties to file their joint claim-construction statement in this format. Appendix 5.2 contains examples of such claim charts.

Many claim terms will not be the focus of summary judgment motions, but are the focus of claims or defenses that will be presented at trial. There can also be collateral reasons for parties to seek construction of terms, such as ensuring that a defendant's future products will be safely outside the scope of an asserted patent. The court should also require the parties to disclose why they are seeking constructions of these other terms.

The court should hold a telephone conference with the parties after they file the list of terms to be construed and the reasons for their submission, prior to the briefing cycle. During this call, the court can state which summary judgment motions it is willing to entertain in connection with the *Markman* proceedings. Moreover, forcing the parties to explain why they need to have terms construed would go a long way toward eliminating unnecessary disputes. Minor disputes over wording choices can also be resolved in this manner. Such telephone conferences can vary in length, from a short call about straightforward matters to a more extended, complex discussion. This telephone conference also provides a further opportunity to discuss whether there are disputed subsidiary facts and how the parties propose presenting evidence.

This process would formally integrate the summary judgment process along with *Markman*. Since claim construction is a matter for the judge (and not a jury), the *Markman* hearing can resolve disputed facts in advance of summary judgment. The court may wish to schedule summary judgment briefing in tandem with claim-construction briefing, or may wish to stagger summary judgment briefing to take place shortly after the *Markman* hearing. Of course, not all case-dispositive motions are ripe for determination before the completion of fact discovery. Accordingly, and to ensure that the court's ruling can comply with the applicable summary judgment standard (i.e., no genuine issue of material fact), the court should be cautious and limited in the types of case-dispositive motions it entertains at the *Markman* stage.

An open question is whether the courts could penalize a party for failing to take advantage of opportunities to bring summary judgment in connection with the *Markman* process. We expect that parties would take advantage of a formalized summary judgment process in connection with *Markman*, and they should be encouraged to do so. However, there are legitimate reasons why parties might want to defer filing a summary judgment motion until later in the case, even where a claim-construction question is at the heart of the dispute. It might be difficult to craft a summary judgment position until the claim-construction ruling issues. Also, it is frequently desirable to close out fact discovery before filing summary judgment motions, to preclude unforeseen facts being "lobbed in" to defeat a summary judgment motion. Courts should address with care any efforts to penalize a party that does not file an early summary judgment motion in connection with the *Markman* process.

5.1.2.1.5 Recommended Approach: Mandatory Disclosure of Terms Requiring Fact-Finding

The Supreme Court's ruling in *Teva* will likely generate disputes over whether particular claim constructions are amenable to fact-finding or resolved by intrinsic evidence. Courts should consider amending their patent local rules and standing orders to require parties to disclose which claim-construction disputes require district court fact-finding prior to the *Markman* hearing. These disclosures could be made at the same time as the exchange of proposed terms for construction (e.g., N.D. Cal. Patent L.R. 4-1) or upon the exchange of preliminary claim constructions and extrinsic evidence (e.g., N.D. Cal. Patent L.R. 4-2). The disclosure would require parties to identify the terms for which district court fact-finding is necessary and the underlying evidence upon which such fact-finding would be based. The parties would also at this time disclose how they propose proffering that evidence for the court's consideration, be it through a live testimony or documentary submission.

There is a risk that parties may take an all-or-nothing approach to the matter, driven by the standard of review on appeal rather than the particular considerations for each term. That is, a party seeking to limit Federal Circuit review might contend that every term rests on disputed questions of fact as supported by an expert declaration that contests every point. Alternatively, parties might seek to expand the effective scope of appellate review by restricting their claim-construction proposal to intrinsic evidence. Early confrontation with these issues can ferret out gamesmanship and enable the court to build a sound record to support its claim-construction rulings.

It is important to recognize that although many terms in patent claims are beyond a district judge's general experience, scientists and engineers have relatively clear understandings within their fields. In fact, many of the disputed terms that are appealed to the Federal Circuit are not technical or scientific terms but common terms that are disputed within the context of the particular patent claim. *See* Anderson & Menell, 108 Nw. U. L. Rev. at 68. Scientists or engineers who take unjustified positions risk having federal judges impugn their credibility. Since their testimony would not occur before a jury, district judges have substantial leeway to press the experts to clarify their positions. Over time, this possibility should have the desired effect of bringing parties closer together in their allegations.

The *Teva* decision places a greater onus on district judges to understand and explain how they parse claim language. The decision affords them greater flexibility to use familiar tools for resolving factual disputes—presentation of evidence and expert testimony. *See* Anderson & Menell, 109 Nw. U. L. Rev. Online at 197–98. At the same time, it demands that they delineate how disputed subsidiary facts relate to the intrinsic evidence. Ultimately, this framework adds to the reliability of the dispute resolution process by bringing better evidence, more scrutiny, and fuller explication to bear on claim construction.

By carefully preparing for *Markman* hearings, selectively using focused expert testimony to resolve disputed subsidiary facts, and clearly explaining their reasoning, district judges have the ability to achieve effective, transparent, and well-reasoned patent claim constructions. As this process takes root, patent litigation will become more predictable and understandable. We can also hope that more cases will settle sooner, especially after *Markman* rulings.

5.1.2.2 Educating the Court About Underlying Science and Technology

As discussed in §§ 5.2.1 and 5.2.3.2.1, claim terms must be interpreted from the perspective of a person having ordinary skill in the art as of the time the invention was made. Thus, the parties will need to educate the court about the science, technology, and the perspective of a person having ordinary skill in the art as of the time period of the invention. The most common vehicle for accomplishing this task is the use of technology tutorials typically done in connection with a *Markman* hearing. Courts occasionally take a significant further step and appoint a technical advisor, special master, or expert for the court. Table 5.2 summarizes the principal characteristics of these educational aids.

Table 5.2
Educating the Court and Court-Appointed Experts

Nature of Expert/ Legal Authority	Process/Role	Procedural Safeguards
1. Tutorial Process	• presented by counsel, experts for each side, or agreed expert • demonstratives often useful (e.g., PowerPoint presentation, simulation video, CD that can be reviewed later)	• typically scheduled within two weeks of *Markman* hearing • usually best to allow each side to make their own presentation, with court actively questioning • advance disclosure (at least 48 hours) of demonstratives • often useful to videotape proceedings for later review
2. Technical Advisor • pursuant to inherent powers. *TechSearch v. Intel*, 286 F.3d 1360 (Fed. Cir. 2002) (approved for use in Markman)	• "sounding board" and tutor who aids the court in understanding "jargon and theory" • not analogous to law clerk because advisor's superior technical knowledge can override judge's prerogative	• fair and open procedure for appointment; address allegations of bias, lack of qualifications • court must clearly define and limit duties in writing • guard against ex parte communications; advisor cannot contribute evidence or conduct independent investigation • make explicit (perhaps through a report or record) the nature and content of the advisor's tutelage concerning technology
3. Special Master • Federal Rule of Civil Procedure 53	• prepares report and recommendations (e.g., proposed claim construction) • court adopts, rejects, or modifies	• parties must be given opportunity to object • court may receive additional evidence • factual and legal issues decided de novo • procedural decisions reviewed for abuse of discretion
4. Expert Witness • Federal Rule of Evidence 706	• instructed by court in writing • provides findings to parties and court • court or any party may call expert as a witness	• court must allow parties to present views • may be deposed by any party

5.1.2.2.1 Technology Tutorials

Technology tutorials can be especially helpful in educating the court about the underlying technology. While the issues that the parties are litigating will always shape tutorials, the goal of the tutorial should be to give the court neutral, useful background information about the technology.

Cases vary widely on the need for technology tutorials. Some cases need little more than a brief introduction by the lawyers at the *Markman* hearing. Others may benefit from a lengthy, separate presentation with animations and live witnesses. With the Supreme Court's recognition in *Teva* that claim construction can entail subsidiary factual findings by the district judge, even in a case where a party has asserted their jury right, the opportunity exists to combine the technology tutorial with a focused evidentiary hearing on disputed subsidiary facts.

A common practice has been to schedule the technology tutorial within two weeks of the *Markman* hearing. It is often best to have the attorneys give the main presentations, with each side's technical expert in attendance for questioning. This approach recognizes that attorneys will generally be the most efficient at tailoring the background technology presentation to the issues the court will confront in *Markman* and throughout the remainder of the case. Having each side's expert in attendance allows the court to ask questions about the science, technical background, and technical terminology. Several courts have successfully utilized what is referred to as the "hot tub" method, in which experts for each side engage in a dialogue. The court moderates the discussion and probes to determine areas of agreement and disagreement. The *Teva* decision authorizes the judge to resolve the dispute based on credibility and corroborating evidence. Courts engaging in such processes should ensure that the testimony becomes part of the record.

Video animations can improve the education process involving complex technologies, which gives the court a tutorial that can be played at any time, including for newly arrived law clerks. However, videos can be costly and time-consuming for the parties and may be less useful than allowing in-court presentations, with the opportunity for live questioning by the court. Some courts videotape in-court tutorials (or use a simple webcam), to achieve the benefits of a live presentation where the court's questions can be answered and a reference copy of the presentation for chambers' use (which captures more than a bare transcript might). The court should ensure that these video recordings are included in the appellate record so as to educate the Federal Circuit about the technology and to enable the Federal Circuit to better understand the basis for the district court's claim construction.

As discussed below, some courts appoint technical experts in patent cases. It is not recommended that the court use a court-appointed expert to deliver the tutorial. Preparing for these tutorials is lengthy and expensive, typically with large investments in graphics and multimedia teaching tools. This function cannot be readily delegated to a court-appointed expert under a cost-sharing agreement by the parties, because the parties would never agree on what should be taught, or how the message should be conveyed. Moreover, allowing a court-appointed expert to present the tutorial would inject substantial uncertainty into the proceedings, and would leave the parties to try to present their own views of the technology through cross-examination of the court-appointed expert (which Federal Rule of Evidence 706 appears to allow), which would detract from the neutral presentation that these tutorials contemplate. It is better to allow each side to present their own view of the technology.

5.1.2.2.1.1 Anticipating the Need for an Appellate Record

It is important to bear in mind that the Federal Circuit faces comparable challenges to those encountered by the district court in understanding the background technology in patent cases. The appellate court lacks the opportunity to hear from science and technology experts about the technology directly. Therefore, it will be valuable to preserve background information in a form that could be useful during appellate review. Tutorial videos prepared by the parties can be particularly valuable. In addition, transcripts of hearings and PowerPoint slides (in notebook and digital format if animated) can help the Federal Circuit comprehend the background science and more fully understand the basis for the district court's claim construction. This will be especially important where the court makes subsidiary factual determinations.

5.1.2.2.2 Court-Appointed Experts

Owing to the challenges of understanding the technical issues in particularly complex patent cases, some courts have turned to the appointment of experts. As reflected in Table 5.2, there are three options: (1) technical advisor; (2) special master; and (3) expert witness. These roles vary significantly. In appointing such an expert, it is important that the court specify the particular role that the expert would serve. *See In re Acacia Media Techs. Corp.*, Nos. M 05-1665 JW, C 05-01114 JW, 2010 U.S. Dist. LEXIS 65297, 2010 WL 2179875, at *4 (N.D. Cal. May 25, 2010) (clarifying initial order which stated simultaneously that the expert was being appointed as an expert pursuant to Federal Rule of Evidence 706 and as a consultant to the court, and specifying that the expert was appointed only as "an advisor to assist it on technical matters," and not as a Rule 706 expert).

5.1.2.2.2.1 Technical Advisor

One option that courts may consider for *Markman* proceedings is to appoint a technical advisor. Because *Markman* proceedings demand that claims be construed from the perspective of a person of ordinary skill in the art, there can be an appropriate role for technically skilled persons to assist the court, particularly in technologically complex cases. *See generally* John Shepard Wiley, Jr., *Taming Patent: Six Steps for Surviving Scary Patent Cases,* 50 UCLA L. Rev. 1413 (2002). The Federal Circuit expressly approved appointing a technical advisor for *Markman* proceedings in *TechSearch LLP v. Intel Corp.*, 286 F.3d 1360 (Fed. Cir. 2002), although the court emphasized the need to establish "safeguards to prevent the technical advisor from introducing new evidence and to assure that the technical advisor does not influence the district court's review of the factual disputes." *Id.* at 1377. Applying Ninth Circuit law, the Federal Circuit noted the following guidelines for appointing a technical advisor: use a fair and open procedure for appointing a neutral technical advisor addressing any allegations of bias, partiality, or lack of qualifications; clearly define and limit the technical advisor's duties in a writing disclosed to all parties; guard against extra-record information; and make explicit, perhaps through a report or record, the nature and content of the technical advisor's tutelage concerning the technology. *Id.* at 1379 (citing *Ass'n of Mexican Am. Educators v. California*, 231 F.3d 572, 611 (9th Cir. 2000) (en banc)). The Federal Circuit cautioned, however, that "district courts should use this inherent authority sparingly and then only in exceptionally technically complicated cases." *Id.* at 1378. (We discuss this option with regard to trial case management in § 8.1.2.4.)

The advisor's proper role is that of a sounding board or tutor who aids the judge's understanding of the technology. This includes explanation of the jargon used in the field, the underlying theory or science of the invention, or other technical aspects of the evidence being presented by the parties. The advisor can also assist the judge's analysis by helping think through critical technical problems. In this latter function, the court must be careful to assure that the decision making is not delegated to the advisor.

A common concern with the appointment of a technical advisor is that the judge may surrender the application of the legal rules of claim construction to the technical expert who could then have undue influence over the proceedings. Although in form the relationship between a judge and a technical advisor is much like the interaction between a judge and law clerk, the former relationship differs in that, because of a judge's knowledge of law, a clerk cannot usurp the judicial role. Unlike the judge's law clerk, who may have undergraduate and possibly some graduate training in the relevant field and understands his or her role in assisting the judge through legal education and familiarity with the judicial system, a technical advisor will typically be a nationally or internationally known scientist or engineer with limited exposure to legal institutions. They are less likely to appreciate the nature of judicial decision making and the unique, constitutionally grounded authority of the court. Perhaps recognizing that parties often do not voluntarily raise these issues to the court, some judges now include in their standard scheduling order a date for parties to submit agreed-upon names of technical advisors.

A related concern with the use of court-appointed advisors for claim construction is that they distance the judge from some of the most important decisions relating to the case. It is essential for the court to engage fully in the interpretation of claim language. These determinations often play a decisive role in the litigation, may require adjustment or further analysis later in the case, and affect the conduct of the trial (e.g., relevance of expert testimony, jury instructions, what arguments can be made to the jury). For this reason, some experienced patent jurists have disavowed the use of advisors in claim construction and caution against their use.

A third concern relates to the transparency of the technical advisor process. The *TechSearch* decision emphasizes the need to guard against extra-record information and make explicit the nature and content of the technical advisor's tutelage on the technology. These principles run counter to using the technical advisor in the same manner as a law clerk, in which the court has informal, off-the-record communication with a member of his or her staff. A technical advisor is not a member of the court's staff. One solution to this concern would be to have all interactions between the judge and the technical advisor in open court with counsel present. Such a procedure, however, could make use of the technical advisor so inconvenient and costly as to render it infeasible. An alternative approach is to have all interactions between the court and the technical advisor transcribed, along with a record made of all correspondence, documents reviewed, and other materials considered by the technical advisor and discussed with the court. A third variation on this alternative, used by at least one court, is to have transcripts of interaction between the court and the technical advisor sealed and released to the parties only after the trial court proceedings have concluded. This approach allows the court some flexibility in its use of the technical advisor while assuring that the parties will have a full opportunity to review that interaction prior to potential appeal.

5.1.2.2.2.2 Special Master

Some courts, pursuant to Federal Rule of Civil Procedure 53, have delegated initial consideration of claim construction to a special master. Such special masters often have general legal training as well as experience with patent law specifically. They might also be familiar with the technical field in question. The special master will typically conduct a claim-construction process with briefing and argument. The special master will then prepare a formal report with recommendations regarding the construction of disputed claim terms. After the parties have had an opportunity to object to that report, the court will often conduct a hearing at which the court may receive additional evidence and then adopt, reject, or modify the recommended claim constructions. For example, a special master for claim construction was appointed with the parties' consent in *Paone v. Microsoft Corp.*, 771 F. Supp. 2d 224, 229 (E.D.N.Y. 2011) (appointing an "experienced and well-regarded patent attorney" as special master for the limited purpose of conducting a *Markman* hearing and issuing a report and recommendation to the court on claim construction). *See also Tech. Licensing Corp. v. Technicolor USA, Inc.*, 2010 U.S. Dist. LEXIS 113292, 2010 WL 4292275, *1 (E.D. Cal. 2010); *Philip M. Adams & Assocs., LLC v. Dell Inc.*, 2010 U.S. Dist. LEXIS 68749, 2010 WL 2733319, *1 (D. Utah 2010) (appointing special master for claim construction over plaintiff's objection).

The use of a special master for claim construction alleviates some of the due process concerns inherent in the use of a technical advisor. The special master does not communicate off the record with the court. On the other hand, the use of a special master runs an even greater risk of distancing the court from the details of claim construction. This limits the court's involvement in some of the most critical aspects of many patent cases and can create problems should claim construction require adjustment later in the case. It may limit the court's ability to gain command over the background science and technology, which could be important later in the case (for example, to address nonobviousness).

5.1.2.2.2.3 Expert Witness

A third option is the formal appointment of an expert pursuant to Federal Rule of Evidence 706. *Cf.* § 2.6.6 (discussing the use of court-appointed damages experts).

This procedure is not usually appropriate for the *Markman* process. It is the court's responsibility to make the ultimate *Markman* determination, even if it appoints a special master. The parties have a significant stake in crafting their presentation of the issues, which is often related to the tutorial process. Furthermore, the process leading up to and the timing of *Markman* decisions caution against the use of a court-appointed expert witness. The list of disputed claim terms will evolve as the case moves to the *Markman* hearing. Selecting and instructing a court-appointed expert could complicate an already-involved and rapidly evolving process. A court-appointed expert for the *Markman* hearing would also create significant redundancy since the parties will have their own experts to the extent such assistance is needed. The court can and should encourage the parties to identify a mutually agreeable expert to educate the court, although experience indicates that parties rarely agree on such a person.

5.1.3 Conduct of the *Markman* Hearing

As courts have experimented with *Markman* hearings, they have had to determine how such proceedings should be characterized and what rules apply.

5.1.3.1 The "Evidentiary" Nature of *Markman* Hearings

The "evidentiary" nature of *Markman* hearings has been hotly contested since their inception. The Supreme Court's *Teva* ruling established that district courts may conduct evidentiary fact-finding to support their claim-construction rulings. However, there is no requirement for district courts to do so—they may base their rulings on evidence intrinsic to the patent, in which case the *Markman* process is a question of law. District courts may also decide to base their rulings on evidence extrinsic to the patent, in which case the subsidiary basis or bases are entitled to deference on appeal.

We can expect an interesting interplay between the district courts and the Federal Circuit as to which terms garner deference on appeal and to what extent. It is clear that if a claim construction is based solely on intrinsic evidence, then it will receive de novo review on appeal. Likewise, if a claim term not explained in the intrinsic record and appears to have meaning to skilled artisans, then it will be necessary to find the meaning of this term through extrinsic evidence "in order to understand, for example, the background science or the meaning of a term in the relevant art during the relevant time period"—in this situation deferential review would govern. *Teva*, 135 S. Ct. at 841.

There will inevitably arise, however, situations where the intrinsic record is sufficient to resolve the claim-construction dispute, and one or both parties marshal expert testimony to buttress their contentions. In this circumstance, the expert testimony may do no more than "pile on" to the intrinsic record. District courts may prefer to rely on that expert testimony to garner deference on appeal. So that the Federal Circuit credits that fact-finding as necessary to the ruling, district courts should make clear that the expert testimony adds to the analysis and is not simply cumulative of the intrinsic record. As noted in § 5.1.2.1.5, advance planning of the fact-finding process, through amendment of the patent local rules' disclosures, may help district courts structure this process and determine in advance if an evidentiary hearing will be necessary.

Extrinsic evidence cannot be used to override the intrinsic evidence. *See* § 5.2.2.1. Likewise, conclusory expert opinions will be disregarded. *See* § 5.2.2.2.2. Thus, deference on appeal may not be available if the Federal Circuit determines that the intrinsic evidence controls. Thus, fact-finding by the district courts should strive to determine if and why the intrinsic evidence is not sufficient to resolve disputed issues.

5.1.3.2 Application of the Federal Rules of Evidence

A frequent and related question is whether, and to what extent, courts should apply the Federal Rules of Evidence in *Markman* proceedings. The dominant and recommended approach is to apply the Federal Rules of Evidence loosely, in part because juries do not hear *Markman* hearings. Furthermore, requiring available witnesses to appear live at a *Markman* hearing and discovery to overcome hearsay and other objections would significantly increase the cost and burden of conducting the hearing. Thus, absent particular concerns about the unreliability of certain forms of proffered evidence, we recommend a liberal approach to applying the Federal Rules of Evidence in *Markman* proceedings, such as allowing use of depositions instead of live testimony and declarations (as long as there has been an opportunity for cross-examination) and freer use of documents without a foundational witness as long as there is no dispute about the document's authenticity.

The court should bear in mind, however, that the evidentiary basis for subsidiary fact-finding will come under closer scrutiny on appeal. This issue did not arise prior to the *Teva* decision, but is now pertinent to evaluation of whether the district court's subsidiary factual findings are "clearly erroneous." Fed. R. Civ. P. 52(a)(6). Therefore, district judges making factual findings as part of their *Markman* rulings should endeavor to build a sound evidentiary record.

5.1.3.3 Safeguards on Extrinsic Evidence

The court should provide safeguards to ensure that extrinsic evidence is reliable. Allowing depositions of experts prior to a *Markman* hearing reduces this risk and may eliminate the need to call witnesses at the *Markman* hearing. If expert testimony occurs, parties should be permitted to cross-examine any witnesses and allow examination into any sources of documentary evidence that may be proffered. Courts need to scrutinize expert submissions and should actively question the opinions of experts. Typically, experts are highly paid consultants, and there is an inherent risk that their opinions will be biased and unreliable. Thus, while it may be extremely probative to hear from persons who are truly experts in the particular field of technology at issue, courts must actively guard against the risk of bias. Cross-examination will usually be sufficient to expose bias and unreliability, and conversely, to confirm that an expert's opinions are sound. Courts may choose to apply a *Daubert* standard for qualifying expert witnesses to present expert opinions in a *Markman* hearing. Because a jury does not hear *Markman* hearings, the need for applying *Daubert* is not as compelling as for a jury trial. It would, however, be within the trial court's discretion to exclude any testimony of a witness whose proffered opinions lack the hallmarks of reliability and relevance that *Daubert* mandates.

5.1.3.4 Evidence of the Accused Device

Another common question is whether, and to what extent, the court should consider the accused device during the *Markman* hearing. In theory, the accused device should have no role in the *Markman* process because the claims should be construed based on the patent language and relevant supporting documentation. Older en banc authority from the Federal Circuit holds that the accused device should not be considered during claim construction. *See SRI Int'l v. Matsushita Elec. of Am.*, 775 F.2d 1107, 1118 (Fed. Cir. 1985) (en banc) ("It is only *after* the claims have been *construed without reference to the accused device* that the claims, as so construed, are applied to the accused device to determine infringement."). More recently, the Federal Circuit expressly approved consideration of the accused device during claim construction. *Wilson Sporting Goods Co. v. Hillerich & Bradsby Co.*, 442 F.3d 1322, 1327 (Fed. Cir. 2006); *Pall Corp. v. Hemasure Inc.*, 181 F.3d 1305, 1308 (Fed. Cir. 1999) ("Although the construction of the claim is independent of the device charged with infringement, it is convenient for the court to concentrate on those aspects of the claim whose relation to the accused device is in dispute."); *see also Every Penny Counts*, 563 F.3d at 1384 (quoting *Aero Prods. Int'l, Inc. v. Intex Recreation Corp.*, 466 F.3d 1000, 1012 n.6 (Fed. Cir. 2006)) ("Although the court revealed an awareness of the accused device, the court's awareness of the accused device is permissible."). As this more recent authority stresses, it is often useful for trial courts to understand the context of the infringement dispute to know what they are deciding when ruling on claim construction. Moreover, knowing the context of the infringement (or validity) dispute gives courts a better sense of whether they even need to construe a term, or if they can simply let the "plain meaning" of a term speak for itself. Nonetheless, the accused device has no relevance to how a person having ordinary skill in the art would interpret claim terms.

5.1.3.5 Evidence of the Prior Art

Relatedly, courts are free to consider the prior art when ruling on claim construction. Prior art may be directly relevant to claim construction, especially where the patent applicant's dialogue with the USPTO concerning the prior art may have given rise to a disclaimer. Also, statements in the patent specification about the prior art may be important evidence for construing claim terms. Even apart from prior art recited in the patent and the prosecution history, it is important for trial courts to have the context of other prior art that will form the basis of an invalidity defense.

Those prior art references may play as large a role in shaping the claim-construction dispute as does the accused device.

5.1.3.6 The Need to Focus *Markman* Proceedings on Claim Interpretation

There are limits on the extent to which the court should consider the accused device and prior art during *Markman* proceedings. The *Markman* case seeks to establish distinct roles for the court and the jury.[1] It is the court's job to perform the legal task of interpreting the scope of the claim terms to the extent possible based upon the patent document from the perspective of a person having ordinary skill in the art. It is the role of the fact-finder (typically the jury) to apply these construed terms to the accused device (to determine infringement) and to the prior art (to determine validity). If the court prejudges infringement or validity in its *Markman* ruling, then the court is subject to reversal for having usurped the role of the jury.[2] *See Am. Piledriving Equip., Inc. v. Geoquip, Inc.*, 637 F.3d 1324 (Fed. Cir. 2011) ("It is well settled that the role of a district court in construing claims is not to redefine claim recitations or to read limitations into the claims to obviate factual questions of infringement and validity but rather to give meaning to the limitations actually contained in the claims, informed by the written description, the prosecution history if in evidence, and any relevant extrinsic evidence."). As we see below, these roles can become blurred in the context of nontechnical claim terms and terms of degree. *See* §§ 5.2.3.1.5.1–5.2.3.1.5.2. Following the *Markman* ruling, the court is free to entertain summary judgment motions that turn on claim construction. As discussed further in Chapter 6, we recommend that courts schedule summary judgment motions that can be resolved on the basis of claim construction simultaneously with claim-construction hearings. Nonetheless, it will be important for the court to avoid trenching upon the jury's role.

---

1. *See MacNeill Eng'g Co. v. Trisport, Ltd.*, 126 F. Supp. 2d 51, 54 n.1 (D. Mass. 2001) ("To open *Markman* hearings to detailed comparisons between the patented and allegedly infringing device creates the unacceptable risk of conflating claim construction (law teaching) with infringement (fact finding). Let's face it, when *Markman* hearings become miniature or full blown infringement trials, the actual *language* of the claim diminishes in importance relative to the *context* of the particular dispute, despite the Supreme Court's admonition that it was the judiciary's particular facility for construing *language* that warranted denoting claim construction as a legal, and hence judicial, function.").

2. *See PPG Indus. v. Guardian Indus. Corp.*, 156 F.3d 1351, 1355 (Fed. Cir. 1998) ("Claims are often drafted using terminology that is not as precise or specific as it might be . . . . That does not mean, however, that a court, under the rubric of claim construction, may give a claim whatever additional precision or specificity is necessary to facilitate a comparison between the claim and the accused product. Rather, after the court has defined the claim with whatever specificity and precision is warranted by the language of the claim and the evidence bearing on the proper construction, the task of determining whether the construed claim reads on the accused product is for the finder of fact.").

5.1.3.7 Sequence of Argument

Courts have broad discretion as to how they conduct *Markman* hearings. Some allocate multiple days to the hearing, while others determine claim construction on the papers. When there is an oral hearing, it may be appropriate to hear from the lawyers on a term-by-term basis. Particularly when there are many terms at issue, hearing each side's positions for each term can help crystallize the dispute for each term. In other cases, it makes sense for each side to give its complete presentation. Allowing each party to do so may be a better way to appreciate the overall themes of a case. Hybrid approaches may work as well, with the court hearing from each side on groups of terms.

It is highly recommended that courts allow the parties to make visual presentations. Multimedia presentations, animations, and other visual aids can be highly instructive tools for teaching the technological concepts and claim-construction principles that shape a dispute. They are also especially helpful in illustrating the particular issues in dispute. To the extent possible, the court should endeavor to preserve this record for appellate review.

Table 5.3 lists some questions that the court may want to ask of the parties during the argument.

Table 5.3
Important Questions During *Markman* Hearing

Why do I need to construe this term?
How does your proposal differ from that of your opponent?
What is the source of ordinary meaning for this term?
Do I need to find an intentional disclaimer (if seeking narrowing construction)?
Does the extrinsic evidence contradict the language of the patent or other intrinsic evidence?
Is the proffered extrinsic evidence simply cumulative of the intrinsic evidence?
Do I need to perform fact-finding to construe this term?

5.1.3.8 Claim Construction in Multidefendant Disputes

Multidefendant disputes pose particular case-management challenges. The defendants may be sued in the same proceeding, or in different proceedings, either before the same judge or in different jurisdictions. The cases may track closely in time, or be staggered by years. Performing claim construction in a manner that fairly accommodates the interests of the plaintiff, the various defendants, and the court is a case-dependent challenge.

Multidefendant disputes have become a far greater case-management challenge with the passage of the America Invents Act. That legislation prohibits joinder of multiple defendants in a single suit for trial unless the defendants are accused of exploiting the "same accused product or process." § 299; *see* § 2.2.2.1.1. Plaintiffs must sue defendants in separate actions absent a common accused product or process, and such matters may not be consolidated for trial. While the statute mandates that each defendant get its own trial, it is silent as to pretrial case management. The motive behind Congress's legislation was to discourage multidefendant suits by making it harder and more costly for nonpracticing entities to wage a litigation campaign against large numbers of defendants at once. It also sought to afford defendants adequate opportunity to present their particular defenses, which was difficult in a large multidefendant trial subject to tight time constraints.

Congress's reform has imposed considerable burdens on the courts. Courts, and consequently plaintiffs, have reacted in a variety of ways. Although no settled procedure has been established, several approaches have emerged, each with its own limitations.

In one approach, each judge will issue his or her own *Markman* ruling, and will handle the litigation on its own separate track. An example is the series of cases brought by MasterObjects against Google, Yahoo!, and eBay. A different judge of the Northern District of California handled each case, and three separate *Markman* rulings were issued. 2013 U.S. Dist. LEXIS 74767, 2013 WL 2319087 (Google); 2013 U.S. Dist. LEXIS 168296, 2013 WL 6185475 (Yahoo!); 2013 U.S. Dist. LEXIS 47001, 2013 WL 1287428 (eBay). While the plaintiff won favorable constructions against Yahoo! and eBay, Google won a case-dispositive construction. When the plaintiff stipulated to noninfringement against Google and appealed, the other courts stayed their actions. When Google's construction was upheld on appeal, all three cases were subsequently dismissed. *MasterObjects, Inc. v. Google Inc.*, 582 F. App'x 893 (Fed. Cir. 2014). Thus, the trailing litigations were stayed and subsequently dismissed, following the developments in the lead case against Google.

In another example, *Body Science v. Boston Scientific*, the five-defendant case filed in the Northern District of Illinois was initially split into five separate litigations in different states. The case-management challenges of five separate litigations predominated, and the case was subsequently recentralized through a multidistrict litigation (MDL) proceeding in Massachusetts, citing discovery coordination and *Markman* consistency as the driving factors. *See In re Body Sci. Patent Litig.*, 883 F. Supp. 2d 1344, 1345 (2012) (MDL No. 2375) ("Centralization, however, will allow a single judge—as opposed to the now five judges in five districts—to preside over discovery relating to the two patents at issue (which will inform and aid the consistent construction of the patents' claims and to consistently rule on challenges to the validity of those patents)."). Having multiple courts each conduct their own pretrial proceedings, including *Markman* hearings, can be criticized as inefficient. Courts can either stay trailing cases for what will likely be prolonged delays while the lead case resolves, or proceed independently, duplicating efforts with a high risk of reaching divergent rulings.

Another approach allows the plaintiff to file multiple suits in a single court and holds the defendants' transfer motions in abeyance until the *Markman* ruling issues. *PersonalWeb Technologies* first employed this approach in litigation against numerous technology companies in the Eastern District of Texas, where, with the approval of the Northern District of California, the Texas court provisionally granted the defendants' transfer motions, to take effect once the *Markman* ruling issued. *See Per-*

sonalWeb Techs., LLC v. Facebook, Inc., 2014 U.S. Dist. LEXIS 4095, 2014 WL 116340 (N.D. Cal. Jan. 13, 2014). This was repeated in the *Norman IP Holdings* litigation, where the plaintiff sued Lexmark in the Eastern District of Texas one day before the America Invents Act (AIA) became law, then sued twenty-two additional defendants shortly thereafter in the same court. The court deferred the defendants' transfer motions through the *Markman* proceedings, citing the administrative challenges of coordinating twenty-three separate proceedings:

> In response to the AIA's joinder provision, plaintiffs now serially file multiple single-defendant (or defendant group) cases involving the same underlying patents. This presents administrative challenges for the Court and, left unchecked, wastes judicial resources by requiring common issues to be addressed individually for each case.

Norman IP Holdings, LLC v. Lexmark Int'l, Inc., 2012 U.S. Dist. LEXIS 112757, 2012 WL 3307942, *4 (E.D. Tex. 2012).

This approach can be criticized for trumping meritorious transfer motions that are deferred until the end of potentially case-dispositive claim-construction proceedings. It also overrides the trend to allow defendants to transfer back to their home districts, as promoted by the Federal Circuit's series of venue rulings in *TS Tech* and its progeny. *In re TS Tech U.S. Corp.*, 551 F.3d 1315 (Fed. Cir. 2008). Nonetheless, the approach of *PersonalWeb* and *Norman IP* does provide a potential mechanism for managing the logistical problems created by Congress's misjoinder reform.

Another approach is to coordinate pretrial management MDL proceedings. *See, e.g., In re Bear Creek Techs., Inc., ('722) Patent Litig.*, 858 F. Supp. 2d 1375 (2012) (MDL No. 2344) (centralizing fourteen actions pending in three districts for pretrial proceedings). Centralizing pretrial proceedings through an MDL transfer may be the best answer for balancing the need for coordinated case management with fairness to the defendant (which may otherwise be eligible for transfer back to a home district) in complex, widespread, multidefendant patent assertions. The selection of a court with expertise in coordinating multidefendant cases could address the concerns associated with deferral of transfer motions as reflected in the *Norman IP* litigation. Furthermore, centralizing proceedings through MDL allows for a more orderly wrap-up of the coordinated proceedings, as opposed to the *Norman IP* approach which terminates upon the court's issuance of the *Markman* order (which may trigger a transfer at an unforeseen time). *See, e.g., In re Protegrity Corp.*, 2015 U.S. Dist. LEXIS 14291, 2015 WL 506373 (MDL No. 2600, Feb. 6, 2015) (centralizing pretrial procedures for seventeen actions in N.D. Cal. to eliminate duplicative discovery and prevent inconsistent pretrial rulings). Like the other approaches discussed above, the MDL approach has its own drawbacks. The pretrial proceedings are conducted in a remote court such that the eventual trial judge might have little or no background in the case.

There are sound justifications for holding consolidated *Markman* hearings, particularly where the plaintiff asserts the same patent against multiple defendants. The intrinsic and extrinsic evidence should be the same in all cases, as will be the universe of prior art that bears on claim construction. The accused devices are generally irrelevant to claim construction. The plaintiff will generally want to conduct only a single *Markman* hearing, and often it will be in the court's interest to hold a single hearing as well.

The defendants' interests may range widely depending on the case. Although the accused devices are not directly relevant to claim scope, the nature of the accused devices certainly affects the terms to be disputed, as well as how the parties shape their proposed constructions. It may be advantageous for the various defendants to be present in a single, consolidated proceeding so that each may be heard when the court first engages in the dispute. Alternatively, having separate proceedings may be best for allowing each defendant to express the unique aspects of its own position. For a defendant in this latter scenario, going second risks that the court may have already settled on a position developed in the earlier case, which the court may be reluctant to change, even if the later case justifies adjustment.

Particularly where cases are pending in separate courts, there may be benefits to holding separate *Markman* hearings, so that each court has an opportunity to assess the claim construction. Claim construction is so foundational to the merits of a case that a court may be reluctant to cede control over the process to a multidistrict proceeding, particularly where different terms may be at issue in the different cases. On the other hand, litigating claim construction through a consolidated MDL proceeding promotes uniformity of claim interpretation across the various actions, which may be important for resolving the overall dispute between the parties and promoting settlement. Having different courts arriving at different constructions renders the disputes more complex, and may drag out the process for determining "who won" until the various conflicting constructions are eventually resolved on appeal. *See, e.g.*, *Am. Piledriving Equip.*, 637 F.3d at 1326–27 (appeal over seven underlying cases in several different jurisdictions, affirming some constructions and reversing others). Thus, whether or not to consolidate the claim construction through a single MDL proceeding depends on the case, and courts have wide discretion to approach consolidation of claim construction as the demands of the case dictate.

5.1.4 The *Markman* Ruling

5.1.4.1 Interrelationship to Jury Instructions

The *Markman* ruling becomes the basis for the court's jury instructions. *AFG Indus., Inc. v. Cardinal IG Co.*, 239 F.3d 1239, 1247 (Fed. Cir. 2001) ("It is critical for trial courts to set forth an express construction of the material claim terms in dispute, in part because the claim construction becomes the basis of the jury instructions, should the case go to trial."). Parties often propose claim constructions that use technical and complex language. Although such proposals may constitute accurate constructions, they are not helpful if read to a jury. Parties should be required to propose constructions in the specific language they want the court to read to the jury. Courts should draft their *Markman* rulings with an eye toward making the claim terms understandable to the jury when the time comes for instructions. In this regard, it is highly recommended that courts end their *Markman* orders with a conclusion that sets forth the exact construction that the jury instructions will use. Any lack of clarity in this regard invites further disputes in the midst of trial during the drafting of jury instructions.

5.1.4.2 Basis for Appellate Review

The court should provide a detailed explanation for the basis for its ruling. This is all the more critical under the Supreme Court's ruling in *Teva*, which provides for deference on review of district court fact-finding. District courts seeking such deference on appeal should deliberately recite factual findings that underlay their constructions. It is only the district courts' fact-finding, not their ultimate constructions, that is entitled to deference on appeal. *See Teva*, 135 S. Ct. at 841 ("The appellate court can still review the district court's ultimate construction of the claim de novo.").

The district court should also scrutinize the factual stipulations that underlie summary judgment motions following or in combination with claim construction. The parties may enter into such stipulations so as to obtain finality of the district court proceedings and secure appellate review (such as the patentee stipulating to noninfringement after receiving a narrow claim construction). If the stipulation is devoid of context, or overly vague and ambiguous, the Federal Circuit may lack the context it needs to resolve the appeal, including making decisions on whether to remand the case. Accordingly, the district court should be vigilant to ensure that any such stipulations provide the necessary facts to justify the finality of the judgment below.[3]

5.1.4.3 Not All Terms Require "Construction"

There is no requirement that a court construe a claim term when there is no genuine dispute about its meaning. *See O2 Micro*, 521 F.3d at 1362. ("[D]istrict courts are not (and should not be) required to construe every limitation present in a patent's asserted claims."). Claim construction aims to define the proper scope of the invention and to give meaning to claim language when the jury might otherwise misunderstand a claim term in the context of the patent and its file history. If a claim term is nontechnical, is in plain English, and derives no special meaning from the patent and its prosecution history, then the court need not function as a thesaurus. *See* § 5.2.3.1. To do so could well encroach upon the fact-finder's domain. The "ordinary" meaning of such terms should speak for itself, and the court should avoid

---

3. Parties do not need to continue asserting their rejected claim construction, post-*Markman*, to preserve the issue for appeal. Rather, it is appropriate for a party to make its subsequent arguments, for example, during pre- or posttrial briefing, within the confines of the district court's construction. *See O2 Micro Int'l*, 521 F.3d at 1359; *Smith & Nephew Inc. v. Arthrex Inc.*, 355 F. App'x 384 (Fed. Cir. 2009). However, a stipulation of infringement that does not state that it is contingent on claim construction will be binding, and cannot be altered by a modified claim construction. *See Fresenius USA Inc. v. Baxter Int'l Inc.*, 582 F.3d 1288, 1304 (Fed. Cir. 2009).

merely paraphrasing claim language with less accurate terminology. *See, e.g., U.S. Surgical Corp. v. Ethicon, Inc.*, 103 F.3d 1554, 1568 (Fed. Cir. 1997) ("Claim construction is a matter of resolution of disputed meanings and technical scope, to clarify and when necessary to explain what the patentee covered by the claims, for use in the determination of infringement. It is not an obligatory exercise in redundancy."); *see also Perfect Web Techs. v. InfoUSA Inc.*, 587 F.3d 1324, 1332 (Fed. Cir. 2009) ("'[A] district court need not construe *undisputed* claim terms prior to issuing a summary judgment of invalidity.'"). By contrast, the terms most appropriate for construction are technical terms for which the jury may not appreciate an "ordinary" meaning. Likewise, when the parties present a fundamental dispute regarding the scope of a claim term, it is the court's duty to resolve it. *Silicon Graphics, Inc. v. ATI Techs., Inc.*, 607 F.3d 784, 798 (Fed. Cir. 2010) (quoting *O2 Micro*, 521 F.3d at 1362); *but see Finjan, Inc. v. Secure Computing Corp.*, 626 F.3d 1197, 1207 (Fed. Cir. 2010) (rejecting the argument that district court "shirked its responsibility to construe a disputed claim term by adopting 'plain and ordinary meaning,'" in part because the court took measures to prevent the jury from reconstruing the term). It is the role of the court to use the *Markman* process to understand the "ordinary" meaning that persons of skill would give to the claim terms in the context of the patent. Using that ordinary meaning, the court should construe the term in light of the intrinsic and noncontradictory extrinsic evidence.

5.1.4.4 The Court May Adopt Its Own Construction

The court is free to devise its own construction of claim terms rather than adopt a construction proposed by either of the parties. However, the consequence of the court issuing its own construction is that it may upset the foundations of the parties' expert reports and any pending motions before the court. This problem may be particularly acute in late-phase *Markman* hearings where the parties' experts may have already rendered reports based on the particular wording of the parties' proposed constructions. In such circumstances, departing from the parties' proposed constructions may throw a case off track by requiring new expert reports and redrafting of case-dispositive motions.

5.1.4.5 Tentative Rulings Prior to the *Markman* Hearing

Many courts report success with issuing tentative rulings prior to the *Markman* hearing. The ability to follow this approach is naturally constrained by the resources of chambers to issue a tentative ruling in advance of the *Markman* hearing. It may also be infeasible where the invention involves complex science and technology. The court may understandably wish to hear from experts and see demonstrative exhibits before opining, even if only tentatively.

A tentative prehearing ruling allows the court to inform the parties of the issues that are most important to the court, in order to most effectively channel the in-court presentations at the *Markman* hearing. This approach enables the court to confirm its understanding of the record and the governing authorities in a direct dialogue with the attorneys. Issuing a tentative ruling prior to the hearing is a good way for the court to clear up any misperceptions that might otherwise result in reversible error. But given that the court may not be familiar with the science and technology at issue and that claim construction can blur the distinction between fact and law, the court should view its tentative position with less conviction than might be the case in other areas of the law.

5.1.5 Amendments to Infringement and Invalidity Contentions

The court's *Markman* ruling can alter the landscape for a party's infringement or invalidity contentions. Accordingly, for those courts that employ patent local rules, or provide for similar provisions in their scheduling orders, it is appropriate to allow limited amendments to a party's infringement or invalidity contentions to account for the *Markman* ruling or other events that may arise during discovery (such as newly discovered prior art, or newly discovered, nonpublic information about the accused devices). *See* N.D. Cal. Patent L.R. 3-6. Such amendments, however, should only be allowed on a showing of good cause. Freely allowing such amendments would invite litigants to change the playing field late in the case and disrupt the orderly framework that the patent local rules are designed to establish.

5.1.6 Interlocutory Appeal of *Markman* Rulings

The Federal Circuit has long resisted reviewing *Markman* rulings until there has been a final judgment of all claims and counterclaims. In the decade following the *Markman* case, various parties attempted to appeal *Markman* rulings prior to obtaining a final judgment on an interlocutory basis without success. Arguments in favor of such early appeals noted that claim construction is a matter of law (during the *Cybor* era) and that obtaining a definitive claim construction from the Federal Circuit could avoid the costs to all parties of a trial on a multitude of issues that hinge on claim construction. Moreover, given the relatively high rate of reversal of claim-construction rulings at the time, trial rulings frequently needed to be vacated when the claim construction changed on appeal, even in part. Thus, parties contended that early appeals of claim-construction rulings should be allowed to avoid expending time and money (including the trial court's own resources) to resolve issues that likely could be disposed of when claim construction is determined on appeal.

Nonetheless, the Federal Circuit denied all interlocutory appeal petitions during the decade following the *Markman* decision and generally discouraged bringing of such appeals. The Federal Circuit was reluctant to accept early appeals of *Markman* rulings in part because claim construction is frequently not finished until a trial is complete. It is routine for additional *Markman* issues to arise during trial—either based on new claim-construction issues, or the all-too-frequent exercise of "construing the construction," when the initial claim construction of a court does not squarely resolve the issues presented for trial. Furthermore, because claim construction implicates so many issues in a case, the Federal Circuit is leery of giving an early ruling on claim construction when still unaware of its implications for other issues. Seeking Federal Circuit review of an interim ruling also disrupts the underlying litigation because such appeals would be handled on the Federal Circuit's regular appeal schedule, without expedited relief.

In 2008, however, the Federal Circuit granted interlocutory appeal of a *Markman* ruling, *see Regents of the Univ. of Cal. v. DakoCytomation Cal., Inc.*, 517 F.3d 1364 (Fed. Cir. 2008), although the circumstances were somewhat unusual. This 2008 ruling has not changed the general rule that the Federal Circuit strongly disfavors interlocutory review of claim-construction rulings. *Portney v. CIBA Vision Corp.*, 401 F. App'x 526, 529 (Fed. Cir. 2010) ("Here, we see no reason to depart from our general practice of waiting until final judgment has issued to resolve ordinary claim construction issues."); *St. Clair Intellectual Prop. Consultants, Inc. v. Nokia Corp.*, 395 F. App'x 707 (Fed. Cir. 2010) (same). Indeed, the Federal Circuit has not accepted any subsequent interlocutory appeals of *Markman* rulings to date. Nonetheless, this case-management option may be appropriate in limited circumstances.

Procedurally, litigants have had the most success obtaining early appellate review when the *Markman* ruling renders the claims noninfringed. The parties may at that point stipulate to noninfringement, and ask the trial court to enter final judgment as to noninfringement under Federal Rule of Civil Procedure 54(b). On occasion, the Federal Circuit has granted review of partial judgments entered under Rule 54(b). *See Lava Trading, Inc. v. Sonic Trading Mgmt., LLC*, 445 F.3d 1348, 1350 (Fed. Cir. 2006). However, because the issues of invalidity and unenforceability generally remain pending below, the Federal Circuit commonly will deny such review. *See Linear Tech. Corp. v. Impala Linear Corp.*, 31 F. App'x 700 (Fed. Cir. 2002). At least one judge has remarked that allowing such piecemeal review of issues "portends chaos in process." *Lava Trading*, 445 F.3d at 1355 (Mayer, J., dissenting). Litigants seeking to invoke such review can maximize their chances by fully describing the basis for noninfringement to allow for meaningful review of that ruling on appeal. *See id.* at 1350. Furthermore, parties can facilitate review by dismissal of remaining claims. *See Nystrom v. TREX Co.*, 339 F.3d 1347, 1351 (Fed. Cir. 2003).

5.1.7 Application of the *Markman* Ruling to Trial

As noted above, the central role of the *Markman* ruling at trial is to define the jury instructions. The *Markman* ruling establishes the claim limitations that must be met to infringe the patent and for the prior art to invalidate the patent. The *Markman* ruling also establishes the scope of the claims that the patent must enable to be valid, and it defines the scope of art that the patentee must have disclosed to the PTO during prosecution. Thus, the *Markman* ruling is critical to most of the substantive matters of patent law in the jury instructions. Having a clear, concise *Markman* ruling, which spells out the final constructions for disputed claim terms, is essential to avoiding disputes at trial over the jury instructions. It is useful to place these constructions in a summary conclusion at the end of an opinion so that they can be readily adapted into jury instructions. Instructions on claim construction must come from the court, and attorneys must not be permitted to reargue claim-construction positions inconsistent with the court's instructions. To do otherwise risks the order of a new trial or reversal. *See CytoLogix*, 424 F.3d at 1172 ("[B]y agreement the parties also presented expert witnesses who testified before the jury regarding claim construction, and counsel argued conflicting claim constructions to the jury. This was improper, and the district court should have refused to allow such testimony despite the agreement of the parties.").

Aside from the actual constructions adopted by the court, which are incorporated into jury instructions, the *Markman* opinion should not be shown to the jury. The *Markman* ruling ordinarily includes language that rejects the claim-construction positions of one of the parties and thus conveying that information to the jury would be prejudicial to the party whose position was rejected. Giving the *Markman* ruling to the jury might also interfere with its analysis of the infringement and invalidity arguments, particularly when (as is common) the *Markman* ruling contains a discussion of the accused device and the prior art.

Since the court will read its construction of terms to the jury, the parties should be required to propose constructions in their *Markman* briefs in the specific language they want the court to read to the jury.

5.2 Analytic Framework and Substantive Principles

As mentioned at the outset of this chapter, the modern practice of claim construction derives from the seminal case of *Markman v. Westview Instruments*, 517 U.S. 370 (1996). It held that the meaning of patent claims is a matter for the court, not the jury, to decide. Although providing some guidance on the approach for construing patent claims, the *Markman* decision spawned many issues relating to the proper framework for determining claim meaning. The Federal Circuit has issued hundreds of opinions since *Markman* addressing this subject. Its approach has shifted over the years and therefore it is critical for courts to ensure that they focus on the most current and authoritative decisions. The Federal Circuit's en banc decision in *Phillips v. AWH Corp.*, 415 F.3d 1303 (Fed. Cir. 2005), stands as the most authoritative synthesis of claim-construction doctrine. While it put to rest some controversies, many core tensions in claim construction persist. Moreover, the decision does not provide a step-by-step approach to construing claims. Our goal in this section of the guide is to provide a systematic process for approaching the *Markman* determination.

This section begins by explaining the process of claim drafting to understand the genesis and evolution of claim terms. It then previews the sources for determining claim meaning and the general hierarchy set forth in *Phillips*. With this background in place, we then offer a structured analysis of claim construction. At the highest level of abstraction, claim construction entails analysis of several threshold questions regarding whether and when a claim term is interpreted and then working through the construal process. The court begins the process with an initial interpretation of the claim term in question based on its own reading. To the extent that the parties identify additional sources of guidance from the intrinsic evidence or extrinsic sources, the court must then systematically work through those sources to reach a proper construction. There are several special cases as well: commonly interpreted terms, means-plus-function claim terms, and mistaken or indefinite claim terms. We also explore the appropriate deference to be accorded prior claim-construction rulings. The section concludes by identifying some common claim-construction pitfalls and by summarizing key processes and substantive issues.

5.2.1 Claim Drafting: The Genesis and Evolution of Claim Terms

Patent claim terms emerge through a process that typically involves multiple contributors who employ at least three distinctive vocabularies—plain English, scientific and/or technical jargon, and the conventions of claim drafting. The court is comfortable with the former but may need assistance interpreting terms that derive from the fields of science and claim drafting. Understanding the process of claim term drafting will ease that semantic challenge.

Figure 5.1 illustrates the drafters, lines of communication, and collaboration leading to the ultimate words used in patent claims. The claim-drafting process begins with the invention and inventor(s). Whether independent or employed in a corporate or university research and development unit, the inventor(s) will in most cases communicate their ideas to a trained patent attorney or agent. That person will typically have some familiarity with the field of invention (although not necessarily to the level of the inventor), as well as substantial training in the drafting of patent applications. Their job is to describe and claim the invention in terms that will satisfy the requirements of the Patent Act. They will seek to write the claims with sufficient specificity to clear the validity hurdles while providing the patentee with significant breadth to cover the foreseeable uses of the invention. As indicated by the two-headed arrow between the inventor and the patent prosecutor, there is often substantial dialogue between the inventor and the drafter before filing the initial application. After that initial filing, however, prosecution of the application and continuations may go on for years. There is often minimal or no interaction between the patent attorney and the inventor during this period, which causes nomenclature to drift and can later complicate claim construction. (This can lead to the anomalous and surprisingly common situation, many years later, in which a court can be called upon to construe a claim term that appears nowhere in the specification.) Whereas the inventor may be steeped in the language of his or her field, the patent drafter uses terms from science as well as claim drafting to achieve a delicate balance of clarity, breadth, and flexibility.

Figure 5.1
Crafting of Patent Claim Terms

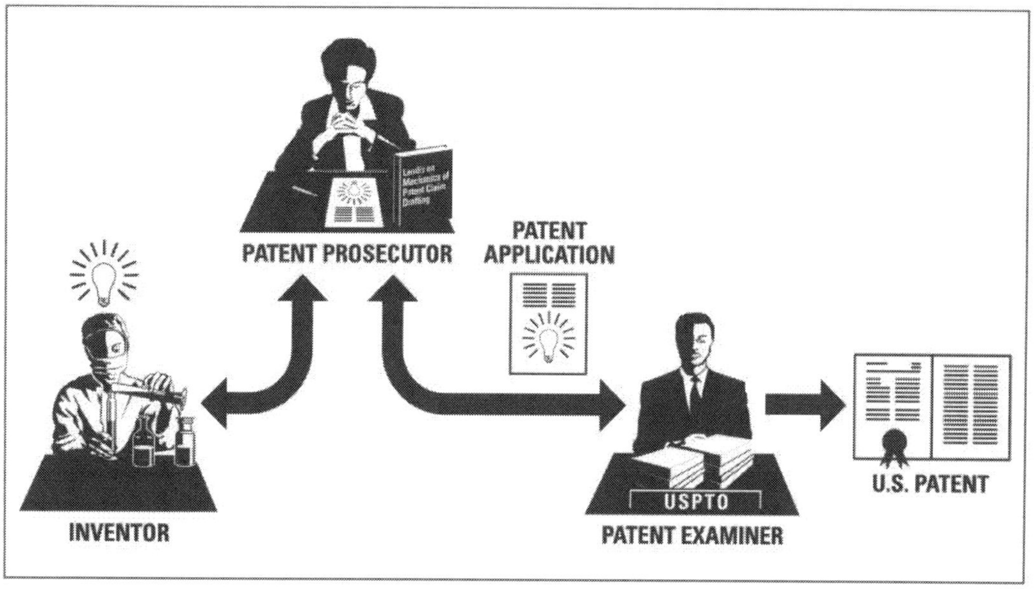

The process of claim drafting does not end when the patent application is submitted. The patent examiner will often play a role in the ultimate claim language of patents. Like the patent prosecutor, examiners have some knowledge of the technical field as well as experience in the process of claim drafting and evaluations. As with the process of application drafting, communication between the prosecutor and the examiner travels in both directions. Patent claims are frequently amended during the prosecution process based on the actions of the examiner. The examiner's focus is on determining that the claims are valid—(1) not anticipated, obvious, or indefinite; and (2) adequately described.

Thus, patent claim language can be an amalgam of multiple vocabularies and perspectives. Patent case law instructs courts to interpret patent claims from the perspective of a person having ordinary skill in the art (i.e., the scientist, technologist, or artisan in the relevant field of invention). This characterization, however, glosses over the role of the patent draftsperson and the examiner in actual claim-drafting practice. Whereas some claim terms—such as "hydroxypropyl, methylcellulose"—undoubtedly derive their meaning from the pertinent technical art, other terms—such as the transitional phrase "comprising"—are better understood from the perspective of the person having ordinary skill in *claim drafting*. Still other terms are simply being used in their plain English sense. Courts need to be sensitive to these distinctions in determining which terms require construction and how to interpret those terms.

5.2.2 Sources for Deriving Claim Meaning

As introduced earlier, *see* § 5.1.3.1, claim construction draws on two general categories of evidence: intrinsic and extrinsic. Chart 5.1 summarizes the main components of these sources.

Chart 5.1
Sources of Evidence for Claim Construction

Intrinsic Evidence

- Patent
- Prosecution history
- Foreign and related patents (and their prosecution histories)
- Prior art that is cited or incorporated by reference in the patent-in-suit and prosecution history

Extrinsic Evidence

- Inventor testimony
- Expert testimony
- Other documentary evidence
- Dictionaries
- Treatises

Prior to the *Phillips* decision, the Federal Circuit doctrine on whether extrinsic evidence could be considered and what role it should play shifted significantly. From 1996 until 2002, consideration of extrinsic evidence beyond educating the court about the technology was heavily disfavored. *See Vitronics Corp. v. Conceptonics, Inc.*, 90 F.3d 1576, 1583 (Fed. Cir. 1996) (finding it was "improper to rely on extrinsic evidence"). Nearly contemporaneous decisions, however, cautioned against such a strong reading. *See Key Pharm. v. Hercon Labs. Corp.*, 161 F.3d 709, 716 (Fed. Cir. 1998) (noting that *Vitronics* "might be misread by some members of the bar as restricting a trial court's ability to hear [extrinsic] evidence. We intend no such thing."). In 2002, the Federal Circuit appeared to elevate dictionaries, a special category of extrinsic evidence, to a central role in claim construction. *See Tex. Dig. Sys., Inc. v. Telegenix, Inc.*, 308 F.3d 1193 (Fed. Cir. 2002). Within a short time, however, the limitations of this approach became apparent:

> The main problem with elevating the dictionary to such prominence is that it focuses the inquiry on the abstract meaning of words rather than on the meaning of claim terms within the context of the patent . . . . [H]eavy reliance on the dictionary divorced from the intrinsic evidence risks transforming the meaning of the claim term to the artisan into the meaning of the term in the abstract, out of its particular context, which is the specification.

Phillips, 415 F.3d at 1321.

Phillips shifted attention back toward the intrinsic record while recognizing that extrinsic evidence can be considered, although with healthy skepticism. Extrinsic evidence may be considered if the court deems it helpful "to educate [itself] regarding the field of invention . . . [and to] determine what a person of ordinary skill in the art would understand claim terms to mean." *Id.* at 1319. The court emphasized, however, that extrinsic evidence must be considered "in the context of the intrinsic evidence[,]" but is "less reliable than the patent and its prosecution history in determining how to read claim terms." *Id.* at 1318–19. The Supreme Court's ruling in *Teva* underscores that extrinsic evidence may be considered, although it reaffirms the principle that intrinsic evidence is paramount in construing patent claims, and extrinsic evidence may not contradict it.

5.2.2.1 Principal Source: Intrinsic Evidence

"Intrinsic" evidence refers to the patent and its file history, including any reexaminations and reissues. Intrinsic evidence also includes related patents and their prosecution histories. In addition, the Federal Circuit generally treats as intrinsic evidence the prior art that is cited or incorporated by reference in the patent-in-suit and prosecution history.

5.2.2.1.1 Prosecution History

Beyond the specification and other claims, an important source of evidence in claim construction is a patent's prosecution history. A "prosecution history" consists of "the complete record of the proceedings before the PTO and includes the prior art cited during the examination of the patent." *Phillips*, 415 F.3d at 1317. During those exchanges, the USPTO will commonly reject the pending patent claims as unpatentable in light of prior art technologies. In response, the patent applicants will typically explain why their claimed inventions are patentable over what had come before. The Federal Circuit cautions that "because the prosecution history represents an ongoing negotiation between the PTO and the applicant, rather than the final product of that negotiation, it often lacks the clarity of the specification and thus is less useful for claim construction purposes." *Id.*

More specifically, the patentee may expressly limit the scope of its patent through disclaimers to avoid prior art. Courts must carefully evaluate such disclaimers during claim construction.

The communications between the applicant and the USPTO may reveal the "ordinary meaning" of a claim term—that is, the communications may show the meaning of a claim term in the context of the patent. *See id.* ("Like the specification, the prosecution history provides evidence of how the PTO and the inventor understood the patent."). For example, in *Nystrom v. TREX Co.*, the prosecution history of the patent confirmed that the claim term "board" in the patent referred to wooden boards, and not plastic boards. *See* 424 F.3d 1136, 1145 (Fed. Cir. 2005); *Hynix Semiconductor Inc. v. Rambus Inc.*, 645 F.3d 1335, 1350 (Fed. Cir. 2011) (interpreting the prosecution history to support a broad interpretation of "bus" because the prosecution history showed that "[a]lthough some of Rambus's claimed inventions require a multiplexing bus, multiplexing is not a requirement in all of Rambus's claims").

5.2.2.1.2 Related and Foreign Applications

Some patents issue from single applications with a single prosecution history. Other patents are members of large families of related patents with a web of underlying patent applications, along with counterparts filed in foreign countries. In the latter instances, when one patent is in suit, parties may find statements in its related patents and patent applications, and in its foreign counterparts, that bear on claim construction. To what extent these statements in related filings impact the construction of the patent in suit is a common dispute in patent litigation.

Where there are a series of patent applications, with the patent in suit issuing from a later filed application, disputes frequently arise over the implications of statements made during prosecution of an earlier filed application (i.e., in a "parent" application). The statements in the parent application are most relevant where the earlier statements address common claim terms with the patent being construed. *Trading Techs. Int'l, Inc. v. Open E Cry, LLC*, 728 F.3d 1309, 1322–23 (Fed. Cir. 2013); *Advanced Cardiovascular Sys., Inc. v. Medtronic, Inc.*, 265 F.3d 1294, 1305–06 (Fed. Cir. 2001). Moreover, where an amendment in a parent application "distinguishes prior art and thereby specifically disclaims a later (though differently worded) limitation in the continuation application," the prosecution disclaimer may apply. *Invitrogen Corp. v. Clontech Labs., Inc.*, 429 F.3d 1052, 1078 (Fed. Cir. 2005). The earlier disclaimer may continue to apply throughout a patent family, particularly if the applicants do not later inform the PTO that they want to rescind the earlier disclaimer. *See Hakim v. Cannon Avent Grp., PLC*, 479 F.3d 1313, 1318 (Fed. Cir. 2007) ("Although a disclaimer made during prosecution can be rescinded, permitting recapture of the disclaimed scope, the prosecution history must be sufficiently clear to inform the examiner that the previous disclaimer, and the prior art that it was made to avoid, may need to be re-visited."). However, the general rule is that when different claim terms are present in the parent and descendant applications, the earlier statements have no bearing on claim construction. *See Ventana Med. Sys., Inc. v. Biogenex Labs., Inc.*, 473 F.3d 1173, 1182 (Fed. Cir. 2006) ("[T]he doctrine of prosecution disclaimer generally does not apply when the claim term in the descendant patent uses different language."); *ResQNet.com, Inc. v. Lansa, Inc.*, 346 F.3d 1374, 1383 (Fed. Cir. 2003) ("Although a parent patent's prosecution history may inform the claim construction of its descendant, the [parent] patent's prosecution history is irrelevant to the meaning of this limitation because the two patents do not share the same claim language."); *Hill-Rom Servs., Inc. v. Stryker Corp.*, 755 F.3d 1367, 1372 (Fed. Cir. 2014) (disregarding statements made in unrelated prosecution history).

Statements to foreign patent offices in counterpart filings may be relevant to construing a U.S. patent where the statements made to the foreign office demonstrate the ordinary meaning of a claim term. *See Starhome GmbH v. AT&T Mobility LLC*, 743 F.3d 849, 858 (Fed. Cir. 2014) (relying on statements to European Patent Office to confirm construction of "intelligent gateway"); *Glaxo Grp. Ltd. v. Ranbaxy Pharm., Inc.*, 262 F.3d 1333, 1337 (Fed. Cir. 2001) (noting that a statement in a related U.K. prosecution history "bolsters this reading" of the claimed "essentially free from crystalline material" limitation in the asserted U.S. patent); *see also Tanabe Seiyaku Co., Ltd. v. U.S. Int'l Trade Comm'n*, 109 F.3d 726, 733 (Fed. Cir. 1997) ("In the present case, the representations made to foreign patent offices are relevant to determine whether a person skilled in the art would consider butanone or other ketones to be interchangeable with acetone in Tanabe's claimed N-alkylation reaction."). However, because the legal requirements for obtaining a patent in other countries may be unique to those countries, statements made to comply with those requirements are generally disregarded in interpreting a U.S. patent. *See Pfizer, Inc. v. Ranbaxy Labs., Ltd.*, 457 F.3d 1284, 1290 (Fed. Cir. 2006) ("[T]he statements made during prosecution of foreign counterparts to the [patent in suit] are irrelevant to claim construction because they were made in response to patentability requirements unique to Danish and European law."); *Apple Inc. v. Motorola, Inc.*, 757 F.3d 1286, 1312 (Fed. Cir. 2014) (explaining that the Federal Circuit will consider "statements made before a foreign patent office when construing claims if they are relevant and not related to unique aspects of foreign patent law," and limiting claim scope based on statements to Japanese patent office).

5.2.2.2 Extrinsic Evidence Is Permissible, but It May Not Contradict or Override Intrinsic Evidence

"Extrinsic evidence" refers to all other types of evidence, including inventor testimony, expert testimony, and documentary evidence of how the patentee and alleged infringer have used the claim terms. Dictionaries are considered to be "extrinsic" evidence. *Phillips*, 415 F.3d at 1318. Judicial decisions from related proceedings may be appropriate extrinsic evidence. *See V-Formation, Inc. v. Benetton Grp. SpA*, 401 F.3d 1307, 1312 (Fed. Cir. 2005) ("The district court properly referred to a related, non-binding judicial opinion to support its independent conclusion in this case."). *Phillips* reaffirmed that the intrinsic evidence is paramount in construing patent claims. Nonetheless, extrinsic evidence can be useful, and *Phillips* and *Teva* confirm that district courts are free to consider extrinsic evidence, including expert testimony, dictionaries, treatises, and other such sources. Litigants continue to argue that it is improper to consider extrinsic evidence in *Markman* rulings, citing *Vitronics*, 90 F.3d 1576. However, the Federal Circuit long ago disavowed any such interpretation of *Vitronics*, and *Phillips* and *Teva* put to rest any suggestion it is wrong to consider extrinsic evidence.

A key to relying on extrinsic evidence is recognizing its limitations. *Phillips* spells out five reasons why extrinsic evidence is inherently less reliable than intrinsic evidence:

> First, extrinsic evidence by definition is not part of the patent and does not have the specification's virtue of being created at the time of patent prosecution for the purpose of explaining the patent's scope and meaning. Second, while claims are construed as they would be understood by a hypothetical person of skill in the art, extrinsic publications may not be written by or for skilled artisans and therefore may not reflect the understanding of a skilled artisan in the field of the patent.

> Third, extrinsic evidence consisting of expert reports and testimony is generated at the time of and for the purpose of litigation and thus can suffer from bias that is not present in intrinsic evidence. . . . Fourth, there is a virtually unbounded universe of potential extrinsic evidence of some marginal relevance that could be brought to bear on any claim construction question . . . . Finally, undue reliance on extrinsic evidence poses the risk that it will be used to change the meaning of claims in derogation of the "indisputable public records consisting of the claims, the specification and the prosecution history," thereby undermining the public notice function of patents.

Phillips, 415 F.3d at 1318–19. Thus, the court must always probe expert testimony for bias and ensure that any expert who offers an opinion is subject to cross-examination. The chief risk of relying on dictionaries, treatises, and other outside documents is pertinence: there is often a gap between how such outside sources characterize a technology and the way a patent presents and claims it. Nonetheless, extrinsic evidence is an increasingly important source for claim construction. *See, e.g.*, *AIA Eng'g Ltd. v. Magotteaux Int'l*, 657 F.3d 1264, 1273–75 (Fed. Cir. 2011) (confirming construction of "homogeneous ceramic composite" based on expert testimony and scholarly treatises); *In re NTP, Inc.*, 654 F.3d 1279, 1289 (Fed. Cir. 2011) (relying on expert testimony that reaffirmed the definition present in specification to justify claim construction).

The Supreme Court's *Teva* decision establishes that extrinsic evidence may establish how a skilled artisan would understand the disputed claim term as of the time of invention. Nonetheless, the extrinsic evidence may not contradict the intrinsic evidence in determining the ultimate claim construction. Thus, the district court should pay special attention to the extent to which the intrinsic evidence constrains the interpretation of disputed claim terms.

5.2.2.2.1 Illustrations of Reliance (and Nonreliance) upon Extrinsic Evidence

Where the specification supports two interpretations of a disputed claim, extrinsic evidence can confirm which interpretation is more consistent with what a person having ordinary skill in the art would have understood at the time of invention. *Phillips* and *Teva* removed any doubt that it might be appropriate to base claim construction on extrinsic evidence. Nonetheless, the Federal Circuit remains highly circumscribed about when it is appropriate to use extrinsic evidence as the source of a proper construction. The Federal Circuit characterized the limited role for extrinsic evidence, saying: "[i]f, and only if, the intrinsic evidence does not establish the meaning of a claim, we can turn to the extrinsic evidence, e.g., inventor testimony, expert testimony, and learned treatises." *Indus. Tech. Research Inst. v. Int'l Trade Comm'n*, 567 F. App'x 914, 917–18 (Fed. Cir. 2014).

The Federal Circuit commonly approves the use of extrinsic evidence to confirm the propriety of a construction that is based in the intrinsic evidence. That is, once the intrinsic evidence has been found to favor a particular construction, it is appropriate to confirm that this construction is consistent with extrinsic evidence.

For example, in *H-W Technology, L.C. v. Overstock.com, Inc.*, 758 F.3d 1329 (Fed. Cir. 2014), the question was whether the claim phrase "user of said phone" was limited to a human, or whether a "thing" could constitute such user. Because the intrinsic evidence indicated that only a human could be such a user, and the extrinsic evidence was mixed, the Federal Circuit agreed that the "user" was limited to a human. *See also Interval Licensing LLC v. AOL, Inc.*, 766 F.3d 1364 (Fed. Cir. 2014) (construing claims based on intrinsic evidence to distinguish "data" from "instructions," and confirming such distinction by resort to extrinsic evidence).

In a dispute over what "homogeneous ceramic composite" meant, the Federal Circuit relied on an engineering textbook that the losing party's expert had introduced. The expert conceded in testimony, supporting the other party's position, that a "composite" could generally be viewed as a multiphase material. *See AIA Eng'g*, 657 F.3d 1264.

In *Conoco Inc. v. Energy & Environmental Int'l*, 460 F.3d 1349, 1362 (Fed. Cir. 2006), the question was whether a "stable" suspension of polymer required sufficient stability to remain suspended when stored for a long period of time, or just stability at the time the suspension was introduced into a pipeline. The court determined from the intrinsic evidence that the appropriate frame of reference was stability at the time the suspension was introduced into the pipeline. The court confirmed its interpretation with the extrinsic evidence, which indicated that all suspensions eventually separate, and found that the appropriate time frame for assessing stability is at the time the suspension is introduced into the pipeline.

Tap Pharmaceutical Products, Inc. v. Owl Pharmaceuticals, L.L.C., 419 F.3d 1346 (Fed. Cir. 2005), also used extrinsic evidence to decide between two plausible interpretations of the specification. *Tap Pharmaceutical* concerned claims to a composition "comprising a copolymer . . . of lactic acid and . . . of glycolic acid." The question was whether the claims were limited to compositions resulting from a polymerization of lactic acid and glycolic acid, or whether the claims also covered the polymer resulting from cyclic precursors that transformed into lactic acid and glycolic acid during polymerization. The district court properly relied on treatises that recognize that copolymers of lactic acid and glycolic acid can be made either by direct polymerization or by ring opening, and on expert testimony that a person of ordinary skill in the art would use the terms "lactic acid" and "glycolic acid" interchangeably with their cyclic analogs. *Id.* at 1349–50.

Attempts to use extrinsic evidence as the *source* for claim constructions are more problematic. Basing the meaning of claim terms on sources external to the patent raises concerns about the notice function of patents. Thus, when extrinsic evidence is used as the source of claim construction, special care must be taken to ensure that the extrinsic evidence is consistent with the patentee's own description of the invention. For example, an appropriate use of extrinsic evidence concerned claims to a "scanner," where the term "scanner" was not defined in the specification, which simply contained one illustrative embodiment having a moving scanner head. *Mass. Inst. of Tech. v. Abacus Software*, 462 F.3d 1344, 1351 (Fed. Cir. 2006). Faced with the question of whether a digital camera qualified as a "scanner," the court turned to dictionaries and concluded that a scanner required "movement between a scanning element and an object being scanned." *Id.* This definition was appropriate because it tracked what the patentee had disclosed in the specification as being a scanner. *Id.*; *see also Boston Sci. Scimed Inc. v. Cordis Corp.*, 554 F.3d 982, 997 (Fed. Cir. 2009) (holding that district court permissibly relied on dictionary definitions of "thrombogenic" to construe "non-thrombogenic" when court's definition was consistent with specification and prosecution history); *Hill-Rom Servs.*, 755 F.3d at 1374 (construing "datalink" broadly to encompass wireless connections, based on expert testimony, when specification was inconclusive)

In a more tenuous example, the Federal Circuit approved the use of expert testimony to set numeric limits on a claim. The claim concerned a pharmaceutical composition with a ratio of "about 1:5" for two chemical components. *Ortho-McNeil Pharm., Inc. v. Caraco Pharm. Labs., Ltd.*, 476 F.3d 1321, 1326–28 (Fed. Cir. 2007). The court reviewed the intrinsic evidence, including claims directed to other ratios, and experimentation disclosed in the specification directed to a range of ratios. It credited the testimony of an expert who opined that "about 1:5" meant "a ratio up to and including 1:7.1 and a ratio down to and including 1:3.6." The Federal Circuit credited the expert testimony, which justified this range as appropriate because it was not statistically different from the claimed ratio of 1:5. *Id.*

A construction based primarily on extrinsic evidence is inappropriate if it contradicts the intrinsic record. For example, in *Vederi, LLC v. Google, Inc.*, 744 F.3d 1376 (Fed. Cir. 2014), Google was sued on its approach for capturing images for StreetView, which records images as a progression of spherical shots. The patent at issue required "images depicting views of objects in a geographic area, the views being substantially elevations of the objects in the geographic area." The district court found the patent was limited to "vertical flat (as opposed to curved or spherical)" depictions of the views, relying largely on extrinsic evidence that defined "elevation" as a vertical plane. The Federal Circuit reversed, finding that the claim term "substantially elevations" accommodated more than planar views, and that the patent's disclosure of using fish-eye lenses confirmed that a strict vertical view was too limiting.

Similarly in *Biagro Western Sales, Inc. v. Grow More, Inc.*, 423 F.3d 1296 (Fed. Cir. 2005), the expert testimony strayed too far from the patent disclosures and sought to reconceptualize the claims. The patent claimed a fertilizer "wherein said phosphorous-containing acid or salt thereof is present in an amount of about 30 to about 40 weight percent." *Id.* at 1302. The amount of phosphorus-containing acid actually present in the accused fertilizer product did not meet the levels stated in the claim, but the patentee tried to use expert testimony to argue that the amount of phosphorous-containing acid in the claim limitation should be read to refer to a "chemical equivalent amount," rather than the amount actually present. In support, the patentee cited fertilizer labeling guidelines and standards and expert declarations, asserting that phosphorus levels in fertilizer are measured by chemically equivalent amounts. This evidence failed to persuade the trial court and the Federal Circuit because Biagro could not tie its measurement approach to the patent's description of the invention. *Id.* at 1303.

It is important to recognize, however, that the Supreme Court's *Teva* decision has altered the framework for considering extrinsic evidence. Therefore, prior Federal Circuit decisions on the role of extrinsic evidence may no longer be valid. District courts can build their claim-construction analysis on the teachings in *Teva.* They should press the parties seeking to introduce extrinsic evidence on how such evidence relates to the intrinsic record.

5.2.2.2.2 Conclusory Expert Opinions Should Be Disregarded

Expert opinions should be grounded both in the intrinsic evidence and by support in other independent, reliable sources. Where these criteria are lacking, the expert opinions should not be relied upon. *SkinMedica, Inc. v. Histogen Inc.*, 727 F.3d 1187 (Fed. Cir. 2013) (quoting *Phillips*, 415 F.3d at 1317) (disregarding expert opinions, explaining that "conclusory, unsupported assertions by experts as to the definition of a claim term are not useful to a court"). Likewise, in *Network Commerce, Inc. v. Microsoft Corp.*, 422 F.3d 1353, 1361 (Fed. Cir. 2005), a patentee sought a construction based upon its expert declaration that a claimed "download component" need not contain a boot program. The expert declaration failed to explain why the passages quoted from the specification supported his opinion and failed to support the expert's conclusion with any reference to industry publications or other independent sources. Accordingly, the declaration was properly disregarded. *Id.*

5.2.3 Claim Construction: Two Stages of Analysis

With that background in place, we are ready to map out the overarching structure of claim construction. Chart 5.2 presents the two distinct steps. Litigants sometimes skip over the first inquiry—whether (and when) claim construction is necessary—and jump right into the complexities of claim construction. Many courts—through patent local rules, *see, e.g.*, N.D. Cal. Patent Local Rules, or case management—focus attention on the threshold issues. Before the court confronts the challenge of construing a claim term, it must consider a series of threshold doctrines and principles that determine whether and when a claim term should be construed.

Chart 5.2
Claim Construction Flowchart

Step 1: Is construction of a claim term required?
Step 2: Interpretation of a claim term

5.2.3.1 Step 1: Is Construction of a Claim Required?

Chart 5.3 presents the series of threshold issues that the court should consider in determining whether and when interpretation of a claim term is appropriate.

Chart 5.3
Step 1: Is Construction of a Claim Term Required?

1. Disputed Meaning That Can Be Derived from the Patent/PHOSITA ("person having ordinary skill in the art") a. Disputed Meaning: Is the meaning of the claim term the subject of legitimate disagreement? *See* § 5.1.4.3. b. Meaning Derivable from the Patent/PHOSITA: For nontechnical terms, is there a special meaning that can be ascertained from the patent? *See* § 5.1.4.3.
2. Priority/Discretion/Timing: Courts have broad discretion to limit and phase claim construction. a. Some courts limit first and usually final *Markman* proceedings to ten terms. b. Court can revisit claim construction; it must eventually construe all legitimately disputed and construable terms before trial. c. Means + function claims (in dispute) must be interpreted to identify corresponding structure, material, or acts. *See* § 5.2.3.5.
3. Issue Preclusion: Deference to Prior *Markman* Ruling a. Issue preclusion cannot be applied offensively against a party who was not represented in prior proceeding, but it can be applied defensively if the four-part test is satisfied. *See* § 5.3. i. Judicial estoppel can be applied where patentee changes positions. ii. Reasoned deference under stare decisis principles. *See* § 5.3.4.
4. Is the Term Amenable to Construction? *See* Table 5.2, § 5.2.3.1.5.

5.2.3.1.1 Is There a Genuine Dispute About the Claim Term?

There is no need to construe terms for the sake of construction. As detailed above, it is recommended that the court order a structured meet-and-confer process to narrow the number of claim terms requiring the court's resolution. Holding a brief telephone conference, prior to claim-construction briefing, at which the parties must articulate the basis for the dispute often further narrows the number of terms.

The mere existence of a dispute on infringement or validity does not mean that claim construction is necessary. Rather, claim construction is necessary to give meaning to claim terms, not to resolve the underlying questions of liability. *See Am. Piledriving Equip.*, 637 F.3d 1324 ("It is well settled that the role of a district court in construing claims is not to redefine claim recitations or to read limitations into the claims to obviate factual questions of infringement and validity but rather to give meaning to the limitations actually contained in the claims, informed by the written description, the prosecution history if in evidence, and any relevant extrinsic evidence.").

5.2.3.1.2 Would Claim Construction Help the Jury?

The point of claim construction is to instruct the jury on what the claim means from the perspective of a person having ordinary skill in the art. For many claim terms, attempting to "construe" the claim language adds little in the way of clarity. Where the perspective of a person having ordinary skill in the art would add nothing to the analysis, there may be no need to construe the terms. Nontechnical terms (e.g., "on" or "above" or "surround") and terms of degree (e.g., "approximately" or "about" or "substantially") may not require construal by the court. Where "construing" a claim term would involve simply substituting a synonym for the claim term, it may be appropriate to allow the claim language to speak for itself.

Construction of a term is clearly appropriate in the case of disputed technical terms, where a person having ordinary skill in the art would bring a distinctive perspective. Of course, in all cases, where the intrinsic and applicable extrinsic evidence further define a term (such as disclaimers, descriptions of "the present invention," and claim differentiation), the court should account for such added evidence in the claim construction. Where the intrinsic evidence and extrinsic evidence do not meaningfully add to the definition of a term, however, it is appropriate (and often preferred) to allow straightforward claim language to stand as is.

5.2.3.1.3 Is Claim Construction a Priority?

The initial *Markman* hearing need not construe all disputed claim terms. Courts increasingly focus the initial *Markman* hearing on no more than about ten "priority" terms, with the expectation that resolving the key terms may dispose of the case. *See* N.D. Cal. Patent Local Rule 4-3(c). Courts are free to revisit any remaining disputes later in the case, but must construe all disputed claim terms before the case is submitted to the jury. How courts wish to balance the priorities of early decision making versus overall completeness will depend on the circumstances of the case.

5.2.3.1.4 Have the Claims Been Construed Before?

There may have been prior proceedings involving the same patents-in-suit or closely related patents. Where there has been a prior construction, the court needs to learn the context of the prior proceedings to determine the impact of doctrines of issue preclusion, claim preclusion, judicial estoppel, and stare decisis. Although the prior proceedings may not be binding in the present litigation, the court should hear from the parties to determine if there are factors that may have preclusive effect or a basis for according deference to the prior claim construction. These important considerations are discussed in § 5.3.

Similarly, in the increasingly common scenario where the patent-in-suit becomes the subject of patent reexamination proceedings, the district court may wish to stay claim construction until those collateral proceedings are resolved. The considerations are addressed in § 4.6.4.

5.2.3.1.5 Is the Term Amenable to Construction?

As illustrated in Table 5.4, claim terms can be categorized into three potentially overlapping general types: (1) lay terms, (2) terms of degree, and (3) technical terms. As discussed previously, *see* §§ 5.1.3.6, 5.1.4.3, not all terms in a claim require construction by the court. It can be improper to construe terms that do not have special meaning that can be derived from the patent.

Table 5.4
Typology of Claim Terms

Type	Lay Terms	Terms of Degree	Technical Terms
Examples	a, above, below, in, surround, to	approximately, essentially, substantial	hydroxypropyl, methylcellulose, cyclic redundancy, oligonucleotide
Amenability to Claim Construction	Such terms are often understood by fact-finder; to construe arguably trenches upon jury's domain, but such terms may have conventional/ established meaning in the technical field.	Such terms are often understood by jury; to construe arguably trenches upon jury's domain. Such terms are inherently contextual. Must be careful not to inappropriately import limitations from specification, but must base interpretation on standard set forth in the specification: if no basis set forth therein, then no basis for construction.	Must be interpreted if meaning is disputed; PHOSITA perspective is essential.
Guide Section	§ 5.2.3.1.5.1	§ 5.2.3.1.5.2	§ 5.2.3.1.5.3

As reflected in Table 5.4, the three types of claim terms are not mutually exclusive, and the question of which category is most appropriate will not always be evident based solely on a reading of the claim. The court will need to examine the intrinsic record to make this assessment. Some plain English terms can have technical meanings in particular fields. For example, the word "inventory" can, depending on the context, be a lay term ("an itemized list of merchandise or supplies" or a "detailed list of all items in stock"). It can also have a more specialized meaning in the field of dry-cleaning process inventions. *See Markman v. Westview Instruments, Inc.*, 52 F.3d 967 (Fed. Cir. 1995) (en banc) (interpreting "inventory" as used in patent claim to mean "articles of clothing" rather than cash or inventory receipts), *aff'd*, 517 U.S. 370 (1996).

Figure 5.2
Landscape of Claim Terms

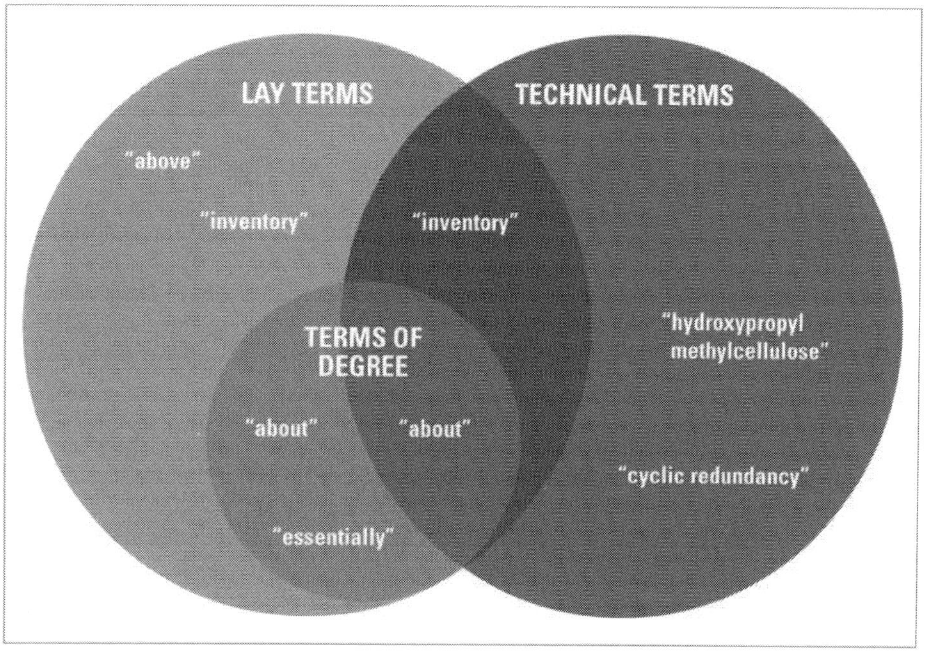

Some technical terms, such as "hydroxypropyl methylcellulose," may well be self-evident. Terms of degree, however, can be ambiguous. For example, the word "about" can obviously have a nontechnical meaning. When used to describe the scope of a particular invention, however, it may well take on meaning that is delimited by intrinsic, and possibly even extrinsic, evidence. *See Ortho-McNeil Pharm.*, 476 F.3d at 1326–28.

5.2.3.1.5.1 Lay Terms

Patent law has long struggled with how precisely claims should be construed. Many claim terms are inherently imprecise. These include terms of degree, such as "substantially," "about," and "approximately," which we deal with separately because they have been the focus of substantial jurisprudence. District courts are commonly asked to give lay terms additional clarity in claim construction. When imprecise language should be left to the jury remains a subtle, confounding, and thorny aspect of patent adjudication.

Efforts to construe lay terms with precision are in some tension with *Markman*'s division of authority between judges and juries. *See Markman*, 517 U.S. at 384. It is the court's role to construe the claims, while it is the jury's role to determine infringement. *Id.* That is, "Step 1" of the infringement analysis is to construe the claims, and "Step 2" is to compare the accused device against the construed claims. Construing terms of degree with more precise language may be error, not only because it "imports limitations" from the specification into the claims, but also because it can impinge on the role of the jury in resolving the question of infringement. The Federal Circuit observed that "line-drawing" questions over what meets the scope of the claims is appropriately left to the jury in some contexts. *See Acumed LLC v. Stryker Corp.*, 483 F.3d 800, 806 (Fed. Cir. 2007) ("[A] sound claim construction need not always purge every shred of ambiguity. The resolution of some line-drawing problems—especially easy ones like this one—is properly left to the trier of fact.").

On the other hand, the Federal Circuit decision in *O2 Micro International* dictates that although "district courts are not (and should not be) required to construe *every* limitation present in a patent's asserted claims," the court must interpret the scope of any claim term for which the parties have presented a "fundamental dispute." 521 F.3d at 1362. In that case, the district court had declined to construe the term "only if" on the ground that it has a well-understood meaning that the jury could apply without judicial interpretation. The parties in the case agreed that "only if" had a common meaning, but the parties disputed the scope of the claim based on this phrase and argued that dispute to the jury. The Federal Circuit vacated the jury verdict and permanent injunction and remanded the case for reconsideration. In view of this decision, the prudent course for district courts will be to construe any claim term—including lay words or phrases—for which there is a legitimate dispute, while keeping in mind that a "plain meaning" construction for certain words and phrases may properly resolve the dispute between the parties. Nonetheless, courts should be skeptical of construing lay terms for which neither party can produce intrinsic evidence indicating a specialized meaning.

5.2.3.1.5.2 Terms of Degree

Courts frequently struggle to construe terms of degree, such as "about," "approximately" and "essentially." This arises for two principal reasons. First, these terms are inherently vague. Second, while these terms have common meaning, they arguably take on a technical meaning within the context of the patent.

Courts must first consider whether these terms should be construed at all, or whether the use of these terms renders the claim invalid for indefiniteness. *See* § 14.3.3.4. Where the terms are not indefinite, they may warrant a definition that provides more particular limits if such words are used in a technical sense or derive meaning from the specification. If the words are not used in a technical sense and the specification does not suggest a standard, the court should not construe the words more precisely but rather leave them for the jury to apply in determining infringement in the context of the accused product or method.

5.2.3.1.5.2.1 Terms of Degree: Potential Indefiniteness

Using terms of degree may render a claim invalid for infiniteness. The definiteness standard requires "clear notice of what is claimed, thereby appris[ing] the public of what is still open to them." *Nautilus, Inc. v. Biosig Instruments, Inc.*, 134 S. Ct. 2120, 2128 (2014). *Nautilus* tightened the definiteness standard, holding that a patent is invalid for indefiniteness if its claims, read in light of the patent specification and file history, fail to inform with reasonable certainty those skilled in the art about the scope of the invention. *Id.* at 2129. The Supreme Court recognized that the definiteness standard "must allow for a modicum of uncertainty" to provide incentives for innovation while avoiding an innovation-discouraging "'zone of uncertainty.'" *Id.* (quoting *United Carbon Co. v. Binney & Smith Co.*, 317 U.S. 228, 236 (1942)). Accordingly, there is no blanket prohibition on terms of degree. *See Interval Licensing LLC v. AOL, Inc.*, 766 F.3d 1364, 1374 (Fed. Cir. 2014).

The Federal Circuit has since reaffirmed its line of cases that terms of degree may be definite where the patent provides enough certainty to one of skill in the art when read in the context of the invention. *See Id.* at 1370 ("[w]e do not understand the Supreme Court to have implied in [*Nautilus*], and we do not hold today, that terms of degree are inherently indefinite. Claim language employing terms of degree has long been found definite where it provided enough certainty to one of skill in the art when read in the context of the invention."); *Biosig Instruments, Inc. v. Nautilus,* Inc., 783 F.3d 1374 (Fed. Cir. 2015) (upholding the validity of the patent at issue in *Nautilus* on remand from the Supreme Court).

While recognizing that the Supreme Court's *Nautilus* ruling has tightened the indefiniteness standard, *see Interval Licensing*, 766 F.3d at 1370–71 (noting that "it is not enough, as some of the language in our prior cases may have suggested, to identify 'some standard for measuring the scope of the phrase'"), the Federal Circuit does not believe that the new standard "'render[s] all of the prior Federal Circuit and district court cases inapplicable' and 'all that is required is that the patent apprise [ordinary-skilled artisans] of the scope of the invention.'" *Nautilus*, 783 F.3d at 1381. (quoting *Freeny v. Apple Inc.*, 2014 U.S. Dist. LEXIS 120446, 2014 WL 4294505, at *4 (E.D. Tex. Aug. 28, 2014) (Bryson, J., sitting by designation). Now, the "claims, when read in light of the specification and the prosecution history, must provide objective boundaries for those of skill in the art." *Interval Licensing*, 766 F.3d at 1370–71.

There are, however, degrees of terms of degree. Some pose more immediate definiteness concerns. "When a 'word of degree' is used, the court must determine whether the patent provides "some standard for measuring that degree." *Nautilus*, 783 F.3d at 1378. (quoting *Enzo Biochem, Inc. v. Applera Corp.*, 599 F.3d 1325, 1332 (Fed. Cir. 2010); *Seattle Box Co., Inc. v. Indus. Crating & Packing, Inc.*, 731 F.2d 818, 826 (Fed. Cir. 1984)). "When a claim limitation is defined in 'purely functional terms,' a determination of whether the limitation is sufficiently definite is 'highly dependent on context (e.g., the disclosure in the specification and the knowledge of a person of ordinary skill in the relevant art area).'" *Nautilus*, 783 F.3d at 1378 (quoting *Halliburton Energy Servs., Inc. v. M-I LLC*, 514 F.3d 1244, 1255 (Fed. Cir. 2008)).

Highly subjective terms are the most susceptible to being declared invalid. For example, the Federal Circuit found a claim directed to a computer display providing that content be shown "in an unobtrusive manner" invalid for indefiniteness. *See Interval Licensing*, 766 F.3d at 1371. Finding this term "purely subjective," the Federal Circuit further noted that the specification provided inconsistent and muddled descriptions of how to apply this term. *Id.*; *see also Datamize, LLC v. Plumtree Software, Inc.*, 417 F.3d 1342, 1352 (Fed. Cir. 2005) (invalidating claim directed to "aesthetically pleasing" display as indefinite, because it is bounded only by the "unpredictable vagaries of any one person's opinion").

More commonplace terms such as "substantially" and "about" permeate patent claims. Accordingly, a fundamental question is how to apply the stricter standard of *Nautilus* against these garden-variety terms of degree. Since *Nautilus*, the Federal Circuit has twice cited with approval its earlier ruling in *Enzo Biochem*, 599 F.3d at 1334–35, which upheld the term "not interfering substantially" where intrinsic evidence provided multiple examples that would allow a skilled artisan to determine whether a particular chemical bond linkage group would "interfer[e] substantially" with hybridization. Thus, courts should look to the intrinsic record for examples to give meaning to these terms of degree.

Section 5.2.4.2 provides further and more general discussion of the claim indefiniteness doctrine.

5.2.3.1.5.2.2 The Court Should Not Delineate Terms of Degree "Where the Patent Provides No Standard"

When the court construes a term of degree, a key question is whether the intrinsic evidence provides some standard for measuring that degree. *Exxon Research & Eng'g Co. v. United States*, 265 F.3d 1371, 1381 (Fed. Cir. 2001) ("When a word of degree is used the district court must determine whether the patent's specification provides some standard for measuring that degree."). Often there may be no such standard, and the Federal Circuit has frequently ruled that it would be error to impose a more exact construction on terms of degree. *See Playtex Prods., Inc. v. Procter & Gamble Co.*, 400 F.3d 901, 907 (Fed. Cir. 2005) ("But the definition of 'substantially flattened surfaces' adopted by the district court introduces a numerical tolerance to the flatness of the gripping area surfaces of the claimed applicator[, which] contradicts the recent precedent of this court, interpreting such terms of degree.") (citing *Cordis Corp. v. Medtronic AVE, Inc.*, 339 F.3d 1352, 1361 (Fed. Cir. 2003) (refusing to impose a precise numeric constraint on the term "substantially uniform thickness") and *Anchor Wall Sys. v. Rockwood Retaining Walls, Inc.*, 340 F.3d 1298, 1311 (Fed. Cir. 2003) (holding that "the phrase 'generally parallel' envisions some amount of deviation from exactly parallel," and that "words of approximation, such as 'generally' and 'substantially,' are descriptive terms commonly used in patent claims to avoid a strict numerical boundary to the specified parameter")). *See also PPG Indus. v. Guardian Indus. Corp.*, 156 F.3d 1351, 1355 (Fed. Cir. 1998) ("Claims are often drafted using terminology that is not as precise or specific as it might be. . . . That does not mean, however, that a court, under the rubric of claim construction, may give a claim whatever additional precision or specificity is necessary to facilitate a comparison between the claim and the accused product."); *Renishaw PLC v. Marposs Societa' per Azioni*, 158 F.3d 1243, 1249 (Fed. Cir. 1998) ("Thus, when a claim term is expressed in general descriptive words, we will not ordinarily limit the term to a numerical range that may appear in the written description or in other claims."); *Acumed*, 483 F.3d at 806 (rejecting argument that the district court's construction of "curved shank" to exclude "sharp corners or sharp angles" renders the construction insufficiently definite since the court did not specify precisely how "sharp" is too sharp).

5.2.3.1.5.2.3 The Appropriate Standard for Defining or Declining to Define Terms of Degree

A standard for measuring a term of degree may come from the patent specification and the working examples. As noted above, one case concerns construction of the term "about 1:5," referring to a pharmaceutical composition having a particular ratio of two components. *Ortho-McNeil Pharm.*, 476 F.3d at 1326–28. The Federal Circuit approved its construction as "a ratio up to and including 1:7.1 and a ratio down to and including 1:3.6." *Id.* at 1328. This construction was derived from the specification, which contained other examples of ratios that were tested and claimed, and from expert testimony, declaring that a range of 1:7.1 and a ratio down to and including 1:3.6 was not statistically different from the stated ratio of 1:5. This case may represent the high-water mark in terms of extrapolating examples from the specification and imposing numerical limits on claim scope, and may suggest a willingness (as discussed above) to credit district court fact-finding based on extrinsic evidence. By contrast, other cases have refused to assign numerical bounds to the scope of the claim term "about." *See Modine Mfg. Co. v. USITC*, 75 F.3d 1545, 1551 (Fed. Cir. 1996) ("It is usually incorrect to read numerical precision into a claim from which it is absent . . . it is a question of technologic fact whether the accused device meets a reasonable meaning of 'about' in the particular circumstances."), *overruled in part by Fresenius Med. Care Holdings, Inc. v. Baxter Int'l, Inc.*, 2006 U.S. Dist. LEXIS 36788, 2006 WL 1469517 (N.D. Cal. May 24, 2006); *see also Lexion Med., LLC v. Northgate Techs., Inc.*, 641 F.3d 1352, 1357 (Fed. Cir. 2011) (affirming infringement of claim phrase "having a temperature within 2°C of the predetermined temperature" by device whose temperature occasionally fluctuated beyond 2°C from the predetermined temperature, based on statements in specification indicating that such fluctuations are intended to be within scope of invention).

A standard for measuring a term of degree may come from the applicant's statements distinguishing the prior art. For example, in *Glaxo Grp. Ltd. v. Ranbaxy Pharms., Inc.*, 262 F.3d 1333, 1337 (Fed. Cir. 2001), the Federal Circuit found that the claim phrase "essentially free of crystalline material" could be properly construed as requiring a crystalline content of less than 10%, based in part on the applicant's descriptions of the prior art. Similarly, in *Biotec Biologische Naturverpackungen GmbH v. Biocorp, Inc.*, 249 F.3d 1341, 1347 (Fed. Cir. 2001), the Federal Circuit approved construing the term "substantially water free" as having a water content below 5% in accordance with statements during prosecution history that distinguished a prior art reference with a water content from 5%–30%.

The construction of a term of degree may also be based on functional properties required by the context of the claim term or other intrinsic evidence. For example, in *Gemtron Corp. v. Saint-Gobain Corp.*, 572 F.3d 1371 (Fed. Cir. 2009), the Federal Circuit considered what was required for an "end edge portion" of a claimed refrigerator shelf to be "relatively resilient" in light of the claim term "relatively resilient end edge portion which temporarily deflects and subsequently rebounds to snap secure." Relying on the claim language and that the specification only discussed resiliency in the context of assembly of the shelf, the court construed the claim to require only that the end edge portion be sufficiently resilient to temporarily deflect and subsequently rebound after glass was inserted into the frame.

However, claim terms, including terms of degree in device or apparatus claims, should not be interpreted to depend on the use of that device absent an express use limitation. For example, the Federal Circuit rejected a construction of "real-time" in the term "displaying real-time data" that required "contextually meaningful delay" because, under this construction, the same apparatus might infringe when used in one activity, but not infringe when used in another. The court explained, "[c]onstruing a non-functional term in an apparatus claim in a way that makes direct infringement turn on the use to which an accused apparatus is later put confuses rather than clarifies, frustrates the ability of both the patentee and potential infringers to ascertain the propriety of particular activities, and is inconsistent with the notice function central to the patent system." *Paragon Solutions, LLC v. Timex Corp.*, 566 F.3d 1075, 1090–91 (Fed. Cir. 2009); *see also Hewlett-Packard Co. v. Bausch & Lomb, Inc.*, 909 F.2d 1464, 1468 (Fed. Cir. 1990) ("[A]pparatus claims cover what a device is, not what a device does.").

Terms of degree frequently do not warrant a more precise construction, and it is often appropriate to pass imprecise terms to the jury in its role as fact-finder. However, the intrinsic evidence may suggest an appropriate standard for providing a more concrete measure of claim scope. The right approach is the one that recognizes the tension between the goals of clarifying claim scope and of avoiding imposing extra limitations on claim language, and then carefully assesses the objective measures that can give standards for the claim terms.

The parties will often say a term of degree needs no construction because it has its "plain and ordinary" or "ordinary and customary" meaning. Courts must probe such positions, because parties often will have fundamentally different views about the "plain and ordinary" meaning of a term. Alternatively, they may use the "plain and ordinary" label to maintain flexibility in their construction of the term. Failure to explore what a party means by the "plain and ordinary" meaning can result in an unresolved construction issue arising during trial.

5.2.3.1.5.3 Technical Terms

When there are genuine disputes about the scope of technical terms, there is no doubt that construction by the court is required. Nonetheless, some technical terms may have a well-established meaning, in which case the definition might be more akin to a glossary definition or perhaps no construction would be necessary. Furthermore, as reflected in Chart 5.4, some lay terms—such as "about"—might have a technical meaning in the context of the patent and hence will require interpretation by the court. *See O2 Micro*, 521 F.3d at 1362 (failure to construe the term "only if" was error where parties disputed its scope).

5.2.3.2 Step 2: Interpretation of Claim Terms

Once it is determined that a term must be construed and is ripe for construal, the court must delve into the complex jurisprudence of interpreting and applying the

Markman decision. Before discussing the disputes that commonly arise in claim construction, it will be useful to state the principles that are generally *not* in dispute. The *Phillips* en banc decision distills these principles and lays out the basic framework for construing patent claims.

A "bedrock principle" of patent law is that "the claims of a patent define the invention to which the patentee is entitled the right to exclude." *Phillips,* 415 F.3d at 1312. The "objective baseline" for construing patent claims is determining "how a person of ordinary skill in the art understands a claim term." *Id.* at 1313. "That starting point is based on the well-settled understanding that inventors are typically persons skilled in the field of the invention and that patents are addressed to and intended to be read by others of skill in the pertinent art." *Id.* Often, other evidence will provide context for characterizing the person having ordinary skill in the art. *See generally* § 14.3.5.3.1 (discussing the standards for determining the characteristics and knowledge of a "person having ordinary skill in the art" (often abbreviated to "PHOSITA")). Temporally, the "ordinary meaning" of a claim term is the meaning that the term would have to a person of ordinary skill in the art "at the time of the invention, i.e., as of the effective filing date of the patent application." *Phillips,* 415 F.3d at 1313. The "effective filing date" is the earlier of the actual filing date or the filing date of an application from which priority is accorded. *See* § 14.3.3.2 n.19. This is significant and can generate evidentiary challenges, because the meaning of scientific and technical terms can change significantly during a patent's lifespan. In the field of digital technology, for example, change can occur rapidly given the exponential rate of advance in computer technology. Litigation over patent claims can occur multiple technological generations after the patent claim term was drafted.

The court's task is to interpret claims through the eyes of a person having ordinary skill in the art field of the invention. That person "is deemed to read the words used in the patent documents with an understanding of their meaning in the field, and to have knowledge of any special meaning and usage in the field." *Phillips,* 415 F.3d at 1313 (quoting *Multiform Desiccants, Inc. v. Medzam, Ltd.,* 133 F.3d 1473, 1477 (Fed. Cir. 1998)). Interpreting patent claims thus requires the court to consider "the same resources as would that person, viz., the patent specification and the prosecution history." *Id.* The proper definition of a claim term is context-dependent. The patent and its prosecution history "usually provide[] the technological and temporal context to enable the court to ascertain the meaning of the claim to a person having ordinary skill in the art at the time of the invention." *Id.* (quoting *V-Formation,* 401 F.3d at 1310). Thus, patent claims are to be interpreted in light of this "intrinsic" evidence (i.e., the patent specification and its prosecution history) as well as pertinent "extrinsic" evidence (i.e., evidence showing the usage of the terms in the field of art).

5.2.3.2.1 Claim-Construction Framework

Figure 5.3 illustrates the starting and ending points for claim construction. We might analogize the claim-construction process to a train line. The first station is the claim itself. "Importantly, the person of ordinary skill in the art is deemed to read the claim term not only in the context of the particular claim in which the disputed term appears, but in the context of the entire patent, including the specification." *See Phil-*

lips, 415 F.3d at 1313. "In some cases, the ordinary meaning of claim language as understood by a person of skill in the art may be readily apparent even to lay judges, and claim construction in such cases involves little more than the application of the widely accepted meaning of commonly understood words . . . . In such circumstances, general purpose dictionaries may be helpful." *Id.* at 1314 (citation omitted).[4] If the term is technical, the court may ascribe little, if any, meaning to the term without substantial background education. Furthermore, "because patentees frequently use terms idiosyncratically, the court looks to 'those sources available to the public that show what a person of skill in the art would have understood disputed claim language to mean.'" *Id.* (citation omitted).

Figure 5.3
Claim-Construction Process: Starting Point and Destination

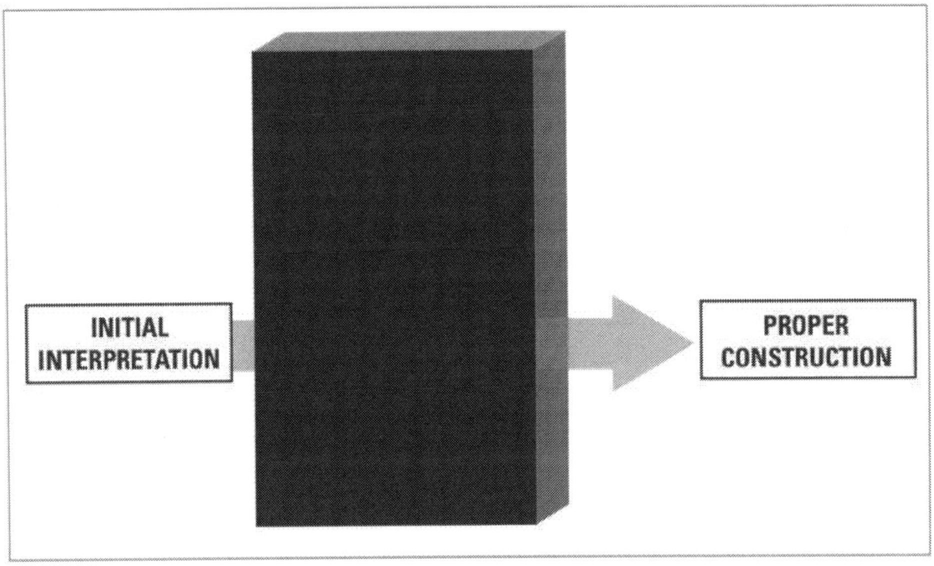

The ultimate destination for this process is the proper construction. This will depend on the appropriate legal standard (the meaning that a person having ordinary skill in the art would attach), the relevant time period (the time of the invention), and the pertinent intrinsic and extrinsic evidence. It may also depend on the jurisprudence of claim construction, such as the doctrine of claim differentiation. A court will develop the proper construction based on a searching review of the intrinsic evidence and any other evidence that the parties present. There are multiple potential "stops" along this track.

Figure 5. illustrates the principal potential stops along the claim-construction line. The parties must inform the court which stations are relevant to interpreting

4. Later in the *Phillips* decision, the Federal Circuit highlighted several pitfalls of relying on dictionaries for claim construction, most notably the tendency toward abstract meaning as opposed to the meaning of claim terms in the context of the patent. *See Phillips*, 415 F.3d at 1319–24; *see also* § 5.4.

the claim and what specific evidence bears on the proposed interpretation. If no evidence is adduced or if the evidence cited is unilluminating, then the court's initial interpretation becomes the proper construction (or the court might deem the claim term as it is). More commonly, the parties will call attention to various sources of meaning from the specification, file wrapper, or extrinsic sources. We explore the jurisprudence relating to this process in what follows.

Figure 5.4
Claim-Construction Process: Inside the Black Box

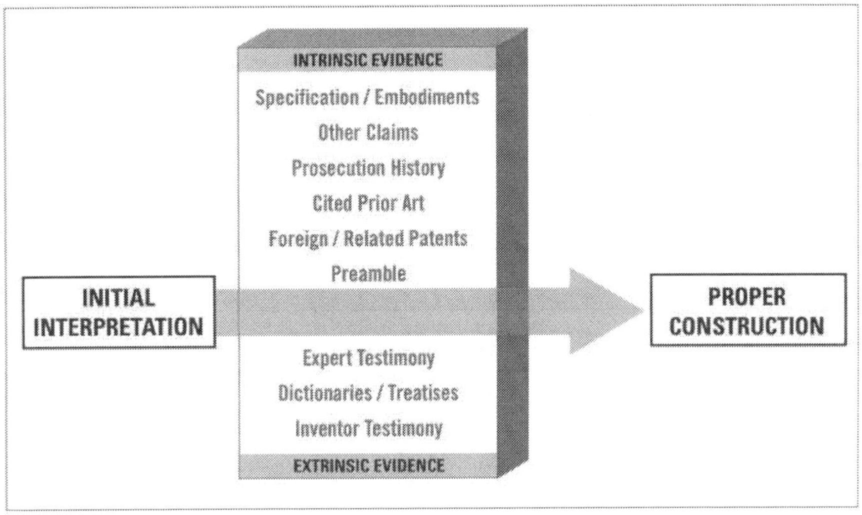

Note that the stations along the claim-construction railroad are aligned vertically but not horizontally. The vertical alignment reflects the priority to be accorded intrinsic evidence. The Federal Circuit has often noted, and the *Phillips* decision affirms, that the specification is the "primary basis for construing the claim" and is in most cases "the best source for understanding a technical term." *See Phillips*, 415 F.3d at 1314 (citations omitted). The sources are not organized horizontally because *Phillips* set forth the principle that "there is no magic formula or catechism for conducting claim construction. Nor is the court barred from considering any particular sources or required to analyze sources in any specific sequence, as long as those sources are not used to contradict claim meaning that is unambiguous in light of the intrinsic evidence." *Id.* at 1324.

Figure 5. frames the substantive analysis. The principles set forth at the top of the chart ground the inquiry. Since the court must construe the term as it would have been understood by a skilled artisan as of the time that the invention was made, a tutorial can be especially useful. An evidentiary hearing or expert declarations might be necessary where the parties dispute the skilled artisan perspective as of the time the invention was made (and within the context of the patent).

With this foundation in place, the court should focus on the claim term in question. As the chart's structure reflects, the inquiry centers on "ordinary meaning." But it is not necessarily the ultimate destination. The proper construction depends on how the patent uses the term. Various doctrines pull toward a narrower or broader construction. Where the intrinsic evidence does not resolve the dispute over claim meaning, the court can look to extrinsic evidence. The subsections that follow examine those forces.

Figure 5.5
Functional Landscape of Claim-Construction Principles and Doctrines

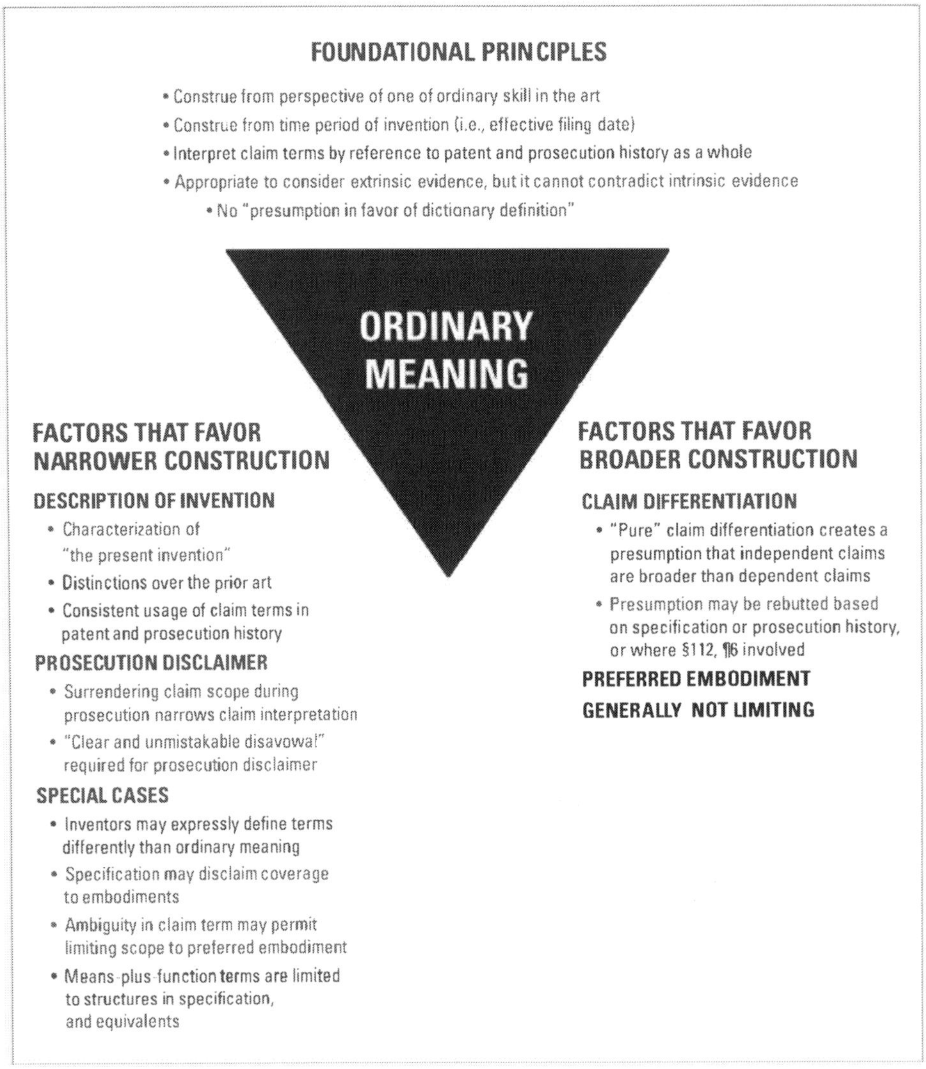

5.2.3.2.2 Starting Point for Analysis: "Ordinary Meaning"

The *Phillips* framework uses "ordinary and customary meaning" as the objective baseline for claim construction. *Phillips*, 415 F.3d at 1312–13. It is important to recognize, however, that even the term "ordinary and customary meaning" has a specialized meaning in patent law. It does not denote the ordinary meaning that a layperson would ascribe to the claim term. Nor does it signify abstract meaning or meaning in a vacuum. Rather, the "ordinary meaning" under *Phillips* is meaning that a person having ordinary skill in the art would attribute to the claim term in the context of the entire patent, including the specification and prosecution history. *Id.* at 1313. *Phillips* recognizes that there may be instances where the specification gives a "special definition" to a claim term that differs from the ordinary and customary meaning of a claim term or that the applicant may have expressly disavowed or disclaimed coverage to the full breadth of the claims under the ordinary and customary meaning. *Id.* at 1316. However, even in those cases where the applicant's statements in the patent and prosecution history do not rise to the level of a "special definition," or a "disavowal" or "disclaimer," *Phillips* recognizes that the proper construction may depart from the ordinary and customary meaning of a claim term.

Phillips reaffirmed that the "starting point" of the analysis is the "ordinary meaning" of the disputed claim terms. However, it overruled prior doctrine on how to determine this ordinary meaning and on the extent to which the ordinary meaning ultimately governs the construction of patent terms. Nonetheless, litigants commonly, and wrongly, attempt to rely on pre-*Phillips* cases that use a now-rejected approach. Because this shift in the law rendered certain lines of authority obsolete, it is important to recognize what *Phillips* changed and which statements from previous case law are no longer valid.

5.2.3.2.2.1 "Presumption of Dictionary Definition" Obsolete

Prior to *Phillips*, a widely applied line of Federal Circuit authority instructed district courts to emphasize dictionary definitions as the source of ordinary meaning. *Tex. Dig. Sys., Inc. v. Telegenix, Inc.*, 308 F.3d 1193, 1204 (Fed. Cir. 2002) (establishing a "presumption in favor of a dictionary definition"). *Texas Digital* instructed district courts to determine the ordinary meaning of claim terms through reference to dictionaries and other sources *before* interpreting the specification. *Id. Texas Digital* established a "heavy presumption" that this dictionary-derived ordinary meaning applied. *Id.* at 1202. Overcoming this presumption required showing that the patentee "has clearly set forth an explicit definition of the term different from its ordinary meaning," or that "the inventor has disavowed or disclaimed scope of coverage, by using words or expressions of manifest exclusion or restriction, representing a clear disavowal of claim scope." *Id.* at 1204. *Phillips* specifically criticized *Texas Digital*'s reliance on dictionaries, which improperly "focuses the inquiry on the abstract meaning of words rather than on the meaning of claim terms within the context of the patent." *Phillips*, 415 F.3d at 1321.

5.2.3.2.2.2 "Heavy Presumption" of Ordinary Meaning

Prior to *Phillips*, the Federal Circuit routinely stated that there is a "heavy presumption" that the ordinary meaning of a patent term governs. *See, e.g., Superguide Corp. v. DirecTV Enters., Inc.*, 358 F.3d 870, 874–75 (Fed. Cir. 2004). When the Federal Circuit articulated its claim-construction methodology in *Phillips*, this "heavy presumption" was omitted. In the years immediately following *Phillips*, this "heavy presumption" language all but disappeared. *But see Elbex Video, Ltd. v. Sensormatic Elecs. Corp.*, 508 F.3d 1366, 1371 (Fed. Cir. 2007). Moreover, the *Phillips* decision expressly rejected the rule of *Texas Digital*, which established a "presumption in favor of a dictionary definition." *Texas Digital*, 308 F.3d at 1204. According to *Phillips*, a reliance on dictionaries in the first instance improperly "focuses the inquiry on the abstract meaning of words rather than on the meaning of claim terms within the context of the patent." *Phillips*, 415 F.3d at 1321. Thus, it appeared that *Phillips* rendered the "heavy presumption" of ordinary meaning obsolete.

Phillips overturned the *Texas Digital* methodology by providing that the meaning of claim terms derives, foremost, from the patent documents themselves. Under *Phillips*, it is the intrinsic record that provides the "technological and temporal context" to determine the meaning of claim terms. *Phillips* refocused the analysis on the invention described in the specification: "The claims are directed to the invention that is described in the specification; they do not have meaning removed from the context from which they arose." *Id.* at 1316 (quoting *Netword, LLC v. Centraal Corp.*, 242 F.3d 1347, 1352 (Fed. Cir. 2001)). Although lawyers commonly cite to language from *Texas Digital*–era case law, those standards are obsolete.

In more recent years, the Federal Circuit has continued to wrestle with this question and appears to be trending back toward a rule that the ordinary meaning will control absent an explicit definition or disavowal. *See Thorner v. Sony Comput. Entm't Am. LLC*, 669 F.3d 1362, 1365 (Fed. Cir. 2012) (holding ordinary meaning should apply unless there is an explicit definition or disavowal). Steadily, the Federal Circuit has now been reintroducing the "heavy presumption" language back into its cases. *See, e.g., Plantronics, Inc. v. Aliph, Inc.*, 724 F.3d 1343, 1350 (Fed. Cir. 2013); *Starhome*, 743 F.3d at 857. Thus, whether such a "heavy presumption" applies remains an open question. The soundest approach is to rely on *Phillips*, which omits such language.

Certain terms, such as technical terms, will tend to derive their meaning from the applicable field of technology, and accordingly their "ordinary meaning" in the field will normally determine the proper claim construction. As a general rule, the more established a claim term is in the relevant technical field, the harder it will be to justify departing from that meaning, absent compelling lexicography or disavowal in the specification or file history. However, other terms, and particularly the more malleable terms that patent attorneys craft, will derive their meaning from the context of the patent document itself.

5.2.3.2.3 Interpreting Claim Language in Light of the Specification

A fundamental challenge in patent law is how to construe claims "in view of the specification." *Phillips*, 415 F.3d at 1315. Tension arises from the competing principles that provide, on the one hand, that "the claims made in the patent are the sole measure of the grant." *Phillips*, 415 F.3d at 1312 (quoting *Aro Mfg. Co. v. Convertible Top Replacement Co.*, 365 U.S. 336, 339 (1961)), and, on the other hand, that a claim term "can be defined only in a way that comports with the instrument as a whole."

Id. at 1316 (quoting *Markman*, 517 U.S. at 389). When and to what extent the terse wording of patent claims should be interpreted in light of thc inventor's other statements in the specification gives rise to a common tension in patent litigation. Indeed, *Phillips* arose out of precisely this type of dispute.

Since *Phillips*, the Federal Circuit has continued to acknowledge the "tightrope" that district courts must walk when construing claims in light of the specification. *See Andersen Corp. v. Fiber Composites, LLC*, 474 F.3d 1361, 1373 (Fed. Cir. 2007). This tightrope was on full display in *Retractable Technologies, Inc. v. Becton, Dickinson & Co.*, 653 F.3d 1296 (Fed. Cir. 2011). There, the majority opinion, authored by Judge Lourie, concluded that the "body" of a syringe was properly construed as limited to a one-piece structure, to the exclusion of two-piece bodies. In the panel dissent, written by Judge Plager, and then in an opinion dissenting from the denial of rehearing en banc (by Judges Moore and Rader), the judges did not believe that the claimed syringe "body" should be limited to a one-piece structure. *Id.*; *see also Retractable Techs. Inc. v. Becton, Dickinson & Co.*, 659 F.3d 1369 (Fed. Cir. 2011) (Moore & Rader, JJ., dissenting)). In many ways, the *Retractable Technologies* case paralleled the dispute in *Phillips*, although this time with the limitation from the specification (i.e., "one-piece") read into the claims. In *Phillips*, the specification's description of the "baffles" at issue was not imposed on the claims. *See id.* at 1371 ("With all due respect to the majority in *Retractable Technologies*, the case is inconsistent with *Phillips*, and we are bound to follow our en banc decision.").

Reconciling the various lines of claim-construction cases is a challenge, and close calls, such as in *Retractable Technologies*, persist. Nonetheless, important guidelines have emerged to govern how to interpret claims in view of the specification. There are several common sources of meaning for claim construction: the preferred embodiments; the manner in which the patentee distinguishes the prior art; the usage of the claim term elsewhere in the patent document (including other claims); disclaimers within the prosecution history; and the preamble. Furthermore, as subsequent sections explore, some commonly used claim terms have become clearer through patent drafting convention and judicial decisions.

5.2.3.2.3.1 The Role of Preferred Embodiments in Claim Construction

Patent specifications typically describe the claimed invention through the use of illustrations or example. In the jargon of patent law, they are characterized as "preferred embodiments." Often the specification will recite a few or even many preferred embodiments of an invention. Claim-construction disputes often center on the import of such illustrations: (1) Must each claim encompass the preferred embodiments? (2) Are the claims limited to the preferred embodiments? (3) Does the number or range of embodiments affect the breadth of the claims? (4) Does ambiguity in a claim term limit its scope to the preferred embodiments? (5) Do characterizations of embodiments as "the invention" or "the present invention" limit the patent accordingly?

5.2.3.2.3.1.1 Claim Scope Generally Includes Preferred Embodiments

The patent claims should generally be construed to encompass the preferred embodiments described in the specification, and it is generally error to adopt a construction that excludes them. *See On-Line Techs., Inc. v. Bodenseewerk Perkin-Elmer GmbH*, 386 F.3d 1133, 1138 (Fed. Cir. 2004) ("[A] claim interpretation that excludes a preferred embodiment from the scope of the claim is rarely, if ever, correct."); *MBO Labs., Inc. v. Becton, Dickinson & Co.*, 474 F.3d 1323, 1333 (Fed. Cir. 2007). Important exceptions to this oft-cited rule apply—such as where there is a clear and unambiguous disclaimer of claim scope in the specification or prosecution history, *see Oatey Co. v. IPS Corp.*, 514 F.3d 1271, 1277 (Fed. Cir. 2008); *N. Am. Container, Inc. v. Plastipak Packaging, Inc.*, 415 F.3d 1335, 1345–46 (Fed. Cir. 2005); *SciMed Life Sys., Inc. v. Advanced Cardiovascular Sys., Inc.*, 242 F.3d 1337, 1344 (Fed. Cir. 2001); *see also* § 5.2.3.2.3, an embodiment is directed to only a subset of claims, *see Helmsderfer v. Bobrick Washroom Equip., Inc.*, 527 F.3d 1379 (Fed. Cir. 2008), or the ordinary meaning simply cannot be stretched to encompass the embodiment. *See also* § 5.2.3.2.3.4 (concerning disclaimers).

There are two primary scenarios in which a claim can properly be construed in a way that excludes an embodiment: (1) where a change occurs in the file history—i.e., the specification remains static during prosecution but the applicant clearly and unambiguously disclaims some claim scope that he or she originally sought during prosecution; and (2) where the specification contains and claims multiple embodiments, a particular claim may not cover a particular embodiment because other claims do. For example, if the claims are sufficiently clear in the usage of claim terms, the construction should follow that usage even if it excludes embodiments within the specification, especially where other claims would encompass those described embodiments. *See Pacing Techs., LLC v. Garmin Int'l, Inc.*, 778 F.3d 1021, 1026 (Fed. Cir. 2015) (approving construction that excludes embodiment where multiple embodiments are disclosed and claim language does not cover that embodiment); *Uship Intellectual Props., LLC v. United States*, 714 F.3d 1311, 1316 (Fed. Cir. 2013) (finding claim scope to automated systems, notwithstanding disclosure of embodiments of manual systems, in view of prosecution disclaimer); *August Tech. Corp. v. Camtek, Ltd.*, 655 F.3d 1278 (Fed. Cir. 2011) (construing "wafer" to mean a physically discrete wafer in view of term usage within claim and in related claims, despite embodiments in specification suggesting that a "wafer" may be each separate circuit on overall wafer).

5.2.3.2.3.1.2 Is the Patent Limited to the Preferred Embodiments?

A common dispute is whether the claim scope should be limited to the embodiments. The mere fact of a particular embodiment being taught (or even "preferred") is generally not sufficient to justify limiting an otherwise broad claim scope to the particular embodiment taught. *See, e.g., GE Lighting Solutions, LLC v. AgriLight, Inc.*, 750 F.3d 1304, 1310 (Fed. Cir. 2014) (reversing claim construction which limited scope of "ICD connector" to features of preferred embodiment); *Azure Networks, LLC v. CSR PLC*, 771 F.3d 1336, 1348 (Fed. Cir. 2014) (reversing claim construction that limited scope of "MAC address" to local address generated by a hub, as taught by embodiments); *Williamson v. Citrix Online, LLC*, 2015 U.S. App. LEXIS 10082, 2015 WL 3687459 at *4 (Fed. Cir. 2015) (reversing construction limited to the disclosed "pictorial map" in view of broader claim language and the lack of disclaimer); *Laryngeal Mask Co. Ltd. v. Ambu S/A*, 618 F.3d 1367, 1371 (Fed. Cir. 2010) (addressing "a difficult case of claim construction," finding that the term "backplate" is not limited to requiring a tube joint described in the specification; court was "mindful that the specification is the single best guide to the meaning of a disputed term" and that the "specification is replete with discussion of a tube joint," but concluded that the term "backplate" was not so limited because only the preferred embodiment indicated that the tube joint "is part of the backplate"); *Agfa Corp. v. Creo Prods., Inc.*, 451 F.3d 1366, 1376–77 (Fed. Cir. 2006) (finding that a claimed "stack" of printing plates was not limited to the particular horizontal stack shown in the specification); *Ormco Corp. v. Align Tech., Inc.*, 463 F.3d 1299, 1306–07 (Fed. Cir. 2006) (finding that a claimed "geometry" of orthodontic teeth was not limited to the geometries of orthodontics shown in the specification); *Acumed*, 483 F.3d at 807 (Fed. Cir. 2007) (finding that a claimed "transverse" hole in a bone nail was not limited to the particular "perpendicular" orientation shown in the specification). The mere fact that the disclosed embodiments of a patented invention have a certain feature does not, by itself, justify limiting the scope of the claims to what is disclosed in the specification. Rather, the fact that the preferred embodiment teaches a certain configuration is just one factor that must be weighed along with other factors such as the clarity of the claim language, the specification's descriptions of the claimed invention, its statements distinguishing the invention from the prior art, and the consistent and uniform usage of claim terms. Other contributing factors include the applicant's statements to the USPTO during patent prosecution and the doctrine of claim differentiation.

Depending on the strength of these other factors, the scale may tip so that the claim is limited to the embodiment disclosed in the specification. *See Pacing Techs.*, 778 F.3d at 1024–25 (Fed. Cir. 2015) (limiting the scope of the claim term "repetitive motion pacing system having data storage and playback" to having certain disclosed features, based on the disclosed object of the invention); *Abbott Labs. v. Sandoz*, 566 F.3d 1282, 1288 (Fed. Cir. 2009) ("[T]he claims cannot 'enlarge what is patented beyond what the inventor has described as the invention.' Thus th[e] court may reach a narrower construction, limited to the embodiment(s) disclosed in the specification, when the claims themselves, the specification, or the prosecution history clearly indicate that the invention encompasses no more than the confined structure or method."); *Am. Piledriving Equip.*, 637 F.3d at 1333 (declining to give the term "eccentric weight portion" a functional description, but instead construing it to include structural elements described in the patent specification, owing to consistent reference throughout the specification to this structure as relating to the invention as a whole); *Edwards Lifesciences LLC v. Cook Inc.*, 582 F.3d 1322, 1327–31 (Fed. Cir. 2009) (limiting the claim term "graft" to mean "intraluminal graft" when "the only devices described in the specification are intraluminal, supporting an interpretation that is consistent with that description"; the specification used the words "graft" and "intraluminal graft" interchangeably; the specification described "intraluminal graft" as the present invention; and neither claim differentiation nor prosecution history required a different construction).

The *Phillips* court acknowledged that "there is sometimes a fine line between reading a claim in light of the specification, and reading a limitation into the claim from the specification." 415 F.3d at 1323 (quoting *Comark Commc'ns, Inc. v. Harris Corp.*, 156 F.3d 1182, 1186–87 (Fed. Cir. 1998)). The Federal Circuit suggested that courts could reasonably and predictably discern this line by focusing on how a person of ordinary skill in the art would understand the claim terms. *Id.* The Federal Circuit has specifically rejected the contention that a court interpreting a patent with only one embodiment must limit the claims of that patent to that embodiment, because § 112 requires that the claims themselves define the limits of a patent and because a person of ordinary skill in the art would rarely do so. *Id.* (construing *Gemstar-TV Guide v. Int'l Trade Comm'n*, 383 F.3d 1352, 1366 (Fed. Cir. 2004)).

The patentee's use of a term within the specification and claims will usually make the distinction between a specification meant to set out specific examples of the invention to disclose how to make and use it, and one in which the claims and embodiments are meant to be strictly coextensive. *Phillips,* 415 F.3d at 1323. District courts should bear in mind, however, that claim drafters routinely avoid providing a clear distinction between embodiments that define the invention and those that merely illustrate it. Through this approach, patentees may get the benefit of a narrow interpretation during prosecution, which might enhance the chances of allowance, while preserving the option of asserting a broad interpretation after the patent issues in enforcement actions. Thus, the "fine line" to which the Federal Circuit refers is often blurred.

5.2.3.2.3.1.3 Does the Number and/or Range of Embodiments Affect the Scope of the Claims?

The Federal Circuit observed in *Phillips* that "although the specification often describes very specific embodiments of the invention, we have repeatedly warned against confining the claims to those embodiments." 415 F.3d at 1323. The court also "expressly rejected the contention that if a patent describes only a single embodiment, the claims of the patent must be construed as being limited to that embodiment." *Id.* Nonetheless, the number and/or range of embodiments may have relevance to the scope of claims. Disputes over how broadly to construe claims in light of the specification trace back to the patent drafter. The patent drafter is the "least cost avoider" in terms of creating a document that can be readily understood and relied on by the public and any courts that may have to interpret it. Scant descriptions of the invention may not necessarily be limiting, but it is uniquely in the power of the patentee to avoid close calls of claim interpretation by clear and detailed descriptions of the full scope of the claimed invention. Just as empirical scientists provide multiple data points to gauge the limits or reach of their theories, it might reasonably be hoped that patentees would likewise express inventions of an empirical nature in a number and range of embodiments if necessary, to convey fully the scope of the claimed invention to the public. Even though a claim is not ordinarily limited to a particular disclosed embodiment, the number and range of embodiments may ultimately affect the scope that can be supported, because those embodiments may inform the court how a person of ordinary skill in the art would understand the claim terms—the issue upon which the court's focus should ultimately remain. *See Phillips*, 415 F.3d at 1323. Proper claim drafting will reduce the burden of, uncertainty surrounding, and need for claim construction.

It may be somewhat ironic, therefore, that claim construction often affords patents supported by a single embodiment with potentially broader scope (ordinary meaning) than more fully illustrated patents. Without as much to consider, the court in the former case is often left with simply the plain language. The principal countervailing force confronting the patentee—the risk that the claim will fail the written description requirement—does not exert much effect as it is often difficult to prove this basis for invalidity. By contrast, patents that are more fully illustrated may provide a clearer basis for construing, and in some cases circumscribing, the scope of the claims. A more balanced middle ground would be to consider the lack of a significant range of illustrative embodiments to be a factor in construing claims based on an empirical foundation. Just as an empirical theory supported by just a single or few examples will be narrower than one supported by a rich and broad range of observations, so the scope of an empirically based invention supported by a single or narrow range of embodiments should, all other factors the same, be understood more narrowly. Such an approach would have the benefit of providing patent drafters with greater incentive to articulate the boundaries of the claimed invention.

It should be noted, however, that claims based upon a conceptual or theoretical foundation may not require disclosure of multiple embodiments to prove their validity or delineate their scope. In such cases, the operative scientific principle will often support and delineate its scope.

5.2.3.2.3.1.4 Does Ambiguity in a Claim Term Limit Its Scope to Preferred Embodiment(s)?

When the claim language is ambiguous, courts look to the specification to determine a reasonable interpretation. *See Rexnord Corp. v. Laitrop Corp.*, 274 F.3d 1336, 1343 (Fed. Cir. 2001) ("[I]f the term or terms chosen by the patentee so deprive the claim of clarity that there is no means by which the scope of the claim may be ascertained by one of ordinary skill in the art from the language used, a court must look to the specification and file history to define the ambiguous term in the first instance.") (internal marks omitted). In *Comark Communications*, 156 F.3d at 1187, the Federal Circuit observed that interpreting claim language in light of the specification is proper when a term is "so amorphous that one of skill in the art can only reconcile the claim language with the inventor's disclosure by recourse to the specification." At the same time, the court cautioned against reading limitations from the specification into the claims (as opposed to interpreting claim language in light of the specification) and declined to do so in that case. *Id.* Nonetheless, courts have on occasion limited claim terms to the preferred embodiments where there is no other way of grounding the ambiguous language. *See Chimie v. PPG Indus., Inc.*, 402 F.3d 1371 (Fed. Cir. 2005).

5.2.3.2.3.1.5 Characterizations of "the Invention" or "the Present Invention"

When the patentee uses descriptive terms such as "the invention" or "the present invention" to describe their claims, then those descriptive embodiments may be definitional. Using such terms as "the present invention is" or "the present invention requires" is viewed as a "disavowal" of broader scope that might otherwise apply. *See Hill-Rom Servs.*, 755 F.3d at 1372("[W]e have held that disclaimer applies when the patentee makes statements such as 'the present invention requires . . .' or 'the present invention is . . .' or 'all embodiments of the present invention are . . .'"). For example, in *Pacing Technologies*, 778 F.3d at 1025, the Federal Circuit found that the specification's repeated use of language identifying the principal and other "object[s] of the present invention" was a clear and unmistakable surrender of claim scope, which justified limiting the scope of the claim term "repetitive motion pacing system having data storage and playback" to having certain disclosed features. The court noted, however, that "the characterization of a feature as 'an object' or 'another object,' or even as a 'principal object,' will not always rise to the level of disclaimer." However, "[i]n this case, where the patent includes a long list of different 'objects of the present invention' that correspond to features positively recited in one or more claims, it seems unlikely that the inventor intended for each claim to be limited to all of the many objects of the invention." The court noted that the patent specification went further by

> including language that constitutes unmistakable disclaimer when considered in the context of the patent as a whole. Immediately following the enumeration of the different objects of the present invention, the '843 patent states that "[t]hose [nineteen listed objects] and other objects and features of the present invention are accomplished, as embodied and fully described herein, by a repetitive motion pacing system that includes . . . a data storage and playback device adapted to producing the sensible tempo." With these words, the patentee does not describe yet another object of the invention—he alerts the reader that the invention accomplishes *all* of its objects and features (the enumerated 19 and all others) . . .

Id.

Likewise, *Honeywell Int'l, Inc. v. ITT Indus., Inc.*, 452 F.3d 1312, 1318 (Fed. Cir. 2006), concerned claims to a "fuel injection system component." Even though the ordinary and customary meaning of a "fuel injection system component" is not limited to a fuel filter, the Federal Circuit found that the proper construction was narrower than that customary meaning and should be limited to a fuel filter. Beyond the fact that all the disclosed embodiments disclosed only fuel filters, the specification repeatedly described the fuel filter as "this invention" and "the present invention." Applying *Phillips,* the court found that there was no need to show that the inventor had "disavowed or disclaimed scope of coverage," as *Texas Digital* had previously set as the standard. *Id.* Rather, the Federal Circuit noted, given the repeated descriptions in the patent specification of "the invention," that "[t]he public is entitled to take the patentee at his word and the word was that the invention is a fuel filter." *Id.; see also Trading Tech. Int'l, Inc. v. eSpeed, Inc.*, 595 F.3d 1340, 1353–54 (Fed. Cir. 2010) (noting that it "takes some comfort against this risk from the inventors' use of the term 'the present invention' rather than 'a preferred embodiment' or just 'an embodiment'"); *Edwards Lifesciences*, 582 F.3d at 1327–31 (limiting the claim term "graft" to mean "intraluminal graft" when "the specification frequently describes an 'intraluminal graft' as 'the present invention' or 'this invention'"); *Andersen*, 474 F.3d at 1367–68 (limiting claim term "composite composition" to pellets in light of statements in specification that are "not descriptions of particular embodiments, but are characterizations directed to the invention as a whole"); *Microsoft Corp. v. Multi-Tech. Sys., Inc.*, 357 F.3d 1340, 1348 (Fed. Cir. 2004) (finding that statements in common specification serve to limit claim language because they "are not limited to describing a preferred embodiment, but more broadly describe the overall inventions of all three patents"); *Alloc, Inc. v. Int'l Trade Comm'n*, 342 F.3d 1361, 1370 (Fed. Cir. 2003) ("[T]his court looks to whether the specification refers to a limitation only as a part of less than all possible embodiments or whether the specification read as a whole suggests that the very character of the invention requires the limitation be a part of every embodiment.").

Nonetheless, the Federal Circuit held in *i4i Limited Partnership v. Microsoft Corp.*, 589 F.3d 1246, 1259-60 (Fed. Cir. 2009), that describing the advantages of the "present invention" does not necessarily limit the claim to systems possessing those advantages. The issue in *i4i* was whether "distinct" storage means required independent manipulation of the metacode map and mapped content. The court held it did not. The specification stated that the "present invention provides the *ability* to work solely on metacodes . . . . Additionally a new map *can* be created based solely on an existing map without requiring the content." *Id.* at 1259. According to the court, these statements were "best understood as describing the advantages of separate storage, the real claim limitation," and, given the permissive language, such as "*ability* to work" and "*can* be created," did not "clearly disclaim systems lacking these benefits." *Id.*

The fact that a specification discloses only a single embodiment does not, by itself, compel limiting claim scope to that embodiment. *Phillips*, 415 F.3d at 1323. There must be additional evidence beyond the disclosure of a single embodiment to justify narrowing a construction to that embodiment. *Agfa*, 451 F.3d at 1376–77. However, the fact that only a single embodiment is shown is a factor that, when taken into consideration with the patentee's description of the invention, may show that the inventor only intended to claim a particular feature as his invention. *See Retractable Techs.*, 653 F.3d at 1304 (holding that the invention is limited to a "single body" syringe based on the patentee's express recitation "that 'the invention' has a body constructed as a single structure, expressly distinguish[es] the invention from the prior art based on this feature, and only disclose[s] embodiment[s] that are expressly limited to having a body that is a single piece."); *Honeywell Int'l*, 452 F.3d at 1318 (limiting scope of "fuel injection system component" to a "fuel filter" because "[t]he written description's detailed discussion of the prior art problem addressed by the patented invention, *viz.*, leakage of non-metal fuel filters in EFI systems, further supports the conclusion that the fuel filter is not a preferred embodiment, but an only embodiment").

5.2.3.2.3.2 Distinctions over the Prior Art

As with descriptions of "the invention," the patentee's manner of distinguishing his invention over the prior art may be definitional. That is, the specification's emphasis on the importance of a particular feature in solving the problems of the prior art is an important factor in defining the claims. These statements that distinguish the claimed invention from the prior art go to the heart of *Phillips*'s instruction to construe claims consistent with a "full understanding of what the inventors actually invented." *Phillips*, 415 F.3d at 1316. The Federal Circuit has found "disclaimer" when "the patent repeatedly disparaged an embodiment as 'antiquated,' having 'inherent inadequacies,' and then detailed the 'deficiencies [that] make it difficult' to use." *See GE Lighting Solutions, Inc.*, 750 F.3d at 1309 (quoting *Chi. Bd. Options Exch., Inc. v. Int'l Sec. Exch., LLC*, 677 F.3d 1361, 1372 (Fed. Cir. 2012)).

For example, in *Inpro II Licensing, S.A.R.L. v. T-Mobile USA, Inc.*, 450 F.3d 1350, 1354–55 (Fed. Cir. 2006), the Federal Circuit affirmed the construction of "host interface" as a "direct parallel bus interface." Among the dispositive factors in this narrow construction were that the only embodiment disclosed was a direct parallel bus interface and that "the specification emphasizes the importance of a parallel connection in solving the problems of the previously used serial connection." *Id.* Since under *Phillips*, there was no need to show that the inventor had disclaimed scope of coverage, T-Mobile obtained a narrowing construction by demonstrating "what the inventor has described as the invention." *Id.* at 1355 (quoting *Netword*, 242 F.3d at 1352); *see also Retractable Techs.*, 653 F.3d at 1305 (limiting scope of syringe "body" to a one-piece body based in part on distinction over prior art syringes composed of multiple pieces).

Statements distinguishing the prior art must be sufficiently clear to warrant a narrowing construction. *Ventana Medical Systems, Inc. v. Biogenex Laboratories, Inc.*, 473 F.3d 1173, 1180–81 (Fed. Cir. 2006) concerned claims to a method of "dispensing" reagents onto a microscope slide. The question was whether "dispensing" was limited to "direct dispensing" (i.e., where the reagent container directly dispenses reagents onto the slide without an intermediary), or whether the claims encompassed the use of an intermediary device to "sip and spit" the reagents from the reagent container onto the slide. The specification contained general criticisms of prior art dispensers, including those using "sip and spit" approaches, as well as those using "direct dispensing" approaches. Because the specification equally criticized both types of prior art dispensers, there was nothing to suggest that the inventor was describing the invention as the use of "direct" instead of "sip and spit" dispensing. Therefore, the Federal Circuit found it was inappropriate to limit the claim scope. *Id.* at 1181 (refusing to narrow claim where challenger "points to only general statements by the inventors indicating that their invention is intended to improve upon prior art staining methods"); *OpenWave Sys., Inc. v. Apple Inc.*, 808 F.3d 509 (Fed.

Cir. 2015) (narrowly construing claim term "mobile device" to exclude communication devices containing a "computer module" based on limiting statements in specification that disparages prior art communication devices containing such "computer modules").

5.2.3.2.3.3 Consistent Usage of Claim Terms

Another claim-construction principle is that the consistent and uniform usage of a claim term in a certain way in the specification may be definitional, showing the "ordinary meaning" of the claim term in the context of the invention. In such circumstances, otherwise broad language in the claim may be limited by the specification's description of the invention. Consistent usage of a claim term in the specification can be definitional even without a showing that there is an "express definition" of the term or a "disclaimer," which the now-overruled *Texas Digital* would have required. For example, the claim term "board" was found to be limited to wooden boards (as opposed to plastic lumber) in light of consistent statements in the specification and prosecution history describing the claimed "boards" as made from wood. *Nystrom*, 424 F.3d at 1145 ("The written description and prosecution history consistently use the term 'board' to refer to wood decking materials cut from a log."); *see also VirnetX, Inc. v. Cisco Sys., Inc.*, 767 F.3d 1308, 1319 (Fed. Cir. 2014) (construing "secure communication link" to require anonymity, based on consistent usage throughout specification).

In *ICU Medical Inc. v. Alaris Medical Systems Inc.*, the Federal Circuit affirmed a construction of "spike" to mean "an elongated structure having a pointed tip for piercing the seal, which tip may be sharp or slightly rounded." 558 F.3d 1368, 1375–76 (Fed. Cir. 2009). The court supported its construction on the ground that "the specification never suggests that the spike can be anything other than pointed" and explained that "adding the functional language 'for piercing the seal' is appropriate because it defines the degree to which the spike must be pointed." *Id.* at 1376; *see also Hologic, Inc. v. SenoRx*, 639 F.3d 1329 (Fed. Cir. 2011) (majority of divided panel construing "asymmetrically located and arranged within the expandable surface" to require the asymmetry be along the longitudinal axis of the balloon when all of the descriptions of the invention describe that type of asymmetry); *Kinetic Concepts, Inc. v. Blue Sky Med. Grp. Inc.*, 554 F.3d 1010, 1018–19 (Fed. Cir 2009) (construing "wound" to exclude pus pockets and infections in the mammary glands when "all of the examples described in the specification involve skin wounds"). *But see Am. Piledriving Equip.*, 637 F.3d 1324 (reversing district court for improperly construing "eccentric weight portion" to require that the portion extend from a particular portion of the gear and in a particular direction, on the ground that these limitations were not part of the inventor's claimed definition of the scope of invention); *Arlington Indus. Inc. v. Bridgeport Fittings*, 632 F.3d 1246 (Fed. Cir. 2011) (declining to construe "spring metal adaptor" to require a split, over dissent which argued that the specification only envisioned adaptors with splits); *Thorner*, 669 F.3d at 1367–68 (refusing to construe "attached to said pad" as limited to either internal or external attachment, because limiting statements in specification were not strong enough to give rise to disavowal); *Falana v. Kent State Univ.*, 669 F.3d 1349, 1354–55 (Fed. Cir.

2012) (finding insufficient force to limiting statements in specification to warrant restricting claims to a compound having a "substantially temperature independent helical twisting power," even though the specification indicates that the invention was narrower than the claim language implied).

5.2.3.2.3.4 Prosecution Disclaimers

Beyond using the prosecution history to ascertain the ordinary meaning of claim terms, the prosecution history can also be used to determine whether there was a "disclaimer" of claim scope. To convince the USPTO to issue patent claims that have been rejected in light of the prior art, patent applicants frequently have to represent that their patent claims do *not* cover certain technologies. These statements are important limitations on claim scope. *Phillips*, 415 F.3d at 1317 ("The purpose of consulting the prosecution history in construing a claim is to exclude any interpretation that was disclaimed during prosecution."). The legal standard for finding a prosecution history disclaimer requires "a clear and unmistakable disavowal of scope during prosecution." *Purdue Pharma L.P. v. Endo Pharm. Inc.*, 438 F.3d 1123, 1136 (Fed. Cir. 2006). For example, in *Uship Intellectual Properties, LLC v. United States*, 714 F.3d 1311, 1316 (Fed. Cir. 2013), the court limited claim scope to automated systems, notwithstanding the specification's disclosed embodiments of manual systems, based on disclaimer in prosecution history. Likewise, in *Atofina v. Great Lakes Chemical Corp.*, 441 F.3d 991, 997 (Fed. Cir. 2006), the Federal Circuit found a prosecution disclaimer to apply, and construed "chromium catalyst" as a catalyst where the only catalytically active material is chromium without the addition of metal oxides or noninert additives. The decision was based on the applicants' statements in the prosecution history which distinguished the claimed invention from the prior art's use of metal oxides and noninert additives, and which emphasized the "criticality of utilizing chromium catalyst alone rather than in combination with other metal components." *Id.*

By contrast, ambiguous statements in the prosecution history do not warrant a disclaimer, particularly when the applicant's statements are similarly subject to multiple interpretations. *SanDisk Corp. v. Memorex Prods., Inc.*, 415 F.3d 1278, 1287 (Fed. Cir. 2005) ("There is no 'clear and unmistakable' disclaimer if a prosecution argument is subject to more than one reasonable interpretation, one of which is consistent with a proffered meaning of the disputed term."). For example, in *Golight, Inc. v. Wal-Mart Stores, Inc.*, 355 F.3d 1327, 1332 (Fed. Cir. 2004), a claim to a "rotating" spotlight was not found subject to a disclaimer, where statements in the prosecution history referring to the spotlight rotating "through 360°" were attributable to other claims, not the claim at issue. *See also LG Elecs., Inc. v. Bizcom Elecs., Inc.*, 453 F.3d 1364, 1373–74 (Fed. Cir. 2006) (finding that prosecution history statements that the prior art did not teach accessing data signals "over a system bus" were not sufficiently clear to justify limiting claims to require claimed signals to travel over a system bus), *reversed on other grounds by Quanta v. LG Elecs.*, 128 S. Ct. 2109 (2008); *Martek Biosciences Corp. v. Nutrinova Inc.*, 579 F.3d 1363 (Fed. Cir. 2009) (finding no prosecution history disclaimer when applicant also distinguished prior art on alternative grounds). Even if prosecution history disclaimer does not apply because there is too much ambiguity, this does not mean that the prosecution history is irrelevant. Rather it can still be used "as support for the construction already discerned from the claim language and confirmed by the written description." *800 Adept, Inc. v. Murex Sec., Ltd.*, 539 F.3d 1354, 1364–65 (Fed. Cir. 2008).

5.2.3.2.4 Looking to Other Claims: The Doctrine of Claim Differentiation

Patents typically contain multiple claims, with variations among the claims describing the patented invention. The doctrine of claim differentiation provides that "each claim in a patent is presumptively different in scope." *RF Del., Inc. v. Pac. Keystone Techs., Inc.*, 326 F.3d 1255, 1263 (Fed. Cir. 2003). The doctrine is based on "the common sense notion that different words or phrases used in separate claims are presumed to indicate that the claims have different meanings and scope." *Andersen*, 474 F.3d at 1369. It also reflects the economic reality that patent fees depend on the number of claims in the patent. Patentees would be disinclined to purchase additional claims if they did not offer a different scope. It is important to recognize, however, that the uncertainties of claim interpretation lead all but the most financially sensitive patent drafters to seek multiple overlapping claims. *See generally* Mark A. Lemley, *The Limits of Claim Differentiation*, 22 Berkeley Tech. L.J. 1389 (2007). Additional claims do not always cover different subject matter. Claim differentiation gives rise to a rebuttable presumption for claim-construction purposes, especially when comparing the scope of an independent claim in view of its dependent claims: "[T]he presence of a dependent claim that adds a particular limitation gives rise to a presumption that the limitation in question is not present in the independent claim." *Phillips*, 415 F.3d at 1315.

"Pure" claim differentiation refers to the situation where there is no meaningful difference between an independent claim and its dependent claim, except for the presence of an added limitation in the dependent claim. In that situation, the presumption is especially strong that the independent claim is *not* restricted by the added limitation in the dependent claim. *GE Lighting Solutions*, 750 F.3d at 1310 (reversing district court construction that imposed features of dependent claims onto independent claim); *Acumed*, 483 F.3d at 806 ("That presumption is especially strong when the limitation in dispute is the only meaningful difference between an independent and dependent claim."). In such situations, construing the independent claim to share that limitation would render the dependent claim "superfluous." *Andersen*, 474 F.3d at 1369–70 ("To the extent that the absence of such difference in meaning and scope would make a claim superfluous, the doctrine of claim differentiation states the presumption that the difference between claims is significant."). The doctrine of claim differentiation has less force when there are additional differences between the independent claim and its dependent claim, such that the dependent claim would not be rendered "superfluous" by limiting the independent claim. *See, e.g.*, *SRAM Corp. v. AD-II Eng'g, Inc.*, 465 F.3d 1351, 1358 (Fed. Cir. 2006) (restricting an independent claim to use of "precision index downshifting" even though this term was present in the dependent claim, when additional differences existed between the independent and dependent claim).

In the case of two independent claims, the doctrine of claim differentiation does not apply because patent drafters are free to, and commonly do, claim an invention using multiple linguistic variations in multiple independent claims. *See, e.g.*, *Andersen Corp.*, 474 F.3d at 1370 (declining to apply claim differentiation to separate groups of claims to "pellets," "linear extrudates," and "composite compositions" where there were other differences varying the scope of the claims); *Curtiss-Wright Flow Control Corp. v. Velan, Inc.*, 438 F.3d 1374, 1380–81 (Fed. Cir. 2006) (recognizing that "[c]laim drafters can also use different terms to define the exact same subject matter."); *Hormone Research Found. v. Genentech, Inc.*, 904 F.2d 1558, 1567 n.15 (Fed. Cir. 1990) ("It is not unusual that separate claims may define the invention using different terminology, especially where (as here) independent claims are involved.").

Even in cases of "pure" claim differentiation where the presumption would apply most strongly, the doctrine can be trumped by other considerations. Claim differentiation "can not broaden claims beyond their correct scope." *Curtiss-Wright*, 438 F.3d at 1380 (quoting *Fantasy Sports Props. v. Sportsline.com*, 287 F.3d 1108, 1115–16 (Fed. Cir. 2002) (quoting *Kraft Foods, Inc. v. International Trading Co.*, 203 F.3d 1362 (Fed. Cir. 2000)). That is, "the written description and prosecution history overcome any presumption arising from the doctrine of claim differentiation." *Andersen*, 474 F.3d at 1369–70; *see also Edwards Lifesciences*, 582 F.3d at 1332 (Fed. Cir. 2009) ("[C]laim differentiation is a rule of thumb that does not trump the clear import of the specification."). For example, where the patent applicant disclaimed subject matter during prosecution to obtain the patent, the patentee cannot attempt to recapture that subject matter through the doctrine of claim differentiation. *See Fantasy Sports Props., Inc. v. Sportsline.com, Inc.*, 287 F.3d 1108, 1115–16 (Fed. Cir. 2002). Likewise, where the limitation in the dependent claim was emphasized during prosecution in order to overcome prior art, it may be appropriate to limit the broader, independent claim to that limitation, thereby trumping the doctrine of claim differentiation. *See ERBE Elektromedizin GmbH v. Canady Tech. LLC*, 629 F.3d 1278, 1286–87 (Fed. Cir. 2010) (limiting "low flow rate" of an independent claim to "less than about 1 liter/minute," as recited in a dependent claim); *see also ICU Med.*, 558 F.3d at 1376 (affirming rejection of claim differentiation argument when dependent claim was added years after the filing date of the original patent and after the introductions of the allegedly infringing products). Given the wide variety of situations where the doctrine of claim differentiation does not apply, the Federal Circuit has cautioned that "[c]laim differentiation is a guide, not a rigid rule." *Laitram Corp. v. Rexnord, Inc.*, 939 F.2d 1533, 1538 (Fed. Cir. 1991).

5.2.3.2.4.1 Presumption of Claim Differentiation May Be Rebutted Based on Specification or Prosecution History Estoppel

Limiting statements in the specification or prosecution history can rebut a broad claim-term interpretation, even if the breadth of that term is reinforced by the doctrine of claim differentiation. *See Seachange Int'l, Inc. v. C-COR, Inc.*, 413 F.3d 1361, 1369 (Fed. Cir. 2005) (noting that claim differentiation is "not a hard and fast rule and will be overcome by a contrary construction dictated by the written description or prosecution history"). For example, in *Regents of the University of California v. DakoCytomation California, Inc.*, 517 F.3d 1364, 1375 (Fed. Cir. 2008), the Federal Circuit approved of a limiting construction on the independent claim term "heterogenous mixture" to exclude repetitive sequences, notwithstanding the presence of dependent claims that do not exclude them. Likewise, in *Retractable Technologies*, 653 F.3d at 1305, the Federal Circuit found the doctrine of claim differentiation to be trumped by statements in the specification that limited a claimed syringe "body" to a one-piece body, especially in view of distinctions made over the prior art.

5.2.3.2.4.2 Presumption of Claim Differentiation Does Not Apply to Means-Plus-Function Claims

As discussed more fully in § 5.2.3.5, means-plus-function claims are limited to the corresponding structures and their equivalents under § 112(f). The statutorily mandated scope of these claims cannot be stretched through resort to claim differentiation. *See, e.g.*, *Cross Med. Prods., Inc. v. Medtronic Sofamor Danek, Inc.*, 424 F.3d 1293, 1304 (Fed. Cir. 2005) ("[A]lthough the doctrine of claim differentiation suggests that claim 5 should be broader than claim 1, any presumption that the claims differ with respect to this feature may be overcome by a contrary construction mandated by the application of § 112[(f)]."); *Laitram*, 939 F.2d at 1538 (holding that the doctrine of claim differentiation yields to an interpretation mandated by § 112(f)).

5.2.3.2.5 Significance of the "Preamble" in Claim Construction

Patent claims commonly have a "preamble" that introduces the claimed invention. Some preambles may be just a few words, while others may be lengthy and detailed. A common dispute is whether the wording of the preamble is a limitation on the scope of the patent. A famously vague standard governs this inquiry: terms in the preamble are limiting when they are "necessary to give life, meaning, and vitality to the claims." *Kropa v. Robie*, 187 F.2d 150, 861 (CCPA 1951). The following principles are used to apply this standard.

Where the preamble is grammatically essential to the claim, the general rule is that it is limiting. *Catalina Mktg. Int'l, Inc. v. Coolsavings.com, Inc.*, 289 F.3d 801, 808–09 (Fed. Cir. 2002). For example, where other terms in the body of the claim derive "antecedent basis" from the preamble, then the preamble is commonly found to be limiting. *Id.* at 808; *see also Bicon, Inc. v. Strauman Co.*, 441 F.3d 945, 952 (Fed. Cir. 2006); *Pacing Techs.*, 778 F.3d at 1023–24. Likewise, where the preamble is "essential to understand limitations or terms in the claim body," it is similarly limiting. *Catalina*, 289 F.3d at 808 (citing *Pitney Bowes, Inc. v. Hewlett-Packard Co.*, 182 F.3d 1298, 1306 (Fed. Cir. 1999)).

If a preamble term is a "necessary and defining aspect of the invention," the preamble is limiting. *On Demand Mach. Corp. v. Ingram Indus., Inc.*, 442 F.3d 1331, 1343 (Fed. Cir. 2006); *see also MBO Labs.*, 474 F.3d at 1330 (interpreting the preamble term "immediately" as limiting, because "[t]he patentee here has clearly indicated via the specification and the prosecution history that the invention provides as an essential feature, immediate needle safety upon removal from the patient."). This principle applies with special force where the language of the preamble was used during prosecution history to distinguish the claimed invention from the prior art. *Catalina*, 289 F.3d at 808; *see also In re Cruciferous Sprout Litig.*, 301 F.3d 1343, 1347–48 (Fed. Cir. 2004) (finding the preamble phrase "rich in glucosinolates" limiting because the patentee relied on the preamble to distinguish the prior art in prosecution).

The countervailing principle is that a preamble is not limiting when the body of the claim "describes a structurally complete invention." *Catalina*, 289 F.3d at 809; *see also Intertool, Ltd. v. Texar Corp.*, 369 F.3d 1289, 1295 (Fed. Cir. 2004) (finding the preamble nonlimiting where the body of the claim described the invention in "complete and exacting structural detail"). Statements of intended uses of an invention are generally *not* limiting. *Catalina*, 289 F.3d at 809; *Ericsson, Inc. v. D-Link Sys., Inc.*, 773 F.3d 1201, 1219 (Fed. Cir. 2014) (declining to limit based on statement of intended use in preamble). This is because "the patentability of apparatus or composition claims depends on the claimed structure, not on the use or purpose of that structure." *Id.* Thus, many cases turn on the question of whether a statement in the preamble describing the purpose of an invention describes a "necessary and defining aspect of the invention" (which is limiting), or is simply a "statement of intended use" (which is not limiting). A review of the Federal Circuit's cases over the past ten years, in cases that litigated the issue of whether to construe the preamble, reveals that the dominant approach in the close cases is to construe the preamble as a limitation.

5.2.3.3 Claim Terms Having Conventional, Presumed, or Established Meanings

Claim terms generally take their meaning from the language of the patent, the prosecution history, and the applicable extrinsic evidence. Some terms, however, have meanings that are derived from conventional usage in claim drafting or prior judicial construction. The case law in this area, however, is notoriously malleable. Take, for example, the term "a" (or "an"). The Federal Circuit "has repeatedly emphasized that an indefinite article 'a' or 'an' in patent parlance carries the meaning of 'one or more' in open-ended claims containing the transitional phrase 'comprising.'" *Baldwin Graphic Sys., Inc. v. Siebert, Inc.*, 512 F.3d 1338, 1342 (Fed. Cir. 2008). The court commented that this interpretation can "best [be] described as a rule, rather than merely as a presumption or even a convention. The exceptions to this rule are extremely limited: a patentee must 'evince[ ] a clear intent' to limit 'a' or 'an' to 'one.' . . . An exception to the general rule that 'a' or 'an' means more than one only arises where the language of the claims themselves, the specification, or the prosecution history necessitate a departure from the rule." *Id.* at 1342–43 (quoting *KCJ Corp. v. Kinetic Concepts, Inc.*, 223 F.3d 1351, 1356 (Fed. Cir. 2000)) (alterations in original).

Just two weeks after stating this "rule," however, the Federal Circuit found that the exception (singular meaning) applied based on the claims and written description in *Tivo, Inc. v. Echostar Communications Corp.*, 516 F.3d 1290, 1303–04 (Fed. Cir. 2008) ("The pertinent claim language refers to 'assembl[ing] said video and audio components into an MPEG stream,' which in context clearly indicates that two separate components are assembled into a single stream, not that the video components are assembled into one stream and the audio components into a second stream."). More recently, the Federal Circuit addressed *Baldwin* directly, holding that "*Baldwin*, however, does not set a hard and fast rule that 'a' always means one or more than one." *Harari v. Lee*, 656 F.3d 1331, 1342 (Fed. Cir. 2011). Thus, even a simple and commonplace word, such as "a," can have divergent meanings, based on the context of the patent and despite the Federal Circuit's best efforts to institute "rules" for its construction. Courts must remain sensitive to the context of patent claims, and avoid rigidly applying what may appear to be an established meaning.

"Transitional phrases" are terms that are used to link the various limitations in a claim. These transitional phrases govern, among other things, whether the claim is "open" or "closed" to the presence of additional elements. Restated, these transitional phrases define whether a claim with defined limitations can be infringed by a device that has additional elements beyond what is specified in the claim. The term "consisting of" is a closed transitional phrase, while the term "comprising" is an open transitional phrase. *See AFG Indus., Inc. v. Cardinal IG Co.*, 239 F.3d 1239, 1244–45 (Fed. Cir. 2001). These terms have established meanings based on decades of consistent use in claim drafting.

Table 5.5, Table 5.6, Table 5.7, and Table 5.8 collect terms that have been commonly construed by the Federal Circuit. As the tables reflect, some of these terms have been construed differently depending on the context. Thus, courts should not woodenly adopt meanings from prior cases. Rather, they should be aware that the Federal Circuit has considered some terms in the past and has, in some cases, attributed general meanings. In every case, however, courts should carefully examine the claim term in context. When a term does not have a clear meaning from the intrinsic evidence, then the jurisprudence may offer useful guidance.

Table 5.5
Commonly Construed Terms—Articles

Term	Meaning	Citation
a, an	Dominant meaning: one or more.	*Baldwin Graphic Sys., Inc. v. Siebert*, 512 F.3d 1338, 1342–43 (Fed. Cir. 2008). *But see Braintree Labs., Inc. v. Novel Labs., Inc.*, 749 F.3d 1349, 1357 (Fed. Cir. 2014).
	However, sometimes means: only one.	*Harari v. Lee*, 656 F.3d 1331 (Fed. Cir. 2011); *Tivo, Inc. v. Echostar Commc'ns Corp.*, 516 F.3d 1290 (Fed. Cir. 2008).
the, said	Indicates identity with a previously used claim term.	*Baldwin Graphic Sys., Inc. v. Siebert, Inc.*, 512 F.3d 1338, 1342–43 (Fed. Cir. 2008).
plurality	At least two.	*York Prods., Inc. v. Cent. Tractor Farm & Family Ctr.*, 99 F.3d 1568, 1575 (Fed. Cir. 1996).

Term	Meaning	Citation
first, second	Distinguishes between repeated instances of an element or limitation.	*Linear Tech. Corp. v. Int'l Trade Comm'n*, 566 F.3d 1049 (Fed. Cir. 2009) (use of claim terms "second circuit" and "third circuit" does not require that the two circuits be entirely distinct, only that each circuit performs its stated functions); *Free Motion Fitness, Inc. v. Cybex Int'l*, 423 F.3d 1343, 1348 (Fed. Cir. 2005); *3M Innovative Props. Co. v. Avery Dennison Corp.*, 350 F.3d 1365, 1371 (Fed. Cir. 2003).

Table 5.6
Commonly Construed Terms—Transitional Phrases

Term	Meaning	Citation
comprising	Is an "open" phrase and allows coverage of technologies that employ additional, unrecited elements.	*AFG Indus., Inc. v. Cardinal IG Co.*, 239 F.3d 1239, 1245 (Fed. Cir. 2001).
containing	Synonymous with "comprising."	*Mars, Inc. v. H.J. Heinz Co.*, 377 F.3d 1369, 1377 (Fed. Cir. 2004).
including	Synonymous with "comprising."	*Amgen Inc. v. Hoechst Marion Roussel, Inc.*, 314 F.3d 1313, 1345 (Fed. Cir. 2003). Note that in *Toro Co. v. White Consol. Indus., Inc.*, 199 F.3d 1295 (Fed. Cir. 1999), the term "including" was found to require permanency of the recited element—i.e., the claim phrase "cover including means for increasing the pressure" required the device's restriction ring to be permanently affixed to and included as part of the air inlet cover, so claims were not literally infringed by device having separate restriction ring that was inserted and removed as a separate part.
having	May be "open" but does not convey an "open" meaning as strongly as "comprising."	*Crystal Semiconductor Corp. v. TriTech Microelectronics Int'l, Inc.*, 246 F.3d 1336 (Fed. Cir. 2001); *Pieczenik v. Dyax Corp.*, 76 F. App'x 293, 296 (Fed. Cir. 2003) (unpublished).
	May be closed, depending on the context of the patent.	*Lampi Corp. v. Am. Power Prods., Inc.*, 228 F.3d 1365, 1376 (Fed. Cir. 2000).

Term	Meaning	Citation
consisting of	Is a "closed" phrase and excludes elements, steps, or ingredients not specified in the claims.	*CIAS, Inc. v. Alliance Gaming Corp.*, 504 F.3d 1356, 1361 (Fed. Cir. 2007); *AFG Indus., Inc. v. Cardinal IG Co.*, 239 F.3d 1239, 1245 (Fed. Cir. 2001).
consisting essentially of	Occupies a middle ground between "open" and "closed" claims and is open to unlisted ingredients that do not materially affect the basic and novel properties of the invention.	*Atlas Powder Co. v. E.I. du Pont De Nemours & Co.*, 750 F.2d 1569, 1574 (Fed. Cir. 1984); *PPG Indus. v. Guardian Indus. Corp.*, 156 F.3d 1351, 1354 (Fed. Cir. 1998).
composed of	Synonymous with "consisting essentially of."	*AFG Indus., Inc. v. Cardinal IG Co.*, 239 F.3d 1239, 1245 (Fed. Cir. 2001).

Table 5.7
Commonly Construed Terms—Terms of Degree

Term	Meaning	Citation
about	Avoids a strict numerical boundary.	*Cen. Admixture Pharmacy Servs., Inc. v. Advanced Cardiac Sols., P.C.*, 482 F.3d 1347, 1355–56 (Fed. Cir. 2007).
essentially	Synonymous with "about."	*Eiselstein v. Frank*, 52 F.3d 1035, 1039 (Fed. Cir. 1995).
substantially	Meaning is highly dependent on intrinsic evidence.	*Deering Precision Instruments, L.L.C. v. Vector Distrib. Sys., Inc.*, 347 F.3d 1314, 1322 (Fed. Cir. 2003) (construing the term "substantially in an imaginary plane."); *Epcon Gas Sys., Inc. v. Bauer Compressors, Inc.*, 279 F.3d 1022 (Fed. Cir. 2002) (construing the terms "substantially constant" and "substantially below"); *Zodiac Pool Care, Inc. v. Hoffinger Indus., Inc.*, 206 F.3d 1408 (Fed. Cir. 2000) (construing the term "substantially inward"); *York Prods., Inc. v. Cent. Tractor Farm & Family Ctr.*, 99 F.3d 1568 (Fed. Cir. 1996) (construing the term "substantially the entire height thereof"); *Tex. Instruments Inc. v. Cypress Semiconductor Corp.*, 90 F.3d 1558 (Fed. Cir. 1996) (construing the term "substantially in the common plane").

Term	Meaning	Citation
up to about	May include or exclude the endpoint, depending on the context. Where the endpoint is numeric (e.g., up to about 10%), the endpoint may be included; whereas, where the endpoint is physical (e.g., painting the wall up to about the door), the endpoint may be excluded.	*AK Steel Corp. v. Sollac*, 344 F.3d 1234 (Fed. Cir. 2003).
surround	To encircle on all sides simultaneously.	*Libman Co. v. Quickie Mfg. Corp.*, 74 F. App'x 900, 904–05 (Fed. Cir. 2003) (unpublished) (heavy reliance on dictionary definition).
in, between, within	Not required to be completely or continuously in, between or within; between may be satisfied even if extension beyond boundaries.	*Foster v. Hallco Mfg. Co.*, 1997 U.S. App. LEXIS 18989, 1997 WL 419391 (Fed. Cir. 1997) (unpublished) (heavy reliance on dictionary definition).
to	When A travels "to" B, it is sufficient to travel on a pathway with B as a destination, possibly visiting intervening components.	*Cybor Corp. v. FAS Techs., Inc.*, 138 F.3d 1448, 1458–59 (Fed. Cir. 1998).
defined	Can be used to mean that one element creates or forms the outline or shape of another element.	*Rival Co. v. Sunbeam Corp.*, 185 F.3d 885 (table) (Fed. Cir. 1999).

Table 5.8
Commonly Construed Terms—Other

Term	Meaning	Citation
whereby	A "whereby" clause that merely states the result of the limitations in the claim adds nothing to the patentability or substance of the claim.	*Hoffer v. Microsoft Corp.*, 405 F.3d 1326, 1329 (Fed. Cir. 2005); *Tex. Instruments Inc. v. U.S. Int'l Trade Comm'n*, 988 F.2d 1165, 1172 (Fed. Cir. 1993).
	However, a "whereby" clause that sets forth a structural limitation and not merely the results achieved by the claimed structure is a positive limitation of the claim.	*Scheinman v. Zalkind*, 112 F.2d 1017, 1019 (C.C.P.A. 1940).
standard, normal, conventional, traditional	Time-dependent terms that are limited to technologies existing at the time of the invention.	*PC Connector Sols. LLC v. SmartDisk Corp.*, 406 F.3d 1359, 1363 (Fed. Cir. 2005).
such as	Of a kind or character about to be indicated, suggested, or exemplified; for instance.	*Catalina Mktg. Int'l v. Coolsavings.com, Inc.*, 289 F.3d 801 (Fed. Cir. 2002).
adapted	Fit for a purpose; capable of a purpose.	*Mattox v. Infotopia, Inc.*, 136 F. App'x 366, 369 (Fed. Cir. 2005) (unpublished).
assembly	A collection of parts to form a structure.	*Kegel Co., Inc. v. AMF Bowling, Inc.*, 127 F.3d 1420, 1427 (Fed. Cir. 1997).
uniform	Having always the same form.	*Middleton, Inc. v. Minn. Mining & Mfg. Co.*, 411 F.3d 1384, 1387 (Fed. Cir. 2002) (reliance on *Texas Digital* and "heavy presumption" rule).
predetermined	Determined beforehand.	*Koito Mfg. Co., Ltd. v. Turn-Key-Tech, LLC*, 381 F.3d 1142, 1147–48 (Fed. Cir. 2004).

5.2.3.4 Interpreting Terms to Preserve Validity

A maxim of patent law is that claims should be construed to preserve their validity. *Phillips*, 415 F.3d at 1327–28. However, the Federal Circuit has "not endorsed a regime in which validity analysis is a regular component of claim construction." *Id.* at 1327. Application of the principle is limited to cases in which, after applying all the available tools of claim construction, the claim remains ambiguous. *Id.* at 1328. A proposed claim construction that preserves validity must be practicable, based on sound claim-construction principles, and must not revise or ignore the explicit language of the claim. *Id.* It must also be reasonable to infer that the USPTO would have recognized that the competing interpretation would have rendered the claim invalid. *Id.*; *Azure Networks, LLC v. CSR PLC*, 771 F.3d 1336, 1354 (Fed. Cir. 2014).

5.2.3.5 Special Case: Means-Plus-Function Claims Limited to Structures in Specification and Equivalents Thereof as of Time of Issuance

A special class of claim language is construed as means-plus-function claim terms. When a party seeks to have a term construed as a means-plus-function term, the analysis is governed by § 112(f) (formerly § 112, ¶ 6):[5]

> An element in a claim for a combination may be expressed as a means or a step for performing a specified function without the recital of structure, material, or acts in support thereof, and such claim shall be construed to cover the corresponding structure, material, or acts described in the specification and equivalents thereof.

When § 112(f) is found to apply to claim language, the claim term is construed by identifying the "function" associated with the claim language, and then identifying the corresponding "structure" in the specification associated with that function. The claim is construed to be limited to those corresponding structures and their equivalents. Thus, parties frequently attempt to invoke § 112(f), as a way to narrow the scope of a patent to the particular technologies disclosed in the specification, or to invalidate the claim when the specification fails to disclose sufficient structure corresponding to the functional claim language. Chart 5.4 sets forth the framework for construing functional claims terms. The court addresses Steps 1, 2A, and 2B as part of claim construction. Step 2C—determining whether the accused device has an identical or equivalent structure to the structure in the patent specification for performing the identified function—is a question of fact for the jury.

5. The nomenclature changed from "§ 112, ¶ 6" to "§ 112(f)" upon passage of the America Invents Act of 2011.

Chart 5.4
Framework for Construing Means-Plus-Function Claims

Step 1: Is term in question "means-plus-function"? Rebuttable Presumption: Inclusion of "means"
• If the term recites "means," then there is a rebuttable presumption that 112(f) governs. • If "means" is not recited, then there is a presumption that 112(f) does not govern, although that presumption may be rebutted by showing that the claim term used is a generic term that does not connote sufficiently definite structure and is tantamount to saying "means."
Step 2: Interpretation Process:
• A. Identify function of term (based on claim-term language, not embodiments). • B. Identify corresponding structure, material, or act based on disclosed embodiments—claim is invalid if there is no disclosure of structures linked to the claimed function. • C. Infringement stage (question of fact): Determine whether the accused device has an identical or equivalent structure (as of the time of issuance of the patent) to that described in the patent specification for performing the function stated in the claim.

5.2.3.5.1 Step 1: Is the Term in Question "Means-Plus-Function"?

When presented with a request to invoke § 112(f), the court must first determine if that section applies. Means-plus-function claiming applies only to "purely functional limitations that do not provide the structure that performs the recited function." *DePuy Spine, Inc. v. Medtronic Sofamor Danek, Inc.*, 469 F.3d 1005, 1023 (Fed. Cir. 2006). There is a rebuttable presumption that § 112(f), applies "[i]f the word 'means' appears in a claim element in association with a function." *Callicrate v. Wadsworth Mfg., Inc.*, 427 F.3d 1361, 1368 (Fed. Cir. 2005). The use of the term "means" in a claim limitation typically implies that the inventor used the means-plus-function claim format, which invokes the associated statutory limits on the literal scope of that claim limitation. *See Greenberg v. Ethicon Endo-Surgery, Inc.*, 91 F.3d 1580, 1584 (Fed. Cir. 1996). Nonetheless, this implication does not apply where the claim language itself provides the structure that performs the recited function. *See Phillips*, 415 F.3d 1303 (finding that a claim limitation stating "means disposed inside the shell for increasing its load bearing capacity comprising internal steel baffles" provides the relevant structure ("internal steel baffles") and hence is not limited to the embodiments in the specification and equivalents thereof); *Cole v. Kimberly-Clark Corp.*, 102 F.3d 524, 531 (Fed. Cir. 1996) (finding that use of the phrase "perforation means" does not invoke § 112(f)).

When a claim limitation lacks the term "means," there is a rebuttable presumption that § 112(f) does not apply. This presumption against construing such limitations under § 112(f) used to be characterized as a "strong" presumption. *See, e.g.*, *Lighting World, Inc. v. Birchwood Lighting, Inc.*, 382 F.3d 1354, 1358 (Fed. Cir. 2004); *Inventio AG v. ThyssenKrupp Elevator Americas Corp.*, 649 F.3d 1350, 1358 (Fed. Cir. 2011). The en banc court thereafter revoked this characterization of the presumption as "strong." *Williamson v. Citrix Online LLC*, 2015 U.S. App. LEXIS 10082, 2015 WL 3687459 at *7 (Fed. Cir. 2015) (en banc). In recharacterizing the presumption, *Williamson* explained the standard for overcoming it, stating that a term lacking "means" will nonetheless be construed under § 112(f) if the "challenger demonstrates that the claim fails to recite sufficiently definite structure or else recites function without reciting sufficient structure for performing that function." *Id.* at *7. The focus is on the claim language as a whole, not just the isolated term that is akin to "means." *Id.* at *8. Generic terms such as "mechanism," "element," "device" and other such terms that do not connote sufficiently definite structure in the context of the overall claim are tantamount to stating "means," and therefore may be construed pursuant to § 112(f) if nothing else in the claim provides sufficient structure. *Id.* at *8. The Federal Circuit has referred to such "black box" words as "nonce" words, although this characterization may breed confusion, considering that "nonce" words are commonly defined as words invented for a particular occasion. *See, e.g.*, American Heritage Dictionary of the English Language, Fifth Edition (2011). Debating the "nonce" label may be unproductive—the focus should remain on whether the term, in the context of the claim as a whole, connotes a class (even a broad class) of specific structures. If so, then the term should not be construed under § 112(f).

The Federal Circuit's decision in *Media Rights Techs. v. Capital One Financial Corp.*, 800 F.3d 1366 (Fed. Cir. 2015) illustrates the effect of *Williamson*. The court found claims reciting a "compliance mechanism" to be governed by § 112(f) for lack of a definite structure, and consequently invalid for indefiniteness owing to the absence of corresponding structure in the specification.

5.2.3.5.2 Step 2: Interpretation of Means-Plus-Function Claim Terms

5.2.3.5.2.1 Step 2A: Identify Claim-Term Function

If § 112(f), applies to a claim term, then the court must first identify the function of that term. It is important to identify the function associated with means-plus-function claim language before identifying the corresponding structure, material, or acts, and not to confuse these two analytically separate steps. *See JVW Enters., Inc. v. Interact Accessories, Inc.*, 424 F.3d 1324, 1330 (Fed. Cir. 2005) ("Determining a claimed function and identifying structure corresponding to that function involve distinct, albeit related, steps that must occur in a particular order."). Errors arise when courts attempt to identify the function of a claimed invention based on its working embodiment, rather than solely based on the claim language. *Id.* Attributing functions to a working device, rather than focusing on the claim language, may wrongly sweep additional functions into the claim. *Id.*

5.2.3.5.2.2 Step 2B: Identify "Corresponding Structure, Material, or Acts"

After identifying the claimed function, the court must identify the corresponding structure in the specification. A proper construction should account for "all structure in the specification corresponding to the claimed function." *Callicrate v. Wadsworth Mfg., Inc.*, 427 F.3d 1361, 1369 (Fed. Cir. 2005). It is error to limit the corresponding structure to just the preferred embodiment. *Id.*

If there is no structure in the specification that corresponds to the claimed function, then the claim is invalid as indefinite, because it cannot be construed. *See, e.g., Williamson*, 2015 U.S. App. LEXIS 10082, 2015 WL 3687459 at *10 (finding claimed "distributed learning control module" governed by § 112(f) and unsupported by structure in specification for lack of an algorithm to perform the claimed function); *Function Media, LLC v. Google, Inc.*, 708 F.3d 1310, 1318 (Fed. Cir. 2013) (finding claimed "means for transmitting" indefinite because "there is no specific algorithm disclosed in prose, as a mathematical formula, in flow charts, or otherwise"); *Robert Bosch, LLC v. Snap-On Inc.*, 769 F.3d 1094, 1100 (Fed. Cir. 2014) (finding claimed "program recognition device" requiring of § 112(f) interpretation, and invalid for lack of structural guidance in specification). Any such finding must be supported by clear and convincing evidence. *See Bancorp Servs., L.L.C. v. Hartford Life Ins. Co.*, 359 F.3d 1367, 1371 (Fed. Cir. 2004).

5.2.3.5.2.3 Step 2C: "Equivalents Thereof"

In addition to structures, materials, or acts of the embodiments described in the patent's specification, the patentee is entitled to "equivalents thereof" as of the time the patent issued. Unlike the determination of function and corresponding structure, material, or acts that are clearly part of claim construction, the "equivalents" issue arises in the context of the infringement determination. The fact-finder must determine whether the means in the accused device or method performs the function stated in the claim in the same or an equivalent manner as the corresponding structures, materials, or acts set forth in the specification. *See Palumbo v. Don-Joy Co.*, 762 F.2d 969 (Fed. Cir. 1985).

5.2.3.5.2.4 Specific Rule for Means-Plus-Function Claims in the Computer Software Context

The Federal Circuit has underscored that computer-based inventions pose special problems for interpreting means-plus-function claims. Merely pointing to a "computer" does not provide sufficient structure in a software or computer means-plus-function claim. Rather, the Federal Circuit has held that "a means-plus-function claim element for which the only disclosed structure is a general purpose computer is invalid if the specification fails to disclose an algorithm for performing the claimed function." *Net MoneyIN, Inc. v. VeriSign, Inc.*, 545 F.3d 1359, 1367 (Fed. Cir. 2008). That is, "if a patentee has invoked computer-implemented means-plus-function claiming, the corresponding structure in the specification for the computer implemented function must be an algorithm unless a general purpose computer is sufficient for performing the function." *Apple v. Motorola*, 757 F.3d 1286, 1298 (Fed. Cir. 2014) (citing *Aristocrat Techs. Australia v. Int'l Game Tech.*, 521 F.3d 1328, 1331 (Fed. Cir. 2008)) (emphasis omitted). The court has explained it is not adequate to "simply describe[] the function to be performed." Rather the specification must describe how the system "ensures those functions are performed." *BlackBoard v. Desire2Learn, Inc.*, 574 F.3d 1371, 1384 (Fed. Cir. 2009). Such an algorithm may be expressed "in any understandable terms including as a mathematical formula, in prose, or as a flow chart, or in any other manner that provides sufficient structure to a person of ordinary skill in the art." *Chi. Bd. Options Exch., Inc. v. Int'l Sec. Exch., LLC*, 748 F.3d 1134, 1141 (Fed. Cir. 2014) (finding specification adequately describes algorithm for "'identifying a counterpart order' on a pro rata basis"); *Triton Tech of Tex., LLC v. Nintendo of Am., Inc.*, 753 F.3d 1375, 1379 (Fed. Cir. 2014) (finding claim to "integrator means" invalid because specification reference to "numerical integration" does not disclose an algorithm—that is, a step-by-step procedure—for performing the claimed function); *Eon Corp. v. AT&T Mobility LLC*, 785 F.3d 616, 624 (Fed. Cir. 2015) (finding means-plus-function claims invalid for lack of disclosure of detailed computer algorithm.)

Furthermore, the Federal Circuit has held that it is irrelevant to the § 112(f) analysis whether a person skilled in the art would know how to write a program to perform the claimed function. This is only relevant to enablement, not indefiniteness. *BlackBoard*, 574 F.3d at 1384–85. When the claim element does not use means-plus-function language, the Federal Circuit does not require disclosure of a particular algorithm. *Apple*, 757 F.3d at 1298 ("The correct inquiry, when 'means' is absent from a limitation, is whether the limitation, read in light of the remaining claim language, specification, prosecution history, and relevant extrinsic evidence, has sufficiently definite structure to a person of ordinary skill in the art," and finding that claim term "heuristic" is sufficiently structural to avoid § 112(f) interpretation).

5.2.4 Product-by-Process Claims

Product claims which include in their limitations the process by which that product is made, for example, a claim to a product "produced by" or "obtainable by" a certain method, are known as "product-by-process" claims. In 2009, the Federal Circuit held en banc that such product-by-process claims must be construed to be limited to products produced by the stated process. *Abbott Labs.*, 566 F.3d at 1291–95.

In doing so, the court reaffirmed its holding in *Atlantic Thermoplastics Co. v. Faytex Corp.*, 970 F.2d 834 (Fed. Cir. 1992) that "process terms in product-by-process claims serve as limitations in determining infringement." *Abbott Laboratories* expressly overruled the conflicting holding of *Scripps Clinic & Research Foundations v. Genentech, Inc.*, 927 F.2d 1565, 1583 (Fed. Cir. 1991), which had held that product-by-process claims were not limited to the product prepared by the process set forth in the claims. The court rejected as "unnecessary and logically unsound" any exception to the rule that limits product-by-process claims to products made by the claimed process in situations in which the structure of the product was unknown and could only be described by the process with which it was made. *Abbott Labs.*, 566 F.3d at 1294–95.

5.2.5 Dysfunctional Claims: Mistakes and Indefiniteness

Courts must occasionally deal with dysfunctional claims. They fall into two principal categories: (1) claims that contain obvious typographical, grammatical, or other errors that render the claim unworkable; and (2) claims that may be indefinite (possibly depending on how it is construed), raising the possibility that the claim is invalid under § 112(b). The former may be obvious from the context and quite possibly due to USPTO oversight. Some mistakes are more intractable and go to the heart of the claimed invention. Deciding whether these mistakes can be fixed at all, who should fix them (the court or the USPTO), and what the consequences of changing the claims are can be challenging.

5.2.5.1 Mistakes

When issues of mistaken claim language arise, the parties often call into question the power of courts to correct mistakes in patents through the claim-construction process. Attempts to correct patents raise the threshold question of whether the district court has legal authority to correct the alleged error or omission or whether such an issue must be brought to the USPTO. The somewhat ambiguous answer is that "courts can continue to correct obvious minor typographical and clerical errors in patents," whereas "major errors are subject only to correction by the PTO." *Novo Indus., L.P. v. Micro Molds Corp.*, 350 F.3d 1348, 1357 (Fed. Cir. 2003).

The general rule is that "[t]he district court can correct an error only if the error is evident from the face of the patent." *See Group One, Ltd. v. Hallmark Cards, Inc.*, 407 F.3d 1297, 1303 (Fed. Cir. 2005). "In deciding whether it had authority to correct a claim, a district court must consider any proposed correction 'from the point of view of one skilled in the art.'" *CBT Flint Partners, LLC v. Return Path, Inc.*, 654 F.3d 1353 (Fed. Cir. 2011) (noting that because all reasonable proposals for the claims would require a computer programmed to "detect and analyze" e-mail, a person of skill in the art would readily know that the meaning of the claim requires insertion of the word "and" between the words "detect" and "analyze"). "A district court can correct a patent only if (1) the correction is not subject to reasonable debate based on consideration of the claim language and the specification *and* (2) the prosecution history does not suggest a different interpretation of the claims." *Novo Indus.*, 350 F.3d at 1357 (emphasis added). Another general rule limiting the corrective power of courts is that "courts may not redraft claims, whether to make them operable or to sustain their validity." *Chef America, Inc. v. Lamb-Weston, Inc.*, 358 F.3d 1371, 1374 (Fed. Cir. 2004).

Whether an error is "evident from the face of the patent" is a matter of frequent dispute. Where the applicant uses an inapt claim term, the applicant is typically held to the wording, even if the intended meaning is abundantly clear. For example, in *Chef America*, the patent dealt with a process for cooking dough. The claim language required "heating the resulting batter-coated dough *to* a temperature in the range of about 400°F to 850°F." *Id.* at 1371 (emphasis added). If the dough is heated "to" that temperature range, it would be burned to a crisp. Heating the dough "at" that temperature range supposedly results in a light, flaky, crispy texture, according to the patent's specification. *See id.* at 1372. Even though it would be nonsensical to require heating the dough "to" 850°F, the court refused to construe the claims otherwise. The Federal Circuit affirmed, which rendered the claims noninfringed. *See id.* at 1373–74.

Courts have somewhat greater leeway to correct administrative errors attributable to the USPTO. Minor errors can be corrected by a district court, even if the prosecution history must be consulted to determine how to fix the error. For example, in *Hoffer v. Microsoft Corp.*, 405 F.3d 1326, 1331 (Fed. Cir. 2005), the Federal Circuit ruled that the district court could have fixed an error in patent-claim numbering that left a dependent claim without a reference to its independent claim, where the appropriate reference was easily determined by reference to the prosecution history. However, where the USPTO printing office omitted a block of claim text from a patent, that error was found to be beyond the district court's corrective powers. *See Grp. One*, 407 F.3d at 1303 ("The prosecution history discloses that the missing language was required to be added by the examiner as a condition for issuance, but one cannot discern what language is missing simply by reading the patent. The district court does not have authority to correct the patent in such circumstances.").

When a district court construes a patent claim to correct an error, that construction is generally retroactive, whereas corrections by the USPTO are prospective. *See Novo Indus*, 350 F.3d at 1356 (noting that a certificate of correction from the USPTO is "only effective for causes of action arising after it was issued"). Thus, litigants have a strong incentive to fix errors through judicial construction as opposed to petitioning the USPTO for a certificate of correction. However, the risk is that if the district court declines to fix the correction, the defective claims may be held invalid for indefiniteness, or may fail for other reasons such as noninfringement. *See, e.g., id.* at 1358 (refusing to correct patent, and holding claim indefinite).

5.2.5.2 Indefiniteness

The potentially dispositive issue of "indefiniteness" is increasingly intertwined with the claim-construction process. "Indefiniteness" is an invalidity defense based on § 112(b), which requires that the claims of a patent "particularly point[ ] out and distinctly claim[ ] the subject matter which the applicant regards as his invention." § 112(b) (formerly § 112, ¶ 2). Explaining the "delicate balance" posed by the definiteness requirement, the Supreme Court recognized that the requirement "must take into account the inherent limitations of language" and allow a "modicum of uncertainty" to allow for appropriate incentives for innovation. *Nautilus, Inc. v. Biosig Instruments, Inc.*, 134 S. Ct. 2120, 2128 (2014). Nonetheless, the Court recognized a patent must be precise enough to afford public notice of claim scope, otherwise there would be a "zone of uncertainty which enterprise and experimentation may enter only at the risk of infringement claims." *Id. Nautilus* reset the legal standard for indefiniteness, elevating it from the Federal Circuit's prior formulation that a claim was indefinite if it was "insolubly ambiguous" and "not amenable to construction." The new standard under *Nautilus* is that the definiteness standard requires that a patent's claims, viewed in light of the specification and prosecution history, must "inform those skilled in the art about the scope of the invention with *reasonable certainty*." *Id.* at 2129 (emphasis added).

Following remand from the Supreme Court, the Federal Circuit emphasized that "general principles of claim construction apply" to assessing invalidity challenges based on claim indefiniteness. *See Biosig Instruments*, 783 F.3d 1378 (quoting *Enzo Biochem*, 599 F.3d at 1332).

Adjudicating indefiniteness poses special case-management challenges, and the right approach will depend on the nature of the particular issues being litigated. The court should address indefiniteness in its scheduling order to establish at which point in the case the parties should raise indefiniteness, whether through claim construction, summary judgment, or trial.

Often, indefiniteness will be most effectively and efficiently resolved in conjunction with claim construction. If the claim scope is too imprecise to tell a skilled artisan its boundaries with reasonable certainty, then it should not be construed and should be held invalid for indefiniteness. Typically the party making the challenge will decline to proffer any construction at all, asserting that the claim cannot be construed. Thus, definiteness is a threshold inquiry within the claim-construction framework.

The indefiniteness inquiry will often fit comfortably into the *Markman* framework. For example, one common indefiniteness argument arises in the context of means-plus-function claims, whereby a party alleges that there is no structure in the specification corresponding to the claimed function. In such circumstances, the court will assess whether there is a sufficient structure in the specification to provide support to the claimed function. Absent such structure, the claim cannot be construed and is indefinite. *See Default Proof Credit Card Sys., Inc. v. Home Depot U.S.A., Inc.*, 412 F.3d 1291, 1302–03 (Fed. Cir. 2005) (invalidating claim for indefiniteness for lack of a structure in the specification corresponding to the claimed function); *Function Media, LLC v. Google, Inc.*, 708 F.3d 1310, 1319 (Fed. Cir. 2013) (invalidating claim for lack of structure in specification showing claimed transmitting function). In some cases, this determination may be clear from the four corners of the patent. In other cases, however, this determination can be fraught with technical complexity and requires substantial expert analysis. *See Ibormeith IP, LLC v. Mercedes-Benz USA, LLC*, 732 F.3d 1376, 1381 (Fed. Cir. 2013) (finding disclosed algorithm in specification insufficient to adequately support claimed "computational means").

Likewise, the court can consider during the *Markman* process whether typographical or other printing errors are sufficiently severe to render the patent uninterpretable. Minor errors are commonly overlooked as long as persons of skill in the art can still understand the claims. *See Energizer Holdings, Inc. v. Int'l Trade Comm'n*, 435 F.3d 1366, 1370 (Fed. Cir. 2006) (refusing to invalidate claim where phrase "said zinc anode" lacked an antecedent basis). However, where entire blocks of text are missing from claims, then the public cannot reasonably be expected to appreciate their scope, and the claims are invalid. *Grp. One*, 407 F.3d at 1302.

Other issues of indefiniteness require a deeper exploration of the subject matter, and may require a mini-trial with extensive testimony from experts. Such disputes should be accounted for well in advance, preferably through the initial case-management order, so that the court may allocate enough time and resources to hear the issue properly. For example, it may be argued that a patent fails to articulate the test for determining if a claim term is infringed, and resolving this dispute may require the court to understand how skilled people in the field would measure various parameters. Exactly such a dispute arose in the Supreme Court's *Teva* case. The "molecular weight" limitation of the patent in suit could be calculated by one of three different approaches. In the challenger's view, because the claim did not say which method of calculation should be used, the claim was indefinite. *See Teva*, 135 S. Ct. at 836. Resolving such disputes requires far more than the textual analysis typically performed at a *Markman* hearing. It requires the court to understand the underlying science and to hear from experts in the field. Typical *Markman* briefing page limits may be insufficient, and this might be best handled on a full-trial record. The parties and the court should come to an early agreement on whether this will be resolved during the *Markman* hearing, and, if so, how to structure that *Markman* hearing to allow a sufficient evidentiary record, or whether to defer this dispute until trial. *See also Honeywell Int'l v. ITC*, 341 F.3d 1332, 1342 (Fed. Cir. 2003) (affirming finding of indefiniteness reached after trial in case involving process for manufacturing synthetic yarn, where "the testing results will necessarily fall within or outside the claim scope depending on the sample preparation method chosen," and "competitors trying to practice the invention or to design around it would be unable to discern the bounds of the invention."); *Halliburton*, 514 F.3d at 1252 (affirming indefiniteness finding after full factual record, because the functional claim term "fragile gel" was ambiguous as to whether it read on the prior art); *Dow Chem. Co. v. Nova Chems. Corp.*, 803 F.3d 620, 632 (Fed. Cir. 2015) (finding claim invalid for indefiniteness after expert testimony showing multiple methods to measure claimed parameter, each of which produced different results, without guidance from specification on which method to select).

Similarly, the court may wish to hear from experts and hold an evidentiary hearing on whether terms of degree and other imprecise terms render the claim invalid for indefiniteness. *See* §§ 5.1.3.1, 5.2.2.2, 5.2.3.1.5.2. For example, a claim requiring an "aesthetically pleasing" interface screen was found indefinite where even the patentee's expert could not articulate how to determine infringement. *Datamize, LLC v. Plumtree Software, Inc.*, 417 F.3d 1342, 1354 (Fed. Cir. 2005); *see also Interval Licensing LLC v. AOL, Inc.*, 766 F.3d 1364 (Fed. Cir. 2014) (finding claim indefinite for use of subjective term "unobtrusive"). Another example is a claim directed to *both* a system and a method of using that system, which is invalid because the public cannot determine the acts that constitute infringement. *IPXL Holdings, L.L.C. v. Amazon.com, Inc.*, 430 F.3d 1377, 1383–84 (Fed. Cir. 2005). These matters are often treated as "claim construction" questions, although they might more aptly be considered a question of whether the claims are indefinite as applied.

Indefiniteness is unique among claim-construction issues in that it carries a burden of proof. Because ruling that a claim cannot be construed means that the claim is invalid, the "presumption of validity," *see* § 282, must be overcome by clear and convincing evidence. *See Bancorp Servs.*, 359 F.3d at 1371. In practice, however, it is difficult to imagine a circumstance in which a court would find that claim term could not be construed for purposes of a *Markman* order but is nonetheless not indefinite by clear and convincing evidence. *See* Anderson & Menell, 109 Nw. U. L. Rev. Online at 198–200 (discussing the interplay of claim construction and indefiniteness post-*Teva*).[6] The Federal Circuit has viewed the standard of review of claim indefiniteness as a pure question of law pursuant to the now-overruled *Cybor* decision. In *Atmel Corp. v. Information Storage Devices, Inc.*, 198 F.3d 1374 (Fed. Cir. 1999), the Federal Circuit reasoned that

> [a] determination of claim indefiniteness is a legal conclusion that is drawn from the court's performance of its duty as the construer of patent claims. *See Personalized Media Commc'ns, LLC v. Int'l Trade Comm'n*, 161 F.3d 696, 705 (Fed. Cir. 1998). Indefiniteness, therefore, like claim construction, is a question of law that we review de novo. *See id.* at 702; *cf. Cybor Corp. v. FAS Techs., Inc.*, 138 F.3d 1448, 1456 (Fed. Cir. 1998) (en banc) (holding that claim construction is a question of law reviewed de novo).

Id. at 1378.

In view of the Supreme Court's rejection of *Cybor*'s de novo standard of review of patent claim construction in *Teva*, there is good reason to believe that a district judge's determination of claim indefiniteness would also fall within the Rule 52(a)(6) framework on which the Supreme Court relied. Under the Supreme Court's *Nautilus* decision, § 112(b) requires that "a patent's claims, viewed in light of the specification and prosecution history, inform those skilled in the art about the scope of the invention with reasonable certainty." Thus, like claim construction, the district judge may well need to hear from skilled artisans and resolve whether the disputed claims are indefinite. Where experts disagree, the court will be required to make subsidiary factual findings based upon the credibility of the witnesses or other tools available to district judges. Hence, the lower court's factual findings are entitled to deference by the Federal Circuit to the extent that the intrinsic evidence does not control.

The *Teva* case also sheds light on the allocation of decision-making authority between judge and jury. The majority confirmed that the Supreme Court used the phrase "within the province of the court" in *Markman* to create a distinct category of rulings with a factual basis that lie outside of the Seventh Amendment right to a jury. Like claim construction, the assessment of claim indefiniteness has no direct antecedent in pre-1791 cases. Moreover, the same functional considerations that led the Court to place claim construction within the province of the court apply to indefiniteness. Therefore, although claim indefiniteness ought not be characterized as a

---

6. In *Nautilus, Inc. v. Biosig Instruments, Inc.*, 134 S. Ct. 2120 (2014), the Supreme Court acknowledged controversy over, but declined to resolve, whether the clear-and-convincing standard applies for proving claim indefiniteness. *See id.* at 2130, n.10.

pure question of law, it nonetheless falls exclusively "within the province of the court."

Even though the question of claim indefiniteness is, like claim construction, a question for the judge and not a jury, the evidentiary standard for invalidity defenses is higher (clear and convincing evidence) than for claim construction (preponderance of the evidence) owing to the Patent Act's presumption of validity. Nonetheless, it is difficult to imagine a scenario in which a judge decides that a term cannot be construed under the preponderance standard but declines to hold that it is indefinite because of the higher clear-and-convincing standard. This seems to be a distinction without a difference, but it would nonetheless be prudent for a district judge to state in finding that the claim is indefinite the court does so by clear and convincing evidence. In essence, the preponderance and clear-and-convincing-evidence standards collapse in this situation.

The upshot of these considerations is that district judges ought to resolve the question of claim indefiniteness at the same stage as claim construction in most cases. Considering indefiniteness and meaning simultaneously will economize judicial resources, simplify patent litigation, and potentially increase settlement where subsidiary factual underpinnings entitle the district judge's resolution to deference on appeal.

5.3 Deference to Prior Claim-Construction Rulings

Where a claim term has been construed in a prior judicial proceeding, it is not uncommon for one or more of the litigants to assert that the court is bound by or, at a minimum, should accord substantial deference to, that prior ruling. Whether, and to what extent, a prior claim-construction ruling is binding in a subsequent proceeding depends on the particular facts of each case, what decision maker provided the prior claim construction (i.e., Federal Circuit, district court, or ITC), and what legal doctrine is being asserted (i.e., issue preclusion, estoppel, or stare decisis).

The Supreme Court's *Markman* decision ostensibly encourages deference to prior claim construction, noting "the importance of uniformity in the treatment of a given patent as a reason to allocate all issues of construction to the court." *Markman*, 517 U.S. at 390. The Supreme Court acknowledged in the next paragraph, however, that "issue preclusion could not be asserted against new and independent infringement defendants even within a given jurisdiction." Nonetheless, following *Markman*, the Federal Circuit "recognize[s] the national *stare decisis* effect that [its] decisions on claim construction have." *Key Pharm. v. Hercon Labs. Corp.*, 161 F.3d 709, 716 (Fed. Cir. 1998); *see also Cybor*, 138 F.3d at 1455 (en banc) ("the Supreme Court endorsed this court's role in providing national uniformity to the construction of a patent claim").

Determining the standards for according deference to prior *Markman* orders and the application of such standards have proven complicated in practice. *See generally Rambus Inc. v. Hynix Semiconductor Inc.*, 569 F. Supp. 2d 946, 965 (N.D. Cal. 2008) (observing that "[s]ince *Markman*, various district courts have taken slightly different approaches to other courts' claim constructions, but despite the Court's suggestion, none has applied *stare decisis*"). Judge Leonard Davis applied stare decisis in the *Eolas* case:

> The issue for reconsideration is a narrow one: whether the Court is bound by the principle of *stare decisis* to adopt the Illinois District Court's construction of "executable application" as affirmed by the Federal Circuit. After a thorough analysis of the case law, the answer is yes.

Eolas Techs., Inc. v. Adobe Sys., Inc., 2011 U.S. Dist. LEXIS 157891 at *5, 2011 WL 11070303 (E.D. Tex. Sept. 23, 2011).

In an effort to promote uniformity and predictability in the treatment of patents, the Supreme Court in *Markman* held that claim construction is decided as a matter of law and is thus subject to the doctrine of stare decisis. *Markman*, 517 U.S. at 390–91 ("[T]reating interpretive issues as purely legal will promote (though it will not guarantee) intrajurisdictional certainty through the application of *stare decisis* . . ."). The Federal Circuit has likewise "recognize[d] the national *stare decisis* effect that [its] decisions on claim construction have." *Key Pharm.*, 161 F.3d at 716.

Parties, sometimes uncritically, invoke a variety of doctrines—claim preclusion, res judicata, issue preclusion, collateral estoppel, judicial estoppel, and/or stare decisis—to attempt to constrain or obviate *Markman* determinations. The application of such doctrines is made all the more complicated by the intermediate nature of *Markman* rulings. *Markman* rulings are a means (construing claim terms) to an end (adjudicating patent validity and infringement or, more commonly, reaching a settlement agreement), not final judgments in and of themselves. An additional complicating factor is the characterization of *Markman* rulings as questions of law. As a result, determining the preclusive effect of such orders requires navigation of overlapping and not entirely cohesive civil procedure doctrines.

Before turning to the particular legal standards for according deference to prior *Markman* determinations, it will be useful to clarify the relevant terminology. There are four distinct concepts: (1) claim preclusion (and the related concept of res judicata); (2) issue preclusion (and the related concepts of collateral and direct estoppel); (3) judicial estoppel; and (4) stare decisis. Issue preclusion, judicial estoppel, and stare decisis are pertinent to the appropriate deference to be accorded prior claim-construction rulings; claim preclusion generally does not come into play in claim construction.

5.3.1 Distinguishing Among Preclusion and Estoppel Doctrines

Although res judicata has historically been interpreted broadly to encompass the binding effect of a judgment in a prior case on claims asserted in pending litigation (and hence encompassing both claim and issue preclusion), the modern trend limits res judicata to claim preclusion. *See* 18 Moore's Federal Practice § 131.10[1][b] (Matthew Bender 3d ed.). "Claim preclusion refers to the effect of a judgment in foreclosing litigation of a matter that never has been litigated, because of a determination that it should have been advanced in an earlier suit. Claim preclusion therefore encompasses the law of merger and bar." *Migra v. Warren City Sch. Dist. Bd. of Educ.*, 465 U.S. 75, 77 n. 1 (1984).[7] When a plaintiff prevails in a lawsuit arising from a particular transaction, all of the claims that the plaintiff raised *or could have raised* "merge" into that judgment and are "barred" from further litigation. See *Waid v. Merrill Area Pub. Sch.*, 91 F.3d 857, 863 (7th Cir. 1996). If the plaintiff attempts to litigate any of those claims again, the judgment itself will serve as a defense. *Markman* rulings do not themselves resolve claims to relief. They merely interpret patent claim terms. Thus, they cannot be said to constitute judgments for the purpose of "claim preclusion" as civil procedure terminology uses the term.

By contrast, the related doctrine of issue preclusion arises with some frequency in *Markman* proceedings. "Issue preclusion refers to the effect of a judgment in foreclosing the relitigation of a matter that has been litigated and decided. This effect is also referred to as direct or collateral estoppel." *Migra*, 465 U.S. at 77 n.1 (1984); *see also Pharmacia & Upjohn Co. v. Mylan Pharm., Inc.*, 170 F.3d 1373, 1379 (Fed. Cir. 1999). Where a patentee (including those in privity) has previously litigated the scope of a patent claim term, a defendant in a subsequent lawsuit relating to the same patent claim term might assert issue preclusion to foreclose relitigation of that matter.[8] The test for issue preclusion, however, is relatively strict and authority splits on its role in the context of prior *Markman* rulings.

Judicial estoppel is an equitable doctrine that precludes a party from adopting a position that is inconsistent with a position taken in a prior lawsuit, whether or not that issue had been actually litigated in the prior proceeding. *See generally* 18 Moore's Federal Practice § 134.30 (Matthew Bender 3d ed.). "Where a party assumes a certain position in a legal proceeding, and succeeds in maintaining that position, he may not thereafter, simply because his interests have changed, assume a contrary position, especially if it be to the prejudice of the party who has acquiesced in the position formerly taken by him." *New Hampshire v. Maine*, 532 U.S. 742, 749 (2001) (quoting *Davis v. Wakelee*, 156 U.S. 680, 689 (1895)). The purpose of the doctrine is "to protect the integrity of the judicial process by prohibiting parties from deliberately changing positions according to the exigencies of the moment." *Id.* at 749–50 (internal marks omitted).

The doctrine of stare decisis promotes adherence to decided matters of law to foster stability and equal treatment. It takes its name from the Latin maxim *stare decisis et non quieta movere* or "to abide by the precedents and not to disturb settled points." The strength of such adherence depends on the source of the prior decision. Stare decisis compels lower courts to follow the decisions of higher courts on ques-

7. The Restatement (Second) of Judgments adheres to the broader definition of res judicata as encompassing both claim and issue preclusion. *See* Restatement (Second) of Judgments, Ch. 3, intro. note (Am. Law Inst. 1982).

8. A patentee cannot use issue preclusion offensively to foreclose a defendant who was not party to that prior litigation from litigating the scope of the patent claim. *See Tex. Instruments, Inc. v. Linear Techs. Corp.*, 182 F. Supp. 2d 580, 590 (E.D. Tex. 2002). Had the Federal Circuit construed that claim term, however, the defendant might be bound under the doctrine of stare decisis. *See* § 5.3.4.

tions of law, whether applied to parties (or those in privity) or complete strangers to the prior proceeding. The decision of a district court is not binding precedent on a different judicial district, the same judicial district, or even the same judge in a different case, under the doctrine of stare decisis. Rather, stare decisis requires only that the later court encountering the issue give consideration and careful analysis to that sister court's decision where applicable to a similar fact pattern. *See United States v. Rodriguez-Pacheco*, 475 F.3d 434, 441 (1st Cir. 2007).

5.3.2 Issue Preclusion/Collateral Estoppel

Issue preclusion most commonly arises in the context of claim construction where a patentee who has previously litigated a patent through a *Markman* ruling seeks a fresh opportunity to construe a claim and an opposing party argues that the prior construction should govern interpretation of the term in question. *Cf. Blonder-Tongue Labs., Inc. v. Univ. of Ill. Found.*, 402 U.S. 313, 333 (1971) (holding that a patentee whose patent is invalidated after "a full and fair" opportunity to litigate its validity is collaterally estopped from relitigating the validity of the patent). The previous litigation might have ended in a settlement agreement, including possibly an order vacating the claim-construction ruling. The courts have divided on what effect, if any, to accord prior claim-construction rulings.

The general standard for issue preclusion requires that the party seeking to foreclose relitigation of an issue proves that: (1) the issue to be precluded is identical to the issue decided in the prior action; (2) the issue was actually litigated in that action; (3) the party against whom collateral estoppel is sought had a full and fair opportunity to litigate the issue in the prior action; and (4) the determination was essential to the final judgment of the prior action. *See Innovad Inc. v. Microsoft Corp.*, 260 F.3d 1326, 1334 (Fed. Cir. 2001) (citing *In re Freeman*, 30 F.3d 1459, 1465 (Fed. Cir. 1994)). Courts apply the collateral estoppel standard of the regional circuit, since issue preclusion is a procedural matter. *See RF Del.*, 326 F.3d at 1261.

5.3.2.1 Identity of Issues

The first prong of the issue preclusion test is satisfied where the patent claims (and claim terms) at issue in the *Markman* proceeding were interpreted in the prior case. *See, e.g.*, *Dynacore Holdings Corp. v. U.S. Philips Corp.*, 243 F. Supp. 2d 31, 35 (S.D.N.Y. 2003) (same patent claims at issue); *Kollmorgen Corp. v. Yaskawa Elec. Corp.*, 147 F. Supp. 2d 464, 466 (W.D. Va. 2001) (same); *Abbott Labs. v. Dey, L.P.*, 110 F. Supp. 2d 667, 669 (N.D. Ill. 2000) ("The claim construction issues disputed in this case are the same issues litigated in the [first] case."). When new claim terms are at issue, then collateral estoppel does not apply. *See, e.g.*, *P.A.T., Co. v. Ultrak, Inc.*, 948 F. Supp. 1518, 1520–21 (D. Kan. 1996). Since different claims within the same patent may use the same language, the "identity of issues" prong may nonetheless be satisfied if the language and context of the language are identical. *See In re Freeman*, 30 F.3d at 1465 n.4; *Aspex Eyewear, Inc. v. Zenni Optical Inc.*, 731 F.3d 1377, 1381 (Fed. Cir. 2013) (affirming application of collateral estoppel when claims with common terms had been previously litigated and found noninfringed by devices materially identical to eyewear in present suit); *e.Digital Corp. v. Futurewei Techs., Inc.*, 772 F.3d 723, 726 (Fed. Cir. 2014) (applying collateral estoppel to reexamined patent, because previously litigated limitation remained, whereas no collateral estoppel applied to unrelated patent). Similarly, since different patents may emanate from the same specification, as in the case of divisional and continuation applications, *see* §§ 14.2.2.3, 14.2.3.2, 14.2.3.3, the "identity of issues" prong may nonetheless be satisfied if the language and context of the language are identical. *See Masco Corp. v. United States*, 49 Fed. Cl. 337 (Ct. Cl. 2001) (applying collateral estoppel to a continuation patent that employed identical claim language relating back to the patent construed in the earlier litigation).

5.3.2.2 Actual Litigation

To satisfy the "actual litigation" prong, the parties to the original litigation must have disputed the claim term at issue, and it must have been adjudicated by the court. *See, e.g., In re Freeman*, 30 F.3d at 1466; *Kollmorgen*, 147 F. Supp. 2d at 466 (stating that the "actually litigated" prong was met after a lengthy *Markman* hearing on the claim construction); *Abbott Labs. v. Dey, L.P.*, 110 F. Supp. 2d at 669–70 (stating the "actually litigated" prong was met because the parties "briefed and argued the issues" before the judge); Restatement (Second) of Judgments § 27 comment d (1980). The "actual litigation" test is not satisfied where an issue was raised but later abandoned, *see* 18 Moore's Federal Practice § 132.03[2][e]; the court in the earlier proceeding declined to rule on the issue, *see id.* § 132.03[4][g]; there is ambiguity as to what was actually litigated and decided, *see id.* § 132.03[2][g]. Courts usually do not consider matters resolved by stipulation to have been actually litigated. *See United States v. Young*, 804 F.2d 116, 118 (8th Cir. 1986) ("A fact established in prior litigation not by judicial resolution but by stipulation has not been 'actually litigated'. . . ."). An exception exists, however, where the parties intend to foreclose future litigation of the issue. *See Hartley v. Mentor Corp.*, 869 F.2d 1469, 1470 (Fed. Cir. 1989); 18 Moore's Federal Practice § 132.03[2][i][ii] (Matthew Bender 3d ed.).

5.3.2.3 Full and Fair Opportunity to Litigate

Issue preclusion requires that the underlying proceeding has afforded the party to be foreclosed from relitigation a full and fair opportunity to litigate. This means that issue preclusion can never be applied against a party not involved (or not in privity with those involved) in the prior proceeding. In *Blonder-Tongue Laboratories*, 402 U.S. at 329–34, the Supreme Court identified a range of factors bearing on whether a patentee had a full and fair chance to litigate the validity of a patent: choice of forum; incentive to litigate; if the issue is obviousness, whether the first validity determination used the standards announced in *Graham v. John Deere Co.*, 383 U.S. 1, 12–24 (1966); whether opinions filed in the first case suggest that the prior case was one of those rare instances where the court or jury failed to grasp the technical subject matter and issues; and whether, without fault of its own, the patentee was deprived of crucial evidence or witnesses in the prior litigation. The Court concluded that there is no "automatic formula" for assessing this prong and that "[i]n the end, decision will necessarily rest on the trial courts' sense of justice and equity." *Id.* at 334. Where the prior court has conducted a *Markman* hearing in which the parties were afforded the ability to present their positions and respond, the "full and fair opportunity to litigate" requirement has been satisfied. *See Kollmorgen*, 147 F. Supp. 2d at 466 (stating that a lengthy *Markman* hearing on the claim construction satisfied the requirement); *TM Patents, L.P. v. IBM Corp.*, 72 F. Supp. 2d 370, 375 (S.D.N.Y. 1999) (noting that both parties agreed that there was a full and fair opportunity to litigate because a *Markman* hearing occurred).

5.3.2.4 Determination Was Essential to the Final Judgment

The final prong of the issue preclusion test has attracted the most controversy in the claim-construction context. It can usefully be divided into two separate inquiries: whether (1) the prior ruling was "final"; and (2) the prior ruling was essential to the judgment.

5.3.2.4.1 Finality

The question of whether a prior claim construction constitutes a final judgment can be characterized along a spectrum. At the easier end of the spectrum, where the court in the prior proceeding interprets the pertinent claim language and issues a final, appealable judgment on validity or infringement, the finality requirement is satisfied. *See, e.g., In re Freeman*, 30 F.3d at 1466 ("[J]udicial statements regarding the scope of patent claims are entitled to collateral estoppel effect in a subsequent infringement suit only to the extent that determination of scope was essential to a final judgment on the question of validity or infringement.") (quoting *A.B. Dick Co. v. Burroughs Corp.*, 713 F.2d 700, 704 (Fed. Cir. 1983)); *Home Diagnostics Inc. v. Lifescan, Inc.*, 120 F. Supp. 2d 864, 870 (N.D. Cal. 2000) (noting there must be a final judgment on validity or infringement for collateral estoppel to apply).

Issue preclusion can also arise out of a ruling granting summary judgment, *see Stevenson v. Sears, Roebuck & Co.*, 713 F.2d 705, 712 (Fed. Cir. 1983); *Sec. People, Inc. v. Medeco Sec. Locks, Inc.*, 59 F. Supp. 2d 1040 (N.D. Cal. 1999), *aff'd mem.*, 243 F.3d 555 (Fed. Cir. 2000), although denial of summary judgment or a grant of partial summary judgment usually does not have preclusive effect. *See Syntex Pharm. Int'l, Ltd. v. K-Line Pharm., Ltd.*, 905 F.2d 1525, 1526 (Fed. Cir. 1990) (noting that an order granting summary judgment of infringement of a patent and denying the alleged infringer's motion for summary judgment of invalidity did not present an appealable final judgment).

Similarly, the Federal Circuit held in *Transonic Systems, Inc. v. Non-Invasive Medical Technologies Corp.*, 75 F. App'x 765, 774 (Fed. Cir. 2003) (unpublished), that claim constructions conducted for purposes of a preliminary injunction ruling are not binding, even in the same litigation. Drawing on the Supreme Court's statement in *University of Texas v. Camenisch*, 451 U.S. 390, 395 (1981), that "findings of fact and conclusions of law made by a court granting a preliminary injunction are not binding at trial on the merits," the Federal Circuit views claim constructions reached during appeals from a grant of a preliminary injunction to be tentative. Hence, these preliminary constructions are not binding on the district court in subsequent proceedings. *See Guttman, Inc. v. Kopykake Enters.*, 302 F.3d 1352, 1361 (Fed. Cir. 2002) ("District courts may engage in a rolling claim construction, in which the court revisits and alters its interpretation of the claim terms as its understanding of the technology evolves."); *Transonic Sys.*, 75 F. App'x at 774. Therefore, claim constructions made in the context of preliminary injunction motions should not be considered final judgments, as the district court remains "at liberty to change the construction of a claim term as the record in a case evolves after a preliminary injunction appeal." *See Transonic Sys.*, 75 F. App'x at 774.

Courts are deeply divided on the issue of finality when the outcome of the prior proceeding is a settlement. Several courts have interpreted the "finality" requirement liberally and functionally, looking to whether the previous judgment is sufficiently firm to be accorded preclusive effect. In *TM Patents*, 72 F. Supp. 2d at 375–77, the defendant sought to hold the patentee to a claim construction rendered in a case resolved through settlement. While recognizing that the settlement did not result in a final, appealable judgment, the court nonetheless determined that the prior claim construction was entitled to preclusive effect. Seeking to elevate substance over form, the court focused on the careful consideration of the issues during the prior litigation and drew upon the Supreme Court's policy ruminations in *Markman*, which emphasized the importance of "uniformity in treatment of a given patent." *See Markman*, 517 U.S. at 390. The court recast "finality" for issue preclusion purposes as whether the prior litigation passed a stage for which there is "no really good reason for permitting [an issue] to be litigated again." *TM Patents*, 72 F. Supp. 2d at 376 (quoting *Lummus Co. v. Commonwealth Oil Ref. Co.*, 297 F.2d 80, 89 (2d Cir. 1961)). The court also noted that the patentee voluntarily entered into the settlement agreement, and the *Markman* ruling was not vacated as part of the settlement.

Although some other courts have since followed *TM Patents*' application of collateral estoppel in the context of settlements following *Markman* rulings, *see, e.g.*, *Edberg v. CPI-The Alternative Supplier, Inc.*, 156 F. Supp. 2d 190 (D. Conn. 2001), a contrary line of cases emerged holding that *Markman* rulings from cases that settled were not final and hence not properly entitled to preclusive effect. *See Lincoln Nat. Life Ins. Co. v. Jackson Nat. Life Ins. Co.*, 2013 U.S. Dist. LEXIS 155502, 2013 WL 5874448 (N.D. Ind. 2013) (declining to apply collateral estoppel against patentee based on prior adverse ruling resolved through settlement); *Kollmorgen*, 147 F. Supp. 2d 464; *Graco Children's Prods., Inc. v. Regalo Int'l*, 77 F. Supp. 2d 660 (E.D. Pa. 1999). The cases read the Supreme Court's policy discussion in the *Markman* case as merely recognizing the importance of uniformity, not changing the fundamental principles for issue preclusion. The *Graco Children's Products* court expressed concern that granting preclusive effect to cases settled after claim constructions might discourage settlement and encourage appeals by patentees who obtained favorable verdicts, but nonetheless needed to correct what they believed to be unduly narrow or otherwise flawed claim constructions.

The preclusive effect of claim-construction rulings in cases resolved by settlement came before the Federal Circuit in *RF Delaware*, 326 F.3d 1255. *See also Dana v. E.S. Originals, Inc.*, 342 F.3d 1320 (Fed. Cir. 2003). Without expressly resolving the district court conflict, the Federal Circuit, applying Eleventh Circuit law, applied a stringent standard to the question of finality: "'if the parties to a suit enter into *an extrajudicial settlement or compromise*, there is no judgment, and future litigation is not barred by *res judicata* or collateral estoppel. . . .'" *RF Del.*, 326 F.3d at 1261 (quoting *Kaspar Wire Works, Inc. v. Leco Eng'g & Mach., Inc.*, 575 F.2d 530, 542 (5th Cir. 1978)). The Federal Circuit drew no implication from the Supreme Court's *Markman* language on which the *TM Patents* court seized. Nonetheless, the court included some language inclined toward a functional approach to finality: "[f]or purposes of issue preclusion . . . , 'final judgment' includes any prior adjudication of an issue in another action that is determined to be sufficiently firm to be accorded conclusive effect." *Id.* at 1261 (quoting *Christo v. Padgett*, 223 F.3d 1324, 1339 n.47 (11th Cir. 2002) (citing Restatement (Second) of Judgments § 13 (1980)). Whether a decision is "sufficiently firm" depends on whether the parties were "fully heard." *Id.* The Federal Circuit noted that the Eleventh Circuit held that a prior district court order issued after an evidentiary hearing satisfied the finality standard because the district court notified the parties of possible preclusive effect, considered the findings final, and entered a final order approving the proposed settlement. *Id.* at 1261 (quoting *Christo v. Padgett*, 223 F.3d at 1339). In *RF Delaware*, the Federal Circuit denied preclusive effect of the earlier *Markman* ruling on the grounds that there was no evidence that a *Markman* hearing had been conducted in the earlier case, the parties did not have notice that the court's order could have preclusive effect, and no final order approving the settlement was ever entered. *Id.*

The Federal Circuit further addressed the preclusive effect of stipulated constructions and settlements in *Pfizer, Inc. v. Teva Pharmaceuticals, USA, Inc.*, 429 F.3d 1364 (Fed. Cir. 2005). Because the parties in the prior proceeding had stipulated that the agreed claim interpretation was for purposes of that litigation only, the Federal Circuit held that the agreement could not preclude litigation in a later case. Looking to jurisprudence on the interpretation of consent decrees, the court declared that "'the scope of a consent decree must be discerned within its four corners' and the conditions upon which a party has consented to waive its right to litigate particular issues 'must be respected.'" *Id.* at 1376 (quoting *United States v. Armour & Co.*, 402 U.S. 673, 682 (1971) and citing *In re Graham*, 973 F.2d 1089, 1097 (3d Cir. 1992) (noting that the Third Circuit defers to the intent of parties concerning the preclusive effect of agreed facts or claims in consent decrees and stipulations)).

5.3.2.4.2 Essential to the Final Judgment

A final requirement for a prior *Markman* ruling to foreclose later interpretation over a claim term is that the earlier construction was essential to the final judgment. When the prior action turns upon resolution of a particular claim term or terms, the court's construction of other claim terms is "merely dictum, and therefore has no issue preclusive effect." *See, e.g.*, *Guardian Media Techs., Ltd. v. Acer Am. Corp.*, 2013 U.S. Dist. LEXIS 63044, 2013 WL 1866901 at *10 (E.D. Tex. 2013) (finding no preclusion where contested term was related to, but not identical to, term that was focus of prior judgment); *Phonometrics, Inc. v. N. Telecom Inc.*, 133 F.3d 1459, 1464 (Fed. Cir. 1998). To have a preclusive effect, the earlier court's interpretation of the particular claim had to be the reason for the previous outcome. *TecSec, Inc. v. IBM Corp.*, 731 F.3d 1336, 1344 (Fed. Cir. 2013) (finding no estoppel where earlier claim construction was not critical to prior appeal); *Jackson Jordan, Inc. v. Plasser Am. Corp.*, 747 F.2d 1567, 1577 (Fed. Cir. 1984).

A related principle is that issues of claim construction that cannot be appealed cannot be accorded preclusive effect. *See Hartley*, 869 F.2d at 1472. Thus, courts will not attach preclusive effect where a patentee loses on the issue of claim interpretation but nonetheless prevails on validity and infringement because the patentee lacked a basis for appealing the *Markman* ruling. *See Graco*, 77 F. Supp. 2d at 664–65; *Schering Corp. v. Amgen, Inc.*, 35 F. Supp. 2d 375, 377 n.2 (D. Del. 1999), *aff'd in part*, 222 F.3d 1347 (Fed. Cir. 2000).

5.3.2.5 Reasoned Deference as a Prudent Approach to Issue Preclusion

In cases in which the basis for applying issue preclusion is open to question, many courts have taken the approach of according prior *Markman* rulings "reasoned deference" in assessing the disputed claim terms. *See, e.g.*, *Finisar Corp. v. DirecTV Group, Inc.*, 523 F.3d 1323, 1329 (Fed. Cir. 2008) (noting that "in the interests of uniformity and correctness," the Federal Circuit "consults the claim analysis of different district courts on the identical terms in the context of the same patent."); *CoStar Realty Information, Inc. v. CIVIX-DDI, LLC*, 2013 U.S. Dist. LEXIS 135448, 2013 WL 5346440 at *5 (N.D. Ill. 2013) ("Courts in this district have stopped short of affording complete deference to prior non-preclusive district court claim constructions, instead giving them the status of only persuasive authority."); *Visto Corp. v. Sproqit Techs., Inc.*, 445 F. Supp. 2d 1104, 1108 (N.D. Cal. 2006). Where no new arguments are offered, no new foundation is laid, and there has been no change in the applicable standards for construing claims, courts generally adopt the prior construction unless it is clearly unsound. Where new argument and evidence is adduced, then the review is more probing and independent. Even in cases in which courts have determined that collateral estoppel applies, they have nonetheless made some independent assessment of claim construction. Thus, even the *TM Patents* court, which held that a *Markman* ruling from an earlier case that settled prior to trial precluded relitigation of claim meaning, used the "reasoned deference" approach as a judicial backstop: "Finally, I have to observe that this issue of collateral estoppel . . . is of marginal practical importance, because I agree with just about everything Judge Young did when he construed the claims in the EMC action." *See TM Patents*, 72 F. Supp. 2d at 370.

5.3.3 Judicial Estoppel

The Federal Circuit has recognized the applicability of the equitable doctrine of judicial estoppel in the context of claim construction. *See Biomedical Patent Mgmt. Corp. v. Cal. Dep't of Health Servs.*, 505 F.3d 1328, 1341 (Fed. Cir. 2007); *Harris Corp. v. Ericsson*, 417 F.3d 1241 (Fed. Cir. 2005); *RF Del.*, 326 F.3d 1255. As an equitable doctrine, the contours of judicial estoppel are relatively flexible. Although "[t]he circumstances under which judicial estoppel may appropriately be invoked are probably not reducible to any general formulation of principle," *Allen v. Zurich Ins. Co.*, 667 F.2d 1162, 1166 (4th Cir. 1982), the Supreme Court has emphasized three factors to consider in determining whether the doctrine applies: (1) whether a party's later position is "clearly inconsistent" with its earlier position; (2) whether the party succeeded in persuading a court to accept that party's earlier position, so that judicial acceptance of an inconsistent position in a later proceeding would create "the perception that either the first or second court was misled"; and (3) whether the party seeking to assert an inconsistent position would derive an unfair advantage or impose an unfair detriment on the opposing party if not estopped. *See New Hampshire v. Maine*, 532 U.S. at 750–51; *Global Sessions LP v. Comerica Bank*, 2014 U.S. Dist. LEXIS 125271, 2014 WL 4415996 at *12 (W.D. Tex. 2014) (finding no judicial estoppel where prior construction was court's construction rather than that the patentee advanced and neither party was free of machinations).

The requirements for judicial estoppel partially overlap with the standard for issue preclusion (such as the element of identity of issues), but there are substantial differences as well. Unlike issue preclusion, judicial estoppel does not require strict mutuality, *Ryan Operations G.P. v. Santiam-Midwest Lumber Co.*, 81 F.3d 355, 360 (3d Cir. 1996) (stating that judicial estoppel does not require privity), or even that the issue had been actually litigated in the prior proceeding. *See Lowery v. Stovall*, 92 F.3d 219, 223 n.3 (4th Cir. 1996). On the other hand, judicial estoppel typically requires strong evidence of improper intent to mislead a tribunal.

Judicial estoppel is also closely related to equitable estoppel. *See id.* Unlike a party asserting equitable estoppel, a party asserting judicial estoppel does not have to prove detrimental reliance because judicial estoppel is designed to protect the integrity of the courts rather than any interests of the litigants. *See Teledyne Indus., Inc. v. NLRB*, 911 F.2d 1214, 1220 (6th Cir. 1990). Therefore, judicial estoppel may apply in a particular case "where neither collateral estoppel nor equitable estoppel . . . would apply." *Allen*, 667 F.2d at 1166–67.

As with issue preclusion and other nonpatent procedural issues, courts apply the standards for judicial estoppel developed by their regional circuit. *See Lampi Corp. v. Am. Power Prods., Inc.*, 228 F.3d 1365, 1377 (Fed. Cir. 2000). Such standards vary across the circuits. For example, although most circuits do not require mutuality of judicial estoppel, some courts limit the doctrine to those who were party to (or in privity with a party to) the prior proceeding. *See Nichols v. Scott*, 69 F.3d 1255, 1272 n.33 (5th Cir. 1995). The relative importance of particular factors varies as well.

Some circuits consider intent—whether the inconsistency in position was for the purpose of gaining unfair advantage—to be most determinative. *See Lowery*, 92 F.3d at 224.[9]

5.3.4 Stare Decisis

Prior to the Supreme Court's *Teva* decision, the Federal Circuit held that lower courts must adhere to prior claim-construction determinations by the Federal Circuit even if the claim construction is applied to a party who was not involved in the prior litigation. *See, e.g., Amgen, Inc. v. F. Hoffmann-La Roche Ltd.*, 494 F. Supp. 2d 54, 60 (D. Mass. 2007); *Tate Access Floors, Inc. v. Interface Architectural Res., Inc.*, 185 F. Supp. 2d 588, 595 (D. Md. 2002); *Wang Labs., Inc. v. Oki Elec. Indus. Co., Ltd.*, 15 F. Supp. 2d 166, 175 (D. Mass. 1998) (holding that a prior Federal Circuit claim construction was binding against a party that was not a party to (or allowed intervention in) prior litigation interpreting the claim term in question). By expressly recognizing a factual component to claim construction, the *Teva* decision casts doubt on this line of cases. Where the basis for the prior Federal Circuit decision is intrinsic evidence, the Federal Circuit's interpretation will typically control. However, litigants who did not participate in the prior case and who have an alternative basis for interpreting the claim are entitled to a fair opportunity to pursue their interpretive analysis.

A claim-construction decision of a district court is not binding precedent on a different judicial district, the same judicial district, or even the same judge in a different case under the doctrine of stare decisis. Rather, stare decisis requires only that the later court encountering the issue give consideration and careful analysis to that sister court's decision where applicable to a similar fact pattern. *See Pinpoint Inc. v. Hotwire, Inc.*, 2013 U.S. Dist. LEXIS 38371, 2013 WL 1174688, *8 (N.D. Ill. 2013); *Amgen, Inc. v. F. Hoffmann-La Roche Ltd.*, 494 F. Supp. 2d 54, 60 (D. Mass. 2007) (citing *Rodriguez-Pacheco*, 475 F.3d at 441); *Tex. Instruments, Inc. v. Linear Techs. Corp.*, 182 F. Supp. 2d 580, 589 (E.D. Tex. 2002); *cf. Finisar*, 523 F.3d at 1329 (noting that "in the interests of uniformity and correctness," the Federal Circuit "consults the claim analysis of different district courts on the identical terms in the context of the same patent."). Courts sometimes accord prior decisions from within their district somewhat greater consideration than those decided outside the district. *See, e.g., Visto*, 445 F. Supp. 2d at 1107–08 (noting that intrajudicial uniformity warrants an even higher level of deference); *Verizon Cal. Inc. v. Ronald A. Katz Tech. Licensing, P.A.*, 326 F. Supp. 2d 1060, 1069 (C.D. Cal. 2003).

---

9. The Federal Circuit holds that judicial estoppel does not normally prevent a party from altering on appeal an unsuccessful position on claim construction that it advocated before the trial court. *See RF Del.*, 326 F.3d at 1262 (quoting *Data Gen. Corp. v. Johnson*, 78 F.3d 1556, 1565 (Fed. Cir. 1996)) ("The doctrine of judicial estoppel is that where a party *successfully* urges a particular position in a legal proceeding, it is estopped from taking a contrary position in a subsequent proceeding where its interests have changed.").

The general rule is that a prior claim-construction decision by the Federal Circuit is binding upon district courts (and future Federal Circuit panels) being asked to construe the same term, in the same patent. *Phonometrics, Inc. v. Westin Hotel Co.*, 350 F.3d 1242, 1244 (Fed. Cir. 2003) ("under principles of *stare decisis*," future Federal Circuit panels "will follow the claim construction set forth by" an earlier panel). The Federal Circuit has in fact "adopted the rule that prior decisions of a panel of the court are binding precedent on subsequent panels unless and until overturned in banc." *Newell Cos. v. Kenney Mfg. Co.*, 864 F.2d 757, 765 (Fed. Cir. 1988). And that rule applies to the construction of claim terms. *See Phonometrics, Inc. v. Economy Inns of Am.*, 349 F.3d 1356, 1363–64 (Fed. Cir. 2003).

The limits of stare decisis are likely to be tested under the AIA's misjoinder regime. Section 299 is producing a proliferation of lawsuits involving the same patents. Furthermore, the *Teva* decision has recognized that claim construction can involve subsidiary factual determinations. Different defendants in separate lawsuits will explore alternative theories and extrinsic evidence, which could result in divergent interpretations. When multiple cases are proceeding in parallel, each with its own claim construction (as allowed by *Teva* and the AIA nonjoinder rule), there is a strong likelihood that the first case to reach the Federal Circuit could upend the constructions reached in the other cases, thereby upsetting the framework of those cases, and requiring a "redo" of expert reports, expert depositions, summary judgment motions, and pretrial proceedings. However, district courts may be reluctant to halt their own proceedings while the lead case in a multijurisdiction suit winds its way through the appellate process. Furthermore, given the likelihood that the claims and constructions at issue in different cases might not be identical, the appeal of the lead case might not resolve the claim-construction disputes of the other pending cases. Therefore, district courts are likely to press onward with their own dockets while the leading case is appealed. After spending considerable resources on trailing cases, those courts may be reluctant to undo their own constructions once the first Federal Circuit opinion is issued. Of course, the myriad ways this could play out requires a case-by-case case-management approach and openness to new solutions, given the fundamental changes in patent law which the AIA and *Teva* have effected.

Just as issue preclusion requires an issue to have been actually *litigated* for collateral estoppel to attach, stipulations of claim meaning may not be entitled to stare decisis effect "because it is only the judiciary—not the parties—that declares what the law is." *Amgen*, 494 F. Supp. 2d at 70. The court in that case noted, however, that "[s]uch agreements, of course, may, where appropriate, implicate judicial estoppel and, where a final judgment occurs, the doctrine of issue preclusion." Also as with issue preclusion, stare decisis applies only to rulings that were necessary to the decision rendered. *See Miken Composites, L.L.C. v. Wilson Sporting Goods Co.*, 515 F.3d 1331, 1338 (Fed. Cir. 2008); *Zenith Radio Corp. v. United States*, 783 F.2d 184, 187 (Fed. Cir. 1986) (holding that stare decisis applied where the resolution of issue was a "necessary predicate" to earlier Federal Circuit ruling).

A distinct tension arises to the extent that courts look to prior *Markman* rulings under the doctrine of stare decisis in circumstances that do not satisfy the more exacting requirements of issue preclusion. In practice, courts have alleviated this strain by affording a party who did not participate in that earlier action a full and fair opportunity to be heard in the later proceeding. At the same time, courts can be mindful of prior rulings. *See Tex. Instruments*, 182 F. Supp. 2d at 590 (E.D. Tex. 2002); *Sears Petroleum & Transp. Corp. v. Archer Daniels Midland Co.*, 2007 U.S. Dist. LEXIS 53576, 2007 WL 2156251, at *8, *12 (N.D.N.Y. July 24, 2007) (stating that "considerable deference should be given to those prior decisions unless overruled or undermined by subsequent legal developments, including intervening case law" before proceeding to consider arguments that had not been heard during prior claim-construction proceedings); *KX Indus., L.P. v. PUR Water Purification Prods., Inc.*, 108 F. Supp. 2d 380, 387 (D. Del. 2000) (holding that it would defer to its prior claim construction, but only "to the extent the parties do not raise new arguments"); *Tex. Instruments*, 182 F. Supp. 2d at 589–90 (expressing concern that refusing to consider a new party's claim-construction arguments raised due process concerns and therefore granting the party's request for a *Markman* hearing); *Townshend Intellectual Prop., L.L.C. v. Broadcom Corp.*, 2008 U.S. Dist LEXIS 7393, 2008 WL 171039 (N.D. Cal. Jan. 18, 2008) (modifying prior claim construction in light of a new party's arguments).

As Judge Whyte has stated, "[t]his general practice accords with the insight that a fresh look at a claim construction can hone a prior court's understanding and construction of a patent." *See Rambus*, 569 F. Supp. 2d at 966. The Federal Circuit has noted that it "would be remiss to overlook another district court's construction of the same claim terms in the same patent as part of [a] separate appeal." *Finisar Corp.*, 523 F.3d at 1329. In that case, the Federal Circuit found a second district court's claim interpretation particularly helpful where it referred to the prior construction, and noted where it disagreed. *See id.* The lesson from *Finisar* is that additional litigation can refine and sharpen courts' understanding of an invention and that a second court should not defer to a prior court's claim construction without questioning its accuracy.

It should be noted, however, that this practice is in tension with the Supreme Court's understanding of stare decisis. *See Payne v. Tenn.*, 501 U.S. 808, 828 (1991) (observing that "[c]onsiderations in favor of *stare decisis* are at their acme in cases involving property and contract rights, where reliance interests are involved"); *Burnet v. Coronado Oil & Gas Co.*, 285 U.S. 393, 406 (1932) (Brandeis, J., dissenting) (noting that "[*s*]*tare decisis* is usually the wise policy, because in most matters it is more important that the applicable rule of law be settled than that it be settled right"); *Genesee Chief v. Fitzhugh*, 53 U.S. 443, 458 (1851) (explaining that "*stare decisis* is the safe and established rule of judicial policy, and should always be adhered to" when dealing with cases establishing rules of property); *Minn. Mining Co. v. Nat'l Mining Co.*, 70 U.S. 332 (1865).

Nonetheless, "while 'most' matters benefit from being settled rather than being settled right, claim construction appears to be an exception." *See Rambus*, 569 F. Supp. 2d at 967. The prevailing notion among the district courts and the Federal Circuit appears to be that it is better to get a claim construction right than it is to get a claim construction settled.

5.3.5 U.S. International Trade Commission Determinations

A growing number of plaintiffs in recent years have concurrently filed complaints in both a U.S. district court and before the U.S. International Trade Commission. As an administrative agency, decisions by the ITC are not binding upon a district court. *See Tex. Instruments Inc. v. Cypress Semiconductor Corp.*, 90 F.3d 1558, 1569 (Fed. Cir. 1996) ("Congress did not intend decisions of the ITC on patent issues to have preclusive effect."). However, as an agency that is highly focused on resolving patent infringement disputes, the rulings of the ITC would ordinarily be conferred substantial persuasive effect. *Id.* ("The district court can attribute whatever persuasive value to the prior ITC decision that it considers justified.").

5.3.6 Patent and Trademark Office Determinations

Often, patents in litigation are also involved in reexamination proceedings before the USPTO. Particularly in these circumstances, the USPTO may have had an opportunity to construe the claims at issue in the district court litigation. However, no deference should be given to claim-construction rulings of the USPTO. The USPTO uses a different standard to construe claims than is appropriate for a district court. Whereas a district court is charged with identifying the proper construction, the USPTO is required to give claims "their broadest reasonable interpretation, consistent with the specification." *In re Swanson*, 540 F.3d 1368, 1377–78 (Fed. Cir. 2008).

5.3.7 Motions to Vacate Claim-Construction Rulings in Connection with Settlement

Claim construction often drives settlement discussions. Parties often resolve their disputes after a claim-construction order has been issued, but prior to entry of final judgment. Occasionally, a patentee may be concerned about potential preclusive effects of an adverse claim-construction ruling in future litigation, and will file either a joint or unopposed motion to vacate that claim-construction ruling in connection with the settlement. While some district courts have granted vacatur in such cases, *see, e.g., Cisco Sys., Inc. v. Telcordia Techs., Inc.*, 590 F. Supp. 2d 828, 830 (E.D. Tex. 2008) (vacating claim-construction order), other courts have denied it on the grounds that it undermines judicial economy and is contrary to public policy. *See, e.g., Allen-Bradley Co. v. Kollmorgen Corp.*, 199 F.R.D. 316, 320 (E.D. Wis. 2001) ("[The] claim construction order, like nearly all court decisions and orders, affects interests beyond those of the parties in the present action. The benefits of settling the present action are, in short, outweighed by the systemic costs that would be incurred by vacating the court's order."); *RE2CON, LLC v. Telfer Oil Co.*, 2013 U.S. Dist. LEXIS 46192, 2013 WL 1325183 at *3 (E.D. Cal. 2013) (declining vacatur).

Although some courts grant vacatur with the goal of facilitating settlement, this practice, especially in patent cases, could be a false economy. It may facilitate the reassertion of weak patents and deprive other courts of the economizing benefits of collateral estoppel. *See* Jeremy W. Bock, *An Empirical Study of Certain Settlement-Related Motions for Vacatur in Patent Cases*, 88 Ind. L. J. 919 (2013) (synthesizing case law and analyzing empirical data on settlement-related motions for vacatur in patent cases over a five-year period); *cf. Lear, Inc. v. Adkins*, 395 U.S. 653, 674 n.19 (1969) (noting "the public's interest in the elimination of specious patents"); *Cardinal Chem. Co. v. Morton Int'l*, 508 U.S. 83, 100 (1993) ("[O]ur prior cases have identified a strong public interest in the finality of judgments in patent litigation."); Jill E. Fisch, *Rewriting History: The Propriety of Eradicating Prior Decisional Law Through Settlement and Vacatur*, 76 Cornell L. Rev. 589, 593 (1991) ("[T]he effect of vacatur on the litigation process extends beyond judicial waste; it perverts the judicial decision into a negotiable commodity, engendering distortion of, and disrespect for, the role of the courts.").

Although there is no Federal Circuit precedent that squarely addresses the merits of a district court's decision on a motion to vacate a claim-construction order, the Supreme Court's decision in *U.S. Bancorp Mortgage Co. v. Bonner Mall Partnership*, 513 U.S. 18 (1994) provides an analytic starting point. The Court denied a settlement-related motion to vacate a final judgment on the ground that vacatur was an "extraordinary remedy" to which equitable entitlement must be shown. *Id.* at 26. Settlement does not justify vacatur in the absence of "exceptional circumstances." *Id.* at 29. The Federal Circuit's guidance on the merits of settlement-related vacatur at the district court level is largely limited to a couple of concurring opinions that provide somewhat differing views. *Compare Ohio Willow Wood Co. v. Thermo-Ply, Inc.*, 629 F.3d 1374, 1376 (Fed. Cir. 2011) (Moore, J., concurring) (extending *U.S. Bancorp* to district courts and observing that "[o]nly in 'exceptional circumstances' should a district court grant vacatur at the request of the litigants") (quoting *U.S. Bancorp*, 513 U.S. at 26.) *with Dana v. E.S. Originals, Inc.*, 342 F.3d 1320, 1328 (Fed. Cir. 2003) (Dyk, J., concurring) (suggesting that *U.S. Bancorp* does not apply to district courts or nonfinal orders).

In general, courts should view with skepticism a request to vacate a claim-construction order in connection with a settlement. Although granting vacatur may be expedient for the particular parties and the court, the public interest and long-term judicial economy may suffer by allowing the patentee "another bite at the apple." The circumstances are, of course, fact-dependent. Accordingly, when presented with a settlement-related motion for vacatur, courts should consider the underlying motives for the settlement, the litigation history of the patent affected by the ruling targeted for vacatur, past patterns of behavior by the patentee, and anticompetitive ramifications, as well as potential effects on third parties.

5.4 Practical Tips for Claim Construction

5.4.1 Recognizing and Avoiding the Pitfalls of Sound-Bite and "Cite"-Bite Advocacy

Patent law is plagued with a surfeit of quotations from Federal Circuit cases that appear to support almost any proposition. The sheer quantity of published opinions that the Federal Circuit has issued over its history is massive. The cases frequently are technically demanding, which can obscure the context around their legal rules. Moreover, important legal shifts over the Federal Circuit's history (most recently in *Phillips*) have rendered entire lines of authority obsolete. The result is that there is a huge trove of case-law sound bites available to litigants that are no longer authoritative, but that are nonetheless cited routinely. This poses an added burden on the courts to recognize what principles are no longer good law. This subsection identifies commonly cited statements from prior cases that are no longer valid, or whose applicability has been sharply limited.

5.4.1.1 "Heavy Presumption of Ordinary Meaning"

As discussed above (*see* §§ 5.2.3.2.2, 5.2.3.2.2.2), *Texas Digital* established a "heavy presumption" that the ordinary meaning of a claim term applies. This standard was routinely cited prior to *Phillips*, but dropped from the Federal Circuit's case law for many years in connection with *Phillips*.[10] *Phillips* did not expressly abrogate the "heavy presumption" standard, and the lack of an express statement from the Federal Circuit disavowing this standard has allowed litigants to continue citing it.

Post-*Phillips*, the Federal Circuit has relied on various standards for departing from the "ordinary meaning" of a term, as discussed herein. Some articulations of the standard, such as applied in *Thorner*, 669 F.3d at 1365–66 (Fed. Cir. 2012), approach a presumption, holding that ordinary meaning should apply unless there is an explicit definition or disavowal of claim scope. Other standards, such as was articulated in *Retractable Technologies*, appear to provide a more flexible framework for determining the proper construction, as discussed herein. More recently, various panels of the Federal Circuit have revived this "heavy presumption" explicitly. *See, e.g.*, *Plantronics*, 724 F.3d at 1350; *Starhome*, 743 F.3d at 857. Courts should be wary of this revival, as it appears to conflict with the methodology approved en banc by *Phillips*.

5.4.1.2 "Presumption in Favor of Dictionary Definition" No Longer Applies

Texas Digital also created a "presumption in favor of a dictionary definition," and held that dictionaries and other such outside sources should be consulted *before* interpreting the patent specification. *Phillips* overruled that approach. *See* § 5.2.3.2.2.1. The court rejected *Texas Digital*'s undue emphasis on dictionaries as a source of ordinary meaning. *Phillips* does not offer a single formula for claim con-

---

10. The last time the Federal Circuit cited this standard prior to *Phillips* was in *Fuji Photo Film Co., Ltd. v. Int'l Trade Comm'n*, 386 F.3d 1095, 1105 (Fed. Cir. 2004). This standard remained absent from Federal Circuit case law until it was cited in *Elbex Video, Ltd. v. Sensormatic Elecs. Corp.*, 508 F.3d 1366, 1371 (Fed. Cir. 2007). This reference appears to be an outlier. There is no indication that the Federal Circuit intended to resuscitate the "heavy presumption" in favor of dictionary meaning.

struction, but broadly instructs that claims must be interpreted consistent with a "full understanding of what the inventors actually invented and intended to envelop with the claim," and that the construction that "stays true to the claim language and most naturally aligns with the patent's description of the invention will be, in the end, the correct construction." *Phillips*, 415 F.3d at 1316. Thus, there is a renewed emphasis on construing claim terms consistent with their usage in the specification.

5.4.1.3 Reliance on Extrinsic Evidence Is Permissible but Cannot Override Intrinsic Evidence

District courts are still reluctant to consider extrinsic evidence, based on *Vitronics*, 90 F.3d at 1583 (Fed. Cir. 1996). That case discouraged trial courts from relying on extrinsic evidence where the intrinsic evidence was sufficiently clear to resolve the claim-construction dispute. *Id.* ("In most situations, an analysis of the intrinsic evidence alone will resolve any ambiguity in a disputed claim term. In such circumstances, it is improper to rely on extrinsic evidence."). *Vitronics* has been interpreted, widely and incorrectly, as a prohibition on extrinsic evidence. The Federal Circuit has consistently backed away from that interpretation, and now *Teva* removes any doubt that extrinsic evidence may be considered during claim construction. It is important to bear in mind, however, that extrinsic evidence cannot be relied upon to override contrary meaning reflected in the specification or other intrinsic evidence. *See Phillips*, 415 F.3d at 1317–18 (noting that extrinsic evidence is "less significant than the intrinsic record" and "less reliable" than intrinsic evidence).

5.4.2 Checklist/Discussion Points for Claim-Construction Hearing

The following summary list reflects key principles for the procedural and substantive elements of *Markman* law.

5.4.2.1 Procedural Aspects

- *Markman Timing*—Recommended approach is to allow sufficient pre-*Markman* discovery and allow identification of claim-construction issues, but sufficient time post-*Markman* to allow *Markman* opinion to issue prior to expert reports.
- *Crystallizing Issues for Markman Hearing*—Courts should order a structured meet-and-confer process in advance of briefing to avoid false disputes and ensure that genuine disputes are properly joined. Courts should use their discretion to prioritize the timing of (and possibly need for) construction of particular claim terms.
- *Consideration of Extrinsic Evidence*—Courts are free to consider extrinsic evidence in support of their *Markman* rulings, but it may not contradict the intrinsic evidence.

- *Fact-Finding*—Courts should ask the parties how the *Markman* hearings should be structured to allow for an evidentiary hearing, if necessary, to build a factual record to allow for deferential review on appeal.

5.4.2.2 Substantive Aspects

- *Threshold Analysis*—Carefully assess what terms require interpretation and what deference, if any, to accord *Markman* rulings of the same patents and claim terms in prior cases.
- *Ordinary Meaning*—The "ordinary meaning" of a claim term is the baseline for claim construction, but there is no longer a "heavy presumption" that it applies. Rather, it is appropriate to depart from the "ordinary" meaning where the intrinsic evidence persuasively demonstrates "what the inventors actually invented and intended to envelop with the claim." *Phillips*, 415 F.3d at 1316.
- *Dictionaries*—There is no "presumption in favor of a dictionary definition." Rather, the proper construction comes foremost from a context-dependent review of the patent and its prosecution history.
- *Departing from Ordinary Meaning*—It may be appropriate to construe a claim term differently than its ordinary meaning when the specification and prosecution history provide reasonable clarity of what the inventors actually intended to claim, including by characterizing the "present invention" to emphasize a particular feature, or distinguishing the prior art in a manner to highlight what the inventors viewed as their invention, or giving a consistent and uniform meaning to terms throughout the patent, among other scenarios.

Appendix 5.1
Joint Claim-Construction Statement Order

UNITED STATES DISTRICT COURT
DISTRICT OF ___________

COMPANY A, Plaintiff, v. COMPANY B, Defendant.	Civil Case No. [CASE NO.] **ORDER** Date: [DATE]

___________, District Judge:

The Court hereby orders the parties to file their joint claim construction statement [pursuant to Local Patent Rule ___] by **[DATE]** and provide the following joint multi-claim chart: Column 1 shall be the claim term to be construed, in rank-order of importance from the most significant to the least significant.

1. Column 2 shall be Plaintiff's proposed construction of the term.
2. Column 3 shall state the impact of Plaintiff's proposed construction of the term on validity or infringement, and whether such construction is case dispositive.
3. Column 4 shall be Defendant's proposed construction of the term.
4. Column 5 shall state the impact of Defendant's proposed construction of the term on validity or infringement, and whether such construction is case dispositive.

IT IS SO ORDERED.

Appendix 5.2
Sample Joint Claim-Construction Charts

UNITED STATES DISTRICT COURT
FOR THE DISTRICT OF NEW JERSEY

IBORMEITH IP, LLC.,	:	Civil Action No. 2:10-CV-05378-FSH-PS
Plaintiff,	:	
	:	**JOINT CLAIM CONSTRUCTION AND**
v.	:	**PREHEARING STATEMENT**
MERCEDES-BENZ USA, LLC and DAIMLER AG,	:	
Defendants.	:	

Plaintiff Ibormeith and Defendants Mercedes-Benz USA, LLC and Daimler AG respectfully submit the following Joint Claim construction and Prehearing Statement. A chart identifying all terms requiring construction and the parties' supporting evidence is attached hereto.

A. LOCAL PATENT RULE 4.3(a) – CONSTRUCTION OF CLAIM TERMS UPON WHICH THE PARTIES AGREE

The parties agree on the construction of the 11th term previously identified as requiring construction. The parties will continue working together to narrow the number of disputed claim terms.

Term No.	Term to be Construed	Plaintiff's Construction	Defendants' Construction
11. (11th claim in chart)	warning indicator (Claim 1)	an audio and/or visual indication of sleepiness provided to the driver	Agree with plaintiff's construction

B. LOCAL PATENT RULE 4.3(b) – PROPOSED CONSTRUCTION OF DISPUTED CLAIM TERMS

Term No.	Term to be Construed	Plaintiff's Construction	Defendants' Construction
1	a sensor for sensing a driver or operator control input (Claim 1)	Plaintiff contends that this is not a means-plus-function clause under Section 112, ¶6. Interpretation: A device that converts a driver's control input to an electrical signal supplying data about the control input.	Defendants contend that this clause is governed by § 112 ¶ 6 and accordingly identify the following structure(s) in the specification which correspond to the function "sensing a driver or operator control input" (which includes hardware and software, and thus also the algorithms used by the software): accelerometer, steering wheel movement sensor, transmission drive shaft sensor, accelerator movement sensor, software and associated algorithms, and equivalents under 112 ¶ 6.
2	control input (Claim 1)	interaction between a driver and the vehicle's controls	"a command from the driver to the vehicle's controls"
3	operational model (Claim 1)	computer software that includes a physiological reference model of driver circadian rhythm pattern(s) and a vehicle operating model or algorithm	Defendants contend that this clause is invalid under § 112 ¶ 2 as indefinite. Alternatively, it shall be construed as: Defendants contend that this clause is governed by § 112 ¶ 6 and accordingly identify the following structure(s) in the specification which correspond to the operating function covering the structure of: processor, computer software, memory, and associated algorithms containing a physiological reference model of driver circadian rhythm patterns and a vehicle operating model or algorithm, as disclosed in the specification and equivalents thereof under 112 ¶ 6.
4	physiological reference model (of driver circadian rhythm pattern(s)) (Claim 1)	data that is based on one or more circadian rhythm patterns that relate to a driver's predisposition to sleepiness	"electronic data regarding those circadian processes of the specific vehicle driver which relate to sleep"
5	circadian rhythm pattern(s) (Claims 1 and 9)	A regular pattern in which the normal human body's biological or physiological activity varies with the time of day, over a 24-hour cycle. Also known as a biorhythm or body clock.	"physiological processes of the human driver or operator which vary with the time of day and occur in approximately 24-hour periods or cycles"

Term No.	Term to be Construed	Plaintiff's Construction	Defendants' Construction
6	operating model or algorithm (Claim 1)	software for computing a decision to provide a warning indication of driver sleepiness	Defendants contend that this clause is invalid under § 112 ¶ 2 as indefinite. Alternatively, it shall be construed as: Defendants contend that this clause is governed by § 112 ¶ 6 and accordingly identify the following structure(s) in the specification which correspond to the function of "operating" including one or more of: processor, memory, software, and associated algorithms as disclosed in one or more of Claim 1; Figs. 4–9; Fig. 21; Tables 8–15, 18, 20, and 24; col. 4, Lines 4–10; col. 8, Lines 29–33; col. 9, Lines 6–16, and equivalents thereof under 112 ¶ 6.
7	computational means for weighting the operational model according to time of day in relation to the driver or operator circadian rhythm pattern(s) and for deriving, from the weighted model, driver or operator sleepiness condition and producing an output determined thereby (Claim 1)	Construction Under Section 112, ¶6 Function: "weighting the operational model according to time of day in relation to the driver or operator circadian rhythm pattern(s)" and "deriving, from the weighted model, driver or operator sleepiness condition and producing an output determined thereby." Structure: processor(s) programmed with software to perform a software algorithm that includes the following steps: obtaining a value of driver predisposition to sleepiness based on the current time of day (in relation to circadian rhythm patterns); obtaining data from one or more sensory or driver inputs; applying weighting factors to the sensory inputs; calculating an adjusted value of driver predisposition to sleepiness; applying the adjusted value to one or more warning threshold values; and outputting a signal if one or more of the thresholds is exceeded; and all equivalents thereof.	Defendants contend that this clause is invalid under § 112 ¶ 2 as indefinite for not providing the specific algorithm(s) associated with the software. Alternatively, it shall be construed as: Function: "weighting the operational model according to time of day in relation to the driver or operator circadian rhythm pattern(s)" and "deriving, from the weighted model, driver or operator sleepiness condition and producing an output determined thereby." Defendants contend that this clause is governed by § 112 ¶ 6 and accordingly identify the following structure(s) in the specification which correspond to the computational means which must include the computer, memory, microprocessor programmed with software, and associated algorithm(s), as disclosed in one or more of the following: Figs. 1, 3–9, 15A–D, 16A–B, 17, 20 and 21; Tables 10–15, 18, 20, and 24; col. 2, Lines 43–47; col. 3, Lines 21–24; col. 3, Lines 39–42; col. 3, Lines 43–49; col. 4, Lines 50–58; col. 5, Lines 3–5; col. 6, Lines 37–39; col. 7, Lines, 62–67; col. 8, Lines 14–17; col. 9, Lines 60–64, and equivalents thereto under 112 ¶ 6.

Term No.	Term to be Construed	Plaintiff's Construction	Defendants' Construction
8	weighting (Claim 1)	Taking into account the relative significance of a factor in a computation	"assigning a quantitative value for the purpose of establishing the relative importance or magnitude of a factor in a computation"
9	weighted model (Claim 1)	refers to the same software used to perform the function of "weighting the operational model according to time of day," which is being interpreted in #7 above; no separate construction is required	No alternative construction is required so long as the "weighted model" refers to the weighted "operational model"
10	sleepiness condition (Claim 1)	a driver's condition or state of sleepiness, drowsiness or lack of alertness	"The state or condition of drowsiness or sleepiness of an individual driver"
12	a sensor for sensing a steering movement, about a reference position (Claim 9)	plaintiff contends that this is <u>not</u> a means-plus-function clause under Section 112, ¶6. Interpretation: A device that converts a driver's movement of the steering wheel to an electrical signal supplying data about the movement of the steering wheel.	Defendants contend that this clause is governed by § 112 ¶ 6 and accordingly identify the following structure(s) in the specification which correspond to the function of sensing a steering movement about a reference position: steering wheel movement sensor as disclosed in Figs. 20 and 21; Tables 1, 2, and 9; col. 8, Lines 41–43, software and associated algorithms, and equivalents under 112 ¶ 6.
13	time of day physiological reference profile (Claim 9)	data that is based on a human's predisposition to sleepiness depending on time of day	"electronic information about those physiological and circadian processes of the vehicle driver which relate to sleep and which occur in approximately 24-hour periods or cycles"
14	predisposition to sleepiness (Claim 9)	tendency or susceptibility to sleepiness, drowsiness or lack of alertness	"an inclination towards drowsiness or sleepiness resulting from the driver or operator's natural circadian rhythm pattern"

Term No.	Term to be Construed	Plaintiff's Construction	Defendants' Construction
15	computational means for computing steering transitions and weighing that computation according to time of day, to provide a warning indication of driver sleepiness. (Claim 9)	Construction under Section 112, ¶6 Function: "computing steering transitions and weighing that computation according to time of day." Structure: processor(s) programmed with software to perform a software algorithm that includes the following steps: using data from the steering movement sensor, determining the frequency of a driver's steering movements (changes in steering angle) and determining a value for any deficit from the expected frequency of an alert driver's steering movements; determining the amplitude of a driver's steering movements (extent of change in steering angle) and determining a value for any surfeit from the expected amplitude of an alert driver's steering movements; obtaining a value of driver predisposition to sleepiness based on the current time of day; calculating a value of driver predisposition to sleepiness taking into account the above values; applying one or more warning threshold values; and outputting a signal if one or more of the thresholds is exceeded to trigger a warning; and all equivalents thereof.	Defendants contend that this clause is invalid under § 112 ¶ 2 as indefinite for not providing the specific algorithm associated with the software. Alternatively, it shall be construed as: Function: "computing steering transitions" and "weighing that computation according to time of day" Defendants contend that this clause is governed by § 112 ¶ 6 and accordingly identify the following structure(s) in the specification which correspond to the computational means which must include the computer, memory, microprocessor programmed with software, and associated algorithms, as disclosed in one or more of the following: Figs. 1, 3–9, 15A–D, 16A–B, 17, 20, and 21; Tables 10–15, 18, 20, and 24; col. 2, Lines 43–47; col. 3, Lines 13-14; col. 3, Lines 39–42; col. 3, Lines 50-53; col. 3, Line 66; col. 4, Line 3; col. 8, Lines 10–17; col. 8, Lines 41–43; col. 9, Lines 60–64, and equivalents
16	steering transitions (Claim 9)	changes in steering wheel angle	This term renders the claim invalid for indefiniteness under § 112 ¶ 2. If the Court sees fit to construe this term, it should mean: "changes in the angular position of the steering wheel of a vehicle that result in a zero crossing"
17	weighing (Claim 9)	taking into account a factor in a computation	"Assigning a quantitative value for the purpose of establishing relative magnitude or importance"

C. LOCAL PATENT RULE 4.3(c) – SIGNIFICANT OR DISPOSITIVE CLAIM TERMS

In accordance with Local Patent Rule 4.3(c), the parties do not believe that any of the disputed claim terms will be case or claim dispositive, or substantially conducive to promoting settlement.

D. LOCAL PATENT RULE 4.3(d) – ANTICIPATED TIME NEEDED FOR CLAIM CONSTRUCTION HEARING

In accordance with Local Patent Rule 4.3(d), the parties agree and respectfully request that the claim construction hearing consist of attorney argument. At this time the parties do not expect to call any expert witnesses for live testimony at the claim construction hearing. The parties estimate that the claim construction hearing will require approximately 3 hours of attorney argument, with 90 minutes allotted to each side.

E. LOCAL PATENT RULE 4.3(e) – IDENTIFICATION OF ANTICIPATED WITNESSES FOR CLAIM CONSTRUCTION HEARING

In accordance with Local Patent Rule 4.3(e), the parties do not anticipate calling any witness in support of the parties' respective claim construction arguments.

Respectfully
submitted,

[Attorneys for Plaintiff]

[Attorneys for Defendants]

Dated: ____________________

IN THE UNITED STATES DISTRICT COURT
FOR THE DISTRICT OF NEW JERSEY

IBORMEITH IP, LLC, Plaintiff, v. MERCEDES-BENZ USA, LLC, and DAIMLER AG, Defendants.	Civil Action No. 10-CV-05378 (FSH) **SUPPLEMENTAL JOINT CLAIM CONSTRUCTION STATEMENT**

Plaintiff Ibormeith and Defendants Mercedes-Benz USA, LLC and Daimler AG respectfully submit the following Supplemental Joint Claim Construction and Prehearing Statement, pursuant to the Court's instructions during the March 26, 2012 telephonic status conference. This document supplements and amends the Original Statement, Docket No. 45-1, dated September 15, 2011.

A. LOCAL PATENT RULE 4.3(a) - CONSTRUCTION OF CLAIM TERMS UPON WHICH THE PARTIES AGREE

The parties continue to agree on the construction of the 11th term originally identified as requiring construction.

Term No.	Term to be Construed	Agreed Construction
11	warning indicator (Claim 1)	an audio and/or visual indication of sleepiness provided to the driver

B. LOCAL PATENT RULES 4.3(b) AND (c) - REVISED LIST OF CLAIM TERMS REQUIRING CONSTRUCTION

Pursuant to the Court's instructions during the March 26, 2012 telephonic status conference, the parties in the above-captioned matter have met-and-conferred to reduce the number of claim terms from U.S. Patent No. 6,313,749 (the '749 patent) requiring construction.

Without waiving any rights, the parties have agreed to remove from the disputed list eleven terms, specifically Term Nos. 1, 2, 4, 5, 8, 9, 10, 12, 13, 14 and 17, from the list in Docket 45-1. The following revised list contains the five remaining disputed terms, Term Nos. 3, 6, 7, 15, and 16 from the original filing. As requested, the parties have attached as Exhibit 1 a chart that lists the terms in order of significance. The revised chart adds the right column, which contains a brief statement of the significance of those terms. Defendants also added text to the column providing their proposed constructions of Term Nos. 7 and 15, which Defendants contend is based on the specification sections cited in the original construction. Plaintiff objects to the additions to Defendants' proposed constructions.

Dated: April 11, 2012

[Attorneys for Plaintiff] **[Attorneys for Defendants]**

NO.	TERM FOR CONSTRUCTION	PLAINTIFF'S CONSTRUCTION	DEFENDANT'S CONSTRUCTION	SIGNIFICANCE
7	Claim 1: "computational means for weighting the operational model according to time of day in relation to the driver or operator circadian rhythm pattern(s) and for deriving, from the weighted model, driver or operator sleepiness condition and producing an output determined thereby"	Construction Under Section 112, ¶ 6 Function: "weighting the operational model according to time of day in relation to the driver or operator circadian rhythm pattern(s)" and "deriving, from the weighted model, driver or operator sleepiness condition and producing an output determined thereby." Structure: processor(s) programmed with software to perform a software algorithm that includes the following steps: obtaining a value of driver predisposition to sleepiness based on the current time of day (in relation to circadian rhythm patterns); obtaining data from one or more sensory or driver inputs; applying weighting factors to the sensory inputs; calculating an adjusted value of driver predisposition to sleepiness; applying the adjusted value to one or more warning threshold values; and outputting a signal if one or more of the thresholds is exceeded; and all equivalents thereof	Defendants contend that this clause is invalid under § 112 ¶ 2 as indefinite for not providing the specific algorithm(s) associated with the software. Alternatively, it shall be construed under § 112 ¶ 6 as: Function: "weighting the operational model according to time of day in relation to the drive or operator circadian rhythm pattern(s)" and "deriving, from the weighted model, driver or operator sleepiness condition and producing an output determined thereby." Structure: computer, memory, microprocessor programmed with software, and the associated algorithms disclosed in the following locations in the specification and equivalents thereto: Figs. 1, 3–9, 15-21; Tables 1–16, 18–24; col. 2, Lines 43–47; col. 3, Lines 21–24, 39–49; col. 4, Lines 50–58; col. 5, Lines 3-5; col. 7, Lines 17–67; col. 8, Lines 1–9, 14–17; col. 9, lines 60–64. The specific algorithms partially disclosed in the cited portions of the specification being: **Algorithm A** 1) Obtain from Figure 3 a circadian score ("S circ") reflecting the driver's predisposition to sleepiness based on the time-of-day;	The "computational means" of claims 1 and 9 require construction as "means-plus-function" limitations under 35 U.S.C. § 112 ¶ 6. These limitations present the greatest level of complexity Defendants' contention that the clause is indefinite would, if adopted, invalidate claim 1. Defendants also believe that adoption of their alternate construction would support a motion for summary judgment of noninfringement of claim 1, but Plaintiff disagrees.

NO.	TERM FOR CONSTRUCTION	PLAINTIFF'S CONSTRUCTION	DEFENDANT'S CONSTRUCTION	SIGNIFICANCE
			2) Adjust the circadian score upward or downward -through addition or subtraction - to account for values reflecting: (i) the age of the driver; (ii) the sex of the driver; (iii) the amount of sleep the driver has had; and (iv) the temperature of the vehicle; 3) If the cumulative score is greater than or equal to "3," use a steering sensor to assess the condition of the road (monotonous or not) and adjust the cumulative score, up or down, accordingly; [Note: the specification does not disclose for Algorithm A how to determine whether a road is monotonous.] 4) Compare the weighted score to the "sleepiness warning thresholds" from Figure 17; 5)If the score exceeds the thresholds, issue a sleepiness warning to the driver. **<u>Algorithm B</u>** 1) Obtain a circadian score ("S circ") of between 0 and 1 that reflects a driver's baseline predisposition to sleepiness in relation to the time of day; [*Note: the specification does not disclose the method of scaling "S circ" between 0 and 1*] 2) Increase (but never decrease) the circadian score by adding a value of between 0 and 1 to	

NO.	TERM FOR CONSTRUCTION	PLAINTIFF'S CONSTRUCTION	DEFENDANT'S CONSTRUCTION	SIGNIFICANCE
			account for the seven factors associated with sleepiness reflected in Table 10: (i) ambient light; (ii) vehicle temperature; (iii) sleep history; (iv) the duration of the trip; (v) the presence of excessive amplitude in corrective steering movements; (vi) the absence of certain corrective steering movements; and (vii) deviation from expected vehicle acceleration and deceleration activity. The weighted score must be between 0 and 1. [*Note: the specification does not disclose the relative importance or value of the sleepiness factors*] 3) Compare the weighted score to one or more predetermined warning thresholds; [*Note: no thresholds are provided in the specification*] 4) Issue a sleepiness warning to the driver if the weighted score exceeds one or more predetermined thresholds and the driver has been operating the vehicle for more than a predetermined period of time. [*Note: the specification does not disclose the predetermined period of time*]	

15	Claim 9: "computational means for computing steering transitions and weighting that computation according to time of day, to provide a warning indication of driver sleepiness"	Construction under Section 112, ¶6 Function: "computing steering transitions and weighing that computation according to time of day." Structure: processor(s) programmed with software algorithm that includes the following steps: using data from the steering movement sensor, determining the frequency of a driver's steering movements (changes in steering angle) and determining a value for any deficit from the expected frequency of an alert driver's steering movements; determining the amplitude of a driver's steering movements (extent of change in steering angle) and determining a value for any surfeit from the expected amplitude of an alert driver's steering movements; obtaining a value of driver predisposition to sleepiness based on the current time of day; calculating a value of driver predisposition to sleepiness taking into account the above values; applying one or more warning threshold values; and outputting a signal if one or more of the thresholds is exceeded to trigger a warning; and all equivalents thereof.	Defendants contend that this clause is invalid under §112 ¶ 2 as indefinite for not providing the specific algorithm associated with the software. Alternatively, it shall be construed under §112 ¶ 6 as: Function: "computing steering transitions" and "weighing that computation according to time of day" Structure: computer, memory, microprocessor programmed with software, and the associated algorithms disclosed in the following locations in the specification, and equivalents thereto: Figures 1, 3–9, 15A–D, 17, 18, 19, 20, 21; Tables 1–4, 6–16, 18–20, 22–24; col. 2, Lines 43–47; col. 3, Lines 13–14; col. 39–42; col. 3, Lines 50–53; col. 3, Line 66 to col. 4, Line 3; col. 4, Lines 50–58; col. 5, Lines 3–5; col. 8, Lines 10–17; col. 8, Lines 35 to col. 9, Line 19; col. 9, Lines 60–64. The specific algorithms partially disclosed in the cited portions of the specification being: **Algorithm C** 1) Establish a reference value reflecting the number of times an alert driver turns the steering wheel across the straight-ahead position ("zero crossings"); 2) Establish a reference value reflecting a measure of the amplitude over time of steering movements by an alert driver;	The "computational means" of claims 1 and 9 require construction as "means plus-function" limitations under 35 U.S.C. §112 ¶ 6. These limitations present the greatest level of complexity. Defendants' contention that the clause is indefinite would, if adopted, invalidate claim 9. Defendants also believe that adoption of their alternate construction would support a motion for summary judgment of noninfringement of claim 9, but Plaintiff disagrees.

			3) Set the straight-ahead steering position as a reference position; 4) Using a steering sensor, calculate a current number of zero crossings over a period of time; [*Note: the specification does not disclose the period of time*] 5) Using a steering sensor, calculate a measure of the current amplitude of steering movements over a period of time; [*Note: the specification does not disclose the period of time*] 6) Compare the number of current zero crossings to the reference value; 7) Compare the current measure of amplitude of steering movements to the reference value; 8) Compare current variability in the amplitude of steering movements to the referenced value; 9) Issue a sleepiness warning if two of the following three conditions occur: (i) the current number of zero crossings is "fewer" than the reference value; (ii) the current measure of amplitude steering movements is "larger" than the reference value; (iii) the current variability in the measure of amplitude is "more" than the reference value. [*Note: claim 9 requires weighting according to time of day, but the specification does not disclose a method for performing such weighting in Algorithm C*]	

			Algorithm D I) Establish a reference value reflecting the number of times the specific driver, when alert, turns the steering wheel across a dynamic reference position (“zero crossings”); 2) Establish a reference value reflecting a measure of the amplitude of steering movements over time by the specific driver; 3) Establish a dynamic reference position, called “ZeroWheel,” according to formula in Table 7; 4) Calculate the current number of times the steering wheel crosses the “Zero Wheel” position during a period of time; 5) Calculate the current measure of the amplitude of the steering movements in relation to the “Zero Wheel” position over a period of time; 6) Calculate the difference between the current number of zero crossings and the reference value to determine the deficit, if any, in current zero crossings; 7) Calculate the difference between the current measure of amplitude of steering movements and the reference value to determine the excess (“surfeit”), if any, in the current measure of amplitude; 8) Weight the results of steps (6) and (7) according to the formulas for “S zerox” and “S rms” in Table 10;	

			9) Add the values of "S zerox" and "S rms" to a circadian score ("S circ") of between 0 and 1, which circadian score is based on the time of day; [*Note: the specification does not disclose the method of scaling "S circ" between 0 and J*] 10) Issue a sleepiness warning to the driver if the sum of step (9) exceeds one or more predetermined thresholds and the driver has been operating the vehicle for more than a predetermined period of time. [*note: no thresholds are provided in the specification*]	
16	Claim 9: "steering transitions"	Changes in steering wheel angle	This term renders the claim invalid for indefiniteness under § 112 ¶2. If the Court sees fit to construe this term, it should mean: "changes in the angular position of the steering wheel of a vehicle that result in a zero crossing"	Defendants' contention that the clause is indefinite would, if adopted, invalidate claim 9. Defendants also believe that adoption of their alternate construction would support a motion for summary judgment of noninfringement of claim 9, but Plaintiff disagrees.
6	Claim 1: "a vehicle or machine operating model or algorithm"	Software for computing a decision to provide a warning indication of driver sleepiness	Defendants contend that this clause is invalid under § 112 ¶2 as indefinite. Alternatively, it shall be construed as: Defendants contend that this clause is invalid under § 112 ¶6 and accordingly identify the following structure(s) in the specification which correspond to the function of "operating" including one or more of: processor, memory, software, and associated algorithms as disclosed in one or more of	Defendants' contention that the clause is indefinite would, if adopted, invalidate claim 1. Defendants also believe that adoption of their alternate construction would support a motion for summary judgment of noninfringement

			Claim 1; Figs. 4–9; Fig. 21; Tables 8–15, 18, 20, and 24; col. 4, Lines 4–10; col. 8, Lines 29–33; col. 9, Lines 6–16, and equivalents thereof under § 112 ¶6.	of claim 1, but Plaintiff disagrees.
3	Claim 1: "operational model"	computer software that includes a physiological reference model of driver circadian rhythm pattern(s) and a vehicle operating model or algorithm	Defendants contend that this clause is invalid under § 112 ¶2 as indefinite. Alternatively, it shall be construed as: Defendants contend that this clause is Governed by § 112 ¶6 and accordingly identify the following structure(s) in the specification which correspond to the operating function covering the structure of: processor, computer software, memory, and associated algorithms containing a physiological reference model of driver circadian rhythm patterns and a vehicle operating model or algorithm, as disclosed in the specification and equivalents thereof under § 112 ¶6.	Defendants' contention that the clause is indefinite would, if adopted, invalidate claim 1. Defendants also believe that adoption of their alternate construction would support a motion for summary judgment of noninfringement of claim 1, but Plaintiff disagrees.

Chapter 6
Summary Judgment

Effective utilization of the summary judgment process is especially important in patent cases because such cases present so many complex issues. Summary judgment can play a critical role in narrowing or simplifying the issues, thereby promoting settlement or simplifying the trial. On the other hand, the summary judgment process in a patent case can put a significant burden on the court, particularly if the parties file numerous, voluminous motions.

The first part of this chapter discusses areas in which courts can promote efficiency in the summary judgment process, and recommends approaches courts have found effective. It also discusses the types of motions that are more and less suited to resolution via summary judgment. The second part of this chapter discusses various substantive issues that often arise during the summary judgment process in patent cases.

6.1 Managing the Summary Judgment Process

In general, effective management of the summary judgment process in patent cases requires an understanding of the types of issues that drive most patent cases and how they typically unfold over the life of a case. It also requires the court to be assertive in case management.

As with any case, the timing of summary judgment motions can be critical. If summary judgment proceedings are held too early for a given case, questions of fact that would have been resolved at a later stage preclude summary judgment. However, deferring summary judgment too long risks wasting the time and resources of the parties and the court on issues that limited discovery could have resolved.

6.1.1 Distinguishing Questions of Law from Questions of Fact

The court "shall grant summary judgment if the movant shows that there is no genuine dispute as to any material fact and the movant is entitled to judgment as a matter of law." Fed. R. Civ. P. 56(a). Thus, pure questions of law, mixed questions of law and fact on which there is no genuine dispute as to any material fact, and undisputed questions of fact are amenable to summary adjudication. *See generally* Gary M. Hnath & Timothy A. Molino, *The Roles of Judges and Juries in Patent Litigation*, 19 Fed. Cir. B.J. 15 (2009–2010); Kevin Casey, Jade Camara, & Nancy Wright, *Standards of Appellate Review in the Federal Circuit: Substance and Semantics*, 11 Fed. Cir. B.J. 279 (2001–2002).

These distinctions are especially subtle in patent litigation, reflecting the complex interplay of fact and law. Furthermore, even though the ultimate claim construction determination is a question of law potentially based on subsidiary questions of fact, *Teva Pharmaceuticals USA, Inc. v. Sandoz, Inc.*, 135 S. Ct. 831 (2015), the subsidiary facts are within the province of the court, *Markman v. Westview Instruments, Inc.*, 517 U.S. 370 (1996), thereby expanding the range of issues that can be resolved on summary judgment. *See* J. Jonas Anderson & Peter S. Menell, *Restoring the Fact/Law Distinction in Patent Claim Construction*, 109 Nw. U. L. Rev. Online 187 (2015).

Table 6.1, Table 6.2, Table 6.3, and Table 6.4 summarize the characterization of patent issues as questions of law, questions of fact, questions of law that are based on underlying questions of fact, and unresolved characterizations. Among the most salient, yet unresolved, fact/law issues is patentable subject matter (§ 101). This area had lain dormant, but has been revived by four recent Supreme Court decisions—*Bilski*, *Mayo*, *Myriad*, and *Alice*. *See* § 14.3.1. While providing conceptual frameworks, these decisions do not provide clear guidance on managing the resolution of patentable subject matter disputes. In particular, it is unclear whether Step 2 of the *Mayo/Alice* framework—whether the claim contains an inventive concept sufficient to transform the ineligible law of nature, natural, phenomena, or abstract idea into a patent-eligible application of the ineligible subject (or, alternatively, whether the application is merely routine or conventional)—turns on factual underpinnings.

Table 6.1
Patent Issues—Questions of Law

Doctrine	Authority
Claim Construction of § 112(f) Claims	*Cardiac Pacemakers, Inc. v. Saint Jude Med., Inc.*, 296 F.3d 1106, 1113 (Fed. Cir. 2002) (means plus function claims); *Linear Tech. Corp. v. Impala Linear Corp.*, 379 F.3d 1311, 1318 (Fed. Cir. 2004) (determining whether a claim language should be interpreted as a mean plus function limitation)
Implied License	*Monsanto Co. v. Scruggs*, 459 F.3d 1328, 1336 (Fed. Cir. 2006)
Repair or Reconstruction	*Fuji Photo Film Co. v. Int'l Trade Comm'n*, 474 F.3d 1281, 1289 (Fed. Cir. 2007)

Doctrine	Authority
Doctrine of Equivalents—Sufficiency of Particularized Elements	*Malta v. Schulmerich Carillons, Inc.*, 952 F.2d 1320, 1331 (Fed. Cir. 1991) (observing that "before a case may be submitted to a jury, a patentee's proof must include substantial evidence of separate and explicit comparison of the claimed and accused devices as to each of the three *Graver Tank* requirements); *Lear Siegler, Inc. v. Sealy Mattress Co.*, 873 F.2d 1422, 1426 (Fed. Cir. 1989); *see also Warner-Jenkinson Co. v. Hilton Davis Chem. Co.*, 520 U.S. 17, 29 (1997) (holding that "[e]ach element contained in a patent claim is deemed material to defining the scope of the patented invention" and that the doctrine of equivalents "must be applied to individual elements of the claim, not to the invention as a whole")
Exception to Doctrine of Equivalents—Prosecution History Estoppel	*Cybor Corp. v. FAS Techs. Inc.*, 138 F.3d 1448, 1460 (Fed. Cir. 1998) (en banc); *Festo Corp. v. Shoketsu Kinzoku Kogyo Kabushiki Co., Ltd.*, 344 F.3d 1359, 1367 (Fed. Cir. 2003)
Exception to Doctrine of Equivalents—"All Elements" Rule/Claim Vitiation Doctrine	*Deere & Co. v. Bush Hog, LLC*, 703 F.3d 1349, 1356–57 (Fed. Cir. 2012); *Charles Mach. Works, Inc. v. Vermeer Mfg. Co.*, 723 F.3d 1376, 1380 (Fed. Cir. 2013)
Exception to Doctrine of Equivalents—Disclosed but Unclaimed Embodiments Dedicated to the Public	*Johnson & Johnston Assocs. Inc. v. R.E. Serv. Co.*, 285 F.3d 1046, 1051–52 (Fed. Cir. 2002) (en banc)
Exception to Doctrine of Equivalents—Scope of Equivalents Cannot Encompass Prior Art	*Wilson Sporting Goods Co. v. David Geoffrey & Assocs.*, 904 F.2d 677 (Fed. Cir. 1990)
Double Patenting	*In re Berg*, 140 F.3d 1428, 1432 (Fed. Cir. 1998); *Georgia-Pacific Corp. v. U.S. Gypsum Co.*, 195 F.3d 1322, 1326 (Fed. Cir. 1999)
Patent Misuse	*B. Braun Med., Inc. v. Abbott Labs.*, 124 F.3d 1419, 1427 (Fed. Cir. 1997) (observing that "the patent misuse doctrine is an extension of the equitable doctrine of unclean hands")
Laches	*A.C. Aukerman Co. v. R.L. Chaides Constr. Co.*, 960 F.2d 1020, 1028 (Fed. Cir. 1992) (en banc); *but see SCA Hygiene Aktiebolag v. First Quality Baby Prods., LLC*, No. 13-1564, 2014 U.S. App. LEXIS 24697, 2014 WL 7460970 (Fed. Cir. Dec. 30, 2014) (granting en banc review that may revisit *Aukerman*)
Equitable Estoppel	*A.C. Aukerman Co. v. R.L. Chaides Constr. Co.*, 960 F.2d 1020, 1028 (Fed. Cir. 1992) (en banc)
Assignor Estoppel	*Carroll Touch, Inc. v. Electro Mech. Sys., Inc.*, 15 F.3d 1573, 1579 (Fed. Cir. 1993)

Doctrine	Authority
Common-Law Experimental Use	*Madey v. Duke Univ.*, 307 F.3d 1351, 1358 (Fed. Cir. 2002)
Injunctive Relief	*eBay Inc. v. MercExchange, LLC*, 547 U.S. 388 (2006)

Table 6.2
Patent Issues—Questions of Fact

Doctrine	Authority
Utility	*Juicy Whip, Inc. v. Orange Bang, Inc.*, 185 F.3d 1364, 1365 (Fed. Cir. 1999)
Novelty (Anticipation) § 102	*Orion IP, LLC v. Hyundai Motor Am.*, 605 F.3d 967, 974 (Fed. Cir. 2010)
Derivations § 102(f)	*Gambro Lundia AB v. Baxter Healthcare Corp.*, 110 F.3d 1573, 1576 (Fed. Cir. 1997)
Written Description § 112	*Fujikawa v. Wattanasin*, 93 F.3d 1559, 1569–70 (Fed. Cir. 1996); *Eiselstein v. Frank*, 52 F.3d 1035, 1038 (Fed. Cir. 1995) ("Compliance with the 'written description' requirement is a question of fact, to be reviewed under the clearly erroneous standard.")
Literal Infringement	*Markman v. Westview Instruments, Inc.*, 517 U.S. 370, 384 (1996); *DSC Commc'n Corp. v. Pulse Commc'ns, Inc.*, 170 F.3d 1354, 1368 (Fed. Cir. 1999) (whether an accused device performs the specific function associated with the § 112(f) means limitation); *In re Hayes Microcomputer Prods.*, 982 F.2d 1527, 1541 (Fed. Cir. 1992); *Moleculon Research Corp. v. CBS, Inc.*, 793 F.2d 1261, 1269–70 (Fed. Cir. 1986)
Doctrine of Equivalents—Determining Equivalency	*Warner-Jenkinson Co. v. Hilton Davis Chem. Co.*, 520 U.S. 17, 38 (1997) (although "noting various legal limitations on the application of the doctrine of equivalents are to be determined by the court, either on a pretrial motion for partial summary judgment or on a motion for judgment as a matter of law at the close of the evidence and after the jury verdict," such as prosecution history estoppel, "all elements" rule, "disclosed by unclaimed embodiments" rule, and rule that scope of equivalents cannot encompass prior art)

Doctrine	Authority
Patent Exhaustion	*Cornell Univ. v. Hewlett-Packard Co.*, 2008 WL 5671886 (N.D.N.Y. 2008) (Rader, J., sitting as a district judge) (Reasoning that "when determining whether a doctrine is legal or equitable, the focus is not solely on the nature of the remedy. The inquiry must also consider the origin of the doctrine. Although case law is scarce with respect to the nature of the patent exhaustion doctrine, the Supreme Court has recognized that patent exhaustion has its roots in the patent law statutory framework. *Bloomer v. McQuewan*, 55 U.S. 539, 549 (1852) ('When he sells the exclusive privilege of making or vending it for use in a particular place, the purchaser buys a portion of the franchise which the patent confers.'). In other words, when the patentee has given up his right to exclude, there is no longer a statutory basis for the patentee to impose restrictions on the subsequent sale or use of the article. Given this statutory framework, it follows that patent exhaustion is a legal doctrine, rather than an equitable one.")
Reverse Doctrine of Equivalents	*Hartness Int'l, Inc. v. Simplimatic Eng'g Co.*, 819 F.2d 1100, 1110, 2 U.S.P.Q.2d 1826, 1833 (Fed. Cir. 1987); *SRI Int'l v. Matsushita Elec. Corp.*, 775 F.2d 1107, 1125 (Fed. Cir. 1985)
Actual Damages	*Cybor Corp. v. FAS Techs., Inc.*, 138 F.3d 1448, 1461 (Fed. Cir. 1998) (en banc)
Lost Profits	*Rite-Hite Corp. v. Kelley Co.*, 56 F.3d 1538, 1543–44 (Fed. Cir. 1995) (en banc)
Reasonable Royalty	*Unisplay, S.A. v. Am. Elec. Sign Co.*, 69 F.3d 512, 517 (Fed. Cir. 1995) ("The determination of the amount of damages based on a reasonable royalty is an issue of fact.")
Willful Infringement—Factual Components	*WBIP, LLC v. Kohler Co.*, __ F.3d __ (Fed. Cir. July 19, 2016) ("We do not interpret [the Supreme Court's decision in *Halo Electronics, Inc., v. Pulse Electronics, Inc.*, No. 14-1513 (June 3, 2016)] as changing the established law that the factual components of the willfulness question should be resolved by the jury" (footnote omitted)). *See* § 7.3.4.5.

Table 6.3
Patent Issues—Questions of Law Based on Underlying Questions of Fact

Doctrine	Authority
Claim Construction in General	*Teva Pharm. USA, Inc. v. Sandoz, Inc.*, 135 S. Ct. 831 (2015) (standard of appellate review); *Markman v. Westview Instruments, Inc.*, 517 U.S. 370 (1996)
Indefinite Claiming § 112(b)	J. Jonas Anderson & Peter S. Menell, *Restoring the Fact/Law Distinction in Patent Claim Construction*, 109 Nw. U. L. Rev. Online 187, 198–200 (2015) (discussing the interplay of claim construction and indefiniteness post-*Teva*); § 5.2.5.2
On-Sale Bar § 102(b)	*Del. Valley Floral Grp., Inc. v. Shaw Rose Nets, LLC*, 597 F.3d 1374, 1379 (Fed. Cir. 2010); *Gemmy Indus. Corp. v. Chrisha Creations Ltd.*, 452 F.3d 1353, 1358 (Fed. Cir. 2006); *Robotic Vision Sys., Inc. v. View Eng'g, Inc.*, 249 F.3d 1307, 1310 (Fed. Cir. 2001) ("Whether an invention was on sale within the meaning of § 102(b) is a question of law that this court reviews *de novo*; however, factual findings underlying a district court's conclusions are subject to the clearly erroneous standard of review.")
Public Use Bar § 102(b)	*Clock Spring, L.P. v. Wrapmaster, Inc.*, 560 F.3d 1317, 1324 (Fed. Cir. 2009); *Motionless Keyboard Co. v. Microsoft Corp.*, 486 F.3d 1376, 1383 (Fed. Cir. 2007)
Printed Publication Bar § 102(b)	*Orion IP, LLC v. Hyundai Motor Am.*, 605 F.3d 967, 974 (Fed. Cir. 2010); *ResQNet.com v. Lansa, Inc.*, 594 F.3d 860, 865 (Fed. Cir. 2010)
Priority of Invention § 102(g)	*Cooper v. Goldfarb*, 154 F.3d 1321, 1327 (Fed. Cir. 1998) ("Priority, conception, and reduction to practice are questions of law which are based on subsidiary factual findings."); *Fujikawa v. Wattanasin*, 93 F.3d 1559, 1564, 1567 (Fed. Cir. 1996) ("The ultimate determination of reduction to practice is a question of law"; "Suppression or concealment is a question of law which we review de novo."); *Checkpoint Sys., Inc. v. U.S. Int'l Trade Comm'n*, 54 F.3d 756, 761 (Fed. Cir. 1995) ("As the parties asserting invalidity, respondents at the ITC bore the burden of establishing, by clear and convincing evidence, facts which support the ultimate legal conclusion of invalidity under § 102(g)."); *Tex. Instruments, Inc. v. Int'l Trade Comm'n*, 871 F.2d 1054, 1068 (Fed. Cir. 1989) (due diligence for priority of invention under 35 U.S.C. § 102(g) is a question of fact)

Doctrine	Authority
Nonobviousness § 103	*KSR Int'l, Co. v. Teleflex, Inc.*, 550 U.S. 398, 427 (2007) ("The ultimate judgment of obviousness is a legal determination."); *Daiichi Sankyo Co., Ltd. v. Apotex, Inc.*, 501 F.3d 1254, 1256 (Fed. Cir. 2007); *Winner Int'l Royalty Corp. v. Wang*, 202 F.3d 1340, 1349 (Fed. Cir. 2000) ("What a reference teaches and whether it teaches toward or away from the claimed invention are questions of fact.") (quoting *In re Bell*, 991 F.2d 781, 784 (Fed. Cir. 1993)); *Sibia Neurosciences, Inc. v. Cadus Pharm. Corp.*, 225 F.3d 1349, 1356 (Fed. Cir. 2000) ("Determining whether there is a suggestion or motivation to modify a prior art reference is one aspect of determining the scope and content of the prior art, a fact question subsidiary to the ultimate conclusion of obviousness."); *Graham v. John Deere Co.*, 383 U.S. 1, 17 (1966) (there are four factual questions underlying the obviousness determination: (1) the scope and content of the prior art is one of the four underlying fact; (2) differences between the subject matter claimed and the prior art; (3) level of ordinary skill in the art; and (4) objective indicia of nonobviousness (secondary considerations))
Prior Inventor	*Solvay S.A. v. Honeywell Int'l, Inc.*, 622 F.3d 1367, 1375 (Fed. Cir. 2010); *Monsanto Co. v. Mycogen Plant Sci., Inc.*, 261 F.3d 1356, 1362 (Fed. Cir. 2001)
Inventorship	*Sewell v. Walters*, 21 F.3d 411, 415 (Fed. Cir. 1994) (inventorship is a question of law with "any facts found . . . in reaching an inventorship holding . . . reviewed for clear error"); *Ethicon, Inc. v. United States Surgical Corp.*, 135 F.3d 1456, 1460 (Fed. Cir. 1998); *Hess v. Adv. Cardiovascular Sys., Inc.*, 106 F.3d 976, 980 (Fed. Cir. 1997) (whether an inventor is improperly named or improperly omitted is a question of fact)
Enablement § 112	*Alza Corp. v. Andrx Pharm., LLC.*, 603 F.3d 935, 939 (Fed. Cir. 2010); *Ortho-McNeil Pharm, Inc. v. Mylan Labs., Inc.*, 520 F.3d 1358, 1365 (Fed. Cir. 2008); *Quaker City Gear Works, Inc. v. Skil Corp.*, 747 F.2d 1446, 1453–54 (Fed. Cir. 1984)
Estoppel Based on Standard Setting	*Rambus Inc. v. Infineon Techs. AG*, 318 F.3d 1081, 1087 n.3 (Fed. Cir. 2003)
Inequitable Conduct	*Therasense, Inc. v. Becton, Dickinson & Co.*, 649 F.3d 1276 (Fed. Cir. 2011) (en banc)

Doctrine	Authority
Enhanced Damages § 284	*Halo Electronics, Inc., v. Pulse Electronics, Inc.*, No. 14-1513 (Supreme Court June 3, 2016) (Although the ultimate resolution is for the court, the decision does not squarely address whether any role remains for the jury). The Federal Circuit has since ruled that the factual components of the willfulness questions should be resolved by the jury. *See WBIP, LLC v. Kohler Co.*, __ F.3d __ (Fed. Cir. July 19, 2016); § 7.3.4.5.

Table 6.4
Patent Issues—Unresolved Characterization

Doctrine	Authority
Statutory Subject Matter § 101	*Mayo Collaborative Servs. v. Prometheus Labs., Inc.*, 132 S. Ct. 1289 (2012); *Assoc. for Molecular Pathology v. Myriad Genetics, Inc.*, 133 S. Ct. 2107 (2013); *Alice Corp. Pty. Ltd. v. CLS Bank Int'l*, 134 S. Ct. 2347 (2014); *Accenture Global Servs., GmbH v. Guidewire Software, Inc.*, 728 F.3d 1336, 1340–41 (Fed. Cir. 2014)
Structural Equivalents Under § 112(f)	*Lockheed Martin Corp. v. Space Sys./Loral, Inc.*, 324 F.3d 1308, 1319 (Fed. Cir. 2003) ("Once a court establishes that a means-plus-function limitation is at issue, it must identify and construe that limitation, thereby determining what the claimed function is, and what structures disclosed in the written description correspond to the 'means' for performing that function."); *Vulcan Eng'g Co. v. Fata Aluminum, Inc.*, 278 F.3d 1366, 1373–76 (Fed. Cir. 2002) (holding that determining a corresponding structure, which includes equivalents to the disclosed structures, is a matter of claim construction); *but see In re Bond*, 910 F.2d 831, 833 (Fed. Cir. 1990) (observing that "structural equivalency under section 112(f) is a question of fact") (citing *Pennwalt Corp. v. Durand-Wayland*, 833 F.2d 931, 933–34 (Fed. Cir. 1987) (en banc)); *Asyst Techs., Inc. v. Empak, Inc.*, 268 F.3d 1364, 1373 (Fed. Cir. 2001) (explaining that whether an accused structure is equivalent to the disclosed structure for purposes of § 112(f) is a question of fact)

6.1.2 Summary Judgment and Claim Construction

Claim construction plays a central role in scheduling and managing summary judgment motions. Generally, the pretrial issues requiring the largest investment of judicial resources in a patent case are claim construction and summary judgment. Furthermore, most of the weighty issues in a patent case—the technical aspects of infringement and most allegations of invalidity—often depend on claim construction. As a result, summary judgment on the main issues in a patent case (infringement and validity) generally cannot be resolved without construing at least some disputed claim terms. For this reason, most courts construe at least the disputed claim terms that the parties have signaled are dispositive of infringement and/or invalidity issues before considering summary judgment motions. Tackling both claim construction and summary judgment at the same time can be daunting, and taking them a step at a time may be prudent in certain cases.

In cases presenting multiple similar and interrelated claim construction disputes, which can generally be resolved using similar evidence, considerable efficiency results from addressing all claim construction issues together in a single proceeding. Resolving claim construction disputes does not by itself resolve a case, unless it fosters settlement or the parties stipulate that claim construction is entirely dispositive of the infringement allegations. Moreover, not all claim construction disputes are essential to resolving a case—sometimes construing just a single disputed claim term is all that is needed to decide a case-dispositive summary judgment motion. In those situations, it can be inefficient to resolve all claim construction disputes before considering summary judgment motions that could obviate further trial court proceedings. Assertive case management can help the court and the parties identify the best approach for each particular case.

The recommendations that follow reflect two guiding principles: (1) summary judgment motions that turn entirely or principally on claim construction should be decided concurrently with claim construction, and (2) where genuine opportunities to resolve or narrow a case early through summary judgment exist, the parties and the court should take advantage of them. Collectively, these recommendations provide a framework for early ("first-track" and "off-track") summary judgment motions through which courts can analyze the specific facts of a case and identify when such motion practice can resolve or substantially narrow the case.

6.1.3 Recommended Dual-Track Approach to Summary Judgment

The tension between devoting judicial and party resources to claim construction while simultaneously preparing for dispositive motions can be productively resolved in many cases by using a dual-track approach to the summary judgment process. On the first (expedited) track are motions that depend primarily on claim construction. On the second track are motions that require resolution of substantial issues beyond claim construction. In some cases, it may be worthwhile to consider summary judgment outside either of these tracks—what we refer to as "off-track" summary judgment motions. Figure 6.1 illustrates the tracks along a timeline.

Figure 6.1
Multitrack Motions for Summary Judgment (MSJ) Process for Patent Cases

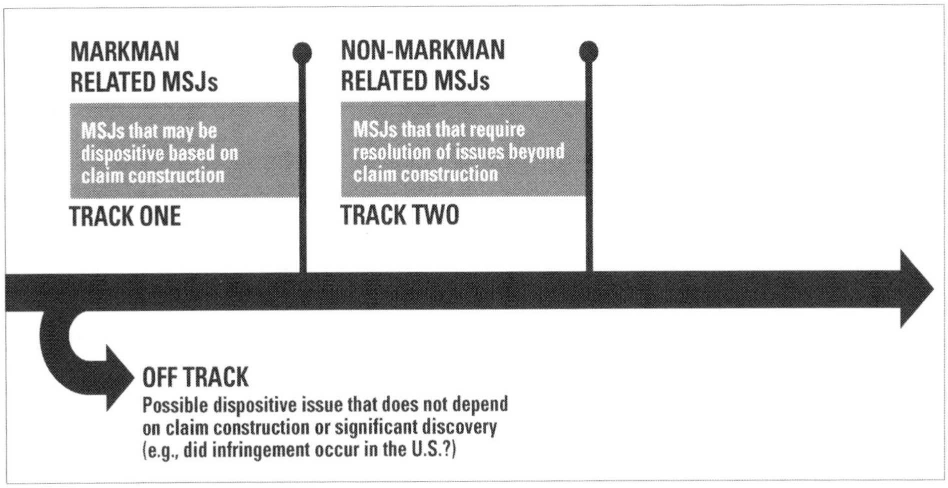

6.1.3.1 "First-Track" Summary Judgment Motions

Since "first-track" motions are based on the resolution of claim construction issues, they most often seek summary judgment of noninfringement. For example, in *Planet Bingo, LLC v. Gametech International, Inc.*, 472 F.3d 1338 (Fed. Cir. 2006), the claims at issue required "establishing a predetermined combination as a winning combination." *Id.* at 1340. The accused bingo machines determined winning combinations after the bingo game began. The parties disputed whether this could be encompassed by the claim term "predetermined." The district court construed "predetermined" to mean a determination made before the game began. This precluded literal infringement. Based on this construction and a finding that making a determination *after* the bingo game began could not be equivalent to making the determination *before* the game began, the district court granted summary judgment of noninfringement. The Federal Circuit affirmed. *Id.* at 1338. In *Planet Bingo*, all that needed to be resolved was the construction of "predetermined" and the issue of what could be "equivalent" to "predetermined"—all other disputes, claim construction or otherwise, were mooted. *See also, e.g., Schoenhaus v. Genesco, Inc.*, 440 F.3d 1354, 1356 (Fed. Cir. 2006) (affirming issuance of a "carefully crafted summary judgment opinion" that "construed two limitations of claim 1 of the patent" in lieu of a claim construction order).

Owing to the interrelationship between claim construction and first-track motions, most first-track motions should be resolved as a part of, or in temporal proximity to, the claim construction process. Courts should first determine whether there are any issues that may be resolved by the construction of a single term or a small set of terms. Where such an issue exists, claim construction and first-track motions should be addressed concurrently. Claim construction is often complex. Counterintuitively, considering first-track motions concurrently with claim construction can *simplify* the claim construction process by focusing the disputes and providing better context with which to understand them. It can also significantly reduce the expenditure of judicial and party resources by eliminating the need to consider all of the parties' claim construction disputes. Indeed, waiting to address such motions until long after claim construction eliminates the potential efficiency of early resolution of the case based on the construction of a single term or a small set of terms. If the court does not prioritize construing crucial terms on which summary judgment could be rendered, the court may address most or all of the claim construction disputes, only to find that only one of those disputes actually mattered to the resolution of the case.

Another benefit of hearing first-track summary judgment motions with claim construction is that it can give the court context for understanding the parties' claim construction disputes. Technically, the accused product is not a factor in claim construction. *Scripps Clinic & Research Found. v. Genentech, Inc.*, 927 F.2d 1565, 1580 (Fed. Cir. 1991) ("The words of the claims are construed independent of the accused product."). Nonetheless, the Federal Circuit has expressly directed district judges to construe claims with an eye to the ultimate issues and disputes in a case. *Id.* ("Of course the particular accused product (or process) is kept in mind, for it is efficient to focus on the construction of only the disputed elements or limitations of the claims."). Indeed, it is "highly undesirable" to consider claim construction issues "without knowledge of the accused devices," *Mass. Inst. of Tech. v. Abacus Software*, 462 F.3d 1344, 1350 (Fed. Cir. 2006), because they provide the "proper context for an accurate claim construction." *Lava Trading, Inc. v. Sonic Trading Mgmt. LLC*, 445 F.3d 1348, 1350 (Fed. Cir. 2006). Summary judgment briefing can also reveal the motives underlying claim construction disputes. Of course, information about the issues in the case need not be provided to the court by summary judgment motions. For example, the court can obtain this information through a tutorial, at a case-management conference, or through the claim construction briefing or hearing.

An alternative is to hear first-track motions prior to the normal claim construction process. If the court determines that a case-dispositive issue turns on the construction of a limited number of terms, it will often make sense to allow a party to file a first-track motion on that issue at an earlier stage of the case and conduct a "mini-*Markman*" in parallel to construe only the terms on which the motion depends. Allowing this flexibility, where the party seeking to file the motion demonstrates that the motion is both viable and likely to resolve or substantially narrow the case, can dramatically reduce the court's (and the parties') investment of time and resources in the case.

6.1.3.2 "Second-Track" Summary Judgment Motions

"Second-track" summary judgment motions involve substantial issues beyond claim construction, and therefore should not normally be considered as part of the claim construction process. Claim construction issues and first-track motions often involve a common set of legal principles and evidence. It makes sense to consider them together. Second-track summary judgment motions involve legal principles and evidence above and beyond the underlying claim construction issues. Moreover, as discussed previously, most courts find that it is best to resolve claim construction issues midway through a case, both to facilitate settlement and so that the parties can prepare for trial knowing what the claim construction is. *See* § 5.1.1. Unless the second-track motion is straightforward and unaffected by claim construction (for example, a challenge to standing, *see* § 2.2.1), making the effort to consider a second-track summary judgment motion before issuing a claim construction order diverts judicial resources from that goal.

6.1.3.3 Implementing a Dual-Track Approach to Summary Judgment

To resolve cases with this dual-track approach, the court must distinguish between the tracks and enforce the distinction. Because of their complexity or the specific facts at issue, some cases do not present realistic opportunities to implement a dual-track approach: claim construction might not drive the dispute; there may be no issues that can be resolved before fact discovery is completed; or factual disputes might obscure those issues at the outset of the case. Courts implementing a dual-track approach can rely on submissions and dialogue with the parties to overcome this latter hurdle. The court must manage the case actively and set expectations early, so that any potential first-track summary judgment motions are identified promptly, vetted by the court to determine whether they are indeed first-track motions, and ultimately briefed prior to or in parallel with the claim construction process. This helps ensure that Fed. R. Civ. P. 56(d) issues do not derail the court's ability to grant a meritorious first-track motion and dispose of the case early.

An essential component of the dual-track process is early notice to the parties of the procedure the court intends to follow. The court should explain the first-track motion concept to the parties in a standing order for patent cases, at the initial case-management conference, or both. Setting proper expectations is especially important where the local rules of a court limit the total number of summary judgment motions or the total number of pages that may be filed with respect to summary judgment motions. For a dual-track approach to be effective, the parties need to know, for example, whether bringing a first-track motion will impede their ability to file a second-track motion later in the case.

To manage the case efficiently, the court should also set a deadline in the case schedule for a summary judgment motion on the first track issues. To avoid unfairness and/or conflicts with Fed. R. Civ. P. 56(d), there should also be a deadline for providing notice to the other party of the basis for any planned first-track motion, including at least the identity of any witnesses who will submit evidence in support of the motion. These deadlines could be the same, provided that the deadline is far enough in advance of the claim construction hearing to allow the opposing party time to perform reasonably necessary discovery, such as deposing the witnesses who submit declarations in support of the first-track motion.

Another way to streamline the process while avoiding Fed. R. Civ. P. 56(d) issues is to require the movant to identify first-track motions early in the case, then require the parties to take discovery on the issues in any first-track motions concurrently with claim construction discovery and disclosures. After this limited discovery is complete, the court can then hear the first-track motions with the claim construction hearing.

Courts must also set expectations to avoid the submission of multiple first-track summary judgment motions. One option is to limit each party to a single first-track motion. Once the briefing is complete, the court could review it and decide whether to consider it along with claim construction. Another option is to require a party to obtain leave of court before filing a first-track motion. This may be the best approach to address the tension that may exist where a jurisdiction only allows one summary judgment motion to be filed without leave. In such jurisdictions, courts should still encourage strong first-track motions, but the court should be clear during the case management conference or in the scheduling order as to whether the first-track motion will be a party's only chance for summary judgment during the course of the case.

Procedurally, the court could require that a party wishing to file a first-track motion submit a two- or three-page letter brief with the court within two weeks of submitting the Joint Claim Construction Statement required under some courts' Patent Local Rules. The letter brief would describe the proposed first-track motion and why it should be heard with claim construction. The court could then evaluate how to proceed. This would also afford the opposing party notice of the basis of the motion, to avoid Fed. R. Civ. P. 56(d) problems.

Appendix 6.1 contains a sample standing order for first-track summary judgment motions. It permits each party to file a single first-track summary judgment motion without leave of court but requires a motion for leave to file additional first-track motions. It is designed to integrate the Patent Local Rules originated by the Northern District of California, although it can be used in any district whether or not the district has adopted a version of those Patent Local Rules. If there are no Patent Local Rules, the court can remove the references in the sample order to those rules. The remaining text in the sample order stands on its own.

6.1.3.4 Recognizing First-Track Summary Judgment Motions

6.1.3.4.1 Noninfringement and Divided Infringement

Noninfringement motions based on a small set of claim terms are the most likely to be first-track motions. This is because a judgment of noninfringement is appropriate if any single claim limitation is not met. *See* § 14.4.1.4. Often, the same or similar claim limitations appear in each of the independent claims. If those claim limitations are not met, literal infringement (and possibly infringement under the Doctrine of Equivalents) cannot be established and the case (or at least some aspects of it) is resolved. Claims that depend on such claims need not be considered because they cannot be infringed if the independent claims are not infringed.

Another area of noninfringement that may be suited to first-track summary judgment motions is where there is divided infringement. The Federal Circuit has emphasized that where an accused infringer does not perform all the steps of an accused method, it cannot be liable for infringement unless it otherwise controls or directs each step of the accused method. *Muniauction, Inc. v. Thomson Corp.*, 532 F.3d 1318 (Fed. Cir. 2008) (reversing a jury verdict of infringement); *BMC Resources,*

Inc. v. Paymentech, LP, 498 F.3d 1373, 1380 (Fed. Cir. 2007) (affirming a judgment of noninfringement). Mere "arms-length cooperation" is not enough to show the necessary control or direction. *BMC*, 498 F.3d at 1381. Instead, "there can only be joint infringement when there is an agency relationship between the parties who perform the method steps or when one party is contractually obligated to the other person to perform the steps." *Akamai Techs., Inc. v. Limelight Networks, Inc.*, 629 F.3d 1311, 1320 (Fed. Cir. 2010), *rev'd on other grounds*, 692 F.3d 1301 (Fed. Cir. 2012) (en banc) (per curiam), *rev'd*, 134 S. Ct. 2111 (2014). The Supreme Court's *Akamai* decision left this rule undisturbed—the Supreme Court declined to review *Muniauction* in reaching its conclusion that "a defendant is not liable for inducing infringement under § 271(b) when no one has directly infringed under § 271(a) or any other statutory provision." *Limelight Networks, Inc. v. Akamai Techs., Inc.*, 134 S. Ct. 2111 (2014). Unless and until *Muniauction* is revisited, divided-infringement noninfringement defenses are prime candidates for first-track motions (or off-track motions, if the issue in a given case does not turn on claim construction).

6.1.3.4.2 Invalidity Challenges Under § 112

While noninfringement motions are the most common first-track summary judgment candidates, invalidity issues under § 112 can often be suitable for resolution in a first-track motion. Especially in the aftermath of the Supreme Court's decisions in *Teva Pharmaceuticals USA, Inc. v. Sandoz, Inc.*, 135 S. Ct. 831 (2015), and *Nautilus, Inc. v. Biosig Instruments, Inc.*, 134 S. Ct. 2120, 2128 (2014), we can expect greater focus on claim indefiniteness determinations. As explored in § 5.2.5.2, claim construction and claim indefiniteness are typically intertwined, making claim indefiniteness potentially ripe for first-track resolution. The considerations that led the Supreme Court to hold in *Markman* that claim construction is a matter for the court (and not a jury) should logically apply to assessing claim indefiniteness. Furthermore, even if the question of claim indefiniteness is subject to a different evidentiary standard (clear and convincing) than claim construction because of § 282's presumption of validity,[1] it is difficult to imagine a scenario in which a judge decides

---

1. In *Nautilus*, the Supreme Court noted, without resolving, controversy over the standard for proving claim indefiniteness:

> As the parties appear to agree, . . . th[e] presumption of validity does not alter the degree of clarity that §112[(b)] demands from patent applicants; to the contrary, it incorporates that definiteness requirement by reference. See §282, ¶2(3) (defenses to infringement actions include "[i]nvalidity of the patent or any claim in suit for failure to comply with . . . any requirement of [§112]").
>
> The parties nonetheless dispute whether factual findings subsidiary to the ultimate issue of definiteness trigger the clear-and-convincing evidence standard and, relatedly, whether deference is due to the PTO's resolution of disputed issues of fact. We leave these questions for another day. The court below treated definiteness as "a legal issue [the] court reviews without deference," 715 F.3d, at 897, and Biosig has not called our attention to any contested factual matter—or PTO determination thereof—pertinent to its infringement claims.

Nautilus, Inc., 134 S. Ct. at 2130, n.10.

that a term could not be construed under the preponderance standard but declines to hold that it is indefinite, owing to the higher threshold for proving invalidity. *See* J. Jonas Anderson & Peter S. Menell, *Restoring the Fact/Law Distinction in Patent Claim Construction*, 109 Nw. U. L. Rev. Online 187, 198–200 (2015) (discussing the interplay of claim construction and indefiniteness post-*Teva*). By contrast, lack of written description is typically less susceptible to early resolution because it often requires factual development through discovery. While written description is a question of fact, a patent can nonetheless be held invalid "on its face" for lack of adequate written description. *Univ. of Rochester v. G.D. Searle & Co.*, 358 F.3d 916, 927 (Fed. Cir. 2004) (describing written description standard and listing cases where a patent was held invalid "on its face" under this standard). Of the § 112 invalidity defenses, enablement is typically the least susceptible to resolution in a first-track motion. Although the ultimate judgment is a question of law, that determination rests on underlying factual issues that often must first be developed through both fact and expert discovery before it is ripe for decision, even where the decision ultimately turns on a claim construction issue. *See, e.g.*, *MagSil Corp. v. Hitachi Global Storage Techs., Inc.*, 687 F.3d 1377 (Fed. Cir. 2012) (stating that enablement is a question of law based on underlying factual findings and affirming summary judgment of non-enablement after the close of fact and expert discovery).

6.1.3.4.3 Invalidity Challenges Under §§ 102 and 103

Whether a summary judgment motion regarding invalidity based on anticipation or obviousness will fall in the first track depends on how many disputes the court needs to resolve, and of what type. Normally, a motion based on anticipation or obviousness will not be a first-track motion because to prove either, the moving party must show that every limitation in every claim is present in the prior art. This typically gives rise to a host of disputes, at least some of which are not governed primarily by claim construction issues. Therefore, these motions are normally not first-track motions. Motions seeking to defeat an anticipation defense are more likely to be first-track motions for the same reasons discussed above with respect to noninfringement—if the patentee can establish the absence of a single element in the allegedly anticipatory reference, the reference does not anticipate. It is possible for a question of anticipation or obviousness to turn in either direction on a small number of issues that are manageable early on in the case. For example, if it is beyond dispute that the patented invention is a specific improvement on a specific prior art device, the validity of the patent may turn on whether the specific improvement is obvious. Now that the Supreme Court has emphasized that obviousness is a legal conclusion for the courts, it is much more likely that, even under the patentee's version of the facts, claimed inventions will be obvious. *See KSR Int'l Co. v. Teleflex, Inc.*, 550 U.S. 398, 425 (2007); *PharmaStem Therapeutics, Inc. v. ViaCell, Inc.*, 491 F.3d 1342, 1362 (Fed. Cir. 2007) (reversing order denying judgment of invalidity based on obviousness); *Tokai Corp. v. Easton Enters., Inc.*, 632 F.3d 1358 (Fed. Cir. 2011) (affirming summary judgment of obviousness); *Odom v. Microsoft Corp.*, 429 F. App'x 967, 2011 U.S. App. LEXIS 9115 (Fed. Cir. 2011) (affirming summary judgment of obviousness); *see also* § 6.2.1.1.2.

6.1.3.4.4 Invalidity Challenges Under § 101

After a long dormancy, patentable subject-matter challenges have become one of the most salient and rapidly evolving areas of patent litigation. From the early 1980s until 2007, invalidity challenges based on patentable subject matter gained little traction. Notwithstanding remarkable advances in computers and biotechnology, the Supreme Court's decisions in *Diamond v. Chakrabarty*, 447 U.S. 303 (1980), and *Diamond v. Diehr*, 450 U.S. 175 (1981), cabined earlier cases that limited the patentability of software-related inventions and opened the patent system to information-age technologies. *See* § 14.3.1.2.3. At the same time, Congress established the Federal Circuit Court of Appeals and it gradually expanded on the *Chakrabarty* and *Diehr* precedents, eventually approving the patent eligibility of DNA sequence claims and business methods. *See* § 14.3.1.2.4. The USPTO lowered the patentability screen accordingly, leading to vast patenting of biotechnology, software, and business methods in the late 1990s and early 2000s.

With growing concerns about the patent system following the bursting of the tech bubble in late 1999, the Federal Circuit gradually opened its doors to § 101 challenges. *See, e.g.*, *In re Nuijten*, 500 F.3d 1346 (Fed. Cir. 2007) (holding that a watermarked electromagnetic signal does not fall into any of the four categories of patent-eligible subject matter); *In re Bilski*, 545 F.3d 943 (Fed. Cir. 2008) (en banc). Beginning in 2010, the Supreme Court reentered the patentable subject matter field, issuing an unprecedented four substantial § 101 decisions—*Bilski v. Kappos*, 561 U.S. 593 (2010); *Mayo Collaborative Services v. Prometheus Laboratories, Inc.*, 132 S. Ct. 1289 (2012); *Association for Molecular Pathology v. Myriad Genetics, Inc.*, 133 S. Ct. 2107 (2013); and *Alice Corp. Pty. Ltd. v. CLS Bank Int'l*, 134 S. Ct. 2347 (2014)—over five terms and substantially reshaping the terrain. *See* § 14.3.1.2.5.

Since these decisions apply retroactively, the lower courts now face a raft of patentable subject matter challenges to patents issued during a period when the PTO applied little to no § 101 screen. Moreover, the Supreme Court's decisions leave some basic and critical questions unresolved. *See* § 14.3.1.3.

The *Alice* decision synthesizes two centuries of jurisprudence into a two-step test:

> Step 1: Does the patent claim a patent-ineligible law of nature, natural phenomena, or abstract idea?
>
> Step 2: If so, does the claim contain an inventive concept sufficient to transform the ineligible law of nature, natural, phenomena, or abstract idea into a patent-eligible application of the ineligible subject matter?

See Alice, 134 S. Ct. at 2355 (attributing the framework to *Mayo*, 132 S. Ct. at 1294–98); § 14.3.1.1. The ultimate question of patentable subject matter appears to be a question of law and, in applying this framework, the Supreme Court has not treated the framework as implicating underlying factual findings. *See id.* at 2355–60. However, it has not explicitly addressed whether this framework does, or could, involve underlying factual findings and, if so, whether those determinations are within the province of the court. Conceptually, both steps of the test could entail subsidiary factual findings in some cases. Under step 1, for example, a court might need to resolve disputes about how laws of nature operate. Under step 2, a court might need to hear expert testimony about whether the *application* of a patent-ineligible law of nature, physical phenomenon, or abstract idea is inventive or merely routine or conventional.

The lower federal courts have only just begun to grapple with these issues. *See DDR Holdings, LLC v. Hotels.com, L.P.*, 773 F.3d 1245 (Fed. Cir. 2014); *Ultramercial, Inc. v. Hulu, LLC*, 772 F.3d 709, 715 (2014); *Ameritox Ltd. v. Millennium Health, LLC*, 2015 U.S. Dist. LEXIS 19665, 2015 WL 728501 (W.D. Wisc. Feb. 18, 2015); *Cal. Inst. of Tech. v. Hughes Commc'ns, Inc.*, 59 F. Supp. 3d 974 (C.D. Cal. 2014); *Cogent Med., Inc. v. Elsevier Inc.*, 2014 U.S. Dist. LEXIS 139856, 2014 WL 4966326 (N.D. Cal. Sept. 30, 2014). The law's evolution is having an impact on interrelated threshold issues: (1) whether claim construction is necessary to the resolution of a § 101 challenge, and (2) what sort of motion should be filed, and when.

Prior to 2010, § 101 challenges were typically asserted at the summary judgment stage. In 2010, following the Supreme Court's decision in *Bilski v. Kappos*, 561 U.S. 593 (2010), accused infringers began to file Rule 12 motions to dispose of certain asserted claims on § 101 grounds at the pleading stage. Over the past several years, the number of cases dismissed at the pleading stage has risen from one in 2012 to eleven in 2014.

The Federal Circuit has stated that "claim construction is not an inviolable prerequisite to a validity determination under § 101," but at the same time has remarked that "it will ordinarily be desirable—and often necessary—to resolve claim construction disputes prior to a § 101 analysis, for the determination of patent eligibility requires a full understanding of the basic character of the claimed subject matter." *Bancorp Servs., L.L.C. v. Sun Life Assurance Co.*, 687 F.3d 1266, 1273–74 (Fed. Cir. 2012). Faced with a body of law that is emerging, and litigation strategies that are evolving, district courts have several options in assessing how to place § 101 motions within a track.

First, the district court may decide a § 101 motion without construing claims where the claim is clearly ineligible under the Supreme Court's teachings. *See, e.g., Fort Props., Inc. v. Am. Master Lease, LLC*, 609 F. Supp. 2d 1052 (C.D. Cal. 2009), *aff'd*, 671 F.3d 1317 (Fed. Cir. 2012) (invalidating claims under § 101 without discussion of claim construction). A court might elect this approach if it were deciding a Rule 12(b)(6) or 12(c) motion, or possibly an "off-track" summary judgment motion. For example, in *Ultramercial, Inc. v. Hulu, LLC*, the Federal Circuit affirmed the district court's grant of the accused infringer's pre-answer motion to dismiss under Rule 12(b)(6) "without formally construing the claims." 772 F.3d 709, 713 (Fed. Cir. 2014). The Federal Circuit stated that it, like the district court, conducted its § 101 analysis "[w]ithout purporting to construe the claims." *Id.* at 714. As litigants test the nascent boundaries of § 101 law and movants attempt to dismiss asserted claims early in litigation on § 101 grounds, however, patentees opposing such motions may increasingly argue that certain claim terms require construction, which in turn relate to factual disputes about the nature of the asserted claims.

In the second approach—which appears more frequently following the Supreme Court's trilogy of § 101 decisions in *Mayo*, *Myriad*, and *Alice*—the district court decides a § 101 motion after considering the non-movant patentee's proposed constructions, but without formal claim construction proceedings. This was, in fact, the posture of *Alice*. 134 S. Ct. at 2360, *aff'g*, *CLS Bank Int'l v. Alice Corp. Pty. Ltd.*, 717 F.3d 1269 (Fed. Cir. 2013), *aff'g*, *CLS Bank Int'l v. Alice Corp. Pty. Ltd.*, 768 F. Supp. 2d 221, 236 n.6 (D.D.C. 2011) ("To have the Court consider CLS's § 101 defense before conducting a possible *Markman* hearing, CLS agreed to assume a construction of claims favorable to Alice.") (internal citation omitted). Similarly, in another case, the Federal Circuit deemed "proper" the district court's grant of a motion to dismiss under Fed. R. Civ. P. 12(b)(6) at the pleading stage, where the court had "construed the terms identified by [the non-movant] 'in the manner most favorable to [the non-movant],'" but without formal claim construction proceedings. *Content Extraction & Transmission LLC v. Wells Fargo Bank, Nat'l Ass'n*, 776 F.3d 1343, 1348–49 (Fed. Cir. 2014). This second approach suggests that even where the non-movant contends that a § 101 defense depends in some way on claim construction, it is often still appropriate to consider a motion at the pleading stage or as an off-track summary judgment motion.

A third approach is for the district court to decide a § 101 motion after a claim construction hearing "to ensure that there are no issues of claim construction that would affect the [c]ourt's legal analysis of the patentability issue." *Loyalty Conversion Sys. Corp. v. Am. Airlines, Inc.*, No. 2:13-CV-655, 2014 U.S. Dist. LEXIS 122244, 2014 WL 4364848, at *4 (E.D. Tex. Sept. 2, 2014) (Bryson, J., sitting by designation). In *Loyalty Conversion*, the district court waited until after the claim construction hearing, even though the § 101 challenge was a motion for judgment on the pleadings pursuant to Fed. R. Civ. P. 12(c). In another case, the district court held a claim construction hearing on the same day as a hearing on the accused infringer's Rule 12(c) motion, and granted the latter, noting that "[t]he Court's claim construction ruling, which is being issued separately today, has no impact on Defendant's Rule 12(c) motion." *buySAFE, Inc. v. Google Inc.*, 964 F. Supp. 2d 331, 333 (D. Del. 2013) *aff'd*, 765 F.3d 1350 (Fed. Cir. 2014). A court following this approach could hear the § 101 issue in a first-track or second-track motion.

As this discussion suggests, the Supreme Court's recent decisions have encouraged parties to file dispositive motions based on § 101 at an increasing rate. At least in part, this results from the Court's decision in *Mayo* and confirmed in *Alice* establishing a two-step framework that simplified the § 101 analysis, making it better suited for early resolution in many cases. Nonetheless, the reach of the Supreme Court's § 101 holdings and how the Federal Circuit will apply them is still in flux. *Compare Ultramercial, Inc. v. Hulu, LLC*, 772 F.3d 709, 715–16 (Fed. Cir. 2014) (finding that the claims fail under § 101 despite computer-implemented limitations that require "updating an activity log, requiring a request from the consumer to view [an] ad, restrictions on public access, and use of the Internet"), *with DDR Holdings, LLC v. Hotels.com, L.P.*, 773 F.3d 1245, 1258–59 (Fed. Cir. 2014) (finding that the claims satisfy § 101 because they did not "broadly and generically claim 'use of the Internet' to perform an abstract business practice (with insignificant added activity)"). Nevertheless, § 101 issues are more susceptible to resolution on summary judgment (or motions under Rules 12(b)(6) or 12(c)) than they were just a few years ago.

To resolve § 101 defenses through early dispositive motions, courts should consider several issues. First, while § 101 issues are susceptible to early resolution in many cases, courts should not assume that first-track or off-track motions are appropriate in every case. Because of the nature of, and substantial attention paid to, the Supreme Court's recent § 101 decisions, there is a danger that dispositive § 101 motions will become (and some would argue, already have become) the motion *du jour*. In other words, as often happens with "hot" issues, parties in some cases can be expected to overreach by suggesting early resolution of § 101 issues where it is unwarranted, for example because it appears that the motion is unlikely to succeed or because it is unlikely to apply to enough of the asserted claims or patents to materially change the scope of the case. Second, and as an important counterpoint, the very characteristics that often make patent claims attractive to patentees in the infringement context, and thus more likely to be asserted in litigation—e.g., broad reach, functional claim terms, generically claimed components—also make a claim more likely to be invalid under § 101. Consequently, experience teaches that the percentage of claims that would appropriately be held invalid under the Supreme Court's § 101 standards is likely higher (and perhaps substantially higher) for claims that are asserted in litigation as compared to all claims in all issued patents, considered in the aggregate. Courts should be careful not to make assumptions either way. They should not assume that a proposed motion should be heard as a first-track or off-track motion simply because it is based on § 101; nor should they assume that the motion is overreaching and, therefore, inappropriate for first-track or off-track resolution simply because it addresses all claims in a patent, or multiple (or even all) patents asserted in the case. Instead, courts should require the party seeking to file a first-track or off-track summary judgment motion to explain the proposed motion, in a letter brief or otherwise, so that the court can evaluate whether the motion is well suited for early resolution in view of the applicable law.

6.1.4 Summary Judgment Independent from Claim Construction (Off-Track)

The discussion above focuses on early summary judgment motions that depend on claim construction. While this typically includes most dispositive issues in a patent case, at least two categories of early summary judgment motions that are not based on claim construction arise with some frequency. First, as discussed above, some dispositive issues (e.g., § 101 invalidity, divided infringement) implicate claim construction in some cases and not in others, depending on the particular facts of the case. Whether tied to claim construction or not, these issues are often ripe for resolution at an early stage for the reasons discussed above.

Second, a few dispositive issues typically do not intersect with claim construction at all. For example, territoriality issues—whether the alleged infringement occurred "in the United States"—usually will not involve claim construction. For such motions, the above first-track/second-track approach does not apply as directly.

Considering a summary judgment motion before issuing a claim construction order can divert the resources of both the court and the parties from resolving the claim construction issues by the mid-point in a case. *See* § 2.1.3.2. In general, however, considering an off-track summary judgment motion before claim construction may make sense if the issue is potentially dispositive of the case as a whole or of a significant issue or issues. Indeed, where it is case dispositive and likely to succeed, a court should consider taking on that motion first, before devoting its time and resources to claim construction. This is especially true for courts that conduct claim construction after discovery closes or immediately before trial, where the savings of time and resources that would result from granting the motion early in the case would be the most substantial.

6.1.5 Streamlining the Summary Judgment Process

No matter when they choose to decide motions for summary judgment, courts can streamline the process in several ways. Table 6.5 summarizes the principal approaches.

Table 6.5
Approaches to Streamlining the Summary Judgment Process

Approach	Advantages	Disadvantages
Letter briefs asking permission to file summary judgment motions	• The court has full view of the possible summary judgment issues and their potential to narrow the case. • The court saves time and effort by prohibiting the filing of weak motions.	• Slightly lengthens the summary judgment process. • The short summary contained in the letter briefing may give the court a distorted picture of the proposed motion.
Limiting the number of summary judgment motions or the total number of pages	• Forces the parties to focus and identify their best arguments to the court; reduces the burden on the court of ruling on a stack of motions.	• Discourages parties from bringing summary judgment motions earlier in the case. • Limits the court's opportunity to dispose of issues prior to trial and create a more manageable trial.
Multiple rounds of summary judgment motions	• May allow additional efficiency by narrowing the issues to be decided at any time.	• May increase the total number of motions filed and encourage parties to file motions on minor issues.

6.1.5.1 Recommended Approach: Letter Briefs Followed by Summary Judgment Motions

Some courts employ a pre-motion letter briefing process to limit the number of summary judgment motions filed by the parties. Each party is required to submit a letter brief summarizing each proposed motion. The court then holds a telephone hearing during which each of the proposed motions is discussed. After this hearing, the court identifies which of the motions may be filed. Some courts allow the parties to file one motion without leave and require leave of court for any motions beyond the first.

The obvious advantage of this approach is that it gives the court an overview of the possible summary judgment issues and their potential to narrow the case. This allows the court to manage its docket with a better understanding of the impact of its decisions. The letter-brief approach allows courts to evaluate a potential first-track or off-track motion to determine whether it would be sensible to decide the proposed motion at an early stage of the case. The court can tailor its limits on summary judgment motions to suit the needs of each particular case.

Disadvantages of the letter-brief approach may include an increase in resources required to manage the case, a somewhat longer summary judgment process, and possible distortion of complex issues by forcing the parties to compress their arguments. However, these risks are small compared to the benefit of not considering a large number of motions, and a more flexible alternative allows the parties to file a single motion without leave of court. In many cases, one motion will be enough and the parties will be content to not file letter briefs requesting leave to file additional motions.

If the parties have competent advocates, they can usually convey enough information to the court in two to three pages and five minutes of oral argument to enable the court to evaluate whether the substance of a proposed motion justifies a full briefing.

6.1.5.2 Limiting the Number of Summary Judgment Motions or the Number of Pages of Summary Judgment Briefing

Some courts limit the number of summary judgment motions the parties can bring during the life of a case; some limit the total number of pages of summary judgment briefing that can be filed; and others implement a limit based on various permutations of the above.

Where a court or jurisdiction limits the number of summary judgment motions that can be brought during the life of a case, or is considering doing so, it should inform the parties early in the case, ideally at the initial case-management conference. Such limitations can affect the parties' litigation strategy and practice. Limiting summary judgment motions in this way has the significant advantage of forcing the parties to focus on and identify their best arguments, and it can significantly reduce the burden on the court. On the other hand, limiting the number of summary judgment motions can reduce the chance for early disposition of the case—because, for example, a party may not be willing to proceed on a potential first-track or off-track motion. This can also limit the court's opportunity to create a more manageable dispute by narrowing the issues early in the case. In general, this approach is not recommended because it lacks flexibility. These issues are magnified where a jurisdiction has a local rule or standing order limiting each party to one summary judgment motion per case. In those instances, the court should evaluate whether the default rule fits each case and should be clear with the parties from the outset about whether it will or will not count a proposed first-track or off-track motion against this limit.

Some courts employ a variation of this approach in which they do not limit the number of summary judgment motions, but instead require all motions to be addressed in a single brief conforming to the usual page limits required by the jurisdiction. This approach does not streamline the summary judgment process. Because parties may bring any number of motions, it does not necessarily reduce the number of issues that the court will have to decide. By limiting each party to a single brief with the usual page limitations, it significantly reduces a party's ability to quote and discuss the importance of evidence supporting the motion. Thus, instead of easing the burden on the court, this approach often results in dense briefs that string-cite evidence, forcing the court to pick through voluminous evidence to reach the merits of the motion. The inefficiencies of this approach are most pronounced when a party brings two or three well-founded motions for summary judgment, but cannot treat any one motion fully. Consequently, we recommend against this variation.

To streamline the process and reduce the burden on the court, but also avoid the issues created by adherence to a strict motion limit or default page limit, some courts consider the potential issues in the case and then limit the total number of pages of summary judgment briefing that can be filed. This hybrid approach requires the parties to select their best arguments and be judicious in the number and scope of motions filed. Nonetheless, it does not arbitrarily limit the number of motions that a party can bring. To determine an appropriate total page limit for briefing, the court should indicate to the parties that it intends to implement such limitations early on in the case, and then during a case-management conference in advance of summary judgment briefing discuss with the parties a reasonable limitation for total pages based on the potential motions in the case. Such a discussion will also help the court evaluate the merits of such motions and establish a reasonable page limitation for the motions that the court will allow the parties to file.

6.1.5.3 Multiple Rounds of Summary Judgment Hearings

In addition to the multi-track approach to summary judgment briefing, other alternatives are also available to make patent cases more manageable and to use judicial resources better. For example, it can be useful to allow or encourage several rounds of summary judgment hearings. This approach makes the most sense in larger cases, in cases where a large number of motions are expected to be filed, or in cases where the parties identify narrow summary judgment motions on issues that require little or no discovery early in the litigation. This approach works best where the first round of motions focuses on issues that can narrow the scope of the case significantly. This allows the court to limit its expenditure of resources on issues that need not be raised later in the case if the issues can be narrowed early. The resolution of major issues early in a case may also encourage settlement.

Another alternative for large patent cases where multiple patents are asserted is to require each patentee to identify "champion" patents and then limit the proceedings to the champion patents until the infringement, invalidity, and other contentions regarding those patents are resolved. In most multi-patent cases, each party should be able to identify its strongest patents and the court may choose to proceed first with these champion patents. This approach may help resolve a case by encouraging settlement if the issues on the strong patents are resolved or narrowed in the early rounds.

A drawback of multiple rounds or multiple hearings is that the approach may increase the total number of motions filed in the case, and it may encourage parties to file motions on minor issues. Another drawback of multiple rounds is the potential delay that it may cause in the case. Thus, where multiple rounds are used, the court should, during the case-management stage, discuss with the parties the number of rounds of summary judgment that it plans to utilize, whether it is open to hearing first-track motions, whether it plans to require the parties to designate champion patents, or whether the court plans to implement any limitations regarding number of pages of briefing or the number of motions. As discussed above, the court can request that the parties notify it of any intended motions early in the case and use that discussion to determine appropriate limits.

6.1.6 The Summary Judgment Hearing

Hearings on motions for summary judgment in patent cases usually present the same issues as other types of cases. However, several issues—the length and division of time, live testimony, the use of graphics, and whether to hold a technology tutorial—raise distinctive concerns in patent cases. Table 6.6 provides the advantages and disadvantages of two approaches to the summary judgment hearing.

Table 6.6
Approaches to the Summary Judgment Hearing

Approach	Advantages	Disadvantages	Examples
Live testimony	• Affords the court the opportunity to hear testimony focused on the issues on which the motion turns.	• Inconsistent with MSJ standard. • Time-consuming. • Invites cumulative testimony.	
Graphics	• May assist the court in understanding complex technical distinctions.	• Invites longer presentations. • Challenging to keep a precise record.	PowerPoint presentations

6.1.6.1 Length and Division of Time

The length of time needed for a summary judgment motion varies widely depending on the court's preferences and the scope and nature of the issues at stake. As an example, a motion seeking summary judgment of infringement implicates a broad scope of issues and may require significantly more time than a motion for summary judgment of noninfringement, which might focus on the absence of a single claim limitation. Typically, whatever time the court allots to the hearing should be divided equally between the parties, and each party should be free to elect how best to use it.

6.1.6.2 Live Testimony

As the factual issues relevant to a motion for summary judgment are sufficiently settled before a motion is brought, live testimony during the hearing is rarely appropriate. Live testimony can be unduly time-consuming and invite cumulative evidence. However, it can be useful in limited circumstances where declarations submitted by the parties do not squarely address each other, creating the perception of a question of material fact when, in reality, one may not exist. In such circumstances, live testimony may allow the court to probe discrepancies in the testimony that may affect whether summary judgment is appropriate.

6.1.6.3 Graphics

Most courts permit the parties to use graphics, such as PowerPoint slides, during their presentations. This can be particularly helpful to the court in patent cases, where visual aids may assist the court in understanding nuanced technical issues. Such presentations help most when they present issues in a functional manner—i.e., through the use of graphical illustrations, charts, and documentary evidence. Where they merely repackage the arguments in briefs with bullet points, such presentations can be inefficient.

6.1.6.4 Technology Tutorial

Because the technology implicated by the patents-in-suit, accused products, and prior art is often complex and unfamiliar to the court, a technology tutorial may clarify the issues to be decided. Whether this should occur in conjunction with summary judgment will depend on the timing of summary judgment relative to claim construction—where technology tutorials are most prevalent, *see* Chapter 5—and the court's needs. If the court holds a tutorial in conjunction with a prior *Markman* hearing, it might not need to hold a second one. The court should nevertheless consider whether the scope of technical issues discussed at the *Markman* stage encompassed the technical information relevant to the summary judgment stage. It often does not because summary judgment frequently implicates a broader set of technical issues. If summary judgment coincides with or precedes claim construction, this weighs in favor of holding a tutorial in connection with the summary judgment hearing. The methodology of the tutorial can take various forms, including a neutral presentation by counsel, a presentation by each party's experts or by a technical advisor to the court, and written submissions by the parties followed by a question-and-answer session. These options are discussed in § 5.1.2.2.

6.1.7 Expert Declarations Filed in Connection with Summary Judgment Motions

Because summary judgment motions in patent cases will typically be both supported and opposed by expert declarations, a central issue in most patent summary judgment motions will be evaluating the extent to which expert declarations create (or fail to create) genuine issues of fact that preclude summary judgment.

6.1.7.1 Some Expert Testimony Cannot Defeat Summary Judgment

6.1.7.1.1 Testimony About Conclusions of Law

Expert opinions directed to a conclusion of law are insufficient to defeat summary judgment. *KSR Int'l Co. v. Teleflex, Inc.*, 550 U.S. 398, 426 (2007) ("To the extent the court understood the *Graham [v. John Deere]* approach to exclude the possibility of summary judgment when an expert provides a conclusory affidavit addressing the question of obviousness, it misunderstood the role expert testimony plays in the analysis.").

Moreover, expert opinions directed to a conclusion of law are generally considered irrelevant because it is the court's role to decide issues of law. However, this distinction can be confusing in patent cases because there are a number of questions of mixed fact and law that may be raised in such cases, for example with respect to obviousness. Courts should, therefore, evaluate carefully the specific opinions that any experts offer to determine whether such opinions are permissible to consider on summary judgment.

6.1.7.1.2 Conclusory Testimony

The conclusory testimony of an expert, at least when standing alone, is not sufficient to defeat summary judgment. *Telemac Cellular Corp. v. Topp Telecom, Inc.*, 247 F.3d 1316 (Fed. Cir. 2001) ("broad conclusory statements offered by *Telemac's* experts are not evidence and are not sufficient to establish a genuine issue of material fact"); *Arthur A. Collins, Inc. v. N. Telecom, Ltd.*, 216 F.3d 1042, 1046 (Fed. Cir. 2000); *In re Dembiczak*, 175 F.3d 994, 999 (Fed. Cir. 1999).

6.1.7.1.3 Testimony Contradicting Clear Disclosure of Prior Art

Expert testimony that purports to contradict the clear disclosure of a prior art reference is insufficient to defeat summary judgment. *Jamesbury Corp. v. Litton In-*

dus. Prods. Inc., 756 F.2d 1556, 1563 (Fed. Cir. 1985) (overturning a jury verdict of anticipation), *overruled in part by A.C. Aukerman Co. v. R.L. Chaides Constr. Co.*, 960 F.2d 1020 (Fed. Cir. 1992).

6.1.7.1.4 Testimony Contradicting Admissions of a Party

In *PharmaStem Therapeutics, Inc. v. ViaCell, Inc.*, 491 F.3d 1342, 1362 (Fed. Cir. 2007), the Federal Circuit refused to give weight to expert testimony proffered by the patentee about the nature of the prior art that contradicted statements in the specification of the patent-in-suit about that art. As a result of these limitations, the mere existence of apparently conflicting expert testimony from both parties does not necessarily mean that questions of material fact preclude summary judgment. For additional limitations on expert testimony, *see* § 7.4.

6.1.7.2 Legal Insufficiency of Expert Testimony

Proffered expert testimony may also fail to navigate patent law's substantive requirements correctly, rendering it of little to no relevance. The most common failing in this regard concerns the timing of the substantive analysis. Whether a patent claim is obvious is measured at the time of invention. Thus, expert opinions about obviousness must focus on what would be known or obvious to a person of ordinary skill *at the time of invention*. But enablement is measured at the time the application was filed, *In re Wands*, 858 F.2d 731, 736–37 (Fed. Cir. 1988); infringement, including equivalency under the doctrine of equivalents, at the time of alleged infringement, *see, e.g., Warner-Jenkinson Co. v. Hilton Davis Chem. Co.*, 520 U.S. 17, 37 (1997); and equivalency under § 112(f), at the time the patent issued, *Al-Site Corp. v. VSI Int'l, Inc.*, 174 F.3d 1308, 1320 (Fed. Cir. 1999). An opinion based on an analysis that focuses on the wrong point in time does not address the substantive standard relevant to the motion. Likewise, an expert opinion about anticipation that does not address whether the asserted prior art reference is enabling may not satisfy the substantive standard. *See, e.g., Forest Labs., Inc. v. Ivax Pharm., Inc.*, 501 F.3d 1263, 1268 (Fed. Cir. 2007). An opinion that fails to address the substantive standard may have little to no probative value. As a result, it may be appropriate to exclude the testimony under Federal Rules of Evidence 402 and 702.

6.1.7.3 Expert Testimony Beyond the Scope of the Expert Report

In patent cases, parties commonly argue that expert testimony regarding summary judgment should be stricken or disallowed because it goes beyond the scope of the expert's reports. This arises in a number of contexts:

- a *Celotex* "failure of proof" argument for summary judgment, based on the absence of opinion or evidence in an expert report, *see, e.g., Telemac Cellular Corp. v. Topp Telecom, Inc.*, 247 F.3d 1316 (Fed. Cir. 2001);
- an argument that a declaration opposing summary judgment should be stricken; and

- expert testimony through declaration that is contrary to deposition testimony.

The consequences of either allowing or disallowing expert testimony that is beyond the scope of the expert's report should be examined carefully. However, courts should keep in mind the Federal Circuit's clear support for allowing the district court discretion to make procedural rulings that are effectively case dispositive. *See O2 Micro Int'l, Ltd. v. Monolithic Power Sys., Inc.*, 467 F.3d 1355, 1368–69 (Fed. Cir. 2006) (finding court did not abuse its discretion in excluding untimely expert reports).

Moreover, it is important for a court to also consider that allowing an expert declaration to stand for a point that is outside the scope of the expert's report on the subject has the practical effect of granting a motion by that party to serve a supplemental expert report. This can be problematic and prejudicial both from a case-management perspective and to the party against whom the declaration has been offered. Where such an expert declaration has been allowed, the scope of the trial will inevitably expand to include testimony on that new point. As discussed in § 7.5.2.3, allowing a supplemental expert report may also unfairly prejudice the party against whom it is offered by raising issues requiring a responsive expert supplementation. Because the substantive underpinnings of validity and infringement are intertwined, a supplemental expert report in the form of a declaration submitted in connection with a motion for summary judgment of noninfringement may justify a responsive supplementation not only on the issue of infringement but also on the issue of validity.

Unfortunately, courts often do not confront this issue. Faced with a request to strike an expert declaration filed in connection with summary judgment, courts commonly remain silent about the request to strike and simply decline to cite the declaration in the opinion. Alternatively, some courts will defer a ruling on the issue until later in the case. These practices should be avoided. They risk basing an important decision on an incomplete record, and they reward a party that failed to proffer a proper, timely report with an unfair advantage. These approaches effectively inject the additional opinions from the declaration into the case, but without any recognition by the court that this has occurred. At best, the receiving party may depose the expert, which will weaken any prejudice argument, and often leads the court to allow the opinions. But the result is often that the party against whom the opinions are offered has little or no opportunity to offer responsive expert opinions, especially because this issue typically arises late in the case. Instead, courts should explicitly address the request to strike as soon as possible and, if the matter is new, either strike that new matter or recognize that the declaration is a supplemental expert report. If the court permits the declaration as a supplementation, it should then provide the receiving party with an opportunity to depose the expert on the supplemental opinions and to offer responsive expert testimony of its own, thus allowing the parties to establish a complete record. Active management by the court will prevent the disclosing party from circumventing the court's schedule and improperly offering belated expert opinions. Section 7.5.2.3 explores these issues further.

6.1.8 Narrowing Trial Issues Through Federal Rule of Civil Procedure 56(g)

Even where summary judgment is not appropriate, summary judgment proceedings may nevertheless be helpful in simplifying a patent case for trial. Federal Rule of Civil Procedure 56(g), as implemented by the 2010 Amendments, states that where "the court does not grant all the relief requested by the motion, it may enter an order stating any material fact—including an item of damages or other relief—that is not genuinely in dispute and treating the fact as established in the case." This provision is particularly useful for patent cases because many of the facts necessary to prove infringement or validity are often undisputed, and this rule can now be used to help narrow the issues in a case.

For example, as discussed in § 14.4.1.4, infringement requires that each claim limitation be present in the accused device. As another example, the same rule applies to anticipation—each claim limitation must be disclosed in the asserted prior art reference. Thus, the party advancing the infringement claim or anticipation defense must present evidence at trial corresponding to each claim limitation. But the party opposing that claim or defense often disputes the presence of only a small subset of these claim elements. If the court can determine, based on the evidence presented at summary judgment, which limitations are undisputed, Fed. R. Civ. P. 56(g) permits it to narrow the infringement or anticipation portion of the trial to only those elements in dispute. This can significantly simplify a trial.

Although a court should apply Fed. R. Civ. P. 56(g) wherever possible, it must do so carefully, considering the scope of the motion and the relative burdens of proof. The court should utilize this rule only where the issues have been joined fully in the summary judgment proceedings. For example, when an accused infringer cites the absence of only one claim limitation in its noninfringement summary judgment motion, it is not necessarily admitting that there are no disputes as to the other limitations. The accused infringer may simply be choosing to move for summary judgment on its strongest noninfringement argument. The same is true of the patentee in the anticipation context. As another example, in some cases the party opposing the motion acknowledges in its briefing or oral argument that certain issues underlying the motion are not disputed. When this happens, a Fed. R. Civ. P. 56(g) order is appropriate.

6.2 Substantive Issues Commonly Raised During Summary Judgment

Some issues in patent cases are more amenable to summary judgment than others. In part, this is because some issues, such as infringement or anticipation, are factual and some, such as obviousness, are primarily legal in nature. There are also different standards of proof: infringement requires only a preponderance of the evidence while invalidity requires clear and convincing evidence. Some motions require a narrow scope of proof while others require that the movant prove a much broader set of facts. For example, noninfringement is more likely to be amenable to summary judgment than infringement, because a patentee must show that each limitation of a claim is found in each accused device. Conversely, an accused infringer need only show the absence of a single limitation to avoid infringement. As a result, the accused infringer's burden on summary judgment is more likely to be satisfied because a narrower scope of proof is required. Finally, some issues are more amenable to summary judgment because the underlying facts are not typically disputed; only the conclusions to be drawn from them are in dispute.

6.2.1 Issues More Amenable to Summary Judgment

This section explores the motions within validity, infringement, and damages that summary judgment can generally resolve.

6.2.1.1 Validity

An accused infringer must prove invalidity by clear and convincing evidence. The Supreme Court has observed that while the standard for proving invalidity does not change, the fact that a material reference was not before the USPTO may make the standard easier to meet. *Microsoft Corp. v. i4i Ltd. P'ship*, 131 S. Ct. 2238, 2251 (2011).

> Simply put, if the PTO did not have all material facts before it, its considered judgment may lose significant force. And, concomitantly, the challenger's burden to persuade the jury of its invalidity defense by clear and convincing evidence may be easier to sustain. In this respect, although we have no occasion to endorse any particular formulation, we note that a jury instruction on the effect of new evidence can, and when requested, most often should be given.

Id. (citations omitted).

In general, the heavy burden for invalidity makes summary judgment on validity issues more likely for patentees than accused infringers. But, as discussed below, the nature of several invalidity defenses often renders them amenable to summary judgment for either party.

6.2.1.1.1 Patentable Subject Matter

The precise contours and character of patentable subject matter limitations are still emerging following the Supreme Court's recent and substantial foray into § 101 law. District courts will need to assess how to learn the pertinent technological background, build an appropriate record, and apply the Supreme Court's somewhat opaque standard. They will also need to determine what role, if any, there is for a jury.

The *Alice* two-step test, *see* § 14.3.1.1, has made § 101 better suited to resolution at the summary judgment stage, or even much earlier. For example, in *buySAFE, Inc. v. Google Inc.*, the Federal Circuit explained that "[a] claim that directly reads on matter in the three identified categories [(laws of nature, natural phenomena, and abstract ideas)] is outside section 101." 765 F.3d 1350, 1353 (Fed. Cir. 2014) (citing *Mayo*, 132 S. Ct. at 1293). But, the panel added, § 101 "also excludes the subject matter of certain claims that by their terms read on a human-made physical thing ('machine, manufacture, or composition of matter') or a human-controlled series of physical acts ('process') rather than laws of nature, natural phenomena, and abstract ideas." *Id.* In that situation, the claim is patent ineligible if "(a) it is 'directed to' matter in one of the three excluded categories and (b) 'the additional elements' do not supply an 'inventive concept' in the physical realm of things and acts—a 'new and useful application' of the ineligible matter in the physical realm—that ensures that the patent is on something 'significantly more than' the ineligible matter itself." *Id.* (quoting *Alice*, 134 S. Ct. at 2355, 2357). The *buySAFE* panel applied that framework to hold that method claims that were "squarely about creating a contractual relationship" were directed to an abstract idea. *Id.* at 1354–55. Other post-*Alice* Federal Circuit decisions have applied the two-step framework toward a variety of claims in a variety of technological contexts. *See, e.g.*, *In re BRCA1- & BRCA2-Based Hereditary Cancer Test Patent Litig.*, 774 F.3d 755, 763 (Fed. Cir. 2014) (holding patent ineligible composition claims directed to DNA primers because they lacked "a unique structure, different from anything found in nature," and method claims directed to screening for alteration of gene because the recited method steps involved abstract ideas and "only routine and conventional steps"); *Content Extraction & Transmission LLC v. Wells Fargo Bank, Nat'l Ass'n*, 776 F.3d 1343, 1346–49 (Fed. Cir. 2014) (holding patent ineligible method claims "drawn to the abstract idea of 1) collecting data, 2) recognizing certain data within the collected data set, and 3) storing that recognized data in a memory").

One rapidly developing area of the law is the application of the *Alice* test to computer- and software-related inventions, where the boundaries between an unpatentable abstract idea and a patentable application of that idea remain unsettled. One tool that courts have used to address such issues is the "machine-or-transformation" test, which states that a claim can be patent-eligible under § 101 if (1) it is tied to a particular machine or apparatus, or (2) if it transforms a particular article into a different state or thing. In *Bilski*, the Supreme Court rejected the machine-or-transformation test as the single broad standard for evaluating subject matter under § 101. It observed that it is nevertheless a "useful and important clue, an investigative tool, for determining whether some claimed inventions are processes under § 101." *Bilski v. Kappos*, 561 U.S. 593, 604 (2009). More recently, the Federal Circuit concluded that the appropriate way to use the machine-or-transformation test is to consider it as part of *Alice's* second step, when evaluating the additional claim elements—separately and in combination with the claim as a whole—to determine whether the result is a patentable application of the unpatentable abstract idea, law of nature, or physical phenomenon. *Ultramercial, Inc. v. Hulu, LLC*, 772 F.3d 709, 716 (Fed. Cir. 2014). In *Bilski*, the Supreme Court also explained that limiting an abstract idea to one field of use or adding token pre- or post-solution steps or components (e.g., conventional steps or components leading up to the abstract idea or following from it) does not make that concept patentable. 561 U.S at 610 (citing *Flook* and *Diehr*).

But, even with these tools, post-*Alice* decisions reflect a varied treatment of machine implementations, particularly in the computing software contexts. On the one hand, the Federal Circuit held patent-ineligible claims directed to "a method of using advertising as an exchange or currency." *Ultramercial*, 772 F.3d at 715. The Federal Circuit concluded that the claims at issue recited an abstract idea, and "simply instruct the practitioner to implement the abstract idea with routine, conventional activity." *Id.* Referencing the machine-or-transformation test, the court concluded that the claim limitations requiring specific computer-based steps, the use of a general purpose computer, and the Internet failed to satisfy that test. *Id.* at 717–18.

On the other hand, the Federal Circuit also applied the *Alice* framework to hold that system claims that "address a business challenge (retaining website visitors)" were patent eligible under *Alice*, noting that those claims were directed to solving "a challenge particular to the Internet." *DDR Holdings, LLC v. Hotels.com, L.P.*, 773 F.3d 1245, 1257 (Fed. Cir. 2014). The court reasoned that the claims at issue did not "merely recite the performance of some business practice known from the pre-Internet world along with the requirement to perform it on the Internet," but rather claimed a solution that "is necessarily rooted in computer technology in order to overcome a problem specifically arising in the realm of computer networks." *Id.* Distinguishing the claims at issue in *Ultramercial*, the *DDR* panel stated that "the claims at issue here specify how interactions with the Internet are manipulated to yield a desired result—a result that overrides the routine and conventional sequence of events ordinarily triggered by the click of a hyperlink." *Id.* at 1258. The court concluded that the claims thus recited a precise and inventive solution, which did not preempt the abstract idea of increasing sales on the Internet by retaining visitors. *Id.* at 1258–59.

Because the application of the *Alice* test is evolving rapidly, particularly in the computing and software contexts, courts facing dispositive motions based on § 101 should be especially careful to identify and consider the most recent decisions applying *Alice* to an analogous factual scenario. For additional considerations about the timing and prevalence of § 101 motions, *see* § 6.1.3.4.4.

6.2.1.1.2 Obviousness

The Supreme Court's decision in *KSR Int'l Co. v. Teleflex, Inc.* clarified the analysis of obviousness in a way that makes this defense appropriate for summary judgment in some circumstances. 550 U.S. 398 (2007). Obviousness is a question of law that is evaluated based on underlying factual questions about the level of skill in the art at the time the invention was made, the scope and content of the prior art, and the differences between the prior art and the asserted claim. *Id.* at 406 (quoting *Graham v. John Deere Co.*, 383 U.S. 1, 17–18 (1966)). These "*Graham* factors" also include secondary indicia, such as commercial success of the invention, a long-felt but unsolved need for the invention, and the failure of others, that may demonstrate that the claimed invention was nonobvious. *Graham*, 383 U.S. at 17–18. However, evidence of secondary indicia are frequently inadequate to establish nonobviousness where either (1) the patentee fails to show the requisite nexus between the secondary indicia and the patent, or (2) the "claimed invention represents no more than the predictable use of prior art elements according to established functions." *Ohio Willow Wood Co. v. Alps South, LLC*, 735 F.3d 1333, 1344 (Fed. Cir. 2013).

In *KSR*, the Court illustrated the application of the *Graham* factors, explaining that:

> When there is a design need or market pressure to solve a problem and there are a finite number of identified, predictable solutions, a person of ordinary skill has good reason to pursue the known options within his or her technical grasp. If this leads to the anticipated success, it is likely the product not of innovation but of ordinary skill and common sense.

KSR, 550 U.S. at 421. Moreover, "most inventions that are obvious were also obvious to try." *Id.* (note, though, that the reverse is not necessarily true). But an obviousness finding requires that the fact-finder consider all of the objective evidence presented by the patentee. *See Plantronics, Inc. v. Aliph, Inc.*, 724 F.3d 1343, 1355 (Fed. Cir. 2013) (reversing finding of nonobviousness on summary judgment and holding improper to conclude patent was invalid as obvious before considering objective indicia of nonobviousness); *Rothman v. Target Corp.*, 556 F.3d 1310, 1322 (Fed. Cir. 2009) (approving district court's charge "that the jury 'must consider' objective indicia of nonobviousness, such as . . . licensing activity").

In addition, *KSR* made clear that an invention may be obvious if it is the product of "common sense," 550 U.S. at 421, but did not illustrate how "common sense" would be established. In *Mintz v. Dietz,* the Federal Circuit explained that "'common sense' is a shorthand label for knowledge so basic that it certainly lies within the skill set of an ordinary artisan." 679 F.3d 1372, 1377 (Fed. Cir. 2012). The court held that it was "clear error" for the district court to (1) merely recite the words "common sense" without any support, and (2) "not consider[] or mak[e] any findings as to [patentee's] evidence showing objective indicia of non-obviousness." *Id.*; *see also Plantronics, Inc.*, 724 F.3d at 1354 ("[obviousness findings] grounded in 'common sense' must contain explicit and clear reasoning providing some rational underpinning why common sense compels a finding of obviousness"). The court subsequently affirmed a district court's finding of invalidity based on "common sense" in *DatCard Sys., Inc. v. PacsGear, Inc.*, even though some limitations were "not clearly present" in the prior art (but were "highly *suggested*"). No. 10-cv-1288-MRP, slip op. at 6 (C.D. Cal. Apr. 1, 2013) (*aff'd DatCard Sys., Inc. v. PacsGear, Inc.*, 550 F. App'x 895 (Fed. Cir. 2014)). The claims were obvious because "[c]ommon sense can provide a reason to combine the teachings of the various references *and* to supply the missing pieces." *Id.*

After the court has construed the claims, the parties typically dispute factual aspects of the *Graham* factors, the ways in which they are sought to be applied consistent with *KSR*, and the legal conclusion to be drawn from them. Such disputes, even if factual in nature, do not necessarily preclude summary judgment. First, factual disputes about the *Graham* factors, even if heated, may not be material. To evaluate the materiality of these disputes, the court can simply assume that the nonmovant's position about the factors is correct, draw inferences most favorable to that party in light of the assumed facts, and then evaluate the motion under that set of facts and inferences. For example, if an accused infringer moves for summary judgment of obviousness and it is apparent that there are factual disputes underlying the motion, the court can assume that the patentee's position on the *Graham* factors is correct and then evaluate obviousness. If the court concludes that the claim is obvious under the patentee's asserted facts, then the dispute about the underlying factors is not material and does not preclude summary judgment. Because obviousness is a question of law, the court does not have to conclude that "no reasonable juror" could find for the patentee, but only that there is clear and convincing evidence that the claimed invention was obvious under the patentee's asserted facts. This was essentially the approach taken by the district court, for example, in *Tokai Corp. v. Easton Enterprises, Inc.*, 632 F.3d 1358 (Fed. Cir. 2011). Specifically, "with regard to the level of skill in the art . . . the parties disagreed sharply. The [district] court determined, however, that the dispute was immaterial, as the court's conclusion on obviousness was the same under either party's asserted level of skill." *Id.* at 1364. The Federal Circuit affirmed the district court's summary judgment of obviousness, observing that, "[s]ince the district court found that the asserted claims would have been obvious to a less sophisticated artisan, then under the facts of this case the court could not have arrived at a different conclusion by adopting the viewpoint of one with greater skill and experience." *Id.* at 1369.

Second, *KSR* makes clear that conflicting expert testimony about the legal conclusions to be drawn from the underlying facts cannot defeat summary judgment. The court made this point explicitly: "To the extent the court understood the *Graham* approach to exclude the possibility of summary judgment when an expert provides a conclusory affidavit addressing the question of obviousness, it misunderstood the role expert testimony plays in the analysis." *KSR*, 550 U.S. at 426. As a question of law, the ultimate conclusion of obviousness or nonobviousness rests with the court. *Id.* Thus the court is *required* to ignore expert opinions about the ultimate legal issue (i.e., whether the claimed combination of limitations was "obvious"), although it should consider opinions directed at the *Graham* factors themselves (e.g., the scope and content of the prior art, and whether it collectively discloses each limitation of a claim).

Procedurally, *KSR* has made summary judgment on the ultimate issue of obviousness easier for either party to obtain. In this regard, *KSR* is equally applicable to other questions of law, such as indefiniteness, and should be considered in those contexts as well. Substantively, *KSR* makes summary judgment of obviousness substantially more accessible for accused infringers than under the old rule, as discussed in § 14.3.5.2. As a result, patentees and accused infringers alike have filed—and won—more obviousness motions than they did before *KSR*. As one example, in *Ohio Willow Wood Co. v. Alps South, LLC*, 735 F.3d 1333 (Fed. Cir. 2013), the Federal Circuit affirmed the district court's use of *KSR's* tools to grant summary determination of obviousness. There, considering claims related to independent claims that another court already held to be obvious, the district court evaluated only the limitations added by the dependent claims—numerical limits on certain characteristics of "gel composition" and "fabric" elements—and found the dependent claims to be obvious. The Federal Circuit affirmed:

> While it is true that [t]he determination of obviousness is made with respect to the subject matter as a whole, not separate pieces of the claim, nothing in the record indicates that confining the otherwise obvious "gel composition" and "fabric" limi-

> tations to the recited numerical limits in the disputed dependent claims was anything other than the exercise of routine skill.

Id. at 1333–34; *see also MySpace, Inc. v. GraphOn Corp.*, 672 F.3d 1250, 1257–58 (Fed. Cir. 2012) (affirming summary judgment of obviousness and finding where "claims share a common term that lies at the heart of the invention," district court's limitation-by-limitation analysis, rather than analysis of claim as a whole, was adequate to support summary judgment); *Unigene Labs, Inc. v. Apotex, Inc.*, 655 F.3d 1352, 1364 (Fed. Cir. 2011) (affirming summary judgment of nonobviousness); *Odom v. Microsoft Corp.*, 429 F. App'x 967, 2011 U.S. App. LEXIS 9115 (Fed. Cir. 2011) (affirming summary judgment of obviousness); *Eisai Co., Ltd. v. Dr. Reddy's Labs, Ltd.*, 533 F.3d 1353, 1355 (Fed. Cir. 2008) (affirming summary judgment of nonobviousness).

6.2.1.1.3 Anticipation

To prove that a patent claim is anticipated, an accused infringer must show by clear and convincing evidence that a single prior art reference contains each limitation of that claim. Conversely, the patentee only needs to show the absence of only one limitation from the prior art disclosure. The combination of this limited showing and the high burden of proof on the accused infringer often combine to make this issue amenable to summary judgment of no anticipation. For the same reasons, summary judgment of anticipation, while possible, is less common.

6.2.1.1.4 Section 112(f) Indefiniteness

Under § 112(f) (formerly § 112, ¶ 6), a patentee can draft its claims in "means-plus-function" form—e.g., claiming a "means for attaching" instead of claiming a nail—so long as it discloses in the specification structure that corresponds to the claimed function. If a patentee fails to disclose corresponding structure within the four corners of the specification, the claim is indefinite. *Budde v. Harley-Davidson, Inc.*, 250 F.3d 1369, 1376 (Fed. Cir. 2001). Note that the Supreme Court's decision in *Nautilus, Inc. v. Biosig Instruments, Inc.*, where it loosened the standard for indefiniteness, did not purport to change (and would not logically alter) the analysis for determining whether a claim is indefinite for failing to comply with § 112(f). *See Nautilus, Inc. v. Biosig Instruments, Inc.*, 134 S. Ct. 2120, 2124 (2014) (rejecting the "insolubly ambiguous" standard in favor of the "reasonable certainty" standard); *Robert Bosch, LLC v. Snap-On, Inc.*, 769 F.3d 1094 (Fed. Cir. 2014) (post-*Nautilus* decision affirming summary judgment of indefiniteness for failure to disclose corresponding structure as required by § 112(f) without referencing *Nautilus* or the "reasonable certainty" standard). Although both types of indefiniteness arise under § 112(b)'s requirement that the claims "particularly point[] out and distinctly claim[] the subject matter" of the invention, to distinguish between the two types we refer to indefiniteness for failure to identify corresponding structure for a means-plus-function or step-plus-function claim as arising "under § 112(f)."

To constitute an adequate corresponding structure, an alleged corresponding structure must be (1) "clearly linked" to the claimed function to which it allegedly corresponds, (2) capable of performing that function, and (3) disclosed within the four corners of the specification (e.g., disclosure in the file history is insufficient). *Budde*, 250 F.3d at 1377. Disputes about whether the specification contains a disclosure adequate to satisfy these requirements are common. For example, in the software context, the parties commonly dispute whether the patent's description of a general-purpose computer operating software that carries out a function provides sufficient structure. This is because, by itself, a general purpose computer is not sufficient structure. *Aristocrat Techs. Austl. Pty. Ltd. v. Int'l Game Tech.*, 521 F.3d 1328, 1333 (Fed. Cir. 2008). Disclosure of an algorithm may suffice, if it is programmed to turn the general-purpose computer into a special-purpose computer, *see id.*, but whether an algorithm in a given patent is sufficiently detailed to do so is often disputed. In this example, as in most cases, this defense depends almost entirely on the disclosure of the specification of the patent-in-suit (though, in some cases, also upon expert testimony concerning the knowledge of one of ordinary skill in the art). Consequently, the range of disputed facts is usually narrow, and the issue typically turns on what conclusions can be drawn from the underlying facts. The disputes about such conclusions are often expressed in competing expert declarations. Because indefiniteness is a question of law, such disputes between experts about the ultimate conclusion do not preclude summary judgment.

6.2.1.1.5 Section 112(b) Indefiniteness Under *Nautilus*

In *Nautilus*, the Supreme Court held that, under the proper standard, "a patent is invalid for indefiniteness if its claims, read in light of the specification delineating the patent, and the prosecution history, fail to inform, with reasonable certainty, those skilled in the art about the scope of the invention." *Nautilus*, 134 S. Ct. at 2124. In *Teva*, the Supreme Court held that claim construction may in some cases require the court to make underlying factual determinations and, in such cases, the district court's underlying factual determinations are to be reviewed for clear error. *Teva Pharm. USA, Inc. v. Sandoz, Inc.*, 135 S. Ct. 831 (2015). The interplay between indefiniteness and claim construction is addressed in § 5.2.5.2, and a discussion of the evolution of the legal standards for indefiniteness appear in § 14.3.3.4. It is worth noting here that in some cases the *Nautilus* and *Teva* decisions are likely to change the posture in which indefiniteness arguments are presented to the court. Historically, indefiniteness was often presented to courts in the first instance in conjunction with claim construction, either through a motion for summary judgment of invalidity filed concurrently with claim construction or more commonly where a party seeks a finding of "indefiniteness" in lieu of a claim construction (and, if successful, files a follow-on motion to convert the finding into a judgment of invalidity). This practice results not only from the natural interplay between claim construction and indefiniteness, but also because the Federal Circuit's now-defunct "insolubly ambiguous" indefiniteness standard—which heightened the focus on whether a claim was capable of construction—effectively mandated that posture for most indefiniteness issues.

By liberalizing the standard for finding that a claim is indefinite, the *Nautilus* decision invites a greater number of indefiniteness challenges at the claim-construction stage. Nonetheless, by shifting the focus of the inquiry from whether a claim is amenable to construction to whether the language reasonably apprises those skilled in the art of the bounds of the invention, *Nautilus* arguably makes at least some forms of indefiniteness less amenable to resolution through claim construction or through a first-track motion.

Indefiniteness disputes can arise in at least three conceptually different scenarios: (1) a claim or claim term is arguably incapable of construction because neither the intrinsic or extrinsic evidence resolves inherent ambiguity; (2) a claim or claim term has a clear meaning, but the clear meaning arguably fails to provide those skilled in the art reasonable certainty about the scope of the invention (e.g., because the meaning results in a subjective determination, because the meaning can be applied in at least two conflicting ways, because the meaning sets a condition that cannot be measured, or because structural elements are claimed in purely functional terms); and/or (3) the parties dispute the claim or claim term meaning and at least one of the proposed constructions arguably fails to provide those skilled in the art reasonable certainty about the scope of the invention.

Scenario 1 presents an issue properly resolved at the claim-construction stage. Claim construction and indefiniteness are both measured from the perspective of a person having ordinary skill in the art at the same point in time, and most underlying factual disputes that affect indefiniteness are likely to be resolved as part of claim construction. Scenarios 2 and 3, however, may be less appropriate for resolution at the claim-construction stage because they implicate factual disputes beyond the type of claim construction fact-finding.

Teva effectively addressed a claim-construction dispute in the context of indefiniteness scenario 3. *See Teva Pharm. USA, Inc. v. Sandoz, Inc.*, 135 S. Ct. 831 (2015). Sandoz defended on the grounds that the patent was invalid because it claimed that Copaxone's active ingredient had "a molecular weight of 5 to 9 kilodaltons." *See id.* at 842. Sandoz argued that there were three methods to determine this weight—peak average molecular weight (the weight of the most prevalent molecule), the weight as calculated by the average weight of all molecules, or the weight as calculated by an average in which heavier molecules count for more—and therefore Teva's failure to specify a precise meaning rendered the claim indefinite. *Id.* at 842–43. Teva's expert testified that skilled artisans would understand the term in question to refer to "peak average molecular weight," which the district judge credited. *Id.*

While this determination is similar to construing the disputed claim term, it answers a distinct factual question. It remains to be seen if claim construction will parallel the claim indefiniteness across the range of cases. Furthermore, claim construction applies a different evidentiary standard (preponderance) than indefiniteness (clear and convincing evidence). As discussed in § 5.2.5.2, there is reason to believe that the standards will largely converge. Moreover, the same rationale that led the Supreme Court to rule in *Markman* that claim construction is a matter for the court (and not a jury) would appear to apply to the claim indefiniteness determination. *See* J. Jonas Anderson & Peter S. Menell, *Restoring the Fact/Law Distinction in Patent Claim Construction*, 109 Nw. U. L. Rev. Online 187, 198–200 (2015) (discussing the interplay of claim construction and indefiniteness post-*Teva*).

Nonetheless, courts should not assume that claim indefiniteness can be resolved through standard claim-construction proceedings. Courts should be careful to identify the precise issues involved in evaluating claim indefiniteness and be sure to afford the parties a fair opportunity to gather and present their evidence.

6.2.1.2 Infringement

As noted above, *see* § 6.2.1, infringement is generally more amenable to summary judgment than is invalidity because of its lower burden of proof (preponderance as opposed to "clear and convincing"). But because a patentee must show that every limitation of an asserted claim is present in the accused device, it is easier to demonstrate factual disputes to preclude summary judgment of infringement. Because the ultimate issue of infringement is one of fact, infringement issues that often require courts to draw inferences from the known facts, such as finding equivalency under § 112(f) and the doctrine of equivalents, are typically not well suited to summary judgment because all such inferences are drawn against the moving party. In contrast, noninfringement and various other issues are often amenable to summary judgment, as discussed below. Of course, in any given case these guidelines may not apply. For example, it is certainly possible that summary judgment of infringement could be appropriate if there are only a few issues in dispute and those issues are effectively resolved as part of claim construction.

6.2.1.2.1 Absence of Literal Infringement

An accused infringer need only show the absence of a single claim limitation from the accused device to avoid literal infringement. Because literal infringement can be defeated on such a narrow ground, motions for summary judgment of noninfringement are common.

6.2.1.2.2 Whether Infringement Under the Doctrine of Equivalents Is Barred by *Festo*

Although infringement under the doctrine of equivalents is a factual question that summary judgment cannot resolve, whether amendments of the patent during prosecution bar the patentee from asserting infringement under the doctrine of equivalents is a legal question well suited to summary judgment. A patentee is barred from asserting infringement under the doctrine of equivalents as to a claim that was amended for reasons of patentability during prosecution unless the asserted equivalent was unforeseeable at the time of the amendment, the amendment bears no more than a tangential relation to the equivalent in question, or there is some other reason suggesting that the patentee could not reasonably have been expected to describe the equivalent. *Festo Corp. v. Shoketsu Kinzoku Kogyo Kabushiki Co.*, 535 U.S. 722, 740–41 (2002); § 14.4.1.4.2.1.2. This inquiry depends largely on facts revealed by the prosecution history for the patent-in-suit. As a result, the court can often decide this issue at the summary judgment stage.

6.2.1.2.3 Whether Infringement Under the Doctrine of Equivalents Would Violate the *Wilson Sporting Goods* Doctrine

In *Wilson Sporting Goods Co. v. David Geoffrey & Assocs.*, the Federal Circuit held that there can be no infringement under the doctrine of equivalents if the asserted equivalents, combined with the remaining elements of the claim, encompass the prior art. 904 F.2d 677, 683 (Fed. Cir. 1990) (*overruled in part on other grounds* by *Cardinal Chem. Co. v. Morton Int'l*, 508 U.S. 83 (1993)); *see* § 14.4.1.4.2.1.3. For example, a patentee might assert that claim limitations one through four are met literally, and limitation five is met under the doctrine of equivalents. *Wilson Sporting Goods* precludes this argument if the prior art discloses literal limitations one through four combined with the element in the accused product that is asserted to be equivalent to claim limitation five. Whether an asserted range of equivalents encompasses the prior art, thus barring the application of the doctrine as advanced by the patentee, is a question of law. *Id.* at 684. Because the court makes the ultimate decision on this issue, it is often amenable to resolution at the summary judgment stage.

6.2.1.2.4 The Actions Accused of Infringement Did/Did Not Occur Within the United States

Under § 271(a), making, using, selling, offering to sell, or importing an infringing product or method *within the United States* constitutes an act of infringement. A single transaction frequently implicates multiple jurisdictions. For example, a widget may be sold by a Tokyo company to an Indiana company pursuant to a contract negotiated in Oslo, with the widgets to be shipped to Indiana f.o.b. Taiwan. In these circumstances, parties often dispute whether the transaction occurred *within the United States* as required by § 271. Parties often style motions about this issue as motions *in limine* relating to damages. For example, the defendant may seek to exclude evidence supporting some of the alleged infringing sales because those sales allegedly occurred in a foreign country. But this issue is properly addressed as one of infringement. Because these motions are substantive, courts should treat them as motions for summary judgment, rather than as *in limine* motions, to ensure that the relevant issues are fully briefed and considered. *See* § 7.5.

Whether an allegedly infringing act occurred within, or outside of, the United States is a question of law. *See N. Am. Philips Corp. v. Lockheed Sanders, Inc.*, 35 F.3d 1576, 1579 (Fed. Cir. 1994). Whether acts occurring within the United States are sufficient to constitute a sale, offer to sell, use, manufacture, or importation is a question of fact. *See, e.g., MEMC Elec. Materials v. Mitsubishi Materials Silicon Corp.*, 420 F.3d 1369, 1375 (Fed. Cir. 2005). Typically, the parties agree that a certain set of events took place in certain locations, but dispute the conclusions to be drawn from these events as they relate to infringement. As a result, both questions—locus of the acts and characterization of the acts—are often amenable to summary judgment.

6.2.1.2.5 The Absence of Evidence of Direct Infringement Bars Claims of Indirect Infringement

Under § 271(b) and (c), a party can be held liable for indirect infringement by contributing to a third party's infringement or by actively inducing a third party to infringe, respectively. To establish indirect infringement, the patentee must prove that specific acts of direct infringement by third parties occurred. *BMC Res., Inc. v. Paymentech, LP*, 498 F.3d 1373, 1380 (Fed. Cir. 2007) (affirming judgment of noninfringement). The analysis of direct infringement is the same for a third party as for a party and so is generally no more or less amenable to summary judgment. But, in some cases, the patentee does not focus its discovery efforts on gathering evidence of direct infringement by third parties. As a result, it is not uncommon for an accused infringer to bring a *Celotex* motion arguing that the patentee plaintiff can show no evidence of the direct infringement by third parties that is a predicate to a finding of indirect infringement against the defendant.

6.2.1.2.6 "Divided" (Joint) Infringement: The Actions Accused of Infringement Are Made by Multiple Parties, Not Just the Accused Infringer

The Federal Circuit has emphasized that where an accused infringer does not itself perform all the steps of an accused method, it cannot be liable for infringement unless it controls or directs performance of each step of the accused method. *Muniauction, Inc. v. Thomson Corp.*, 532 F.3d 1318 (Fed. Cir. 2008) (reversing a jury verdict of infringement); *BMC Res., Inc.*, 498 F.3d at 1380. Mere "arms-length cooperation" is not enough to show the necessary control or direction. *BMC Res., Inc.*, 498 F.3d at 1381. Indeed, the Federal Circuit set forth the bright line rule that "there can only be joint infringement when there is an agency relationship between the parties who perform the method steps or when one party is contractually obligated to the other person to perform the steps." *Akamai Techs., Inc. v. Limelight Networks, Inc.*, 629 F.3d 1311, 1320 (Fed. Cir. 2010), *rev'd on other grounds*, 692 F.3d 1301 (Fed. Cir. 2012) (en banc) (per curiam), *rev'd*, 134 S. Ct. 2111 (2014).

In 2012, the Federal Circuit sitting en banc reversed the *Akamai* decision without revisiting the § 271(a) direct infringement case law and instead held that a party could be liable for induced infringement under § 271(b), even when there is no direct infringement by a single entity under § 271(a). *Limelight Networks, Inc. v. Akamai Techs., Inc.*, 134 S. Ct. 2111 (2014). That holding was reversed by the Supreme Court, which held that a defendant is not "liable for inducing infringement under § 271(b) when no one has directly infringed under § 271(a) or any other statutory provision." *Id.* at 2115. In reaching its decision, the Supreme Court declined to review the *Muniauction* decision and assumed without deciding that the Federal Circuit's holding in *Muniauction* was correct. *Id.* at 2120. Thus, at present, *Muniauction*'s "single actor" rule for method claims controls.

By contrast, the same "single entity" rule does not appear to apply to apparatus claims. *See, e.g., Centillion Data Sys., LLC v. Qwest Commc'ns Int'l, Inc.*, 631 F.3d 1279, 1285 (Fed. Cir. 2011) ("The customer puts the system as a whole into service, *i.e.*, controls the system and obtains benefit from it . . . . By causing the system as a whole to perform this processing and obtaining the benefit of the result, the customer has 'used' the system under § 271(a).").

Additionally, and for either an apparatus or method claim, the law is clear that "'[a] patentee can usually structure a claim to capture infringement by a single party,' by 'focus[ing] on one entity.'" *Uniloc USA, Inc. v. Microsoft Corp.*, 632 F.3d 1292, 1309 (Fed. Cir. 2011) (citing *BMC Res., Inc. v. Paymentech, L.P.*, 498 F.3d 1373, 1381 (Fed. Cir. 2007)). "That other parties are necessary to complete the environment in which the claimed element functions does not necessarily divide the infringement between the necessary parties." *Uniloc*, 632 F.3d at 1309 (noting a claim may require two parties to function, but may be infringed by just the one who uses the claimed invention). Thus, in some circumstances, a claim may recite multiple actors without presenting a divided infringement issue.

When a party other than the accused infringer performs one or more of the steps in a method claim, the issue of whether that step is performed under the direction or control of the accused infringer may be amenable to summary judgment. The issue is so narrow in scope that the material facts may not be in dispute. Thus, summary judgment may be appropriate if those facts establish that a third party performed at least one step of the method outside the control or direction of the accused infringer.

6.2.1.2.7 Absence of Evidence Showing the Required Mental State for Indirect Infringement

There was, for some time, debate about the mental state required for indirect infringement. The Supreme Court clarified the standard for inducement in *Global-Tech Appliances, Inc. v. SEB S.A.*, 131 S. Ct. 2060 (2011), holding that "induced infringement under § 271(b) requires knowledge that the induced acts constitute infringement" of the asserted patent. *Id.* at 2068. In reaching this conclusion, the Court relied on—and embraced—its oft-overlooked decision in *Aro Manufacturing Co., Inc. v. Convertible Top Replacement Co.* (*Aro II*), 377 U.S. 476 (1964), which addresses the mental state for contributory infringement under § 271(c). There, a majority of the Court held "that § 271(c) does require a showing that the alleged contributory infringer knew that the combination for which his component was especially designed was both patented and infringing." *Id.* at 488; *see also Global-Tech*, 131 S. Ct. at 2067–68 (discussing *Aro II* and holding that § 271(b) and (c) require the "same knowledge"—that the induced act or combination to which the alleged infringer contributed was infringing.)

The Supreme Court's clarification of the mental state for inducement and contributory infringement made disputes about whether the alleged indirect infringer possessed the requisite mental state more amenable to summary judgment. For example, where the patentee can point to no evidence showing that the alleged infringer had knowledge of the patent when the acts occurred, summary judgment may be appropriate. Likewise, where an accused infringer can show that, even though it had knowledge of the patent, it had a good-faith belief that the allegedly infringing acts or combinations did not, in fact, infringe, summary judgment may also be appropriate.

6.2.1.2.8 License and Exhaustion Defenses

Patent licenses and the doctrine of patent exhaustion create a constellation of defenses that are often amenable to summary judgment. A straightforward license defense arises when an accused infringer asserts that the acts alleged to infringe are covered by a valid license to the patent-in-suit. While the defense often involves some factual issues, such factual disputes are often limited and the primary issues in dispute are typically legal—whether a valid license contract exists, whether that contract covers both the patent-in-suit and the acts accused of infringement, and so forth. Likewise, an implied license defense—where, typically, the purchaser of a licensed product is accused of infringement based on its use or incorporation of that product into another product—is at its core a series of contractual questions focused on the rights granted by the patentee to the component manufacturer, and on the scope of rights "sold" by the component manufacturer to the downstream customer now accused of infringement. Patent exhaustion, a closely related (and often conflated) defense that arises when the patentee seeks to double-dip by enforcing its rights against both an upstream and downstream entity with respect to the same product, presents similar issues. Because each of these defenses typically involves a confined set of facts and presents legal or equitable issues that are decided by the Court, they can often be resolved, one way or the other, on summary judgment.

6.2.1.3 Damages

Many substantive issues within the damages sphere require the fact finder to draw factual conclusions from disputed evidence and so are not particularly well-suited for resolution on summary judgment. There are, however, a number of exceptions.

First, under § 287, damages against the infringer begin to accrue (1) upon actual notice of the patent or (2) upon constructive notice of the patent. When a patentee sells products embodying the invention, constructive notice can be established by marking those products with the patent number. When method claims are asserted, the marking requirement may not apply, and the patentee may be able to accrue damages from the time the patent issued. *See, e.g., Hanson v. Alpine Ski Area, Inc.*, 718 F.2d 1075, 1082–83 (Fed. Cir. 1983). There is often little dispute about whether the patentee sells an embodying product, has marked that product with the patent number, or has provided actual notice of the patent to the accused infringer prior to suit. Thus, courts are not typically asked to address the factual question whether a patentee satisfied the marking requirement. Instead, the parties typically dispute whether, given the nature of the asserted and non-asserted claims in the patent-in-suit, marking was required at all. This is a narrow, legal issue that can often be decided at the summary judgment stage.

Second, when one side's expert relies on improper *legal* theories, it may be possible to adjudicate damages issues through pretrial motion practice. For example, when a party seeks the benefit of the entire market value rule without evidence that "the patented feature creates the basis for customer demand or substantially create[s] the value of the component parts" it may be possible (and advisable) to rule on the issue prior to trial. *See Uniloc USA, Inc. v. Microsoft Corp.*, 632 F.3d 1292 (Fed. Cir. 2011). Similarly, where a party improperly relies on the "25% Rule" as a methodology to calculate a reasonable royalty, a court should consider ruling prior to trial on this issue. *See id.* at 1315 (holding as a matter of law that the 25% rule of thumb is a fundamentally flawed tool for determining a baseline royalty rate in a hypothetical negotiation, therefore evidence relying on that rule is inadmissible). A court should also consider ruling prior to trial on an improper application of the Nash Bargaining Solution in which a party fails to "sufficiently establish[] that the premises of the theorem actually apply to the facts of the case at hand," because such a use would be an "inappropriate 'rule of thumb.'" *VirnetX, Inc. v. Cisco Sys., Inc.*, 767 F.3d 1308, 1332–34 (Fed. Cir. 2014); *see also Robocast, Inc. v. Microsoft Corp.*, No. 10-1055-RGA, 2014 U.S. Dist. LEXIS 10745, 2014 WL 350062 (D. Del. Jan. 29, 2014) (ruling on application of Nash bargaining and reliance on licenses not technologically comparable); *Oracle Am., Inc. v. Google Inc.*, 798 F. Supp. 2d 1111 (N.D. Cal. 2011) (excluding conjoint analysis where the expert included three patented features among the seven studied features, failed to include important non-patented features among the seven tested features, and failed to provide any reasonable criteria for the selection).

6.2.2 Issues Less Amenable to Summary Judgment

The issues least amenable to summary judgment are typically those that have at least two of the following characteristics: (1) require a high burden of proof; (2) are questions of fact; (3) are broad issues requiring the movant to establish a wide range of facts; and (4) involve subjects about which the underlying facts are typically disputed.

For example, the contention that a patent claim is anticipated combines the high clear-and-convincing burden of proof with the requirement that the accused infringer establish that a single reference contains a disclosure of every limitation of the claim. This normally involves proving a wide range of facts in the face of vehement disagreement from the patentee, though of course in some cases anticipation may be an issue that is essentially resolved as a result of a broad claim construction. Infringement under the doctrine of equivalents has a different combination of characteristics: It is a factual question that requires the fact finder to draw inferences from the underlying facts, and the parties typically rely heavily on conflicting expert opinions about whether the differences between the claim limitation and asserted equivalent are insubstantial. Again, however, in some cases the doctrine of equivalents may be an issue that is essentially resolved as a result of a broad claim construction.

The equitable issues of laches and estoppel typically involve heavily disputed underlying facts. The invalidity defenses of enablement and written description combine a high burden of proof with the fact that the parties typically rely on conflicting expert testimony about what a person having ordinary skill in the art would have understood about the patent's disclosure. As a result of these characteristics, these issues are less amenable to summary judgment.

Another issue generally less amenable to summary judgment is a claim of inequitable conduct. This is particularly true in light of the Federal Circuit's en banc decision in *Therasense, Inc. v. Becton, Dickinson & Co.*, 649 F.3d 1276 (Fed. Cir. 2011). In *Therasense*, the court set forth heightened standards for both parts of the two-part standard for an inequitable conduct defense. To satisfy the first part, the accused infringer must show, by clear and convincing evidence, that the patentee "acted with the specific intent to deceive the [Patent Office]." *Id.* at 1290. In cases where the alleged misconduct was the nondisclosure of prior art, the accused infringer "must prove by clear and convincing evidence that the applicant knew of the [prior art] reference, knew that it was material, and made a deliberate decision to withhold it." *Id.* To satisfy the second part of the test, the accused infringer must prove, by clear and convincing evidence, that the misconduct was "but-for" material. In the context of nondisclosure, but-for materiality means that "the [Patent Office] would not have allowed a claim had it been aware of the undisclosed prior art." *Id.* at 1291. *Therasense* provides one exception to but-for materiality—"[w]hen the patentee has engaged in affirmative acts of egregious misconduct, such as the filing of an unmistakably false affidavit, the misconduct is material." *Id.* at 1292.

Because the standard is high and the inquiry is fact-intensive, inequitable conduct can seldom be affirmatively established on summary judgment. A patentee, however, can more easily establish a lack of inequitable conduct on summary judgment in light of the heightened standard. For example, in the nondisclosure context, even where materiality and knowledge are established, the claim will not survive without evidence sufficient to draw the inference that the material was withheld with the specific intent to deceive the Patent Office—even high materiality is insufficient to give rise to an inference where there is no evidence of intent. *See, e.g.*, *1st Media, LLC v. Elec. Arts, Inc.*, 694 F.3d 1367, 1373–74 (Fed. Cir. 2012) (reversing a district court judgment of inequitable conduct following a bench trial, despite the district court's finding that the withheld references were material and that the named inventor and his prosecution attorney knew that they were material, because there was "no direct evidence that [the inventor and prosecuting attorney] intended to deceive the PTO"). But where some evidence of the specific intent to deceive exists, particularly in the context of misrepresentations made to the Patent Office, an inequitable conduct defense may be difficult to resolve on summary judgment. *See, e.g.*, *Ohio Willow Wood Co. v. Alps S., LLC*, 735 F.3d at 1350–51 (reversing summary judgment of no inequitable conduct where the record contained evidence sufficient to find but-for materiality of withheld material, where counsel repeatedly made false representations in arguments to Board of Patent Appeals and Interferences, and where the fact that the repeated misrepresentations were directly refuted by evidence in the attorneys' possession was sufficient to support an inference of intent to deceive, but observing that "[w]e leave it to the district court to determine if the inference of deceptive intent that we hold could be drawn when viewing the evidence in a light most favorable to Alps remains after assessing the credibility of OWW's witnesses"). Because the issue of intent turns on the credibility of witnesses, inequitable conduct is difficult to resolve on summary judgment absent a complete failure of proof as to one of the elements of the defense.

In a significant shift, willfulness is now also less amenable to summary judgment. As prior editions of this Guide explained, for nearly a decade courts applied the two-prong willfulness test set forth in *In re Seagate Technology, LLC*, 497 F.3d 1360 (Fed. Cir. 2007). To satisfy the first prong, *Seagate* required the patentee to prove by "clear and convincing evidence that the infringer acted despite an objectively high likelihood that its actions constituted infringement of a valid patent," *Id.* at 1371. The Federal Circuit equated this prong with an "objective baselessness" standard, and "[i]f an objective litigant could conclude that the [defenses were] reasonably calculated to elicit a favorable outcome" they were not objectively baseless under § 285 and, for the same reason, *Seagate*'s objective test would not be satisfied." *Bard Peripheral Vascular, Inc. v. W.L. Gore & Assocs., Inc.*, 682 F.3d 1003, 1007 (Fed. Cir. 2012). In short, if any of the defendant's defenses were not baseless, willfulness failed as a matter of law, regardless of whether the patentee could satisfy the second ("subjective intent") prong. This made willfulness very susceptible to summary judgment.

In 2016, the Supreme Court rejected the "unduly rigid" *Seagate* test in *Halo Electronics, Inc., v. Pulse Electronics, Inc.*, No. 14-1513, slip op. at 9-11, 15 (Supreme Court, June 3, 2016). In its place, the Court held that, like most aspects of patent litigation, willfulness requires proof by a preponderance of the evidence, not clear and convincing evidence. *Id.* at 12. And it embraced the AIA's amendments to § 284 that bar patentees from relying on a defendant's decision not to seek an opinion of counsel to prove willfulness. *Id.* at 14. Beyond these clear pronouncements, the Supreme Court provided only general guidelines about the standard for willfulness and enhanced damages, leaving much room for interpretation. For example, the Court delinked enhanced damages from willfulness by observing that willfulness is not a per se requirement for enhanced damages. At the same time, the Court observed that enhanced damages are generally appropriate only in egregious cases typified by willful misconduct. *Id.* at 11. Thus, willfulness will continue to play a central role in awarding enhanced damages. The Court did not identify what other factors might warrant enhanced damages, opening up leeway for litigants and district judges to flesh out appropriate circumstances.

As to the standard for awarding enhanced damages, the Court painted with broad strokes—damages should not be enhanced in "garden-variety" infringement cases and are "generally . . . reserved for egregious cases typified by willful misconduct," but "none of this is to say that enhanced damages must follow a finding of egregious misconduct." *Id.* at 11, 15. Although courts will need to work through the contours of these guidelines, what is clear is that the new standard is fact-intensive: "courts should continue to take into account the particular circumstances of each case in deciding whether to award damages, and in what amount." *Id.* at 11. Given the fact-intensive nature of the inquiry, and—at least in the short term—the uncertainty about how these new guidelines should be applied, willful infringement is not well-suited for resolution by summary judgment in most cases.

Appendix 6.1
Sample Standing Order Setting a Schedule for First-Track Summary Judgment Motions

IN THE UNITED STATES DISTRICT COURT
FOR THE DISTRICT OF ______________

COMPANY, INC.,

Plaintiff,

vs. CASE NO. X

ANOTHER COMPANY, INC.,

Defendant.

STANDING ORDER RE: CLAIM CONSTRUCTION SCHEDULING

It is hereby **ORDERED** that the following deadlines are in effect for all patent infringement cases before the Court absent further order of this Court:

80 days prior to CC hearing date	**[N.D. Cal. Patent L.R. 4-3]** Joint Claim Construction and Prehearing Statement due. Parties shall jointly submit a claim construction chart that sets forth construction of those terms on which the parties agree; each party's proposed constructions of each disputed term, together with an identification of all references from the specification or prosecution history that each party contends support its construction; an identification of the terms whose construction will be most significant to the resolution of the case up to a maximum of 10. **Notice of Intent to File Summary Judgment Motion Based On Claim Construction Due.** A party that believes summary judgment can be granted based in whole or in primary part on the resolution of a claim construction dispute, and that wishes to file a motion for summary judgment to be heard in conjunction with claim construction, shall file a notice with the Court. The notice shall be no longer than 3 pages and shall (1) identify the claim construction dispute on which the summary judgment motion depends and (2) provide a brief summary of the party's basis for believing that summary judgment can be granted based in whole or in primary part on resolution of that claim construction dispute. A party may not identify (or file) more than one summary judgment motion to be heard in conjunction with claim construction without leave of court. If a party wishes to obtain leave of court to file more than one motion, it must file a motion seeking leave no later than 30 days prior this deadline.

65 days prior to CC hearing date	**Motion for Summary Judgment Due.** Any summary judgment motions to be heard with claim construction must be filed.
50 days prior to CC hearing date	**[N.D. Cal. Patent L.R. 4-4]** Discovery Deadline—Claim Construction Issues. The parties shall complete all discovery relating to claim construction, including any depositions with respect to claim construction of any witnesses, including experts.
45 days prior to CC hearing date	**Discovery Deadline—Opposition to Summary Judgment with Claim Construction.** The non-moving party shall complete all discovery relating to any summary judgment motion filed to be heard with claim construction, including any depositions of any witnesses, including experts, offering declarations in support of such summary judgment motions.
35 days prior to CC hearing date	**[N.D. Cal. Patent L.R. 4-5(a)]** Opening brief regarding claim construction due from party claiming patent infringement. **Summary Judgment Opposition Due.** Opposition brief due for any summary judgment motions to be heard with claim construction.
21 days prior to CC hearing date	**[N.D. Cal. Patent L.R. 4-5(b)]** Responsive brief regarding claim construction due from party defending against claim of patent infringement. **Discovery Deadline—Summary Judgment with Claim Construction.** The moving party shall complete all discovery relating to any summary judgment motion filed to be heard with claim construction, including any depositions of any witnesses, including experts, offering declarations in opposition to such summary judgment motions.
14 days prior to CC hearing date	Parties to file a notice with the Court stating the estimated amount of time requested for the claim construction hearing. The Court will notify the parties if it is unable to accommodate this request. **[N.D. Cal. Patent L.R. 4-5(c)]**—Reply brief regarding claim construction due from party claiming patent infringement. **Summary Judgment Reply Due.** Reply brief due for any summary judgment motions to be heard with claim construction.
CC hearing date	The Claim Construction Hearing set by the Court. The Court will hear any Motion for Summary Judgment filed in compliance with the deadlines in this Order in conjunction with the Claim Construction Hearing or shortly thereafter. The Court will notify the parties if the hearing will be separate from the Claim Construction Hearing.

Appendix A
Patent Glossary

Note: Many of these definitions are derived from the USPTO glossary, available at http://www.uspto.gov/main/glossary/index.html.

abandonment: A patent application becomes abandoned for failure to file a complete and proper reply within the time period provided under 37 C.F.R. § 1.134 and § 1.136 unless an office action indicates otherwise. Abandonment may be either of the invention or of an application. An abandoned application, in accordance with 37 C.F.R. §§ 1.135 and 1.138, is one which is removed from the Patent Office docket of pending applications. *See* § 14.3.4.1.6.

abstract of the disclosure: A concise statement of the technical disclosure, including that which is new in the art to which the invention pertains.

agent (practitioner, representative): One who is not an attorney but is authorized to act for or in place of the applicant(s) before the USPTO, that is, an individual who is registered to practice before the USPTO.

all-limitation rule (all-elements rule): A doctrine requiring that an allegedly infringing device contain every element of a claim to establish infringement, either literally or under the doctrine of equivalents. *See* § 14.4.1.4.2.1.1.

analogous art (pertinent art, relevant art): In a nonobviousness analysis, art that a person having ordinary skill in the art would have consulted in attempting to solve the problem addressed by the innovation. Analogous art must be either within the same field of endeavor as the invention, or from a different field but reasonably pertinent to the same problem. *See* § 14.3.5.3.2.

antedate (swearing behind a reference): A procedure whereby a patent applicant can establish an invention date earlier than the effective date of prior art that has been cited against his claims in a rejection for non-obviousness (§ 103) or lack of novelty (§§ 102(a) or (e)).

anticipation: A single prior art reference anticipates a claim when it contains all the elements of the claim. The claim is rejected for lack of novelty under § 102.

assignment: A transfer of ownership of a patent application or patent from one entity to another. Record all assignments with the USPTO Assignment Services Division to maintain clear title to pending patent applications and patents.

benefit claim: The claiming by an applicant in a nonprovisional application of a benefit of an invention disclosed in a prior-filed, co-pending (under examination at the same time), provisional, or nonprovisional application, or international application designating the United States for the purposes of securing an earlier effective filing date for the nonprovisional application.

best mode: The specification must set forth the best mode, or preferred embodiment, contemplated by the inventor at the time of filing, of making and using his or her invention (§ 112), or the patent may be declared invalid. *See* § 14.3.3.3. The AIA eliminated failure to set forth best mode as a basis for patent invalidity.

blocking patent: Two or more patented inventions block each other when one cannot be practiced without infringing the other, and vice versa. Blocking patents often arise when an improvement on an invention is patented: the improvement cannot be practiced without infringing the original patent, and the original inventor cannot practice the improvement without infringing the improvement patent. The parties commonly agree to a cross-license to resolve the issue.

central claiming: A claiming regime in which a claim recites the preferred embodiment of the invention but is deemed to cover a range of equivalents to that preferred embodiment.

Certificate of Correction: Minor errors in an issued patent can be corrected with a Certificate of Correction. *See* § 254 (correction of USPTO mistake); § 255 (correction of applicant mistake).

claim restriction: A discretely claimed component of a patent claim. *See also element.*

claim vitiation: An accused device cannot be infringing if it would effectively vitiate (or eliminate) any claim limitation. This doctrine is a corollary of the all-elements rule. *See* § 14.4.1.4.2.1.1.1.

claims: Claims delineate the patented invention. The patent specification must conclude with a claim or claims particularly pointing out and distinctly claiming the subject matter that the applicant regards as his or her invention or discovery.

classification: Patents are classified by a system using a three-digit class and a three-digit subclass to describe every similar grouping of patent art. Multiple classification codes may describe a single invention.

combination patent: A patent granted for an invention that unites existing components in a novel way.

composed of (used when defining the scope of a claim): A transitional phrase that is interpreted in the same manner as either *consisting of* or *consisting essentially of*, depending on the facts of the particular case.

comprising (used when defining the scope of a claim): A transitional phrase that is synonymous with *including, containing* or *characterized by*; is inclusive or open-ended and does not exclude additional, unrecited elements or method steps. *Comprising* is a term of art used in claim language that means that the named elements are essential in describing the invention.

conception: The formation in the mind of the inventor of the definite and permanent idea of the complete invention that is thereafter reduced to practice. *See* § 14.3.4.1.2.1.

consisting essentially of (used when defining the scope of a claim): A transitional phrase that limits the scope of a claim to the specified materials or steps and those that do not materially affect the basic and novel characteristics of the claimed invention. For the purposes of searching for and applying prior art under §§ 102 and 103, absent a clear indication in the specification or claims of what the basic and novel characteristics actually are, *consisting essentially of* will be construed as equivalent to *comprising*.

consisting of (used when defining the scope of a claim): A transitional phrase that is closed and excludes any element, step, or ingredient not specified in the claim.

continuation: A second application for the same invention claimed in a prior nonprovisional application and filed before the first application becomes abandoned or patented.

continuation-in-part (CIP): An application filed during the lifetime of an earlier nonprovisional application that repeats some substantial portion or all of the earlier nonprovisional application and adds matter not disclosed in the earlier nonprovisional application. *See* § 14.2.3.4.

contributory infringement: Section 271(c) imposes liability when a party "offers to sell or sell within the United States or imports into the United States a component of a patented machine, manufacture, combination or composition, or a material or apparatus for use in practicing a patented process, constituting a material part of the invention, knowing the same to be especially made or especially adapted for use in an infringement of such patent, and not a staple article or commodity of commerce suitable for substantial noninfringing use, shall be liable as a contributory infringer." *See* § 14.4.1.3.2.

counterpart: An application filed in a foreign patent office that is substantially similar to the patent application filed with the USPTO and is based on some or all of the same invention. The two applications would generally have the same applicant.

covered business method review (CBMR): The America Invents Act instituted a variant of the postgrant review process for business method patents of all filing dates. Patent validity can be challenged on any ground, and covered business method review is broader than inter partes review. *See* § 14.2.5.8.1.

critical date: The date one year prior to the date a patent application is filed. The patent will be invalid for lack of novelty if the invention was in public use in the United States, or patented or described anywhere in the world, prior to the critical date. *See* § 102(b); § 14.3.4.1.5.

declaration (of inventor): A document in which an applicant for patent declares that he or she (1) made or authorized the application, (2) believes that he or she is the original inventor or an original joint inventor of a claimed invention in the application; and (3) acknowledges that any willful false statement made in the declaration is punishable under 18 U.S.C. § 1001 by fine or imprisonment of not more than five (5) years, or both. These requirements apply to applications filed after September 15, 2012. *See* M.P.E.P § 602.01(a)–(b). For applications filed prior to that date, the declaration also required the inventor's country of citizenship. An oath or declaration must be filed in each nonprovisional patent application.

definiteness: Shorthand for the requirement, under § 112(b), that the claims particularly point out and distinctly claim the subject matter that the applicant regards as his or her invention. *See* § 14.3.3.4.

dependent claim: A claim that refers back to and further limits a preceding dependent or independent claim. A dependent claim includes by reference every limitation of the claim from which it depends.

derivation proceeding: The AIA established this new proceeding to allow an inventor to challenge an earlier-filed third-party application or patent claiming subject matter that was derived from the inventor's own work. This proceeding partially substitutes for interference proceedings. *See* § 14.3.4.2.5.

design patent: A patent for a new, original, and ornamental design for an article of manufacture.

designation: A selection made by the applicant, in the Request for an International Application filed under the Patent Cooperation Treaty (PCT), as to the countries in which protection for an invention is desired.

diligence: To establish a conception date as the date of invention, the inventor must have worked diligently following conception to reduce the invention to practice. In the course of an interference, a party can establish its conception date as the date of invention by showing reasonable diligence from before the other's conception until their own reduction to practice date. *See* § 102(g); § 14.3.4.1.2.3.

direct infringement: A person is liable for direct infringement if he or she "without authority makes, uses, offers to sell, or sells any patented invention, within the United States or imports into the United States any patented invention during the term of the patent therefore." § 271(a). An accused infringer's intent is immaterial, as patent infringement is a strict liability offense. *See* § 14.4.1.1.

disclaimer: There are two types of disclaimers under § 253: statutory disclaimers and terminal disclaimers. A patentee may make a statutory disclaimer of any complete claim, stating therein the extent of his or her interest in such patent. A patentee may make a terminal disclaimer to disclaim or dedicate to the public the remaining time of the term of the patent granted. A terminal disclaimer may be filed for the purpose of overcoming a judicially created double-patenting rejection. Disclaimers are required to be in writing and recorded in the USPTO, and are considered part of the original patent to the extent of the interest actually possessed by the disclaimant and by those claiming under him or her.

disclosure: In return for a patent, the inventor gives as consideration a complete disclosure of the invention for which protection is sought. *See* § 14.3.3.

divisional application: A later application for an independent or distinct invention disclosing and claiming only a portion of the subject matter disclosed in the earlier or parent application.

doctrine of equivalents: A judicially developed principle for finding patent infringement when the accused process or product falls outside the literal scope of the patent claims. The essential objective inquiry is: "Does the accused product or process contain elements equivalent to each claimed element of the patented invention?" *See* § 14.4.1.4.2.

double patenting: An inventor may not obtain claims in more than one patent directed either to the same invention or an obvious variation of the same invention. A rejection by the USPTO based on obviousness can be overcome by filing a terminal disclaimer stating that the additional patents will expire on the same date as the first patent. A terminal disclaimer, therefore, eliminates any improper extension of the initial patent term. *See* § 14.4.2.4.1.

effective filing date: The filing date of an earlier-filed application accorded under §§ 119/365(a)/365(b) (foreign filing or domestic provisional application), 120/365(c) (earlier U.S. filing date), or 121 (divisional applications), or if none of these sections is satisfied, the actual filing date of the patent.

electronic file wrapper: A system that provides a way to access electronic copies of the correspondence, documents, and other pertinent records used in considering a particular patent application.

element: A discretely claimed component of a patent claim. *See also claim restriction.*

embodiment: A manner in which an invention can be made, used, practiced, or expressed. *See best mode.*

enablement: The specification must describe in "full, clear, concise, and exact terms" how to make and use the invention such that any person skilled in the art can do so without undue experimentation. *See* § 14.3.3.2.

ex parte reexamination: A procedure whereby patentees and third parties can seek reexamination of issued patents. *See* § 14.2.5.5.2.

experimental use: Experimental use has two distinct meanings within patent law. First, experimental use is an exception to the public-use statutory bar under § 102(b). So long as the public use was to test or experiment with the invention, it is not counted in computing the one-year statutory bar. Second, experimental use is a defense to infringement and requires that the construction and use of the patented invention be for scientific purposes only. *See* § 14.3.4.1.5.1.

express abandonment: *See abandonment.*

file wrapper: The folder into which papers for a particular application are collected and maintained. It contains a complete record of proceedings in the USPTO from the filing of the initial patent application to the issued patent. The file wrapper of a patent application that is maintained by the USPTO is the official record.

file wrapper estoppel: *See prosecution history estoppel.*

filing date: The date of receipt in the USPTO of an application which includes (1) a specification containing a description and, if the application is a nonprovisional application, at least one claim, and (2) any required drawings.

final office action: A USPTO action on the second or any subsequent examination or consideration by an examiner that is intended to close the prosecution of a nonprovisional patent application.

First Sale Doctrine/Exhaustion Principle: The first unrestricted sale of a patented product exhausts the patentee's control over that product, and it can be resold and repaired without implicating the patent owner's rights. This is a form of implied license. *See* § 14.4.2.2.1.1.

grace period: The one-year period between the critical date and the filing date, during which the invention may be offered for sale or used publicly in the United States, or described in a printed publication or patented anywhere in the world without invalidating the patent under § 102(b).

***Handgards* claim**: An antitrust counterclaim to a patent infringement suit, alleging that the patentee either knew the patent was invalid or was not being infringed. *See Handgards, Inc. v. Ethicon, Inc.*, 601 F.2d 986 (9th Cir. 1979).

having (used when defining the scope of a claim): A transitional phrase that is synonymous with *including*, *containing*, or *characterized by*; is inclusive or open-ended and does not exclude additional, unrecited elements or method steps.

improvement patent: A patent based on an improvement to a preexisting invention.

indefiniteness: *See definiteness.*

independent claim: A claim that does not refer back to or depend on another claim.

indirect infringement: Indirect infringement covers conduct by a person who assists or supports another's direct infringement of a patented invention. Direct infringement must be established as a predicate for each act of indirect infringement. *See* § 14.4.1.3.

inducement: Section 271(b) provides that "[w]hoever actively induces infringement of a patent shall be liable as an infringer." A finding of inducement requires that a patent owner establish evidence of culpable conduct directed toward encouraging another's infringement. *See* § 14.4.1.3.1.

inequitable conduct: Where a patent applicant breaches the duty to prosecute a patent application in good faith and candor. *See* 37 C.F.R. § 1.56; *see also* § 14.4.2.3.1.

information disclosure statement (IDS): A list of patents, publications, U.S. applications, or other information submitted for consideration by the USPTO in a nonprovisional patent application filed under § 111(a) to comply with applicant's duty to submit information that is material to the patentability of the claimed invention. *See* § 14.2.2.1.

inter partes reexamination: A procedure allowing third parties to seek invalidation by the USPTO of patents granted on applications filed on or after November 29, 1999. It was phased out beginning on September 16, 2011, and replaced by the AIA's inter partes review procedure. *See* § 14.2.5.5.3.

inter partes review (IPR): A procedure established by the AIA for third parties to seek invalidation of patents. *See* § 14.2.5.6.

interference: A proceeding, typically conducted before the Board of Patent Appeals and Interferences or in certain circumstances before a district court, to determine priority of invention between a pending application and/or one or more unexpired patents.

intervening rights: Claims that were modified at reissue, for any reason, are subject to a reliance-type interest (intervening rights). Third parties may rely on the claims of an issued patent. *See* § 14.2.5.4.2.2.

invention: Any art or process, machine, manufacture, design, or composition of matter, or any new and useful improvement thereof, or any variety of plant, which is or may be patentable under the patent laws of the United States.

invention date: The date either on which an invention is reduced to practice or conceived, so long as the inventor can show reasonable diligence from conception until reduction to practice.

issue date: The date that a patent application becomes a U.S. patent. The issue date is the date that patent rights can be exercised.

***Jepson* claim format**: A claim containing a preamble explaining the current state of the art, followed by a description of the claimed patentable improvement.

joint infringement: Liability for joint infringement can be found only where one party controlled or directed each step in the process. *See* § 14.4.1.3.3.

joint inventor: An inventor who is named with at least one other inventor in a patent application, wherein each inventor contributes to the conception of the invention set forth in at least one claim in a patent application.

laches: An equitable defense that the plaintiff unreasonably delayed in asserting an infringement claim. If a patentee files suit more than six years after he or she became (or reasonably should have become) aware of the alleged infringement, a presumption of laches arises, and the patentee must establish legitimate reasons for the delay. This defense does not bar the plaintiff's action entirely, but prevents the recovery of any damages accrued prior to the filing of the action. *See* § 14.4.2.3.4.

license: An agreement between a patent owner and a licensee that the patent owner will not sue the licensee for acts that would otherwise constitute infringement.

limitation: A component of an invention described in a patent claim. *See element.*

literal infringement: Literal infringement requires an accused device to satisfy every element of the asserted patent claim precisely. *See* § 14.4.1.4.1.

***Markush* claim format**: A *Markush* claim claims a genus of inventions in a single claim where the family of inventions all share a common trait, for example, "a chemical compound of the formula COOH–CH2-R, where R is selected from the group consisting of ________." *Markush* claims normally do not occur outside of the field of chemistry.

means-plus-function claim format: A means-plus-function claim defines one or more elements of the claim as a "means for [performing a function]." This special type of limitation is interpreted to cover the structure(s) described in the specification for performing the claimed function as well as equivalents of that/those structure(s) as of the time of filing. *See* § 112(f); § 14.4.1.4.1.1.

method claim: A claim covering a way of doing something, typically conveyed as a series of steps.

multiple dependent claim: A dependent claim that further limits and refers back in the alternative to more than one preceding independent or dependent claim. Acceptable multiple dependent claims shall refer to preceding claims using the terms *or*, *any one of*, *one of*, *any of*, *either*. A multiple dependent claim may not depend on another multiple dependent claim, either directly or indirectly.

national stage application: An application that has entered the national phase of the Patent Cooperation Treaty by the fulfillment of certain requirements in a national patent office. Such an application is filed under § 371 in the United States and is referred to as a "371 application."

new matter: Information in an amendment to a pending patent that departs from the original disclosure. Under § 132, amendments cannot introduce new matter into the disclosure of the invention.

nonfinal office action: An office action made by the examiner where the applicant is entitled to reply and request reconsideration or further examination, with or without making an amendment.

nonobviousness: The requirement that to be patentable, an invention be sufficiently different from the prior art that, at the time it was made, it would not have been obvious to a person having ordinary skill in the art. *See* § 14.3.5.

nonpatent literature: Documents and publications that are not patents or published patent applications but are cited as references for being relevant in a patent prosecution. For example, a magazine article or doctoral thesis relevant to a claimed invention might be cited as nonpatent literature. Typically, references cited in an application are grouped into domestic patents and patent application publications, foreign patents, and nonpatent literature.

nonprovisional application: The "regular" type of patent applications, as distinct from provisional applications filed under § 111(b), often referred to simply as "applications." *See* § 14.2.2.2.1.

nonresponsive amendment: An amendment filed by the applicant that does not fully respond to the examiner's office action in accordance with 37 C.F.R. § 1.111.

normal publication: Regular 18-month publication or redacted publication of a nonprovisional application.

notice: The practice of marking a patented article with the word *patent* followed by the patent number. Without notice, the patentee may recover only for damages that occurred after the infringer received a charge of patent infringement.

notice of abandonment: A written notification from the USPTO that an application has been declared abandoned or, in other words, is no longer pending. If the application was abandoned unintentionally or due to USPTO error, the applicant has a deadline of two months from the issue date of the notice of abandonment to file either (1) a petition to revive the application or (2) a request to reinstate the application.

notice of allowance: A notification to the applicant that he or she is entitled to a patent under the law and requesting payment of a specified issue fee (and possibly a publication fee as well) within three months (non-extendable) from the mailing date of the notice of allowance.

notice of references cited (also known as a PTO-892 form): A list of relevant references cited by a patent examiner in an office action. The following are some examples of such references: domestic patents, domestic patent application publications, foreign patents or patent publications, publications, electronic documents, and affidavits.

novelty: The requirement under § 102 that an invention be sufficiently new relative to the prior art. *See* § 14.3.4.

oath: *See declaration (of inventor).*

obviousness: *See nonobviousness.*

office action: The patent examiner's responses to the patent application and subsequent amendments.

on-sale bar: Section 102(b) specifies an on-sale bar, such that if an invention has been on sale for over one year, it is no longer patentable. *See* § 14.3.4.1.5.2.

opposition: A procedure allowing a third party to request a patent application's refusal or an issued patent's annulment.

original application: *Original* is used in the patent statute and rules to refer to an application that is not a reissue application. An original application may be a first filing or a continuing application.

parent application: The term *parent* is applied to an earlier application of the inventor disclosing a given invention.

patent: A quasi-property right granted by the government of the United States to an inventor "to exclude others from making, using, offering for sale, or selling the invention throughout the United States or importing the invention into the United States" for a limited time in exchange for public disclosure of the invention.

Patent Cooperation Treaty (PCT): A mechanism by which an applicant can file a single application that, when certain requirements have been fulfilled, is equivalent to a regular national filing in each designated country. There are currently over 130 PCT contracting states.

patent pending: A phrase that often appears on manufactured items. It means that someone has applied for a patent on an invention that is contained in the manufactured item. It serves as a warning that a patent may issue that would cover the item and that copiers should be careful because they might infringe if the patent issues. Once the patent issues, the patent owner will stop using the phrase "patent pending" and start using a phrase such as "covered by U.S. Patent Number XXXXXXX."

patent term: The period of time during which a patent is enforceable. For patent applications filed after June 8, 1995, the expiration date is twenty years from the earliest effective filing date, subject to various extensions for delays occurring during prosecution and regulatory approval for drug-related patents. *See* § 14.2.4.

Patent Trial and Appeal Board (PTAB): The AIA created this administrative body to replace the Board of Patent Appeals and Interferences (BPAI). It hears appeals by a patent applicant from a USPTO patent examiner's final refusal to allow a patent application or adverse decision in an ex parte patent reexamination proceeding, inter partes and postgrant review proceedings filed by a party challenging the validity of an issued patent, derivation proceedings filed by a subsequent patent applicant claiming that an earlier patent applicant for the same invention derived the invention from the subsequent patent applicant, and interference proceedings to determine the first inventor of an invention commenced before September 16, 2012. PTAB decisions concerning inter partes and postgrant reviews and ex parte reexamination proceedings may be appealed only to the U.S. Court of Appeals for the Federal Circuit. In several circumstances, a civil action against the USPTO in the U.S. District Court for the Eastern District of Virginia may be instituted after a final

PTAB decision: (1) where a patent applicant is dissatisfied with a PTAB decision concerning the final rejection of the patent application unless the applicant has appealed to the Federal Circuit (*see* § 145); (2) in a derivation proceeding where the losing party initially filed a notice of appeal from the PTAB decision to the Federal Circuit, the adverse party may request that further proceedings instead be conducted in the Eastern District of Virginia (*see* AIA § 7); and (3) where a party is dissatisfied with the decision in an interference proceeding over which the PTAB has jurisdiction, unless that party has appealed to the Federal Circuit (*see* § 146).

peripheral claiming: A regime in which an applicant delineates the precise boundaries of the claimed area of exclusivity, in contrast to central claiming in which the applicant defines the claim directly.

person: For purposes of small entity determination, a person is defined as any inventor or other individual (e.g., an individual to whom an inventor has transferred some rights in the invention) who has not assigned, granted, conveyed, or licensed, and is under no obligation under contract or law to assign, grant, convey, or license any rights in the invention.

person having ordinary skill in the art (PHOSITA): A hypothetical person with knowledge of all analogous art from whose perspective nonobviousness, written description, and enablement are analyzed. *See* §§ 103, 112; *see also* §§ 14.3.3, 14.3.5.3.1.

petition to make special (PTMS): An applicant may petition the USPTO to examine his or her application ahead of other pending applications. A petition to make special may be granted on the basis of an inventor's age or poor health, that the patent will enable manufacture of the invention, is presently being infringed, relates to certain fields including superconductivity, HIV/AIDS, and counter-terrorism, or several other reasons.

post-grant review (PGR): Under this new procedure added by the AIA, third parties may file a petition seeking to cancel one or more patent claims within nine months of a patent's issue or reissue date. *See* § 14.2.5.8.

preferred embodiment: How the inventor sets forth the best mode for carrying out the claimed invention in the application.

printed publication: A reference that is sufficiently accessible to the public interested in the invention. *See* § 14.3.4.1.1.2.

prior art: The general category of technologies and events against which novelty and nonobviousness are evaluated. What qualifies as prior art is specified in §§ 102 and 103.

priority claim: Claims under §§ 119(a)–(e) and 120 for the benefit of the filing date of earlier filed applications.

priority date: The first filing of a patent application anywhere in the world describing an enabled invention usually establishes the priority date for that invention. *See* § 14.2.2.2.3.

pro se: Used to designate an independent inventor who has elected to file an application by himself or herself without the services of a licensed representative.

prosecution: The process for applying for and obtaining a patent from the USPTO.

prosecution history estoppel: A doctrine that prevents a patentee from obtaining coverage through the doctrine of equivalents over subject matter that was surrendered during prosecution. *See* § 14.4.1.4.2.1.2.

provisional application: A provisional application for patent is a U.S. national application for patent filed in the USPTO under § 111(b), which allows filing without a formal patent claim, oath or declaration, or any information disclosure (prior art) statement. A provisional application can establish an early effective filing date in a nonprovisional patent application filed under § 111(a) and automatically becomes abandoned after one year. It also allows the term *patent pending* to be applied. *See* § 14.2.2.2.4.

reads on: An accused device, manufacture, composition, or process "reads on" (and hence infringes) a patent claim if it embodies each of the claim limitations. Similarly, a patent claim "reads on" a prior art reference (and hence is invalid) if the prior art reference contains each of the claim limitations.

reasonable diligence: First-to-conceive inventor must have been reasonably diligent in working to reduce the invention to practice between the time "just prior" to the later inventor's date of conception until the first-to-conceive inventor's reduction to practice. Reasonable diligence is only at issue when the inventor was first to conceive but second to reduce to practice. *See* § 14.3.4.1.2.3.

recapture rule: Bars a patentee from seeking reissue claims that regain subject matter that was surrendered to obtain allowance during the original prosecution. *See* § 14.2.5.4.2.1. This rule is similar to prosecution history estoppel. *See* § 14.4.1.4.2.1.2.

record copy: Original copy of an international application filed under the Patent Cooperation Treaty maintained by the International Bureau of the World Intellectual Property Organization.

redacted publication: A patent application publication that omits material that was present in the specification or claims of the nonprovisional patent application filed in the USPTO. *See* 37 C.F.R. § 1.217 and MPEP § 1132.

reduction to practice: Following conception, reduction to practice is the final step in the inventive process. Reduction to practice can be actual (by constructing a physical embodiment of the invention) or constructive (by filing a patent application that satisfies the disclosure requirements of § 112). *See* § 14.3.4.1.2.2.

reexamination proceeding: At any time during the enforceability of a patent, any person may file a request for the USPTO to conduct a second examination of any claim of the patent on the basis of prior art patents or printed publications which that person states to be pertinent and applicable to the patent and believes to have a bearing on the patentability (*see* 37 C.F.R. § 1.501). For the request for reexamination to be granted, a substantial new question of patentability must be present with regard to at least one patent claim. The request must be in writing and must be accompanied by payment of a reexamination request filing fee as set forth in 37 C.F.R. § 1.20(c). *See* § 14.2.5.5.

reference: *See prior art.*

reissue application: An application for a patent to take the place of an unexpired patent that is defective in one or more particulars. Resissues may narrow or broaden the application. *See* § 14.2.5.4.

rejoinder: The returning to active consideration of claims previously withdrawn from consideration to due to a restriction requirement—i.e., a determination by the USPTO that an application contains more than one invention.

request for continued examination (RCE): A request filed in an application in which prosecution is closed (e.g., the application is under final rejection or a notice of allowance) that is filed to reopen prosecution and continue examination of the application.

restriction: If two or more independent and distinct inventions are claimed in a single application, the examiner may require the applicant to elect a single invention to which the claims will be restricted. This requirement is known as a requirement for restriction (also known as a requirement for division). Such requirement will normally be made before any action on the merits; however, it may be made at any time before final action (final rejection).

reverse doctrine of equivalents: A doctrine excusing infringement where an accused device literally infringes a patent, but should nonetheless be excused because it substantially differs in operative principle and results. Although it has not been applied in over a century to excuse infringement, it continues to be raised. *See* § 14.4.1.4.3.

specification: A written description of the invention and the manner and process of making and using the same.

statutory disclaimer: *See disclaimer.*

submarine patent: An informal term for a patent that is intentionally delayed in prosecution by the applicant to let an infringing user continue to develop its business, with the intention of claiming later-invented technology once the patent finally "surfaces" from the PTO. As of November 29, 2000, most patent applications must be published within eighteen months of filing, so submarine patents have become less common.

substitute patent application: An application that is, in essence, a duplicate of a prior application by the same applicant abandoned before the filing of the substitute application. A substitute application does not obtain the benefit of the filing date of the prior application.

supplemental Examination: A procedure added by the AIA authorizing a patentee to seek further consideration of additional information relevant to patentability. *See* § 14.2.5.3.

terminal disclaimer: *See disclaimer.*

utility: To be patentable, an invention must have specific, substantial, and credible utility. *See* § 14.3.2.

***Walker Process* claim**: An antitrust counterclaim to a patent infringement suit, alleging that the patent was fraudulently obtained so as to exert monopolistic power and is therefore invalid. *See Walker Process Equip., Inc. v. Food Mach. & Chem. Corp.*, 382 U.S. 172 (1965).

written description: The portion of a patent specification, as required by § 112(a), describing the background of the invention, a summary of the invention, and a detailed description of the invention. The patentee must convey with reasonable clarity to those skilled in the art that, as of the filing date sought, he or she was in possession of the invention, and the written description must enable a person having ordinary skill in the art to practice the invention without undue experimentation. *See* § 14.3.3.1.

Appendix B
Acronyms

AIA: America Invents Act
AIPA: American Inventors Protection Act of 1999
AIPLA: American Intellectual Property Law Association
ANDA: Abbreviated New Drug Application
AOUSC: Administrative Office of the United States Courts
AU: (Group) Art Unit
BLA: Biologic License Application
BPAI: Board of Patent Appeals and Interferences
BPCIA: Biologics Price Competition and Innovation Act
CAPC: civil action to obtain patent certainty
CBM: covered business method
CBMR: covered business method review
CC: claim construction
CCPA: United States Court of Customs and Patent Appeals
CIP: continuation-in-part
CMC: case-management conference
CPA: continued prosecution application
CRU: Central Reexamination Unit
DOE: Doctrine of Equivalents
EAST: examiner automated search tools
EFD: effective filing date
EFS: electronic filing system
ePAS: Electronic Patent Assignment System
EPO: European Patent Office
ESD: examination support document
ESI: electronically stored information
FAR: Federal Acquisitions Regulations
FCBA: Federal Circuit Bar Association
FDA: Food and Drug Administration
FDCA: Food, Drug, and Cosmetic Act
FRAND: fair, reasonable and non-discriminatory
FTC: Federal Trade Commission
FTF: first-to-file
FTI: first-to-invent
GAU: Group Art Unit
IDS: information disclosure statement
INID: Internationally agreed Numbers for the Identification of bibliographic Data
IPR: inter partes review
IT: information technology
ITC: International Trade Commission

JMDL: Judicial Panel on Multidistrict Litigation
JSPR: joint preliminary status report
MDL: multidistrict litigation
MPEP: Manual of Patent Examining Procedure
MSJ: motion for summary judgment
NCE: new chemical entity
NDA: new drug application
NOA: notice of allowance
NPE: nonpracticing entity
NPL: non-patent literature
OG: Official Gazette
OIPE: Office of Initial Patent Examination
PAIR: Patent Application Information Retrieval
PCT: Patent Cooperation Treaty
PGR: postgrant review
PHOSITA: person having ordinary skill in the art
PHSA: Public Health and Safety Act
PLR(s): patent local rule(s)
PPA: Plant Patent Act
PTA: patent term adjustment
PTAB: Patent Trial and Appeal Board
PTE: patent term extension
PTMS: petition to make special
PTO: Patent and Trademark Office
PVP: plant variety protection
PVPA: Plant Variety Protection Act
RAND: reasonable and nondiscriminatory
RCE: request for continued examination
RCFC: Rules of the United States Court of Federal Claims
RLD: Reference Listed Drug
SEP: standard-essential patents
SNQ: substantial new question of patentability
SSO: standard setting organization
TD: terminal disclaimer
TSM: teaching, suggestion, or motivation
UPOV: Convention of the International Union for the Protection of New Plant Varieties
USITC: United States International Trade Commission
USPTO: United States Patent and Trademark Office
WIPO: World Intellectual Property Organization
WTO: World Trade Organization

Table of Cases

Author Biographies

Peter S. Menell is the Koret Professor of Law at the University of California, Berkeley School of Law, where he specializes in intellectual property law. In 1995, he co-founded the Berkeley Center for Law & Technology, which has been instrumental in Berkeley Law being named the top intellectual property program in the nation for nearly two decades. Professor Menell earned his B.S. from M.I.T., M.A. and Ph.D. in Economics from Stanford University, and J.D. from Harvard Law School, where he served as an editor of the *Harvard Law Review*. After graduating from law school, he clerked for Judge Jon O. Newman of the Court of Appeals for the Second Circuit. Professor Menell has written more than 70 articles and 10 books, including *Intellectual Property in the New Technological Age* (with R. Merges and M. Lemley, now in its eighth edition, 2016) and *Software and Internet Law* (with M. Lemley, R. Merges, P. Samuelson, and B. Carver, 4th ed. 2011). Professor Menell has organized more than 50 intellectual property education programs for the Federal Judicial Center since 1998. Professor Menell founded and supervises the *Annual Review of Law and Technology* (now in its nineteenth year, published by the *Berkeley Technology Law Journal*). He has advised the U.S. Congress, federal agencies, state attorneys general, and technology and entertainment companies on a wide range of intellectual property and antitrust matters. He is a member of the District of New Jersey Local Patent Rules Advisory Committee and the Court of Federal Claims Advisory Council. He served from 2012–2013 as one of the inaugural scholars in the USPTO's Thomas Alva Edison Visiting Professionals Program.

Lynn H. Pasahow is a partner in the Litigation Group at Fenwick & West, where he specializes in patent litigation. He has represented cutting-edge technology companies and universities and their Nobel laureate and other inventors in patent and other intellectual property litigation in the software, Internet, and biotech industries. Mr. Pasahow is a coauthor, with Judge William W Schwarzer, of *Civil Discovery: A Guide to Efficient Practice*. He co-teaches an intellectual property course at the University of California, San Francisco, and regularly lectures about intellectual property law subjects to groups that have included the Federal Judicial Center, the American Association for the Advancement of Science, the American Law Institute, the Practising Law Institute, and the University of California, Berkeley School of Law. Mr. Pasahow earned his B.A. from Stanford University and his J.D. from the University of California, Berkeley School of Law.

James Pooley advises clients on patent and trade secret matters in Silicon Valley. He served from 2009 through 2014 as deputy director general, Innovation and Technology Section, at the World Intellectual Property Organization (WIPO). Prior to that appointment, Mr. Pooley was a partner at Morrison and Foerster, where he specialized in intellectual property and technology-related commercial litigation. Mr. Pooley is the author of the treatise *Trade Secrets* (Law Journal Press), *Secrets: Managing Information Assets in the Age of Cyberespionage* (Verus Press 2015), and numerous other professional publications in the field of intellectual property. He is a former president of the American Intellectual Property Law Association and the National Inventors Hall of Fame. Mr. Pooley has taught as an adjunct professor of law at the University of California, Berkeley School of Law. He is a fellow of the California Council on Science and Technology and a member of the National Academy of Sciences Committee on Intellectual Property Rights. Mr. Pooley conceived and scripted an instructional video for jurors in patent cases that was produced by the Federal Judicial Center. Mr. Pooley earned his B.A. from Lafayette College and his J.D. from Columbia University School of Law.

Matthew D. Powers is the lead partner at Tensegrity Law Group, LLP. He is one of the nation's most experienced patent trial lawyers. He has litigated and tried cases in jurisdictions nationwide involving a wide range of technologies, including semiconductor, biomedical, computer, computer peripherals, cellular, holographic, digital media and specialty chemical products. He has published articles on various aspects of intellectual property law and litigation. Mr. Powers has taught as an adjunct professor of law at the University of California, Berkeley School of Law. Mr. Powers earned his B.S. from Northwestern University and his J.D. from Harvard Law School.

Steven C. Carlson is managing partner in the Silicon Valley office of Kasowitz, Benson, Torres & Friedman LLP, where he specializes in patent litigation. He served as a judicial law clerk to Judge Roderick R. McKelvie of the U.S. District Court for the District of Delaware and to Judge Paul R. Michel of the U.S. Court of Appeals for the Federal Circuit. He earned his B.A. from Reed College and his J.D. from Yale Law School, where he served as an editor of the *Yale Law Journal.*

Jeffrey G. Homrig is a partner in the Silicon Valley office of Latham & Watkins LLP. He has extensive experience as a litigator and trial lawyer in complex and high-stakes patent cases for leading technology companies. He graduated from University of California, Berkeley School of Law, and holds a B.A. from the University of California, Berkeley.

George F. Pappas is a partner at Covington & Burling LLP, where he specializes in patent litigation. He is a fellow of the American College of Trial Lawyers and the chair of its Complex Litigation Committee. He also chairs the Editorial Committee and is one of the coauthors of *Anatomy of a Patent Case* (2d ed. 2012), published in conjunction with the Federal Judicial Center. He received his undergraduate and law degrees from the University of Maryland.

Carolyn Chang is a partner at Fenwick & West's Silicon Valley office, where she specializes in patent litigation. She received her B.A. from the University of California, Berkeley, and her J.D. from the University of California, Hastings College of the Law.

Colette Reiner Mayer is a partner at Morrison & Foerster's Silicon Valley office, where she specializes in patent litigation. She earned her B.S. from M.I.T. and her J.D. from Cardozo School of Law.

Marc David Peters is a partner at Morrison & Foerster's Silicon Valley office, where he specializes in patent and trade secret litigation. He earned his B.A. from Harvard University, his M.A. and Ph.D. in Physics from the University of California, Berkeley, and his J.D. from Stanford Law School.

Collaborator Profiles

Anita Choi is an associate at Morrison & Foerster's Silicon Valley office, where she focuses on clean technology, biofuels, agricultural biotechnology, life sciences, biotechnology, pharmaceuticals, molecular diagnostics, and material sciences. She earned her B.S. from the California Institute of Technology, her M.B.A. from the Wharton School of Business, and her J.D. from the University of Pennsylvania Law School.

John Fargo serves as the director of the Intellectual Property Staff within the Commercial Litigation Branch of the Civil Division at the U.S. Department of Justice. He specializes in intellectual property litigation at the Federal Court of Claims. He earned his B.S. in Industrial Engineering and his J.D. at the State University of New York at Buffalo.

Michael Sawyer is an associate in the Washington, D.C., office of Covington & Burling where he specializes in patent litigation. He served as a judicial law clerk to Judge William C. Bryson of the U.S. Court of Appeals for the Federal Circuit. He earned his B.S. in Computer Science and Mathematics at the University of Scranton and his J.D. from the University of California, Berkeley School of Law.

Allison A. Schmitt currently serves as a law clerk to the Honorable Stanley R. Chesler at the U.S. District Court for the District of New Jersey, after which she will be clerking for Judge Kathleen M. O'Malley of the U.S. Court of Appeals for the Federal Circuit. She earned her B.S. in Chemistry and Biochemistry from the University of Washington, her Ph.D. in Chemistry from Duke University, and her J.D. from the University of California, Berkeley School of Law.

Michael R. Ward is a partner at Morrison & Foerster's San Francisco office, where he specializes in intellectual property relating to plants and biotechnology. He earned his B.S. from the University of California, Berkeley, his M.S. in Agronomy and Ph.D. in Plant Physiology/Biochemistry from the University of California, Davis, and his J.D. from Golden Gate University School of Law.

Patricia Young is an associate at Latham & Watkins LLP, where she specializes in patent litigation. She received her S.B. from M.I.T. and her J.D. from Harvard Law School.

Made in United States
Orlando, FL
10 November 2026

90506336R00317